# READINGS IN LATE ANTIQUITY

"This is a wonderful anthology. Clear, accessible, and vividly engaging, it presents the panoply of Late Antique life from east to west, from city to village, from the powerful to the humble, from transcendent hopes to ordinary burdens – a world to explore, relish, and ponder."

Susan Ashbrook Harvey, *Brown University*

"Unusually comprehensive and enterprising in its selections, this sourcebook will give an entire new generation a choice and a challenge."

Peter Brown, *Princeton University*

Late Antiquity (*c*. 250–650) witnessed the transition from Classical Antiquity to the Middle Ages in the Mediterranean and Near Eastern worlds. Christianity displaced polytheism over a wide area, offering new definitions of identity and community. The Roman Empire collapsed in western Europe to be replaced by new Germanic kingdoms. In the East, Byzantium emerged, while the Persian Empire reached its apogee and collapsed. Arab armies carrying the banner of Islam reshaped the political map and brought the Late Antique era to a close.

This sourcebook illustrates the dramatic political, social and religious transformations of Late Antiquity through the words of the men and women who experienced them. Drawing from Greek, Latin, Syriac, Hebrew, Coptic, Persian, Arabic, and Armenian sources, the carefully chosen passages illuminate the lives of emperors, abbesses, aristocrats, slaves, children, barbarian chieftains, and saints. The Roman Empire is kept at the centre of the discussion, with chapters devoted to its government, cities, army, law, medicine, domestic life, philosophy, and its Jewish population. Further chapters deal with the peoples who surrounded the Roman state: Persians, Huns, northern barbarians, and the followers of Islam.

This revised and updated second edition provides an expanded view of Late Antiquity with a new chapter on domestic life, as well extra material throughout, including passages that appear for the first time in English translation. *Readings in Late Antiquity* is the only sourcebook that covers such a wide range of topics over the full breadth of the Late Antique period.

**Michael Maas** is Professor of History and Classical Studies at Rice University, USA, where he teaches ancient history. His research focuses on Late Antiquity. His most recent books are *The Cambridge Companion to the Age of Justinian* (2005) and *Exegesis in the Early Byzantine Mediterranean* (2003).

# ROUTLEDGE SOURCEBOOKS FOR THE ANCIENT WORLD

READINGS IN LATE ANTIQUITY
Second edition
*Michael Maas*

GREEK AND ROMAN EDUCATION
*Mark Joyal, J.C. Yardley and Iain McDougall*

THE REPUBLICAN ROMAN ARMY
*Michael M. Sage*

THE STORY OF ATHENS
*Phillip Harding*

ROMAN SOCIAL HISTORY
*Tim Parkin and Arthur Pomeroy*

DEATH IN ANCIENT ROME
*Valerie Hope*

ANCIENT ROME
*Matthew Dillon and Lynda Garland*

SEXUALITY IN GREEK AND ROMAN LITERATURE
*Marguerite Johnson and Terry Ryan*

ATHENIAN POLITICAL ORATORY
*David Phillips*

POMPEII
*Alison E. Cooley and M.G.L. Cooley*

GREEK SCIENCE OF THE HELLENISTIC ERA
*Georgia Irby-Massie and Paul Keyser*

WOMEN AND LAW IN THE ROMAN EMPIRE
*Judith Evans Grubbs*

WARFARE IN ANCIENT GREECE
*Michael M. Sage*

READINGS IN LATE ANTIQUITY
*Michael Maas*

THE GOVERNMENT OF THE ROMAN EMPIRE
*Barbara Levick*

PAGANS AND CHRISTIANS IN LATE ANTIQUITY
*A.D. Lee*

ANCIENT GREECE
Second edition
*Matthew Dillon and Lynda Garland*

ANCIENT GREEK LAWS
*Ilias Arnaoutoglou*

TRIALS FROM CLASSICAL ATHENS
*Christopher Carey*

GREEK AND ROMAN TECHNOLOGY
*John Humphrey, John Oleson and Andrew Sherwood*

ROMAN ITALY 388 BC–AD 200
*Kathryn Lomas*

THE ROMAN ARMY 31 BC–AD 337
*Brian Campbell*

THE ROMAN HOUSEHOLD
*Jane F. Gardner and Thomas Wiedemann*

ATHENIAN POLITICS
*G.R. Stanton*

GREEK AND ROMAN SLAVERY
*Thomas Wiedemann*


FORTHCOMING:

ANCIENT GREECE
Third edition
*Matthew Dillon and Lynda Garland*

ANCIENT CITY OF ROME
*Christopher Smith, J.C.N. Coulston, Hazel Dodge*

WOMEN OF THE ANCIENT NEAR EAST
*Mark Chavalas*

GREEK RELIGION
*Emma Stafford and Karen Stears*

# READINGS IN LATE ANTIQUITY

## A Sourcebook

### Second edition

## *Michael Maas*

Routledge
Taylor & Francis Group

LONDON AND NEW YORK

First published 2000
by Routledge

Reprinted 2003

This second edition published 2010 by
Routledge
2 Park Square, Milton Park, Abingdon, Oxon OX14 4RN

Simultaneously published in the USA and Canada
by Routledge
270 Madison Ave., New York, NY 100016

*Routledge is an imprint of the Taylor & Francis Group, an informa business*

Typeset in Times New Roman by
Keystroke, Tettenhall, Wolverhampton
Printed and bound in Great Britain by
CPI Antony Rowe, Chippenham, Wiltshire

*British Library Cataloguing in Publication Data*
A catalogue record for this book is available from the British Library

*Library of Congress Cataloguing in Publication Data*
Maas, Michael, 1951–
Readings in late antiquity : a sourcebook / Michael Maas.
p. cm.
"Simultaneously published in the USA and Canada"–T.p. verso.
Includes bibliographical references and indexes.
1. Rome–History–Empire, 284–476–Sources. 2. Byzantine Empire–Civilization–To
527–Sources. 3. Byzantine Empire–Civilization–527–1081–Sources. I. Title.
DG78.M22 2009
937′.06–dc22
2009042117

ISBN10: 0–415–47336–5 (hbk)
ISBN10: 0–415–47337–3 (pbk)

ISBN13 978–0–415–47336–1 (hbk)
ISBN13 978–0–415–47337–8 (pbk)

# CONTENTS

| | | |
|---|---|---|
| **Maps** | | xliii |
| **Introduction to the first edition** | | lxiii |
| **Introduction to the second edition** | | lxvii |
| **Acknowledgments** | | lxix |
| **Chronology** | | lxxi |
| **Late Antique rulers** | | lxxv |
| **Permissions** | | lxxxiii |
| 1 | The Roman Empire: ruler and administration | 1 |
| 2 | Cities | 37 |
| 3 | The Roman army | 78 |
| 4 | Christianity | 110 |
| 5 | Polytheism | 174 |
| 6 | Jews | 201 |
| 7 | Women | 224 |
| 8 | Domestic life | 240 |
| 9 | Law | 285 |
| 10 | Medicine | 297 |
| 11 | Philosophy | 311 |
| 12 | Sasanian Persia | 327 |
| 13 | Invaders and successor states | 345 |
| 14 | Steppe peoples and Slavs | 371 |
| 15 | Islam | 387 |
| | **Appendix: Late Antiquity on the Web** | 408 |
| | **Index of ancient sources** | 410 |
| | **Index** | 416 |

# EXTENDED CONTENTS

A list of passages new to the second edition may be found on the Routledge website: http://www.routledge.com/books/Readings-in-Late-Antiquity-isbn 9780415473378

| | | |
|---|---|---|
| **1** | **The Roman Empire: ruler and administration** | **1** |
| *1.1* | *Introduction* | *1* |
| *1.2* | *The emperor and the imperial office* | *2* |
| *1.2.1* | *The emperor comes to town*<br>AMMIANUS MARCELLINUS, *HISTORY* 16.10.5–10<br>AMMIANUS MARCELLINUS, *HISTORY* 22.2.3–5 | *2* |
| *1.2.2* | *Imperial acclamations*<br>THEODOSIAN CODE, "MINUTES OF THE SENATE," 5 | *3* |
| *1.2.3* | *Court ritual*<br>CYRIL OF SCYTHOPOLIS, *LIFE OF SABAS* 71 | *5* |
| *1.2.4* | *Cautious advice for an all-powerful monarch*<br>AGAPETUS, *EXPOSITION* 1, 2, 30, 35, 37 | *5* |
| *1.2.5* | *The emperor's role in war and peace*<br>SYNESIUS OF CYRENE, *ON KINGSHIP* 16 | *6* |
| *1.2.6* | *Ruler cult*<br>GREGORY OF NAZIANZUS, *ORATION* 4.80 | *7* |
| *1.2.7* | *The emperor as the embodiment of law*<br>THEMISTIUS, *ORATION* 19 (227D, 228A) | *7* |
| *1.2.8* | *The Christian emperor looks to heaven*<br>EUSEBIUS, *LIFE OF CONSTANTINE* 4.15 | *8* |
| *1.2.9* | *The image of the emperor*<br>THEOPHILUS, *A HOMILY ON THE VIRGIN* | *8* |
| *1.2.10* | *The imperial right to interfere in church affairs*<br>OSSIUS OF CORDOBA, LETTER TO CONSTANTIUS II,<br>QUOTED BY ATHANASIUS, *HISTORY OF THE ARIANS* 44, 6–8 | *9* |

*1.2.11*  *The emperor as priest – Justinian's view*  9
JUSTINIAN, *NOVEL* 6 (MARCH 6, 535)

*1.2.12*  *Challenging Justinian's interference in church affairs*  10
FACUNDUS OF HERMIONE, *IN DEFENSE OF THE THREE*
*CHAPTERS* 12.3

*1.2.13*  *The emperor as the source of instability*  10
PROCOPIUS, *SECRET HISTORY* 3.1 AND 5.1

*1.3*  **Imperial administration**  *11*

*1.3.1*  *Diocletian's reforms*  11
LACTANTIUS, *ON THE DEATH OF THE PERSECUTORS* 7.1–8

*1.3.2*  *An able emperor relies on his advisory council*  12
AMMIANUS MARCELLINUS, *HISTORY* 15.5.12–14

*1.3.3*  *A top official's close ties to the monarch*  13
CASSIODORUS, *DOCUMENTS* 6.5

*1.3.4*  *A hierarchy of administrators supervised by the emperor*  14
THEODOSIAN CODE 1.15.1

*1.3.5*  *Entrance requirements for the bureaucracy*  15
THEODOSIAN CODE 7.2.1

*1.3.6*  *The honor of serving the emperor*  15
THE GREEK ANTHOLOGY 16.48

*1.3.7*  *Bishops in the imperial administration*  15
JUSTINIAN, *EDICT 1*, PREFACE

*1.3.8*  *Access to the emperor for all citizens*  16
THEODOSIAN CODE 1.5.1

*1.3.9*  *A new aristocracy of service*  17
BASIL OF CAESAREA, *LETTER* 299

*1.3.10*  *Corruption and suffering in the provinces*  17
JOHN LYDUS, *ON THE MAGISTRACIES OF THE ROMAN*
*STATE* 3.59

*1.3.11*  *A picture of the Roman Empire*  18
EUMENIUS, *FOR THE RESTORATION OF THE SCHOOLS* .20–.21

*1.3.12*  *The condition and use of Roman roads*  19
THEODOSIAN CODE 15.3.4

*1.3.13*   *Roman roads after Rome*                                      19
CASSIODORUS, *VARIAE* XII.18
GREGORY OF TOURS, *THE HISTORY OF THE FRANKS* VI.11

**1.4**   **Economic life**                                             **20**

*1.4.1*   *Diocletian's Edict on Maximum Prices*                         21
DIOCLETIAN, *EDICT ON MAXIMUM PRICES*, PREAMBLE

*1.4.2*   *Justinian's Edict on the Regulation of Skilled Labor*         22
JUSTINIAN, *EDICT 6*, "ON THE REGULATION OF SKILLED
LABOR," PREFACE, 1

*1.4.3*   *The colossal wealth of aristocrats*                           23
OLYMPIODORUS OF THEBES, *FRAGMENT* 41.2

*1.4.4*   *What to do with wealth?*                                      23
ANONYMOUS, *ON RICHES* 6.3, 20.1–2

*1.4.5*   *Poverty*                                                      24
LIBANIUS, *ORATION* 7.1–3

*1.4.6*   *Natural disasters and local economies*                       25
LIBANIUS, *ORATION* 18.289, 293

*1.4.7*   *Famine*                                                       25
PSEUDO-JOSHUA THE STYLITE, *CHRONICLE* 38–42

*1.4.8*   *The emperor steps in*                                         26
ANONYMOUS ORATOR, *SPEECH OF THANKS TO
CONSTANTINE* 5–6

*1.4.9*   *The great estates and the rise of patrons*                   28
*THEODOSIAN CODE* 11.24.2
JUSTINIAN, CODE II.54.1

*1.4.10*   *Exploitation of peasant farmers in Syria and Egypt*         28
JOHN CHRYSOSTOM, *HOMILY ON MATTHEW* 61.3

*1.4.11*   *Dependence upon a landlord on an Egyptian estate*           29
*OXYRHYNCHUS PAPYRUS* I.130, LINES 1–10

*1.4.12*   *The colonate*                                               30
JUSTINIAN, *CODE* 11.48.23.2

*1.4.13*   *A patron from the outside*                                  30
*HISTORY OF THE MONKS IN EGYPT* 8.30–1

*1.4.14*   *Who is the best patron?*                                          31
          MIDRASH HA-GADDOL, DEUTERONOMY 32:9

*1.4.15*   *Landlocked peasants*                                              31
          SYNESIUS, EPISTLES 148

*1.4.16*   *Slavery is taken for granted*                                     32
          BASIL OF CAESAREA, ON THE HOLY SPIRIT 20

*1.4.17*   *Slaves in the law*                                                33
          JUSTINIAN, INSTITUTES 1.3–5

*1.4.18*   *Slavery, the wage of sin*                                         34
          AUGUSTINE, CITY OF GOD 19.15

*1.4.19*   *An international trade in humans*                                 34
          AUGUSTINE, LETTER 10.2

          *Further reading*                                                   35

**2**      **Cities**                                                         **37**
**2.1**    **Introduction**                                                   *37*
**2.2**    **City administration**                                           *37*

*2.2.1*    *The importance of city senators*                                  37
          THEODOSIAN CODE 12.1.144, 184

*2.2.2*    *The generosity of city senators*                                  38
          LIBANIUS, ORATION 11, "IN PRAISE OF ANTIOCH," 133–7

*2.2.3*    *Praises for a city's patron*                                      39
          APHRODISIAS, INSCRIPTION 83

*2.2.4*    *Imperial administrators and cities*                               40
          APHRODISIAS, INSCRIPTION 40

*2.3*      *City life*                                                        *40*

*2.3.1*    *The individual character of a city: Alexandria*                   40
          DESCRIPTION OF THE ENTIRE WORLD 35–7

*2.3.2*    *Urban rioting*                                                    41
          GERONTIUS, LIFE OF MELANIA THE YOUNGER 19

*2.3.3*    *An emperor almost falls: the Nika Riots*                          41
          PROCOPIUS, HISTORY OF THE WARS 1.24.1–2, 7–10

*2.3.4*    *The people of Rome expect entertainment*                          42
          SYMMACHUS, OFFICIAL DISPATCH 6

*2.3.5*  *Celebrity charioteers*                                              43
AGATHIAS, "ON PORPHYRIUS OF THE BLUE FACTION,"
*GREEK ANTHOLOGY* 16.380

*2.3.6*  *Spilling blood for entertainment*                                   43
SEBEOS, *HISTORY* 10

*2.3.7*  *The end of gladiatorial combat*                                     44
*THEODOSIAN CODE* 15.12.1

*2.3.8*  *Christian condemnation of public entertainments*                    45
JOHN CHRYSOSTOM, *HOMILY ON MATTHEW* 37.6

*2.3.9*  *Theodora on stage*                                                  45
PROCOPIUS, *SECRET HISTORY* 9.20–2

*2.3.10*  *Festivals and calendars*                                           45
JOHN MALALAS, *THE CHRONICLE* 7.7

*2.3.11*  *Taking a bath*                                                     46
INSCRIPTION OF THE EMPRESS EUDOCIA
CLEMENT OF ALEXANDRIA, *PAEDAGOGUS* 3.9

*2.3.12*  *The odor of sanctity*                                              47
PSEUDO-ATHANASIUS, *PATROLOGIA GRAECA* 28.264

**2.4**  **The city of Rome**                                                **47**

*2.4.1*  *Rome in old age*                                                    48
AMMIANUS MARCELLINUS, *HISTORY* 14.6.3–6

*2.4.2*  *Rome, center of the world*                                          48
RUTILIUS NAMATIANUS, "A VOYAGE HOME TO GAUL,"
LINES 37–66

*2.4.3*  *Rome's countless wonders*                                           49
ZACHARIAH OF MITYLENE, *THE SYRIAC CHRONICLE* 10–16

**2.5**  **Rome becomes a Christian center**                                 **50**

*2.5.1*  *A martyr foresees Rome's Christian future*                          50
PRUDENTIUS, *ON THE CROWNS OF THE MARTYRS* 2.1–20,
413–562

*2.5.2*  *Christian citizens of Rome*                                         52
PRUDENTIUS, *AGAINST SYMMACHUS*, 506–25, 565, 578, 587

2.5.3   Rome's temples abandoned                                    53
        PAULINUS OF NOLA, *POEM* 19.53–75

2.5.4   The primacy of the bishop of Rome                           53
        POPE LEO I, *SERMON* 3

2.5.5   Protecting and restoring Rome's buildings                   54
        *CORPUS OF LATIN INSCRIPTIONS* 6.1189

2.5.6   A quarry for builders                                       55
        MAJORIAN, *NOVEL* 4

**2.6     The sack of Rome, AD 410**                                **56**

2.6.1   The first shocking news                                     56
        JEROME, *LETTER* 127.12

2.6.2   Rome's place in God's plan: the Eusebian background         56
        EUSEBIUS, *TRICENNIAL ORATION: ON CHRIST'S SEPULCHRE*
        16.4–6

2.6.3   Pagans blame Christians                                     57
        AUGUSTINE, *CITY OF GOD* 2.3

2.6.4   "Nothing had happened": Orosius' explanation               57
        OROSIUS, *HISTORY AGAINST THE PAGANS* 7.39–41

2.6.5   Augustine on the sacred significance of Rome                58
        AUGUSTINE, *CITY OF GOD* 18.53

**2.7     Constantinople**                                          **59**

2.7.1   Founding the new Rome                                       59
        *EASTER CHRONICLE* 1 (AD 328)

2.7.2   Advancing against the East                                  60
        PROCOPIUS, *ON BUILDINGS* 1.2.1–19

2.7.3   Justinian's Saint Sophia – a temple to rival Solomon's      61
        PROCOPIUS, *ON BUILDINGS* 1.1.23, 24, 27, 47–9

2.7.4   Belisarius celebrates a triumph                            61
        PROCOPIUS, *HISTORY OF THE WARS* 4.9.1–14

2.7.5   The center of Constantinople                                63
        PROCOPIUS, *ON BUILDINGS* 1.10.10–20

2.7.6   Christian theory of empire                                  64
        PAUL THE SILENTIARY, *DESCRIPTION OF HAGIA SOPHIA*

**2.8**    **Secular and Christian education**    **66**

2.8.1    *Educating an elite*    66
AUGUSTINE, *CONFESSIONS* 2.3.5

2.8.2    *Training for imperial service*    67
JOHN LYDUS, *ON THE MAGISTRACIES OF THE ROMAN STATE* 3.26

2.8.3    *Honor your teachers!*    67
AGATHIAS, *GREEK ANTHOLOGY* 16.36

2.8.4    *Julian on proper education*    68
JULIAN, *LETTER* 36

2.8.5    *Christ or Cicero? Jerome's choice*    69
JEROME, *LETTER* 22.30 TO EUSTOCHIUM

2.8.6    *Should Christian students read the pagan classics?*    70
BASIL OF CAESAREA, *ADDRESS TO YOUNG MEN ON READING PROFANE LITERATURE*

2.8.7    *No place for secular literature*    71
POPE GREGORY THE GREAT, *LETTER* 2.24 TO BISHOP DESIDERIUS OF VIENNE

2.8.8    *Students murder a Christian schoolmaster*    71
PRUDENTIUS, *ON THE CROWNS OF THE MARTYRS* 9.5–60

2.8.9    *Christian curriculum taught on a Roman model – in Syria*    72
JUNILLUS AFRICANUS, *THE BASIC TEACHINGS OF DIVINE LAW*, INTRODUCTION

2.8.10    *Reducing teachers' salaries*    73
PROCOPIUS, *SECRET HISTORY* 26.5

2.8.11    *Interpreting the Bible*    73
BASIL OF CAESAREA, *HOMILY* 10.1, "A PSALM ON THE LOT OF THE JUST MAN"
BASIL OF CAESAREA, *HOMILY* 11.4

2.8.12    *Preserving classical and Christian learning*    74
CASSIODORUS, *AN INTRODUCTION TO DIVINE AND HUMAN READINGS* I.1, 5–6

2.8.13    *Searching for a teacher: the case of Ananias of Shirak*    75
ANANIAS OF SHIRAK, *AUTOBIOGRAPHY*

     *Further reading*    77

| | | |
|---|---|---|
| **3** | **The Roman army** | **78** |
| *3.1* | *Introduction* | *78* |
| *3.2* | *Reorganization of the army* | *79* |

*3.2.1*   *The decline of border defenses: Constantine's fault?*   79
ZOSIMUS, *NEW HISTORY* 2.34

*3.3*   ***The army in the field***   ***80***

*3.3.1*   *Elephants vs. legionaries*   80
AMMIANUS MARCELLINUS, *HISTORY* 25.6.1–4

*3.3.2*   *Guarding the emperor*   81
AMMIANUS MARCELLINUS, *HISTORY* 17.13.8–10

*3.3.3*   *Training the cavalry*   81
MAURICE, *TREATISE ON STRATEGY* 1.2

*3.3.4*   *The navy*   82
THEOPHANES, *CHRONICLE*, AM 5961, AD 468–469

*3.3.5*   *Border troops*   83
THEODOSIUS, *NOVEL* 4.1

*3.3.6*   *Border forts*   83
ANONYMOUS, *ON STRATEGY* 9

*3.3.7*   *River frontier patrols*   84
*THEODOSIAN CODE* 7.17.1, "RIVER PATROL CRAFT ON
THE DANUBE"

*3.3.8*   *Raiding*   85
AMMIANUS MARCELLINUS, *HISTORY* 17.1.5–7

*3.3.9*   *How to establish frontier defense*   86
JUSTINIAN, *CODE* 1.27.2.4, 8

*3.3.10*   *Border defense crumbles on the Danube*   86
EUGIPPIUS, *THE LIFE OF SAINT SEVERIN* 20.1

*3.3.11*   *The siege of Amida – a lucky escape*   87
AMMIANUS MARCELLINUS, *HISTORY* 19.2.7–11; 19.4.1;
19.8.4–9

*3.3.12*   *Military medicine*   88
VEGETIUS, *EPITOME OF MILITARY SCIENCE* 3.2, "HOW
THE ARMY'S HEALTH IS CONTROLLED"

3.3.13  *The wounded after a battle*                                    89
        AMMIANUS MARCELLINUS, *HISTORY* 19.2.15

3.3.14  *Rewards after a battle*                                        90
        THEOPHYLACT SIMOCATTA, *HISTORY* 2.6.10–12

**3.4**    ***Soldiers within the empire***                            **90**
3.4.1   *Soldiers protect civilian life*                               90
        ABBINAEUS, *ARCHIVE* 45

3.4.2   *Soldiers need discipline*                                     91
        SYNESIUS, *ON KINGSHIP* 18

3.4.3   *An extortion racket in Syria*                                 91
        LIBANIUS, *ORATION* 47, "ON PROTECTION SYSTEMS,"
        1, 3–12, 2.17, 18

3.4.4   *Tax collection*                                               94
        ABBINAEUS, *ARCHIVE* 3

**3.5**    ***Manpower shortages and the problems of recruitment***    **95**
3.5.1   *Recruits*                                                     95
        VEGETIUS, *EPITOME OF MILITARY SCIENCE* 1.2–4, "FROM
        WHAT REGIONS RECRUITS SHOULD BE LEVIED"

3.5.2   *Sons of soldiers must enlist*                                 96
        *THEODOSIAN CODE* 7.1.5

3.5.3   *Enforced recruitment and draft evasion*                      96
        *THEODOSIAN CODE* 7.13.1
        *THEODOSIAN CODE* 7.13.5
        *THEODOSIAN CODE* 17.18.1

3.5.4   *Slaves are permitted to enlist*                              97
        *THEODOSIAN CODE* 7.13.16

3.5.5   *Exemptions from military service*                            97
        *THEODOSIAN CODE* 13.3.3

**3.6**    **Non-Roman recruits**                                      **97**
3.6.1   *Barbarian federates*                                         97
        AMMIANUS MARCELLINUS, *HISTORY* 17.13.3

3.6.2   *The history of federates*                                    98
        PROCOPIUS, *HISTORY OF THE WARS* 3.11.1–5

| | | |
|---|---|---|
| *3.6.3* | *Recruiting grounds and imperial borders*<br>ZOSIMUS, *NEW HISTORY* 4.12 | 98 |
| **3.7** | **Payment and billeting** | **99** |
| *3.7.1* | *How were soldiers paid?*<br>AMMIANUS MARCELLINUS, *HISTORY* 20.4.17–18 | 99 |
| *3.7.2* | *Billeting*<br>*THEODOSIAN CODE* 7.8.5 | 99 |
| *3.7.3* | *Billeting Goths in Edessa*<br>PSEUDO JOSHUA THE STYLITE, *CHRONICLE* 93–4 | 100 |
| **3.8** | **The practice of war** | **101** |
| *3.8.1* | *Strategy, tactics and training*<br>VEGETIUS, *EPITOME OF MILITARY SCIENCE* 1.1 | 101 |
| *3.8.2* | *Discipline and punishment*<br>ZOSIMUS, *NEW HISTORY* 3.3.4–5 | 102 |
| *3.8.3* | *The rules of war*<br>VEGETIUS, *EPITOME OF MILITARY SCIENCE* 3.26 | 102 |
| *3.8.4* | *The danger of fighting pitched battle*<br>MAURICE, *TREATISE ON STRATEGY* 8.2.4 | 103 |
| *3.8.5* | *Prayers and battle*<br>MAURICE, *TREATISE ON STRATEGY* 2.18 | 103 |
| *3.8.6* | *Military anthropology*<br>MAURICE, *TREATISE ON STRATEGY* 11.3 | 104 |
| **3.9** | **Christians in the army** | **105** |
| *3.9.1* | *The passion of Saint Marcellus*<br>*THE ACTS OF MARCELLUS* 250–9 | 105 |
| *3.9.2* | *Saint Martin refuses to fight*<br>SULPICIUS SEVERUS, *THE LIFE OF SAINT MARTIN OF TOURS* 2 | 106 |
| *3.9.3* | *Just war*<br>AUGUSTINE, *AGAINST FAUSTUS* 22.74–5 | 107 |
| *3.9.4* | *The Christian military vocation*<br>AUGUSTINE, *LETTER* 189.2.4, 6 | 108 |

| | | |
|---|---|---|
| 3.9.5 | *Regimental priests*<br>THEODORET, *LETTER* 2 | 108 |
| | *Further reading* | 109 |
| **4** | **Christianity** | **110** |
| *4.1* | *Introduction* | *110* |
| *4.2* | *Conversions* | *111* |
| 4.2.1 | *God helps Constantine: "In this sign you will conquer"*<br>EUSEBIUS, *LIFE OF CONSTANTINE* 1.29 | 111 |
| 4.2.2 | *"Through divine inspiration"*<br>ARCH OF CONSTANTINE, INSCRIPTION | 112 |
| 4.2.3 | *The last Vestal Virgin*<br>PRUDENTIUS, *ON THE CROWNS OF THE MARTYRS* 2.517–28 | 112 |
| 4.2.4 | *Antony rejects the world*<br>ATHANASIUS, *LIFE OF ANTONY* 2–3 | 113 |
| 4.2.5 | *A voice in the garden leads Augustine to conversion*<br>AUGUSTINE, *CONFESSIONS* 8.12.29 | 113 |
| 4.2.6 | *Christian peace after a busy public life*<br>PAULINUS OF NOLA, *LETTER* 5.4 | 114 |
| 4.2.7 | *A Frankish king accepts Catholicism*<br>GREGORY OF TOURS, *THE HISTORY OF THE FRANKS* 2.30 | 115 |
| 4.2.8 | *Patrick goes to Ireland*<br>SAINT PATRICK, *THE CONFESSION* 1.1, 2, 17, 23, 41, 42, 50, 52 | 115 |
| *4.3* | *Church and state* | *117* |
| 4.3.1 | *The Edict of Milan*<br>LACTANTIUS, *ON THE DEATH OF THE PERSECUTORS* 48.1–11 | 117 |
| 4.3.2 | *Massacre at Thessalonica*<br>AMBROSE, *LETTER* 51.4, 6, 11, 13 | 119 |
| *4.4* | *Bishops* | *120* |
| 4.4.1 | *Bishops as administrators*<br>COUNCIL OF NICAEA, *CANON* 4 (325); SYNOD OF ANTIOCH,<br>*CANON* 9 (341) | 120 |

4.4.2  Augustine chooses his successor  121
AUGUSTINE, "THE ELECTION OF ERACLIUS," *ACTA
ECCLESIASTICA, LETTER* 213.1–7

4.4.3  Public debate: Augustine vs. a Manichaean  121
AUGUSTINE, *DISPUTATION AGAINST FORTUNATUS* 1, 35–7

4.4.4  How should a bishop behave?  123
POPE GREGORY THE GREAT, *BOOK OF PASTORAL RULE* 2.1

4.4.5  A bishop demands respect, even from an empress  124
PHILOSTORGIUS, *SUDA*, A 254, LEONTIUS

4.4.6  Constantine and the bickering bishops  124
SOCRATES SCHOLASTICUS, *ECCLESIASTICAL HISTORY* 1.34

4.4.7  Vicious debate at a church council  126
GREGORY OF NAZIANZUS, *CONCERNING HIS OWN LIFE*
1680–9

4.4.8  The consequences of losing: Nestorius describes his
enemies  126
NESTORIUS, *THE BAZAAR OF HERACLEIDES* 2.1

4.4.9  An archbishop's schedule of bribes  128
CYRIL OF ALEXANDRIA, *LETTER* 96

4.4.10  Legal functions of bishops  130
*THEODOSIAN CODE* 1.27.1

4.4.11  Giving up a quiet life to become Pope  130
POPE GREGORY THE GREAT, *LETTER* 1.5, TO PRINCESS
THEOCTISTA

4.5  **Theology**  131

4.5.1  Arius and the human nature of Christ  131
ARIUS, *LETTER TO ALEXANDER OF ALEXANDRIA* 2–5

4.5.2  The Nicene Creed  132
"THE CREED OF NICAEA"

4.5.3  Nestorius' heresy  132
NESTORIUS, *SECOND LETTER TO CYRIL*

4.5.4  Christ's two natures unified  133
POPE LEO I, *SERMON* 54.2

4.5.5   *Mary and the virgin birth*                                    134
        ROMANOS THE MELODIST, *ON THE PRESENTATION IN
        THE TEMPLE*, STROPHES 3, 4

4.5.6   *The Council of Chalcedon and Nestorianism*                    135
        THE COUNCIL OF CHALCEDON, *DEFINITION OF THE FAITH*

4.5.7   *The government forbids heresy*                                 135
        THEODOSIAN CODE, 16.5.5

4.5.8   *Pelagius on salvation*                                         136
        AUGUSTINE, *ON HERESIES 88*

4.5.9   *The* Tome *of Leo*                                             137
        POPE LEO I, *LETTER* 28.4

4.5.10  *The* Henotikon *of Zeno*                                       138
        THE HENOTIKON: LETTER OF ZENO TO THE BISHOPS,
        MONKS AND LAITY OF EGYPT (EVAGRIUS, *ECCLESIASTICAL
        HISTORY* 111.14)

4.5.11  *An apology for differences of opinion among Christians*        139
        EVAGRIUS, *ECCLESIASTICAL HISTORY* 11

4.5.12  *Justinian on orthodoxy*                                        140
        JUSTINIAN, *AGAINST THE MONOPHYSITES*, CONCLUSION

4.5.13  *The "Three Chapters" Controversy*                              141
        FACUNDUS OF HERMIONE, *IN DEFENSE OF THE THREE
        CHAPTERS* 12.3

**4.6**    **Martyrs and relics**                                      **142**

4.6.1   *The martyrdom of Timothy of Gaza*                             142
        EUSEBIUS, *THE MARTYRS OF PALESTINE* 3.1

4.6.2   *Mar Kardagh: a martyr in Persia*                             143
        THE HISTORY OF THE HEROIC DEEDS OF MAR KARDAGH
        THE VICTORIOUS MARTYR, 1, 65–9

4.6.3   *Relics of martyrs*                                            144
        PRUDENTIUS, *ON THE CROWNS OF THE MARTYRS* 5.333–44

4.6.4   *Martyrs in church art*                                        144
        PRUDENTIUS, *ON THE CROWNS OF THE MARTYRS* 11.123–34

4.6.5   *Violation of tombs in search of relics*                       145
        THEODOSIAN CODE 9.17.7

| | | |
|---|---|---|
| 4.6.6 | *Send me the head of Saint Paul!*<br>POPE GREGORY THE GREAT, *LETTER* 30 | 145 |
| **4.7** | **Pilgrimage and relics** | **146** |
| 4.7.1 | *Relics in Jerusalem*<br>CYRIL OF JERUSALEM, *LETTER TO THE EMPEROR*<br>*CONSTANTIUS* 3–5 | 146 |
| 4.7.2 | *Constantine and Jerusalem's holy sites*<br>EUSEBIUS, *LIFE OF CONSTANTINE* 3.25, 27–9 | 147 |
| 4.7.3 | *Paula – a pious Roman aristocrat in Jerusalem*<br>JEROME, *LETTER* 108 TO EUSTOCHIUM | 148 |
| 4.7.4 | *Egeria visits the Cross*<br>EGERIA, *TRAVELS* 36.5, 37.1–3 | 148 |
| 4.7.5 | *The Piacenza Pilgrim*<br>*THE PIACENZA PILGRIM* 1, 5, 11, 12, 18–20 | 149 |
| 4.7.6 | *Heraclius restores the Cross to Jerusalem*<br>SEBEOS, *HISTORY*, CH. 29, VERSE 99 | 151 |
| **4.8** | **Asceticism** | **152** |
| 4.8.1 | *The Devil tempts Antony*<br>ATHANASIUS, *LIFE OF ANTONY* 5–7 | 152 |
| 4.8.2 | *Extreme asceticism*<br>CANONS OF THE COUNCIL OF GANGRA 343 | 153 |
| 4.8.3 | *Simeon the Stylite: public ascetic acts draw crowds*<br>BEDJAN, *THE HEROIC DEEDS OF MAR SIMEON, THE CHIEF*<br>*OF THE ANCHORITES (ACTS OF MARTYRS AND SAINTS)* | 154 |
| 4.8.4 | *The death of Simeon*<br>JACOB OF SERUG, *HOMILY ON SIMEON THE STYLITE*<br>65 5–6, 659–60, 664–5 | 155 |
| 4.8.5 | *John Cassian's rules for monastic life*<br>JOHN CASSIAN, *INSTITUTES* 1.2, 4.5 | 157 |
| 4.8.6 | *Benedict on the twelve degrees of humility*<br>SAINT BENEDICT, *RULE FOR MONASTERIES* 7 | 157 |
| 4.8.7 | *The difficulties of monastic life*<br>ROMANOS THE MELODIST, *ON CHRISTIAN LIFE*, STROPHES<br>22, 23, 25 | 160 |

4.8.8   *Female founders of monasteries*                    161
        SERGIA, *NARRATION CONCERNING SAINT OLYMPIAS*
        1, 4, 5, 9

4.8.9   *Advice to young nuns*                              162
        EVAGRIUS PONTICUS, *ADVICE TO A YOUNG WOMAN*

4.8.10  *Monks on a rampage: the destructive side of piety*  163

**4.9     Liturgy and prayer**                              **163**

4.9.1   *Celebration of the Eucharist*                      163
        THE DIVINE LITURGY 9.1

4.9.2   *Prayers, priests and the people*                   164
        JOHN CHRYSOSTOM, *ON THE SECOND LETTER TO THE*
        *CORINTHIANS*, P. 61, XVIII, COL. 527

4.9.3   *The Akathistos Hymn*                               164
        *AKATHISTOS HYMN*, PROOIMION

**4.10    Calendars and apocalyptic literature**            **165**

4.10.1  *No litigation on Sundays*                          165
        *THEODOSIAN CODE* 2.8.1

4.10.2  *"Anno Domini" – the Christian calendar begins*     165
        DIONYSIUS EXIGUUS, *LETTER TO BISHOP PETRONIUS*
        (*PATROLOGIA LATINA* 67.487)

4.10.3  *Providential history*                              166

4.10.4  *Apocalyptic: the oracle of Baalbek*               166
        *THE ORACLE OF BAALBEK*, LINES 136–227

4.10.5  *Arabs in apocalyptic vision*                       168
        *APOCALYPSE OF PSEUDO-METHODIUS*, "CHILDREN OF
        ISHMAEL," 11.1–15

**4.11    Reading the Bible**                               **169**

4.11.1  *Translating the Bible*                             169
        AUGUSTINE, *LETTER* 71

4.11.2  *Pope Gregory explains the Bible*                   171
        POPE GREGORY I, *MORALIA* 20.1.1

| | | |
|---|---|---|
| 4.11.3 | *Teaching the Bible through paintings in church* | 171 |
| | PAULINUS OF NOLA, *CARMINA* XXVII, 512–95 | |
| | *Further reading* | 172 |
| **5** | **Polytheism** | **174** |
| **5.1** | **Introduction** | **174** |
| **5.2** | **Varieties of religious experience** | **175** |
| 5.2.1 | *A prayer to Hecate* | 175 |
| | HYMN TO SELENE-HECATE ARTEMIS FROM A GREEK MAGICAL HANDBOOK | |
| 5.2.2 | *Divination* | 175 |
| | SORTES SANGALLENSES 6, 14, 54, 57–60, 88, 106–7 | |
| 5.2.3 | *Oracles* | 178 |
| | AMMIANUS MARCELLINUS, *HISTORY* 29.1.29–32 | |
| 5.2.4 | *The cult of Isis* | 179 |
| | FIRMICUS MATERNUS, *THE ERROR OF THE PAGAN RELIGIONS* 2.3–6 | |
| 5.2.5 | *The mysteries of Attis* | 180 |
| | FIRMICUS MATERNUS, *THE ERROR OF THE PAGAN RELIGIONS* 22 | |
| 5.2.6 | *Sacrificing a bull to Mithras* | 180 |
| | CORPUS OF LATIN INSCRIPTIONS 6.510; H. DESSAU, INSCRIPTIONES LATINAE SELECTAE II 1 (1902) NO. 4152 | |
| 5.2.7 | *The art and effects of prayer* | 181 |
| | IAMBLICHUS, *ON THE MYSTERIES* 5.26 | |
| 5.2.8 | *The importance of sacrifice* | 182 |
| | SALLUSTIUS, *CONCERNING THE GODS AND THE UNIVERSE* 15, 16 | |
| 5.2.9 | *Worship in the countryside* | 183 |
| | MAXIMUS OF TURIN, *SERMON* 107 | |
| 5.2.10 | *The end of the Secular Games* | 183 |
| | ZOSIMUS, *NEW HISTORY* 2.7 | |
| 5.2.11 | *Manichaeism* | 183 |
| | PRAYER OF THE EMANATIONS | |

5.2.12   *Imperial edict against Manichaeism*                              185
         COMPARISON OF MOSAIC AND ROMAN LAW 15.3

**5.3**    **Suppression of polytheism**                                   **186**

5.3.1    *Roman legislation against polytheist practices*                  186
         JUSTINIAN, *CODE* I.11.1–2, 4–7; *THEODOSIAN CODE*
         16.10.4, 9, 17, 20, 24

5.3.2    *Christian resentment of pagan sacrifice*                         188
         SHENUTE, *OPEN LETTER TO A PAGAN NOTABLE*

5.3.3    *Destroying the temples*                                          189
         ZACHARIAH, BISHOP OF MITYLENE, *LIFE OF SEVERUS*
         27–35

5.3.4    *Churches built on pagan sites: the temple of Zeus Marnas*
         *in Gaza*                                                         189
         MARK THE DEACON, *LIFE OF PORPHYRY* 75–6, 78

5.3.5    *Saint Nicholas chops down sacred trees*                          190
         *THE LIFE OF SAINT NICHOLAS OF SION* 15, 16, 18

5.3.6    *"Pagan" residues*                                               192
         POPE LEO I, *SERMON* 27.4

5.3.7    *Non-religious festivals suppressed*                              192
         COUNCIL "IN TRULLO" (691–692), CANON 62

**5.4**    **Difficulties of conversion**                                  **193**

5.4.1    *Neither pagan nor Christian*                                     193
         JOHN OF EPHESUS, *LIFE OF SIMEON THE MOUNTAINEER*

5.4.2    *Tell your peasants what to do*                                   193
         POPE GREGORY THE GREAT, *LETTER* 423

5.4.3    *Conversion, class, and coercion*                                 194
         POPE GREGORY THE GREAT, *LETTER* 9.204

5.4.4    *Mass conversions as imperial policy*                             194
         JOHN OF EPHESUS, *ECCLESIASTICAL HISTORY* (FRAGMENT)

5.4.5    *Purge of intellectuals at Constantinople*                        195
         JOHN OF EPHESUS, *ECCLESIASTICAL HISTORY* (FRAGMENT)

5.4.6    *Polytheists fight back*                                          195
         AUGUSTINE, *LETTER* 50

*5.4.7*   *Julian the Apostate and the Antiochenes*          196
          AMMIANUS MARCELLINUS, *HISTORY* 22.14.3

*5.4.8*   *Angry at the monks*                                197
          LIBANIUS, *ORATION* 30 8–11, "FOR THE TEMPLES"

*5.4.9*   *Obstacles to travel*                               198
          MARK THE DEACON, *LIFE OF PORPHYRY, BISHOP OF
          GAZA* 17

*5.4.10*  *Resistance in North Africa*                        198
          AUGUSTINE, *LETTER* 91

*5.4.11*  *The Altar of Victory dispute*                      199
          SYMMACHUS, *OFFICIAL DISPATCH* 3.8–10

          *Further reading*                                   200

**6**     **Jews**                                            **201**
**6.1**   **Introduction**                                    **201**
**6.2**   **Discrimination against Jews in Roman law**        **202**

*6.2.1*   *Jews may not circumcise Christian slaves*          202
          *THEODOSIAN CODE* 16.9.1 [JUSTINIAN, *CODE* 1.10.1]

*6.2.2*   *Jews and Christians may not marry one another*     202
          *THEODOSIAN CODE* 3.7.2 [JUSTINIAN, *CODE* 1.9.5]

*6.2.3*   *Christians may not become Jews*                    202
          *THEODOSIAN CODE* 16.8.7 [JUSTINIAN, *CODE* 1.7.1]

*6.2.4*   *Trials in Jewish courts*                           203
          *THEODOSIAN CODE* 2.1.10

*6.2.5*   *Jews allowed in municipal senates*                 203
          *THEODOSIAN CODE* 16.8.3

*6.2.6*   *Should translations of the Bible be used in synagogue
          worship?*                                           203
          JUSTINIAN, *NOVEL* 146, PREAMBLE

*6.2.7*   *Discrimination in church law*                      204
          ELVIRA CHURCH COUNCIL, *CANONS* 16, 49, 50

*6.2.8*   *Imperial protection of the Jewish community:
          synagogues and property rights*                    205
          *THEODOSIAN CODE* 16.8.20 [JUSTINIAN, *CODE* 1.9.10.13]

6.2.9    *The State reserves the right of punishment for itself*                    205
         THEODOSIAN CODE 16.8.21 [JUSTINIAN, *CODE* 1.9.10.14]

6.2.10   *Ambrose challenges the emperor: the Callinicum affair*                    205
         AMBROSE, *LETTER* 40 1, 2, 6, 10, 13, 20, 21

6.2.11   *Julian and the temple in Jerusalem*                                       207
         JULIAN, *LETTER* 51, "TO THE COMMUNITY OF THE JEWS"

**6.3**      **Christian justification of anti-Jewish behavior**                        **208**

6.3.1    *What did Jews do wrong in Christian eyes?*                                 208
         AUGUSTINE, *CITY OF GOD* 4.34

6.3.2    *Christian attraction to Judaism is condemned*                             208
         JOHN CHRYSOSTOM, *HOMILY AGAINST THE JEWS* 1.3, 1.5

6.3.3    *Forced conversion*                                                        209
         SEVERUS OF MINORCA, *LETTER ON THE CONVERSION*
         *OF THE JEWS* 3.6–7, 6.1–4, 13.1–14, 24.1.10, 30. 1–2

6.3.4    *Disappointment with a false Messiah – and conversion*                     211
         SOCRATES SCHOLASTICUS, *ECCLESIASTICAL HISTORY* 38

6.3.5    *Conversion to Islam*                                                      212
         IBN HISHAM, *BIOGRAPHY OF MUHAMMAD*, VOL. 1, 516–17

**6.4**      **Jewish resistance**                                                      **213**

6.4.1    *Jewish anger at converts*                                                 214
         THEODOSIAN CODE 16.8.1

6.4.2    *Destruction of the symbols of persecution*                               214
         THEODOSIAN CODE 16.8.18

6.4.3    *Jews defend Naples in 535*                                                214
         PROCOPIUS, *HISTORY OF THE WARS* 5.8.41–3, 10.24–6

6.4.4    *Jews help the Persians take Jerusalem*                                    215
         ANTIOCHUS STRATEGOS, *THE SACK OF JERUSALEM*

**6.5**      **Daily life in Jewish communities**                                       **216**

6.5.1    *Self-government*                                                          216
         THE BABYLONIAN TALMUD, SANHEDRIN 4B–5A

6.5.2    *Jews lose self-government: the end of the patriarchate*                   216
         THEODOSIAN CODE 16.8.29 [JUSTINIAN, *CODE* 1.9 16]

6.5.3   Education                                                          217
        THE JERUSALEM TALMUD, HAGIGAH 1.7.76C

6.5.4   Interpreting the Law                                               217
        THE BABYLONIAN TALMUD, YEBAMOTH 15, 114B

6.5.5   Sabbath worship at sea                                             218
        SYNESIUS OF CYRENE, LETTER 4, "TO HIS BROTHER"

6.5.6   Legal differences between men and women, c.500                     219
        THE BABYLONIAN TALMUD, KIDDUSHIN 29 A–B

6.5.7   Public lives of women                                              220
        APAMAEA SYNAGOGUE FLOOR MOSAIC INSCRIPTION

6.5.8   Hebrew liturgy in synagogues                                       220
        ELEAZAR BEN KALLIR, BATTLE BETWEEN BEHEMOTH
        AND LEVIATHAN

6.5.9   Mourning the destruction of the Temple                             221
        ANONYMOUS, DIRGE FOR THE NINTH OF AV

6.5.10  Jews in the Islamic world                                          222
        QURAN, SURAS 9.29, 5.51

        Further reading                                                    222

7       Women                                                              224
7.1     Introduction                                                       224
7.2     Powerful women                                                     224

7.2.1   Helena – empress and Church benefactor                             224
        SOZOMEN, ECCLESIASTICAL HISTORY 2.2

7.2.2   The empress refuses to panic: Theodora during the
        Nika Riot                                                          225
        PROCOPIUS, HISTORY OF THE WARS 1.24.32–8

7.2.3   Aristocratic female virtues                                        226
        CORPUS OF LATIN INSCRIPTIONS, 6.1755, ROME

7.2.4   Death of a scholar: Hypatia of Alexandria                          226
        DAMASCIUS, LIFE OF ISIDORE, FRAGMENT 102

7.3     Christianity and women                                            227

7.3.1   Olympias – aristocratic habits and spiritual values               227
        THE LIFE OF OLYMPIAS 2, 5

7.3.2   *The generosity and leadership of Melania the Younger*          228
        LIFE OF MELANIA THE YOUNGER 22, 23, 30, 35

7.3.3   *Defying family expectations in Ireland*          229
        SAINT PATRICK, *DECLARATION* 42

7.3.4   *Saint Pelagia the Harlot: sin and salvation*          230
        THE LIFE OF SAINT PELAGIA THE HARLOT 4–7, 18, 20–6, 53

7.3.5   *Tarbo, a Christian martyr in Persia*          232
        PERSIAN MARTYRS, "THE MARTYRDOM OF TARBO,
        HER SISTER, AND HER SERVANT," 254–60

**7.4**     **Male attitudes**          **235**

7.4.1   *Daughters of Eve*          235
        AMBROSE, *COMMENTARY ON PAUL'S FIRST LETTER TO*
        *THE CORINTHIANS* 148

7.4.2   *The pain of abandoning a concubine*          236
        AUGUSTINE, *CONFESSIONS* 6.15.25
        AUGUSTINE, *THE GOOD IN MARRIAGE* 5.5.376–7

**7.5**     **Legal status**          **237**

7.5.1   *Women's right to prosecute in court*          237
        THEODOSIAN CODE 9.1.3

7.5.2   *The new status of celibacy*          237
        THEODOSIAN CODE 8.16.1

7.5.3   *Protecting women*          237
        THEODOSIAN CODE 15.8.2 [JUSTINIAN, *CODE* 11.40.6]

7.5.4   *Legitimacy and inheritance*          238
        JUSTINIAN, *CODE* 6.57.5

7.5.5   *Women benefit from Roman law*          238
        JUSTINIAN, *NOVEL* 21.1

        *Further reading*          239

**8**       **Domestic life**          **240**
**8.1**     **Introduction**          **240**
**8.2**     **Sexuality, procreation, and birth**          **240**

8.2.1   *Sexual intercourse*          240
        AUGUSTINE, *ON CHRIST'S GRACE AND ORIGINAL SIN*
        2.38.43

| | | |
|---|---|---|
| 8.2.2 | *Conception* | 241 |
| | NEMESIUS OF EMESA, *ON THE NATURE OF MAN* 25 | |
| 8.2.3 | *Abortion and contraception* | 241 |
| | CAESARIUS OF ARLES, *SERMON* 44.2 | |
| 8.2.4 | *Childbirth's pains* | 242 |
| | EPHREM THE SYRIAN, *HYMN ON PARADISE* 8.8 | |
| 8.2.5 | *Women's bodies and bearing children* | 242 |
| | PSEUDO-ATHANASIUS, *LIFE OF SYNCLETICA* 42 | |
| 8.2.6 | *Naming a baby girl* | 242 |
| | *MILITARY PAPYRUS* 2.84 | |
| 8.2.7 | *Exposure of unwanted infants* | 243 |
| | JUSTINIAN, *DIGEST* 25.3.4 | |
| | BASIL OF CAESAREA, *LETTER* 199.33 | |
| **8.3** | **Children** | **243** |
| 8.3.1 | *Raising abandoned children* | 243 |
| | *THEODOSIAN CODE* 5.9.1 | |
| 8.3.2 | *Parents prevented from selling their children* | 243 |
| | *THEODOSIAN CODE* 11.27.2 | |
| 8.3.3 | *Girls* | 244 |
| | JEROME, *LETTER* 128 | |
| 8.3.4 | *The benefits of beating children* | 245 |
| | AUGUSTINE, *LETTER* 104, PL 33 | |
| 8.3.5 | *A father's care for his son's education* | 245 |
| | SYMMACHUS, *LETTER* 3.20 | |
| 8.3.6 | *A teenager's love of learning* | 245 |
| | LIBANIUS, *AUTOBIOGRAPHY* 4, 5, 8, 19, 21, 22 | |
| 8.3.7 | *A grandfather's advice about study and relaxation* | 247 |
| | AUSONIUS, *EPISTLES* 22 | |
| **8.4** | **Marriage and divorce** | **248** |
| 8.4.1 | *Adolescence and betrothal* | 248 |
| | GREGORY OF NYSSA, *VITA MACRINAE* 4–5 | |
| 8.4.2 | *Aristocratic courtship* | 249 |
| | JEROME, *LETTER* 127 | |

*8.4.3*  *Penalties for failing to marry are abolished*   249
THEODOSIAN CODE 8.16.1

*8.4.4*  *Astrology and different sorts of marriage*   250
FIRMICUS MATERNUS, *MATHESIS* 7.14

*8.4.5*  *Betrothal*   251
THEODOSIAN CODE 3.5.1

*8.4.6*  *Prenuptial agreements*   251
JOHN CHRYSOSTOM, *PATROLOGIA GRAECA* 51, 226–7

*8.4.7*  *Dowry*   251
THE DOWRY OF GEMINIA JANUARILLA

*8.4.8*  *Traditional wedding ceremonies*   252
JOHN CHRYSOSTOM, *SERMON ON MARRIAGE*

*8.4.9*  *Forbidden marriage*   252
THEODOSIAN CODE 3.12.1–2

*8.4.10*  *Adultery*   253
THEODOSIAN CODE 9.7.1

*8.4.11*  *A husband returns from captivity*   253
POPE LEO I, *EPISTLE* 159.1–4

*8.4.12*  *A wife returns from captivity*   255
POPE INNOCENT I, *EPISTLE 36 (PATROLOGIA LATINA* 30: 602–3)

*8.4.13*  *Marriage and divorce*   255
JUSTINIAN, *NOVEL* 22.3–7

*8.4.14*  *Women's right to divorce*   257
THEODOSIAN CODE 3.16.1

*8.4.15*  *A father decides for his daughter*   257
OXYRHYNCHUS PAPYRUS I.129 (6TH CENTURY)

*8.4.16*  *Jerome defends a woman who decides to divorce*   258
JEROME, *LETTER* 77.2–3

*8.5*  ***Life in the Roman household***   ***259***

*8.5.1*  *Slaves in the household*   259
OXYRHYNCHUS PAPYRUS VI.939 (4TH CENTURY)

*8.5.2*  *Responsibilities of the wife of a Roman senator*   260
ANONYMOUS, *TO GREGORIA* 18

8.5.3    *Female modesty, rings, and the household*    261
CLEMENT OF ALEXANDRIA, *PAEDAGOGUS* 3.11

8.5.4    *Mother–daughter tensions in the same household*    262
JEROME, *LETTER* 117

8.5.5    *The married life of Augustine's parents*    262
AUGUSTINE, *CONFESSIONS* 9.9.19

8.5.6    *Mothers-in-law*    263
*PRIVATE LETTER*

**8.6**    **The house itself**    **264**

8.6.1    *Farmhouse*    264
ILLUSTRATION: FARMHOUSE AT HORVAT SUSIYA

8.6.2    *Townhouse*    265
ILLUSTRATION: TOWNHOUSE IN THE CITY OF PERGAMON

8.6.3    *Mansion*    265
ILLUSTRATION: MANSION IN THUBURBO MAIUS

8.6.4    *Villa*    265
ILLUSTRATION: LULLINGSTONE VILLA

8.6.5    *Buying a house*    268
AMBROSE, *ON PSALM 118 EXPOSITIO SERMO 13, LITTERA* "MEM" 7

8.6.6    *Amulet to protect a house*    268
OXYRHYNCHUS PAPYRUS 1060

8.6.7    *The sign of the cross, an emblem of protection*    269
JOHN CHRYSOSTOM, *AGAINST JEWS AND NON-CHRISTIANS* 9
*LINTEL OF A HOUSE IN SYRIA*

8.6.8    *Household gods*    269
AUGUSTINE, *CITY OF GOD* 4.11

**8.7**    **The end of life**    **270**

8.7.1    *The problems of old age*    270
MAXIMIAN, *ELEGIACS* 1.1–16, 153–66, 191–204, 279–92

8.7.2    *The will of Gregory of Nazianzus*    272
GREGORY OF NAZIANZUS, *WILL*

8.7.3    *The death and funeral of Proclus the Philosopher*    275
MARINUS, *LIFE OF PROCLUS* 36–7

8.7.4    *Christian funerals*                                      276
         *APOSTOLIC CONSTITUTIONS* 6.30.2
         JEROME, *LETTER* 77.11

8.7.5    *Burials and grave inscriptions*                          277
         *A MOTHER'S GRIEF*
         *THE GRAVE OF A PAGAN COUPLE*
         *A CHRISTIAN EPITAPH*

8.7.6    *Remembering the dead*                                    280
         AUSONIUS, *PARENTALIA* 1, 9, 10

8.7.7    *What next? The afterlife in Late Antiquity*              282
         *EPITAPH*
         EPHREM THE SYRIAN, *HYMN ON PARADISE* VIII, VERSES
         2, 3, 4, 7, 11

         *Further reading*                                        284

**9       Law**                                                  **285**
**9.1    *Introduction***                                        **285**

9.1.1    *What is law?*                                           285
         JUSTINIAN, *INSTITUTES* 1.1

9.1.2    *Legal education*                                        286
         JUSTINIAN, *DIGEST, THE WHOLE BODY OF LAW* 1–2, 6–7

9.1.3    *A hostile view of lawyers*                              287
         AMMIANUS MARCELLINUS, *HISTORY* 30.4.9–11, 13–15, 19

9.1.4    *Judges must be supervised*                              289
         *THEODOSIAN CODE* 1.5.9

9.1.5    *The right of appeal*                                    289
         *THEODOSIAN CODE* 1.5.1

9.1.6    *Law courts closed on Sunday*                            289
         *THEODOSIAN CODE* 2.8.1

9.1.7    *Codifications and reform*                               290
         JUSTINIAN, *CODE*, "THE FIRST PREFACE"

9.1.8    *Jurisprudence*                                          290
         JUSTINIAN, *DIGEST* 4, 12

| | | |
|---|---|---|
| **9.2** | **Christianity and the law** | **291** |
| *9.2.1* | *Why is legislation always necessary?* | 291 |
| | JUSTINIAN, *NOVEL* 84, PREFACE (539) | |
| | JUSTINIAN, *NOVEL* 73, PREFACE (538) | |
| *9.2.2* | *Local law dies out* | 292 |
| | JUSTINIAN, *NOVEL* 21 | |
| *9.2.3* | *The comparison of Roman and Mosaic law* | 293 |
| | THE COMPARISON OF ROMAN AND MOSAIC LAW 15 | |
| *9.2.4* | *The Syro-Roman Law Book* | 294 |
| | THE SYRO-ROMAN LAW BOOK, INTRODUCTION | |
| **9.3** | **Torture** | **295** |
| | AUGUSTINE, *CITY OF GOD AGAINST THE PAGANS*, 19.6 | |
| | *Further reading* | 296 |
| **10** | **Medicine** | **297** |
| **10.1** | **Introduction** | **297** |
| **10.2** | **The medical profession** | **297** |
| *10.2.1* | *What is medicine?* | 297 |
| | ISIDORE OF SEVILLE, *ON MEDICINE* 1.1–2; 4.1–2; 5.2–3; 9.1, 2, 3, 5; 13.1–5 | |
| *10.2.2* | *Medical experience vs. received opinion* | 299 |
| | ALEXANDER OF TRALLES, *ON VISCOUS HUMORS AND THICK MASSES FOUND IN THE LUNG* 5, 4 | |
| *10.2.3* | *A great physician* | 300 |
| | EUNAPIUS OF SARDIS, *LIVES OF THE PHILOSOPHERS (IONICUS)* 499.2–3 | |
| *10.2.4* | *Military physicians* | 300 |
| | AMMIANUS MARCELLINUS, *HISTORY* 19.2.15 | |
| *10.2.5* | *Faith healing* | 301 |
| | GREGORY OF TOURS, *THE MIRACLE OF SAINT MARTIN* 2.1, 4.36 | |
| *10.2.6* | *A medical specialist* | 301 |
| | GEORGE THE MONK, *LIFE OF THEODORE OF SYKEON* 145–6 | |

**10.3**    ***Care of the sick and cures***                                302

10.3.1   *Hospitals*                                                          302
         THE LIFE AND VIRTUES OF THE HOLY BISHOP MASONA
         5.3.2–9

10.3.2   *House calls*                                                        303
         THE DEATH AND MIRACLES OF THE BISHOPS OF MERIDA
         4.2.6–13

10.3.3   *Baths*                                                              304
         PAUL OF AEGINA, THE SEVEN BOOKS OF PAUL OF AEGINA,
         VOL. 1, SECTION 51, "ON BATHS"

10.3.4   *Magical healing*                                                    304
         SEFER HA-RAZIM [BOOK OF MYSTERIES] 1.28–3.4

10.3.5   *Dieting*                                                            305
         CAELIUS AURELIANUS, ON ACUTE DISEASES AND CHRONIC
         DISEASES 11.129, 132–8

**10.4**    ***Plague***                                                     307

10.4.1   *The Great Plague*                                                   307
         EVAGRIUS, ECCLESIASTICAL HISTORY 29

10.4.2   *The Plague strikes Constantinople*                                  308
         PROCOPIUS, HISTORY OF THE WARS 2.22–23.1

10.4.3   *Plague in Gaul*                                                     309
         GREGORY OF TOURS, THE HISTORY OF THE FRANKS 5.34

10.4.4   *Farmers avoid plague-ridden cities*                                 309
         THE LIFE OF SAINT NICHOLAS OF SION 52

         *Further reading*                                                    310

**11**      **Philosophy**                                                   311
**11.1**    **Introduction**                                                311

11.1.1   *Plotinus and "the One"*                                             311
         PLOTINUS, ENNEAD 5.4.1.5–16

11.1.2   *The three hypostases: the One, Nous, and Soul*                      312
         PLOTINUS, ENNEAD 5.2.1

11.1.3   *A philosophical life*                                               312
         PORPHYRY, ON THE LIFE OF PLOTINUS AND THE ORDER
         OF HIS BOOKS 1, 9

*11.1.4*  *Intellectual beauty and contemplation*  313
PLOTINUS, *ENNEAD* 5.8.4

*11.1.5*  *Julian's Hymn to Helios, god of the sun*  314
JULIAN, *HYMN TO KING HELIOS, DEDICATED TO SALLUST*
130, 132, 133
JULIAN, *HYMN TO THE MOTHER OF THE GODS* 180

*11.1.6*  *Pythagoras, the guide*  315
IAMBLICHUS, *THE EXHORTATION TO PHILOSOPHY* 1

*11.1.7*  *The art of theurgy*  316
IAMBLICHUS, *ON THE MYSTERIES* 2.12, 5.23

*11.1.8*  *The life and education of Proclus*  317
MARINOS OF NEAPOLIS, *LIFE OF PROCLUS* 8–13, 19, 21, 29

*11.1.9*  *Athenian philosophers go to Persia*  319
AGATHIAS, *THE HISTORIES* 2.30.3–7, 2.31.1–4

*11.1.10* *Philoponus and the creation of the world*  320
SIMPLICIUS, *ON THE HEAVENS* 119.7–9

*11.1.11* *The consolation of philosophy*  321
BOETHIUS, *THE CONSOLATION OF PHILOSOPHY* 1.2–3, 1.6–7

*11.1.12* *Martianus Capella on the shape of the universe*  324
MARTIANUS CAPELLA, *THE MARRIAGE OF PHILOLOGY
AND MERCURY* 8.814

*11.1.13* *Macrobius on the descent of the soul*  325
MACROBIUS, *COMMENTARY ON THE DREAM OF SCIPIO*
1.12.1–2, 4, 7, 9, 16, 17

*Further reading*  326

**12**   **Sasanian Persia**  **327**
*12.1*   *Introduction*  *327*

*12.1.1*  *The ideal Sasanian monarch*  327
*TANSAR'S LETTER TO GUSHNASP* 1–3, 12–13, 22–3, 27, 44

*12.1.2*  *The Zoroastrian creed*  330
*THE BOOK OF THE COUNSEL OF ZARTUSHT* 2–8

*12.1.3*  *The struggle of light and darkness*  331
*GREATER CREATION* 1.1–39

| | | |
|---|---|---|
| 12.1.4 | *A trip to Hell and Heaven* | 332 |
| | ARDA VIRAZ, *A VISION OF HEAVEN AND HELL* 6.3.8–12, 15, 18 | |
| 12.1.5 | *Expansion of Zoroastrianism* | 334 |
| | INSCRIPTION OF KIRDIR AT THE KAABA OF ZOROASTER, LINES 11–13 | |
| 12.1.6 | *Christians in Roman–Persian negotiations* | 335 |
| | EUSEBIUS, *LIFE OF CONSTANTINE* 4.8–13 | |
| 12.1.7 | *Julian's fatal invasion of Mesopotamia* | 336 |
| | AMMIANUS MARCELLINUS, *HISTORY* 24.7.1, 3–6 | |
| 12.1.8 | *The Persians sack Amida* | 336 |
| | ZACHARIAH OF MITYLENE, *SYRIAC CHRONICLE* 7.3–4 | |
| 12.1.9 | *The reforms of Khusro Anushirwan* | 338 |
| | IBN MISKAWAYH, *THE EXPERIENCES OF THE NATIONS* | |
| 12.1.10 | *An Armenian obituary of Khusro* | 339 |
| | *KHUSRO'S OBITUARY* | |
| 12.1.11 | *Huns: a common enemy* | 340 |
| | PROCOPIUS, *HISTORY OF THE WARS* 2.10.19–24 | |
| 12.1.12 | *Justinian breaks Persia's silk monopoly* | 340 |
| | PROCOPIUS, *HISTORY OF THE WARS* 8.17.1–8 | |
| 12.1.13 | *Roman hostility in the later sixth century* | 341 |
| | AGATHIAS, *THE HISTORIES* 2.24.5, 2.25.3 | |
| 12.1.14 | *The siege of Constantinople in 626* | 341 |
| | *EASTER CHRONICLE* (AD 626) | |
| 12.1.15 | *Heraclius triumphant* | 342 |
| | *EASTER CHRONICLE* (AD 628) | |
| 12.1.16 | *The Cross restored to Jerusalem* | 343 |
| | THEOPHANES, *CHRONICLE* (AM 6120) | |
| | *Further reading* | 344 |
| **13** | **Invaders and successor states** | **345** |
| *13.1* | *Introduction* | *345* |
| 13.1.1 | *Early Visigothic communities* | 346 |
| | *THE PASSION OF SAINT SABA* 3.3–5 | |

*13.1.2 Adrianople: an unexpected catastrophe in 378*
AMMIANUS MARCELLINUS, *HISTORY* 31.4.1–6
346

*13.1.3 Destruction of Visigothic draftees*
AMMIANUS MARCELLINUS, *HISTORY* 31.16.8
347

*13.1.4 Visigothic quarrels*
ZOSIMUS, *NEW HISTORY* 4.56
348

*13.1.5 Improving relations with Rome*
OROSIUS, *HISTORY AGAINST THE PAGANS* 7.43
348

*13.1.6 Settlement of the Goths in Aquitania*
PAULINUS OF PELLA, *EUCHARISTICUS* 564–81
349

*13.1.7 A Frankish prince*
SIDONIUS APOLLINARIS, *LETTER* 4.20
350

*13.1.8 An Italian ambassador at the Visigothic court*
ENNODIUS, *LIFE OF SAINT EPIPHANIUS*
351

*13.1.9 How strange to learn "German"!*
SIDONIUS, *LETTER* 5.5
352

*13.1.10 Romans deserve their fate! The interpretation of
Salvian of Marseilles*
SALVIAN, *ON THE GOVERNANCE OF GOD* 5.4–7
353

*13.1.11 Theoderic's wise rule in Italy*
THE ANONYMUS VALESIANUS 12.65–7, 69–73
354

*13.1.12 Theoderic's New World Order*
CASSIODORUS, *VARIAE* III.3
CASSIODORUS, *VARIAE* III.4
355

*13.1.13 Tensions of acculturation*
PROCOPIUS, *HISTORY OF THE WARS* 5.2.6–19
356

*13.1.14 Care for the Roman legacy*
CASSIODORUS, *OFFICIAL CORRESPONDENCE* 3.9
357

*13.1.15 Vandalism*
VICTOR OF VITA, *HISTORY OF THE PERSECUTION IN THE
PROVINCE OF AFRICA*, "THE CHARITY OF DEOGRATIAS,
BISHOP OF CARTHAGE, TO THE CAPTIVES BROUGHT
FROM ROME BY THE VANDALS," 1.24–6
358

*13.1.16* *Saint Severinus – hero of a crumbling frontier*     359
EUGIPPIUS, *THE LIFE OF SAINT SEVERINUS* 24.1, 4.1–5

*13.1.17* *The end of Roman Britain*     360
GILDAS, *ON THE RUIN OF BRITAIN* 24

*13.1.18* *"Barbarian" law codes*     361
THE BURGUNDIAN CODE, PREFACE 1, 2, 3, 8, 13; 2.1, 2

*13.1.19* *The rise of the Franks*     362
GREGORY OF TOURS, *THE HISTORY OF THE FRANKS* 2.27

*13.1.20* *Venantius Fortunatus*     363
VENANTIUS FORTUNATUS *POEMS*

**13.2** **Ethnogenesis: Where and how did ancient peoples come into being?**     **366**

*13.2.1* *The origin of the Goths*     367
JORDANES, *THE GOTHIC HISTORY*, 4.25–29

*13.2.2* *Maintaining tribal identity*     367
PROCOPIUS, *HISTORY OF THE WARS*, 7.2.1–3

*13.2.3* *A view of the Franks from Constantinople*     368
AGATHIAS, *HISTORIES*, I.2.1; 1.2.3–4

*13.2.4* *What gives different peoples their distinguishing characteristics?*     368
ISIDORE OF SEVILLE, *ETYMOLOGIES* 9.2.105

*Further reading*     369

**14** **Steppe peoples and Slavs**     **371**
**14.1** **Introduction**     **371**
**14.2** **Huns**     **371**

*14.2.1* *Huns: unknown and terrible invaders*     371
AMMIANUS MARCELLINUS, *HISTORY* 31.2.1–12

*14.2.2* *Attila at home*     373
PRISCUS, *FRAGMENT* 11.2

*14.2.3* *Attila looks west*     376
GREGORY OF TOURS, *THE HISTORY OF THE FRANKS* 2.6–7

*14.2.4* *Why didn't Attila sack Rome?*     377
PROSPER, *EPITOMA CHRONICON* FOR THE YEAR 452

14.2.5   *A war of images*                                               377
PRISCUS, *FRAGMENT* 22.3

14.2.6   *The death and burial of Attila*                                 377
PRISCUS, *FRAGMENT* 24.1

14.2.7   *After Attila's death*                                           378
JORDANES, *GETICA L*, 261 = PRISCUS FR. 25

14.2.8   *Hun raiding in the Middle East*                                 379
THE BOOK OF CALIPHS (*CSCO SCRIPT. SYR.* SER. 3, VOL. 4.2,
LEIPZIG, 1904), 106

14.2.9   *Huns force Romans and Persians to co-operate*                  379
PROCOPIUS, *HISTORY OF THE WARS* 2.10.19–24

14.2.10 *Conversion of Huns and imperial ritual*                         380
NIKEPHOROS, *SHORT HISTORY AFTER THE REIGN OF
MAURICE* 9

**14.3**     ***Avars***                                                 380

14.3.1   *Characteristics of Avar society*                               381
MAURICE, *TREATISE ON STRATEGY* 11.2

14.3.2   *Avars at the Byzantine court*                                   381
FLAVIUS CRESCONIUS CORIPPUS, *IN PRAISE OF JUSTIN 11*,
3.191–270

14.3.3   *Persians and Avars attack Constantinople*                      383
NIKEPHOROS, *SHORT HISTORY AFTER THE REIGN OF
MAURICE* 13

**14.4**     ***Turks***                                                 **383**

14.4.1   *An embassy to the Turks*                                        383
MENANDER THE GUARDSMAN, *FRAGMENT* 19.1

**14.5**     ***Slavs***                                                 **385**

14.5.1   *A glimpse of early Slavic society*                             385
MAURICE, *TREATISE ON STRATEGY* 11.4

*Further reading*                                                        386

| | | |
|---|---|---|
| **15** | **Islam** | **387** |
| *15.1* | *Introduction* | *387* |
| *15.2* | *Arabs before Islam* | *387* |

*15.2.1*  *Pre-Islamic oral poetry: a death lament*   387
AL-KHANSA, "LAMENT FOR A BROTHER"

*15.2.2*  *Warrior virtues*   388
QAIS IBN AL-KHATIM, "THE DAY OF BU'ATH"

*15.2.3*  *Arab allies of dangerous superpowers*   389
PROCOPIUS, *HISTORY OF THE WARS*, "AL-MUNDHIR
(ALAMOUNDARAS)," 1.17.40–7

*15.2.4*  *Arabian religion before Islam*   390
IBN AL-KALBI, *THE BOOK OF IDOLS* 3–23

*15.3*  *Muhammad and the Quran*   *391*

*15.3.1*  *God and His praise*   391
QURAN, SURA 1.1–7, "THE OPENING" (REVEALED AT MECCA)

*15.3.2*  *God is transcendent*   392
QURAN, SURA 2.255, "THE COW" (REVEALED AT
AL-MADINAH)

*15.3.3*  *God's judgment*   392
QURAN, SURA 81.1–21, "THE OVERTHROWING" (REVEALED
AT MECCA)

*15.3.4*  *God's apostle*   393
QURAN, SURA 18.57–8, "THE CAVE" (REVEALED AT MECCA)

*15.3.5*  *A criticism of Christianity*   393
QURAN, SURA 112, "THE UNITY" (REVEALED AT MECCA)

*15.3.6*  *The prophetic tradition*   393
QURAN, SURA 3.84–5, "THE FAMILY OF IMRAN"

*15.3.7*  *God's message*   394
QURAN, SURA 10.38–9, "JONAH" (REVEALED AT MECCA)

*15.3.8*  *Rewards after death*   394
QURAN, SURA 29.57–8, "THE SPIDER"

*15.3.9*  *From oral tradition to written text: how the Quran was
assembled*   394
AL-BUKHARI, *SAHIH* 3.392–4

15.3.10  *Muhammad's ordinance for Medina*                          395
MUHAMMAD'S ORDINANCE FOR MEDINA

15.3.11  *The Pact of 'Umar*                                        396
AL-TURTUSHI, *SIRAJ AL-MULUK* 229–30

15.3.12  *Rules of war*                                             397
AL-TABARI, *THE HISTORY OF THE PROPHETS AND KINGS*
1.1850

15.3.13  *Substitute soldiers*                                      398
POEM ON THE CALL TO ARMS

15.3.14  *Conquest by treaty*                                       398
AL-BALADHURI, *THE BOOK OF THE CONQUEST OF THE
REGIONS*

15.3.15  *A Christian's explanation of Islam before the capture
of Jerusalem*                                                       399
SOPHRONIUS OF JERUSALEM, *SERMON ON THE EPIPHANY*

15.3.16  *Jerusalem surrenders, 636*                                399
AL-TABARI, *THE HISTORY OF THE PROPHETS AND KINGS*
1.2050

15.3.17  *A clear choice for Jews: Arabs welcomed to Hebron*        400
TREATISE ON THE RELICS OF THE PATRIARCHS AT HEBRON

15.3.18  *Christian collusion*                                      400
JOHN, BISHOP OF NIKIU, *THE CHRONICLE*, 120.17–28

15.3.19  *The new managers*                                         402
LETTER OF QORRA, GOVERNOR OF EGYPT

15.3.20  *Mosques, symbols of imperial power*                       402
AL-MUQADDASI, *THE BEST DIVISIONS FOR KNOWLEDGE
OF THE REGIONS*

15.3.21  *Arabic, the new administrative language*                  403
AL-BALADHURI, *THE BOOK OF THE CONQUESTS OF
THE REGIONS*

15.3.22  *Muslims reach Ethiopia*                                   403
IBN ISHAQ, *BIOGRAPHY OF MUHAMMAD*

15.3.23  *Islam in Samaritan eyes*                                  404
THE CONTINUATIO OF THE CHRONICLE OF ABU AL-FATH 1.1

*15.3.24 An early non-Muslim view of Muhammad*       405
      THE INSTRUCTION OF JACOB, WHO WAS RECENTLY BAPTIZED

*15.3.25 Disaster for the Romans*       406
      THEOPHANES, *CHRONICLE* AM 6121, 6122 (AD 628/9)

      *Further reading*       407

# MAPS

1 The world of Late Antiquity, *c.*300–*c.*400     xliv
2 The Roman Empire in Late Antiquity     xlv
3 Dioceses, prefectures and provinces of the Roman Empire
   according to the Notitia Dignitatum (about AD 425)     xlvi
4 The Roman Empire: approximate travel times and vine and
   olive cultivation     xlvii
5 The Eastern Mediterranean     xlviii
6 Northern Mesopotamia     xlix
7 City of Rome about AD 500: churches and public buildings     l
8 Constantinople     li
9 Jerusalem, AD 326–638     lii
10 Caesarea Maritima     liii
11 Palestine in the sixth century     liv
12 Empire of the Huns under Attila about 450     lv
   Empire of the Avars about 560     lv
13 Germanic kingdoms about AD 525     lvi
14 The Danube in the time of Severinus     lvii
15 The plague in the sixth century: first wave 541–544     lviii
   The plague in the sixth century: second wave 557–561;
   third wave 570–574     lviii
16 The Red Sea and Arabia before the rise of Islam     lix
17 The Mediterranean world and the expansion of Islam,
   about AD 700     lx
18 The Sasanian Empire     lxi

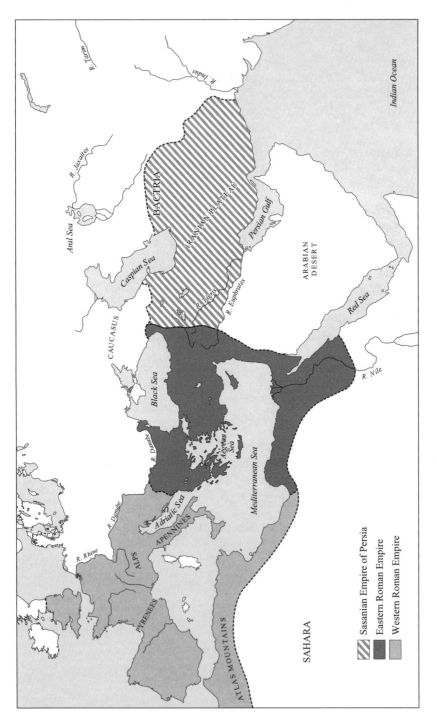

*Map 1* The world of Late Antiquity *c.*300–*c.*400

Sasanian Empire of Persia

Eastern Roman Empire

Western Roman Empire

R. Tarim

R. Indus

Indian Ocean

R. Jaxartes

BACTRIA

IRANIAN PLATEAU

Persian Gulf

Aral Sea

Caspian Sea

ARABIAN DESERT

R. Tigris

R. Euphrates

Red Sea

CAUCASUS

Black Sea

R. Nile

R. Danube

Aegean Sea

Mediterranean Sea

Adriatic Sea

APENNINES

R. Danube

ALPS

R. Rhine

PYRENEES

SAHARA

ATLAS MOUNTAINS

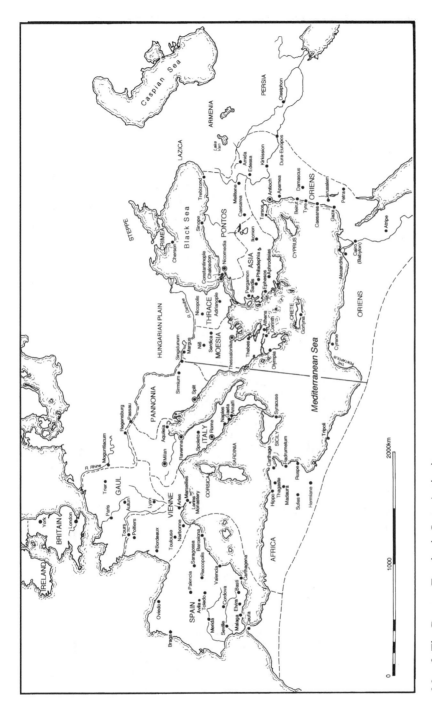

*Map 2* The Roman Empire in Late Antiquity

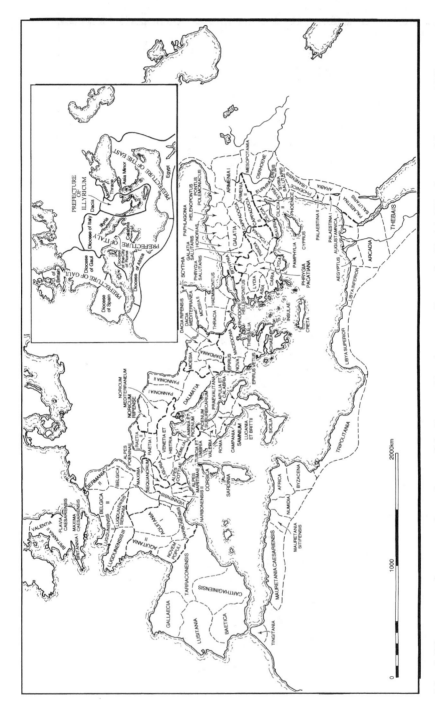

*Map 3* Dioceses, prefectures and provinces of the Roman Empire according to the Notitia Dignitatum (about AD 425)

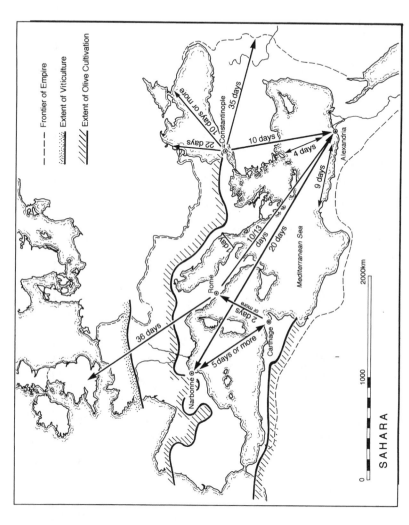

*Map 4*  The Roman Empire: approximate travel times and vine and olive cultivation

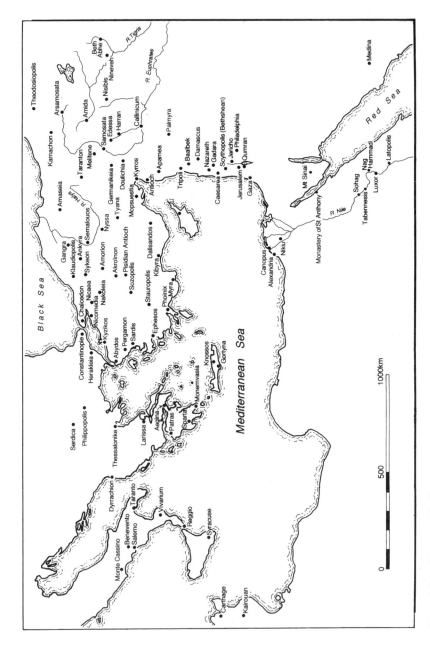

*Map 5* The Eastern Mediterranean

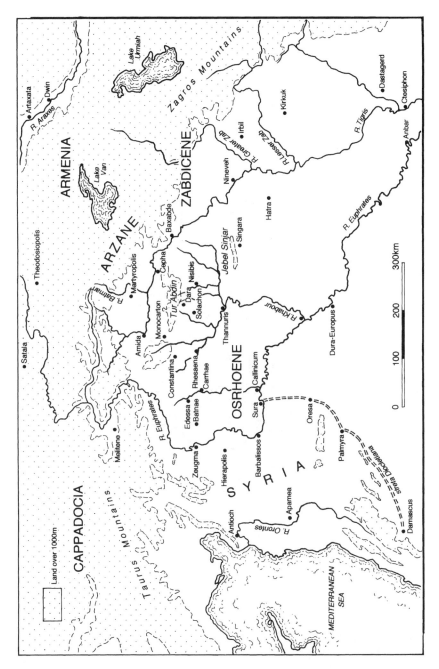

*Map 6* Northern Mesopotamia

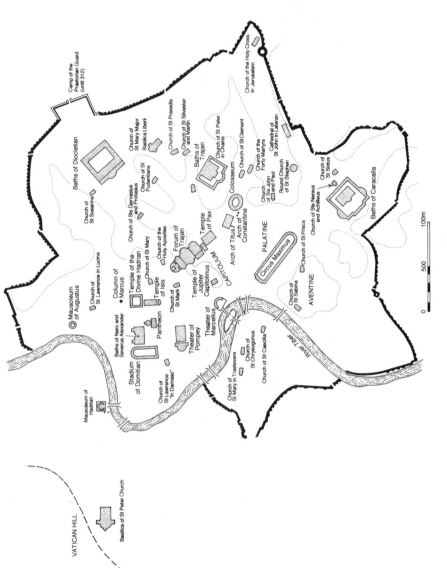

*Map 7* City of Rome about AD 500: churches and public buildings

VATICAN HILL

Basilica of St Peter Church

Mausoleum of Hadrian

Church of St Lawrence "in Damaso"

Stadium of Domitian

Pantheon

Baths of Nero and Severus Alexander

Church of St Lawrence in Lucina

Mausoleum of Augustus

Church of St Susanna

Baths of Diocletian

Camp of the Praetorian Guard (until 312)

Column of Marcus

Temple of the Divine Hadrian

Church of St Mary

Church of the Holy Apostles

Temple of Isis

Temple of Jupiter Capitolinus

Forum of Trajan

Temple of Pax

Church of Sts Gervasius and Protasius

Church of St Pudentiana

Church of St Mark

Theater of Pompey

Theater of Marcellus

CAPITOLIUM

Arch of Titus

Arch of Constantine

Church of St Mary in Trastevere

Church of St Chrysogonus

Church of St Caecilia

River Tiber

Church of St Praxedis

Church of St Mary Major

Basilica Liberii

Church of St Silvester and Martin

Church of St Peter in Chains

Church of St Clement

Baths of Trajan

Colosseum

Church of the Forty Martyrs

Round Church of St Stephen

Church of Sts John and Paul

Cathedral of St John in Lateran

Church of St Sixtus

PALATINE

Circus Maximus

Church of St Prisca

Church of St Sabina

AVENTINE

Church of Sts Nereus and Achilleus

Baths of Caracalla

Church of the Holy Cross in Jerusalem

0        500        100m

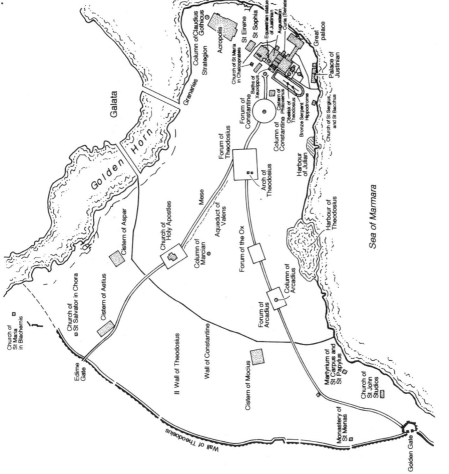

*Map 8* Constantinople

Gate

St Stephen's
Church

Eudocia's
Palace

Church of the
Paralytic

St Stephen's Gate

Jericho
Gate

Tomb
of the
Virgin

Church of
St Serapion

Pool of Israel

Gethsemane
Church

Streets with
Colonnade
(Cardo)

Church of Our Lady
of the Spasm

Remains of
Antonia Fortress

MOUNT OF OLIVES

Church of
St George

Golden Gate

Theodorus
Monastery

Church of the
Holy Sepulchre

Remains of
Temple of Jupiter

Monastery of
the Spoudaeans

Gate

Church of Sts
Cosmas and
Damian

St
Sophia's
church

Baptistery

Pool of the
Patriarch

Forum

Temple Site

Church of John
the Baptist

David's Gate

Bath
House

Bath House

Monks' Quarters
in Northern Zion

Monks' dwellings

New Church
of St Mary

Church of
St Menas

Jeremiah's
Grotto

Residential
Quarter

VALLEY OF JEHOSHAPAT
(Kidron Valley)

Residential
Quarter

Basilica of
Holy Zion

Church of St Stephen

St Peter's Church

Eudocia's
Church

Siloam
Pool

Church

VALLEY OF HINNOM

Burial Cave of
Zion Church

0        250        500m

*Map 9*   Jerusalem, AD 326–638

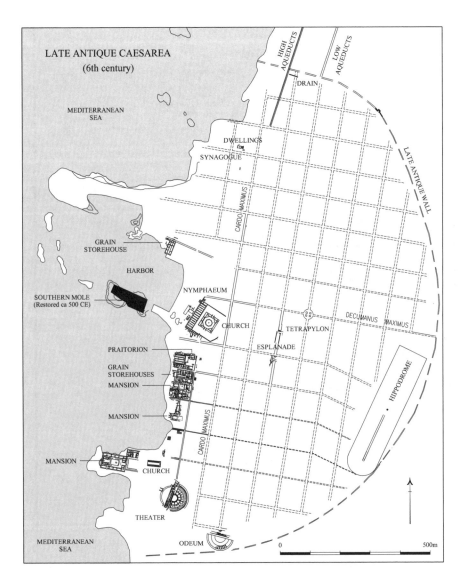

## LATE ANTIQUE CAESAREA
### (6th century)

HIGH AQUEDUCTS

LOW AQUEDUCTS

DRAIN

MEDITERRANEAN
SEA

LATE ANTIQUE WALL

DWELLINGS

SYNAGOGUE

CARDO MAXIMUS

GRAIN
STOREHOUSE

HARBOR

NYMPHAEUM

SOUTHERN MOLE
(Restored ca 500 CE)

DECUMANUS MAXIMUS

CHURCH

TETRAPYLON

ESPLANADE

PRAITORION

GRAIN
STOREHOUSES

MANSION

HIPPODROME

MANSION

CARDO MAXIMUS

MANSION

CHURCH

THEATER

MEDITERRANEAN
SEA

ODEUM

0                    500m

*Map 10*  Caesarea Maritima

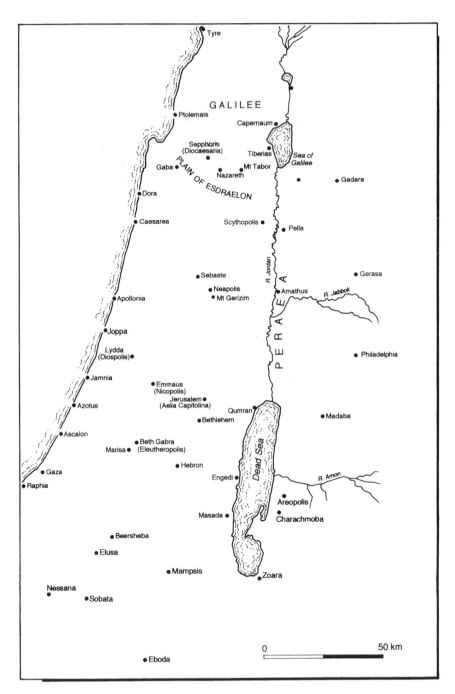

*Map 11* Palestine in the sixth century

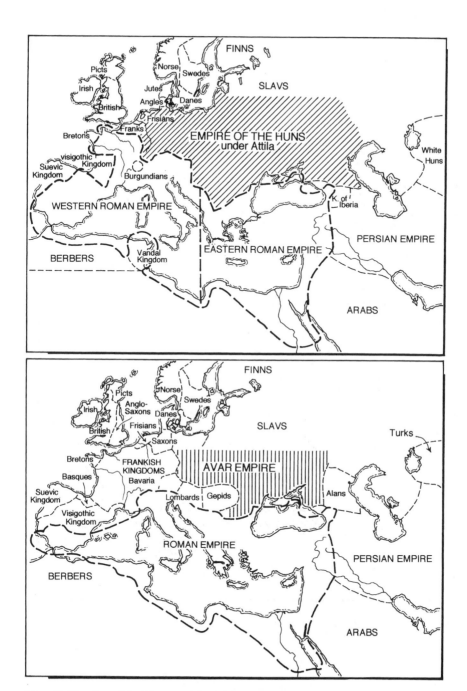

*Map 12* Empire of the Huns under Attila about 450
Empire of the Avars about 560

*Map 13* Germanic kingdoms about AD 525

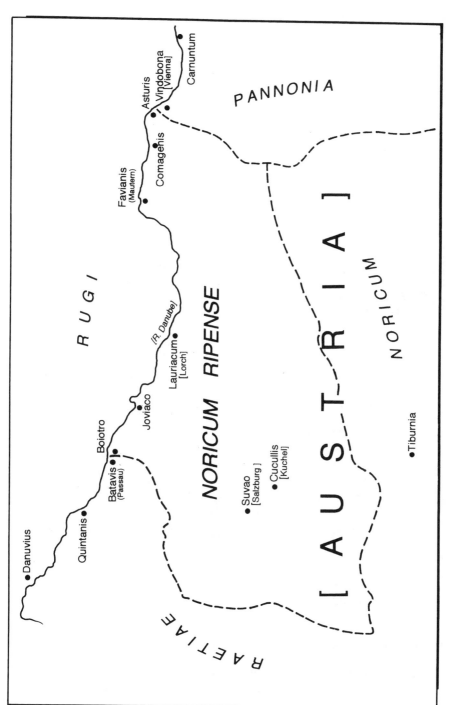

*Map 14* The Danube in the time of Severinus

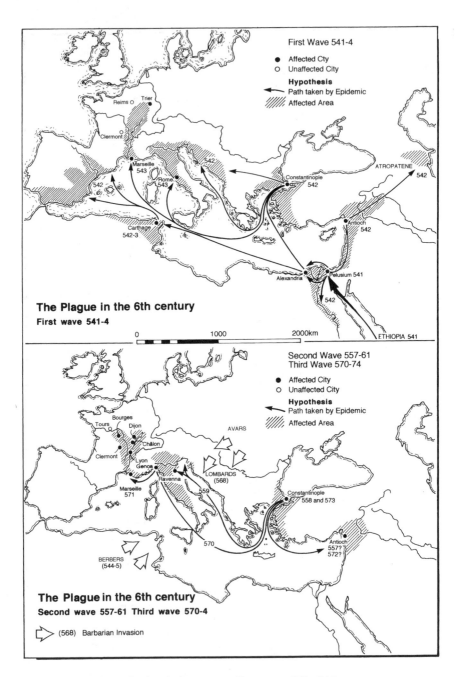

First Wave 541-4

● Affected Cty
○ Unaffected City

**Hypothesis**
← Path taken by Epidemic
▨ Affected Area

Reims ○    Trier

Clermont ○

Marseille
543

Rome
543

542

542

542

Carthage
542-3

Constantinople
542

ATROPATENE
542

Antioch
542

Alexandria    Pelusium 541

542

**The Plague in the 6th century**
**First wave 541-4**

0          1000          2000km

ETHIOPIA 541

Second Wave 557-61
Third Wave 570-74

● Affected City
○ Unaffected City

**Hypothesis**
← Path taken by Epidemic
▨ Affected Area

Bourges
Tours ○    Dijon
Châlon
Clermont ○
Lyon
Genoa
Ravenna
Marseille
571

AVARS

LOMBARDS
(568)

559

570

Constantinople
558 and 573

Antioch
557?
572?

BERBERS
(544-5)

**The Plague in the 6th century**
**Second wave 557-61 Third wave 570-4**

▷ (568) Barbarian Invasion

*Map 15* The plague in the sixth century: first wave 541–544
The plague in the sixth century: second wave 557–561; third wave
570–574

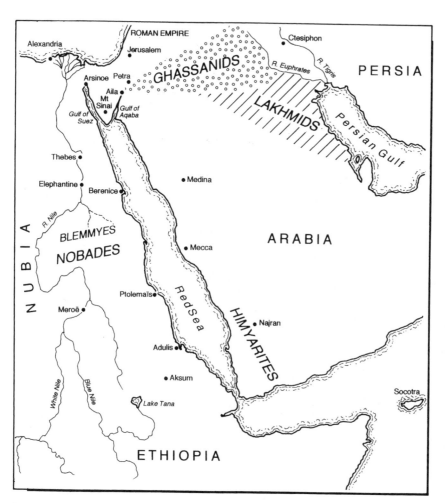

*Map 16* The Red Sea and Arabia before the rise of Islam

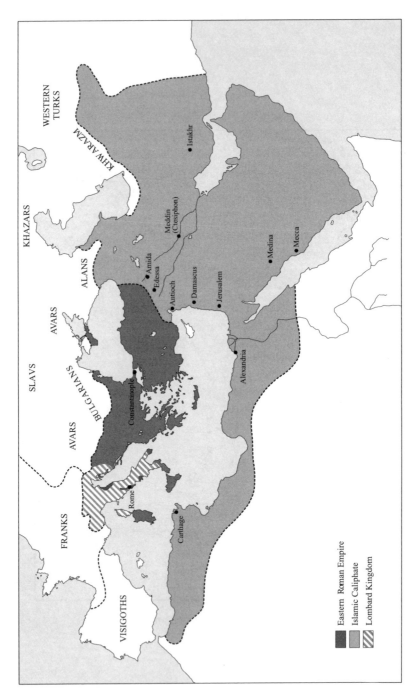

*Map 17* The Mediterranean world and the expansion of Islam, about AD 700

Eastern Roman Empire

Islamic Caliphate

Lombard Kingdom

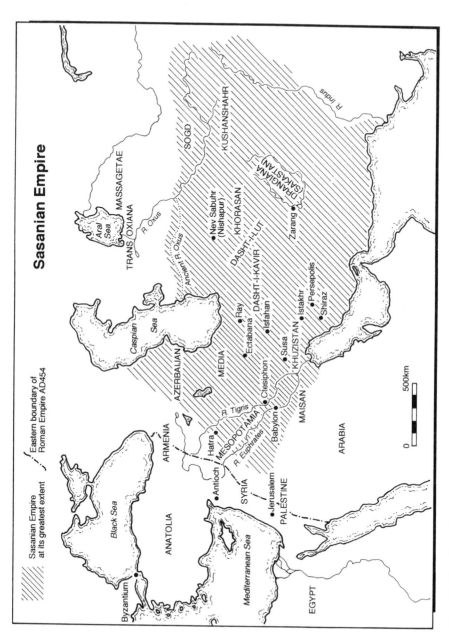

## Sasanian Empire

Sasanian Empire
at its greatest extent

Eastern boundary of
Roman Empire AD454

*Map 18* The Sasanian Empire

# INTRODUCTION TO THE
# FIRST EDITION

The excerpts from ancient authors in this book illustrate a range of topics that I have taught over the last fifteen years in courses on Late Antiquity. While preparing course packets for my classes, I have been continually surprised at how many Late Antique sources have been translated, and how widely dispersed they are in books and journals, some difficult to find in a small library. This Reader is meant to meet the need for an introductory college textbook of sources that pulls some of this material together. Late Antiquity is a fairly new field of study, and there is no one collection of translated sources that touches on its many aspects. It is my hope that colleagues in other universities will find this a convenient and useful compendium, and that our students will find the material a provocative starting point for deeper investigations.

By Late Antiquity I mean the period stretching roughly from Diocletian's reforms in the late third century to the rise of Islam in the seventh and covering a swath across Europe and the Middle East. Late Antiquity embraces a broad range of cultures and political and religious systems over a long time span. Scholars of this material in earlier generations have tended not to cross disciplinary boundaries and have used other periodizations, such as Late Roman, Early Medieval, and Early Byzantine. The passages included here are not meant to constitute a documentary history of the period; that would take many volumes. They are intended to be suggestive and not exhaustive, and though they are linked topically, I have not strung them together into a continuous narrative. Instead, I invite interested readers to dip into the material that most appeals to them and not to read the book cover to cover. Sections of the Reader can be used as appropriate, and broader interpretive narratives can be developed in the classroom through lectures and discussions.

The focus of the book is on the Roman Empire, which lay at the heart of the late antique world, and I presume that most instructors will approach Late Antiquity from a Roman perspective. The chapters are arranged in two groups. The first addresses the Roman world directly, with long chapters on the Roman Empire, the Roman army, Christianity, Jews, and Polytheism, and shorter chapters on women, Philosophy, law and medicine. Late Antiquity, however, is now conventionally understood to be more than the later Roman Empire, and so I have included short chapters on neighboring groups, Persia, Islam, peoples of the steppe and Slavs, and Germanic invaders and successor states. Because collections of material on medieval

Europe are readily available, I have not provided any material on Merovingian Gaul other than Gregory of Tours' account of Clovis' conversion and the spread of the plague in Gaul. Readers must look elsewhere for Lombards, Anglo-Saxons and substantial material on the early Slavs. The selections reflect my concerns in introductory courses. I have tried to include old favorites sure to be on most syllabi (e.g., the "Edict of Milan"; the battle of Adrianople; the Nicene Creed), as well as passages that I have often wished I had at hand but did not (e.g., the *Henotikon* of Zeno; Dionysius Exiguus on AD dating). Some of the material will be brand new to English speakers (e.g., an early Samaritan response to Islam; the Syriac martyrdom of Mar Kardagh). All translations of the *Theodosian Code* and the *Novels* of Valentinian and Majorian are from Clyde Pharr, trans., *The Theodosian Code and Novels and the Sirmondian Constitutions* (New York: Greenwood Press, 1959), except where otherwise indicated.

Each chapter includes a general introduction, full bibliographic information about the translation, a very brief introduction for every source to aid students wishing to pursue a topic further, and a few suggestions for further reading at the end. I have included only material in English, and references are for the most part to books and articles published since the appearance of Averil Cameron's two books that are now the standard college textbooks for the period: *The Later Roman Empire* (Harvard, 1993) and *The Mediterranean World in Late Antiquity* (Routledge, 1993). These two works include annotated bibliographies and very helpful notes. Students are also encouraged to consult the following standard works:

Peter Brown, *The World of Late Antiquity* (1971); Peter Brown, *The Rise of Western Christendom. Triumph and Diversity* (1996); Judith Herrin, *The Formation of Christendom* (1987); A.H.M. Jones, *The Later Roman Empire* (1964); Warren Treadgold, *A History of the Byzantine State and Society* (1997); *The Oxford Classical Dictionary*, 3rd edn, ed. Simon Hornblower and Antony Spawforth (1996); *The Oxford Dictionary of Byzantium* (1991); *Encyclopedia of Early Christianity* (1997); *Dictionary of Late Antiquity*, ed. Peter Brown, Glenn Bowersock, and Oleg Grabar (forthcoming); *Cambridge Ancient History*, vol. 14 (1998); *Encyclopedia of the Early Church*, ed. Angelo Di Berardino, trans. Adrian Walford (1992); *Atlas of the Roman World*, ed. John Matthews and Tim Cornell; *Atlas of the Early Christian World*, ed. Mary E. Hedlund and H.H. Rowley (1966); *The Oxford Dictionary of the Christian Church*, 3rd edn, ed. F.L. Cross and E.A. Livingstone (1997); Dan Bahat, *The Illustrated Atlas of Jerusalem* (1990); *Atlas of Classical History*, ed. Richard J.A. Talbert (1985).

Most of the passages included here have already been published (permissions are given on pp. lxxxiii–lxxxviii). Several translations appear for the first time. I am very grateful to Milka Rubin, Susanna Elm, and Joel Walker for excerpts *13.3.22*, *3.8.8* and *3.6.2*, which are taken from works in progress. If no translator is listed, the translation is mine. The translations of all the other sources appear as originally published, and I have not tried to impose a uniform style upon them. I have, however, taken the liberty of standardizing spelling of proper names and place names as much as seemed practical. I have also occasionally made very minor changes in translation to make the passages more readable for my students. In particular I have eliminated most parentheses and included the readings suggested by the translators. I have eliminated diacritical marks except the "ayn" from the Arabic. I have changed pronouns to proper nouns on occasion and translated foreign terms into English, even if this produces some imprecision. Most of the time Latinized spellings have been retained. Titles of ancient works are given in English. Occasionally brief glosses are added in the text, marked by [square brackets]. In the interest of saving space, the standard editions of the Greek, Latin, Syriac, Arabic, Hebrew, Persian, Ethiopic, and Armenian texts have not been provided. This information can be found by consulting the translated source of each passage, which is given in every case.

It has been a pleasure and an education to choose these sources and prepare them for a general audience. If reading them excites curiosity and encourages further reading in some aspect of the Late Antique world, the book will have done its job.

# INTRODUCTION TO THE
# SECOND EDITION

This volume is an expanded version of *Readings in Late Antiquity* as it appeared in 2000. A number of new passages have been added throughout the book. They are indicated with an asterisk in the table of contents. A new chapter, "Chapter 8: Domestic life," has been added at the suggestion of William Klingshirn, to whom I am most grateful for the idea of the chapter and for many suggestions for its content. The passages tell stories that in my experience have interested students and provoked discussion. They are not intended to provide a complete overview of the Late Antique period. My hope continues to be that instructors will be able to pick from among this broad selection to suit the purposes of their particular classes.

In the decade that has passed since this book first went to press, the study of Late Antiquity has flourished, resulting in a very large number of excellent articles and monographs. The reading lists at the end of each chapter contain only a select few of these publications. I have chosen only English titles since this book is intended for Anglophone students. All of the suggested titles contain further bibliographies that will help students carry their interests further.

Several important new books have appeared that should be frequently consulted. These supplement the list given on p. lxiv of this book, in the Introduction to the first edition. They are *The Cambridge Ancient History, Volume 13: the Late Empire, AD 337–425*, ed. Averil Cameron and Peter Garnsey (Cambridge: Cambridge University Press, 1998); *The Cambridge Ancient History, Volume 14: Late Antiquity: Empire and Successors, AD 425–600*, ed. Averil Cameron, Bryan Ward-Perkins, and Michael Whitby (Cambridge: Cambridge University Press, 2001); *The New Cambridge Medieval History, Volume 1: c.500–c.700*, ed. Paul Fouracre (Cambridge: Cambridge University Press, 2006); *The Cambridge History of the Byzantine Empire c.500–1492*, ed. Jonathan Shepard (Cambridge: Cambridge University Press, 2008); Brown, Peter, *The Rise of Western Christendom*, 2nd edn. (Malden, MA: Blackwell Publishing, 2003); Mitchell, Stephen, *A History of the Later Roman Empire, AD 284–641: The Transformation of the Ancient World* (Malden, MA: Blackwell Publishing, 2007). Students should also take note of Talbert, Richard J.A., ed., *The Barrington Atlas of the Classical World* (Princeton, NJ: Princeton University Press, 2000); and the new *Journal of Late Antiquity* that began publication in 2008. The *Journal of Roman Studies* and the *Journal of Roman Archaeology* now regularly carry articles and reviews on Late Antique topics.

Translations are my own if not otherwise indicated.

# ACKNOWLEDGMENTS

I wish to thank the following colleagues and friends for their expert assistance: Joseph Alchermes, Sam Barnish, Jay Bregman, Susanna Elm, Hugh Elton, Geoffrey Greatrex, Susan Ashbrook Harvey, Matthias Henze, Martha Jenks, Matthew Koeffler, Rudi Lindner, Ralph Mathisen, Danielle Raneft, Claudia Rapp, Milka Rubin, Michele Salzman, Paula Sanders, and Joel Walker. An anonymous reader read the entire manuscript and made many helpful suggestions, as did Peter Brown, mentor and friend for twenty years. The Interlibrary Loan Staff at Rice University efficiently provided mountains of books and photocopies. I am grateful to Dean Judith Brown and Gale Stokes for providing some funds to pay for student assistance and to David Zetoony, Lisa Gabriel, Mark Lewis, Rick Sawyer, Rob Britten, Liz Lehman, Isabel Valdez, Nicole Williams, Tammy Whitlock, Matthew Thompson, and Mary Summers for their help of different sorts. I owe special thanks to my father J. J. Maas, who generously underwrote the cost of publishers' permissions, and to Jean Brusher, editor in the Rice History Department, for her assistance. Most of all I am grateful to my peerless assistant Anandi Sheth (Rice '99), who helped in the preparation of this manuscript from its beginning to the very end.

## Acknowledgments for the second edition

Several friends have contributed their own translations to this volume. I wish to thank Peter Bell, Carlos Galvao-Sobrinho, William Klingshirn, Scott McGill, Joseph Pucci, and Kristina Sessa for their generosity and helpful suggestions.

I have benefited from advice from many friends, in particular Kim Bowes, Kate Cooper, Kenneth Holum, Anna Iamim, Gavin Kelly, Helmut Reimitz, Michele Salzman, Paula Sanders, Peter Sarris, Tina Sessa, Jonathan Shepard, and Ed Watts, to all of whom I offer my sincere gratitude. Special thanks go to Daniel Abosso, who prepared an up-to-date "Late Antiquity on the Web" list; to Maya Maskarinec, my long-distance research assistant, for invaluable contributions throughout this project; to Danielle Boss, for gathering permissions; and to Julia Layard Miller, for editorial assistance in creating and submitting the new manuscript. Once again it is a pleasure to acknowledge the expertise of the Interlibrary Loan staff at Rice University as well as that of the library staff at Dumbarton Oaks, where I worked during the last two weeks of August, 2008. Kate Mertes prepared the index with remarkable efficiency and speed, for which I am very grateful. I am happy to express my thanks to Richard Stoneman, who encouraged me to undertake the second edition, and to Matt Gibbons and Lalle Pursglove of Routledge and all the staff at Keystroke, with whose assistance the book was completed.

# CHRONOLOGY

| | |
|---|---|
| 216–277 | Mani |
| 224 | Sasanian Empire founded |
| 238–270s | Crisis in Roman Empire |
| 250–330 | Arius |
| 263–340 | Eusebius of Caesarea |
| 270 | Antony goes into the desert |
| | Plotinus dies |
| 284–305 | Diocletian |
| 301 | Edict on Maximum Prices |
| 303 | Great persecution of Christians |
| c.305 | Porphyry dies |
| 306–337 | Constantine |
| 312 | Battle of Milvian Bridge |
| 313 | Edict of Milan |
| 324 | Constantine defeats Licinius and takes over the eastern empire |
| 325 | Council of Nicea |
| c.325 | Iamblichus dies |
| 330 | Dedication of Constantinople |
| 337–361 | Constantius |
| 355–361 | Julian in Gaul |
| c.356–361 | *Life of Antony* appears |
| 359 | Shapur II takes Amida |
| 361–363 | Julian the Apostate |
| 364–375 | Valentinian (West) |
| 364–378 | Valens (East) |
| 378 | Battle of Adrianople |
| 379–395 | Theodosius I |
| 382 | Goths settled as federates: Altar of Victory removed from Roman Senate house |
| 387 | Augustine's conversion in Milan |
| | "Riot of the Statues" at Antioch |
| 388 | Callinicum affair |

| 392 | Revolt of Eugenius |
| 394 | Battle of River Frigidus |
| 395 | Augustine, bishop of Hippo |
| 395–423 | Honorius (West) |
| 395–408 | Arcadius (East) |
| 396–459 | Simon Stylites |
| 398 | John Chrysostom, bishop of Constantinople |
| 355–431 | Paulinus of Nola |
| 400 | Monastery of Lerins founded |
| 404 | John Chrysostom deposed |
| 406 | Vandals, Alans, Sueves cross Rhine |
| 407–411 | Constantine III (Britain) |
| 408 | Death of Stilicho |
| 408–450 | Theodosius II |
| 410 | Roman troops leave Britain |
| | Alaric sacks Rome |
| 412–444 | Cyril of Alexandria |
| 416 | Orosius, *History against the Pagans* |
| 418 | Visigoths settled in Aquitania |
| 420 | John Cassian, *Institutes* |
| 420–490 | Patrick |
| 425–455 | Valentinian III |
| 429–439 | Vandals conquer North Africa |
| 429 | End of the Jewish patriarchate |
| 430–480 | Sidonius Apollinaris |
| 431 | Council of Ephesus |
| 434–453 | Attila |
| 438 | Theodosian Code |
| 440–461 | Pope Leo |
| 450–457 | Marcian (East) |
| 451 | Attila invades Gaul |
| | Council of Chalcedon |
| 454–482 | Severinus in Noricum |
| 455–457 | Avitus (West) |
| 455 | Vandals sack Rome |
| 457–474 | Leo (East) |
| 468 | Expedition against Vandals fails |
| 474–491 | Zeno (East) |
| 476 | Romulus Augustulus deposed |
| 476–493 | Odovacar rules Italy |
| 481–511 | Clovis |
| 485 | Proclus dies |
| 490 | Salic Law |
| 490–583 | Cassiodorus |

| | |
|---|---|
| 491–518 | Anastasius |
| 493–526 | Theodoric the Ostrogoth rules Italy |
| c.500 | Pseudo-Dionysius the Areopagite |
| 502–542 | Caesarius of Arles |
| 507 | Franks defeat Visigoths at Battle of Vouille |
| 507–588 | John of Ephesus |
| 511 | Eugippius, *Life of Severinus of Noricum* |
| 518–527 | Justin I |
| 520 | Gildas, *On the Ruin of Britain* |
| 524 | Boethius, *Consolation of Philosophy* |
| 527–533 | Justinian's *Code, Digest, Institutes* |
| 527–565 | Justinian |
| 529 | John Philoponus attacks Aristotle's view of matter |
| | Benedict at Monte Cassino |
| | Academy at Athens closed |
| 530–579 | Khusro I Anoshirwan (Chosroes) |
| 532 | Nika Riots in Constantinople |
| 533–561 | Justinian's reconquests in West |
| 537 | Church of Saint Sophia (Holy Wisdom) completed in Constantinople |
| 538–594 | Gregory of Tours |
| 542 | Plague begins |
| | Jacob Baradaeus establishes Monophysite Church |
| 550s | Slavs enter Balkans |
| 553 | *Three Chapters* Controversy ends |
| 560–536 | Isidore of Seville |
| 568 | Lombards invade Italy |
| 570–632 | Muhammad |
| 578–582 | Tiberius II |
| 580s | Avar empire takes shape |
| 582–602 | Maurice |
| 589 | Visigoths convert from Arianism to Catholicism |
| 590–604 | Pope Gregory the Great |
| 591 | Maurice restores Khusro II |
| 597 | Augustine begins conversion of Britain |
| 602–610 | Phocas |
| 610 | Muhammad begins to receive Quran |
| 610–641 | Heraclius |
| 614 | Persians sack Jerusalem |
| 622 | Muhammad leaves Mecca for Medina (Hijra) |
| 626 | Avars and Persians besiege Constantinople |
| 630 | Heraclius restores True Cross to Jerusalem |
| 632 | Muhammad dies |
| 634–650s | Arabs conquer Syria, Egypt, and Persia |
| 636 | Battle of the River Yarmuk |

| | |
|---|---|
| 638 | Arabs take Jerusalem |
| 640 | Arabs conquer Egypt |
| 660 | Quran written down |
| 692 | Dome of the Rock built in Jerusalem |
| 698 | Arabs conquer Carthage |
| 699 | Arabic replaces Greek in administration of Caliphate |

# LATE ANTIQUE RULERS

## Roman emperors (222–811)

**(Usurpers are in *italics*)**

| | |
|---|---|
| 222–235 | Severus Alexander |
| 235–238 | Maximinus Thrax |
| 238 | Gordian I |
| 238 | Gordian II |
| 238 | Pupienus |
| 238 | Balbinus |
| 238–244 | Gordian III |
| 240 | *Sabinianus* |
| 244–249 | Philip the Arab |
| 248 | *Pacatianus* |
| 248 | *Jotapian* |
| 248 | *Silbannacus* |
| 249–251 | Decius |
| 249–252 | *Priscus* |
| 250 | *Licinianus* |
| 251 | Herennius Etruscus |
| 251 | Hostilian |
| 251–253 | Tribonianus Gallus |
| 251–253 | Volusianus |
| 253 | Aemilianus |
| 253–260 | Valerian I |
| 253–268 | Gallienus |
| 260 | *Saloninus* |
| 258 *or* 260 | *Ingenuus* |
| 260 | *Regalianus* |
| 260–261 | *Macrianus Major* |
| 260–261 | *Macrianus Minor* |
| 260–261 | *Quietus* |

| | |
|---|---|
| 261–261 or 262 | *Mussius Aemilianus* |
| 268 | *Aureolus* |

## Gallic empire

| | |
|---|---|
| 260–268 | Postumus |
| 269 | Laelianus |
| 269 | Marius |
| 269–271 | Victorinus |
| 270–271 | *Domitianus* |
| 271–274 | Tetricus I |

## Illyrian emperors

| | |
|---|---|
| 268–270 | Claudius II Gothicus |
| 270 | Quintillus |
| 270–275 | Aurelian |
| 271 | *Septimius* |
| 275–276 | Tacitus |
| 276 | Florianus |
| 276–282 | Probus |
| 280 | *Saturninus* |
| 280 | *Proculus* |
| 280 | *Bonosus* |
| 282–283 | Carus |
| 283–285 | Carinus |
| 283–284 | Numerian |

## Britannic empire

| | |
|---|---|
| 286–293 | Carausius |
| 293–297 | Allectus |

## Tetrarchy and Constantinian dynasty

| | | |
|---|---|---|
| 284–305 | Diocletian | Co-emperor with Maximian |
| 286–306 | Maximian | Co-emperor with Diocletian |
| 305–306 | Constantius Chlorus | Co-emperor with Galerius |
| 305–311 | Galerius | Co-emperor with Constantius I Chlorus and then Severus II |
| 306–307 | Severus II | Co-emperor with Galerius |
| 307–308 | Maximian | |
| 306–312 | Maxentius | |
| 306–337 | Constantine | |

| | | |
|---|---|---|
| 308 | *Domitius Alexander* | |
| 308–324 | Licinius | Co-emperor |
| 310–313 | Maximinus Daia | Co-emperor |
| 316–317 | Valerius Valens | Co-emperor with Licinius |
| 324 | Martinianus | Co-emperor with Licinius |
| 337–340 | Constantine II | Co-emperor |
| 337–361 | Constantius II | Co-emperor |
| 337–350 | Constans I | |
| 350–353 | *Magnentius* | |
| c.350 | Vetranio | |
| c.350 | *Nepotianus* | |
| 361–363 | Julian | |
| 363–364 | Jovian | |

## Valentinian dynasty

| | | |
|---|---|---|
| 364–375 | Valentinian I | Emperor in the west |
| 365–378 | Valens | Emperor in the east |
| 365–366 | *Procopius* | |
| 375–383 | Gratian | |
| 375–392 | Valentinian II | |
| 379 | Theodosius I | Co-emperor |
| 383–388 | Magnus Maximus | |
| c.386–388 | *Flavius Victor* | |
| 392–394 | *Eugenius* | |
| 394–395 | Theodosius I | |
| 383–395 | Arcadius | |
| 393–395 | Honorius | |

## Western empire

| | | |
|---|---|---|
| 395–423 | Honorius | Co-emperor with Constantius III (421) |
| 407–411 | *Constantine III* | |
| 409–411 | *Constans II* | Co-ruler with Constantine III |
| 409–410 | *Priscus Attalus* | |
| 409–411 | *Maximus* | |
| 411–413 | *Jovinus* | |
| 412–413 | *Sebastianus* | Co-ruler with Jovinus |
| 414–415 | *Priscus Attalus* | |
| 421 | Constantius III | Co-emperor with Honorius |
| 423–425 | *Joannes* | |
| 425–455 | Valentinian III | |
| 455 | Petronius Maximus | |

| | |
|---|---|
| 455–456 | Avitus |
| 457–461 | Majorian |
| 461–465 | Libius Severus |
| 467–472 | Anthemius |
| 472 | Olybrius |
| 473–474 | Glycerius |
| 474–480 | Julius Nepos |
| 475–476 | Romulus Augustulus |

### Eastern empire

| | |
|---|---|
| 395–408 | Arcadius |
| 408–450 | Theodosius II |
| 425–455 | Valentinian III |
| 450–457 | Marcian |
| 457–474 | Leo I |
| 474 | Leo II |
| 474–491 | Zeno |
| 475–476 | Basiliscus |
| 491–518 | Anastasius |
| 518–527 | Justin I |
| 527–565 | Justinian |
| 565–578 | Justin II |
| 578–582 | Tiberius II |
| 582–602 | Maurice |
| 602–610 | Phocas |
| 610–641 | Heraclius |
| 641 | Constantine II |
| 641 | Heraclonas (Heracleon) |
| 641–668 | Constantine III (Constans II) |

## Persian emperors (226–628)

| | |
|---|---|
| 226?–241? | Ardashir I |
| 241–272? | Shapur I |
| 272–273 | Hormizd Ardashir |
| 273–276 | Vahram I |
| 276–293 | Vahram II |
| 293 | Vahram III |
| 293–302 | Narseh |
| 302–309 | Hormizd II |
| 309–379 | Shapur II |
| 379–383 | Ardashir II |
| 383–388 | Shapur III |

| | |
|---|---|
| 388–399 | Vahram IV |
| 399–420 | Yazdgerd I |
| 420–439 | Vahram V |
| 439–457 | Yazdgerd II |
| 457–459 | Hormizd III |
| 459–484 | Peroz I |
| 484–488 | Valash (Balash) |
| 488–531 | Kavadh I |
| 496–498 | Zamasp (Djamasp) |
| 531–579 | Khusro I |
| 579–590 | Hormizd IV |
| 590–591 | Vahram Chobin |
| 590–628 | Khusro II |
| 590–591 | Vahram VI |
| 591–592 | Bistam |
| 593 | Hormizd V |
| 628 | Kavadh II |
| 628–630 | Ardashir III |
| 629 | Peroz II |
| 630 | Shahrbaraz |
| 630–631 | Boran |
| 631–632 | Hormizd VI |
| 631–651 | Yazdegerd |

## Popes of Rome (314–655)

| | |
|---|---|
| 314–335 | Sylvester |
| 336 | Mark |
| 337–352 | Julius I |
| 352–366 | Liberius |
| 366–384 | Damasus I |
| 384–399 | Siricius |
| 399–401 | Anastasius I |
| 401–417 | Innocent I |
| 417–418 | Zosimus |
| 418–422 | Boniface I |
| 422–432 | Celestine I |
| 432–440 | Sixtus III |
| 440–461 | Leo I |
| 461–468 | Hilarius |
| 468–483 | Simplicius |
| 483–492 | Felix III (II) |
| 492–496 | Gelasius I |
| 496–498 | Anastasius II |

| | |
|---|---|
| 498–514 | Symmachus |
| 514–523 | Hormisdas |
| 523–526 | John I |
| 526–530 | Felix IV (III) |
| 530–532 | Boniface II |
| 533–535 | John II |
| 535–536 | Agapetus I |
| 536–537 | Silverius |
| 537–555 | Vigilius |
| 556–561 | Pelagius I |
| 561–574 | John III |
| 575–579 | Benedict I |
| 579–590 | Pelagius II |
| 590–604 | Gregory I |
| 604–606 | Sabinianus |
| 607 | Boniface III |
| 608–615 | Boniface IV |
| 615–618 | Deodatus I |
| 619–625 | Boniface V |
| 625–638 | Honorius I |
| 640 | Severinus |
| 640–642 | John IV |
| 642–649 | Theodore I |
| 649–655 | Martin I |

## Orthodox patriarchs of Constantinople (315–655)

| | |
|---|---|
| 315–327? | Metrophanes |
| 327?–340 | Alexandros |
| 340–341 | Paul I |
| 341–342 | Eusebios |
| 342–344 | Paul I (again) |
| 342–348 | Makedonios I |
| 348–350 | Paul I (again) |
| 350–360 | Makedonios I (again) |
| 360–369 | Eudoxios |
| 369–379 | Demophilos |
| 369–370 | Evagrios |
| 379–381 | Gregorios I |
| 381 | Maximos |
| 381–397 | Nektarios |
| 398–404 | John I, Chrysostom |
| 404–405 | Arsakios |
| 405 (406?)–425 | Antikos |

| 426–427 | Sisinnios I |
|---|---|
| 428–431 | Nestorios |
| 431–434 | Maximianos |
| 434–447 | Proklos |
| 447–449 | Phlabianos |
| 449–458 | Anatolios |
| 458–471 | Gennadios I |
| 471–489 | Akakios |
| 489–490 | Phrabitas |
| 490–496 | Euphemios |
| 496–511 | Makedonios II |
| 511–518 | Timotheos I |
| 518–520 | John II Kappadokes |
| 520–536 | Epiphanios |
| 536 | Anthimos I |
| 536–552 | Menas |
| 552–565 | Eutychios |
| 565–577 | John III Antiocheus |
| 577–582 | Eutychios (again) |
| 582–595 | John IV Nesteutes |
| 595–606 | Kyriakos |
| 607–610 | Thomas I |
| 610–638 | Sergios |
| 638–641, 654 | Pyrrhos I |
| 641–653 | Paul II |

# PERMISSIONS

I would like to thank the following presses for permission to quote passages of more than 400 words from the following books:

Allen and Unwin, Armstrong, A.H., *Plotinus*, 1953.

American Oriental Society, Torrey, Charles C. and Hanns Oertel, eds, *Journal of the American Oriental Society*, 35.2 (1915).

American Philosophical Society, Downey, Glanville, trans., "Libanius' Oration in Praise of Antioch (Oration XI)." *Proceedings of the American Philosophical Society*, 103.5 (1959); Sharpe, William D., trans., "Isidore of Seville." *Transactions of the American Philosophical Society*, 54.2 (1964).

AMS Press, Hamilton, F.J. and E.W. Brooks, trans., Zachariah of Mitylene, *The Syriac Chronicle*, 1899, reprint 1979.

Ares Publishers, Oikonomides, A.M., trans., Marinos of Neapolis, *Life of Proclus*, 1977.

Aris and Phillips, Wilkinson, John, *Jerusalem Pilgrims Before the Crusades*, 1977.

Athlone Press, Cameron, Averil, ed., Corippus, *In Laudem Jiustini Augusti Minoris*, 1976.

Augsburg Fortress, Rusch, William, ed., *The Trinitarian Controversy*, 1979; Daly, Robert J. and Burns, J. Patout, *Christians in the Military*, 1985; Kraemer, Ross, *Maenads, Martyrs, and Monasteries*, 1988.

Australian Association of Byzantine Studies, Ridley, Ronald, *Zosimus. New History*, 1982.

Bar-Ilan University Press, Sperber, Daniel, *Roman Palestine: The Land*, 1978.

Broadview Press, Murray, Alexander C., *From Roman to Merovingian Gaul. A Reader*, 2000.

Cambridge University Press, Frend, W.H.C., *The Rise of the Monophysite Movement: Chapters in the History of the Church in the 5th and 6th Centuries*,

1972; Gardner, Iain and Samuel N.C. Lieu, *Manichaean Texts from the Roman Empire*, 2004; Sarris, Peter, trans., *Economy and Society in the Age of Justinian*, 2006.

Catholic University of America Press, Gavin, Joseph N., trans., *The Vitae Sanctorum Patrum Emeretensium. Text and Translation*, 1946; Parsons, Sister Wilfred, trans., *Saint Augustine: Letters*, vol. l, ed. Roy Joseph Deferrari, 1951 (vol. 12 of *The Fathers of the Church*); Cook, Genevieve Marie, trans., Ennodius, *Life of St. Epiphanius*, ed. Roy J. Deferrari, *Early Christian Biographies*, 1952 (vol. 15 of *The Fathers of the Church*); Wood, Simon P., trans., *Clement of Alexandria. Christ the Educator*, 1954 (vol. 23 of *The Fathers of the Church*).

Centre for Byzantine, Ottoman, and Modern Greek Studies, The University of Birmingham, Ware, Kallistos and Rosemary Morris, "Teaching the Faith," in *Church and People in Byzantium*, 1990.

Columbia University Press, Jones, Leslie Webber, trans., *Cassiodorus, An Introduction to Divine and Human Readings*, 1946; Lewis, Naphtali and Meyer Reinhold, eds, *Roman Civilization: Selected Readings*, vol. 2, 1990; Stahl, William Harris, trans., Macrobius, *Commentary on the Dream of Scipio*, 1952.

Cornell University Press, Birks, Peter and Grant McLeod, trans., *Justinian's "Institutes,"* 1987. Introduction and translation ©1987 by Peter Birks and Grant McLeod. Reproduced from *Justinian's "Institutes,"* translated with an introduction by Peter Birks and Grant McLeod with the Latin text by Paul Krueger. Used by permission of the American publisher, Cornell University Press.

Craik, Elizabeth, ed., and Jill Harries, "Treasure in Heaven: Properties and Inheritance among Senators of Late Rome," in *Marriage and Property*, Aberdeen, 1984.

Darwin Press, Levy-Rubin, Milka, *The Continuatio of the Samaritan Chronicle of Abu al-Fath in Late Antiquity and Early Islam*, eds A. Cameron and L. Conrad, 2002; Rubin, Zeev, "The Reforms of Khosro Anushirwan," in *The Byzantine and Early Islamic Near East III: States, Resources, and Armies*, ed. Averil Cameron, 1992.

Duckworth, Mercken, H.P.F. "The Greek Commentators on Aristotle's Ethics," in *Aristotle Transformed*, Richard Sorabji, ed., 1990; Wildberg, Christian, *Philoponus, Against Aristotle, on the Eternity of the World*, 1987; Birks, Peter and Grant McLeod, *Justinian's "Institutes,"* 1987.

Dumbarton Oaks Press, Dennis, George T., trans., "The Anonymous Byzantine Treatise on Strategy," in *Three Byzantine Military Treatises*, 1985; Alexander, Paul J., *The Oracle of Baalbek: The Tiburtine Sibyl in Greek Dress*, 1967.

Edwin Mellon, Clark, Elizabeth A., "Sergia's Narration" and "Life of Olympias," in *Jerome, Chrysostom, and Friends: Essays and Translations*, 1979.

Eerdmans Publishing Co., Zenos, A.C., trans., Socrates Scholasticus, *Ecclesiastical History* (vol. 2 of *The Nicene and Post-Nicene Fathers*, eds. Philip Schaff and Henry Wace, 1979).

Estonian Evangelical Lutheran Church in America, Vööbus, Arthur, *The Syro-Roman Law Book*, vol. 2, 1983.

Fordham University Press, Dvornik, Francis, *Byzantium and the Roman Primacy*, 1966.

Fortress Press, Helgeland, John and Robert Daly, eds., *Christians and the Military: The Early Experience*, 1985. Reprinted from *Christians and the Military* by John Helgeland, Robert J. Daly, and J. Patout Burns, copyright 1985 Fortress Press. Used by permission of Augsburg Fortress; Norris, Richard A. Jr., ed., *The Christological Controversy*, 1980. Reprinted from *The Christological Controversy*, edited by Richard A. Norris, Jr., copyright 1980 Fortress Press. Used by permission of Augsburg Fortress; Rusch, William G., ed. and trans., *The Trinitarian Controversy*, 1979. Reprinted from *The Trinitarian Controversy*, edited by William Rusch, copyright 1979 Fortress Press. Used by permission of Augsburg Fortress.

Francis Cairns, Blockley, R.C., trans., *The History of Menander the Guardsman*, 1985; Blockley, R.C., trans., *The Fragmentary Classicising Historians of the Later Roman Empire: Eunapius, Olympiodorus, Priscus and Malchus*, 1983.

Greenwood Press, New York, Clyde Pharr, trans., *The Theodosian Code and Novels and the Sirmondian Constitutions* (1969).

Harvard University Press and the Loeb Classical Library, Norman, A.F., trans., *Libanius: Autobiography and Selected Letters*, vol. l, 1992; Norman, A.F., trans., *Libanius: Selected Works*, vol. 2, 1969; 1977; Robinson, George W., trans., Eugippius, *The Life of Saint Severinus*, 1914; Thomson, H.J., trans., *Prudentius*, vol. 2, 1953; Dewing, H.P, trans., *Procopius, History of the Wars*, vol. 2, 1916; Rolfe, John C., trans., *Ammianus Marcellinus*, vols 1 and 3, 1956; Rolfe, John C., trans., "Excerpta Valesiana," in *Ammianus Marcellinus*, vol. 3, 1956; Wright, Wilmer Cave, trans., *The Works of the Emperor Julian*, vol. 1 (1913), and vol. 3 (1923).

Hellenic College Press, Ševčenko, Ihor and Nancy Patterson Ševčenko, trans., *The Life of St. Nicholas of Sion*, 1984.

Hendrickson Publishers, James Barmby, trans., Gregory the Great, *Selected Epistles* (vol. 12 of *Nicene and Post-Nicene Fathers*, eds. Philip Schaff and Henry Wace, 1885/1995); Newman, Albert H., trans., Augustine, *The Anti-Manichaean Writings* (vol. 4 of *Nicene and Post-Nicene Fathers*, eds. Philip Schaff and Henry Wace, 1887/1994); Schaff, Philip and Henry Wace, eds,. *Leo the Great, Gregory the Great* (vol. 12 of *Nicene and Post-Nicene Fathers*, 1994); Schaff, Philip and Henry Wace, eds., *Jerome, Selected Works* (vol. 6 of *Nicene and Post-Nicene Fathers*, 1994).

Istituto Italiano per il Medio ed Estremo Oriente, Boyce, Mary, *The Letter of Tansar*, 1968.

Jewish Publication Society, Stillman, Norman A., *The Jews of Arab Lands: A History and Source Book*, 1979.

Jewish Theological Seminary of America, Leveine, Lee, *The Galilee in Late Antiquity*, 1992.

Johns Hopkins Press, MacKinney, Loren C., *Early Medieval Medicine*, 1937.

Liberal Arts Press, Grant, Frederick C., *Hellenistic Religions: The Age of Syncretism*, 1953.

Liturgical Press, Doyle, Leonard J., *St. Benedict's Rule for Monasteries*, 1948.

Liverpool University Press, Barnish, S.J.B., *The Variae of Magnus Aurelius Cassiodorus Senator*, 1992; Palmer, Andrew and Sebastian Brock, *The Seventh Century in the West-Syrian Chronicle*, 1993; Bell, Peter, *Political Voices in the Age of Justinian*, 2009; *Vegetius: Epitome of Military Science*, 1993, trans. N.P. Milner, *Chronicon Paschale 284–628 AD*, trans. Michael Whitby and Mary Whitby, 1989.

Missionary Society of St. Paul the Apostle in the State of New York, and Paulist Press, Gregg, Robert C., trans., *Athanasius*, 1980.

Newman Press, Forbes, Clarence A., trans., *Firmicus Maternus: The Error of Pagan Religions*, 1970.

New Advent, excerpts from *Nicene and Post-Nicene Fathers*, Second Series, vol. XII, ed. Philip Schaff, 1890, revised and edited by Kevin Knight; Jerome, *Letter* 77, trans. Kevin Knight, 2008.

Oxford (Clarendon Press), Nestorius, *The Bazaar of Heracleides*, trans. G.R. Driver and Leonard Hodgson, 1925.

Oxford University Press, Guillaume, A., trans., *The Life of Muhammad*, 1955; Fitzgerald, Augustine, trans., *The Letters of Synesius of Cyrene*, 1926; Creed, J.L., trans., Lactantius, *On the Death of the Persecutors*, 1984; Van Dam, Raymond, "Self-Representation in the Will of Gregory of Nazianzus." *Journal of Theological Studies* 46.1, 1995; Bradbury, Scott, trans., *Severus of Minorca: Letter on the Conversion of the Jews*, 1996.

Penguin Books, Watts, V.E., trans., Boethius, *The Consolation of Philosophy*, 1969; Lewis Thorpe, trans., Gregory of Tours, *The History of the Franks*, 1974; Isbell, Harold, trans., *The Last Poets of Imperial Rome*, 1982; Carmi, T., ed., *The Penguin Book of Hebrew Verse*, 1981.

Phanes Press, Guthrie, Kenneth Sylvan, trans., *Proclus's Biography, Hymns and Works: Master-Key Edition: Putting the Reader in Full Command of the Whole*

PERMISSIONS

University of Chicago Press, Chicago, Illinois, U.S.A.; Boyce, Mary, *Textual Sources for the Study of Zoroastrianism*, 1984.

University of Michigan Press, Waddell, Helen, trans., *The Desert Fathers*, 1971.

University of Pennsylvania Press, Drew, Katherine Fischer, trans., *The Burgundian Code*, 1972; Dennis, George T., trans., *Maurice's Strategikon: Handbook of Byzantine Military Strategy*, 1984.

University of Toronto Press, Mango, Cyril, *The Art of the Byzantine Empire, 312–1453*, 1986.

Walker, Lewis, Bernard, ed., *Islam from the Prophet Muhammad to the Capture of Constantinople*, vol. 2: *Religion and Society*, 1974.

Williams and Norgate, Charles, R.H., trans., *The Chronicle* of *John, Bishop of Nikiou*, 1916.

The editor and publisher gratefully acknowledge all copyright holders who have granted permission to reproduce their work. While considerable effort has been made to trace and contact all copyright holders, this has not always been possible. Any errors and omissions will be corrected at the earliest opportunity, if notified.

# 1

# THE ROMAN EMPIRE:
# RULER AND ADMINISTRATION

## 1.1 Introduction

At the beginning of the fourth century, the Roman Empire controlled western Europe between the Atlantic and the Rhine and Danube Rivers, Britain, a swath of land across North Africa to Egypt, Anatolia, and the territories of the Middle East as far as Armenia and Syria. Nearly fifty thousand miles of roads combined with the maritime routes of the Mediterranean to link imperial territories and enable the circulation of troops, merchandise, and ideas. Armies patrolled the edges of the empire or waited further inland to strike at invaders. The inhabitants of the Roman Empire in Late Antiquity spoke many dialects and languages in addition to Latin and Greek, hundreds of small economic regions prospered, over a thousand cities dotted the landscape, and countless gods received the prayers of their followers. This tumultuous enterprise was held together by the emperor, who served as a symbol of unity and authority as well as the commander of overwhelming military force.

This chapter has three general parts. It begins with the emperor and the imperial office and the theories of power that supported it. The second section gives passages illustrating the imperial administrative system: the chain of command that linked the governing officials of the state to the emperor and his chief officers. It also shows the patrons (monks, generals, urban aristocrats) who could intervene in the system on behalf of their dependants. The third section deals with aspects of economic life within the Roman Empire. Romans did not have a sophisticated notion of economics, and their writers did not often address economic matters directly. Nevertheless, it is possible to present some legislation that grappled with inflation. Endemic poverty in the city and countryside rendered daily life quite harsh for the majority of the population, as will be seen in examples below that illustrate the condition of the peasantry and its growing dependence for protection upon landed magnates who controlled their lives. No one challenged the institution of slavery or concerned themselves to any degree with the condition of the millions of slaves throughout the empire.

## 1.2 The emperor and the imperial office

In Late Antiquity the Roman emperor stood at the very center of society. No one questioned his authority or right to rule; he was the ultimate human source of all earthly power. An ever more elaborate ritual life developed around the figure of the emperor to mark his unique status. Though acted out primarily in the great capitals where the emperor held court, many ceremonies also took place in cities throughout the land.

The growth of imperial autocracy gained momentum with the grafting of Christian ideas of divine legitimization to older, well-established Roman theories of imperial rule. As God's chosen agent, the emperor tried to make his earthly kingdom the image of the kingdom of heaven. Heavy responsibilities accompanied the imperial office, for failure to rule justly in accordance with Roman law could bring divine retribution upon the emperor and his subjects alike. Under this pressure aggressive emperors like Constantine and Justinian emphasized their role as *de facto* bishops and leaders of the faith. This stance often made the relation of the emperor to the Christian church a contested issue.

### 1.2.1 The emperor comes to town

The ceremony of the *adventus* (arrival) marked an emperor's arrival at a city and played a regular part of imperial ritual in Late Antiquity. It combined both careful planning and spontaneous activity, giving the city the opportunity to display its loyalty and the emperor a chance to present himself to the public. Here, the historian Ammianus Marcellinus gives two eyewitness examples: the emperor Constantius II's first visit to the city of Rome in 357, and the emperor Julian's arrival in Constantinople to take the throne in 362.

*1.*

Ammianus Marcellinus, *History* 16.10.5–10
[*Ammianus Marcellinus*, vol. I, trans. John C. Rolfe (London: Heinemann, 1956) pp. 245, 247]

> ... when Constantius was nearing the city, as he beheld with calm countenance the dutiful attendance of the senate and the august likenesses of the patrician stock, he thought ... that the sanctuary of the whole world was present before him. And when he turned from them to the populace, he was amazed to see in what crowds men of every type had flocked from all quarters to Rome. And as if he were planning to overawe the Euphrates with a show of arms, or the Rhine, while the standards preceded him on each side, he himself sat alone upon a golden chariot in the resplendent blaze of shimmering precious stones, whose mingled glitter seemed to form a sort of shifting light. And behind the manifold others that preceded him he was surrounded by dragons woven out of purple thread and bound to the golden and jewelled tops of spears, with wide mouths open to the breeze and hence hissing as if roused by anger, and leaving their tails winding in the wind. And there marched on either side twin lines of infantrymen

2

with shields and crests gleaming with glittering rays, clad in shining mail, and scattered among them were the full armoured cavalry . . . Accordingly being saluted as Augustus with favouring shouts, while hills and shores thundered out the roar, he never stirred, but showed himself as calm and imperturbable as he was commonly seen in his provinces. For he both stooped when passing through lofty gates (although he was very short), and as if his neck were in a vice, he kept the gaze of his eyes straight ahead, and turned his face neither to right nor to left, but (as if he were a clay figure) neither did he nod when the wheel jolted, nor was he ever seen to spit, or to wipe or rub his face or nose, or move his hands about.

2.

Ammianus Marcellinus, *History* 22.2.3–5
[Sabine MacCormack, *Art and Ceremony in Late Antiquity* (Berkeley: University of California Press, 1981) p. 47]

Julian hastened [from Philippopolis] yet more exalted, in some chariot, as it were, of Triptolemus, which, because of its swiftness is, in the ancient tales, imagined to have been drawn by winged serpents of the air. In this way, feared by land and sea, and held up by no delay, he entered Heraclea . . . When this became known at Constantinople, all ages and sexes poured forth as though they were going to see someone sent down from heaven. So he was received . . . with the respectful attendance of the Senate and the universal acclaim of the people; being accompanied by rows of citizens and soldiers, he was escorted as though in a line of battle, and the eyes of all were turned on him not just with a fixed gaze, but with great wonder. For, it seemed closer to a dream that a young man, short of stature but distinguished by great deeds, should, after the bloodstained destruction of kings and nations, after a progress of unheard-of speed from city to city, increasing in wealth and strength wherever he went, have seized all places more easily than rumour flies, and should at last have taken up the empire with the assent of heaven.

## 1.2.2 *Imperial acclamations*

Highly formalized cheering played a part in celebrating the emperor. The Roman Senate chanted these acclamations in 438 in the Roman Senate House to honor Theodosius II (and Valentinian III) on the completion of the Theodosian Law Code.
*Theodosian Code*, "Minutes of the Senate," 5

[The assembly shouted:]
"Augustuses of Augustuses, the greatest of Augustuses!"
    [Repeated eight times]
"God gave You to us! God save You for us!"
    [Repeated twenty-seven times]
"As Roman Emperors, pious and felicitous may You rule for many years!"
    [Repeated twenty-two times]

"For the good of the human race, for the good of the Senate, for the good of the State, for the good of all!"

[Repeated twenty-four times]

"Our hope is in You, You are our salvation!"

[Repeated twenty-six times]

"May it please our Augustuses to live forever!"

[Repeated twenty-two times]

"May You pacify the world and triumph here in person!"

[Repeated twenty-four times]

"These are the prayers of the Senate, these are the prayers of the Roman people!"

[Repeated ten times]

"Dearer than our children, dearer than our parents!"

[Repeated sixteen times]

"Suppressors of informers, suppressors of chicanery!"

[Repeated twenty-eight times]

"Through You our honors, through You our patrimonies, through You our all!"

[Repeated twenty-eight times]

"Through You our military strength, through You our laws!"

[Repeated twenty times]

"We give thanks for this regulation of Yours!"

[Repeated twenty-three times]

"You have removed the ambiguities of the imperial constitutions!"

[Repeated twenty-three times]

"Pious emperors thus wisely plan!"

[Repeated twenty-six times]

"You wisely provide for lawsuits, You provide for the public peace!"

[Repeated twenty-five times]

"Let many copies of the Code be made to be kept in the governmental offices!"

[Repeated ten times]

"Let them be kept under seal in the public bureaus!"

[Repeated twenty times]

"In order that the established laws may not be falsified, let many copies be made!"

[Repeated twenty-five times]

"In order that the established laws may not be falsified, let all copies be written out in letters [without abbreviations]!"

[Repeated eighteen times]

"To this copy which will be made by the constitutionaries let no annotations upon the law be added!"

[Repeated twelve times]

"We request that copies to be kept in the imperial bureaus shall be made at public expense!"

[Repeated sixteen times]

4

### 1.2.3  Court ritual

When Sabas, a poor but prestigious monk from Palestine, went to Constantinople to ask for remission of taxes in Palestine in the wake of a destructive Samaritan revolt, Justinian (527–565) ignored the complicated choreography of court ceremonial and hurried to greet him. This gesture emphasized the emperor's piety in a calculated and dramatic fashion.

Cyril of Scythopolis, *Life of Sabas*, ch. 71
[Cyril of Scythopolis, *Lives of the Monks of Palestine*, trans. R.M. Price (Kalamazoo, MI: Cistercian Pub., 1991) pp. 182–3]

> The patriarch having sent letters in advance to the emperor announcing godly Sabas' arrival, our divinely protected emperor [Justinian], overjoyed, sent the imperial galleys to meet him . . . As he entered the palace with the bishops and came within the curtain, God opened the emperor's eyes; he saw the radiance of divine favour in the shape of a crown blazing forth and emitting sunlike beams from the head of the old man. Running up, Justinian greeted him with reverence, kissing his godly head with tears of joy; on obtaining his blessing, he took from Sabas' hand the petition from Palestine . . .

### 1.2.4  Cautious advice for an all-powerful monarch

Agapetus, a deacon at the cathedral of Saint Sophia in Constantinople, wrote a book of advice, the *Exposition*, for the emperor Justinian during the early years of his reign. This treatise explains that the emperor's job is to imitate God's heavenly rule through personal piety by maintaining the just rule of law in the empire. Agapetus' work draws from the fourth century bishop Eusebius, who adapted Hellenistic ideas of kingship to the ideology of a Christian empire. Works like the *Exposition* (called "Mirrors for Princes") were one way for subjects to remind their monarch of the need to rule fairly.

Agapetus, *Exposition* 1, 2, 30, 35, 37
[Ernest Barker, *Social and Political Thought in Byzantium from Justinian I to the Last Palaeologus* (Oxford: Oxford University Press, 1957) pp. 54–5, 58–9]

> 1. Having a dignity which is set above all other honours, Sire, you render above all to God, who gave you that dignity; inasmuch as He gave you the sceptre of earthly power after the likeness of the heavenly kingdom, to the end that you should instruct men to hold fast the cause of justice, and should punish the howling of those who rage against that cause, being yourself under the kingship of the law of justice and lawfully king of those who are subject to you.

> 2. Like the man at the helm of the ship, the mind of the king, with its many eyes, is always on the watch, keeping a firm hold on the rudder of enforcement of law and sweeping away by its might the currents of lawlessness, to the end that the ship of the State of the world may not run into the waves of injustice.

30. Being entrusted by God with the office of kingship on earth, do not employ wrong-doers in the management of affairs; for he who has given wrong-doers their power will owe an account to God for what they have wrongly done. Therefore let the appointment of officials be made after strict examination.

35. Consider yourself to be surely and truly a king when you rule with the consent of your subjects. For a subject people which is unconsenting revolts when it finds an opportunity; but a people which is attached to its sovereign by the bonds of good will keep firm and true in its obedience to him.

37. He who has attained to great authority should imitate, so far as he can, the Giver of that authority. If in any way he bears the image of God, Who is over all, and if through Him he holds rule over all, he will imitate God best if he thinks that nothing is more precious than mercy.

### 1.2.5  The emperor's role in war and peace

Synesius of Cyrene, a politically active philosopher and bishop at the beginning of the fifth century, believed the emperor must be both warrior and peacemaker. This coincided with a new phase in the eastern empire lasting for about two centuries – that of non-military emperors. Their concentration on civilian administration rather than direct engagement in military affairs contributed to the survival of the empire in the east.

Synesius of Cyrene, *On Kingship* 16
[*The Essays and Hymns of Synesius of Cyrene*, vol. 1, trans. Augustine Fitzgerald (London: Humphrey Milford/Oxford University Press, 1926) p. 140]

16. Now the warlike king may be above all a man of peace, for to him alone who is able to inflict injury upon the evildoer is it given to keep the peace. For my own part I should say that the king has, all in all, gained most applause as a peacemaker who, although desiring injustice to none, is nevertheless provided with the power to escape injury at the hands of others; for if he does not war, he will certainly be warred against. Peace is a happier state than war, because the preparations of war are actually made with a view to peace. The end in view would justly be preferred to those things which exist on its account. Thus it is well that the king give himself up to each half of his command in turn, that the body politic divided into two estates, that of the armed men and that of the unarmed; and after consorting with his fighting men, he should visit cities and country districts to which, by the use of the military, we have granted fearless possession of their farms and civic rights. He will visit again and again in his tours as many races and as many cities as possible; and whatever portion of his Empire he does not reach, even to that he will devote his attention in what is apparently an effective and excellent way.

### *1.2.6 Ruler cult*

Christianity accommodated the Roman tradition of ruler cult by making the emperor God's special agent. Although demoted from divine status himself, the emperor maintained a central position in the Christian theory of empire. Gregory of Nazianzus (329–c.390), who became bishop of Constantinople in 380, was one of the most influential voices in the Greek church. His description of ruler cult indicates that the power possessed by emperors was a unique, divine gift and so was worthy of public veneration. This passage shows how ruler cult maintained its presence in a Christian environment.

Gregory of Nazianzus, *Oration* 4.80

[Francis Dvornik, *Early Christian and Byzantine Political Philosophy, Origins and Background* II (Washington, DC: Dumbarton Oaks Press, 1966) pp. 686–7]

> It is an axiom of royal practice, observed, if not by all other men among whom royalty exists, certainly by the Romans, that the rulers should be publicly honored by their statues. Neither their crowns and diadems and bright purple, nor the number of their bodyguards, nor the multitude of their subjects is sufficient to establish their sovereignty; but they need also adoration in order to seem more supreme: not only the adoration directed to them personally, but also that made to their images and portraits, in order that a greater and more perfect honor be rendered to them. Emperors vary in what they like to see represented with their likenesses in these portraits: some love to see themselves with the more prominent cities offering them gifts; others, with victories crowning their heads; others, with the magistracies adorned with the insignia of office adoring them; others, in the act of killing animals in feats of archery; others, with subjugated barbarians lying prostrate under their feet or being exterminated in various ways. It is not that they love only the reality of the deeds of which they are so proud, but also their representation in works of art.

### *1.2.7 The emperor as the embodiment of law*

Themistius was a non-Christian rhetorician of such talent that he prospered under Christian emperors of the mid-fourth century. He was a bridge between Christian emperors and the urban aristocracies of the eastern empire, for whose recruitment into the new Senate at Constantinople he was made responsible. As a member of the Senate and then Prefect of Constantinople, he gave advice to emperors. In an oration praising Theodosius I for pardoning rebellious subjects in Antioch whom the law condemned to death, he developed the idea that the emperor not only stood above the law but was the embodiment of the law itself – the "animate" or "incarnate" law. Christian theology of empire found this idea entirely acceptable.

Themistius, *Oration* 19 (227d, 228a)

[Francis Dvornik, *Early Christian and Byzantine Political Philosophy. Origins and Background* II (Washington, DC: Dumbarton Oaks Press, 1966) p. 623]

Here we see men returning to life from the depths of Hades. The law had sent them there, but the master of the law recalled them thence. He knew that the excellence of the judge and that of the emperor are not the same: it befits the one to obey, the other to amend the laws and to mitigate what in them is hard and cruel. For he is the animate law, not merely a law laid down in permanent and unchangeable terms. This means that God sent kings to the earth to serve men as refuge from an immovable law to the safety of the animate and living law.

### 1.2.8 The Christian emperor looks to heaven

Like other emperors before him, Constantine the Great (306–337) left his carefully crafted image not only on statues but also on coins and public buildings throughout the empire. The following passage describes how in this way his Christian piety could be seen by all his subjects.

Eusebius, *Life of Constantine* 4.15

[Philip Schaff and Henry Wace, eds., *Nicene and Post-Nicene Fathers: Life of Constantine the Great*, vol. I, second series (Peabody, MA: Hendrickson Pubs, 1994) p. 544]

> How deeply his soul was impressed by the power of divine faith may be understood from the circumstance that he directed his likeness to be stamped on the golden coin of the empire with the eyes uplifted as in the posture of prayer to God: and this money became current throughout the Roman world. His portrait also at full length was placed over the entrance gates of the palaces in some cities, the eyes upraised to heaven, and the hands outspread as if in prayer.

### 1.2.9 The image of the emperor

Theophilus, archbishop of Alexandria from 385 to 412, compares the imperial image to an icon of Mary, the mother of Jesus. He shows how a painting of the emperor could serve as a point of refuge and a guarantor of a citizen's right to trial. Such images were found in cities throughout the empire.

Theophilus, *A Homily on the Virgin*

[William H. Worrel, ed., *The Coptic Manuscripts in the Freer Collection* (New York: The Macmillan Company, 1923) pp. 359–79, here p. 375]

> If the image of the emperor of this world when painted is set up in the midst of the market-place, becoming a protection to the whole city, and if violence is committed against anyone, and he goes and takes hold of the image of the emperor, then no man will be able to oppose him, even though the emperor is naught but a mortal man; and he is taken to a court of law. Let us therefore, my beloved (parishioners), honor the icon of Our Lady (Mary), the veritable queen.

### 1.2.10  The imperial right to interfere in church affairs

Clergymen might appeal to the emperor to intervene in church affairs if they thought he shared their doctrinal position and would further their cause. The fourth-century Spanish bishop Ossius (Hosius) of Cordoba, who was a Nicene Christian, advised emperor Constantius II, an Arian, of the proper relation between church and state: hands off. The long struggle between the Church hierarchy and the imperial office was underway already by the middle of the fourth century.

Ossius of Cordoba, Letter to Constantius II, quoted by Athanasius, *History of the Arians* 44, 6–8

[Timothy D. Barnes, *Athanasius and Constantius: Theology and Politics in the Constantinian Empire* (Cambridge, MA: Harvard University Press, 1993) p. 175]

> Stop, I beg you, and remember that you are a mortal man: fear the day of judgment and keep yourself pure for it. Do not intrude yourself into the affairs of the church, and do not give us advice about these matters but rather receive instruction on them from us. God has given you kingship, but has entrusted us with what belongs to the church. Just as the man who tries to steal your position as emperor contradicts God who has placed you there, so too you should be afraid of becoming guilty of great offense by putting the affairs of the church under your control. It is written: "Render unto Caesar the things that are Caesar's, and unto God those that are God's" (Matthew 22.21). Hence neither do we bishops have the right to rule over the world nor do you, Emperor, have the right to officiate in Church.

### 1.2.11  The emperor as priest – Justinian's view

In theory, Justinian (527–565) respected the difference between the priesthood and the imperial office, as he explains in a law of 535. Here he describes the proper relation of civil and religious obligations of the emperor.

Justinian, *Novel* 6 (March 6, 535)

[Francis Dvornik, *Byzantium and the Roman Primacy* (New York: Fordham University Press, 1966) p. 72]

> The two greatest gifts which God in His infinite goodness has granted men are the Priesthood and the Empire. The priesthood takes care of divine interests and the empire of human interests of which it has supervision. Both powers emanate from the same principle and bring human life to its perfection. It is for this reason that the emperors have nothing closer to their hearts than the honor of priests because they pray continually to God for the emperors. When the clergy shows a proper spirit and devotes itself entirely to God, and the emperor governs the state which is entrusted to him, then a harmony results which is most profitable to the human race. So it is then that the true divine teachings and the honor of the clergy are the first among our preoccupations.

### *1.2.12 Challenging Justinian's interference in church affairs*

When Justinian attempted to impose a definition of the faith upon the North African church during the *Three Chapters* Controversy (543–553), he received a stiff rebuke from Bishop Facundus of Hermione. This churchman insisted that establishing Christological norms was the business of the priesthood, not the emperor. Facundus illustrated his message with the biblical story of King Oziah (2 Chronicles 26:16ff) who overstepped the bounds of his office and was punished by God.

Facundus of Hermione, *In Defense of the Three Chapters* 12.3

[Francis Dvornik, *Early Christian and Byzantine Political Philosophy. Origins and Background* II (Washington, DC: Dumbarton Oaks Press, 1966) p. 826]

> One should remember the fate of Oziah who ruled over many nations, rose to fame, and felt such pride in his heart that he placed incense on the altar, which was the exclusive privilege of the priests and sons of Aaron. For this sin his impudent face, which had lost all sense of reverence, was stricken with leprosy. Our very humble Prince knows that Oziah did not go unpunished for daring to sacrifice and usurp the function of a priest, even of the second order: all the more should he know that he will not escape punishment for discussing the essentials of the Christian faith, which he cannot do; or for making new canons, which is the privilege of the priests of the first order when a number of them are gathered together.

### *1.2.13 The emperor as the source of instability*

The all-powerful emperor could be blamed for all the empire's woes just as easily as for its triumphs. Procopius of Caesarea's viciously hostile portrait of Justinian in his *Secret History* was not a psychotic aberration but the obverse of his treatment of the emperor in the panegyrical *Buildings* and *Wars*. It reveals dread of the chaotic innovation that a demonic emperor might bring about. Such criticism of the emperor recurred in late antique writing.

Procopius, *Secret History* 3.1 and 5.1

[Procopius, *Secret History*, trans. G.A. Williamson (Harmondsworth: Penguin Books, 1988) pp. 94, 130]

> [3.1] When Justinian ascended the throne it took him a very little while to bring everything into confusion. Things hitherto forbidden by law were one by one brought into public life, while established customs were swept away wholesale, as if he had been invested with the forms of majesty on condition that he would change all things to new forms. Long established offices were abolished, and new ones set up to run the nation's business; the laws of the land and the organization of the army were treated in the same way, not because justice required it or the general interest urged him to it, but merely that everything might have a new look and might be associated with his name. If there was anything which he was not in a position to transform then and there, even so he would at least attach his own name to it.

[5.1] That the emperor was not a man but, as I have already pointed out, a demon in human shape, could be demonstrated by considering the magnitude of the calamities which he brought on the human race. For it is by the immensity of what he accomplishes that the power of the doer is manifested. To make any accurate estimate of the number of lives destroyed by this man would never, it seems to me, be within the power of any living being other than God. For sooner could one number all the sands than the hosts of men destroyed by this potentate. But making a rough estimate of the area which has been denuded of its inhabitants I suggest that a million million lost their lives.

## 1.3 Imperial administration

In Late Antiquity the small imperial administrative system of the early empire gave way to a highly centralized, hugely expensive and oppressive bureaucracy controlled by the emperor. Diocletian's reforms (284–305) increased the number of provinces and gave each a separate civil and military administration. A complicated chain of command linked the vastly increased number of civil and military administrators to the imperial court, and a merciless system of tax collection developed to meet the increased costs of administration. As the chief executive officer of the state, the emperor supervised the great administrative bureaus of the empire. Drawing their authority from him, these bureaus managed the daily affairs of the empire. The administrative system drew talented men into imperial service from across the empire and rewarded them with an elaborate system of honors. The imperial bureaucracy gradually displaced the older urban administrative apparatus.

### 1.3.1 Diocletian's reforms

Lactantius (c.240–c.320), a Christian teacher and writer who suffered during Diocletian's persecutions, describes the reforms that were the foundation of the Late Antique governmental system. Obvious hatred of Diocletian distorts Lactantius' account, which should not be accepted uncritically. Nevertheless, Lactantius remains a starting point for understanding the major changes of Diocletian's regime. The administrative system that he developed is known as the Tetrarchy because it involved four men: two senior rulers called Augustus, and two junior rulers called Caesar. Each governed a quarter of the empire. (See *1.4.1, 3.2.1*, pages 21 and 79.)

Lactantius, *On the Death of the Persecutors* 7.1–8
[Lactantius, *De Mortibus Persecutorum*, ed. and trans. J.L. Creed (Oxford: Oxford University Press, 1984) pp. 11–13]

> Diocletian was an author of crimes and a deviser of evils; he ruined everything and could not even keep his hands from God. In his greed and anxiety he turned the whole world upside down. He appointed three men to share his rule, dividing the world into four parts and multiplying the armies, since each of the

four strove to have a far larger number of troops than previous emperors had had when they were governing the state alone. The number of recipients began to exceed the number of contributors by so much that, with farmers' resources exhausted by the enormous size of the requisitions, fields became deserted and cultivated land was turned into forest. To ensure that terror was universal, provinces too were cut into fragments; many governors and even more officials were imposed on individual regions, almost on individual cities, and to these were added numerous accountants, controllers, and prefects' deputies. The activities of all these people were very rarely civil; they engaged only in repeated condemnations and confiscations, and in exacting endless resources – and the exactions were not just frequent, they were incessant, and involved insupportable injustices. And how could the arrangements for raising soldiers be endured?

The same Diocletian with his insatiable greed was never willing that his treasuries should be depleted; he was always amassing surplus wealth and funds for largess so that he could keep what he was storing complete and inviolate. Since too by his various misdeeds he was causing an immense rise in prices, he tried to fix by law the prices of goods put up for sale. Much blood was then shed over small and cheap items; in the general alarm nothing appeared for sale, and the rise in prices got much worse until, after many had met their deaths, sheer necessity led to the repeal of the law.

In addition, Diocletian had a limitless passion for building, which led to an equally limitless scouring of the provinces to raise workers, craftsmen, wagons, and whatever is necessary for building operations. Here he built basilicas, there a circus, a mint, an arms-factory, here he built a house for his wife, there one for his daughter . . .

### 1.3.2 An able emperor relies on his advisory council

In 355 corrupt officials sought to frame Silvanus, the military commander in Gaul, for treason. Emperor Constantius II got wind of the plot and investigated. We see the emperor and his advisory council at work, punishing the wrongdoers. Unfortunately, Silvanus did not learn of being cleared of charges against him in time, and driven by fear, he proclaimed himself emperor – a fatal mistake.

Ammianus Marcellinus, *History* 15.5.12–14

[*Ammianus Marcellinus*, vol. I, trans. John C. Rolfe (Cambridge, MA: Harvard University Press, 1956) pp. 141, 143]

12. And on learning this, the emperor decided that the matter should be investigated searchingly through the medium of his council and all his officers. And when the judges had taken their seats, Florentius, son of Nigrinianus, at the time deputy master of the offices, on scrutinizing the script with greater care, and finding a kind of shadow, as it were, of the former letters, perceived what had been done, namely, that the earlier text had been tampered with and

other matter added quite different from what Silvanus had dictated, in accordance with the intention of this patched-up forgery. 13. Accordingly, when this cloud of deceit had broken away, the emperor, learning of the events from a faithful report, deprived the prefect of his powers, and gave orders that he should be put under examination; but he was acquitted through an energetic conspiracy of many persons. Eusebius, however, former count of the privy purse, on being put upon the rack, admitted that this had been set on foot with his cognizance. 14. Aedesius, who maintained with stout denial that he had known nothing of what was done, got off scot-free. And so at the close of the business all those were acquitted whom the incriminating report had forced to be produced for trial . . .

### 1.3.3 A top official's close ties to the monarch

The chief legal magistrate of the empire was the Quaestor. A definition of the responsibilities of this office, and the special ties of the Quaestor to the ruler, comes from the pen of Cassiodorus, an Italian aristocrat who served the Ostrogothic ruler Theoderic in the early sixth century. Although the speaking voice is that of Theoderic, for whom Cassiodorus wrote, the definition of the office and the sentiments about ruling that accompany it are fully Roman. Cassiodorus had held the office himself, and he wished to emphasize Theoderic's respect for proper Roman procedures.

Cassiodorus, *Documents* 6.5

[*The Variae of Magnus Aurelius Cassiodorus Senator*, trans. S.J.B. Barnish (Liverpool: Liverpool University Press, 1992) pp. 96–7]

1. If honours gain in distinction the more they enjoy my gaze, if the ruler's frequent presence shows his affection, so no magistrate can be more glorious than he who is admitted to a share in my counsels. For to others I entrust the procurement of the public revenues, to others the hearing of lawsuits, to others the rights of my estates. The Quaestorship I value as the words of my tongue, and take it wholeheartedly to myself. 2. Of necessity, this office is linked intimately to my thoughts, that it may speak in its own words what it knows as my sentiments; it discards its own will and judgment, and so absorbs the purpose of my mind that you would think its discourse really came from me. How hard it is for the subject to assume the speech of the ruler, to be able to express what may be supposed my own, and, advanced to public honour, to create a noble lie. 3. Think of the honour and responsibility you have in equal measure. If I am in any doubt, I ask the Quaestor, who is a treasury of public reputation, a store-room of the laws, ever ready for the unexpected; and, as Tully [Cicero], the master of eloquence, puts it, nothing "seems more remarkable than the ability, by speech, to hold men's minds, to attract their inclinations, to drive them whither, or to lead them whence he wills" [Cicero, *De Oratore* I.30]. For, if it is the proper part of the orator to speak with gravity and style that he may move the

minds of the judges, how much more eloquent must he be who is known to admonish the people with their prince's mouth that they should love the right, hate the wrong, praise good men without ceasing, and zealously denounce the evil. So, punishment may be given a holiday where the power of eloquence prevails. He must imitate the ancients with intelligence; he must correct the morals of others, and preserve his own with due integrity.

4. Finally, the Quaestor must be such a man as it befits to bear the image of a prince. For if, as is often the case, I should chance to hear a case from documents, how great will be the authority of that tongue which can prime the royal wits under the public eye? Legal skill and cautious speech must accompany him, so that no one shall criticize what the prince may happen to decide. Moreover, he will need a resolute spirit, so that no bribes and no threats may carry him from the path of justice. 5. For, in the preservation of equity, I, who should still be obeyed, suffer myself to be contradicted. But take heed to bring forward such legal learning that you may expound all things fitly on request. Other offices, indeed, may seek the help of legal assessors, but yours gives its counsels to the prince.

And therefore, prompted by the fame of your wisdom and eloquence, for this indiction, I allot you, by God's favour, the Quaestorship, the glory of letters, the temple of social order [*civilitas*], the begetter of every honour, the home of self-restraint, and seat of all virtues; so act that you strive to be equal to the duties just described.

6. For to you, the provinces transmit their petitions; from you, the Senate seeks the aid of the laws; from you experts request the justice they have learnt; and you must satisfy all those who may demand legal help from me. But, while doing all this, you must be carried away by no pride, gnawed by no grudge, never pleased by the misfortunes of others, since what is hateful to the prince cannot be right for the Quaestor. Wield a prince's power with a subject's rank. Ennobled as my mouth-piece, so speak that you may still think yourself due to render account before my judgment seat, where a man will either be condemned and receive his reward, or be praised and gain the glory of his upright ways.

### 1.3.4 A hierarchy of administrators supervised by the emperor

A controlled chain of command was basic to the success of the Late Antique administrative system. Constantine (312–337) did away with the Tetrarchy of Diocletian and asserted supreme rule for himself, but he maintained the administrative subdivisions of the state. Here Constantine gives instructions to his vicars, the officials in charge of dioceses. A diocese included a number of provinces, so the vicar (referred to by his honorific title "Your Gravity") was superior to a governor.

*Theodosian Code* 1.15.1

> The Office of Vicar
> In order that Your Gravity, occupied as you are with other duties, may not be burdened with a huge mass of such rescripts, it is Our pleasure to enjoin upon

Your Gravity those cases only in which a more powerful person can oppress an inferior or lesser judge or cases in which a matter arises of the kind that is not permitted to be terminated in the court of the governor, or cases which, although they have long been handled by the aforesaid governors, must now be terminated before you. [Constantine, 325]

### 1.3.5  Entrance requirements for the bureaucracy

Great care was taken that members of the imperial service met certain standards. This law of 383 indicates the continuing importance of social status in the administrative mentality.

*Theodosian Code* 7.2.1

> Whenever any man supposes that he should offer himself for imperial service, examination shall immediately be made of his birth status and of every aspect of his legal status, so that he cannot misrepresent his home, his family, or his parents. He shall not be given credence in this matter, however, except with the supporting testimony of the rank of Most Honorable. For in this way it will come about that no persons shall evade service in the municipal councils and no persons shall aspire to imperial service except those who are found by such a careful inquiry to be completely free both by birth and by the legal status of their lives. [Gratian, Valentinian and Theodosius 383]

### 1.3.6  The honor of serving the emperor

Service in the imperial bureaucracy conferred great honor. This poem, inscribed on a statue base, celebrates the achievements of Proculus (died *c.*526) who served as the Quaestor and earned the consulship under Justin I.

*The Greek Anthology* 16.48

["The Greek Anthology" 16.48, trans. Cyril Mango, in *The Art of the Byzantine Empire, 312–1453* (Englewood Cliffs, NJ: Prentice-Hall Inc., 1972) p. 46]

> I am Proculus, the son of Paul, a native of Byzantium, who was snatched in my flower by the Imperial court and placed in the hall of Justice that I may be the faithful spokesman of the mighty Emperor. This bronze proclaims the reward of my labors. Father and son enjoyed similar honors, yet the son surpassed his begetter by winning the consular staffs.

### 1.3.7  Bishops in the imperial administration

Justinian's *Edict 1* of 535 illustrates the important role that bishops gradually came to play in imperial administration after the reign of Constantine. Justinian requires that provincial bishops report to him any illegalities performed by civil administrators. In this way the church took a formal place in his program of provincial reform.

Justinian, *Edict 1*, Preface
[*The Thirteen Edicts of Justinian* (translated and annotated), William Sims
Thurman, Dissertation, University of Texas, Austin, 1964, pp. 1–2]

EDICT 1: ADDRESSED TO THE MOST DEVOUT BISHOPS AND MOST
HOLY PATRIARCHS EVERYWHERE ON EARTH.
*Preface.*
Since we serve as guardians of the commonwealth that God has entrusted to
our care and since we strive that our subjects live under completely equitable
conditions, we have drafted the subjoined edict which we deem proper to
announce to Your Holiness and through you to all the persons of your province.
Therefore it shall be the duty of Your Reverence and of all the other bishops to
enforce these provisions and to inform us if the provincial governors violate
any point, so that none of the laws that we have reverently and justly decreed
may be slighted. For if we pity our subjects because they, in addition to the
payment of fiscal taxes, have also suffered enormous injustices on account of
extortion on the part of their governors because of the sales that are made of
provincial governorships, and if we strive to eliminate such sales through the
subjoined edict, while you negligently fail to denounce them to us, this edict
will be consecrated to our Lord God, but you shall render an account to him for
the injustice done by others, if any injury is inflicted on your parishioners
without our being informed of it. Moreover, since you are present in your
region and exert yourselves in defense of both them and all who live elsewhere,
you must inform us of both those who rightly administer their offices and of
those who violate this our edict, so that in cognizance of each we may punish
the latter and reward the former. After this edict has been posted in public and
is thus published to all, it shall be taken into the most holy church and deposited
with the sacred vessels, as being itself consecrated to God and written for the
preservation of men whom He has created. You would also do something
preferable and expedient for all your parishioners, if you should engrave it on
wooden tablets or on stone and post it within the porticoes of the most holy
church, and thus make it easy for all men to read and acquire a knowledge of
what we have decreed.

### 1.3.8 Access to the emperor for all citizens

Despite the rigidly hierarchical organization of authority, the right of access to the
emperor by all citizens (a holdover from the early empire) remained a possibility. In
this law of 325, Constantine explains the principle to his Praetorian Prefect, who has
the responsibility of deciding whether to forward appeals to the emperor. (See *9.1.5*,
page 289.)
*Theodosian Code* 1.5.1

By edict We remind all provincials that, if they have been treated with
contempt when appealing to their own governors, they shall have the right to

appeal to Your Gravity, so that, if it should appear that this mistreatment occurred by the fault or negligence of the governors, Your Gravity shall immediately refer the matter to Our Wisdom, in order that it may be possible for such governors to be fittingly punished.

### 1.3.9 A new aristocracy of service

In the general recovery of the empire following the reforms of Diocletian in the late third century, a new aristocracy gradually developed in the Roman Empire. These new magnates combined service to (and rewards from) the emperor with accumulation of wealth and property at the local level. Men of senatorial rank had the responsibility of making sure the collection of taxes went smoothly in the regions of their influence. The opportunities for corruption were enormous and seldom missed. By avoiding payment of their own taxes, they grew wealthier – but the empire suffered. In the following letter, Bishop Basil of Caesarea praises the unusual rectitude of a high-ranking official whose job it was to evaluate property for taxation.

Basil of Caesarea, *Letter* 299

[*Saint Basil: Letters*, vol. 2, trans. A.C. Way (Washington, DC: Catholic University of America Press, 1951) p. 290]

> You wrote to me, although I was already aware of it, that you are dissatisfied with the administering of public affairs . . . For men who are engaged in financial affairs, looking toward wealth and agitated about this present glory, it is considered the greatest blessing to get control of some power by which they will be able to treat their friends well, to ward off their enemies, and to obtain for themselves what they desire. But you are not such a one. Impossible! You, who even voluntarily withdrew from civil power although it was so great, and, when it was possible for you to rule over the city as over one home, you chose a life simple and quiet, considering that not having trouble or causing it for others was worth more than the value others put upon being disagreeable.

### 1.3.10 Corruption and suffering in the provinces

Abuses of power were never eliminated. Here John the Lydian, an imperial civil servant in Constantinople under Justinian, describes an imperial official's brutal oppression of leading citizens in his hometown, Philadelphia in Lydia. Lydus calls this corrupt man "the Cyclops" and "Salmoneus," two evil figures from Greek mythology. (See *3.4.3*, page 91.)

John Lydus, *On the Magistracies of the Roman State* 3.59

[Anastasius C. Bandy, *Ioannes Lydus on Powers* or *The Magistracies of the Roman State* (Philadelphia: The American Philosophical Society, 1983) pp. 225, 227]

> 59. If only he had been most guilty to this degree and not also of sufferings and acts of terror against the subjects beyond the point of tragedy. Now, though I shudder to recount his obviously very numerous deeds of defilement (they are

countless, so that naturally they and they alone can fill up very large volumes of grief), I shall tell at this point the tragic tale of one act of his perpetrated for the sake of money. A certain Petronius in my Philadelphia, a man worthy of account and distinguished for family, property, and learning – this man was the possessor of precious stones from his ancestors, which were numerous and at the same time kept from the sight of private individuals because of their beauty and size. The Cyclops had him seized and had irons put around him, and proceeded to have him mercilessly scourged, while naked, with rods by barbarians, having shut him up in his mules' barn . . . Just as soon as this had become known, "the city stirred itself in alarm and pressed its hands to its eyes," and the people began wailing aloud, not having the courage either to help the one being racked to shreds or to conciliate the Fiend. The city's bishop, however, accompanied by all the priests, took up even the sacred scriptures and hastened to him, having intended to conciliate him through them. The Salmoneus, who regarded even God on a par with mankind, ordered them to go on stage and perform their own rites, not restraining himself at all from mentioning, by the obscene words which he had uttered, such to wit licentious acts as happen to be performed in brothels. And the symbols of God were present, uncovered and visible to all, and the pontifex [the bishop] who was being insulted along with them was lamenting bitterly, seeing the Deity dishonorably disregarded in this way. Petronius, however, because he regarded God above his own property, sent home, had all that he owned brought, including also the aforementioned stones, and had them cast at the outer door of the Cyclops . . .

### 1.3.11 A picture of the Roman Empire

During the reign of the emperor Diocletian, Eumenius of Autun, a rhetorician and bureaucrat in Gaul, delivered an oration to the governor of the province asking for Autun's school of rhetoric to be rebuilt. He asked that a map be repainted on the walls that would both teach the students geography and celebrate the might of the Roman Empire.

Eumenius, *For the Restoration of the Schools* .20–.21
[C.E.V. Nixon and Barbara Saylor Rodgers, trans., *In Praise of Later Roman Emperors: The Panegyrici Latini* (Berkeley: University of California Press, 1994) pp. 171–7]

Then let those funds, Your Excellency, allotted to me by the best masters of all virtues, be given to this institution devoted to learning and eloquence, that as we give thanks for the rest of the advantages in our lives in the temples of the gods who support them, so let us celebrate the unique regard of the same gods for letters in the ancient temple of literature.

Further, in its porticoes let the young men see and contemplate daily every land and all the seas and whatever cities, peoples, nations, the unconquered rulers either restore by affection or conquer by valor or restrain by fear. Since for the purpose of instructing the youth, to have them learn more clearly with their eyes what they comprehend less readily by their ears, there are pictured in that place, as I believe you have seen yourself, the sites of all locations with their names, their extent, and the distances between them, the sources and terminations of all the rivers, the curves of all the shores, and the Ocean, both where its circuit girds the earth and where its pressure breaks into it. Here let the most noble accomplishments of the bravest Emperors be recalled through representations of the separate regions, while the twin rivers [Euphrates and Tigris] of Persia and the thirsty fields of Libya and the recurred horns of the Rhine and the many-cleft mouth of the Nile are seen again as eager messengers constantly arrive.

Meanwhile the minds of the people gazing upon each of these places will imagine Egypt, its madness given over, peacefully subject to your clemency, Diocletian Augustus, or you, invincible Maximian, hurling lightning upon the smitten hordes of the Moors, or beneath your right hand, lord Constantius, Batavia and Britannia raising up their muddied heads from woods and waves, or you, Maximian Caesar (Galerius), trampling upon Persian bows and quivers. For now, now at last, it is a delight to see a picture of the world, since we see nothing in it which is not ours.

### 1.3.12 The condition and use of Roman roads

Over fifty thousand miles of roads bound the Empire together at the height of its power, but by Late Antiquity many of them had fallen into disrepair. With the exception of a military highway on the eastern frontier built by Diocletian, new construction of roads ceased. Organized road maintenance became a local rather than an imperial responsibility, causing emperors to remind provincial leaders to fulfill their obligations, as this law of 399 illustrates. Regular repair of roads ceased by the early fifth century.

*Theodosian Code* 15.3.4

It was, indeed, formerly established that the patrimonies of illustrious dignitaries should be considered exempt from the construction and repair of roads. But on account of the immense ruin of the highways, it is our will that all persons, with helpful devotion, shall eagerly desire to hasten to the repair of the public roads. [Arcadius and Honorius, 399]

### 1.3.13 Roman roads after Rome

*1.*

Theoderic I, the Ostrogothic ruler of Italy (r. 471–526), faced problems of road maintenance. In the following passage the king's chief official, Cassiodorus, orders another official to repair the Flaminian Way, one of the great highways of Roman Italy.

Cassiodorus, *Variae* XII.18

[*The Letters of Cassiodorus: Being a Condensed Translation of the Variae Epistolae of Magnus Aurelius Cassiodorus Senator*, trans. Thomas Hodgkin (London: Henry Frowde, 1886). Available online on Project Gutenberg.]

> Great is the reward of those who serve Kings efficiently; as severe is the punishment of those who neglect their duties towards them. How delightful is it to journey without obstacles over a well-made road, to pass doubtful places without fear, to ascend mountainous steeps by a gentle incline, to have no fear of the planking of a bridge when one crosses it, and in short to accomplish one's journey so that everything happens to one's liking!
>
> This is the pleasure which you can now prepare for your Sovereign. Therefore, as the Flaminian Way is furrowed by the action of torrents, join the yawning chasms by the broadest of bridges; clear away the rough woods which choke the sides of the highway; procure the stipulated number of post-horses, and see that they have all the points which are required in a good steed; collect the designated quantities of provisions without plundering the peasants. A failure in any one of these particulars will ruin your whole service.

### 2.

Even in poor condition, Roman roads continued to be used. The following extract from Gregory of Tours' *History of the Franks*, composed in the new Frankish kingdom in the late sixth century, describes the strategy of King Guntram of Burgundy (561–592) during one of the many wars with other Frankish kings of his day.

Gregory of Tours, *The History of the Franks* VI.11

[Gregory of Tours, *The History of the Franks*, trans. Lewis Thorpe (Harmondsworth: Penguin Books, 1974) pp. 341–2]

> Now that he had made peace with Chilperic, Childebert sent envoys to King Guntram to say that he must return that half of Marseilles which Childebert had given to him after the death of his father. If Guntram would not agree, he must know that holding on to this half of the city would cost him dear. Guntram refused. He had the roads blocked, so that no one should find the way open to cross his kingdom.

## 1.4 Economic life

In recent years, much scholarly attention has been directed to changes in the economic life of the Roman Empire in Late Antiquity. Archaeological evidence has yielded many insights, while new information has been wrung from the limited ancient written documents. Scholars note many local regional economic communities linked in various degrees to one another to create rather fragile economic superstructures. General trends also included a growing dependency of large segments of the peasantry upon wealthy landowners, and in some areas, the decline of urban life. An extensive reorganization of the economy begun by Diocletian in the late third century led to a prosperous empire in the fourth, but this did not last. Such factors as war and invasion, heavy taxation on the peasantry – and failure to pay taxes by wealthy landholders, plague, and breakdown of trade are given as "tipping factors" that caused economic crises across the empire. In the course of the fifth century and later, the economies of the western provinces declined, but in the East, which was spared the destructive invasions of the fifth century, the Roman economy in many regions continued to be fairly robust well into the sixth century.

### 1.4.1 Diocletian's Edict on Maximum Prices

In 296 Diocletian overhauled the tax system and introduced a new coinage in order to combat the economic chaos of previous decades. In order to put a ceiling on prices, which had gone out of control due to unrestrained inflation, Diocletian (with the support of the other Tetrarchs) decreed fixed limits to prices and wages in the empire. The death penalty could be imposed on offenders. It is possible that he was responding to the petitions of soldiers and that the imperial court itself produced a "mini-inflation" wherever it was located, thereby increasing the number of complaints sent to him. This edict was published in 301, but because of its impracticality was revoked by 305. It demonstrates the desperate measures that the emperor could take to try to control the economy. (See *1.3.1*, page 11.)

Diocletian, *Edict on Maximum Prices*, preamble
[Naphtali Lewis and Meyer Reinhold, eds., *Roman Civilization: Selected Readings*, vol. II (New York: Columbia University Press, 1990) pp. 422, 423]

> If the excesses perpetrated by persons of unlimited and frenzied avarice could be checked by some self-restraint – this avarice which rushes for gain and profit with no thought for mankind . . .; or if the general welfare could endure without harm this riotous license by which, in its unfortunate state, it is being very seriously injured every day, the situation could perhaps be faced with dissembling and silence, with the hope that human forbearance might alleviate the cruel and pitiable situation. But the only desire of these uncontrolled madmen is to have no thought for the common need. Among the unscrupulous, the immoderate, and the avaricious it is considered almost a creed . . . to desist from plundering the wealth of all only when necessity compels them. Through their extreme need, moreover, some persons have become acutely aware of their most unfortunate situation, and can no longer close their eyes to it. Therefore we, who are the protectors of the human race, are agreed, as we view the situation, that decisive legislation is necessary, so that the long-hoped-for solutions which mankind itself could not provide may, by the remedies provided by our foresight, be vouchsafed for the general betterment of all . . .
>
> We hasten, therefore, to apply the remedies long demanded by the situation, satisfied that no one can complain that our intervention with regulations is untimely or unnecessary, trivial or unimportant. These measures are directed

against the unscrupulous, who have perceived in our silence of so many years a lesson in restraint but have been unwilling to imitate it. For who is so insensitive and so devoid of human feeling that he can be unaware or has not perceived that uncontrolled prices are widespread in the sales taking place in the markets and in the daily life of the cities? Nor is the uncurbed passion for profiteering lessened either by abundant supplies or by fruitful years . . .

It is our pleasure, therefore, that the prices listed in the subjoined schedule be held in observance in the whole of our Empire . . .

It is our pleasure that anyone who resists the measures of this statute shall be subject to a capital penalty for daring to do so. And let no one consider the statute harsh, since there is at hand a ready protection from danger in the observance of moderation . . . We therefore exhort the loyalty of all, so that a regulation instituted for the public good may be observed with willing obedience and due scruple, especially as it is seen that by a statute of this kind provision has been made, not for single municipalities and peoples and provinces but for the whole world . . .

The prices for the sale of individual items which no one may exceed are listed below.

### 1.4.2  Justinian's Edict on the Regulation of Skilled Labor

Controlling prices remained a problem for imperial officials. Diocletian's efforts were mirrored by Justinian in 544 as he sought to combat the financial repercussions of the plague.

Justinian, *Edict* 6, "On the Regulation of Skilled Labor," Preface, 1
[*The Thirteen Edicts of Justinian*, trans. William Sims Thurman (Dissertation, University of Texas, Austin, 1964) pp. 12–14]

We learn that pursuant to the chastening that we have received in the benevolence of our Lord God, persons engaged in business and professions, as well as artisans of various crafts, and agriculturalists, not to mention the merchant seamen, have abandoned themselves to avarice and demand double and triple prices and wages that are contrary to the custom prevalent from antiquity, although these persons should rather have been improved by this calamity.

1. It is therefore our decision to forbid such covetous greed on the part of everyone through a sacred imperial edict. In the future no businessman, workman, or artisan in any occupation, trade, or agricultural pursuit shall dare to charge a higher price or wage than that of the custom prevalent from antiquity. We also order those who make estimates for construction, cultivation and other works not to calculate any raise in pay for the workmen, but that they adhere to the old original custom. We order those who act as employers and also those who purchase any kind of products to adhere to this carefully. For we do not concede to them the right to furnish any amount in excess of the established customary fee. Those who charge any more than the custom prevalent from antiquity must know that they shall be compelled to pay a triple

amount to the fisc, if they should be convicted of taking or giving more than the original regulation prescribes. We order Your Excellency and the most glorious prefect of this blessed city to examine this matter and to enforce this law. For it is our will that through you those who have violated this our regulation shall be fined with the designated penalty and subjected to punishments. A penalty of 5 pounds of gold shall be imposed upon your subordinate office staff, if they neglect any of our instructions.

23 March, 544

### 1.4.3 The colossal wealth of aristocrats

The inequality of wealth between the very rich and the very poor in the Roman Empire cannot be overstated. In this passage written in the late fourth century, the historian Olympiodorus of Thebes describes the enormous sums spent by aristocrats in Rome to celebrate their holding of government offices. (See *1.4.13*, page 30.)

Olympiodorus of Thebes, *Fragment* 41.2

[Roger Blockley, *The Fragmentary Classicising Historians of the Later Roman Empire: Eunapius, Olympiodorus, Priscus and Malchus* (Liverpool: F. Cairns, 1983) p. 205]

> Many of the Roman households received an income of 4,000 pounds of gold per year from their properties, not including grain, wine and other produce, which if sold, would have amounted to one-third of the income in gold. The income of the households at Rome of the second class was 1,000 or 1,500 pounds of gold. When Probus, the son of Olybrius, celebrated his praetorship during the reign of the usurper John (423–425), he spent 1,200 pounds of gold. Before the capture of Rome, Symmachus the orator, a senator of middling wealth, spent 2,000 pounds when his son Symmachus celebrated his praetorship. Maximus, one of the wealthy men, spent 4,000 pounds on his son's praetorship. The praetors celebrated their festivals for seven days.

### 1.4.4 What to do with wealth?

In the Gospel of Matthew, Jesus told a young man, "If you wish to be perfect, go, sell your possessions, and give the money to the poor, and you will have treasure in heaven; then come, follow me." Christians grappled with how literally this injunction should be taken. At one extreme it underlay the ascetic lifestyle of the monastic movement. Other Christians wished to remain "in the world" as they followed Jesus' teachings. The anonymous text below, written in the second decade of the fifth century, rejected untrammeled greed and advocated keeping only enough money for the necessities of life.

Anonymous, *On Riches* 6.3, 20.1–2

[B.R. Rees, *The Letters of Pelagius and his Followers* (Rochester: Boydell & Brewer, 1991) pp. 179–80; 209]

6.3 All this time you convince yourself that it is from God that you receive what in fact you either procure with your ill-gotten gains or acquire at the price of shameful sycophancy and oft-repeated acts of obeisance, bowing your head to the ground and addressing as "Lord" one whom you scorn, while he, the trafficker in offices, also scorns you, and sometimes you glory in being called "honourable," though the only true honour is that which is paid to moral character, not that acquired by money or shameful servitude.

20.1 But I must not ignore either the excessively subtle and refined ingenuity of those who think themselves religious and are reckoned to be despisers of the world by themselves and by ignorant people because they go about in more lowly attire, taking no pleasure in possessing ornaments or gold or silver or in display of more costly metal, and yet keep all their possessions hidden away in their treasuries and, motivated by sheer greed, retain possession of what they disdain to use in the eyes of men merely in order to enjoy a worthless reputation.

20.2 But I have sons, you will say, for whom I want to keep all my possessions . . . What then are we saying? That you should completely disinherit your sons? Far from it! Rather, that you should leave them no more than their nature requires. For how can you be said to love them, if you are seen to confer on them something which will only harm them?

### 1.4.5 *Poverty*

The orator Libanius (died 394) described the poverty to be seen in his beloved Antioch, the grandest city in Syria. Christian writers echoed similar sentiments as awareness of poverty and compassion for the poor took a new place in public discourse during the fourth century.

Libanius, *Oration* 7.1–3
[Translated by Carlos Galvao-Sobrinho]

Yesterday at night a man grieved and lamented as he counted the number of beggars. Some of them stood upright; others were too frail to stand. Some were so weak they could not even sit up. Many were mutilated. The emaciated beggars looked worse than the dead. The man said it is a most pitiable sight to see these people enduring the cold dressed only in rags, wearing nothing but a scrap of cloth. Some have their arms and legs bare from their shoulders and groin. Others have no part of their bodies covered. Unceasingly, they ask to be given something from passers-by, and they are content if they receive not only a piece of bread but also when they get a penny. While this man weeps for the poor and calls them wretched, another haughtily walks by, leaving the bath-house under the shining light of the lamps on his way to dinners lacking nothing but ambrosia and nectar.

## 1.4.6  Natural disasters and local economies

Local agricultural economies were of quite a small scale and highly vulnerable to natural disasters. Libanius describes the consequences of a drought brought about by nature, which he grandiloquently suggests felt indignant at the emperor Julian's death.

Libanius, *Oration* 18.289, 293

[Libanius, *Selected Works*, vol. I, trans. A.F. Norman (Cambridge, MA: Harvard University Press, 1969) pp. 475, 477]

> (289) Everywhere is full of carpetbaggers – lands, islands, villages, cities, markets, harbours and back streets. Houses and slaves are put up for sale, foster parents, nurses, attendants, even the tombs of their ancestors. Everywhere there is poverty, beggary and tears; farmers think it better to be beggars than farmers, and the man who gives alms today is tomorrow himself in need of alms . . . (293) but from the seasons have come famine and plague, afflicting man and beast alike, as though it is not right that creatures upon earth should flourish once [the emperor Julian] has departed.

## 1.4.7  Famine

Though famines were rare, they hit hard. This account of a famine in northern Syria at the turn of the sixth century illuminates the plight of the victims and how the authorities took steps to alleviate the suffering.

Pseudo-Joshua the Stylite, *Chronicle* 38–42

[W. Wright, *The Chronicle of Joshua the Stylite* (Cambridge: Cambridge University Press, 1882) pp. 27–31]

> 38. The year 811 [499–500]. In the month of Adar [March] of this year the locusts came upon us out of the ground, so that, because of their number, we imagined that not only had the eggs that were in the ground been hatched to our harm, but that the very air was vomiting them against us, and that they were descending from the sky upon us. When they were only able to crawl, they devoured and consumed all the Arab territory and all that of Rasain and Tella and Edessa. But after they were able to fly, the stretch of their radii was from the border of Assyria to the western sea [the Mediterranean] and they went north as far as the boundary of the Ortaye. They ate up and desolated these districts and utterly consumed everything that was in them . . . Presently, in the month of Nisan [April] there began to be a dearth of grain and of everything else, and four modii of wheat were sold for a dinar. In the months of Khaziran [June] and Tammuz [July] the inhabitants of these districts were reduced to all sorts of shifts to live. They sowed millet for their own use but it did not thrive. Before the year came to an end, misery from hunger had reduced the people to beggary, so that they sold their property for half its worth, horses, and oxen and sheep and pits. And because the locusts devoured all the crop, and left neither

pasture nor food for man or beast, many forsook their native places and removed to other districts of the north and west. And the sick who were in the village, as well as the old men and boys and women and infants, and those who were tortured by hunger, being unable to walk far and go to distant places, entered into the cities to get a livelihood by begging; thus many villages and hamlets were left destitute of inhabitants.

39. ... At this time our father (Mar) Peter set out to visit the emperor (at Constantinople), in order to beg him to remit the tax. The governor, however, laid hold of the landed proprietors, and used great violence to them and extorted it from them, so that, before the bishop could persuade the emperor, the governor had sent the money to the capital. When the emperor saw that the money had arrived, he did not like to remit it; but, in order not to send our father away empty, he remitted two folles [coins of little worth] to the villagers, and the price which they were paying whilst he freed the citizens from the obligation of drawing water for the Greek soldiery.

40. The governor himself too set out to visit the emperor, girt with his sword, and left Eusebius to hold his post and govern the city. When this Eusebius saw that the bakers were not sufficient to make bread for the market, because of the multitude of country people, of whom the city was full, and because of the poor who had no bread in their houses, he gave an order that everyone who chose might make bread and sell it in the market.

41. The year 812 [AD 500–501]. In this year, after the vintage, wine was sold at the rate of six measures for a dinar, and a kap of raisins for three hundred numia. The famine was sore in the villages and in the city; for those who were left in the villages were eating bitter-vetches, and others were frying the withered fallen grapes and eating them, though even of them there was not enough to satisfy them. And those who were in the city were wandering about the streets, picking up the stalks and leaves of vegetables, all filthy with mud, and eating them. They were sleeping in the porticoes and streets, and wailing by night and day from the pangs of hunger; and their bodies wasted away, and they were in a sad plight, and became like jackals because of the leanness of their bodies. The whole city was full of them, and they began to die in the porticoes and in the streets.

42. After the governor Demosthenes had gone up to the emperor, he informed him of this calamity; and the emperor gave him no small sum of money to distribute among the poor. And when he came back from his presence to Edessa, he sealed many of them on their necks with leaden seals, and gave each of them a pound of bread a day. Still, however, they were not able to live, because they were tortured by the pangs of hunger, which wasted them away.

### 1.4.8 The emperor steps in

Imperial intervention into local economic crises could avert disaster. This panegyric to Constantine describes how in 311 he saved the community of the Aedui in Gaul by temporarily halting their taxes.

Anonymous Orator, *Speech of Thanks to Constantine* 5–6
[C.E.V. Nixon and Barbara Saylor Rodgers, *In Praise of Later Roman Emperors: The Panegyrici Latini* (Berkeley: University of California Press, 1994) pp. 272–6]

(5) I have related, Emperor, how well deserving were the Aedui of your succor; it follows that I should relate how grievously they were afflicted . . . as doctors pre-eminent in their skill do not disdain to inspect the wounds which they treat, so may you now listen for a little while to the burdens of the Aedui which you have relieved. For you cannot achieve praise for clemency without undergoing a feeling of pity. That city lay prostrate, not so much because of the collapse of its walls as because of the exhaustion of its strength, from the time when the harshness of the new census drained it of life. But a complaint could not be made with justice, since we were both in possession of the fields which had been registered and bound by the common formula of the Gallic census, we who can be compared to no one in our fortunes. So much the more, Emperor, do we thank your clemency, who by freely granting remedies made us seem to have obtained justly what we could not rightly have sought.

(6) For we have, as I have said, both the number of persons which was recorded, and the amount of land, but both are rendered worthless owing to the inactivity of men and the treachery of the earth. For where are we going to find a field or a farmer comparable to those of the Remi, the Nervii or even of our closest neighbors the Tricasses, whose returns match their labor? Although one would fairly pardon the cultivators themselves, whom it irks to labor without profit, if a field which never meets its expenses is abandoned out of necessity, especially when you consider the poverty of the country folk, for whom there was no possibility either of draining water off their land or cutting back the woods, reeling under their debts as they were. Thus whatever was once tolerably fertile land has now either degenerated into swamps or been choked with brambles. Indeed even that famous district, the Arebrignian, is spoken about with empty envy, for cultivation of the vine is conspicuous in only one place; for the rest of it, by contrast, is impassable because of forests and rocks, the dens of untroubled wild beasts. That plain, moreover, which lies under it and extends as far as the Saône was indeed once a delightful spot, as I hear, when uninterrupted cultivation throughout the properties of individual proprietors carried away the overflow from springs in open channels. Now, however, that their courses have been blocked because of desolation, whatever had been very fertile because it was low-lying has been converted into marshes with deep holes.

Finally the vineyards themselves, at which the ignorant marvel, have grown so decayed with age that they scarcely respond any longer to cultivation. The roots of the vines, the age of which we do not now know, are bound by having been layered a thousand times, and prevent the trenches from reaching the required depth, and the very shoots that they send out are not buried but merely covered, to be washed out by rains and scorched by the sun. Nor can we mark out a place anywhere for new vines, as is customary in Aquitania and other

27

provinces, since higher up the rocks are unbroken, and below the low-lying land is subject to frosts.

## 1.4.9 The great estates and the rise of patrons

The increasing imperial demand for revenues that followed Diocletian's reforms had a marked impact on the rural peasantry, whose labor produced taxable revenues for the state. The imperial bureaucracy took steps to register all land and manpower in the empire and then bind workers to their places of registration so that they could be taxed regularly. Sometimes the fiscal burdens were too heavy, and peasants sought the protection of powerful landowners who were not their legitimate employers, even if doing so entailed limits on their own freedom. The government objected to the resulting loss of revenues and the power of influential landowners. (See *2.2.3*, page 39.)

The first law below indicates an imperial effort to stop the flight of farm workers to protectors who were not their legitimate employers. This is a sign that the patronage system on great estates was underway already in the fourth century. The second law, dating to the reign of Leo (457–474), but maintained in the *Code of Justinian*, shows that entire villages could become implicated in the patronage system and that this was still a problem in the sixth century.

*Theodosian Code* 11.24.2
[Peter Sarris, *Economy and Society in the Age of Justinian* (Cambridge: Cambridge University Press, 2006) p. 187]

> Farmers are to refrain from resorting to patronage and they shall be subjected to punishment if by audacious contrivances they should seek such assistance for themselves . . . And as for those who lavish their patronage, for each one of the landholdings, however many they are found to have received, they will have to pay twenty-five pounds of gold. [Valentinian, Valens, and Gratian, 368 or 370]

Justinian, *Code* II.54.1
[Peter Sarris, *Economy and Society in the Age of Justinian* (Cambridge: Cambridge University Press, 2006) p. 192]

> If, after this imperial law of ours, anyone should flee to the patronage of any person whatsoever, thereby harming and defrauding the fulfillment of this public obligation, the agreement made for this purpose shall have no validity, be it under the outward appearance of a gift, or sale, or contract of employment, or any other contractual form whatsoever . . . and the villages and properties of those that have taken recourse to patronage shall suffer public confiscation.

## 1.4.10 Exploitation of peasant farmers in Syria and Egypt

John Chrysostom, the Patriarch of Constantinople from 398 to 404, was a native of Antioch in Syria. He spoke out against the exploitation of Syrian peasants who labored on vast estates owned by wealthy landlords. The workers suffered, but their efforts helped make the Late Antique period one of economic growth in the eastern Mediterranean.

John Chrysostom, *Homily on Matthew* 61.3
[Peter Sarris, *Economy and Society in the Age of Justinian* (Cambridge: Cambridge University Press, 2006) p. 196]

> [The landlords of Antioch] impose unceasing and intolerable payments on [the peasants], and require of them laborious services . . . What sight could be more pitiable than when having toiled the whole winter through in frost and rain, spent with work, the peasants return with empty hands and even in debt, dreading and fearing more than this ruin and more than hunger, the torments inflicted by the overseers, the seizures, the demand notes, the arrests, the inescapable forced labour?

### 1.4.11 Dependence upon a landlord on an Egyptian estate

Sometime around 550, an unfortunate tenant farmer in Egypt named Anoup wrote to his "kind lord," the enormously rich and influential aristocrat and patron of countless estates, Flavius Apion III. Faced with financial ruin, Anoup had no choice but to throw himself on the mercy of the mighty Apion family. It was in the interest of the Apions to help this farmer, whose family had worked for several generations on Apion properties. Their mutual interdependence increased the power of the Apion family. Similar arrangements were common throughout Mediterranean lands as great landowning families increased the scale of their holdings and consolidated their power.

This in turn led to new forms of estate management in which landowners no longer simply leased land to tenant farmers as had been the case before Diocletian. Now, a bi-partite system emerged in which peasants were granted allotments of land in return for payment of rent. At the same time they would also be expected to work regularly on centrally organized land owned solely by local aristocrats.

*Oxyrhynchus Papyrus* I.130, lines 1–10
[Peter Sarris, *Economy and Society in the Age of Justinian* (Cambridge: Cambridge University Press, 2006) p. 72]

> No injustice or wickedness has ever attached to the glorious household of my kind lord, but it is ever full of mercy and overflowing to supply the needs of others. On account of this, I the wretched slave of my good lord wish to bring it to your lordship's knowledge by this present entreaty for mercy that I serve my kind lord as my fathers and forefathers did before me and pay the taxes every year. And by the will of God in the past eleventh and tenth indictions my cattle died, and I borrowed the not inconsiderable amount of 15 *solidi* [gold pieces] so as to be able to buy the same number of cattle. Yet when I approached my kind lord and asked for pity in my straits, those belonging to my lord refused to do my lord's bidding. For unless your pity extends to me, my lord, I cannot stay on my

*ktema* [farm allotment] and fulfill my services with regard to the properties of the estate. But I beseech and urge your lordship to command that mercy be shown to me because of the disaster that has overtaken me.

### 1.4.12 The colonate

A new type of tenant peasantry emerged in Late Antiquity, the colonate. While still free Roman citizens, these peasants (called *coloni* as well as other terms) could not leave their farms permanently, but their landlords could not evict them either. *Coloni* had many obligations to their landlords and limited control of their own possessions. Not all peasants were *coloni*, and it was possible to leave the status of *colonus*. The complex ties of economic dependency embedded in this institution anticipated the development of feudal structures in medieval Europe. This law of Justinian describes basic aspects of the colonate.

Justinian, *Code* 11.48.23.2

[Roth Clausing, *The Roman Colonate* (New York: Columbia University Press, 1925) p. 24]

> Let the proprietors take care that they inflict no innovation nor violence upon the *coloni*. For if the proprietors are guilty of any such action, the *moderator* [governor] of the province himself shall take complete charge of the matter; and he shall see that the *coloni* are recompensed for any injury which they have received, and that the old customary rent is observed. This law applies not only to the actual *coloni* but to their posterity of whatever age or sex; and we decree that the offspring of the *coloni* once born on the estate shall always remain in possession under exactly the same conditions which we have defined for their ancestors on the estates of others.

### 1.4.13 A patron from the outside

Holy men who belonged to neither the local nor the imperial hierarchy functioned well as patrons of villages which dotted the rural hinterlands of cities. (See *1.4.3*, page 23.)

*History of the Monks in Egypt* 8.30–1

[Alan K. Bowman, *Egypt after the Pharaohs from 332BC–AD642: From Alexander to the Arab Conquest* (Berkeley and Los Angeles: University of California Press, 1986) p. 129]

> Not long afterwards two villages came into armed conflict with each other in a dispute concerning the ownership of land. When Apollo [a monk] was informed of this, he went down to them at once to restore peace among them . . .

[*In another instance*]

> Apollo said to the brigand, "If you obey me, my friend, I shall ask my master to forgive you your sins." When the brigand heard this he did not hesitate. He

threw down his arms and clasped the saint's knees. Then Apollo, having become a mediator of peace, restored to each person his property.

### 1.4.14 Who is the best patron?

Finding an appropriate patron could mean survival for a community. The following excerpt from a fourth-century Jewish commentary on Deuteronomy gives a parable from Palestine that spells out various options. (See *2.4.3*, page 49; *3.4.3*, page 91.)

*Midrash Ha-Gaddol*, Deuteronomy 32:9

[Daniel Sperber, *Roman Palestine 200–400; The Land: Crisis and Change in Agrarian Society Reflected in Rabbinic Sources* (Ramat-Gan: Bar-Ilan University Press, 1978) p. 69]

> To what is this similar? It is like unto a king who entered into a city and everyone in his entourage entered it with him, governors, dukes, and commanders. Some made of the governor their patron, some of the duke, some of the chief of the army. There was one clever fellow there. He said: All these people are under the authority of the king, and cannot prevent him from doing whatever he may wish to do. But he can prevent them from doing what they wish to do. I shall choose as my patron none other than the king who can prevent all others from doing anything he objects to.

### 1.4.15 Landlocked peasants

For the sophisticated and well-traveled aristocrat Synesius of Cyrene (*c.*373–*c.*414), a neo-Platonic philosopher who became a bishop in the town of Ptolemais in Libya after 410, the limited horizons of uneducated peasants were a source of considerable amusement. Here he tells a friend about peasants in his neighborhood who are so far from the sea and so ignorant that they refuse to believe in the existence of fish.

Synesius, *Epistles* 148

[*The Letters of Synesius of Cyrene*, trans. Augustine Fitzgerald (London: Humphrey Milford/Oxford University Press, 1926) pp. 243–8]

> To Olympius
> As a matter of fact, I do not live near the sea, and I rarely come to the harbor. I have moved up country to the southern extremity of the Cyrenaica, and my neighbors are such men as Odysseus was in quest of, when he steered from Ithaca, to appease the wrath of Poseidon, in obedience of the oracle.
> Men, who know not of the sea, nor eat food mixed with salt. But do not think that I am exaggerating when I say that people here do not take to the sea, even for the purpose of getting their salt, nor yet suppose that thus they eat their meat and cakes unsalted. We have, I swear by holy Hestia, at a distance to the south less than that which separates us from the sea to the north, a native salt which comes from the earth and which we call Ammon's salt. It collects under a scab, as it were, of crumbling stone, and when this scab, which conceals it, has been

removed, it is easy enough to scoop out the depths with one's hand or with a shovel, and the lumps that you may take up in this manner are salt, pleasant both to look at and to taste.

Do not think it sophistical vanity on my part, this account of the salts found in this country. Rustic people such as we are the last to harbor vain glory. But you express a wish to learn from me about everything in my part of the world; therefore be prepared for a loquacious letter, that you may pay the penalty for your untimely curiosity. At the same time, what is foreign to anyone is difficult of credence. A Syrian will not easily acknowledge the existence of salt from the earth, very much as people here are hard to convince when I answer questions about ships, sails, and the sea.

You may remember that once when I was studying philosophy with you, I looked out upon this very thing, the sea, and the great deep lake which stretches from Pharos to Canopus. One ship was being towed in; another was moving with all sails set; another was propelled by oars. You laughed at me when I compared this last one to a centipede. Now the people here are in the same state of mind as we ourselves, whenever we listen to tales in the world beyond Thule, whatever Thule may be, which gives to those who have crossed it freedom to lie about it without criticism or censure. Even if they admit what is told them about vessels, or only seem to laugh at it, at all events they stoutly refuse to believe that the sea too is able to nourish mankind. According to their idea, this privilege belongs to mother earth alone.

On one occasion, when they refused to believe in the existence of fish, I took a certain jar, and dashing it against a stone, showed them plenty of salted fish from Egypt, on which they said they were the bodies of evil snakes, sprang up and took to flight, for they suspected that the spines were as dangerous as the poison of serpent's fang. Then the oldest and most intelligent of them all said that he found it difficult to believe that salt water could produce anything good and fit to eat, since spring water, excellent though it be to drink, produces nothing except frogs and leeches, which not even a madman would taste. And yet their ignorance is natural.

### 1.4.16 Slavery is taken for granted

Slavery pervaded Late Antique society and was generally accepted without question. Here Basil of Caesarea, a bishop of the late fourth century, gives a Christian interpretation of the institution.

Basil of Caesarea, *On the Holy Spirit* 20

[Peter Garnsey, *Ideas of Slavery from Aristotle to Augustine* (Cambridge: Cambridge University Press, 1996) p. 45]

> Some say that the Spirit is neither master nor slave, but like a freeman. What miserable nonsense! What pitiful audacity! What shall I lament, their ignorance or their blasphemy? They insult the dogmas pertaining to the divine nature by

confining them within human categories. They think they see differences of dignity among men, and then apply such variation to the ineffable nature of God. Do they not realize that even among men, no one is a slave by nature? Men are brought under the yoke of slavery either because they are captured in battle or else they sell themselves into slavery owing to poverty; as the Egyptians became the slaves of Pharaoh. Sometimes, by a wise and inscrutable providence, worthless children are commanded by their father to serve their more intelligent brothers and sisters. Any upright person investigating the circumstances would realize that such situations bring much benefit, and are not a sentence of condemnation for those involved. It is better for a man who lacks intelligence and self-control to become another's possession. Governed by his master's intelligence, he will become like a chariot driven by a skilled horseman, or a ship with a seasoned sailor at the tiller. That is why Jacob obtained his father's blessing and became Esau's master: so that this foolish son, who had no intelligence properly to guide him, might profit from his prudent brother, even against his will. Canaan became "a slave of slaves to this brother", because his father Ham was void of understanding, unable to teach his son any virtue. That is why men become slaves, but those who escape poverty, war, or the need of a guardian, are free. And even though one man is called a master, and another a slave, we are all the possessions of our Creator; we all share the rank of slave.

### 1.4.17  Slaves in the law

The *Institutes* state the main principles of the law of persons – the distinction between free people and slaves.

Justinian, *Institutes* 1.3–5

[*Justinian's Institutes*, trans. Peter Birks and Grant McLeod (Ithaca, NY: Cornell University Press, 1987) pp. 39, 41]

### 1.3 THE LAW OF PERSONS

The main classification in the law of persons is this: all men are either free or slaves. 1. Liberty – the Latin "libertas" gives us "liberi", free men – denotes a man's natural ability to do what he wants as long as the law or some other force does not prevent him. 2. Slavery on the other hand is an institution of the law of all peoples; it makes a man the property of another, contrary to the law of nature . . . 4. They are either born slaves or enslaved afterwards. The offspring of slave women are born slaves. Enslavement can happen under the law of all peoples, by capture; or under the law of the state, as when a free man over twenty allows himself to be sold to share the price. The legal condition of all slaves is the same. 5. Among free men there are many distinctions. Free men are either free-born or freed.

33

## 1.4 THE FREE-BORN

A person is free-born if he is free at the moment of his birth, whether he is the child of a marriage between two free-born people, or is born to freed people, or to a couple one of whom is free-born and the other is freed. Equally he is free-born if his mother is free and his father a slave. The same is true if his mother is free and his father unknown because he was conceived casually. It is enough for the mother to be free at the time of the birth even though a slave at conception. Even the other way around, with the mother free at conception but a slave by the birth, it is accepted that the child is born free. The reason is that the mother's calamity should not prejudice the baby in her womb.

## 1.5 FREEDMEN

A freedman is someone who has been manumitted from lawful slavery. Manumission is the grant of freedom. As the word implies, while a man is a slave he is gripped in the hand of his owner and in his power; by release from that grip he becomes free . . . We have given all freedmen Roman citizenship irrespective of shortcoming as to the age of the slave manumitted or of the owner manumitting or in the mode of manumission, all of which used to be material. We have added considerably to the ways in which slaves can acquire freedom with Roman citizenship. That is the only kind of freedom nowadays.

### 1.4.18 Slavery, the wage of sin

For Augustine, slavery was God's harsh judgment.
Augustine, *City of God* 19.15
[David Knowles, ed., *Augustine: City of God* (New York: Penguin, 1981) p. 875]

> The first cause of slavery, then, is sin, whereby man was subjected to man in the condition of bondage; and this can only happen by the judgment of God, with whom there is no injustice, and who knows how to allot different punishments according to the deserts of the offenders.

### 1.4.19 An international trade in humans

Slave dealers thrived throughout the empire. Here Augustine describes the depredations of slavers in the provinces of Roman North Africa (not sub-Saharan) in the early 420s.
Augustine, *Letter* 10.2
[Peter Garnsey, *Ideas of Slavery from Aristotle to Augustine* (Cambridge: Cambridge University Press, 1996) pp. 60–1]

> There are so many of those in Africa who are commonly called "slave dealers" that they seem to be draining Africa of much of its human population

and transferring their "merchandise" to the provinces across the sea. Almost all of these are free persons. Only a few are found to have been sold by their parents, and these people buy them, not as Roman laws permit, as indentured servants for a period of twenty-five years, but in fact they buy them as slaves and sell them across the sea as slaves. True slaves are sold by their masters only rarely. Now from this bunch of merchants has grown up a multitude of pillaging and corrupting "dealers" so that in herds, shouting, in frightening military or barbarian attire they invade sparsely populated and remote rural areas and they violently carry off those whom they would sell to the merchants . . .

# Further reading

Bagnall, Roger, *Egypt in Late Antiquity* (Princeton, NJ: Princeton University Press, 1993)

Banaji, Jairus, *Agrarian Change in Late Antiquity: Gold, Labour, and Aristocratic Dominance* (Oxford: Oxford University Press, 2007)

Barnwell, P.S., *Emperor, Prefects, and Kings: The Roman West, 395–565* (London: Duckworth, 1992)

Brown, Peter, *The World of Late Antiquity, AD 150–750* (New York: W.W. Norton, 1971)

Brown, Peter, *The Rise of Western Christendom. Triumph and Diversity*, 2nd edn. (London: Blackwell, 2003)

Cameron, Averil, *The Later Roman Empire: A.D. 284–430* (Cambridge, MA: Harvard University Press, 1993)

Cameron, Averil, *The Mediterranean World in Late Antiquity, A.D. 395–600* (London: Routledge, 1993)

Cameron, Averil and Peter Garnsey, eds., *The Cambridge Ancient History*, vol. 13: *The Late Empire, AD 337–425* (Cambridge: Cambridge University Press, 1998)

Cameron, Averil, Bryan Ward-Perkins, and Michael Whitby, eds., *The Cambridge Ancient History*, vol. 14: *Late Antiquity: Empire and Successors, A.D. 425–600* (Cambridge: Cambridge University Press, 2001)

Corcoran, Simon, *The Empire of the Tetrarchs. Imperial Pronouncements and Government* (Oxford: Oxford University Press, 1996)

Drake, H.A., ed., *Violence in Late Antiquity: Perceptions and Practices* (Aldershot, England: Ashgate, 2006)

Ellis, Linda, Frank Kidner, and Gillian Clark, *Shifting Frontiers IV: Travel, Communication and Geography in Late Antiquity* (San Francisco: San Francisco State University, 2001)

Fowden, Garth, *Empire to Commonwealth: Consequences of Monotheism in Late Antiquity* (Princeton, NJ: Princeton University Press, 1993)

Garnsey, Peter, *Ideas of Slavery from Aristotle to Augustine* (Cambridge: Cambridge University Press, 1996)

Lee, A.D., *Information and Frontiers. Roman Foreign Relations in Late Antiquity* (Cambridge: Cambridge University Press, 1993)

Matthews, John, *The Roman Empire of Ammianus* (London: Duckworth, 1989)

McCormick, Michael, *Eternal Victory: Triumphal Rulership in Late Antiquity, Byzantium, and the Early Medieval West* (Cambridge: Cambridge University Press, 1986)

McCormick, Michael, *Origins of the European Economy: Communications and Commerce, A.D. 300–900* (Cambridge: Cambridge University Press, 2001)

Pohl, Walter, Ian Wood, and Helmut Reimitz, *The Transformation of Frontiers from Late Antiquity to the Carolingians* (Leiden, Boston: Brill, 2001)

Sarris, Peter, *Economy and Society in the Age of Justinian* (Cambridge: Cambridge University Press, 2006)

Sarris, Peter and Jairus Banaji, eds., *Aristocrats, Peasants and the Transformation of Rural Society, c.400–800* [Special Issue]. *Journal of Agrarian Change* 9.1 (2009)

Treadgold, Warren, *A History of the Byzantine State and Society* (Stanford, CA: Stanford University Press, 1997)

Ward-Perkins, Bryan, "Land, Labour, and Settlement," and "Specialized Production and Exchange," in *The Cambridge Ancient History*, vol. 14, ed. Averil Cameron, Bryan Ward-Perkins, and Michael Whitby (Cambridge: Cambridge University Press, 2001) pp. 315–45 and pp. 346–91

Webster, Leslie, and Michelle Brown, eds, *The Transformation of the Roman World* (Berkeley: University of California Press, 1997)

Whittow, Mark, *The Making of Byzantium, 600–1025* (Berkeley: University of California Press, 1996)

Wickham, Chris, *Framing the Early Middle Ages: Europe and the Mediterranean 400–800* (Oxford: Oxford University Press, 2005)

# 2

# CITIES

## 2.1 Introduction

For Romans, civilized life meant urban life. In the approximately fifteen hundred cities that dotted the imperial map, basic values of imperial culture found expression. Most cities numbered only 10,000–50,000 inhabitants fed by the agricultural hinterlands that surrounded them. Only a handful of resplendent cities, such as Rome, Constantinople, Alexandria, and Antioch, had populations nearing half a million. In the course of the Late Antique centuries, urban culture changed across the empire for economic, political, and above all religious reasons. Some aspects of city life from earlier periods persisted, but the advent of Christianity had a profound effect on traditional patterns of behavior and public life and on the urban fabric itself.

This chapter illustrates different aspects of urban life throughout the empire: city administration and the honors and liabilities that accompanied it; the patterns of formal education that shaped community leaders; the many bawdy and exciting entertainments that amused the populace; and riots among the disaffected poor who constituted the majority of every city's population.

The city of Rome receives special attention as the imperial city against which all other Roman communities were measured in terms of wealth, honor, and prestige. In addition to its size and the magnificence of its public buildings and spaces, it played a role in historical thought and the popular imagination as the symbol of the empire's destiny – so much so that when Visigoths sacked the city in 410, pagans and Christians argued passionately about the meaning of the event. As the New Rome, the city of Constantinople (modern Istanbul in Turkey), inaugurated by emperor Constantine, displaced the city of Rome in political and economic importance, becoming the center point of a developing Christian state – medieval Byzantium. Various aspects of life in the New Rome are illustrated below.

## 2.2 City administration

### 2.2.1 The importance of city senators

Cities were the points at which the imperial administration connected with local cultures and skimmed off the wealth generated by peasants in the vast countryside.

Decurions, the local aristocrats who filled the cities' senates, played such an important role in tax collection for the state that they could not be permitted to abandon their traditional roles. For all but a few of the very wealthiest men, these financial obligations made being a decurion a terrible burden rather than a great honor. By the late sixth century bureaucrats serving the central imperial bureaucracy had absorbed most of the obligations of the decurions, and city senates fell out of use.

*Theodosian Code* 12.1.144, 184

> 12.1.44 In order that decurions may not wander abroad for a long time or join the imperial service, to the fraud of the municipalities, unless they return to their own municipalities within five years, their property shall be assigned to their municipal councils for performing the compulsory public services and bearing the burdens of their municipalities. [Arcadius and Honorius, 395]

> 12.1.184 Children of decurions and of gubernatorial apparitors must follow their own birth status, no matter when they may be born, whether before the prerogative and the expressed time of the imperial service that has been undertaken or after the period has elapsed, since it is enough that exemption has been granted by Our Clemency to their parents as a remuneration. [Honorius and Theodosius, 423]

### 2.2.2 The generosity of city senators

In the Roman Empire the leading men of every city competed in bringing benefits to their communities. They paid for public buildings of all sorts, sponsored public entertainments, and provided food in times of want. These benefactions, called liturgies, brought honor to their donors. As service in city senates became an ever-greater burden in the course of the fifth and sixth centuries, this sort of traditional generosity declined. Here Libanius, the fourth-century rhetor and civic patron of Antioch, describes the system at its best.

Libanius, *Oration* 11, "In Praise of Antioch," 133–7

["Libanius' Oration in Praise of Antioch (Oration 11)," trans. Glanville Downey, *Proceedings of the American Philosophical Society*, 103.5 (Philadelphia: The American Philosophical Society, 1959) p. 667]

> First let us look at the senate, since the whole structure of the city is based upon this as upon a root. This one alone is the greatest of those which exist everywhere, and the best, composed of men who can reckon up their fathers and grandfathers and great-grandfathers, and even beyond that, in the same rank, men who had their forebears as teachers of good will toward the city, each one of whom understood, when he took over his property, that it was necessary to hold his property for the common benefit. For these men inherited their ancestral property by their good fortune, and spent it freely through their generosity, and through their industry they acquired many possessions; and just as the foundations of their wealth were blameless, they used it with all magnificence for the liturgies, avoiding poverty through their prudence, taking

greater pleasure in spending for the benefit of the city than others take in amassing wealth, meeting expense so lavishly that there was fear lest they be brought to indigence, and making their outlays in varied forms, sometimes supporting the populace in times of need and wiping out the failures of the soil through their gifts, and always enriching the whole city through the enjoyment of baths and the pleasures of spectacles, introducing their sons, while they themselves were still living, to the bearing of liturgies; and by their magnificent generosity turning into occasions for spending money the immunities granted to them by the laws, spending their own wealth more lavishly than men who had never yet borne a liturgy. For the feeling which elsewhere follows upon gain is here joined instead with spending, and a wealthy man would be more ashamed of fleeing a liturgy than he would be of diminishing his property through his liturgies. As though they had some god as a surety that whatever they lay out, double gain will come from Good Fortune, they spend lavishly on horse races and gymnastic contests, some according to their means, others more than is suitable for their means. The object which each of those engaged in the liturgies strives for is to surpass his predecessor and to make rivalry impossible for his successor, and to bring forth in fairer fashion the things which are customarily performed, while adding new features to those which have been traditional. Among us alone is there more competition over the undertaking of liturgies than there is among others in escaping them, and many men have often through expenditures sought to win their way to this honor, joining expense to expense, and making their way to the second outlay by means of the first, not purchasing, by means of small expenditures, an escape from greater ones, but by many outlays making their way to the spending of more.

### 2.2.3 Praises for a city's patron

The following inscription from Aphrodisias, a city in southwest Asia Minor, erected sometime in the late sixth century, praises Albinus, an aristocratic patron of the city, and sketches the hierarchy of powers at work in the city. (See also *1.4.9–1.4.14*, pages 28–31.)

Aphrodisias, Inscription 83
[Charlotte Roueché, *Aphrodisias in Late Antiquity* (London: Society for the Promotion of Roman Studies, 1989) p. 129]

God is one, for the whole world! Many years for the emperors! Many years for the eparchs! Many years for the Senate! Many years for the metropolis! . . . Albinus – Hurrah for the builder of the stoa! Lord, lover of your country, remain for us! Your buildings are an eternal reminder, Albinus . . . Most Distinguished Albinus . . . Albinus, behold what you have given! The whole city says this: "Throw your enemies in the river! May the great God provide this!" Hurrah for the Most Distinguished Albinus, to the Senate! . . . envy does not vanquish fortune. Hurrah for Albinus, the builder of this work also! You have disregarded wealth and obtained glory, Most Distinguished Albinus. Most Distinguished Albinus, like your ancestors a lover of your country, may you receive plenty. Providing . . . for the city, he is acclaimed . . . also. With your buildings you have made the city brilliant, Albinus, lover of your country. The whole city, having acclaimed you with one voice, says: "He who forgets you, Most Distinguished Albinus, does not know God." The fortune of the city triumphs!

### 2.2.4 Imperial administrators and cities

By the fifth century city senates had begun to decline in importance. Men in the imperial bureaucracy increasingly took on the traditional responsibilities of city aristocrats to maintain public buildings, provide entertainments and champion cities at court. The following inscription from Aphrodisias indicates the sort of public honors that such patrons might attain. Dulcitius, a governor in the late fourth century, restored the gate of the agora of Aphrodisias. In this fanciful inscription the gate itself speaks his praise:

Aphrodisias, Inscription 40

[Charlotte Roueché, *Aphrodisias in Late Antiquity* (London: Society for the Promotion of Roman Studies, 1989) p. 129]

> Stranger, sing of Dulcitius, the governor, giver of games and founder and lover of honour, and Maioumarch [Patron of the Festival of Maiouma], who, stretching out his strong hand, raised me too, who had suffered for unnumbered years.

## 2.3 City life

### 2.3.1 The individual character of a city: Alexandria

While a standard repertoire of buildings and activities bound together urban experience across the empire, individual cities prided themselves on their distinctive attributes. One of the most glorious cities of the Mediterranean was Alexandria in the Nile delta in Egypt. This description, written in the mid-fourth century, tells of the city's particular characteristics.

*Description of the Entire World* 35–7

["Expositio Totius Mundi," *Seminarium Kondakovium*, 8, trans. A.A. Vasiliev (Madison, WI, 1935) pp. 12–13]

> 35. Alexandria is a very great city, famous for her arrangement, abounding in all advantages and rich in food; she eats three kinds of fish, something which no other province has – river fish, lake fish, and sea fish. All kinds either of perfumes or any other barbarian merchandise abound in the city. Beyond the extreme part of Thebais there is the people of the Indians, and receiving everything, Alexandria stands above all. The gods are devoutly worshipped, and the Temple of Serapis is there, the unique and wonderful spectacle of the

whole world; nowhere on earth is to be found such a building or such symmetry of the temple or such rites of worship. It seems that first place is adjudged to this temple in all countries.

36. In addition to all those advantages Alexandria possesses one thing which is produced nowhere but in Alexandria and her district; without this neither her courts of justice nor private business can be directed; indeed without this very thing the whole race of men could hardly exist. What is this which is so lauded by us? The paper which she makes herself and exports to the whole world, showing this useful thing to all; only Alexandria possesses this above all cities and provinces, but without envy she gives her advantages to others. She also possesses the favour of the Nile more than all the rest of the province. This Nile river, flowing down in the summer, waters the whole earth and prepares it for sowing; those who sow the earth bountifully are filled with great blessing. For them one measure makes one hundred and twenty measures. In such a way the soil yields every year and is profitable to all the provinces. For Constantinople ... is for the most part fed by Alexandria; likewise the eastern regions are supplied, especially on account of the army of the Emperor and the war with the Persians; because no other province can suffice for that purpose but the divine Egypt.

### 2.3.2 Urban rioting

With no formal say in their own governance, urban crowds sometimes turned to violence to give voice to their needs. Public officials were particularly vulnerable. This riot occurred in Rome in 408, when Visigoths were menacing the city.
Gerontius, *Life of Melania the Younger* 19
[Jill Harries, "'Treasure in heaven': Property and inheritance among Senators of Late Rome," in *Marriage and Property*, ed. Elizabeth M. Craik (Aberdeen: Aberdeen University Press, 1984) p. 67]

And when they were leaving Rome, the Prefect of the City, a man of strong pagan convictions, resolved in concert with the whole Senate that their goods should be vindicated to the public treasury. He was pressing on with putting this plan early into effect when, by the Providence of God, the people rose against him because of a bread shortage; and thus he was maltreated and lynched in the heart of the city and all the rest were terrified into holding their peace.

### 2.3.3 An emperor almost falls: the Nika Riots

During the "Nika Riots" (532) the emperor Justinian almost fled Constantinople. Only a massacre at the Hippodrome put an end to the disorder. (See also *7.2.2*, page 225.)
Procopius, *History of the Wars* 1.24.1–2, 7–10
[Procopius, *History of the Wars*, vol. I, trans. H.B. Dewing (Cambridge, MA: Harvard University Press, 1971) pp. 219, 221, 223]

At this same time an insurrection broke out unexpectedly in Byzantium among the populace, and, contrary to expectation, it proved to be a very serious affair, and ended in great harm to the people and to the senate, as the following account will show. In every city the population has been divided for a long time past into the Blue and the Green factions; but within comparatively recent times it has come about that, for the sake of these names and the seats which the rival factions occupy in watching the games, they spend their money and abandon their bodies to the most cruel tortures, and even do not think it unworthy to die a most shameful death . . .

But at this time the officers of the city administration in Byzantium were leading away to death some of the rioters. But the members of the two factions, conspiring together and declaring a truce with each other, seized the prisoners and then straightaway entered the prison and released all those who were in confinement there, whether they had been condemned on a charge of stirring up sedition, or for any other unlawful act. And all the attendants in the service of the city government were killed indiscriminately; meanwhile, all of the citizens who were sane-minded were fleeing to the opposite mainland; and fire was applied to the city as if it had fallen under the hand of an enemy. The sanctuary of Sophia and the baths of Zeuxippus, and the portion of the imperial residence from the propylaea as far as the so-called House of Ares were destroyed by fire, and besides these both the great colonnades which extended as far as the market place which bears the name of Constantine, in addition to many houses of wealthy men and a vast amount of treasure. During this time the emperor and his consort with a few members of the senate shut themselves up in the palace and remained quietly there. Now the watchword which the populace passed around to one another was "Nika," and the insurrection has been called by this name up to the present time.

### 2.3.4 The people of Rome expect entertainment

Symmachus, the prefect of Rome in 384, wrote to the emperors Theodosius I and Valentinian II urging them in the strongest terms to provide the entertainments that the people of Rome expected as their right.

Symmachus, *Official Dispatch* 6
[R.H. Barrow, *Prefect and Emperor. The Relationes of Symmachus A.D. 384* (Oxford: Clarendon Press, 1973) p. 57]

The Roman people look for outstanding benefactions from your Divinities, but, my Lords Emperors, it now asks again for those which your Eternities voluntarily promised: for it regards them as owed. Not that it feels any doubt that they are to be rendered to it – for we can trust nothing with greater confidence than the undertaking of good emperors – but it does not wish, by not making an immediate demand, to give the impression of dissatisfaction with what is offered. 2. And so it begs that your Clemencies, after granting those subsidies which your generosity has made towards our sustenance, should furnish also the enjoyments of chariot races and dramatic performances to be held in the circus and in Pompey's theatre. The city delights in these entertainments and your promise has awakened anticipation. 3. Every day messengers are awaited to confirm that these promised shows will soon arrive at the city; reports on charioteers and on horses are being collected; every conveyance, every ship is rumoured to have brought in theatrical artists. Nevertheless it is affection for your Perennities, not avidity for entertainment, that has whetted the longings of the populace. Give for this moment what is asked of you so that in the future room may be left for all the other things which without limit you will bestow.

### 2.3.5  Celebrity charioteers

City populations throughout the empire had an obsession with chariot races. Successful charioteers attained celebrity status. Paintings of the greatest charioteers with accompanying inscriptions adorned even the imperial box at the Hippodrome in Constantinople. The Blues were one of the great racing teams, and Porphyrius one of the most beloved charioteers of the sixth century.

Agathias, "On Porphyrius of the Blue Faction," *Greek Anthology* 16.380
[Cyril Mango, *The Art of the Byzantine Empire 312–1453* (Englewood Cliffs, NJ: Prentice-Hall Inc., 1972) p. 49]

> Having overcome on earth every other charioteer, Porphyrius, the wonder of the Blue faction, has been nobly carried up to race even in the air. This man, who has vanquished all the chariot-drivers of the world, mounts up that he may race with the Sun.

### 2.3.6  Spilling blood for entertainment

The martyr stories of Christian saints vividly describe the cruelty of public entertainment. The following account from the seventh-century Armenian historian Sebeos describes the ordeal of Smbat.

Sebeos, *History* 10
[*Sebeos' History*, trans. Robert Bedrosian (New York: Sources of the Armenian Tradition, 1985) pp. 56–8]

> In that period imperial ambassadors arrived with edicts. They seized Smbat and seven other men and took them before the emperor. Investigating them in front of the multitudinous public, the verdict was passed that Smbat be stripped and thrown into the circus. Smbat possessed a gigantic size; he was handsome, tall of stature, broad-shouldered and hard in body as a fist, or the ground. He then was mighty and martial and had displayed his bravery and force in numerous wars. Such was his strength that once when riding on a large and powerful horse, passing through a dense forest of pines and other strong trees, Smbat seized a branch of the tree, energetically wrapped his torso and legs around the

horse's middle and lifted the horse bodily from the ground. When all the troops saw this they were awestruck with wonder.

So they stripped Smbat, dressed him in trousers and threw him into the circus to be eaten by the beasts. They released a bear on him. As soon as the bear was opposite him, Smbat shouted in a great voice, attacked the bear, punched its forehead with his fist and killed it on the spot. Second, they released a bull on him. Smbat seized the bull by the horns, shouted powerfully and, when the bull wearied of the fight, Smbat wrenched its neck and crushed both horns on the bull's head. The bull weakened, and drawing back, took to flight. But Smbat ran after the bull and seized it by its tail and worked on the hoof of one of its legs. The hoof came off in his hand, and the bull fled from him, lacking a hoof on one leg. The third time, they released a lion on him. When the lion was attacking him, Smbat was aided by the Lord, for he seized the lion by the ear and jumped astride it. Seizing the throat, he choked and killed the lion. Then the clamor of the vast mob filled the place, and they sought the emperor's mercy on Smbat.

Tired from the combat, Smbat sat on the dead lion to rest a little. The emperor's wife threw herself at the emperor's feet, requesting mercy for him, for previously the man had been dear to the emperor and to his wife and the emperor had styled him his adopted son. The emperor was astounded by the man's strength and endurance; and when he heard the entreaties of his wife and all the palace, he ordered that Smbat be pardoned.

Then they took him to the bath for washing. They washed and clothed him, invited him to dine at court, and revived him with food. After a short time, not because of any evil will of the emperor, but from the slander of envious people, the emperor ordered Smbat's men placed on a boat and exiled to a distant island. From there he ordered that they be taken to Africa with the Armenians among them, and Smbat among the troops there in camp.

### 2.3.7 *The end of gladiatorial combat*

Influenced by Christian abhorrence of the sport, Constantine tried to end gladiatorial games in 325. The combats proved hard to suppress, however, and later emperors also issued laws against the games. Gladiator fights probably never occurred in Constantinople. In the city of Rome, however, gladiatorial training schools and combats lasted until the turn of the fifth century. References to gladiatorial games cease after this time in both East and West.

*Theodosian Code* 15.12.1

> Emperor Constantine Augustus to Maximus, Praetorian Prefect. Bloody spectacles displease Us amid public peace and domestic tranquility. Wherefore, since We wholly forbid the existence of gladiators, You shall cause those persons who, perchance, on account of some crime, customarily sustained that condition and sentence, to serve rather in the mines, so that they will assume the penalty for their crimes without shedding their blood. [Constantine, 325]

### 2.3.8  Christian condemnation of public entertainments

John Chrysostom, bishop of Constantinople (398–404), threw a wet blanket over the many pleasures of attending the theater.

John Chrysostom, *Homily on Matthew* 37.6
[Eunice Dauterman Maguire, Henry Maguire, and Maggie J. Duncan-Flowers, *Art and Holy Power in the Early Christian House* (Urbana and Chicago: University of Illinois Press, 1989) p. 221]

> There you will find obscene language, and even more obscene postures, and the same kind of hairstyles, gaits, clothes, and voices, as well as softness of limbs, sidelong glances, pipes and flutes, plays and pantomimes, and in short, everything full of the utmost licentiousness.

### 2.3.9  Theodora on stage

Audiences enjoyed watching sex play of all sorts on the public stage. Here Procopius describes a most unusual burlesque act performed in Constantinople in the early sixth century. The performer, Theodora, caught the eye of Justinian – and went on to become empress.

Procopius, *Secret History* 9.20–2
[*Procopius, The Secret History*, trans. G.A. Williamson (New York: Penguin Books, 1966) pp. 84–5]

> Often in the theater, too, in full view of all the people she would throw off her clothes and stand naked in their midst, having only a g-string about her private parts and her groin – not, however, because she was ashamed to expose these also to the public, but because no one is allowed to appear there absolutely naked: a g-string round the groin is compulsory. With this minimum covering she would spread herself out and lie face upwards on the floor. Servants on whom this task had been imposed would sprinkle barley grains over her private parts, and geese trained for the purpose used to pick them off one by one with their bills and swallow them. Theodora, so far from blushing when she stood up again, actually seemed to be proud of this performance.

### 2.3.10  Festivals and calendars

The calendar year marked dozens of holidays. One of them was the Brumalia, an immensely popular, time-honored celebration that predated Christianity. At these festivities, associated with the winter solstice, people held dinner parties and wished their friends a long life. In the sixth century the pious Justinian celebrated the Brumalia lavishly in association with his consulship – with no thought of religious impropriety. By the end of the seventh century, however, the Brumalia and many other traditional festivals had been suppressed by churchmen. John Malalas, the sixth-century historian from Antioch, includes the fictional character "Romus" – a founder of Rome – in his description of the Brumalia.

John Malalas, *The Chronicle* 7.7
[*The Chronicle of John Malalas*, trans. E. Jeffreys *et al.* (*Byzantina Australiensia* 4, Melbourne, 1986) p. 95]

Because of this Romus devised what is known as the Brumalia, declaring, it is said, that the emperor of the time must entertain his entire senate and officials and all who serve in the palace, since they are persons of consequence, during the winter when there is a respite from fighting. He began by inviting and entertaining first those whose names began with alpha, and so on, right to the last letter; he ordered his senate to entertain in the same way. They too entertained the whole army, and those they wanted. . . . This custom of the Brumalia has persisted in the Roman state to the present day.

### 2.3.11 *Taking a bath*

All cities had public bath houses where people met to exercise, swim, and gossip. Baths also were a regular part of medical therapies. Some baths had specific purposes, as the empress Eudocia describes in her account of her pilgrimages to Jerusalem in 438–439. The second excerpt, written in the late second century, provides a Christian perspective on bathing for pleasure. (See also *10.3.3*, page 304.)

*1.*

Inscription of the Empress Eudocia
[Judith Green and Yoram Tsafrir, "Greek Inscriptions from Hammat Gader: A Poem by the Empress Eudocia and Two Building Inscriptions," *Israel Exploration Journal*, vol. 32, nos 2–3 (1982) p. 84]

We came to the city which is called Gadara . . . In that area, three miles from the city, are hot springs which are called the baths of Elijah, where lepers are cleansed who have their meals from the inn there at public expense. In the evening the baths are filled. In front of the furnace of water is a large tank. When it is filled, all the openings are closed, and they are sent inside through a back door with lights and incense and they sit in that tank the whole night. When they have fallen asleep that person who is to be cured sees a certain vision and when he has told it, the baths themselves are not used for seven days and within seven days he is cleansed.

*2.*

Clement of Alexandria, *Paedagogus* 3.9
[*Clement of Alexandria. Christ the Educator*, trans. Simon P. Wood (Fathers of the Church, vol. XXIII (New York: Fathers of the Church, 1954) pp. 237–8]

There are four reasons prompting us to frequent the baths (it was at this point that I digressed a while back in my discussion): either for cleanliness, for warmth, for health, or for the satisfaction of pleasure. We must not think of bathing for pleasure, because we must ruthlessly expel all unworthy pleasure. Women may make use of the bath for the sake of cleanliness and of health; men, only for the sake of their health. The motive of seeking warmth is scarcely urgent, since we can find relief from cold in other ways.

The continued use of baths undermines a man's strength, weakening the muscles of his body and often inducing lassitude and even fainting spells. Bodies drink up water in a definite way in the baths, like trees, not only by mouth, but also, as they say, through the pores of the whole body. A proof of this is that, often, when a man has been thirsty, his thirst is quenched on entering the water. Therefore, if the bath has no real benefit to offer, it should be completely avoided. The ancients called it a fulling shop for men, since it wrinkles the body before time, and forces the body to become old early; in much the way that iron is tempered by heat, the flesh is made soft by heat. We need to be hardened, as it were, by being doused in cold.

We ought not bathe on every occasion, either, but if at times we are too hungry, or too full, we should omit it. As a matter of fact, [it should be adjusted] to the age of the individual, and to the season of the year. It is not useful at all times, nor to everyone at all times, as those versed in these things agree. Due proportion is sufficient guide for us; we call upon it for help in every part of our life. Again, we should not linger in the bath so long that we will need someone to lead us out by the hand, nor should we loiter long or frequently in it, as we might in the public square. Finally, to have a score of servants pouring water over one is grievously to offend a neighbor; it is a sign of one far advanced in self-indulgence and unwilling to understand that the bath should be common, on an equal footing to all who bathe there.

### 2.3.12  The odor of sanctity

From an ascetic point of view avoiding baths was a good thing since too much attention to the body was immodest. This fifth-century text encourages virgins to avoid bathing.

Pseudo-Athanasius, *Patrologia Graeca* 28.264
[Gillian Clark, *Women in Late Antiquity* (Oxford: Clarendon Press, 1993) p. 93]

Do not go to the baths, if you are healthy, without great need; do not immerse your whole body in water, for you are consecrated to the Lord. Do not defile your body with anything worldly, but wash only your face, your hands and your feet. When you wash your face, do not use both hands, or rub your cheeks, or apply herbs or nitre or such: worldly women do that. Wash in pure water.

## 2.4  The city of Rome

Displaced by more strategically located cities such as Trier, Milan, Antioch, and eventually Constantinople, the city of Rome ceased to be the administrative capital of the Roman Empire during Late Antiquity. The Senate continued to meet there, however, and venerable civic rituals continued to be celebrated in its lavish setting. In the century following Constantine's conversion in 312, Rome very slowly took on a Christian face. Non-Christian traditionalists resiliently defended the city's classical buildings and literary heritage, and Christian leaders eventually learned to protect Rome's classical legacy as well. Sacked by Visigoths (410) and Vandals (454), and the site of vicious battles between Goths and the armies of Justinian that came to "restore" Italy to the empire in the mid-sixth century, Rome shrank in numbers of inhabitants and saw many of its finest buildings destroyed. By 600 Rome had become a city of ruins, memories – and the home of a vigorous papacy.

### 2.4.1 Rome in old age

Ammianus Marcellinus (c.330–after 391), the last major Roman historian to write in Latin, describes Rome as a city no longer in her prime, but nevertheless respected everywhere.

Ammianus Marcellinus, *History* 14.6.3–6
[*Ammianus Marcellinus*, vol. I, trans. John C. Rolfe (Cambridge, MA: Harvard University Press, 1956) pp. 37, 39]

> At the time when Rome first began to rise into a position of world-wide splendor, destined to live so long as men shall exist, in order that she might grow to a towering stature, Virtue and Fortune, ordinarily at variance, formed a pact of eternal peace; for if either one of them had failed her, Rome had not come to complete supremacy. Her people, from the very cradle to the end of their childhood, a period of about three hundred years, carried on wars about her walls. Then, entering upon adult life, after many toilsome wars, they crossed the Alps and the sea. Grown to youth and manhood, from every region which the vast globe includes, they brought back laurels and triumphs. And now, declining into old age, and often owing victory to its name alone, it has come to a quieter period of life. Thus the venerable city, after humbling the proud necks of savage nations, and making laws, the everlasting foundations and moorings of liberty, like a thrifty parent, wise and wealthy, has entrusted the management of her inheritance to the Caesars, as to her children . . . Throughout all regions and parts of the earth she is accepted as mistress and queen; everywhere the white hair for the senators and their authority are revered and the name of the Roman people is respected and honored.

### 2.4.2 Rome, center of the world

For Rutilius Namatianus, a Latin poet who wrote a poem about his sea voyage home to Gaul from Rome in 416, the city of Rome and the empire that it symbolized remained the center of the world. Even in the difficult days of the early fifth century when imperial control of western Europe was collapsing, the poet could celebrate Rome as "queen of the world and brightest jewel in the vault of heaven." His decision to sail home rather than to risk the danger of travel on highways where bands of Goths might be encountered reflects the failed power of the imperial government in Italy.

Rutilius Namatianus, "A Voyage Home to Gaul," lines 37–66
[J. Wight Duff and Arnold M. Duff, eds., *Minor Latin Poets* (London: Heinemann, 1904) pp. 767–8]

> I have chosen the sea, since roads by land, if on the level, are flooded by rivers; if on higher ground, are beset with rocks. Since Tuscany and since the Aurelian highway, after suffering the outrages of Goths with fire or sword, can no longer control forest with homestead or river with bridge, it is better to entrust my sails to the wayward sea. Repeated kisses I imprint on the gates I have to leave; unwillingly my feet cross the honoured threshold. In tears I beseech pardon (for my departure) and offer a sacrifice of praise, so far as weeping allows the words to run: "Listen, O fairest queen of thy world, Rome, welcomed amid the starry skies, listen, though mother of men and mother of gods, thanks to thy temples we are not far from heaven: thee do we chant, and shall, while destiny allows, forever chant. None can be safe if forgetful of thee. Sooner shall guilty oblivion whelm the sun than the honour due to thee quit my heart; for thy benefits extend as far as the sun's rays, where the circling Ocean-flood bounds the world. For thee the very Sun-god who holdeth all together doth revolve: his steeds that rise in thy domains he puts in thy domains to rest. Thee Africa hath not stayed with scorching sands, nor hath the Bear (the North) armed with its native cold, repulsed thee. As far as living Nature hath stretched towards the poles, so far hath earth opened a path for thy valour. For nations far apart thou hast made a single fatherland; under thy dominion captivity hath meant profit even for those who knew not justice: and by offering to the vanquished a share on thine own justice, thou hast made a city of what was erstwhile a world.

### 2.4.3 *Rome's countless wonders*

The sixth-century chronicler Zachariah of Mitylene offers a portrait of the city of Rome in simple, quantitative terms. His original Greek text survives only in Syriac. Whether or not Zachariah's list is accurate, it shows that Rome's splendor cannot be matched.

Zachariah of Mitylene, *The Syriac Chronicle* 10.16
[Zachariah of Mitylene, *The Syriac Chronicle*, trans. F.J. Hamilton and E.W. Brooks (London: Methuen & Co., 1899/reprinted 1979) pp. 317–19]

> Now the description of the decorations of the city, given shortly, is as follows, with respect to the wealth of its inhabitants, and their great and pre-eminent prosperity, and their grand and glorious objects of luxury and pleasure, as in a great city of wonderful beauty. Now its pre-eminent decorations are as follows, not to speak of the splendour inside the houses and the beautiful formation of the columns in their halls and of their colonnades and of their staircases, and their lofty height, as in the city of wonderful beauty. It contains 24 churches of

the blessed apostles, Catholic churches. It contains 2 great basilicas where the king sits and the senators are assembled before him every day. It contains 324 great spacious streets. It contains 2 great capitols. It contains 80 golden gods. It contains 64 ivory gods. It contains 46,603 dwelling-houses. It contains 1,797 houses of magnates. It contains 1,352 reservoirs pouring forth water. It contains 274 bakers, who are constantly making and distributing annonae [free grain] to the inhabitants of the city, besides those who make and sell in the city. It contains 5,000 cemeteries, where they lay out and bury. It contains 31 great marble pedestals. It contains 3,785 bronze statues of kings and magistrates. It contains, moreover, 25 bronze statues of Abraham, Sarah, and Hagar, and of the kings of the house of David, which Vespasian the king brought up when he sacked Jerusalem, and the gates of Jerusalem and other bronze objects. It contains 2 colossal statues. It contains 2 columns of shells. It contains 2 circuses. It contains 2 theatres . . . It contains 2 amphitheatres. It contains 4 granaries. It contains 11 nymphaea. It contains 22 great and mighty bronze horses. It contains 926 baths. It contains 4 police stations. It contains 14 guardsmen's barracks. It contains 2 sets of special bronze horses. It contains 45 brothels. It contains 2,300 public oil-warehouses. It contains 291 prisons. It contains 254 public places or privies in the city precincts. It contains 673 watchmen, who guard the city, and the men who command them all are 7. The gates of the city are 37. Now the circumference of the whole city is 216,036 feet, which is 40 miles; the diameter of the city from east to west is 12 miles, and from north to south 12 miles.

But God is faithful, who will make its second prosperity greater than its first, because great is the glory of all the might of the dominion of the Romans.

## 2.5  Rome becomes a Christian center

### 2.5.1  A martyr foresees Rome's Christian future

Prudentius (Aurelius Prudentius Clemens, 348–c.408) had a career as an imperial administrator in Spain before turning to writing Christian poetry about 395. His poem about the martyrdom of Saint Laurence (d. 258) describes the transformation of the city of Rome into a Christian capital. After introductory remarks, Prudentius puts a prayer in Laurence's mouth (as he is being tortured to death) about Rome's Christian future.

Prudentius, *On the Crowns of the Martyrs* 2.1–20, 413–562
[Brian Croke and Jill Harries, *Religious Conflict in Fourth Century Rome: A Documentary Study* (Sydney: Sydney University Press, 1982) pp. 6–9]

Rome, the former mother of temples but now given over to Christ, under Laurence's leadership you have prevailed and triumph over barbarians' rites. You had already subdued proud kings, reined in nations and now you impose on monstrous idols the yoke of your empire. One glory alone among all her prizes the city of the toga lacked, to conquer foul Jupiter by the taming of savage paganism, a glory won not by the mere brute strength of a Cossus, a Camillus or a Caesar but by the not unbloody struggle of the martyr Laurence. Faith fought under arms and did not spare her own blood; for by death she destroyed death and for her own sake sacrificed herself.

[Laurence's prayer]

"O Christ, the one name, splendour and strength of the Father, creator of heaven and earth, guardian of these walls, you have placed Rome's sceptre supreme over all things, ordaining that the world shall serve the toga of Quirinus [i.e., Roman rule] and submit to her armies, so that you could tame the habits and practices, speech, character and worship of disparate peoples under one system of laws; see how all mankind has passed to the kingdom of Remus and, although unlike in their practices before, now shares the same language and beliefs. This was resolved so that the rule of the Christian name might all the more bind all lands together with a single bond. Grant, Christ, the prayer of your Romans that the city through which you have brought all into a single religion may be Christian. All members of the empire are henceforth allied in the one creed. The conquered world is growing peaceful; peaceful too let its capital be. Let her see her separated regions join us in one state of grace. Let Rome's founder, Romulus, become a member of the faith and Numa [a mythological king of Rome] himself become a believer. The Trojan aberration still confuses the senate of Catos, and honours at secret hearths the Phrygians' exiled deities. Two-faced Janus and Sterculus – I shudder to name so many of the fathers' monstrosities – and old Saturn's festal day are worshipped by the senate. Wipe out this shame, O Christ. Send down your servant, Gabriel, so that blind and strange Iulus may recognize the true God. We possess already the most trustworthy pledges of that hope, for already the two princes of the apostles [Peter and Paul] reign here, the one who summoned the gentiles, the other who occupies the foremost throne and opens up the gates of eternity which are in his charge. Away with you, adulterous Jupiter, defiled by incest with your sister, leave Rome to be free and flee her people who are now Christ's. Paul casts you from our bounds; Peter's blood banishes you and Nero's deed hurts you, his armourer. I foresee that in the future there shall come an emperor [Theodosius I], a servant of God, to forbid Rome to be a slave to shameful abominations of religious rites, to close and bar the temples, lock the ivory doors, destroy the cursed entrances, barring them with bolts of brass. Then at last shall marble shine clean and unstained with blood, the bronzes now seen as idols shall stand purified of guilt."

His prayer ended and with it his bondage to the flesh; his spirit broke out eagerly when his speech was done. Some senators whom the martyr's amazing freedom had persuaded to follow Christ raised his body and carried it on their shoulders. The spirit [i.e., of Laurence] suddenly penetrated their inmost hearts and induced them to reject former frivolities for the love of God on high. From that day, the worship of shameful gods waned: fewer people gathered at their shrines while there was a rush to the judgment seat of Christ . . . That death of the holy martyr was in truth the death of the temples, and Vesta, powerless, saw the Palladian Lares [ancients gods that protected Roman households] safely abandoned. Those Romans formerly accustomed to pray at Numa's cup now throng the halls of Christ which re-echo with the martyr's name in hymns. The very men who were the senate's pride, formerly priests of the Lupercal or *flamines*, fondly kiss the thresholds of the apostles and martyrs. Illustrious families, men and women of noble birth, dedicate their high-born children with prayers before our eyes. A priest who once wore the headbands of pagan ritual is marked with the sign of the Cross and into your own church, Laurence, there enters a Vestal, Claudia.

Three, four, even seven times blessed is the resident of Rome who at close quarters pays honour to you and the dwelling-place where your bones rest; he is permitted to kneel close by and weep tears upon the place, press his breast to the ground and quietly pour out his prayers . . . Admitted to heaven as a citizen of the indescribable city, on the citadel of the immortal senate you, O Laurence, wear the civic crown. I picture the martyr shining with precious jewels, he whom heavenly Rome has elected a perpetual consul. The power entrusted to you, the magnitude of the duty given you, is displayed in the rejoicing of the [Roman] citizens whose petitions you grant.

### 2.5.2  Christian citizens of Rome

Prudentius' treatise *Against Symmachus*, completed in 402, may coincide with a trip the poet made to Rome. It describes how Rome in her old age turned to Christianity, and how nearly all its residents from the most eminent senators to the humblest tenement dwellers have turned their backs on pagan worship.

Prudentius, *Against Symmachus*, 506–25, 565, 578, 587

[Brian Croke and Jill Harries, *Religious Conflict in Fourth Century Rome: A Documentary Study* (Sydney: Sydney University Press, 1982) pp. 66–7]

By edicts such as these was the City educated to abandon her old errors and shook the dark clouds from her wrinkled face. The nobles were now ready to try the paths of eternity and, at their great-souled leader's bidding, to follow Christ and place their hopes in everlasting life. Then, in her old age, for the first time Rome, keen to learn, blushed at her own history; now is she shamed of time past and hates the years gone by together with their religious ceremonies. As soon as she, recalling how the fields bordering the ditches of her walls have been soaked with just men's innocent blood, sees around her a thousand reproachful tombs, still more deeply does she repent her cruel judgment, her uncontrolled assertion of power, her over-violent anger in the cause of a shameful religion. She desires to compensate for the dreadful wounds inflicted through injuring justice by offering obedience, though late, and asking forgiveness. In order to absolve her great empire of the charge of cruelty in her past rejection of holiness she searches after the atonement indicated to her and converts to faith in Christ with total devotion.

... One may count hundreds of ancient noble houses who have turned to the banner of Christ and raised themselves from the vast depths of shameful idolatry. If the city has any identity it lies in these men; if the more eminent order of men create a country's character, these men do so, when the will of the people is one with theirs and the common people and the powerful are united. Look again at the illustrious hall where sits the light of our state; only with difficulty will you find a few minds still clouded with pagan frivolities, tentatively clinging to their worn-out rituals, choosing to keep to the darkness, though it is banished, and shutting their eyes to the glorious noonday sun ... Now turn and look at the people. How few there are who do not spurn Jupiter's bloodstained altar ... Do we still doubt that Rome is dedicated to you, Christ, that she has passed under your laws, with all her people and her most eminent citizens, wills to extend her earthly kingdom beyond the stars of the great and lofty heaven.

### 2.5.3 Rome's temples abandoned

This poem by Paulinus of Nola (see *4.2.6*, page 114) about the saving force of Christianity paints a picture of Rome transformed by Christian practice. It was written to honor the birthday of Saint Felix of Nola on January 13, 405. (See also 4.2.3, page 112.)

Paulinus of Nola, *Poem* 19.53–75

[Brian Croke and Jill Harries, *Religious Conflict in Fourth Century Rome: A Documentary Study* (Sydney: Sydney University Press, 1982) pp. 9–10]

Then [God] put Peter and Paul in the city of Rome because the capital of the world, being driven insane by her many vices and blinded by her darkness, needed the chief doctors ... As the faith grows stronger, error is overcome and will fall away, and with hardly anyone left in the power of evil and death, all Rome acknowledges the name of Christ and mocks Numa's [a mythological king of Rome] fantasies and the Sibyl's prophecies. Among the numerous flocks of the supreme God the devout crowd responds to the holy shepherds with a glad Amen. The sacred cry strikes to heaven with praises of the eternal Lord and the pinnacle of the Capitol totters with the shock. The neglected images in the empty temples tremble when struck by the pious voices, and are overthrown by the name of Christ. Terrified demons abandon their deserted shrines. The envious Serpent pale with rages struggles in vain, his lips blood-stained, bemoaning with this hungry throat the redemption of man, and at the same time now, with unavailing groans, the predator writhes around his dry altars cheated of the blood of sacrificial cattle.

### 2.5.4 The primacy of the bishop of Rome

After a slow development, the claims of the bishop of Rome to spiritual and legal primacy in the Church were clearly expressed by the middle of the fifth century.

Christ's words to the apostle Simon, "Thou art Peter [Petrus], and upon this rock [*petram*] will I build my church, and the gates of Hell shall not prevail against it. And I will give the keys of the kingdom of heaven . . .", provided legitimacy to the bishop of Rome. The medieval papacy built upon this foundation. In the following excerpt from a sermon delivered about 450, Pope Leo I (440–461) stated the "Petrine Doctrine" with confidence.

Pope Leo I, *Sermon 3*

[Pope Leo I, *Sermon 3*, trans. C.L. Feltoe in *A Select Library of Nicene and Post-Nicene Fathers of the Christian Church*, series 2, vol. XII, eds. Philip Schaff and Henry Wace (Grand Rapids, MI: Eerdmans,1955) pp. 116–18]

> Now that the mystery of this divine priesthood has descended to human agency, it runs not by the line of birth, nor is that which flesh and blood created, chosen, but without regard to the privilege of paternity and succession by inheritance, those men are received by the Church as its rulers whom the Holy Ghost prepares: so that in the people of God's adoption, the whole body of which is priestly and royal, it is not the prerogative of earthly origin which obtains the unction, but the condescension of Divine grace which creates the bishop.
>
> The dispensation of Truth therefore abides, and the blessed Peter persevering in the strength of the Rock, which he has received, has not abandoned the helm of the Church, which he undertook. For he was ordained before the rest in such a way that from his being called the Rock, from his being pronounced the Foundation, from his being constituted the Doorkeeper of the kingdom of heaven, from his being set as the Umpire to bind and to loose, whose judgments shall retain their validity in heaven, from all these mystical titles we might know the nature of his association with Christ. And still today he more fully and effectually performs what is entrusted to him, and carries out every part of his duty and charge in Him and with Him, through Whom he has been glorified. And so if anything is rightly done and rightly decreed by us; if anything, if anything is won from the mercy of God by our daily supplications, it is of his work and merits whose power lives and whose authority prevails in his See.
>
> . . . For though the whole Church, which is in all the world, ought to abound in all virtues, yet you especially, above all people, it becomes to excel in deeds of piety, because founded as you are on the very citadel of the Apostolic Rock, not only has our Lord Jesus Christ redeemed you in common with all men, but the blessed Apostle Peter has instructed you far beyond all men. Through the same Christ our Lord.

### 2.5.5 Protecting and restoring Rome's buildings

Maintaining the infrastructure of the city of Rome was a huge task. The following inscription from the Porta Maggiore in Rome was erected during the reigns of Arcadius and Honorius at the turn of the fifth century to commemorate a successful clean-up campaign. Restoration was an imperial virtue.

*Corpus of Latin Inscriptions* 6.1189
[Donald R. Dudley, *Urbs Roma. A Sourcebook of Classical Texts on the City and its Monuments* (London: Phaidon Press, 1967) p. 36]

> The Senate and People of Rome set this up to the Imperial Caesars, our Lords the two princes Arcadius and Honorius, victorious, triumphant, ever Augusti, to commemorate the restoration of the walls, gates, and towers of the Eternal City, after the removal of huge quantities of rubble. At the suggestion of the distinguished and noble Count Stilicho, Master of both of the Armed Forces, their statues were set up to preserve the memory of their name. Flavius Macrobius Longinianus, City Prefect, devoted to their majesty and divine power, was in charge of the work.

## 2.5.6 A quarry for builders

In 458 the emperor Majorian issued a law to protect the ancient buildings of Rome.
Majorian, *Novel* 4

> While We rule the State, it is Our will to correct the practice whose commission We have long detested, whereby the appearance of the venerable City is marred. Indeed, it is manifest that the public buildings, in which the adornment of the entire City of Rome consists, are being destroyed everywhere by the punishable recommendation of the office of the Prefect of the City. While it is pretended that the stones are necessary for public works, the beautiful structures of the ancient buildings are being scattered, and in order that something small may be repaired, great things are being destroyed. Hence the occasion now arises that also each and every person who is constructing a private edifice, through the favoritism of the judges who are situated in the City, does not hesitate to take presumptuously and to transfer the necessary materials from the public places, although those things which belong to the splendor of the cities ought to be preserved by civic affection, even under the necessity of repair.
>
> Therefore, by this general law We sanction that all the buildings that have been founded by the ancients as temples and as other monuments and that were constructed for the public use or pleasure shall not be destroyed by any person, and that it shall transpire that a judge who should decree that this be done shall be punished by the payment of fifty pounds of gold. If his apparitors and accountants should obey him when he so orders and should not resist him in any way by their own recommendation, they shall be subjected to the punishment of cudgeling, and they shall also be mutilated by the loss of their hands, through which the monuments of the ancients that should be preserved are desecrated. [Leo and Majorian, 458]

## 2.6 The sack of Rome, AD 410

The sack of Rome, the "Eternal City," in 410 by Alaric the Visigoth raised many questions. Was Christianity to blame for halting the rituals which had kept the empire safe for centuries? Or was the sack the fault of pagans who refused to accept Christianity and so incurred the wrath of the Christian God? Was the Christian God punishing sinning Christians? Or was it meaningless to discuss the mysterious divine will in such terms at all? The following selections illustrate different points of view.

### 2.6.1 The first shocking news

The world seemed upside down to Jerome in the Holy Land when he first heard of the capture of Rome in 410.

Jerome, *Letter* 127.12

[*Select Letters of St Jerome*, trans. F.A. Wright (London: Heinemann, 1954) p. 463]

> While these things were taking place in Jebus [Jerusalem], a dreadful rumor reached us from the West. We heard that Rome was besieged, that the citizens were buying their safety with gold, and that when they had been thus despoiled they were again beleaguered, so as to lose not only their substance but their lives. The speaker's voice failed and sobs interrupted his utterance. The city which had taken the whole world was itself taken; nay, it fell by famine before it fell by the sword, and there were but a few found to be made prisoners. The rage of hunger had recourse to impious food; men tore one another's limbs, and the mother did not spare the baby at her breast, taking again within her body that which her body had just brought forth.

### 2.6.2 Rome's place in God's plan: the Eusebian background

For Bishop Eusebius of Caesarea (*c.*263–*c.*339), Rome's existence had a place in a divine historical plan, as shown in this passage composed in 336 to celebrate Constantine's thirtieth year on the throne. Eusebius' perspective was widely accepted in the Christian community, but the Visigothic capture of the city challenged their assumptions. (See also *4.10.3*, page 166.)

Eusebius, *Tricennial Oration: On Christ's Sepulchre* 16.4–6

[H.A. Drake, *In Praise of Constantine. A Historical Study and New Translation of Eusebius' Tricennial Orations* (Los Angeles: University of California Press, 1975) p. 120]

> 16.4 At the same time, one empire also flowered everywhere, the Roman, and the eternally implacable and irreconcilable enmity of nations was completely resolved. And as the knowledge of One God was imparted to all men and one manner of piety, the salutary teaching of Christ, in the same way at one and the same time a single sovereign arose for the entire Roman Empire and a deep peace took hold of the totality. Together at the same critical moment, as if from

a single divine will, two beneficial shoots were produced for mankind: the empire of the Romans and the teachings of true worship.

16.5 ... But two great powers – the Roman Empire, which became a monarchy at that time, and the teachings of Christ – proceeding as if from a single starting point, at once tamed and reconciled all to friendship. Thus each blossomed at the same time and place as the other.

16.6 For while the power of Our Savior destroyed the polyarchy and polytheism of the demons and heralded the one kingdom of God to Greeks and barbarians and all men to the farthest extent of the earth, the Roman Empire, now that the causes of the manifold governments had been abolished, subdued the visible governments, in order to merge the entire race into one unity and concord. Already it has united most of the various peoples, and it is further destined to obtain all those not yet united, right up to the very limits of the inhabited world. For with divine power the salutary instruction prepares the way for it and causes everything to be smooth.

### 2.6.3 Pagans blame Christians

In his monumental work *City of God* (written from 413 to 425), Augustine, bishop of Hippo and greatest intellect of the Latin Church in Late Antiquity, summarizes pagan argument and points to historical facts which could contradict their thesis.

Augustine, *City of God* 2.3

[Augustine, *Concerning the City of God Against the Pagans*, trans. Henry Bettenson (New York: Penguin, 1972) p. 50]

> You must bear in mind that in mentioning these facts I am still dealing with the ignorant, the people whose stupidity has given rise to the popular proverb, "No rain! It's all the fault of the Christians." The well-educated who are fond of history are readily acquainted with these facts, but they wish to inflame the hatred of the illiterate mobs against us, and so they pretend not to know the facts, and do their best to support the vulgar notion that the disasters which are bound to fall on humanity during a given period and over a given area are to be laid at the door of Christianity, which, in opposition to their gods, is being extended everywhere with immense prestige and unexampled popularity.
>
> So let us help them to recall the many and various disasters which over-whelmed the Roman State before Christ's incarnation – before his name became known to the nations, and received that honour which arouses their ineffectual envy.

### 2.6.4 "Nothing had happened": Orosius' explanation

Writing to silence pagan critics, Orosius, a pupil of Augustine, found it easy in 416 to play down the significance of the sack of Rome. Attributing the sack to God's anger, he suggested that disasters at least as severe had occurred before the empire was Christian.

Orosius, *History Against the Pagans* 7.39–41
[*Seven Books Against the Pagans*, trans. I.W. Raymond (New York: Columbia University Press, 1936) pp. 387, 388, 390]

> 7.39 Alaric appeared before trembling Rome, laid siege, spread confusion, and broke into the City. He first, however, gave orders that all those who had taken refuge in sacred places, especially in the basilicas of the holy Apostles Peter and Paul, should be permitted to remain inviolate and unmolested; he allowed his men to devote themselves to plunder as much as they wished, but he gave orders that they should refrain from bloodshed. A further proof that the storming of the City was due to the wrath of God rather than to the bravery of the enemy is shown by the fact that the blessed Innocent, the bishop of Rome, who at that time was at Ravenna, through the hidden providence of God, even as Lot the Just was withdrawn from the Sodomites, did not witness the destruction of the sinful populace . . .
>
> 7.40 It was in the one thousand one hundred and sixty-fourth year of the City that Alaric stormed Rome. Although the memory of the event is still fresh, anyone who saw the numbers of the Romans themselves and listened to their talk would think that "nothing had happened," as they themselves admit, unless perhaps he were to notice some charred ruins still remaining.
>
> 7.41 . . . Because the judgments of God are inscrutable and we can neither know them all nor explain those we know, let me state briefly that the rebuke of our Judge and God, in whatever form it may take, is justly undergone by those who know and likewise by those who know not.

## 2.6.5 *Augustine on the sacred significance of Rome*

In *City of God* (written between 413 and 426), Augustine offers a new interpretation of the sack of Rome. He rejects the popular Christian idea that the creation of a Christian Roman Empire was an inevitable step in God's plan for human salvation, and that Christianity's success on the surface was the fulfillment of biblical prophecy. Instead he argues that neither Rome's distress nor Christian triumphs held sacred significance. The only event that mattered after Jesus' resurrection would be Judgment Day. In this way, Augustine disconnects Roman imperial history from salvation history.

Augustine, *City of God* 18.53
[Augustine, *Concerning the City of God Against the Pagans*, trans. Henry Bettenson (New York: Penguin, 1981) p. 838]

> That last persecution, to be sure, which will be inflicted by Antichrist, will be extinguished by Jesus himself, present in person. For the Scripture says that "he will kill him with the breath of his mouth and annihilate him by the splendor of his coming." Here the usual question is, "When will this happen?" But the question is completely ill-timed. For had it been in our interest to know this, who could have been a better informant than the master, God himself, when the

disciples asked him? For they did not keep silent about it with him, but put the question to him in person, "Lord, is this the time when you are going to restore the sovereignty to Israel?" But he replied, "It is not for you to know the times which the Father has reserved for his own control." Now in fact they had not asked about the hour or the day or the year, but about the time, when they were given this answer. It is in vain, therefore, that we try to reckon and put a limit to the number of years that remain for this world, since we hear from the mouth of Truth that it is not for us to know this. And yet some have asserted that 400, 500 or as much as 1,000 years may be completed between the Lord's ascension and his final coming. But to show how each of them supports his opinion would take too long; and in any case it is unnecessary, for they make use of human conjectures, and quote no decisive evidence from the authority of canonical Scripture. In fact, to all those who make such calculations on this subject comes the command, "Relax your fingers, and give them a rest." And it comes from him who says, "It is not for you to know the times, which the Father has reserved for his own control." [Acts 1:6–7]

## 2.7 Constantinople

### 2.7.1 Founding the new Rome

Constantine founded a new imperial capital, Constantinople, on the site of the city of Byzantium on the western side of the Bosporus, adorning it with art and architectural treasures brought from Rome and cities throughout the empire. The city of Rome provided the model for his New Rome. The traditional date of Constantine's foundation is 324, but historians are not in agreement about this. The sixth century source from which the passage below is taken gives a date of 328. A formal dedication ceremony for the city occurred in May, 330.

*Easter Chronicle* 1 (AD 328)
[*Chronicon Paschale: 284–628 AD*, trans. Michael Whitby and Mary Whitby (Liverpool: Liverpool University Press, 1989) pp. 15, 16]

In the time of the aforementioned consuls, Constantine the celebrated emperor departed from Rome and, while staying at Nicomedia metropolis of Bithynia, made visitations for a long time to Byzantium. He renewed the first wall of the city of Byzas, and after making considerable extensions also to the same wall he joined them to the ancient wall of the city and named it Constantinople; he also completed the Hippodrome, adorning it with works in bronze and with every excellence, and made in it a box for imperial viewing in likeness of the one which is in Rome. And he made a great Palace near the same Hippodrome, and the ascent from the Palace to the box in the Hippodrome by way of the Kochlias [spiral staircase], as it is called. And he also built a forum which was large and exceedingly fine; and he set in the middle a great porphyry column of Theban stone worthy of admiration, and he set on top of the same column a great statue of himself with rays of light on his head, a work in bronze which he had brought from Phrygia. The same emperor Constantine secretly took away from Rome the Palladium, as it is called, and placed it in the Forum built by him, beneath the column of his monument, as certain of the Byzantines say who have heard it by tradition. And after making bloodless sacrifice, he named the Tyche [the guardian spirit] of the city renewed by him Anthusa.

### 2.7.2  Advancing against the East

One of the noteworthy monuments in Constantinople was the great equestrian statue of Justinian (527–565). The statue defiantly faced Persia, not the new kingdoms of the West – a hint of where emperors in Constantinople located the real enemy in the sixth century.

Procopius, *On Buildings* 1.2.1–19

[Cyril Mango, *The Art of the Byzantine Empire, 312–1453* (Englewood Cliffs, NJ: Prentice-Hall Inc., 1972) pp. 110–11]

In front of the Senate House there happened to be a public square; this square the people of Byzantium call the Augustaion. Here seven courses of stone are laid in a square, all joined together in sequence, but each course receding and falling short with regard to the one beneath it in such a way that each stone set in a projecting position becomes a step and the people who gather there can sit upon them as on seats. At the top of the stones there rises a pillar of extraordinary height, not all of one piece, but composed of large blocks in circular courses, cut at an angle on their inner faces and joined to one another by the skill of the masons. Finest bronze, cast into panels and wreaths, encompasses the stones on all sides, both binding them securely together and covering them with adornment, and simulating the form of a column nearly throughout, but especially at the top and base. This bronze is in color softer than pure gold, while in value it does not fall much short of an equal weight of silver. At the summit of the column stands a huge bronze horse turned towards the east, a most noteworthy sight. He seems to be about to advance and to be vigorously pressing forward. Indeed, he lifts up his left front foot as if about to step on the ground before him, while the other is planted on the stone above which he stands as though to take the next step. The hind feet he draws together so as to have them in readiness when it is time to set them in motion. Upon this horse is mounted a bronze image of the Emperor like a colossus. And the image is clad like Achilles, for that is how they call the costume he wears. He is shod in ankle boots and has no greaves on his legs. Furthermore, he wears a cuirass in heroic fashion and his head is covered with a helmet which gives the impression of swaying, and a kind of radiance flashes forth from there. One might say in poetic style that this was the Autumn star. He gazes towards the rising sun, steering his course, I suppose, against the Persians. In his left hand he holds a globe, by which the sculptor has signified that the whole earth and sea were subject to him, yet he carries neither sword nor spear nor any other weapon, but a cross surmounts his globe, by virtue of which alone he has won the kingship and victory in war. Stretching forth his right hand towards the regions of the East and spreading out his fingers, he commands the barbarians that dwell there to remain at home and not to advance any further.

### 2.7.3 Justinian's Saint Sophia – a temple to rival Solomon's

Imperial patronage filled Constantinople with magnificent houses of worship. Procopius describes the construction of the Church of Saint Sophia (Holy Wisdom) by Justinian in 532–537. This church dominated the center of Constantinople and was thought to rival Solomon's temple in Jerusalem described in the Bible.

Procopius, *On Buildings* 1.1.23, 24, 27, 47–9

[Cyril Mango, *The Art of the Byzantine Empire, 312–1453* (Englewood Cliffs, NJ: Prentice-Hall Inc., 1972) pp. 72, 74, 75]

> The Emperor, disregarding all considerations of expense, hastened to begin construction and raised craftsmen from the whole world. It was Anthemius of Tralles, the most learned man in the discipline called engineering, not only of all his contemporaries, but also as compared to those who had lived long before him, who ministered to the Emperor's zeal by regulating the work of the builders and preparing in advance designs of what was going to be built.
>
> . . . So the church has been made a spectacle of great beauty, stupendous to those who see it and altogether incredible to those who hear of it . . .
>
> . . . Rising above this circle is an enormous spherical dome which makes the building exceptionally beautiful. It seems not to be founded on solid masonry, but to be suspended from heaven by that golden chain and so covers the space. All of these elements, marvellously fitted together in mid-air, suspended from one another and reposing only on the parts adjacent to them, produce a unified and most remarkable harmony in the work, and yet do not allow the spectators to rest their gaze upon any one of them for a length of time, but each detail readily draws and attracts the eye to itself. Thus the vision constantly shifts round, and the beholders are quite unable to select any particular element which they might admire more than all the others. No matter how much they concentrate their attention on this side and that, and examine everything with contracted eyebrows, they are unable to understand the craftsmanship and always depart from there amazed by the perplexing spectacle.

### 2.7.4 Belisarius celebrates a triumph

Since Rome's earliest days, triumphant generals had led victory parades through Rome to the Temple of Jupiter on the Capitoline hill to celebrate their achievement and show off their booty. In the imperial period triumphs of this sort became a prerogative of emperors alone. In 534 Justinian permitted Belisarius the honor of a triumphal procession in the Hippodrome in Constantinople, the new Rome, to celebrate the conquest of the Vandal kingdom in North Africa. Although the triumph was celebrated in an archaizing fashion, it reflected the current reality of Justinian's authority. Belisarius performed formal obeisance (proskynesis) before the emperor just as the defeated Vandal king was obliged to do, demonstrating that everyone, enemy and citizen alike, was equally subject to the emperor. By sparing the life of the Vandal king, Justinian emphasized his magnanimity and mercy.

Procopius, *History of the Wars* 4.9.1–14

[Procopius, *History of the Wars*, trans. H.P. Dewing (Cambridge, MA: Harvard University Press, 1916) pp. 279, 281, 282]

> Belisarius, upon reaching Byzantium with Gelimer and the Vandals, was counted worthy to receive such honours, as in former times were assigned to those generals of the Romans who had won the greatest and most noteworthy victories. And a period of about six hundred years had now passed since anyone had attained these honours, except, indeed, Titus and Trajan, and such other emperors as had led armies against some barbarian nation and had been victorious. For he displayed the spoils and slaves from the war in the midst of the city and led a procession which the Romans call a "triumph," not, however, in the ancient manner, but going on foot from his own house to the hippodrome and then again from the barriers until he reached the place where the imperial throne is. And there was booty, – first of all, whatever articles are wont to be set apart for the royal service, – thrones of gold and carriages in which it is customary for a king's consort to ride, and much jewelry made of precious stones, and golden drinking cups, and all the other things which are useful for the royal table. And there was also silver weighing many thousands of talents and all the royal treasure amounting to an exceedingly great sum (for Gizeric had despoiled the Palatium in Rome . . .), and among these were the treasures of the Jews, which Titus, the son of Vespasian, together with certain others, had brought to Rome after the capture of Jerusalem . . . And there were slaves in the triumph, among whom was Gelimer himself, wearing some sort of a purple garment upon his shoulders, and all his family, and as many of the Vandals as were very tall and fair of body. And when Gelimer reached the hippodrome and saw the emperor sitting upon a lofty seat and the people standing on either side and realized as he looked about in what an evil plight he was, he neither wept nor cried out, but ceased not saying over in the words of the Hebrew Scripture: "Vanity of vanities, all is vanity." And when he came before the emperor's seat, they stripped off the purple garment, and compelled him to do obeisance to the Emperor Justinian. This also Belisarius did, as being a suppliant of the emperor along with him. And the Emperor Justinian and the Empress Theodora . . . [gave to Gelimer] lands not to be despised in Galatia and permitted him to live there together with his family. However, Gelimer was by no means enrolled among the patricians, since he was unwilling to change from the faith of Arius.

## 2.7.5  The center of Constantinople

In his panegyrical work *On Buildings* Procopius offers a description of the grand public spaces and palatial structures of the New Rome at the middle of the sixth century. The brilliant mosaic in the Bronze Gate, or Chalke, the vestibule of the imperial palace, shows Justinian and Theodora welcoming Belisarius back in triumph from reconquering North Africa and Italy in the emperor's name.

Procopius, *On Buildings* 1.10.10–20

[Cyril Mango, *The Art of the Byzantine Empire, 312–1453* (Toronto: University of Toronto Press, 1986) pp. 108–10]

There is in front of the Palace a square bordered by colonnades which the people of Byzantium call Augustaion . . . To the east of this square stands the Senate House, a work of the emperor Justinian surpassing description by reason of the magnificence of its entire construction . . . Six columns stand in front of it, two of which have between them the wall of the Senate House that faces west, while the other four are set slightly forward; all of them are white in appearance, while as regards size, they are, I believe, the biggest columns in the whole world. The columns form a portico, the roof of which curves into a vault, while the whole upper part of the portico is decorated with beautiful marble of the same kind as the columns and is wonderfully set off by a multitude of statues that stand above it.

Nor far from this square is the residence of the Emperor. Nearly the whole Palace has been constructed anew by the Emperor Justinian, but it is impossible to describe it in words . . . We know the lion by his claw, as the proverb has it; so also will my readers know the impressiveness of the Palace from its vestibule . . . This vestibule, then, which is called Chalke [the Bronze Gate], is of the following kind. Four straight walls, as high as heaven, are set in a rectangle, and they are in all respects similar to one another, except that the two facing south and north, respectively, are slightly shorter than the others. Near each corner there projects an eminence of carefully worked stones, rising together with the wall from the ground to the top, and while being four-sided, it is joined to the wall on one of its sides; far from breaking up the beautiful space, it adds a kind of adornment thanks to the harmony of similar proportions. Above these elements rise eight arches, four of them sustaining the central part of the roof which curves into the form of a suspended cupola, while the others, two to the south and two to the north, lean onto the adjoining walls and lift up the vaulted roof that hangs between them. The entire ceiling prides itself on its pictures, affixed here not by means of wax poured on in melted form, but composed of tiny mosaic cubes adorned with various colors. These simulate all kinds of subjects including human figures; I shall now describe the nature of these pictures. On either side are war and battle, and numerous cities are being captured, some in Italy, others in Libya. The Emperor is victorious through his lieutenant, the general Belisarius, who returns to the Emperor, his whole army intact, and offers him booty, namely kings and kingdoms and all other things that are prized by men. In the center stand the Emperor and the Empress Theodora, both seeming to rejoice as they celebrate their victory over the kings of the Vandals and the Goths, who approach them as captives of war being led into bondage. They are surrounded by the Roman Senate, one and all in festive mood. This is indicated by the mosaic cubes which on their faces take on a joyful bloom. So they smile proudly as they offer the Emperor divine honors because of the magnitude of his achievements. The whole interior up to the mosaic of the ceiling is revetted with beautiful marbles, not only the upright surfaces, but the entire floor as well. Some of these are Spartan stone resembling emerald, others imitate the flame of fire. Most of them, however, are white in color, not plain, but having at intervals a tracery of wavy blue lines.

## 2.7.6 Christian theory of empire

Part of the dome of the great Church of the Holy Wisdom (Hagia Sophia) in Constantinople collapsed in 558 but was soon rebuilt. Paul the Silentiary, an aristocratic courtier (a "silentiary"), composed a poem, the *Description*, that he delivered in the presence of the emperor Justinian and the patriarch Eutychius during the rededication ceremonies between December 24, 562 and January 6, 563. Paul's poem contains two panegyrics of the emperor and the patriarch that provide a succinct exposition of imperial ideology and illustrate how the emperor wished himself and his projects to be seen. The first extract below emphasizes the scale of the empire Justinian has re-established – with the help of God, which has also saved him from a recent conspiracy and enables him to intercede with God on behalf of his subjects, and his late wife Theodora to intercede with God on his behalf. The second excerpt underlines the status of Constantinople as the "New Rome," and its superiority to her "mother," "Old Rome," illustrating his policy of "imperial renewal." The third excerpt praises the patriarch in terms that underscore the partnership that Justinian sought to achieve with ecclesiastical authority.

Paul the Silentiary, *Description of Hagia Sophia*
[Peter Bell, *Political Voices in the Age of Justinian* (Liverpool: Liverpool University Press, 2009)]

> **1.** (1) Is it possible to find a day greater than now, on which both God and the Emperor are honoured? It is impossible to name one. We know that Christ is Master; yes, we know it absolutely. For you make this known by your words, (5) Mightiest One, even to barbarians. As a result, you have Him to hand as a collaborator in your deeds: in making laws, founding cities, raising temples [i.e. churches], taking up arms (should the need arise), arranging truces and checking conflicts. (10) From this, Victory is inherent in your labours like an emblem. Is it not true that, to the West, we must traverse the whole earth and come to the Ocean, to find the boundary of your power? While to the East, do you not now make all men yours? (15) Some you routed in battle; others before it came to this; and have you not held every Libyan in slavery long

since? From this, you escape from diseases serenely, against all expectation. (20) From this, as one would expect, you always pass by hidden dangers with knowledge, Mightiest One, protected not by spears or shields, but by the very hand of God.

I admire you, Almighty One, for your good courage, I admire you for your judgement and your faith. The ambush [of a recent conspiracy] was laid, (25) the sword at the ready, the appointed day at hand; the conspirators had already passed within the palace and were grasping the inner door. Next they intended to dash against your throne. But you realised this and had known long since; (30) so you remained steadfast and had faith in Him alone who is your champion – I mean God – through whom you are victorious in all things. And you did not fail in your objective. For what followed? The leader of the ambush fell by his own hand, (35) for Justice was not willing to preserve him. For She knew clearly from the tyrants who had often experienced it, that if you had him in your power alive, you would for certain turn straight to pity and mercy; you conquer all mankind in these too. (40) With compassion for the errors of life, you have groaned often at our transgressions, Best of Men. Often you moisten your kindly eye with tears, as kings will, grieving on our behalf. Especially when on seeing lack of self-control, life's housemate (45), you release everyone from their evil debts, like God, and run to forgiveness. You make petitions to yourself when the magnitude of the accusations does not allow others (50) to begin their entreaties. Indeed, you never allow another to exercise the pity which is pre-eminently yours. And, through the impious effrontery of our actions, you have occasion for intercession above.

Does he not take up arms against God Himself, (55) the man who is not willing for this emperor to rule, a man who is gentle and kindly, and who gives benefits in moderation to friends and non-friends alike. This saves you. This makes the soul of the empress, Mighty Master, she who is blessed, all-excellent, lovely and all-wise (60), to intercede with God on your behalf; she whom you had as a pious collaborator, when she was alive.

**2.** (145) But come, fruitful Rome, and garland our life-giving emperor, clothing him abundantly with pure hymns . . . (150) because, by raising this measure-less temple about your arm, he has made you more brilliant than your mother on the Tiber. Give way, I say, renowned Roman Capitol, give way! My emperor has so far overtopped that wonder as great God is superior to an idol! (155) And so I desire, in honey-voiced measures, that you, Anthusa of the golden tunic [i.e. Rome], sing of your Sceptre-bearer. For indeed, not only did our lord, equipping his hand with weapons, enslave innumerable barbarians with his shield-piercing spear, so that they would bow their untamed necks to your yoke-straps, and cower before the yoke of your justice; but even (160) black Envy himself, shrieking insolently, sank down beneath the bow of the emperor, protector of the city, and, torn by a shower of arrows, thudded down, and by his fall hollowed out the dust. But you too, first born Latin Rome, come, (165) singing a song in harmony with fresh-budding Rome;

come, rejoicing that you see your child surpassing her mother, for this is the delight of parents.

**3.** (968) Let us direct our song towards the august Priest. The hymn too for its part is in some respect yours, Lord . . . (974) For when, Sceptre-bearer, in the fecund counsel of your mind, you appointed the great Initiate to your sanctuary . . . (977) immediately you bound on the wreath of victory for your labours in protecting the city . . . (979) But also, Most-hymned Father, Leader of the Holy Temple, grant me a loving ear. By your seal, the glory of the emperor is protected; by your prayers, winged Victory has subjected the nations to the yoke of your sovereignty which preserves cities. And some, who exulted in clashing shields, the spear brings beneath the emperor's feet, but (985) countless other barbarian-speaking nations of the earth have gathered at Rome, because they have heard of the holiness, Thrice-prayed-for one, of your serenity. Just lately I saw the divine court thronged by black-limbed men. Enchanted by your divinely-inspired voice, they voluntarily bowed both soul and neck (990) to the Heavenly and Earthly thrones. Wretched are those who have not received your hand upon their head, the hand which drives away sins hard to withstand, the hand which supports the impoverished, the hand which is the nurse of orphans and assuager of all distress. (995) For indeed, from birth, temperance and modesty have united you to holy ways of heavenly hope. Your meals and your divinely-inspired purpose are both simple; simple is the bright gleam of your eyes, simple the steps of your feet and a simple word moves your lips. (1000) You do not cultivate a downcast, lowering, gloomy brow; you foster a heart which rejoices in Christ, and bear a kindly, gracious radiance; and, on your countenance, a gentle smile furrows your august cheeks. You bear these things as signs of your gentle-minded heart; for, seated unshaken in untumultuous serenity, you are inaccessible to the quick steps of anger (1005). You have shaken off all the woes of material cares, but, opening up your kindly heart as a channel of piety, you direct a sympathetic eye towards human sufferings . . . (1027) May you continue to foster the realm of my emperor, Blessed One, by your prayers; and may you continue to cleanse from Rome which neighbours the sea every stain of sinful-minded life.

## 2.8 Secular and Christian education

### 2.8.1 Educating an elite

Secular education was the route to success in the public world for a smart, poor boy with ambitious parents. With such training he might rise very high in the meritocratic imperial bureaucracy. Augustine describes his own education in late fourth-century North Africa.

Augustine, *Confessions* 2.3.5

[*Saint Augustine, Confessions*, trans. Henry Chadwick (New York: Oxford University Press, 1992) p. 26]

During my sixteenth year there was an interruption in my studies. I was recalled from Madauros, the nearby town where I had first lived away from home to learn literature and oratory. During that time funds were gathered in preparation for a more distant absence at Carthage, for which my father had more enthusiasm than cash, since he was a citizen of Thagaste with very modest resources . . . At that time everybody was full of praise for my father because he spent money on his son beyond the means of his estate, when that was necessary to finance an education entailing a long journey. Many citizens of far greater wealth did nothing of the kind for their children. But this same father did not care what character before you I was developing, or how chaste I was so long as I possessed a cultured tongue . . .

## 2.8.2 Training for imperial service

In the early sixth century, another provincial, John the Lydian, combined education with preparation for the civil bureaucracy in Constantinople. He pulled strings to get ahead. Pedantry and a superficial knowledge of philosophy were no hindrance to advancement.

John Lydus, *On the Magistracies of the Roman State* 3.26
[John Lydus, *Ioannes Lydus on Powers* or *The Magistracies of the Roman State*, trans. Anastasius C. Bandy (Philadelphia: The American Philosophical Society, 1983) pp. 173, 175]

When I was twenty-one years of age . . . I came to this blessed city from my native Philadelphia . . . and after I had pondered many matters with myself, I resolved to join the *memoriales* of the court and to gird myself up for service with them. In order, however, that I might not seem to suffer the loss of the intervening time, I decided to frequent a philosopher's school. The leading teacher at that time was Agapius, about whom the poet Christodorus in his one-volume work *On the Disciples of the Great Proclus* even says thus: "Agapius is assuredly last but the first of all." As I was going through the rudiments of the Aristotelian doctrines, I had the good fortune to hear also some lectures on Platonic philosophy under him. Fortune, however, having planned to thrust me rather into this service [the Praetorian Prefecture] advanced Zoticus, a countryman of mine and one who liked me immensely, to the prefecture of the praetoria under Anastasius, the most clement of all emperors. Because he was able not only to persuade but even to compel me, he enrolled me among the speedwriters of the magistracy, in which also the very gentle Ammianus, late nephew to my father, happened to be excelling.

## 2.8.3 Honor your teachers!

Teachers received public honors. This poem by Agathias, written in Constantinople in the mid-sixth century, recalls Heraklamon, a professor from Pergamon, whose painted portrait was put on public display. The translation captures the rather stilted tone of the poem – a sign of sophisticated literary skill.

Agathias, *Greek Anthology* 16.36

[Cyril Mango, *The Art of the Byzantine Empire, 312–1453* (Englewood Cliffs, NJ: Prentice-Hall Inc., 1972) p. 119]

> Mayest thou forgive that we have not erected for you images, long overdue for thy speeches and agile eloquence. Now, however, because of thy labors and concern on behalf of the city, we have set up this painting of thee, O Heraklamon. If the honor is too small, do not blame us: for in this manner we are wont to reward our good men.

### 2.8.4 *Julian on proper education*

The emperor Julian "the Apostate," writing in 362, attempted to prevent Christians from teaching the traditional curriculum. He argued that it was fundamentally dishonest to teach material in which one did not believe.

Julian, *Letter* 36

[*The Works of the Emperor Julian*, vol. III, trans. W.C. Wright (Cambridge, MA: Harvard University Press) pp. 117–23]

> I hold that a proper education results, not in laboriously acquired symmetry of phrases and language, but in a healthy condition of mind, I mean a mind that has understanding and true opinions about things good and evil, honorable and base. Therefore, when a man thinks one thing and teaches his pupils another, in my opinion he fails to educate exactly in proportion as he fails to be an honest man . . . I think it is absurd that men [the poets and orators of Greece who acknowledged that the gods had inspired them and who expound the works of these writers] should dishonor the gods whom they used to honor. Yet, though I think this is absurd, I do not say that they ought to change their opinions and then instruct the young. But I give them this choice; either not to teach what they do not think admirable, or if they wish to teach, let them first really persuade their pupils that neither Homer nor Hesiod nor any of these writers whom they expound and have declared to be guilty of impiety, folly and error in regard to the gods, is such as they declare. For since they make a livelihood and receive pay from the works of these writers, they thereby confess that they are most shamefully greedy of gain, and that for the sake of a few drachmas they would put up with anything . . . If they believe that those whose interpreters they are and for whom they sit, so to speak, in the seat of the prophets, were wise men, let them be the first to emulate their piety towards the gods. If, however, they think that those writers were in error with respect to the most honored gods, then let them betake themselves to the churches of the Galileans to expound Matthew and Luke, since you Galileans are obeying them when you ordain that men shall refrain from temple-worship. For my part, I would say that your ears and your tongues might be "born anew," as you would say,

as regards these things in which may I ever have part, and all who think and act as is pleasing to me. For religious and secular teachers let there be a general ordinance to this effect: Any youth who wishes to attend the schools is not excluded; nor indeed would it be reasonable to shut out from the best way boys who are still too ignorant to know which way to turn, and to overawe them into being led against their will, as one cures the insane, except that we concede indulgence to all for this sort of disease. For we ought, I think, to teach, but not to punish the demented.

## 2.8.5  Christ or Cicero? Jerome's choice

For many churchmen educated to appreciate the refinements of classical literary style, the Bible in its different translations could seem stylistically crude. In this letter written in 384, Jerome describes the crisis of conscience caused by his devotion to secular Latin literature.

Jerome, *Letter* 22.30 to Eustochium

[Jerome, *Letters and Selected Works. Nicene and Post-Nicene Fathers*, second series vol. VI, ed. Philip Schaff and Henry Wace (Grand Rapids, MI: Eerdmans, 1893/1995)]

Many years ago, when for the kingdom of heaven's sake, I had cut myself off from home, parents, sister, relations, and – harder still – from the dainty food to which I had become accustomed; and when I was on my way to Jerusalem to wage my warfare, I still could not bring myself to forgo the library which I had formed for myself at Rome with great care and toil. And so, miserable man that I was, I would fast only that I might afterwards read Cicero. After many nights spent in vigil, after floods of tears called from my inmost heart, after the recollection of my past sins, I would once more take up Plautus. And when at times I returned to my right mind, and began to read the prophets, their style seemed rude and repellent. I failed to see the light with my blinded eyes; but I attributed the fault not to them, but to the sun. While the old serpent was still making me his plaything, about the middle of Lent a deep-seated fever fell upon my weakened body, and while it destroyed my rest completely – the story seems hardly credible – it so wasted my unhappy frame that scarcely anything was left me but skin and bone. Meantime preparations for my funeral went on; my body grew gradually colder, and the warmth of life lingered only in my throbbing breast. Suddenly I was caught up in the spirit and dragged before the judgment seat of the Judge; and here the light was so bright, and those who stood around were so radiant, that I cast myself upon the ground and did not dare to look up. Asked who and what I was I replied: "I am a Christian." But He who presided said: "Thou liest, thou art a follower of Cicero and not of Christ. For 'where thy treasure is, there will thy heart be also.' " Instantly I became dumb, and amid the strokes of the lash – for He had ordered me to be scourged – I was tortured more severely still by the fire of conscience, considering with myself that verse, "In the grave who shall give thee thanks?"

Yet for all that I began to cry and to bewail myself, saying: "Have mercy upon me, O Lord, have mercy upon me." ... At last the bystanders, falling down before the knees of Him who presided, prayed that He would have pity on my youth and that He would give me space to repent of my error. He might still, they urged, inflict torture on me, should I ever again read the works of the gentiles. Under the stress of that awful moment I should have been ready to make even still larger promises than these. Accordingly I made oath and called upon His name, saying: "Lord, if ever again I possess worldly books, or if ever again I read such, I have denied Thee." Dismissed, then, on taking this oath, I returned to the upper world, and, to the surprise of all, I opened upon them eyes so drenched with tears that my distress served to convince even the incredulous ... May it never, hereafter, be my lot to fall under such inquisition! I profess that my shoulders were black and blue, that I felt the bruises long after I awoke from my sleep, and thenceforth I read the books of God with a zeal greater than I had previously given to the books of men.

### 2.8.6 *Should Christian students read the pagan classics?*

What would be the place of classical literature and learning within a Christian environment? Toward the end of his life, Basil the Great (*c*.330–379), bishop of Caesarea in Cappadocia and one of the most influential voices of Greek Christianity, wrote of the dangers and benefits of studying the classics.

Basil of Caesarea, *Address to Young Men on Reading Profane Literature*
[George A. Jackson, *Early Christian Literature Primers* (*The Post-Nicene Greek Fathers*, vol. III; New York: D. Appleton and Co., 1883) pp. 94–5]

It is sufficiently proved that this pagan learning is not without use to the soul. Consequently, we now say in what manner it is needful for you to share in it. First, to commence with the works of the poets, as they offer discourses of every kind, the mind is not to fix upon all things in their order. When they show you a good man, whether they recount his actions or his words, it is necessary to love him, to take him for a model, and to make all effort to resemble him. Do they offer the example of a bad man? It is necessary to shun the imitating of such, shutting your ears, as they say that Ulysses did, so as not to hear the songs of the sirens. For the habit of hearing words contrary to virtue leads to the practice of vice. It is necessary, then, to watch incessantly in guarding our souls, lest that, charmed by the attraction of the words, we receive in our ignorance some bad impressions, and with the honey introduce into our bosoms poisonous fluids. Thus, we do not approve the poets when they put into the mouths of their characters revilings and sarcasm, when they depict love or drunkenness, or when they make happiness to consist in a table well served and effeminate songs. Still less should we listen to them discoursing of their gods ... I am able to say as much of the historians. As to the orators, we should keep ourselves from imitating their art of lying: for falsehood can never become us, neither in the tribunal nor in anything – us, who have chosen the true and right way of life. But we should collect carefully the recitals of these authors when we see there the praise of virtue or the condemnation of vice. We rejoice only in the perfume and the colors of flowers, while the bees know how to find in them honey: so those who are not content to seek for the agreeable and the seducing in the works of the pagans, are able even to find in them treasures for the soul.

### 2.8.7 No place for secular literature

Gregory the Great, Pope from 590 to 604, took a hard line against secular literature in a letter written in 601 to Bishop Desiderius of Vienne.

Pope Gregory the Great, *Letter* 2.24 to Bishop Desiderius of Vienne
[Jeffrey Richards, *Consul of God. The Life and Times of Gregory the Great* (London: Routledge, 1980) p. 28]

> A report has reached us, which we cannot mention without shame, that you are lecturing on profane literature to certain friends. This fills me with such grief and vehement disgust that my former opinion of you has been turned to mourning and sorrow. For the same mouth cannot sing the praises of Jupiter and the praises of Christ. Consider yourself how offensive, how abominable a thing it is for a bishop to recite verses which are unfit even to be recited by a religious layman . . . If hereafter it is clearly established that the information I received was false, and that you are not applying yourself to the idle vanities of secular literature, I shall render thanks to God, who has not allowed your heart to be polluted by the blasphemous praises of unspeakable men.

### 2.8.8 Students murder a Christian schoolmaster

Prudentius (348–post 405) tells the chilling tale of a Christian schoolmaster murdered by his pagan students.

Prudentius, *On the Crowns of the Martyrs* 9.5–60
[*Prudentius*, vol. II, trans. H.J. Thomson (Cambridge, MA: Harvard University Press, 1953) pp. 221, 223, 225]

> I was bowed to the ground before the tomb which the holy martyr Cassian honours with his consecrated body; and while in tears I was thinking of my sins and all my life's distresses and stinging pains, I lifted my face towards heaven, and there stood confronting me a picture of the martyr painted in colours, bearing a thousand wounds, all his parts torn, and showing his skin broken with tiny pricks. Countless boys round about (a pitiful sight!) were stabbing and piercing his body with the little styles with which they used to run over their wax tablets, writing down the droning lesson in school. I appealed to the verger and he said: "What you are looking at, stranger, is no vain old wife's tale. The picture tells the story of what happened; it is recorded in books and displays the honest assurance of the olden time. He had been in charge of a school for boys and sat as a teacher of reading and writing with a great throng round him,

and he was skilled in putting every word in short signs and following speech quickly with swift pricks on the wax. But at times the young mob, feeling his teaching harsh and stern, were moved with anger and fear, for the teacher is ever distasteful to the youthful learner and childhood never takes kindly to training. Now there came a cruel tempest battering the faith and pressing hard on the people devoted to the Christian glory. The governor of the flock of pupils was dragged from the midst of his class because he had scornfully refused to worship at the altars, and when the contrivers of punishments asked of what profession this man of such high and unruly spirit was, they answered: 'He teaches a company of young children, giving them their first lessons in writing down words with signs invented for the purpose.' 'Take him away,' he cried, 'take him away a prisoner, and make the children a present of the man who used to flog them. Let them make sport of him as they please, give them leave to mangle him at will, let them give their hands a holiday and dip them in their master's blood. It is a pleasant thought that the strict teacher should himself furnish sport to the pupils he has too much held down.'

"So he is stripped of his garments and his hands are tied behind his back, and all the band are there, armed with their sharp styles. All the hatred long conceived in silent resentment they each vent now, burning with gall that has at last found freedom. Some throw their brittle tablets and break them against his face, the wood flying in fragments when it strikes his brow, the wax-covered boxwood splitting with a loud crack as it is dashed on his blood-stained cheeks, the broken slab wet and red from the blow. Others again launch at him the sharp iron pricks, the end with which by scratching strokes the wax is written upon, and the end with which the letters that have been cut are rubbed out and the roughened surface once more made into a smooth, glossy space. With the one the confessor of Christ is stabbed, with the other he is cut; the one end enters the soft flesh, the other splits the skin. Two hundred hands together have pierced him all over his body, and from all these wounds at once the blood is dripping."

### 2.8.9 Christian curriculum taught on a Roman model – in Syria

In the introduction to his book on biblical exegesis, Junillus, the chief legal official of Justinian from 541/2 to 546, responded to the request of a visiting North African bishop for information about religious instruction. Junillus describes the systematic religious instruction offered in Nisibis, a center of Christian learning in Syria. Taking this as a model, his own book follows an orderly structure intended to help beginners in the study of biblical interpretation.

Junillus Africanus, *The Basic Teachings of Divine Law*, Introduction
[Michael Maas, *Exegesis and Empire in the Early Byzantine Mediterranean. Junillus Africanus and the Instituta Regularia Divinae Legis*, with a contribution by Edward G. Mathews, Jr. (Tübingen: Mohr Siebeck, 2003) pp. 119–21]

As is your custom, you asked whether there might be someone among the Greeks who burned with a passion for the divine books. I replied to this question that I had seen a certain man called Paul, a Persian by origin, who was educated at the Syrian School in the city of Nisibis, where the Divine Law is taught in a disciplined and orderly fashion by public teachers in the same way that in a secular education grammar and rhetoric are taught in our cities. Then, when you asked repeatedly if I possessed any of his works I said that I had read a certain book of his, entitled *Rules*, that he used to introduce his students to the preliminary, literal meaning of divine scriptures before he exposed them to more serious explanation. His purpose was that they might initially come to understand the purpose and arrangement of these very principles which operate in Divine Law, so that they might be taught not in a haphazard and confused way but one by one in an orderly manner.

## 2.8.10  Reducing teachers' salaries

Although Justinian took measures to maintain teachers in Carthage and Rome after the reconquest, his reduction of the salaries of pagan educators in Constantinople symbolized the demise of secular education funded by the state. Here Procopius attacks Justinian's "downsizing" in education.

Procopius, *Secret History* 26.5

[*Procopius*, vol. VI: *The Anecdota or Secret History*, trans. H.B. Dewing (Cambridge, MA: Harvard University Press, 1935) p. 303]

Nay more, he also caused physicians and teachers of free-born children to be in want of the necessities of life. For the allowances of free maintenance which former Emperors had decreed should be given to men of these professions from the public funds he cancelled entirely.

## 2.8.11  Interpreting the Bible

Different approaches to interpreting the Bible's layers of meaning (e.g. allegorical, literal, spiritual) developed in Late Antiquity. One approach was to find references that anticipated the New Testament in the Hebrew Bible. At the beginning of his *Homily* 10 Basil of Caesarea describes how Scripture might be used.

Basil of Caesarea, *Homily* 10.1, "A Psalm on the Lot of the Just Man"

[*The Fathers of the Church: Saint Basil, Exegetic Homilies*, trans. Sister Agnes Clare Way (Washington, DC: Catholic University of America Press, 1963) pp. 151–2]

All Scripture is inspired by God and is useful, composed by the Spirit for this reason, namely, that we men, each and all of us, as if in a general hospital for souls, may select the remedy for his own condition. For, it says, "care will make the greatest sin to cease." Now, the prophets teach one thing, historians another, the law something else, and the form of advice found in the proverbs something different still. But, the Book of Psalms has taken over what is profitable from all. It foretells coming events; it recalls history; it frames laws for life; it suggests what must be done; and, in general, it is the common treasury of good doctrine, carefully finding what is suitable for each one. The old wounds of souls it cures completely, and to the recently wounded it brings speedy improvements; the diseased it treats and the unharmed it preserves. On the whole, it effaces, as far as is possible, the passions, which subtly exercise dominion over souls during the lifetime of man, and it does this with a certain orderly persuasion and sweetness which produces sound thoughts.

In *Homily* 11.4 he explains a sentence of Psalm 7.

Basil of Caesarea, *Homily* 11.4

[*The Fathers of the Church: Saint Basil, Exegetic Homilies*, trans. Sister Agnes Clare Way (Washington, DC: Catholic University of America Press, 1963) p. 171]

"The Lord will judge the people." Words about judgment are scattered in many places in Scripture, as most cogent and essential for the teaching of true religion to those who believe in God through Jesus Christ. Since the words concerning the judgment are written with various meanings, they seem to hold some confusion for those who do not accurately distinguish the meanings. "He who believes in me is not judged; but he who does not believe is already judged."

## 2.8.12 *Preserving classical and Christian learning*

Also in the sixth century, Cassiodorus, the worldly statesman at Theoderic's court and the cleric who founded the monastery at Vivarium in southern Italy, described a well-integrated education of Christian as well as secular materials. As a result of his beliefs, a great deal of classical literature was copied and preserved in this and other monasteries.

Cassiodorus, *An Introduction to Divine and Human Readings* I.1, 5–6

[Cassiodorus, *An Introduction to Divine and Human Readings*, trans. Leslie Webber Jones (New York: Columbia University Press, 1946) pp. 67–70]

1. Perceiving that the schools were swarming with students because of a great longing for secular letters (a great part of mankind believed that through these schools it attained worldly wisdom), I was, I confess, extremely sorry that the Divine Scriptures had no public teachers, since worldly authors were rich in instruction beyond doubt most distinguished. I strove with the most holy Agapetus, bishop of the city of Rome, to collect subscriptions and to have Christian rather than secular schools receive professors in the city of Rome, just as the custom is said to have existed for a long time at Alexandria and is said even now to be zealously cultivated by the Hebrews in Nisibis, a city of the Syrians, that thereby the soul might obtain eternal salvation and the tongue of

the faithful might be adorned with a holy and completely faultless eloquence. But although my ardent desire could in no way have been fulfilled because of the struggles that seethed and raged excessively in the Italian realm, inasmuch as a peaceful affair has no place in anxious times, I was driven by divine charity to this device, namely, in the place of a teacher to prepare for you under the Lord's guidance these introductory books; through which, in my opinion, the unbroken line of the Divine Scriptures and the compendious knowledge of secular letters might with the Lord's beneficence be related – books not at all fluent, perhaps, since in them is found, not studied eloquence, but indispensable narration; to be sure, they are extremely useful, since through them one learns the indicated origin of both the salvation of the soul and secular knowledge. In them I commit to you, not my own learning, but the words of men of former times, which it is right to praise and glorious to proclaim for future generations, for whatever is said about men of former times by way of praise of the Lord is not considered hateful display. Add to this the fact that one is pleased with a venerable teacher if one consults him frequently; moreover, whenever one desires to have recourse to such teachers, one will find no harshness in them.

5. In the first book, therefore, present and ready you have masters of a bygone generation to teach you not so much by their tongues as by your eyes. Wisely then, studious brothers, restrain your eager desires, learning in the proper order what should be read . . .

6. In the second book, which concerns the arts and disciplines of liberal letters, a few things ought, of course, to be culled; here, however, one would make a mistake with less danger if in making it he preserved his faith steadfast. Moreover, whatever will be found in the Divine Scriptures concerning such matters will generally be better understood because of previous knowledge. For it is agreed that in the origin of spiritual wisdom, as it were, evidences of these matters were sown abroad in the manner of seeds, which instructors in secular letters later most wisely transferred to their own rules; we have shown our approval of this action in a suitable place, perhaps in our expounding of the Psalter.

### 2.8.13 Searching for a teacher: the case of Ananias of Shirak

By the mid-seventh century, education had become even harder to find. The "thrice blessed" Armenian scholar Ananias of Shirak (600–665) describes his desire for secular learning – and the difficulty of obtaining it in Armenia.

Ananias of Shirak, *Autobiography*

[Ananias of Shirak, *Autobiography*, trans. F.C. Conybeare (in *Byzantinische Zeitschrift* 6, 1897) pp. 572–3]

> I, Ananias Shirakvantzi, am he who collected the literature of our race of Armenians, and was learned in divine writ; and day by day I enlightened the eyes of my mind according to the word of the psalmist. And I was for ever hearing of the blessedness of the wise and of those who seek after wisdom;

even as it is commanded by Solomon: "Do thou acquire knowledge and wisdom, and continue to drive away ignorance, calling darkness her parent. If thou expel knowledge, then will I also expel thee." And I was in dread of these threats, and I desired to attain unto blessedness and longed for wisdom. But I was very wanting in the art of counting, and I reflected that no discourse is in keeping with wisdom in the absence of number, which I regarded as the mother of all philosophies. And among the Armenians I found no man who was learned in this science, nor in their land did I find any books of science. So I set out to go to Greece and I came to Theodoupolis, and I found there a reasonable man, learned in the writings of the church who was named Eliazar. He told me that there was a certain man who was a mathematician in the region of fourth Armenia, Christodotus his name. And I went and spent with him a space of six months. And I saw that he had not the whole science, but only a smattering of it; so I went on thence to Constantinople; and those of my acquaintance who were there met me and said to me: Why have you embarked upon such a long and toilsome journey; when Tychicus the teacher of Byzantium is near to us on the coast of Pontus, which is called Trebizond. He is full of wisdom and has a knowledge of Armenian literature and is well known to the princes. And I said: How do you know this? And they said: We saw many travellers going to him, because of his very great knowledge.

But we now had as a fellow voyager Philagrius, the deacon of the patriarch of Constantinople, who was taking many youths to him for instruction. On hearing this I glorified God, who thus fulfilled the desire of his servant, according to the saying: "Seek ye and ye shall find." And when I had come, I found him at the shrine of Saint Eugenia. And I announced my coming to him; and he received me with joy and said: I thank God for sending thee in search of wisdom; that thou mayest use these sciences in the diocese of St. Gregory; and I am the more glad, that that land takes its instruction from myself. For in my youth I was a good deal in Armenia, and there was ignorance in the land. And the teacher Tychicus unto whom I went, loved me as his son and schooled me in all his thoughts. And the lord gave me grace, and I learned fully the art of mathematics, so that the pupils in the royal court were envious of me. And I lived with him eight years, and read and learned many writings which were not translated into our tongue. For he had an enormous library, secret books and open, ecclesiastical and profane, scientific and historical, medical and chronological. But I need not enumerate them in detail, for there is no book which was not found with him, and in translating he had such grace as comes from the holy spirit; for when he desired to translate Greek books into Armenian, he did not do it hesitatingly like other translators, for he understood the Armenian tongue, as he did Armenian letters. And he told me how he came to know the Armenian tongue and to acquire such wisdom. He told me that when he was a young man in Trebizond he had been in the court of John the Warrior, and he served in Armenia, and spent a long time there until the reign of Maurice, during which he became acquainted with the tongue and the literature.

# Further reading

Bassett, Sarah, *The Urban Image of Late Antique Constantinople* (Cambridge: Cambridge University Press, 2004)

Brogiolo, G.P. and Bryan Ward-Perkins, *The Idea and Ideal of the Town between Late Antiquity and the Early Middle Ages* (Leiden, Boston, Cologne: Brill, 1999)

Curran, John, *Pagan City and Christian Capital. Rome in the Fourth Century* (Oxford: Clarendon Press, 2000)

Harris, William, ed., *The Transformation of Urbs Roma. Journal of Roman Archaeology Supplement* (1998)

Holum, Kenneth, "The Classical City in the Sixth Century," in M. Maas, ed., *The Cambridge Companion to the Age of Justinian* (Cambridge: Cambridge University Press, 2005)

Lançon, Bertrand, *Rome in Late Antiquity: AD 313–604*, trans. Antonia Neville (Edinburgh: Edinburgh University Press, 2000)

Lavan, Luke, ed., *Recent Research in Late Antique Urbanism. Journal of Roman Archaeology, Supplementary Series Number 42* (Portsmouth, RI: Journal of Roman Archaeology, 2001)

Liebeschuetz, J.H.W.G., *The Decline and Fall of the Roman City* (Oxford: Oxford University Press, 2001)

Lim, Richard, *Public Disputation, Power, and Social Order in Antiquity* (Berkeley: University of California Press, 1995)

Mango, Cyril, *Byzantium: The Empire of New Rome* (New York: University of California Press, 1980)

Rich, John, ed., *The City in Late Antiquity* (London: Routledge, 1992)

# 3

# THE ROMAN ARMY

## 3.1 Introduction

The Roman army played a fundamental role in the life of the empire in Late Antiquity, laying claim to a greater share of men and resources than ever before. As had been the case since the reign of Augustus at the beginning of the empire, control of the army continued to be the emperor's first concern. In the eastern empire subordination of the military to the state apparatus was achieved and the army remained a powerful institution, but in the West the army fell out of imperial control in the fifth century and formed the nucleus of new post-Roman regimes.

Military disasters preoccupied Rome's leaders from the end of the Severan dynasty (235) to the rise of Diocletian (284). During this half century of chronic civil war and foreign invasion the state nearly foundered, but hard and useful lessons were learned. When Diocletian, who had risen from the ranks himself, seized power he drew on the experience of previous soldier emperors to institute far-reaching military reforms. He greatly increased the size of the army, renewed massive defense of the empire's perimeters, and continued using the elite mobile field army (the *comitatenses*). To prevent usurpation and to strengthen the chain of command, Diocletian doubled the number of provinces and separated military and administrative offices within them. He introduced a rigorous new tax system to raise funds for the vastly increased military and civilian bureaucracies. Need for soldiers had to be measured against need for revenues. Constantine (306–337) continued to build on the military reforms of the Tetrarchy. He created a large, highly mobile field army with higher pay and greater privileges than those of frontier troops, whose role was reduced. Two new commanders, the *Magister Equitum* (Master of Cavalry) and *Magister Militum* (Master of Soldiers), directed these forces, and they remained important figures throughout Late Antiquity.

These changes served the empire very well through most of the fourth century, but difficulties in recruitment and growing reliance on foreign troops anticipated the military crises of the next century. Valens' defeat by an army of Goths at Adrianople in 378 and the consequent enrollment of Gothic troops in the Roman army under their own native commanders represents an ominous shift in military affairs. In particular, the extent of barbarian recruitment and the degree of authority maintained over the army by the state became a critical issue. Competition among generals continued to fragment the West. A series of military dictators managed affairs in the West, and the Roman army slowly disappeared. Intense pressures from the Huns drove different groups into the empire, and by the mid-fifth century Britain, North Africa, Spain, and much of Gaul were irretrievably lost to the Roman state. In the East, however, civilian control was maintained over foreign recruits, new recruiting grounds within the empire were exploited, and the state prospered sufficiently to attempt expeditions of reconquest under Leo (465–466; 470) and Justinian (533–552). The size of the army was reduced due to plague and other factors, however, and new strategies of defense, finance, and diplomacy developed. Forces continued to decline in number. By Justinian's day military forces totaled perhaps 150,000. In the 620s Heraclius forged a new army that he led to victory against Persia in 627. Nevertheless, Islamic armies easily overran Egypt and large portions of the Near East in the seventh century.

In addition to waging war against all sorts of invaders, maintaining a watch on the borders, and protecting the emperor, imperial troops also assisted in tax collection and served as a sort of police force.

As the size of armies declined in the sixth and seventh centuries in the East, careful preparation for battle and cunning became the hallmarks of a highly professional army. Training troops remained a high priority, and a variety of military handbooks survive to show how tactics and training were understood. A growing reliance upon cavalry, especially heavily armed cavalry as a highly mobile strike force, was a significant development.

A few Christian soldiers were martyred in the pre-Constantinian period, and the Roman army remained largely pagan well into the fourth century because most troops were recruited from the unconverted pagan countryside. Constantine's battlefield conversion to Christianity, however, marked the beginning of an inescapable change, and though some concessions had to be made to military leaders, imperial legislation against pagans rid the army of non-Christians. Because church leaders such as Augustine and Jerome endorsed military service to Christian emperors, Christian traditions of non-violence yielded to the idea of the "just war." Justinian (527–565) initiated his wars of reconquest to restore Chalcedonian Orthodoxy to lands ruled by Arians while Heraclius' campaigns against Persia were cast virtually as crusades.

## 3.2 Reorganization of the army

### 3.2.1 The decline of border defenses: Constantine's fault?

Constantine's military policies built upon those of Diocletian and earlier third-century emperors. Zosimus, a pagan writing in the late fifth century, objected to Constantine's reforms because of the emperor's Christianity. In this passage from his New History, Zosimus criticizes Constantine's de-emphasis of border defense as a first step in the ruin of the entire empire. (See *1.3.1*, page 11.)

Zosimus, *New History* 2.34

[*Zosimus*, trans. Ronald Ridley (Canberra: Australian Association for Byzantine Studies, 1982) p. 39]

Constantine did something else which gave the barbarians unhindered access to the Roman empire. By the forethought of Diocletian, the frontiers of the empire everywhere were covered, as I have stated, with cities, garrisons and fortifications which housed the whole army. Consequently it was impossible for the barbarians to cross the frontier because they were confronted at every point by forces capable of resisting their attacks. (2) Constantine destroyed this security by removing most of the troops from the frontiers and stationing them in cities which did not need assistance, thus both stripping of protection those being molested by the barbarians and subjecting the cities left alone by them to the outrages of the soldiers, so that henceforth most have become deserted. Moreover he enervated the troops by allowing them to devote themselves to shows and luxuries. In plain terms, Constantine was the origin and beginning of the present destruction of the empire.

## 3.3 The army in the field

The Roman army in Late Antiquity had two main parts. The elite central field forces, called *comitatenses*, included both cavalry and infantry and bore the main battlefield responsibilities. They were commanded by emperors themselves (though not as a rule during the fifth and sixth centuries) or by Masters of Soldiers. Cavalrymen were often recruited from non-Roman peoples. Infantry regiments drew from Roman citizens as well as from men beyond the borders. The second part comprised the *limitanei*, commanded by counts (*comites*) or dukes (*duces*). These troops, charged with border defense, gradually declined in mobility and effectiveness and disappeared in the East by the end of the sixth century.

### 3.3.1 Elephants vs. legionaries

The fourth-century military historian Ammianus Marcellinus describes some of the unusual fighting conditions encountered by Roman troops returning from Persia following the death of Emperor Julian in 363.

Ammianus Marcellinus, *History* 25.6.1–4

[*Ammianus Marcellinus*, vol. II, trans. John C. Rolfe (London: Heinemann, 1956) p. 523]

> While these arrangements were being made on both sides, in Jovian's behalf victims were killed, and when the entrails were inspected it was announced that he would ruin everything if he remained within the rampart of his camp (as he thought of doing), but would be victor if he marched out. But when we accordingly were just beginning to leave, the Persians attacked us, with the elephants in front. By the unapproachable and frightful stench of these brutes horses and men were at first thrown into confusion, but the Jovian Legion and Herculian Legion, after killing a few of the beasts, bravely resisted the mailclad horsemen. Then the legions of the Jovii and the Victores came to the aid of their struggling companions and slew two elephants, along with a considerable

number of the enemy. On our left wing some valiant warriors fell, Julianus, Macrobius and Maximus, tribunes of the legions which then held first place in our army. Having buried these men as well as the pressing conditions allowed, when towards nightfall we were coming at rapid pace to a fortress called Sumere, we recognized the corpse of Anatolius lying in the road . . .

### 3.3.2 Guarding the emperor

Again Ammianus describes a difficult moment during Constantius' campaigns against the Sarmatians in 358. The Praetorian Guard protected their emperor.
Ammianus Marcellinus, *History* 17.13.8–10
[*Ammianus Marcellinus*, vol. I, trans. John C. Rolfe (Cambridge, MA: Harvard University Press, 1956) pp. 385, 387]

> When the day was now declining to evening and the waning light warned them to do away with delay, the Roman soldiers lifted up their standards and rushed upon the enemy in a fiery attack. Thereupon the foe massed themselves together, and, huddled in close order, directed all their attack against the emperor himself, who, as was said, stood on higher ground, charging upon him with fierce looks and savage cries. The furious madness of this onset so angered our army that it could not brook it, and as the savages hotly menaced the emperor . . ., they took the form of a wedge . . . and scattered them with a hot charge. Then on the right our infantry slaughtered the bands of their infantry, while on the left our cavalry poured into the nimble squadrons of their cavalry. The praetorian cohort, which stood before the emperor and was carefully guarding him, fell upon the breasts of the resisting foe, and then upon their backs as they took to flight.

### 3.3.3 Training the cavalry

With the decline of border defenses, the need for a highly mobile strike force became paramount, and so the use of cavalry units grew in importance (though not necessarily in number) in the late-Roman army. Proper equipment was essential for cavalrymen to fight successfully. The frequent mention of the nomadic Avars in this passage from Maurice's *Treatise on Strategy*, written in the late sixth century, indicates the influence of these steppe nomads on shaping Roman military organization and strategy. Stirrups and horned saddles bore the weight of heavily armed riders.
Maurice, *Treatise on Strategy* 1.2
[*Maurice's Strategikon: Handbook of Byzantine Military Strategy*, trans. George T. Dennis (Philadelphia: University of Pennsylvania Press, 1984) p. 12]

> With individual training progressing satisfactorily, the soldiers must be armed by their commanding officers. The proper equipment needed on campaign may be gotten ready in the leisure of winter quarters. Each soldier should have the equipment corresponding to his rank and his pay and perquisites . . . They

should have hooded coats of mail reaching to their ankles, which can be caught up by thongs and rings, along with carrying cases; helmets with small plumes on top; bows suited to the strength of each man, and not above it, more in fact on the weaker side, cases broad enough so that when necessary they can fit the strung bows in them, with spare bow strings in their saddle bags; quivers with covers holding about thirty or forty arrows; in their baldrics small files and awls; cavalry lances of that Avar type with leather thongs in the middle of the shaft and with pennons; swords; round neck pieces of the Avar type made with linen fringes outside and wool inside. Young foreigners unskilled with the bow should have lances and shields. It is not a bad idea for the bucellarii troops [i.e., elite divisions] to make use of iron gauntlets and small tassels hanging from the back straps and the breast straps of the horses, as well as small pennons hanging from their own shoulders over the coats of mail. For the more handsome the soldier is in his armament, the more confidence he gains in himself and the more fear he inspires in the enemy.

Apart from the foreigners, all the younger Romans up to the age of forty must definitely be required to possess bow and quiver, whether they be expert archers or just average. They should possess two lances so as to have a spare at hand in case the first one misses. Unskilled men should use lighter bows. Given enough time, even those who do not know how to shoot will learn, for it is essential that they do so.

The horses, especially those of the officers and the other special troops, in particular those in the front ranks of the battle line, should have protective pieces of iron armor about their heads and breast plates of iron or felt, or else breast and neck coverings such as the Avars use.

The saddles should have large and thick cloths; the bridles should be of good quality; attached to the saddles should be two iron stirrups, a lasso with thong, hobble, a saddle bag large enough to hold three or four days' rations for the soldier when needed. There should be four tassels on the back strap, one on top of the head, and one under the chin . . .

Each squad should have a tent, as well as sickles and axes to meet any contingency. It is well to have the tents of the Avar type, which combine practicality with good appearance.

### 3.3.4 The navy

Large-scale naval expeditions were rare. In 468 Emperor Leo sent a huge force in an unsuccessful attempt to reconquer North Africa from the Vandals. This account, which comes at second hand from a fifth-century source, exaggerates the number of ships and the costs of the expedition.

Theophanes, *Chronicle*, AM 5961, AD 468–469

[*The Chronicle of Theophanes Confessor: Byzantine and Near Eastern History, AD 284–813*, trans. Cyril Mango and Roger Scott (Oxford: Clarendon Press, 1997) p. 180]

In this year the Emperor Leo equipped and sent out a big fleet against Gizerich who ruled the Africans. For after the death of Marcian, Gizerich had committed many terrible things against the territories under the Empire of the Romans, plundering, taking many prisoners and destroying the cities. And so the emperor, moved by zeal, gathered 100,000 ships from the entire eastern sea, filled them with armies and weapons, and sent them against Gizerich. Indeed they say that he spent one hundred and thirty thousand pounds of gold on this expedition.

### 3.3.5 Border troops

During their long history, border troops had acquired many names, but they are referred to in the sources primarily as *limitanei*. These forces were mostly stationed along the perimeter of the empire, but they sometimes were deployed within provinces to protect against unruly tribesmen and bandits. After Diocletian they declined in prestige though they continued to perform important functions on a regional basis. The following law of 438 indicates imperial concern for their welfare.

Theodosius, *Novel* 4.1

> The welfare of the border militia demands the support and assistance of Our Clemency, since they are said to be afflicted by the complaints of certain persons and by the fact that they are being produced before various judges, so that as between private life and military science they are born to neither. Add to this the fact that they are compelled to unlearn the use of arms for the observance of the forum of a civilian office, and they are strangers in an alien life, inexperienced in litigation, ignorant of the court actions which are instituted by shameless eloquence and popular doctrines. These facts were brought to Our knowledge by the report of the Sublime Anatolius, Master of Both Branches of the Military Service throughout the Orient. Wherefore We do not allow any further that the loss of so great an advantage shall be disregarded, since it is evident by the regulations of Our ancestors that whatever territory is included within the power of the Roman name is defended from the incursions of the barbarians by the rampart of the frontier.
>
> On account of these circumstances We sanction by a law destined to live in all the ages that throughout all the region of the Orient from the farthest solitudes, no soldier of a duke, no soldier of the border militia, who with difficulty and hardship withstands the misery of hunger by means of his meager emoluments, shall be produced at all in Our most sacred imperial court, either by the sacred imperial order of Our Divinity or by Our divine imperial response . . . [Theodosius and Valentinian, 438]

### 3.3.6 Border forts

Often *limitanei* were stationed in forts located at strategic points on the frontier, and the positioning and maintenance of fortifications and the management of soldiers' private lives became a fine art, as an anonymous sixth-century military treatise reveals.

Anonymous, *On Strategy* 9

[George T. Dennis, ed., *The Anonymous Byzantine Treatise on Strategy*, in *Three Byzantine Military Treatises* (Washington, DC: Dumbarton Oaks Press, 1985) p. 29]

> Forts are used for several purposes: first, to observe the approach of the enemy; second, to receive deserters from the enemy; third, to hold back any fugitives from our own side. The fourth is to facilitate assembly for raids against outlying enemy territories. These are undertaken not so much for plunder as for finding out what the enemy are doing and what plans they are making against us.
>
> These forts should be erected near the frontier and not far from the route the enemy are expected to take, so that any hostile advance will not go undetected by the garrison. They should not be located too much out in the open. If they are, the enemy, taking advantage of the ground, could keep them under observation from very close up to a great distance and so prevent any of our men, if need arise, from entering the fort or from leaving it when they wish.
>
> Natural strength as well as technical skill should assure the defense of the forts. Valuables should not be stored in them, nor should too many men be assembled there. These may lead the enemy to invest the place for a long time. This would make it difficult for us to assemble our own troops for action, whereas it would be an easy matter for the enemy to get ready to move out.
>
> The garrison in each fort should have a commanding officer entrusted with complete responsibility for the post. He should be conspicuous for his religious character as well as for all the other qualifications one expects in an officer. The men in the garrison should not have their wives and children with them. Most of them should be left in a different province, so that love of them may not tempt the men to go over to the enemy or otherwise jeopardize the security of the fort. Soldiers should not stay too long in these posts, but should be relieved at regular intervals. One group may return home, while another comes in from their homes to the fort. Still, if a fort is extremely strong, so that there is no danger of its being besieged, and we can keep it provisioned without any problem, then there is no reason why the men cannot have their families reside there with them.
>
> We must not entrust the safety of these forts or assign to their garrisons men who have once been captured by the enemy or who have relatives imprisoned by them or who have been caught and convicted of some crime. Under all circumstances the forts must have a good supply of food and water, enough to last through any possible siege by the enemy.

### 3.3.7 River frontier patrols

Naval flotillas, deployed primarily along the Rhine and Danube Rivers, were also part of the border forces. This law of Theodosius II and Honorius demonstrates the importance placed upon them through the severity of punishment for their neglect.

*Theodosian Code* 7.17.1, "River Patrol Craft on the Danube"

We decree that there shall be assigned to the Moesian border ninety river patrol craft of recent construction and that ten more shall be added to these by the repair of old craft; and on the Scythian border, which is rather widespread and extensive, there shall be assigned one hundred and ten such new craft, with fifteen added by the restoration of antiquated ones. The stipulation shall be observed that each year hereafter by the renovation of old craft, four reconnaissance patrol craft and ten inshore patrol craft shall be constructed on the Moesian border, but on the Scythian border five reconnaissance patrol craft and twelve inshore patrol craft shall be constructed entirely new. These shall be equipped with all their weapons and supplies at the instance of the duke and shall be constructed on the responsibility of his office staff. With this supplement of reconstructed craft, the restoration of the entire number of craft decreed shall be speedily completed within seven years, and Your Sublimity, by your industry, shall arrange from what sources the assembly and construction of these craft must be procured. [Theodosius, 412]

### 3.3.8 Raiding

Roman forces engaged in small-scale raiding to intimidate enemy forces. In this passage, Roman troops have crossed the Rhine in 357 to ravage the territory of the Alamanni. Though enemies of Rome, these people lived in Roman-style houses.
Ammianus Marcellinus, *History* 17.1.5–7
[*Ammianus Marcellinus*, vol. I, trans. John C. Rolfe (Cambridge, MA: Harvard University Press, 1956) p. 307]

This arrangement thus made, at the very break of day the savages were seen drawn up along the hill-tops, and the soldiers in high spirits were led up to the higher ground; but they found no one there (since the enemy, suspecting this, had hastily decamped), and then great columns of smoke were seen at a distance, revealing that our men had burst in and were devastating the enemy's territory. This action broke the Germans' spirit, and abandoning the ambuscades which they had laid for our men in narrow and dangerous places, they fled across the river, Menus by name, to bear aid to their kinsfolk. For, as is apt to happen in times of doubt and confusion, they were panic-stricken by the raid of our cavalry on the one side, and on the other by the sudden onset of our infantry, who had rowed up the river in their boats; and with their knowledge of the ground they had quick recourse to flight. Upon their departure our soldiers marched on undisturbed and plundered farms rich in cattle and crops, sparing none; and having dragged out the captives, they set fire to and burned down all the houses, which were built quite carefully in Roman fashion.

### 3.3.9  How to establish frontier defense

In the following law of 534, Justinian instructs his general Belisarius on the function and arrangement of troops on the frontier of the former Roman territories newly reconquered from the Vandals in North Africa.

Justinian, *Code* 1.27.2.4, 8

[*The Civil Law*, trans. S.P. Scott (Cincinnati, OH: Central Trust, 1932) pp. 133–4]

> (4) Let those men to whose care the defence of the provinces has been entrusted be vigilant and protect our subjects from being injured by incursions of the enemy, and be ready to implore the aid of God, by day and by night, and exert all their efforts to extend the boundaries of the provinces of Africa to that point where the Roman Empire had its limits before the invasion of the Vandals and the Moors, and where the ancient guards were posted, as is shown by the forts and defences; and, moreover, let them, by all means, hasten to enclose and fortify those cities which formerly were situated near the fortifications which were erected when those regions were under Roman domination, when with God's assistance the enemy was expelled from the said provinces. And, let them dispatch officers and soldiers to those points where their boundaries were situated at a time when all the provinces of Africa formed a part of the Roman Empire, as, with the aid of God, through whose favor they have been restored to Us, We hope speedily to be successful . . .

> (8) In order to maintain the boundaries it seemed necessary to Us that other soldiers, in addition to those in the camps, should be posted along them, who could defend the camps and cities situated there, as well as cultivate the soil; so that other inhabitants of the provinces, seeing them there, might betake themselves to those places. We have made a list of the number of soldiers to be appointed to guard the frontiers, to enable Your Excellency, in accordance with the said list which We send to you, to make provision for their distribution through the camps and other places; so that, if you should find suitable detachments in the provinces, or where a military force was formerly stationed, you can fix the number of frontier guards for each boundary; and if any trouble should arise, these soldiers can, with their leaders, and without the aid of those in the camps, defend the points where they have been distributed; and neither they themselves nor their officers should extend the boundaries; and all this must be done in such a way that the aforesaid frontier guards may not be subjected to any expense by their officers and the latter may not fraudulently convert any of their pay to their own use. [Honorius and Theodosius, 412]

### 3.3.10  Border defense crumbles on the Danube

*The Life of Saint Severin* describes the collapse of the Danubian border under pressure from tribes which were themselves being pushed by the Huns. The following passage, written in Italy in 511 by Severin's disciple Eugippius, an Italian monk, describes the disappearance of the unpaid Roman garrison in a small border town. (See *13.1.16*, page 359.)

Eugippius, *The Life of Saint Severin* 20.1

[*The Fathers of the Church: Eugippius, The Life of Saint Severin*, trans. Ludwig Bieler (Washington, DC: The Catholic University Press, 1965) p. 78]

> At the time when the Roman Empire was still in existence, the soldiers of many towns were supported by public money for their watch along the wall. When this arrangement ceased, the military formations were dissolved and, at the same time, the wall was allowed to break down. The garrison of Batavis, however, still held out. Some of these had gone to Italy to fetch for their comrades the last payment, but on their way they had been routed by the barbarians, and nobody knew. One day when St. Severin was reading in his cell, he suddenly closed the book and began to sigh heavily and to shed tears. He told those who were present to go speedily to the river, which, as he declared, was at that hour red with human blood. And at that moment, the news arrived that the bodies of the said soldiers had been washed ashore by the current of the river.

### 3.3.11 The siege of Amida – a lucky escape

Ammianus Marcellinus witnessed the siege of Amida in 359. He describes the miseries endured by the soldiers and townspeople as the Persians attacked. When Amida finally fell to the Persian forces – the Persian king himself took part in the fighting – Ammianus was lucky to escape with a few companions.

Ammianus Marcellinus, *History* 19.2.7–11; 19.4.1; 19.8.4–9

[*Ammianus Marcellinus*, vol. I, trans. John C. Rolfe (Cambridge, MA: Harvard University Press, 1956) pp. 479, 481, 487, 509, 511, 513]

> 19.2.7 Then heads were shattered, as masses of stone, hurled from the scorpions, crushed many of the enemy; others were pierced by arrows, some were struck down by spears and the ground strewn with their bodies, while others that were only wounded retreated in headlong flight to their companions. 8. No less was the grief and no fewer the deaths in the city, since a thick cloud of arrows in compact mass darkened the air, while the artillery which the Persians had acquired from the plunder of Singara inflicted still more wounds. 9. For the defenders, recovering their strength and returning in relays to the contest they had abandoned, when wounded in their great ardour for defense fell with destructive results; or if only mangled, they overturned in their writhing those who stood next to them, or at any rate, so long as they remained alive kept calling for those who had the skill to pull out the arrows implanted in their bodies. 10. Thus slaughter was piled upon slaughter and prolonged to the very end of the day, nor was it lessened even by the darkness of evening, with such great determination did both sides fight. 11. And so the night watches were passed under the burden of arms, while the hills re-echoed from the shouts

rising from both sides, as our men praised the power of Constantius Caesar as lord of the world and the universe, and the Persians called Sapor "saansaan" and "pirosen," which being interpreted is "king of kings" and "victor in wars" . . .

19.4.1 But within the city, where the quantity of corpses scattered through the streets was too great to admit of burial, a plague was added to so many ills, fostered by the contagious infection of maggot-infested bodies, the steaming heat, and the weakness of the populace from various causes . . .

19.8.4–9 . . . And now the city was filled with the eager rush of the enemy's forces, and since all hope of defence or of flight was cut off, armed and unarmed alike without distinction of sex were slaughtered like so many cattle. 5. Therefore when the darkness of evening was coming on and a large number of our soldiers, although adverse fortune still struggled against them, were joined in battle and thus kept busy, I hid with two others in a secluded part of the city, and under cover of a dark night made my escape through a postern gate at which no guard was kept; and, aided by my familiarity with desert places and by the speed of my companions, I at length reached the tenth milestone. 6. At the post-house there we got a little rest, and when we were making ready to go farther and I was already unequal to the excessive walking, to which as a gentleman I was unused, I met a terrible sight, which however furnished me a most timely relief, worn out as I was by extreme weariness. 7. A groom, mounted on a runaway horse without saddle or bit, in order not to fall off had tied the rein by which, in the usual manner, the horse was guided, tightly to his left hand; and afterwards, being thrown off and unable to loose the knot, he was torn limb from limb as he was dragged through desert places and woods, while the animal, exhausted by running, was held back by the weight of the dead body; so I caught it and making timely use of the service of its back, with those same companions I with difficulty reached some springs of sulphurous water, naturally hot. 8. And since the heat had caused us parching thirst, for a long time we went slowly about looking for water. And we fortunately found a deep well, but it was neither possible to go down into it because of its depth, nor were there ropes at hand; so taught by extreme need, we cut the linen garments in which we were clad into long strips and from them made a great rope. To the extreme end of this we tied the cap which one of us wore under his helmet, and when this was let down by the rope and sucked up the water after the manner of a sponge, it readily quenched the thirst by which we were tormented. 9. From there we quickly made our way to the Euphrates river . . .

### 3.3.12  Military medicine

Military medicine involved both preventive planning and battlefield activity. Here Vegetius, a military author of the late fourth century, explains how the health of the army might be taken care of. (See also Chapter 10, Medicine.)

Vegetius, *Epitome of Military Science* 3.2, "How the Army's Health is Controlled"
[*Vegetius: Epitome of Military Science*, trans. N.P. Milner (Liverpool: Liverpool University Press, 1993) pp. 64, 65]

3.2 Next I shall explain a subject to which special thought must be devoted – how the army's health is preserved – that is, by means of site, water-supply, season, medicine and exercise. By "site" I mean that soldiers should not camp in pestilential areas near unhealthy marshes, nor in arid plains and hills, lacking tree-cover, nor without tents in summer. They should not move out too late in the day and fall sick from sunstroke and marching-fatigue, but rather start a march before dawn, reaching the destination in the heat of the day. They should not in severe winter weather march by night through snow and ice, or suffer from shortage of firewood or an inadequate supply of clothes. For a soldier who is forced to be cold is not likely to be healthy or fit for an expedition. Neither should the army use bad or marsh water, for bad drinking-water, like poison, causes disease in the drinkers. To be sure, it requires constant vigilance on the part of officers and tribunes and of the Count who holds the senior command to see that ordinary soldiers who fall sick from this cause may be nursed back to health with suitable food and tended by the doctors' art. It is hard for those who are fighting both a war and disease.

But military experts considered that daily exercises in arms were more conducive to soldiers' health than doctors. So they wished that the infantry be trained without cease, under cover when rainy or snowing, in the exercise-field on the rest of the days. Similarly they gave orders that cavalry should constantly train themselves and their horses not only in the plains, but also over precipitous places and courses made very difficult with gaping ditches, so that nothing unfamiliar might meet them in the stress of battle. From this it is appreciated how zealously an army should always be trained in the art of war, since the habit of work may bring it both health in the camp, and victory in the field.

If a multitude of soldiers stays too long in autumn or summer in the same place, then drinking-water contaminated by pollution of the water supply and air tainted by the foul smell itself give rise to a most deadly disease. This can only be prevented by frequent changes of camp.

### 3.3.13  The wounded after a battle

Doctors faced grisly responsibilities among the wounded after a battle, as Ammianus describes at the siege of Amida.
Ammianus Marcellinus, *History* 19.2.15
[*Ammianus Marcellinus*, vol. I, trans. John C. Rolfe (London: Heinemann; Cambridge, MA: Harvard University Press, 1958) p. 483]

See *10.2.4*, page 300, for passage text.

### 3.3.14  Rewards after a battle

The seventh-century historian Theophylact Simocatta describes the aftermath of a victorious battle. Philippicus rewards his troops in a military parade and makes provisions for the wounded.

Theophylact Simocatta, *History* 2.6.10–12

[*The History of Theophylact Simocatta*, trans. Michael and Mary Whitby (Oxford: Clarendon Press, 1986) p. 51]

> On the next day the general held a review of the soldiery: he favoured the wounded with gifts, gold and silver decoration was a reward for courageous spirit, and he weighed out the recompense according to the extent of the perils. For some people received promotion as a prize for fortitude, another man a Persian horse, fine in appearance yet good in battle, another a silver helmet and quiver, another a shield, breastplate, and spears. The Romans inherited possessions equal to the battle's inheritance of corpses. But at midday the general dismissed the parade and dispatched the wounded to the cities and nearby forts, so as to heal and soothe the pangs of their wounds through the gentle sorcery of the works of Asclepius.

## 3.4  Soldiers within the empire

### 3.4.1  Soldiers protect civilian life

In addition to military responsibilities, soldiers could also have police responsibilities in the districts in which they were stationed. In the following petition from Egypt, written in 343, a veteran and his wife request that Abbinaeus, the local commander, take action against burglars.

Abbinaeus, *Archive* 45

[H.I. Bell *et al.*, eds., *The Abbinaeus Archive* (Oxford: Clarendon Press, 1962) p. 102]

> To Flavius Abinnaeus, commandant of the troops in the camp of Dionysias from Flavius Priscus, veteran, honourably discharged, and Alia his wife, daughter of Heron, soldier in the Imperial suite, landowners in the village of Philagris. On the twenty-fifth day of the present month of Payni, Sir, in my absence, while my wife was left alone in the house, certain evildoers in the manner of robbers attacked the house by night and making a subterranean passage carried off all that I myself and my wife possessed. Wherefore I ask and beseech your humanity to apprehend the officials of the village and compel them to present before you the persons guilty of the robbery, and then to bring our statement to the knowledge of our lord the Duke; for his function it is to take vengeance on the perpetrators of such outrages. And obtaining this we shall acknowledge our gratitude to you, Sir. Farewell.

### 3.4.2  Soldiers need discipline

Soldiers could be an extremely disruptive force in provincial life; their abuses of the unarmed population among whom they were billeted were constant and often notorious. Synesius, an influential aristocrat and scholar of the early fifth century, included a plea for control of soldiers in his treatise *On Kingship*, written in Constantinople in the late 390s.

Synesius, *On Kingship* 18

[*The Essays and Hymns of Synesius of Cyrene*, vol. 1, trans. Augustine Fitzgerald (London: Humphrey Milford/Oxford University Press, 1930) p. 141]

> First of all, let the soldiers be enjoined to show consideration to the city populations, and to the rural also, and to be as little as possible a burden to them, remembering the duties they have undertaken on their account. For the king fights in their defence, and enlists men to fight in order that the prosperity of the town and the countryside may be preserved. Whosoever, therefore, keeps the foreign enemy from me, but does not himself treat me with justice, such a man as this seems to me in no wise to differ from a dog who pursues wolves as far away as possible for no other reason than that he may himself slaughter the flock at his leisure, whereas in his fill of milk he has received the due reward of his guardianship. True peace, therefore, comes if the soldiers have been trained to treat civilians as brothers, and only to take what the regulations permit.

### 3.4.3  An extortion racket in Syria

Libanius wrote an outraged plea to the emperor (*c.*392), complaining of the brutal protection rackets established by soldiers in the vicinity of Antioch, where military landholdings may have been especially dense. As a leading citizen he could easily reach the ear of the emperor to speak on behalf of his community. He did not welcome rival patrons from the military sphere. In addition to revealing the abuse of citizens by soldiers, his *Oration* 47 reveals the importance of patronage networks, the dependence of farmers upon high-placed landlords and protectors, the plight of city councilors, and the attitudes of the very wealthy toward their dependants. Military abuses threatened the traditional civilian patronage networks of the late empire which Libanius represents. (See *1.3.10*, *1.4.14*, pages 17 and 31.)

Libanius, *Oration* 47, "On Protection Systems," 1, 3–12, 2.17, 18

[*Libanius, Selected Works*, vol. II, trans. A.F. Norman (Cambridge, MA: Harvard University Press, 1977) pp. 501, 503, 507, 509, 511, 517]

> Had I not seen in the long space of time and in countless matters, Sire, your joy in the well-being of your subjects and your desire that none should suffer wrong at the hands of anyone, I would perhaps have counseled myself to keep silence and would not seek to upset or inconvenience my reluctant hearer. However, your good nature inspires me with the confidence that, by the remarks I am about to make, I will please you, carry conviction with you, and

win for myself a name for loyalty, and so it is with pleasure and eagerness that I have come to outline a policy which will be regarded as yours rather than mine, since you give force to any words uttered by translating them into action, and without that argument would be in vain. . . . 3. For your commanders in chief and for the officers of the regiments they command, both one and all, my wish is for them success and a happy life, but without making any illicit gain or causing others to behave with complete lack of scruple – misconduct such as is rife at present. Listen, Sire, and learn. 4. There exist large villages, belonging to many owners. These have recourse to the soldiery stationed in them, not so as to avoid trouble but so as to be able to cause it. And the payment comes from the produce of the land – wheat, barley, the fruit of the trees, or else bullion or gold coin. So, protected by their arms, the donors have purchased for themselves complete license. And now they inflict toil and trouble upon their neighbours by encroaching on their lands, cutting down the trees, looting, slaughtering and butchering the cattle, and feasting themselves on it. When the one-time owners bewail the sight, they make merry and laugh at them, and so far from showing fear that anybody should get to know of it, they cap their misdeeds with threats and the promise not to refrain from anything else at all. 5. A sorry tale this, Sire, you think: but you have not heard the worst of it yet, at least if their daughters are more important than goats or sheep – for they don't keep their hands off them either. So what need, then, to mention the beatings and the insults, how the women grab women by the hair and ill-treat them, how they make wells useless for their owners with the stuff they throw into them, or how they rob them of their flow of river water, and by this means of their gardens too, while they maintain soldiers, some more, some less, in the midst of their villages, and these for the most part loll about or doze after their fill of wine and meat, with the result that if any of the victims loses his temper or defends himself, and one of soldiers happens to be hit too, then it is death for the one who struck him, and not the slightest chance of an excuse for him. He must knuckle under to a soldier, however drunk, and put up with anything; and the laws in this instance are a dead letter. 6. This is what has turned peasants into brigands; this is what has put into their hands the steel – not the steel beloved of the land but that which kills. For, as their power grows by means of the military billeted among them, their recklessness also increases, and the local police turn on such as these the proverbial blind eye, since they know that if they help the down-trodden victims it will cost them dear because of their protector. This in fact is the term they apply to those many rascals, though it is properly applicable, I feel, to those who, in the provision of legitimate assistance, succour the wronged and helpless, and make them secure.

7. This kind of protection, however, produces results exactly the reverse. It provides the motive force for injuring others – among them the collectors of taxes, too. I wanted them here to support me and to complain of their sufferings. It would certainly be to the accompaniment of the tears of men who have been reduced from wealth to poverty. Do you want to know, Sire, how

this comes about? Well, those whose task and duty it is, go to collect the tribute to these villages which are fenced and defended around by generals. Then they present their demands, nicely at first and in a tone of restraint, but, being met with contempt and ridicule, with increasing anger and raised voice, as is to be expected when people do not receive their proper due. Then they threaten the village headmen, but to no purpose since such are inferior to those who exploit the villages. Then they lay hands on them and arrest them, but the villagers reveal their armoury of stones. 8. So the gatherers collect wounds instead of tithes and make their way back to town, revealing what they have suffered by the blood on their clothes. They have none to take up the cudgels for them, for the influence of the person who has taken the protection money forbids this, and the poor devils are told that they must pay up or be flogged until they drop. Since they are forced to do so, and despair of any revenue from their estates and fear more wounds, and since they have no ready supply of gold or silver, they tearfully offer for sale their maidservants, their attendants, the sons of their foster-parents, while they grasp the knees of the seller in entreaty. 9. They go to their farms, too, not, as before, with their children in family parties, but with the prospective purchasers to sell them. A common table is set out before them, but the seller sees the price of his land turn into tax money. On leaving his father's, sometimes his grandfather's estates, he gazes back at their tombs, kisses his hand to them in a final gesture, begs their pardon, and so departs. Then his concern is for the maintenance of himself, his wife and his children, and when none is anywhere forthcoming, the need to beg ensues. 10. So a councillor is erased from the council: no sponge wipes out his name: he no longer has the property. This is what reduces the councils instead of increasing them, and makes the numbers in every one less instead of more. And this is a loss to the whole town. Indeed, if it is otherwise successful, but things go wrong in this respect, all else suffers and especially the fortune of the empire, for its well-being or its ruin depends upon its subjects. So the town councils suffer harm because of this fine protection-system and the towns suffer harm because of that done to their councils, and the fighting forces again because of that done to the towns. And the fighting forces you must not ignore, Sire, for it is through them that you can inflict and not suffer defeat, inspire and not feel fear. So suppress such a system of protection as this which our enemies would want us to have.

11. But the quest for a protector is not peculiar to those estates which belong to many landowners who each possess a small area, but also to those who have a single owner. These too have recourse to the hireling and pay the price, but at the owner's cost, and they provide their gifts from what they deprive him of. Yet these villages belong to men of standing, too, people capable of offering a protecting hand to the distressed. But, to be sure, it is in quest of committing mischief, not in avoidance of suffering it, that the villages buy the aid of certain individuals. They employ it over a long period of time, even against their landlords, though the land needs working; they look on them with wrathful eye,

as if they work as they like, are beyond compulsion, and will not put a hand to the soil, unless they persuade themselves. 12. The first to behave with such impudence soon have plenty of followers to imitate their bad example. Then, the one party begins proceedings and files charges, but the others have protectors, even in argument. And the protector is more influential than the laws, so that what is to be seen is a pitiful spectacle – protests from the peasantry, the bandying of high words, a crowd of lawyers, legal arguments, decisions, and the winning of the case . . .

2.17. Moreover, from the other estates those who do not have their way clear for such excesses, many of them deserting their wives and children, scuttle to those persons of influence, such towers of strength, to enjoy their illegal power to the full. And even if the accuser be a member of the general's train, he tells him that he will deal with the offender, and off he goes, leaving the accuser floored. 18. Whose job is it, then, to put a stop to evasions like this and whose to preserve their estates for those who inherited them? The task is yours, Sire. It is proper that this bounty should come from you. It is for you to feel some concern and to provide the cure and not to ignore the growing spread of spite. In fact, this has already been ignored for long enough already; a stop must surely be put to it.

### 3.4.4  Tax collection

Often detachments of soldiers assisted in the unpopular responsibility of tax collection for the imperial government. In the following papyrus from the Abbinaeus archive (342–351), Abinnaeus receives instructions – and a veiled threat – from the Overseer of the Imperial Domains to send troops to assist in revenue collection.

Abbinaeus, *Archive* 3

[H.I. Bell *et al.*, eds., *The Abbinaeus Archive* (Oxford: Clarendon Press, 1962) p. 40]

> Flavius Macarius the most illustrious Overseer of the Imperial Domains to Flavius Abinnaeus, prefect of the camp of Dionysias, greeting: His Excellency my lord Flavius Felicissimus the most illustrious Count and Duke, making provision for the imperial revenues, has given orders to my heedfulness that a military detachment should be furnished from the troops under your command for the collection of the Imperial taxes. See to it zealously therefore that in accordance with the instructions given to you by my said lord the most illustrious Duke and also by my lord the most illustrious Catholicus, knowing that if you should refuse to send them it will be brought to the knowledge of my said lord the Duke that you have impeded the collection of the Imperial revenues. I pray for your health, my lord and brother, for many years.

## 3.5 Manpower shortages and the problems of recruitment

### 3.5.1 Recruits

After the reforms of Diocletian and Constantine, the Roman army consisted of between 300,000 and 600,000 men. This would have required at least 15,000 new recruits per year, and perhaps twice that number. Most soldiers served for twenty years, while border troops not in legions served an additional four years. The military handbook of Vegetius discusses the sources of the best soldiers and principles of recruitment. (See also *13.2.4*, page 368.)

Vegetius, *Epitome of Military Science* 1.2–4, "From What Regions Recruits Should be Levied"

[*Vegetius: Epitome of Military Science*, trans. N.P. Milner (Liverpool: Liverpool University Press, 1993) pp. 3, 4, 5]

1.2 The order of our subject demands that the first part should treat of the provinces and peoples from which recruits should be levied. Now it is common knowledge that cowards and brave men are born in all places. However, nation surpasses nation in warfare, and climate exerts an enormous influence on the strength of minds and bodies. In this connection let us not omit what has won the approval of the most learned men. They tell us that all peoples that are near the sun, being parched by great heat, are more intelligent but have less blood, and therefore lack steadiness and confidence to fight at close quarters, because those who are conscious of having less blood are afraid of wounds. On the other hand, the peoples of the north, remote from the sun's heat, are less intelligent, but having a superabundance of blood are readiest for wars. Recruits should therefore be raised from the more temperate climes. The plenteousness of their blood supplies a contempt for wounds and death, and intelligence cannot be lacking either which preserves discipline in camp and is of no little assistance with counsel in battle.

3. The next question is to consider whether a recruit from the country or from the city is more useful. On this subject I think that it could never have been doubted that the rural populace is better suited for arms. They are nurtured under the open sky in a life of work, enduring the sun, careless of shade, unacquainted with bathhouses, ignorant of luxury, simple-souled, content with a little, with limbs toughened to endure every kind of toil, and for whom wielding iron, digging a fosse and carrying a burden is what they are used to from the country.

4. At what age recruits should be approved: next let us examine at what age it is appropriate to levy soldiers. Indeed if ancient custom is to be retained, everyone knows that those entering puberty should be brought to the levy. For those things are taught not only more quickly but even more completely which are learned from boyhood. Secondly military alacrity, jumping and running should be attempted before the body stiffens with age. For it is speed which, with training, makes a brave warrior. Adolescents are the ones to recruit . . .

### 3.5.2  Sons of soldiers must enlist

The sons of soldiers were required by law to enlist.
*Theodosian Code* 7.1.5

> We again call to the practice of war and to the camp the sons of those men
> who have continued steadfast in military service. We shall confer on these
> sons also the same advantages of terms of service as are enjoyed by those
> men of the second military rank who perform especially salutary service to the
> State. But if weakness of health or condition of body or smallness of stature
> should exempt some of them from the condition of armed imperial service, We
> order them to perform imperial service in other offices. [Valentinian and
> Valens, 364]

### 3.5.3  Enforced recruitment and draft evasion

Many imperial laws dealt with issues of recruitment. Chief concerns were that the
social hierarchy be preserved so that the tax system would be maintained and that
deserters be fiercely punished. The following excerpts from the *Theodosian Code*
illustrate these points.
*Theodosian Code* 7.13.1

> Whenever recruits are to be presented for service, they shall not be approved
> unless their birth status is investigated in the presence of the decurions. The
> assurance, however, shall be denied to the decurions that any person who is
> avoiding imperial service may perhaps escape the service by assuming the title
> of decurion. Leaders of the auxiliary shock troops shall not be granted license
> to receive a recruit, of course, unless the judge should first be informed and
> should write a reply as to whether or not the recruit is a decurion. Recruits shall
> be chosen for imperial service from their nineteenth year. [Constantius, 353]

*Theodosian Code* 7.13.5

> If any person should be found to have caused damage to his body by cutting
> off his fingers to avoid the oaths of military service, he shall be consumed in
> avenging flames, and his master, if he should not prevent him, shall be stricken
> by a severe penalty. [Valentinian and Valens, *c.*368]

*Theodosian Code* 17.18.1

> If a deserter should be apprehended on the premises of any person whatever
> and if such person is of plebeian and lowly status, he shall know that he will be
> punished by the penalty of labor in the mines. If, however, he should be a
> person of some higher status or rank, he shall be informed that he will be fined
> half of his property . . . [Valentinian and Valens, 365]

### 3.5.4 Slaves are permitted to enlist

*Theodosian Code* 7.13.16

> In the matter of defense against hostile attacks, We order that consideration be given not only to the legal status of soldiers, but also to their physical strength. Although We believe that freeborn persons are aroused by love of country, We exhort slaves also, by the authority of this edict, that as soon as possible they shall offer themselves for the labors of war, and if they receive their arms as men fit for military service, they shall obtain the reward of freedom, and they shall also receive two gold pieces each for travel money. Especially, of course, do We urge this service upon the slaves of those persons who are retained in the armed imperial service, and likewise upon the slaves of federated allies and of conquered peoples, since it is evident that they are making war also along with their masters. [Arcadius, Honorius, Theodosius II, 406]

### 3.5.5 Exemptions from military service

Certain professions were free from military responsibilities altogether.

*Theodosian Code* 13.3.3

> In confirmation of the special grants of imperial favor by previous sainted Emperors, We command that physicians and professors of literature and also their wives and their children shall be free from the performance of every obligatory and compulsory public service. They shall not be held subject to the duties of military service nor receive quartered persons nor perform any compulsory public service, so that they may more easily train many persons in the liberal studies and the aforesaid arts. [Constantine, 333]

## 3.6 Non-Roman recruits

Foreigners were a significant source of Roman military manpower. They might volunteer as individuals or groups, or as prisoners of war be forced into the army. Many were settled by treaty (precise terms varied considerably) within imperial borders. In the fourth and fifth centuries about 25 percent of the ranks were of non-Roman origin. Archaeologists debate how quickly these groups assimilated into the larger Roman population. The regions north of the Rhine and Danube provided most foreign recruits. In the eastern empire Armenians and other groups from the Caucasus region became important sources of manpower. Arabs, Persians, and various "barbarian" groups enlisted in the army as well. There was no significant manpower shortage at the time of the fall of the western half of the empire. (See also Chapter 13.)

### 3.6.1 Barbarian federates

Foreign tribes often made treaties (*foedera*) with the imperial government and in return for providing military service were given land within the empire. The term "federate" came to refer to elite non-Roman troops recruited for service to the empire by about the early fifth century. By the sixth century, the ranks of the "federates" were open to men from within the empire as well as foreigners. Ammianus describes typical circumstances that produced federate allies; in this case the Limigantes, a Sarmatian people, submit to Constantius II in 358.

Ammianus Marcellinus, *History* 17.13.3

[*Ammianus Marcellinus*, vol. I, trans. John C. Rolfe (Cambridge, MA: Harvard University Press, 1956) p. 383]

> Accordingly, suspecting that the weight of war would be directed against them, the Limigantes got ready wiles and arms and entreaties. But at the first sight of our army, as if smitten by a stroke of lightning and anticipating the utmost, after having pleaded for life they promised a yearly tribute, a levy of their able youth, and slavery; but they were ready, as they showed by gestures and expression, to refuse if they should be ordered to move elsewhere, trusting to the protection of the situation in which they had established themselves in security, after driving out their masters.

### 3.6.2 The history of federates

Procopius gives a sketch of the history of federate soldiers as he understands it from the point of view of Constantinople in the sixth century.

Procopius, *History of the Wars* 3.11.1–5

[*Procopius*, vol. II, trans. H.B. Dewing (Cambridge, MA: Harvard University Press, 1916) pp. 101, 103]

> The emperor, meanwhile . . . was preparing four hundred soldiers with Cyril as commander, who were to assist Godas in guarding the island. And with them he also had in readiness for the expedition against Carthage, ten thousand foot-soldiers, and five thousand horsemen, gathered from the regular troops and from the "foederati" [federates]. Now at an earlier time only barbarians were enlisted among the federates, those, namely, who had come into the Roman political system, not in the condition of slaves, since they had not been conquered by the Romans, but on the basis of complete equality. For the Romans call treaties with their enemies "foedera." But at the present time there is nothing to prevent anyone from assuming this name, since time will by no means consent to keep names attached to the things to which they were formerly applied, but conditions are ever changing about according to the desire of the men who control them, and men pay little heed to the meaning which they originally attached to a name.

### 3.6.3 Recruiting grounds and imperial borders

Archaeologists find it difficult to distinguish among the populations on either side of the northern Roman border in Late Antiquity. Here Zosimus reveals that the fighting men from either side easily found a place together in the Roman army in 367–369.

Zosimus, *New History* 4.12

[*Zosimus: New History*, trans. Ronald Ridley (Canberra: Australian Association for Byzantine Studies, 1982) p. 75]

> While Valens was engaged in preparations, the emperor Valentinian, after successfully handling the German situation, thought he ought to ensure the future security of the Gallic provinces. So levying a vast army of young men, both barbarians living near the Rhine and farmers from the Roman provinces, he enrolled them in the legions and trained them so thoroughly for war that, through fear of their drill and experience, none of the people beyond the Rhine disturbed the Roman cities for nine whole years.

## 3.7 Payment and billeting

### 3.7.1 How were soldiers paid?

Until the fifth century rations were paid in kind, and after that paid for by a cash equivalent. Soldiers received a small annual stipend, often in arrears, and also donatives, which were cash gifts presented whenever a new emperor reached the throne and at five-year intervals thereafter. On retirement, soldiers received land or cash. When Julian was chosen by his soldiers to be emperor he was forced to grant them a stipend, as Ammianus Marcellinus describes.

Ammianus Marcellinus, *History* 20.4.17–18

[*Ammianus Marcellinus*, vol. II, trans. John C. Rolfe (Cambridge, MA: Harvard University Press, 1956) p. 27]

> After this the shouts of his soldiers continued nonetheless on every side, and since all insisted with one and the same ardor and with loud and urgent outcries mingled with abuse and insults, Caesar Julian was compelled to consent. Then, placed upon an infantryman's shield and raised on high, he was hailed by all as Augustus and bidden to bring out a diadem . . . a man called Maurus . . . took off the neck chain which he wore as carrier of the dragon [standard] and boldly placed it on Julian's head. Julian, driven to the extremity of compulsion, and perceiving that he could not avoid imminent danger if he persisted in his resistance, promised each man five gold pieces and a pound of silver.

### 3.7.2 Billeting

Particularly in the cities of the eastern empire, soldiers were routinely billeted in the houses of private citizens, although retired high officials had some exceptions. Government regulations attempted to prevent abuses by the soldiers and by the landlords with uneven success as the following law demonstrates.

*Theodosian Code 7.8.5*

In any city in which We Ourselves may be or in which those persons who perform imperial service for Us may sojourn, We remove all injustice both on the part of Our quartering officers and of the persons quartered. One third of a house shall be assigned to a quartered person, and the owner shall possess two thirds of his house and his own in full confidence and security, to the extent that when the house has been thus divided into three parts, the owner shall have the first opportunity to choose his portion, and the person quartered shall obtain whichever part he wishes second, while the third part shall be left for the owner. For it is the full measure of equity and justice that the person who enjoys possession by the right of succession or who had the good fortune to have purchased or built his home should have the portion of his own particular choice and also the remaining third portion.

1. Workshops that are assigned to trade shall not be subjected to the annoyance of the aforesaid division but shall be undisturbed, free, and protected from every annoyance of compulsory quartering . . . [Arcadius and Honorius, 398]

### 3.7.3 Billeting Goths in Edessa

When in the early sixth century the imperial prefect Romanus decided that it was unfair that the common citizens of Edessa bear the full brunt of billeting Goth soldiers, the Goths grew angry at the amount of supplies he allotted them and attempted to kill him. As a result he backed down and the Goths continued their abusive behavior among the townspeople.

Pseudo-Joshua the Stylite, *Chronicle* 93–4

[W. Wright, trans., *The Chronicle of Joshua the Stylite* (Cambridge: Cambridge University Press, 1882) pp. 71–2]

93. But the common people were murmuring, and crying out and saying, "The Goths ought not to be billeted upon us, but upon the landed proprietors, because they have been benefited by this remission." The prefect gave orders that their request should be granted. When this began to be done, all the grandees of the city assembled unto the Duke Romanus and asked of him, saying, "Let your highness give orders what each of these Goths should receive by the month, lest, when they enter the houses of wealthy people, they plunder them as they have plundered the common people." He granted their request, and ordered that they should receive a measure of oil per month, and two hundred pounds of wood, and a bed and bedding between each two of them.

94. When the Goths heard this order, they ran to attack the Duke in the house of the family of Barsa and to kill him. As they were ascending the stairs of his lodging, he heard the sound of their tumult and uproar, and perceived what they wanted to do. He quickly put on his armour, and took up his weapons, and drew his sword, and stood at the upper door of the house in which he lodged. He did not however kill any one of the Goths, but (merely)

kept brandishing his sword and hindering the first that came up from forcing their way in upon him. Thus a great many people occupied the stairs of the house, as thy holiness well knoweth. When therefore the first who had gone up were unable to get in, because of their fear of the sword, and those behind were pressing upon them, many men occupied the stairs; and because of the weight they broke and fell upon them. A few of them were killed, but many had their limbs broken and were maimed, so that they could not be cured again. When Romanus had found an opportunity because of this accident, he fled upon the roof from one house to another and made his escape; but he said nothing more to them, and for this reason they remained where they were billeted, behaving exactly as they pleased for there was nothing to check them or restrain or admonish them.

## 3.8 The practice of war

### 3.8.1 Strategy, tactics and training

In the four centuries between Diocletian and Heraclius, Roman strategy and tactics adapted to new enemies, new military technologies, and changed resources of manpower. Tactical handbooks continued to be produced which gave advice on all aspects of military activity. Careful training and logistical expertise lost few battles and won many wars. By 700 avoiding pitched battles where the outcome was not certain had become the order of the day. Vegetius, who wrote a handbook of military science c.384–389, understood Roman military success in terms of good training.

Vegetius, *Epitome of Military Science* 1.1, "That the Romans Conquered all Peoples Solely Because of their Military Training"

[*Vegetius: Epitome of Military Science*, trans. N.P. Milner (Liverpool: Liverpool University Press, 1993) pp. 2–3]

> In every battle it is not numbers and untaught bravery so much as skill and training that generally produce the victory. For we see no other explanation of the conquest of the world by the Roman People than their drill-at-arms, camp-discipline and military expertise. How else could small Roman forces have availed against hordes of Gauls? How could small stature have ventured to confront Germanic tallness? That the Spaniards surpassed our men not only in numbers but in physical strength is obvious. To Africans' treachery and money we have always been unequal. No one has doubted that we are defeated by the arts and intelligence of the Greeks. But what succeeded against all of them was careful selection of recruits, instruction in the roles, so to speak, of war, toughening in daily exercises, prior acquaintance in field practice with all possible eventualities in war and battle, and strict punishment of cowardice. Scientific knowledge of warfare nurtures courage in battle. No one is afraid to do what he is confident of having learned well. A small force which is highly trained in the conflicts of war is more apt to victory: a raw and untrained horde is always exposed to slaughter.

### 3.8.2 Discipline and punishment

With discipline at a premium, punishment was harsh. Zosimus describes an unusual response taken by Julian when discipline broke down among some of his troops during a battle in 357.

Zosimus, *New History* 3.3.4–5

[*Zosimus: New History*, trans. Ronald Ridley (Canberra: Australian Association for Byzantine Studies, 1952) p. 50]

> And I ought not to omit what Caesar (Julian) did after this victory. He had a troop of six hundred horses, well trained in war, on whose strength and experience he so relied that he hazarded many of his hopes with them. When the battle began, the whole army fell upon the enemy with maximum enthusiasm so that the Roman army was gaining considerable advantage, but these alone broke ranks and fled, and even though Caesar himself and a few others rode after them and called them back to share in the victory, they would not have any part in the battle. (5) Caesar was therefore very properly angry with them because, as far as they were concerned, they had abandoned their countrymen to the barbarians, but he did not impose on them the penalty defined by law; rather he dressed them in women's clothing and led them through the camp to expel them, thinking this a punishment worse than death for manly soldiers. And the result was advantageous for both him and them; for in the second war against the Germans, they remembered the disgrace visited upon them and were almost the only troops who fought bravely.

### 3.8.3 The rules of war

Vegetius spells out the rules of war.

Vegetius, *Epitome of Military Science* 3.26, "General Rules of War"

[*Vegetius: Epitome of Military Science*, trans. N.P. Milner (Liverpool: Liverpool University Press, 1993) pp. 108, 109, 110, 111]

> In all battles the terms of campaign are such that what benefits you harms the enemy, and what helps him always hinders you. Therefore we ought never to do or omit to do anything at his bidding, but carry out only that which we judge useful to ourselves. For you begin to be against yourself if you copy what he has done in his own interest, and likewise whatever you attempt for your side will be against him if he choose to imitate it.
>
> In war, he who spends more time watching in outposts and puts more effort into training soldiers, will be less subject to danger.
>
> A soldier should never be led into battle unless you have made trial of him first.
>
> It is preferable to subdue an enemy by famine, raids and terror, than in battle where fortune tends to have more influence than bravery.
>
> No plans are better than those you carry out without the enemy's knowledge in advance.

Opportunity in war is usually of greater value than bravery.

Soliciting and taking in enemy soldiers, if they come in good faith, is greatly to be relied on, because desertions harm the enemy more than casualties.

It is preferable to keep additional reserves behind the line than to spread the soldiers too widely.

It is difficult to beat someone who can form a true estimate of his own and the enemy's forces.

Bravery is of more value than numbers.

Terrain is often of more value than bravery.

Few men are born naturally brave; hard work and good training makes many so.

An army is improved by work, enfeebled by inactivity . . .

Discuss with many what you should do, but what you are going to do discuss with as few and as trustworthy as possible, or rather with yourself alone.

Soldiers are corrected by fear and punishment in camp, on campaign hope and rewards make them behave better.

Good generals never engage in a general engagement except when opportunity offers, or under great necessity.

A great strategy is to press the enemy more with famine than with the sword.

The mode in which you are going to give battle should not become known to the enemy, lest they make moves to resist with any counter measures.

### 3.8.4  The danger of fighting pitched battle

A military handbook, *The Strategikon*, written in the late sixth century and usually attributed to the emperor Maurice (582–602), draws its information from battlefield experience. This passage advises generals to avoid pitched battles. It is safer to harm an enemy by tricks or other means than to risk losing a major confrontation.

Maurice, *Treatise on Strategy* 8.2.4

[*Maurice's Strategikon: Handbook of Byzantine Military Strategy*, trans. George T. Dennis (Philadelphia: University of Pennsylvania Press, 1984) p. 83]

It is well to hurt the enemy by deceit, by raids, or by hunger, and never be enticed into a pitched battle, which is a demonstration more of luck than of bravery.

### 3.8.5  Prayers and battle

Even battle cries did not escape the scrutiny of military thinkers.

Maurice, *Treatise on Strategy* 2.18, "The Battle Cry Sometimes Used"

[*Maurice's Strategikon: Handbook of Byzantine Military Strategy*, trans. George T. Dennis (Philadelphia: University of Pennsylvania Press, 1984) pp. 33–4]

The battle cry, "Nobiscum" (With us!), which it was customary to shout when beginning the charge is, in our opinion, extremely dangerous and harmful.

Shouting it at that moment may cause the ranks to break up. For because of the shout, the more timid soldiers in approaching really close combat may hesitate before the clash, while the bolder, roused to anger, may rashly push forward and break ranks.

. . . Instead of the shout, prayers should be said in camp on the actual day of battle before anyone goes out the gate. All, led by the priests, the general, and the other officers, should recite the "Kyrie eleison" (Lord have mercy) for some time in unison. Then, in hopes of success, each [contingent] should shout the "Nobiscum Deus" (God is with us) three times as it marches out of camp. As soon as the army leaves the camp to form for battle, absolute silence should prevail, and no unnecessary word should be spoken. For this keeps the army in better order, and the commands of the officers are more readily understood. The full spirit of the charge is conveyed by the very circumstances, the necessary closing of ranks, and the presence of the enemy, and no other sign is needed. But when the army closes with the enemy, it is not a bad idea for the men to shout and cheer, especially the rear ranks, to unnerve the enemy and stir up our own troops.

### 3.8.6 Military anthropology

Roman professional soldiers appreciated the differences among the fighting methods of their enemies, and there developed a sort of military ethnography. In the following passages, *The Strategikon* notes the characteristics of different sorts of enemies. (See section *13.2*, page 366.)

Maurice, *Treatise on Strategy* 11.3, "Dealing With the Light-Haired Peoples, Such as the Franks, Lombards, and Others Like Them"

(*Maurice's Strategikon: Handbook of Byzantine Military Strategy*, trans. George T. Dennis (Philadelphia: University of Pennsylvania Press, 1984) p. 119]

The light-haired races place great value on freedom. They are bold and undaunted in battle. Daring and impetuous as they are, they consider any timidity and even a short retreat as a disgrace. They calmly despise death as they fight violently in hand-to-hand combat either on horseback or on foot. If they are hard-pressed in cavalry actions, they dismount at a single prearranged sign and line up on foot. Although only a few against many horsemen, they do not shrink from the fight. They are armed with shields, lances, and short swords slung from their shoulders. They prefer fighting on foot and rapid charges.

Whether on foot or on horseback they draw up for battle, not in any fixed measure and formation, or in regiments or divisions, but according to tribes, their kinship with one another, and common interest . . .

## 3.9 Christians in the army

### 3.9.1 The passion of Saint Marcellus

Perhaps nowhere can the change in relation of Christians to the Roman state be seen more dramatically than in military affairs. Before Constantine, some men preferred martyrdom to shedding blood as a soldier. By the beginning of the fifth century, however, Augustine and other fathers of the church developed theories that justified warfare. The excerpts that follow illustrate these extreme positions. A typical military martyr was Marcellus, executed in 298 in North Africa. The author lists the emperors incorrectly.

*The Acts of Marcellus* 250–9

[John Helgeland, Robert Daly, and J. Patout Burns, eds., *Christians and the Military: The Early Experience* (Philadelphia: Fortress Press, 1985) pp. 60–1]

Just before the first day of August, in the consulship of Faustus and Gallus in the camp of the legion VII Gemina, Marcellus of the city of Hasta Regia was brought in, and Fortunatus said:

"Why did you decide to take off your belt and throw it down with your sword and your staff?"

"I have already told you," Marcellus replied. "Before the standards of this legion when you were celebrating the holiday of your empire I answered publicly and in a loud voice confessed that I was a Christian, and that I could not fight by any other oath, but solely for the Lord Christ Jesus, Son of God almighty."

"I cannot conceal your rash act," said Fortunatus, "and hence I shall report this to the sacred ears of our lords Diocletian and Maximian, the most invincible Augusti, and to the most noble Caesars, Constantine and Licinius. But you shall be handed over to the court of the praetorian prefect, the lord Aurelius Agricolanus, under the guard of the soldier Caecilius Arva."

On 30 October in the consulship of Faustus and Gallus at Tingis, when Marcellus of the city of Hasta Regia was brought in, one of the court secretaries announced: "Here before the court is Marcellus, whom the governor Fortunatus has handed over to your jurisdiction. He is submitted to your Excellency. There is also a letter here from Fortunatus, which I shall read with your permission."

Agricolanus said: "Read it."

The court clerk said: "It has already been read."

Agricolanus said: "Did you say the things reported in the governor's official proceedings?"

"I did," replied Marcellus.

Agricolanus said: "Did you serve as a centurion of the first cohort?"

"I did," replied Saint Marcellus.

"What madness came over you," said Agricolanus, "that you should renounce your military oath and say such things?"

Saint Marcellus replied: "There is no madness in him who fears God."

Agricolanus said: "You did say all that is contained in the governor's proceedings?"

"I did," replied Saint Marcellus.

Agricolanus said: "You did throw down your weapons?"

"I did," replied Saint Marcellus, "for it is not proper for a Christian, who fears Christ the Lord, to fight for the troubles of this world."

"Since this is the case," said Agricolanus, "Marcellus' deeds must be punished in accordance with military procedure." Then he spoke as follows:

"Whereas Marcellus has publicly rejected and defiled the oath of the centurion's rank in which he served, and has, according to the governor's court records, uttered certain words full of madness, we hereby decree that he be executed by the sword."

After these words were spoken, Marcellus was beheaded and thus won the martyr's palm that he desired, in the reign of our Lord Jesus Christ, who has received his martyr in peace: to him is honour, glory, valour, and power for ever. Amen.

### 3.9.2 Saint Martin refuses to fight

The most famous late Roman evader of military service became a saint. *The Life of Saint Martin of Tours* describes how this son of a pagan veteran resisted the call to arms.

Sulpicius Severus, *The Life of Saint Martin of Tours* 2

[*Sulpicius Severus*, trans. Bernard M. Peebles, *The Fathers of the Church*, vol. 7 (New York: Fathers of the Church, 1949) pp. 105–6]

Martin himself, entering the military service in his youth, served in the cavalry of the imperial guard under Emperor Constantius, and subsequently under Emperor Julian. Yet, this was not of his own accord, for, from almost his first years, he aspired rather to the service of God, his saintly childhood foreshadowing the nobility of his youth. When he was ten years old, against the wish of his parents, he took refuge in a church and demanded to be made a catechumen. With a complete and remarkable dedication to the work of God, he longed, at the age of twelve, for the desert, and would indeed have satisfied his wish if the weakness of his years had not stood in the way. With his spirit, none the less, ever drawn toward monasteries or the church, he even then in boyhood was reflecting upon what later his devotion was to fulfill. But when an imperial edict was issued, requiring sons of veterans to be enrolled for military service, he was handed over by his father, who was hostile toward his spiritual actions. Martin was fifteen years old when, arrested and in chains, he was subjected to the military oath. He satisfied himself with the service of a single slave. Yet, by a reversal of roles, it was the master who was the servant. This went so far that Martin generally took off the other's boots, and cleaned them himself. They would take their meals together, Martin, however, usually doing the serving.

He was three years under arms before his baptism, yet free from those vices in which such men are commonly involved.

### 3.9.3 Just war

Augustine, writing when the church had become closely associated with the state, interpreted a soldier's responsibility very differently. In 397, responding to Faustus, a Manichaean, Augustine argued that a soldier who fights out of loyalty to a ruler and is not influenced by evil passions is fighting justly – even if his ruler is not.

Augustine, *Against Faustus* 22.74–5

[John Helgeland, Robert Daly, and J. Patout Burns, eds., *Christians and the Military: The Early Experience* (Philadelphia: Fortress Press, 1985) pp. 81–2]

22.74. What, indeed is wrong with war? That people die who will eventually die anyway so that those who survive may be subdued in peace? A coward complains of this but it does not bother religious people. No, the true evils in warfare are the desire to inflict damage, the cruelty of revenge, disquiet and implacability of spirit, the savagery of rebellion, the lust for domination, and other such things. Indeed, often enough good men are commanded by God or a lawful ruler to wage war precisely in order to punish these things in the face of violent resistance . . .

75. When humans undertake war, the person responsible and the reasons for acting are quite important. The natural order which is directed to peace among mortals requires that the ruler take counsel and initiate war; once war has been commanded, the soldiers should serve in it to promote the general peace and safety. No one must ever question the rightness of a war which is waged on God's command, since not even that which is undertaken from human greed can cause any real harm either to the incorruptible God or to any of his holy ones. God commands war to drive out, to crush or to subjugate the pride of mortals. Suffering war exercises the patience of his saints, humbles them and helps them to accept his fatherly correction. No one has any power over them unless it is given from above. All power comes from God's command or permission. Thus a just man may rightly fight for the order of civil peace even if he serves under the command of a ruler who is himself irreligious. What he is commanded to do is either clearly not contrary or not clearly contrary to God's precept. The evil of giving the command might make the king guilty but the order of obedience would keep the soldier innocent. How much more innocently, therefore, might a person engage in war when he is commanded to fight by God, who can never command anything improperly, as anyone who serves him cannot fail to realize.

### 3.9.4 The Christian military vocation

Replying to a letter from Boniface, the military governor of Numidia in 421, Augustine describes the Christian military vocation.

Augustine, *Letter* 189.2.4, 6

[John Helgeland, Robert Daly, and J. Patout Burns, eds., *Christians and the Military: The Early Experience* (Philadelphia: Fortress Press, 1985) pp. 76–7]

> 4. Do not suppose that a person who serves in the army cannot be pleasing to God. The holy David, a soldier, was given high praise by our Lord. Many of the just men of his time were also soldiers. Another soldier, the centurion, said to the Lord, "I am not worthy to have you enter under my roof but only speak a word and my servant will be healed. I, indeed, am a man subject to authority and have soldiers under me. I say to one, 'Go' and he goes; to another, 'Come' and he comes; to my servant 'Do this' and he does it." The Lord said to him, "Amen, I say to you, I have not found such faith in Israel" [Matt. 8: 8–10] . . .
> 6. When you are arming yourself for battle, therefore, let this thought be foremost in your mind: even your bodily strength is God's gift. Think about God's gift in this way and do not use it against God. Once you have given your word, you must keep it to the opponent against whom you wage war and all the more to your friend for whom you fight. You must always have peace as your objective and regard war as forced upon you, so that God may free you from this necessity and preserve you in peace. Peace is not sought in order to stir up war; war is waged to secure the peace. You must, therefore, be a peacemaker even in waging war so that by your conquest you may lead those you subdue to the enjoyment of peace. "Blessed are the peacemakers," says the Lord, "for they shall be called children of God" [Matt. 5: 9]. How sweet is human peace for the temporal prosperity of mortals; yet how much the sweeter is that eternal peace for the eternal salvation of the angels. May it be necessity, therefore, not your own desire, which destroys your attacking enemy. As you respond with ferocity to the rebelling and resisting, so do you owe compassion to the defeated and captured, especially when you no longer fear a disturbance of the peace.

### 3.9.5 Regimental priests

By the fifth century, priests regularly accompanied armies.

Theodoret, *Letter* 2

[A.H.M. Jones, "Military Chaplains in the Roman Army," *Harvard Theological Review* 46 (1953) pp. 239–40]

> To Eusebius, Bishop of Ancyra:
> . . . The priesthood direct not only provinces, cities, villages, estates, and farms; but the regiments of soldiers stationed in cities and villages too have consecrated shepherds. Among these is the discreet deacon Agapetus, who

claims as his city the metropolis of our province, and has been appointed to guide a military regiment in things divine. That is why he has started for Thrace, for his unit happens to be stationed there.

## Further reading

Cameron, Averil, ed., *The Byzantine and Early Islamic Near East*, III: *States, Resources and Armies* (Princeton, NJ: Darwin Press, 1995)

de Blois, Lukas and Elio Lo Cascio, eds., with the aid of Olivia Hekster and Gerda de Kleijn, *Impact of the Roman Army (200 BC–AD 476: Economic, Social, Political, Religious, and Cultural Aspects. Proceedings of the Sixth Workshop of the International Network Impact of Empire (Roman Empire, 200 BC–AD 476)*, Capri, March 29–April 2, 2005 (Leiden, Boston: Brill, 2007)

Elton, Hugh, *Frontiers of the Roman Empire* (London: Batsford, 1996)

Elton, Hugh, *Warfare in Roman Europe, AD 350–425* (Oxford: Oxford University Press, 1996)

Erdkamp, Paul, *A Companion to the Roman Army* (Malden, MA: Blackwell, 2007)

French, D.H. and C.S. Lightfoot, eds., *The Eastern Frontier of the Roman Empire* (Oxford: Oxford University Press, 1989)

Halsall, Guy, *Warfare and Society in the Barbarian West, 450–900* (London: Routledge, 2003)

Kaegi, Walter E., *Byzantine Military Unrest, 471–843: An Interpretation* (Amsterdam, 1981)

Lee, A.D., *War in Late Antiquity. A Social History.* (Malden, MA: Blackwell Publishing, 2007)

MacMullen, Ramsay, *Soldier and Civilian in the Late Roman Empire* (Cambridge, MA, 1963)

Sabin, Philip, Hans Van Wees, and Michael Whitby, *The Cambridge History of Greek and Roman Warfare*, vol. II: *Rome from the Late Republic to the Late Empire* (Cambridge: Cambridge University Press, 2007)

Southern, Pat, and Karen Ramsey Dixon, *The Late Roman Army* (London: Batsford, 1996)

Treadgold, Warren, *Byzantium and Its Army, 284–1081* (Stanford, CA: Stanford University Press, 1995)

# 4

# CHRISTIANITY

## 4.1 Introduction

When Constantine converted to Christianity in 312, he could not have foreseen that the population of the lands that he ruled from Britain to Syria would be predominantly Christian by the mid-seventh century. Charting the rapid spread of the religion and the societal realignments that accompanied it requires a look at a variety of subjects illustrated by the documents below. There is no single explanation for the spread of Christianity.

First of all, the phenomenon of conversion to Christianity deserves attention, for not everyone accepted the faith for the same reasons or with the same understanding of what becoming Christian meant. In theory, at least, conversion involved making a change in what an individual "was," and that did not mean the same thing for warlords like Constantine and Clovis the Frank as it did for an intellectual like Augustine or the millions of ordinary women and men who decided – or were forced – to become Christian. Every day in Late Antiquity a host of people became Christian, and for a host of reasons. Some people who were already Christian chose to follow their faith more seriously.

Since the religion included a moral vision and expected changes in behavior among its adherents, definitions of acceptable practice were contested. Sacrificing to Zeus was an obvious taboo, but the status of the intellectual legacy of Mediterranean antiquity remained in question.

It is misleading to think of Christianity as a monolithic entity in antiquity. Divisions among its adherents were as many and as contentious as today. Fierce debates raged about the nature of Christ and the relationship of the elements of the Trinity, with different groups identifying themselves in terms of these arguments. Consequently, "proper" interpretation of Scripture reached new heights of sophistication. With imperial ideology wedded to Christianity, issues of orthodoxy and heterodoxy became matters of state. Relations between emperors and the bishops of Rome, Constantinople, Alexandria, and the other great episcopal sees often flared up as state power and church authority reached accommodations of different sorts. The idea that the state should sponsor missionary activity grew slowly. By the mid-sixth century forced conversion at home and diplomatic efforts aimed at conversion abroad had become matters of policy.

Ascetic forms of Christianity, which entailed the radical devaluation of the body in pursuit of access to God, came to the fore in Late Antiquity. Organized monastic centers suddenly dotted the landscape where men and women might "leave" the world and pursue lives of humility and devotion to God – under the close supervision of abbots and abbesses. Often endowed by wealthy individuals, monasteries and convents were a genuinely new phenomenon. Ascetic values also deeply affected many people who remained "in the world" of everyday life.

Another sudden development after Constantine was the spread of pilgrimage to religious sites, especially in Palestine, where the events of Jesus' life had transpired, and where relics might be venerated. A new "sacred landscape" developed as well throughout the Roman Empire and beyond to mark the places where holy individuals lived and miraculous events occurred. Churches and associated religious processions cut across urban space in new ways, changing the rhythms of daily life. Christianity contributed new ways of organizing the passage of time: Sundays, new festivals to mark the passage of the year, and even the "AD" system of dating years started in Late Antiquity.

Christianity began in the Roman Empire, but one did not have to be Roman to be Christian. Different sorts of Christianity spilled over the imperial borders and offered models of community that long outlasted Rome.

## 4.2 Conversions

People of many backgrounds became Christians for many reasons ranging from the self-serving to the deeply spiritual. The different circumstances of conversion illustrate how Christianity encountered every sort of person, and how the religion itself gained social definition in return.

### 4.2.1 God helps Constantine: "In this sign you will conquer"

Having previous experience of revelation from Apollo, Constantine appreciated the significance of an injunction from Christ, "In this sign you will conquer," on the eve of the battle for Rome against Maxentius in 312. When Constantine won, Christianity took a giant step forward to becoming the sole licit religion of the state. Eusebius of Caesarea describes Constantine's experience some years later. His account of Constantine's miraculous vision became the standard account.

Eusebius, *Life of Constantine* 1.29

[Philip Schaff and Henry Wace, eds., *Nicene and Post-Nicene Fathers*, vol. I: *Life of Constantine the Great*, second series (Peabody, MA: Hendrickson Publishers, 1995) p. 490]

> *How the Christ of God appeared to him in his Sleep, and commanded him to use in his Wars a Standard made in the Form of the Cross.*
>
> Constantine said, moreover, that he doubted within himself what the import of this apparition could be. And while he continued to ponder and reason on its meaning, night suddenly came on; then in his sleep the Christ of God appeared

to him with the same sign which he had seen in the heavens, and commanded him to make a likeness of that sign which he had seen in the heavens, and to use it as a safeguard in all engagements with his enemies.

### 4.2.2 *"Through divine inspiration"*

In 315 the Arch of Constantine was dedicated in Rome, just three years after his victory over Maxentius. The Roman Senate, which commissioned the arch, was not Christian, and the inscription upon it treads a delicate line in attributing Constantine's victory to an unnamed god.

Arch of Constantine, Inscription
[Kurt Weitzmann, ed., *Age of Spirituality: Late Antique Early Christian Art, Third to Seventh Century* (New York: Princeton University Press, 1979) p. 67]

> To the Emperor Caesar Flavius Constantine Maximus
> Pius Felix Augustus, the Senate and the Roman People,
> Since through divine inspiration and great wisdom
> He has delivered the state from the tyrant
> And his party by his army and noble arms,
> Dedicate this arch, decorated with triumphal insignia.

### 4.2.3 *The last Vestal Virgin*

With a few words addressed to Saint Laurence, who had been martyred in Rome in the first century, Prudentius, a Christian Latin poet of the late fourth century, notes a conversion of alarming significance: Claudia, the High Priestess of the Vestal Virgins (the very ancient and only female priesthood in Rome), became a Christian in 394 when the cult was abandoned. When this daughter of Rome's lofty aristocracy adopted the new faith, her name was erased from a memorial inscription that praised her modesty and chastity in her religious role. The inscription was found on a statue base near the House of Vesta in the Roman Forum during excavations in the nineteenth century. (See also *2.5.3*, page 53.)

Prudentius, *On the Crowns of the Martyrs* 2.517–28
[*Prudentius*, vol. II, trans. H.J. Thomson (Cambridge, MA: Harvard University Press, 1953) p. 139]

> The very ornaments of the Senate, men who once served in the festival of the Lupercalia, or as priests, now eagerly kiss the thresholds of apostles and martyrs. We see distinguished families, where both sides are high born, dedicate their dear ones, their noble children. The priest who once wore the headbands is admitted to receive the sign of the cross and, Laurence, a Vestal Virgin Claudia enters your church.

### 4.2.4 Antony rejects the world

In Athanasius' *Life of Antony*, we meet the founding father of Egyptian asceticism. Although already Christian, the young Antony turned to a more rigorously ascetic religiosity when he heard the Gospel read. This was the first step in the development of Egyptian monasticism. Athanasius' account written *c.*356–361 became influential among monks everywhere. (See also *4.8.1*, page 152.)

Athanasius, *Life of Antony* 2–3

[*Athanasius: The Life of Antony and the Letter to Marcellinus*, trans. Robert C. Gregg (New York: Paulist Press, 1980) pp. 31–2]

> 2. He was left alone, after his parents' death, with one quite young sister. He was about eighteen or even twenty years old, and he was responsible both for the home and his sister. Six months had not passed since the death of his parents when, going to the Lord's house as usual and gathering his thoughts, he considered while he walked how the apostles, forsaking everything, followed the Savior, and how in Acts some sold what they possessed and took the proceeds and placed them at the feet of the apostles for distribution among those in need, and what great hope is stored up for such people in heaven. He went into the church pondering these things, and just then it happened that the Gospel was being read, and he heard the Lord saying to the rich man, *If you would be perfect, go, sell what you possess and give to the poor, and you will have treasure in heaven.* It was as if by God's design he held the saints in his recollection, and as if the passage were read on his account. Immediately Antony went out from the Lord's house and gave to the townspeople the possessions he had from his forebears (three hundred fertile and very beautiful parcels of land), so that they would not disturb him or his sister in the least. And selling all the rest that was portable, when he collected sufficient money, he donated it to the poor, keeping a few things for his sister.
>
> 3. But when, entering the Lord's house once more, he heard in the Gospel the Lord saying, *Do not be anxious about tomorrow,* he could not remain any longer, but going out he gave those remaining possessions also to the needy. Placing his sister in the charge of respected and trusted virgins, and giving her over to the convent for rearing, he devoted himself from then on to the discipline rather than the household, giving heed to himself and patiently training himself.

### 4.2.5 A voice in the garden leads Augustine to conversion

For Augustine (354–430), full acceptance of Christianity came only after the most painful searching of his own soul. He discovered that he needed the aid of God to make the leap to faith. God's grace, not intellectual reason, was the real agent of his conversion.

Augustine, *Confessions* 8.12.29

[*Saint Augustine, Confessions*, trans. Henry Chadwick (New York: Oxford University Press, 1991) pp. 152–3]

As I was saying this and weeping in the bitter agony of my heart, suddenly I heard a voice from the nearby house chanting as if it might be a boy or a girl (I do not know which), saying and repeating over and over again "Pick up and read, pick up and read." At once my countenance changed, and I began to think intently whether there might be some sort of children's game in which such a chant is used. But I could not remember having heard of one. I checked the flood of tears and stood up. I interpreted it solely as a divine command to me to open the book and read the first chapter I might find. For I had heard how Antony happened to be present at the gospel reading, and took it as an admonition addressed to himself when the words were read: "Go, sell all you have, give to the poor, and you shall have treasure in heaven; and come, follow me" (Matt. 19:21). By such an inspired utterance he was immediately "converted to you" (Ps. 50:15). So I hurried back to the place where Alypius was sitting. There I had put down the book of the apostle when I got up. I seized it, opened it and in silence read the first passage on which my eyes lit: "Not in riots and drunken parties, not in eroticism and indecencies, not in strife and rivalry, but put on the Lord Jesus Christ and make no provision for the flesh in its lusts" (Rom. 13:13–14). I neither wished nor needed to read further. At once, with the last words of this sentence, it was as if a light of relief from all anxiety flooded into my heart. All the shadows of doubt were dispelled.

## 4.2.6 Christian peace after a busy public life

After enduring many tragedies in his personal life, the Christian aristocrat Paulinus of Nola sold his gigantic estates in Gaul and Spain by 395 and accepted a more serious Christian life. He became a monk in a south Italian monastery. His turn to asceticism represents a rejection of his past life and the many tiresome burdens of secular responsibility.

Paulinus of Nola, *Letter* 5.4

[Jill Harries, "'Treasure in Heaven.' Properties and Inheritance Among Senators of Late Rome," in Elizabeth M. Craik, ed., *Marriage and Property* (Aberdeen: Aberdeen University Press, 1984) p. 63]

But advancing age and a character loaded with honours from its early years brought deeper seriousness in maturity, and besides, the weakening of my body and the drying up of my flesh wore away my eagerness for pleasures. Moreover, my mortal life itself often exercised in trials and difficulties created in me a hatred of disturbance and increased my cultivation of religion in my need for hope and fear of uncertainty. And so, undistracted by public affairs and far removed from the clatter of the forum, I celebrate rural leisure and the Church in the pleasant and peaceful seclusion of my home . . .

### 4.2.7 A Frankish king accepts Catholicism

When the Franks became Catholics, the full integration of Roman provincial populations and Germanic rulers could finally proceed in Gaul. There was no longer a
religious barrier between "Romans" and "barbarians" as was the case in Ostrogothic
Italy or the Visigothic kingdom. In 496, Clovis, the mighty king of the Franks,
followed the lead of his wife, Clotild, and accepted Christianity.

Gregory of Tours, *The History of the Franks* 2.30

[Gregory of Tours, *History of the Franks*, trans. Lewis Thorpe (New York:
Penguin, 1977) p. 143]

> (30). Queen Clotild continued to pray that her husband might recognize the
> true God and give up his idol-worship. Nothing could persuade him to accept
> Christianity. Finally war broke out against the Alamanni and in this conflict he
> was forced by necessity to accept what he had refused of his own free will. It
> so turned out that when the two armies met on the battlefield there was great
> slaughter and the troops of Clovis were rapidly being annihilated. He raised his
> eyes to heaven when he saw this, felt compunction in his heart and was moved
> to tears. "Jesus Christ," he said, "you who Clotild maintains to be the son of
> the living God, you who deign to give help to those in travail and victory to
> those who trust in you, in faith I beg the glory of your help. If you will give me
> victory over my enemies, and if I may have evidence of that miraculous power
> which the people dedicated to your name say that they have experienced, then
> I will believe in you and I will be baptized in your name. I have called upon my
> own gods, but, as I see only too clearly, they have no intention of helping me.
> I therefore cannot believe that they possess any power, for they do not come to
> the assistance of those who trust in them. I now call upon you. I want to believe
> in you, but I must first be saved from my enemies." Even as he said this the
> Alamanni turned their backs and began to run away. As soon as they saw that
> their King was killed, they submitted to Clovis. "We beg you," they said, "to
> put an end to this slaughter. We are prepared to obey you." Clovis stopped the
> war. He made a speech in which he called for peace. Then he went home. He
> told the Queen how he had won a victory by calling on the name of Christ. This
> happened in the fifteenth year of his reign.

### 4.2.8 Patrick goes to Ireland

The most famous of all Late Antique missionaries was Patrick, who brought
Christianity to Ireland in the middle of the fifth century. He narrates the adventures
of his life in a compelling narrative.

Saint Patrick, *The Confession* 1.1, 2, 17, 23, 41, 42, 50, 52

[A.B.E. Hood, ed., *St. Patrick: His Writings and Muirchu's Life* (London:
Phillimore, 1978) pp. 41, 44, 45, 50, 52]

> 1. I, Patrick the sinner, quite uncultivated and the least of all the faithful and
> utterly despicable to many, had as my father the deacon Calpornius, son of the

late Potitus, a priest, who belonged to the town of Bannavem Taberniae; he had a small estate nearby, and it was there that I was taken captive. I was then about sixteen years old. I did not know the true God and I was taken into captivity in Ireland with so many thousands; and we deserved it, because we drew away from God and did not keep His commandments and did not obey our priests who kept reminding us of our salvation; and the Lord brought on us the fury of His anger and scattered us among many peoples even to the ends of the earth, where now I in my insignificance find myself among foreigners.

2. And there the Lord opened up my awareness of my unbelief, so that I might, however late, remember my faults and turn with all my heart to the Lord my God, who had regard for my lowly estate and took pity on my youth and ignorance and watched over me before I knew Him and before I learned sense or could distinguish between good and evil and who protected me and comforted me as a father might his son . . .

16. Now after I reached Ireland, well, I pastured the flocks every day and I used to pray many times a day; more and more did my love of God and my fear of Him increase, and my faith grew and my spirit was stirred, and as a result I would say up to a hundred prayers in one day, and almost as many at night; I would even stay in the forests and on the mountain and would wake to pray before dawn in all weathers, snow, frost, rain; and I felt no harm and there was no listlessness in me – as I now realize, it was because the Spirit was fervent within me.

17. And it was in fact there that one night while asleep I heard a voice saying to me: "You do well to fast, since you will soon be going to your home country;" and again, very shortly after, I heard this prophecy: "See, your ship is ready." And it was not near at hand but was perhaps two hundred miles away, and I had never been there and did not know a living soul there. And then I soon ran away and abandoned the man with whom I had been for six years, and I came in God's strength, for He granted me a successful journey and I had nothing to fear, till I reached that ship . . .

23. And again a few years later I was in Britain with my kinsfolk, and they welcomed me as a son and asked me earnestly not to go off anywhere and leave them this time, after the great tribulations which I had been through. And it was there that I saw one night in a vision a man coming as it were from Ireland (his name was Victoricus), with countless letters, and he gave me one of them, and I read the heading of the letter, "The Voice of the Irish," and as I read these opening words aloud, I imagined at that very instant that I heard the voice of those who were beside the forest of Foclut which is near the western sea; and thus they cried, as though with one voice: "We beg you, holy boy, to come and walk again among us;" and I was stung with remorse in my heart and could not read on, and so I awoke. Thanks be to God, that after so many years the Lord bestowed on them according to their cry . . .

41. And how has it lately come about in Ireland that those who never had any knowledge of God but up till now always worshipped idols and abominations

are now called the people of the Lord and the sons of God, and sons and daughters of Irish underkings are seen to be monks and virgins of Christ?

42. And there was also a blessed lady of native Irish birth and high rank, very beautiful and grown up, whom I baptised; and a few days later she found some reason to come to us and indicated that she had received a message from an angel of God, and the angel had urged her too to become a virgin of Christ and to draw near to God. Thanks be to God, six days later she most commendably and enthusiastically took up that same course that all virgins of God also do – not with their fathers' consent; no, they endure persecution and their own parents' unfair reproaches, and yet their number grows larger and larger (and we do not know the numbers of our family of faith who have been reborn there), not to mention widows and the self-denying. But it is the women kept in slavery who suffer especially; they even have to endure constant threats and terrorisation; but the Lord has given grace to many of His handmaidens, for though they are forbidden to do so, they resolutely follow His example . . .

50. But perhaps when I baptised so many thousands I hoped for even a halfpenny from any of them? Tell me, and I will give it back. Or when the Lord everywhere ordained clergy through someone as ordinary as me and I conferred on each of them his function freely, if I asked any of them for even so much as the price of my shoe, tell it against me, and I shall give it back to you . . .

52. From time to time I gave presents to the kings, quite apart from the payments I made to their sons who travel with me; however, they arrested me and my companions and that day were extremely eager to kill me, but my time had not yet come; they seized everything that they found on us and put me in irons; and fourteen days later the Lord released me from their power, and we had restored to us all our belongings for God's sake and the sake of the close friends whom we previously acquired.

53. But you know from experience how much I have paid to those who administered justice in all the districts, whom I was in the habit of visiting. I reckon that I must have dispensed to them the price of fifteen men at the least, so that you may enjoy me and I always enjoy you in God. I have no regrets; indeed I am not satisfied with that – I still spend and I will spend more. The Lord has it in His power to grant me afterwards that I may spend myself for your souls.

## 4.3 Church and state

### 4.3.1 The Edict of Milan

In 313 Constantine, who ruled the western provinces, and Licinius, who ruled in the east, met in Milan, where they issued a decree granting freedom of worship to all religions, including Christianity. Some scholars doubt the authenticity of the so-called "Edict of Milan," but Lactantius' discussion has given it wide currency.

Lactantius, *On the Death of the Persecutors* 48.1–11
[Lactantius, *On the Death of the Persecutors*, trans. J.L. Creed (New York: Oxford University Press, 1984) pp. 71, 73]

When I, Constantine Augustus, and I, Licinius Augustus, happily met at Milan and had under consideration all matters which concerned the public advantage and safety, we thought that, among all the other things that we saw would benefit the majority of men, the arrangements which above all needed to be made were those which ensured reverence for the Divinity, so that we might grant both to Christians and to all men freedom to follow whatever religion each one wished, in order that whatever divinity there is in the seat of heaven may be appeased and made propitious towards us and towards all who have been set under our power. We thought therefore that in accordance with salutary and most correct reasoning we ought to follow the policy of regarding this opportunity as one not to be denied to anyone at all, whether he wished to give his mind to the observances of the Christians or to that religion which he felt was most fitting to himself, so that the supreme Divinity, whose religion we obey with free minds, may be able to show in all matters His accustomed favour and benevolence towards us. For this reason we wish your Devotedness to know that we have resolved that, all the conditions which were contained in letters previously sent to your office about the Christian name being completely set aside, those measures should be repealed which seemed utterly inauspicious and foreign to our clemency, and that each individual one of those who share this same wish to observe the religion of the Christians should freely and straightforwardly hasten to do so without any anxiety or interference. We thought that this should be very fully communicated to your Solicitude, so that you should know that we have given a free and absolute permission to these same Christians to practice their religion. And when you perceive that this indulgence has been accorded by us to these people, your Devotedness understands that others too have been granted a similarly open and free permission to follow their own religion and worship as befits the peacefulness of our times, so that each man may have a free opportunity to engage in whatever worship he has chosen. This we have done to ensure that no cult or religion may seem to have been impaired by us.

We have also decided that we should decree as follows about the Christians as a body: if, during the period that has passed, any appear to have purchased either from our treasury or from anyone else those places in which the Christians had previously been accustomed to assemble, and about which before now a definite rule had been laid down in the letters that were sent to your office, they should now restore these same places to the Christians without receiving any money for them or making any request for payment, and without any question of obstruction or equivocation; those who received such places as a gift should return them in the same way but the more speedily to these same Christians; both those who bought them and those who received them as gifts should, if they seek something from our benevolence, make a request of the deputy for their interests to be consulted by our clemency. All these places must forthwith be handed over to the body of the Christians through your intervention and without any delay.

And since these same Christians are known to have possessed not only the places in which they had the habit of assembling but other property too which belongs by right to their body – that is, to the churches not to individuals – you will order all this property, in accordance with the law which we have explained above, to be given back without any equivocation or dispute at all to these same Christians, that is to their body and assemblies, preserving always the principle stated above, that those who restore this same property as we have enjoined without receiving a price for it may hope to secure indemnity from our benevolence. In all these matters you will be bound to offer the aforesaid body of Christians your most effective support so that our instructions can be the more rapidly carried out and the interests of public tranquility thereby served in this matter too by our clemency.

### 4.3.2 Massacre at Thessalonica

Ambrose wielded great influence while bishop of Milan (373–397). In 390 he forced the emperor to do penance for massacring thousands of civilians in Thessalonica. (See also *6.2.10*, page 205.)

Ambrose, *Letter* 51.4, 6, 11, 13

[J. Stevenson, *Creeds, Councils, and Controversies. Documents Illustrative of the History of the Church AD 337–461* (London: SPCK, 1966) pp. 140–1]

Listen, august Emperor. I cannot deny that you have a zeal for the faith; I do confess that you have the fear of God. But you have a natural vehemence, which, if soothed, you quickly turn to mercy; if anyone stirs it up, you rouse it so much more that you can scarcely restrain it. Would that if no one soothes it, at least no one may inflame it! To yourself I willingly entrust it, you restrain yourself, and overcome your natural vehemence by the love of piety . . .

A deed has been done in the city of the Thessalonians which has no parallel, and which I was not able to prevent happening; a deed which, indeed, I had before said would be most atrocious when I so often petitioned against it, and which you yourself show by revoking it too late you consider to be heinous, this I could not extenuate when done. When the news first reached me, a synod had met because of the arrival of the Gallic bishops. There was not one who did not lament it, not one who thought lightly of it; your being in fellowship with Ambrose was no excuse for your deed. Blame for what had been done would have been heaped more and more on me, had no one said that your reconciliation to our God was necessary.

I have written this, not in order to confound you, but that the examples of these kings may stir you up to put away this sin from your kingdom, for you will do it away by humbling your soul before God. You are a man, and temptation has come upon you; conquer it. Sin is not done away but by tears and penitence. Neither angel can do it, nor archangel. The Lord himself, who alone can say "I am with you" if we have sinned, does not forgive any but those who repent . . .

I, indeed, though a debtor to your kindness in all other things, for which I cannot be ungrateful, that kindness which has surpassed that of many emperors, and has been equalled by one only; I, I say, have no cause for a charge of contumacy against you, but have cause for fear; I dare not offer the sacrifice [the sacraments] if you intend to be present. Is that which is not allowed after shedding the blood of one innocent person, allowed after shedding the blood of many? I do not think so . . .

## 4.4 Bishops

### 4.4.1 Bishops as administrators

The role of bishops in Roman society expanded during Late Antiquity. As the leaders of their communities, bishops adjudicated disputes on matters of doctrine and discipline, performed many administrative functions, and managed ecclesiastical properties. When important matters required, they came together in Synods or Councils to make decisions. Constantine granted them certain judicial functions, and their role in secular affairs grew rapidly.

Council of Nicaea, *Canon* 4 (325); Synod of Antioch, *Canon* 9 (341)
[Francis Dvornik, *Byzantium and the Roman Primacy* (New York: Fordham University Press, 1966) pp. 31, 32]

#### Council of Nicaea, Canon 4

Each new bishop should be installed by the group of bishops resident in the province. If it is not possible for the bishops to come together because of pressing difficulties or because of the distances involved, then at least three bishops of the province shall come together and, after having obtained the written agreement of the other bishops, they shall proceed to the consecration. It belongs to the metropolitan of each province to confirm what has been done.

#### Synod of Antioch, Canon 9

The bishops of each province should remember that the bishop resident in the capital should occupy himself with all of the province and should exercise surveillance over the whole. Any person with matters to be taken care of, from anywhere in the province must go to the capital. For this reason, it is decreed that the bishop of the capital should have precedence over all the other bishops and they shall not undertake any serious matter without consulting him. This is in accord with the ancient canons of our Fathers.

### 4.4.2 Augustine chooses his successor

Augustine describes the highly emotional selection of Eraclius to be his successor as bishop of Hippo in September 426. He addressed a large assembly with these moving words.

Augustine, "The Election of Eraclius," *Acta Ecclesiastica, Letter* 213.1–7
[F. van der Meer, *Augustine the Bishop: The Life and Work of a Father of the Church*, trans. Brian Battershaw and G.R. Lamb (London: Sheed and Ward, 1961) pp. 270, 271]

> God willed that I should come to this town as a young man, but now my youth is past and I am an old one. I know only too well that when a bishop dies his Church is liable to be disturbed by the scheming of quarrelsome and self-seeking men, and I must have a care that things which I have to my sorrow been compelled to witness shall, in so far as I can prevent it, not become the portion of this town . . . So now, in order to forestall any possible complaint, I desire to make known my own wishes to you all, for these wishes are, as I honestly believe, in accordance with the will of God. I wish the priest Eraclius to be my successor.

[Twenty-three times the people (who had been taken completely by surprise) called out, "Thanks to God! Praised be Christ!" followed by "Christ, hear us! Long live Augustine!" sixteen times. And then eight times, "Father, bishop!" Finally Augustine concluded his remarks:]

> It is not necessary that I should say anything in praise of Eraclius. I admire his wisdom, but will spare his modesty. It is enough that you all know him, and I will only say that I know my desire is the same as your own, and that if I did not know this I could now put it to the test. However that may be, my wish is now made plain, and this is the thing that, despite my frosty old age, I ask of God with glowing prayers in which I request and direct you to join. May God melt all your minds together into the unity of the peace of Christ, and then confirm them in the conviction which he has created in our own. He has sent us this man. May he protect him and keep him without blemish or reproach, so that he who in my life has been my joy may exercise my office after my death. You see that the secretaries are taking note of all we say, and that they also note what you say yourselves, so that neither my words nor yours "fall to the ground"; and in order to make it all more plain we will immediately have this matter entered in the Church records, for I should like to see this matter settled, as far as it is possible to settle finally any human thing.

### 4.4.3 Public debate: Augustine vs. a Manichaean

Bishops led the struggle with non-believers on the local level. In August 392, Augustine engaged in a public debate with his former friend Fortunatus, a Manichaean, in the hall of a bath house. Augustine's rhetorical training and personal knowledge of Manichaeism worked to his advantage. After two days of debate he had reduced Fortunatus to silence and driven him from town for good. Such debates were a common occurrence in Late Antique cities. (See also *5.2.12*, page 185.)

Augustine, *Disputation against Fortunatus* 1, 35–7

[Augustine, *The Anti-Manichaean Writings*, trans. Albert H. Newman (*Nicene and Post-Nicene Fathers*, vol. 4, ed. Philip Schaff and Henry Wace (Grand Rapids, MI: Eerdmans, 1887/1994)) pp. 113–14, 123–47

1. Augustine said: I now regard as error what formerly I regarded as truth. I desire to hear from you who are present whether my supposition is correct. First of all I regard it as the height of error to believe that Almighty God, in whom is our one hope, is in any part either violable, or contaminable, or corruptible. This I know your heresy affirms, not indeed in the words that I now use; for when you are questioned you confess that God is incorruptible, and absolutely inviolable, and incontaminable; but when you begin to expound the rest of your system, we are compelled to declare Him corruptible, penetrable, contaminable. For you say that another race of darkness, whatever it may be, has rebelled against the kingdom of God; but that Almighty God, when He saw what ruin and desolation threatened his domains, unless he should make some opposition to the adverse race and resist it, sent this virtue, from whose commingling with evil and the race of darkness the world was framed. Hence it is that here good souls labor, serve, err, are corrupted: that they may see the need of a liberator, who should purge them from error, loose them from this commingling with evil, and liberate them from servitude. I think it impious to believe that Almighty God ever feared any adverse race, or was under necessity to precipitate us into afflictions.

Fortunatus said: Because I know that you have been in our midst, that is, have lived as an adherent among the Manichaeans, these are the principles of our faith. The matter now to be considered is our mode of living, the falsely alleged crimes for which we are maltreated. Therefore let the good men present hear from you whether these things with which we are charged and which we have thrown in our teeth are true or false. For from your instruction, and from your exposition and explanation, they will have been able to gain more correct information about our mode of life, if it shall have been set forth by you . . .

35. Augustine said: And did God omnipotent, merciful and supreme, that He might impose a restraint on contrary nature, wish it to be limited so that He might make us unrestrained?

Fortunatus said: But so He calls us back to Himself.

36. Augustine said: If he recalls to Himself from an unrestrained state, if from sin, from error, from misery, what need was there for the soul to suffer so great evils through so long a time till the world ends? Since God by whom you say it was sent could in no way suffer injury.

Fortunatus said: What then am I to say?

37. Augustine said: I know that you have nothing to say, and that I, when I was among you, never found anything to say on this question, and that I was thus admonished from on high to leave that error and to be converted to the Catholic faith or rather to recall it, by the indulgence of Him who did not permit me to inhere for ever in this fallacy. But if you confess that you have nothing to reply, I will expound the Catholic faith to all those hearing and investigating, seeing that they are believers, if they permit and wish.

Fortunatus said: Without prejudice to my profession I might say: when I shall have reconsidered with my superiors the things that have been opposed by you, if they fail to respond to this question of mine, which is now in like manner proposed to me by you, it will be in my contemplation (since I desire my soul to be liberated by an assured faith) to come to the investigation of this thing that you have proposed to me and that you promise you will show).

Augustine said: Thanks be to God.

### 4.4.4  How should a bishop behave?

The *Book of Pastoral Rule* written by Pope Gregory I (590–604) became a model for bishops of his own day and throughout the Middle Ages. He refers to bishops as "rulers" because of their position of authority over their congregations.

Pope Gregory the Great, *Book of Pastoral Rule* 2.1

[Gregory the Great, *Book of Pastoral Rule*, trans. J. Barmby, *Library of Nicene and Post-Nicene Fathers*, second series, vol. XII (Grand Rapids, MI: Eerdmans, 1895/1995) p. 9]

The conduct of a prelate ought so far to transcend the conduct of the people as the life of a shepherd is wont to exalt him above the flock. For one whose estimation is such that the people are called his flock is bound anxiously to consider what great necessity is laid upon him to maintain rectitude. It is necessary, then, that in thought he should be pure, in action chief; discreet in keeping silence, profitable in speech; a near neighbor to every one in sympathy, exalted above all in contemplation; a familiar friend of good livers through humility, unbending against the vices of evil-doers through zeal for righteousness; not relaxing in his care for what is inward from being occupied in outward things, nor neglecting to provide for outward things in his solicitude for what is inward. But the things which we have thus briefly touched on let us now unfold and discuss more at length . . .

. . . Supreme rule, then, is ordered well, when he who presides lords it over vices, rather than his brethren. But, when superiors correct their delinquent subordinates, it remains for them anxiously to take heed how far, while in right of their authority they smite faults with due discipline, they still, through custody of humility, acknowledge themselves to be on a par with the very brethren who are corrected . . .

It is to be borne in mind also, that it is right for good rulers to desire to please men; but this in order to draw their neighbors by the sweetness of their own character to affection for the truth; not that they should long to be themselves loved, but should make affection for themselves as a sort of road by which to lead the hearts of their hearers to the love of the Creator. For it is indeed difficult for a preacher who is not loved, however well he may preach, to be willingly listened to. He, then, who is over others, ought to study to be loved to the end that he may be listened to . . .

### 4.4.5  A bishop demands respect, even from an empress

Leontius of Antioch was a mid-fourth-century Arian bishop as famous as much for his outspokenness as for his attempts to steer a middle course between Arian and Orthodox sensibilities. In this passage taken from a church history he does not hesitate to chastise the empress on matters of deference.

Philostorgius, *Suda*, A 254, Leontius

[Philostorgius, *Church History*, trans. Philip R. Amidon (Leiden, Boston: Brill, 2007) pp. 96–7]

He was equally free with everyone in his attitude and quite outspoken. Once when a council was being held and Eusebia, Constantius' wife, was putting on airs and receiving the reverence of the bishops, he alone made little of her and stayed home. She was annoyed at this and felt angry, and sent a message to him to complain and to coax him with promises, saying, "I will build a great church for you and furnish it lavishly if you visit me." But he replied, "If you should decide to do something like that, your majesty, then realize that you would be benefiting your own soul no less than me. But if you wished to receive a visit in a way that would maintain the respect due to bishops, then when I entered, you would come down at once from your lofty throne, advance to meet me respectfully, bow your head to my hands, and request my blessings. Then I would be seated when I bade you by giving the signal. If you agreed to this, I would pay you a visit. Otherwise, you could not give the gifts so many or so great that we would transgress the sacred law of the priesthood by surrendering the honor due to bishops."

When Eusebia received this reply, she grew furious and considered it insufferable that she should be addressed by Leontius in this way. Quite under the sway of anger, her womanish ill-temper and impulsive spirit gave vent to a continuous stream of threats, and, relating to her husband what had happened, she urged him to exact punishment for it. But he for his part praised the freedom of attitude Leontius had shown, calmed his wife's anger, and sent her back to the women's quarters.

### 4.4.6  Constantine and the bickering bishops

Unsophisticated in the workings of ecclesiastical debate, Emperor Constantine grew frustrated at the machinations of bishops of different factions. He ordered the bishops who had convened at Tyre in 335 to gather in his presence to review the charges laid against Athanasius, a critic of the teachings of Arius.

Socrates Scholasticus, *Ecclesiastical History* 1.34

[Socrates Scholasticus, *Ecclesiastical History*, trans. A.C. Zenos (*Nicene and Post-Nicene Fathers*, second series, vol. II (Grand Rapids, MI: Eerdmans, 1979) pp. 32–3]

Victor Constantine Maximus Augustus, to the bishops convened at Tyre:

I am indeed ignorant of the decisions which have been made by your Council with so much turbulence and storm: but the truth seems to have been perverted by some tumultuous and disorderly proceedings: because, that is to say, in your mutual love of contention, which you seem desirous of perpetuating, you disregard the consideration of those things which are acceptable to God. It will, however, I trust, be the work of Divine Providence to dissipate the mischief resulting from this jealous rivalry, as soon as they shall have been detected; and to make it apparent to us, whether ye who have been convened have had regard to truth, and whether your decisions on the subjects which have been submitted to your judgment have been made apart from partiality or prejudice. Wherefore it is indispensable that you should all without delay attend upon my piety, that you may yourselves give a strict account of your transactions. For what reason I have deemed it proper to write thus, and to summon you before me, you will learn from what follows. As I was making my entry into the city which bears our name, in this our most flourishing home, Constantinople, – and it happened that I was riding on horseback at the time, – suddenly the Bishop Athanasius, with certain ecclesiastics whom he had around him, presented himself so unexpectedly in our path, as to produce an occasion of consternation. For the Omniscient God is my witness that at first sight I did not recognize him until some of my attendants, in answer to my enquiry, informed me, as was very natural, both who he was, and what injustice he had suffered. At that time indeed I neither conversed, nor held any communication with him. But as he repeatedly entreated an audience, and I had not only refused it, but almost ordered that he should be removed from my presence, he said with greater boldness, that he petitioned for nothing more than that you might be summoned hither, in order that in our presence, he, driven by necessity to such a course, might have a fair opportunity afforded him of complaining of his wrongs. Wherefore as this seems reasonable, and consistent with the equity of my government, I willingly gave instructions that these things should be written to you. My command therefore is, that all, as many as composed the Synod convened at Tyre, should forthwith hasten to the court of our clemency, in order that from the facts themselves you may make clear the purity and integrity of your decision in my presence, whom you cannot but own to be a true servant of God. It is in consequence of the acts of my religious service towards God that peace is everywhere reigning; and that the name of God is sincerely had in reverence even among the barbarians themselves, who until now were ignorant of the truth. Now it is evident that he who knows not the truth, does not have a true knowledge of God also: yet, as I before said, even the barbarians on my account, who am a genuine servant of God, have acknowledged and learned to worship him, whom they have perceived in very deed protecting and caring for me everywhere. So that from dread of us chiefly, they have been thus brought to the knowledge of the true God whom they now worship. Nevertheless we who pretend to have a religious veneration for (I will not say who guard) the holy mysteries of his church, we, I say, do nothing but what tends to discord and animosity, and to speak plainly, to the destruction of the human race. But hasten, as I have already said, all of you to us as speedily as possible: and be assured that I shall endeavor with all my power to cause that what is contained in the Divine Law may be preserved inviolate, on which neither stigma nor reproach shall be able to fasten itself; and this will come to pass when its enemies, who under cover of the sacred profession introduce numerous and diversified blasphemies, are dispersed, broken to pieces, and altogether annihilated.

### 4.4.7 Vicious debate at a church council

Gregory of Nazianzus (bishop of Constantinople 380–381) was a prolific writer and a staunch defender of Nicene orthodoxy. His bitter remarks about the reactions of fellow churchmen to one of his own orations give a vivid impression of the sometimes vicious debate at church councils.

Gregory of Nazianzus, *Concerning His Own Life* 1680–9
[Saint Gregory of Nazianzus, *Three Poems*, trans. Denis Molaise Meehan, *Fathers of the Church*, vol. 75 (Washington, DC: Catholic University of America Press, 1987) p. 123]

My speech was the signal for screams on every side from that flock of crows all massed together. The horde of young men, a new-fangled party, gave the impression of dust churned up by a whirlwind during a storm. In their confused chattering not even a ruler backed by reverential fear and authority could have managed to reason with them. They were like a swarm of wasps suddenly darting up in one's face and, far from attempting to chasten them, the august assembly of the elders actually joined the demonstration.

### 4.4.8 The consequences of losing: Nestorius describes his enemies

Because of the condemnation of his beliefs, the writings of Nestorius, bishop of Constantinople from 428 to 431, were destroyed by his doctrinal adversaries. A Syriac translation of his *Bazaar of Heracleides* survives and provides Nestorius' views of how he was treated by the other contentious bishops at the Council of Ephesus in 431 at which his writings were condemned. (See also *4.5.3*, page 132.)

Nestorius, *The Bazaar of Heracleides* 2.1
[Nestorius, *The Bazaar of Heracleides* trans. G.R. Driver and Leonard Hodgson
(Oxford: Clarendon Press, 1925) pp. 265–7, 277–8]

Yet after they have examined [my words] with all exactitude, as though Christ
were seeing [them], they have condemned me without having found difficulty
over anything or having quarrelled and without having established anything by
question or by answer; but they were hastening in order that those who were
about to come might not overtake them, that is, the Council of the East, which
was near, and those from Rome. Neither have they examined nor even have
they read; and, as I indeed suppose, even the things too which they have written
they have written afterwards; the days and the time itself sufficed not for the
writing and the signing. For it was apparent that they were signing against
me gladly and freely, even without a cause; for not one indeed of them has
written the cause on account of which they have deprived me, except only this
man [who is] wise and intelligent above all men and able to say something
intelligible, that is Acacius of Melitene: because he has not confessed that God
the Word died, he was worthy to be deprived, since he has made Divine
Scripture to lie and further because he has calumniated Cyril with having
said that God the Word died, when he had not [so] said; and he has also made
the Scripture to lie, teaching that the birth and the suffering concerned not the
divinity but the humanity, and he has calumniated also the very writings of the
holy and godly bishop, Cyril, as though they call God the Word passible
[capable of suffering], a thing which neither he nor any other of those who
think piously have dared to say . . .

Now on one of these [points] and not upon two of them it was right that I
should be accused; but they were accepting against me contrary [charges] and
in the greatness of their preoccupation they were not willing to break off that
with which they were engaged, but they were zealous to withdraw themselves
and to dissent, that they might not come under the judgment of the judges. But
they disclaimed [us] as enemies in such wise as to prove their preoccupation
and their anxiety and to be thought fearful by the bishops who were present and
who were absent; and they did all things such as take place in wars. And the
[followers] of the Egyptian and those of Memnon, by whom they were aided,
were going round the city, girded and armed with rods, stiff-necked men, who
rushed upon them with the clamour of barbarians and forcibly emitted from
their nostrils a spirit of anger with fearful cries at no great distance, breathing
[anger] without self-control, with all pride, against those whom they knew to be
not in agreement with the things which were done by them. They were taking
bells round the city and were kindling fire in many places and handing round
documents of various kinds; and all those things which were taking place were
[matters] of astonishment and of fear, so that they blocked all the ways and
made every one flee and not be seen, and were behaving arbitrarily, giving way
to drunkenness and to intoxication and to a disgraceful outcry. And there was

none hindering, nor even bringing succour, and thus [men] were amazed. But all of it was being done against us, and for this reason we made use of the succour of the Emperor and of the authority of the Strategi [Generals], who were angered at the things which were done, though they let them be.

But there came the bishop of Antioch with many other bishops, whom they were seeking to win over to agree with them in what was unjustly and boldly done; and they named themselves an Ecumenical Council. And after they knew the things which were being boldly done and their disgraceful audacity and their sudden war and the vehemence of the madness wherewith they were intentionally doing all things, they degraded from their episcopal rank the organizers of this disorder, who had raised up all this evil; yea, I mean Cyril and Memnon. But for the rest of their organizers, they laid them under anathema, because they had discharged naught of the work of the episcopate, as persons who have made use not of the object and traditions, but [only] of the authority of the episcopate. And, in order that they might not deny or dissemble what was done against them, they wrote their deprivation in all parts of the city, that there might be for all of them witnesses that they had deprived them and for what reasons they had deprived them. They made these things known unto the Emperor through the letters of the Council, and their boldness in all of them and the war which had taken place after the fashion of barbarians. And for this reason also they allowed them not to pray in the apostolic church of Saint John, but [brought it about] that persons stoned them, and they hardly escaped and were rescued, and they said also the cause wherefore they made bold to do this: that whatever had caused this disturbance and division in the churches might not be examined by the Council.

[When the emperor Theodosius deposed Nestorius in July 431, in the prelude to the Council of Ephesus, crowds of people in Constantinople who favored Nestorius' opponent, Cyril of Alexandria, chanted slogans in the street.]

But after it was known that the intention of the Emperor had been overcome by them [the supporters of Cyril] all the heretics, who had formerly been deprived by me, took part with them, and all with one mouth were alike proclaiming my anathema, taking courage from anything that had taken place, in every part of the city, but especially in the parts by the sanctuary, in such wise as to add unto themselves crowds of the people to commit iniquity without reverence; and thus they took courage, clapping the hands and saying naught else except "God the Word died".

### 4.4.9 An archbishop's schedule of bribes

Cyril, the influential patriarch of Alexandria from 412 to 444, wrote widely on biblical interpretation and was deeply involved in Christological polemic and day-to-day politics. The wealth of Alexandria provided the cash for him to play for very high stakes. This letter provides a schedule of bribes to be given to people who could further Cyril's political aims; on one diplomatic trip to Constantinople he spent about 2,500 pounds of gold in this way – enough to feed 45,000 poor people for a year. It illustrates how high-level churchmen were involved in corrupt patronage networks, the workings of the court, and doctrinal disputes.

Cyril of Alexandria, *Letter* 96

[St. Cyril of Alexandria, *Letters 51–110*, trans. John I. McEnerney *The Fathers of the Church*, vol. 77 (Washington, DC: Catholic University of America Press, 1987) pp. 151–3]

(1) To Paul the Prefect: four larger wool rugs, two moderate wool rugs, four place covers, four table cloths, six larger *bila* [rugs or curtains], six medium sized *bila*, six stool covers, twelve for doors, two larger caldrons, four ivory chairs, two ivory stools, four *persoina* [pews?], two larger tables, two ostriches [pieces of furniture?]; and in order that he would help us in the cause about those matters which were written to him: fifty pounds of gold.

(2) And to his domestic, one wool rug, two rugs, four *bila*, two stool covers, and one hundred gold coins.

(3) To Marcella, the chambermaid, the same as was dispatched to him, and that she would persuade Augusta by asking her: fifty pounds of gold . . .

(5) To the prefect Chryseros, that he would cease to oppose us, we were forced to dispatch double amounts: six larger wool rugs, four moderate rugs, four larger rugs, eight place covers, six table cloths, six large *bila* rugs, six medium sized *bila*, six stool covers, twelve for chairs, four larger caldrons, four ivory chairs, four ivory stools, six *persoina*, four larger tables, six ostriches; and if he shall have acted in accordance with what was written to him by the most magnificent Aristolaus with the lord Claudianus intervening as mediator: two hundred pounds of gold.

(6) And to Solomon, his domestic, two larger wool rugs, four place covers, four table cloths, four *bila*, four stool covers, six covers for chairs, six caldrons, two ivory chairs, two ostriches; and just as was written to lord Claudianus, so he may use persuasion to forward the proposal: fifty pounds of gold.

(7) To lady Heleniana, who is [the wife] of the prefect of the praetorian guard, the same in all things which were dispatched to Chryseros, so also to her; and in order that the prefect, persuaded by her, would help us: one hundred pounds of gold. As to her assessor, Florentinus, just as the things sent to Solomon, equally the same also to him and fifty pounds of gold.

(8) And to the other chamberlains customary suppliant gifts have been dispatched.

To Romanus the chamberlain: four larger wool rugs, four place covers, four stool covers, six covers for chairs, two caldrons, two ivory chairs; and so that he would aid in our cause: thirty pounds of gold.

### 4.4.10 Legal functions of bishops

Constantine gave bishops legal authority to judge cases if either party in the suit desired to be tried in an episcopal court. Such decisions were binding, not open to appeal, and had to be enforced by the civil authorities. The entry of bishops into the governing structure of the empire marked an important step in the creation of a Christian-Roman society.

*Theodosian Code* 1.27.1

> Pursuant to his own authority, a judge must observe that if an action should be brought before an episcopal court, he shall maintain silence, and if any person should desire him to transfer his case to the jurisdiction of the Christian law and to observe that kind of court, he shall be heard, even though the action had been instituted before the judge, and whatever may be adjudged by them shall be held as sacred; provided, however, that there shall be no such usurpation of authority in that one of the litigants should proceed to the aforementioned tribunal and should report back his own unrestricted choice of a tribunal. For the judge must have the unimpaired right of jurisdiction of the case that is pending before him, in order that he may pronounce his decision, after full credit is given to all the facts as presented. [Constantine, c.318]

### 4.4.11 Giving up a quiet life to become Pope

Gregory the Great, the vigorous bishop of Rome from 590 to 604, professed reluctance at being raised to the papal throne. Once there he did much to shape the medieval papacy.

Pope Gregory the Great, *Letter* 1.5, to Princess Theoctista
[Jeffrey Richards, *Consul of God: The Life and Times of Gregory the Great* (London/Boston, MA: Routledge and Kegan Paul, 1980) pp. 42–3]

> Under the pretense of being made a bishop, I am brought back into the world; for I am now more in bondage than ever I was as a layman. I have lost the deep joy of my quiet, and while I seem outwardly to have risen, I am inwardly falling down. Wherefore I grieve that I am driven far from the face of my maker. It used to be my daily aim to put myself beyond the world, beyond the flesh; to expel all corporeal forms from the eyes of the soul and to behold in the spirit the blessedness of heaven . . . But from this height I have been suddenly cast down by the whirlwind of this trial. I have fallen into fear and trembling, for, though I dread nothing for myself, I am greatly afraid for those who are committed to my charge. I am tossed to and fro with the waves of business, I am overwhelmed with its storms . . . When my business is done, I try to return to my inner thoughts but cannot, for I am driven away by vain tumultuous thoughts. I loved the beauty of the contemplative life . . . but by some judgment, I know not what, I have been wedded . . . to the active life. Behold my most serene lord the Emperor has ordered an ape to become a lion.

## 4.5 Theology

Disagreement about the relation of the divinity in Christ to the divinity of the Father proved exceptionally divisive in the Late Antique church. Defining the Trinity and explaining the unity as well as the distinctiveness of its elements preoccupied churchmen and provided the intellectual foundations of sectarian divisions among Christian communities. When rivalries among the great episcopal sees combined with the coercive force of the state, defining doctrine – and enforcing it – became matters of the highest significance.

### 4.5.1 Arius and the human nature of Christ

Arius (died 336), an Alexandrian deacon, taught that Christ was not coeternal with God because he was created after God and so was subordinate to and less than God. Arianism stressed the human nature of Christ and denied the incarnation of God as man. His teachings spread widely.

Arius, *Letter to Alexander of Alexandria* 2–5

[William G. Rusch, trans. and ed., *The Trinitarian Controversy* (Philadelphia: Fortress Press, 1980) pp. 31–2]

(2) Our faith, from our ancestors, which we have learned also from you, is this. We know one God – alone unbegotten, alone everlasting, alone without beginning, alone true, alone possessing immortality, alone wise, alone good, alone master, judge of all, manager, director, immutable and unchangeable, just and good, God of Law, Prophets, and New Testament – who begot an only-begotten Son before eternal times, through whom he made the ages and everything. But he begot him not in appearance but in truth, having submitted him to his own will, an immutable and unchangeable perfect creature of God, (3) but not as one of the creatures – an offspring, but not as one of those born – nor as Valentinus decreed that the offspring of the Father is an emanation, nor as Manes propounded that the offspring of the Father is part of the same substance, nor as Sabellius, who divides the monad, says "Father-and-Son," nor as Hieracas believes a light from a light as a lamp divided into two; nor is he the one who was before, later begotten or created into a Son as you yourself also, Blessed Pope, very often have forbidden throughout the midst of the church and in council those who teach these things. But, as we say, he was created by the will of God before times and ages, and he received life, being, and glories from the Father as the Father has shared them with him. (4) For the Father, having given to him the inheritance of all, did not deprive himself of those things which he has in himself without generation, for he is the source of all. Thus there are three *hypostases*. God being the cause of all is without beginning, most alone; but the Son, begotten by the Father, created and founded before the ages, was not before he was begotten. Rather, the Son begotten timelessly before everything, alone was caused to subsist by the Father. For he is not everlasting or co-everlasting or unbegotten with the

Father. Nor does he have being with the Father, as certain individuals mention things relatively and bring into the discussion two unbegotten causes. Bur God is thus before all as a monad and cause. Therefore he is also before the Son, as we have learned from you when you preached throughout the midst of the church.

(5) Therefore, insofar as he has from God being, glories, and life, and all things have been handed over to him, thus God is his cause. For he, as his God and being before him, rules him. But if "from him" [Rom. 11:36] and "from the womb" [Ps. 110:3] and "I came from the Father and I come" [John 16:28] are thought by some to signify that he is a part of him and an emanation, the Father will be according to them compounded, divided, mutable and a body, and, as far as they are concerned, the incorporeal God suffers things suitable to the body.

### 4.5.2 *The Nicene Creed*

In 325, Arius was condemned at the Council of Nicaea. The Nicene Creed states the Synod's theology.

"The Creed of Nicaea"
[William G. Rusch, trans. and ed., *The Trinitarian Controversy* (Philadelphia: Fortress Press, 1980) p. 49]

> We believe in one God, Father, all-sovereign, maker of all things seen and unseen; and in one Lord Jesus Christ, the Son of God, begotten from the Father as only-begotten, that is, from the substance of the Father, God from God, light from light, true God from true God, begotten, not made, *homoousios* with the Father, through whom all things came into existence, the things in heaven and the things on the earth, who because of us men and our salvation came down and was incarnated, made man, suffered, and arose on the third day, ascended into heaven, comes to judge the living and the dead; and in one Holy Spirit. And those who say "there was once when he was not" or "he was not before he was begotten" or "he came into existence from nothing" or who affirm that the Son of God is of another *hypostasis* or substance, or a creature, or mutable or subject to change, such ones the catholic and apostolic church pronounces accursed and separated from the church.

### 4.5.3 *Nestorius' heresy*

Nestorius, bishop of Constantinople (428–431), denied that Jesus the man was the son of God and objected to referring to Mary as *Theotokos*, or Mother of God. In his second letter to Cyril of Alexandria, Nestorius defends his ideas. (See also 4.4.8, page 126.)

Nestorius, *Second Letter to Cyril*
[Richard A. Norris, Jr., trans. and ed., *The Christological Controversy* (Philadelphia: Fortress Press, 1980) pp. 137–9]

Everywhere in Holy Scripture, whenever mention is made of the saving dispensation of the Lord, what is conveyed to us is the birth and suffering not of the deity but of the humanity of Christ, so that by a more exact manner of speech the holy Virgin is called Mother of Christ, not Mother of God. Listen to these words of the Gospels: "The book of the birth of Jesus Christ, son of David, son of Abraham" [Matt. 1:1]. It is obvious that the son of David was not the divine Logos. And hear another witness, if it seems right: "Jacob begat Joseph, the husband of Mary, of whom was born Jesus who is called Christ" [Matt. 1:16]. Consider another voice bearing witness for us: "The birth of Jesus Christ was on this wise, for when his mother Mary was betrothed to Joseph, she was discovered to have conceived in her womb by the Holy Spirit" [Matt. 1:18]. Shall I suppose that the deity of the Only Begotten is a creature of the Spirit? And what shall it mean that "the mother of Jesus was there" [John 2:1]? And again, "with Mary the mother of Jesus" [Acts 1:14]; and "that which is born in her is of the Holy Spirit" [Matt. 1:20]; and "Take the child and his mother and flee into Egypt" [Matt. 2:13]; and "concerning his Son, who was born of the seed of David according to the flesh" [Rom. 1:3]; and again this, concerning the passion: "God sent his Son in the likeness of sinful flesh, and because of sin, and condemned sin in the flesh" [Rom. 8:3]; and again, "Christ died for our sins" [1 Cor. 15:3]; and "Christ suffered in the flesh" [1 Pet. 4:1]; and "This is," not my deity, but "my body which is broken for you" [1 Cor. 11:24] – and thousands of other statements warning the human race not to think that the deity of the Son is a new thing, or susceptible to bodily passion, but rather the flesh which is united to the nature of the Godhead.

That is why Christ calls himself both Lord and son of David. He says, "'What do you think about the Christ? Whose son is he?' They say to him, 'David's.' Jesus answered and said to them, 'How then does David, speaking in the Spirit, call him Lord, saying, "The lord said to my Lord, 'Sit on my right hand'"?'" [Matt. 22:42–44], because he is entirely the son of David according to the flesh but Lord according to the deity. The body therefore is the temple of the Son's deity, and a temple united to it by a complete and divine conjunction, so that the nature of the deity associates itself with the things belonging to the body, and the body is acknowledged to be noble and worthy of the wonders related in the Gospels.

To attribute also to him, in the name of this association, the characteristics of the flesh that has been conjoined with him – I mean birth and suffering and death – is, my brother, either the work of a mind which truly errs in the fashion of the Greeks or that of a mind diseased with the insane heresy of Arius and Apollinaris and the others . . .

### 4.5.4 Christ's two natures unified

Pope Leo's Palm Sunday sermon in 442 anticipates the discussions that led to the Council of Chalcedon and the decisions made there in 451.

Pope Leo I, *Sermon* 54.2
[*Fathers of the Church: St. Leo the Great: Sermons*, trans. Jane Patricia Freeland and Agnes Josephine Conway (Washington, DC: The Catholic University of America Press, 1996) p. 233]

(2) In everything that pertains to the Passion of our Lord Jesus Christ, dearly beloved, Catholic Faith has handed this down, has demanded this. We need to know that two natures have come together in our Redeemer, and that, while its own characteristics remain, so great a unity of the two substances came about that, from the time when – as the course of human nature demanded – "the Word was made flesh" in the womb of the Blessed Virgin, we cannot think of him as God without that which is man, nor can we think of him as man without that which is God.

Each nature expresses its own truth in its own distinct actions, but neither separates itself from its connection with the other. Neither one lacks anything there, but the whole lowliness is in his majesty, while the whole majesty is in his lowliness. Unity brings no confusion, nor does the distinctiveness ruin the unity . . . One is subject to suffering, the other inviolable.

Yet reproach belongs to the very one to whom glory belongs also. It is the same Person in weakness who is also in strength; the same Person is capable of death who is also victor over death. God took on the whole man and bound himself to man and man to himself by the plan of his mercy and power, in such a way that each nature is in the other and neither crosses over into the other from its own distinctiveness.

### 4.5.5 Mary and the virgin birth

In a beautiful hymn of the mid-sixth century, Romanos the Melodist depicts Mary pondering the miracle of her virgin motherhood.
Romanos the Melodist, *On the Presentation in the Temple*, strophes 3, 4
[*Kontakia of Romanos, Byzantine Melodist*, vol. 1: *On the Person of Christ*, trans. Marjorie Carpenter (Columbia: University of Missouri Press, 1970) p. 40]

*Strophe 3:*
While the angels sang hymns to the lover of men, Mary advanced,
Holding Him in her arms;
And she pondered on how she became mother and remained a virgin,
For she realized that the birth was supernatural; she was awed and she trembled.
Meditating on these things, she said to herself:
MARY: "How shall I find a name for Thee, my son?
For if I call Thee the man I see Thou art, yet Thou art more than man.
Thou hast kept my virginity unsullied,
Thou, the only friend of man."

*Strophe 4:*
MARY: "Shall I call Thee perfect man? But I know that Thy conception was divine,
For no mortal man
Was ever conceived without intercourse and seed as Thou, O blameless One.
And if I call Thee God, I am amazed at seeing Thee in every respect like me,
For Thou hast no traits which differ from those of man,
Yet Thou wast conceived and born without sin."

### 4.5.6 The Council of Chalcedon and Nestorianism

The Council of Chalcedon (October 8–31, 451) drew together bishops mostly from the East to determine further Christological issues raised by Nestorianism. The Council defined the two natures of Christ as inviolably united in one person *(hypostasis)* without confusion, division, separation or change.

The Council of Chalcedon, *Definition of the Faith*
[Richard A. Norris, Jr., trans. and ed., *The Christological Controversy* (Philadelphia: Fortress Press, 1980) pp. 156–7]

> We believe in one God, Father, Ruler of all, the maker of heaven and earth and of all things seen and unseen.
>
> And in one Lord Jesus Christ, the only-begotten Son of God, begotten from the Father before all ages, true God from true God, begotten not made, of one essence with the Father; through whom all things were made; who for us human beings and for our salvation came down and was incarnate and became human; and suffered, and rose on the third day and went up into the heavens and is seated at the right hand of the Father, and is coming to judge the living and the dead.
>
> And in the Holy Spirit.
>
> But those who say, "There was a 'when' when he was not" and "Before he was begotten he did not exist" and "He came into existence out of nothing," or who say that the Son of God is "from another hypostasis or essence," or "mutable" or "alterable" – them the catholic and apostolic church anathematizes . . .

### 4.5.7 The government forbids heresy

Christian communities had differed in theology, custom, and ritual practice since their beginnings in the first century. They often disagreed on basic definitions of the faith, on what texts should be considered canonical, and on who had the right to interpret those texts. As various communities grew in importance, their leaders regularly made claims to possessing the truth about the religion. Individuals and communities that held opposing beliefs could dismiss and persecute one another as "heretical." When the Roman state became associated with Christianity in the course of the fourth century, the Christian community with which the emperor associated himself, generally called "orthodox" or correct, gained access to tremendous coercive power. Consequently the definition of orthodox belief and practice became a concern of the Roman government. In the following law, issued in 379, the emperors forbade all heresies, claiming divine and imperial authority. Argument about orthodoxy and heresy continues to this day.

*Theodosian Code*, 16.5.5

> All heresies are forbidden by both divine and imperial laws and shall forever cease. If any profane man by his punishable teachings should weaken the concept of God, he shall have the right to know such noxious doctrines only for himself but shall not reveal them to others to their hurt. If any person by a renewed death [i.e. the death of sin] should corrupt bodies that have been redeemed by the venerable baptismal font, by taking away the effect of that ceremony which he repeats, he shall know such doctrines for himself alone, and he shall not ruin others by his nefarious teaching. All teachers and ministers alike of this perverse superstition shall abstain from the gathering places of a doctrine already condemned, whether they defame the name of bishop by the assumption of such priestly office, or, that which is almost the same, they belie religion with the appellation of priests, or also if they call themselves deacons, although they may not even be considered Christians. Finally, the rescript that was recently issued at Sirmium shall be annulled, and there shall remain only those enactments pertaining to Catholic doctrine which were decreed by Our father of eternal memory and which We ourselves commanded by an equally manifold order, which will survive forever. [Gratian, Valentinian, and Theodosius, 379]

### 4.5.8 Pelagius on salvation

Pelagius (*c*.354–420/7) taught that humans were free to choose between good and evil, and he opposed ideas of predestination. By placing responsibility on men and women, he relegated divine grace and the sacraments to a secondary role in attaining salvation. Augustine was his most powerful opponent.

Augustine, *On Heresies* 88

[J. Stevenson, ed., *Creeds, Councils, and Controversies. Documents Illustrative of the History of the Church, AD* 337–461 (London: SPCK, 1966) pp. 224–5]

> The Pelagian heresy, at this present time the most recent of all, owes its rise to the monk Pelagius. Caelestius followed him so closely as his teacher, that their adherents are also called Caelestians. These men are such opponents of the grace of God . . . that without it, as they believe, man can do all the commandments of God . . .
>
> After a time, Pelagius was accused by the brethren of ascribing nothing to the grace of God for the purpose of keeping his commandments. He admitted the charge so far as, not indeed to put grace before free will, but to supplant it

by faithless cunning, and to say that it was given to men in order that what they are commanded to do by their free will they may the more easily be able to accomplish with the help of grace. Of course, by saying "the more easily be able" he wished it to be believed that, though with more difficulty, still men are able without grace, to do the commandments of God . . . they say that the grace of God, whereby we are delivered from irreligion, is given us according to our merits. This (doctrine), indeed, Pelagius, at his trial before the bishops in Palestine, when he was afraid of being condemned, was forced to condemn; but, in his later writings, he is found to teach it. They even go as far as to say that the life of the righteous in this world has no sin, and thus the Church of Christ in this mortal state is so perfected as to be altogether without spot or wrinkle . . .

They also deny that infants, born according to Adam after the flesh, contract by their first (*i.e.* natural) birth the infection of the ancient death. So they assert that they are born without any bond of original sin: with the result, of course, that there is in them nothing that has to be released at their Second (or New) Birth . . . Several other things are charged against them. But these are especially the points on which it may be understood how all, or nearly all, the rest depend.

### 4.5.9 *The* Tome *of Leo*

In his famous *Tome* (449), Pope Leo I declared that the incarnate Christ was a single Person in whom two perfect natures could be distinguished. This dogmatic statement linked Rome and Constantinople against Alexandria in support of the Council of Chalcedon. The *Tome* circulated widely, and in the sixth century was the basis for attempts to reunite Monophysitism (also called Miaphysitism) and Chalcedonianism.

Pope Leo I, *Letter* 28.4

[J. Stevenson, ed., *Creeds, Councils, and Controversies. Documents Illustrative of the History of the Church, AD* 337–461 (London: SPCK, 1966) pp. 318–19]

The Son of God, therefore, coming down from his seat in heaven, and yet not withdrawing from his Father's glory, born after a new order by a new mode of birth, enters this lower world. In a new order – because invisible in what belongs to himself he became visible in what belongs to us, and he, the incomprehensible, willed to be comprehended, abiding before time, he began to exist in time; the Lord of the Universe, drawing a shadow over the immensity of his majesty, took the form of a servant; the impassible God did not abhor to become man, subject to suffering, and, immortal as he is, to become subject to the laws of death; but he was born by a new kind of birth, inasmuch as inviolate virginity, which knew not the desire of the flesh, furnished the substance of flesh. Our Lord took from his mother nature, not sin; nor in our Lord Jesus Christ, born of a virgin's womb, is the nature unlike ours because his birth was wonderful. For he that is true God is true man; nor in this unity is there any unreality, while the lowliness of the manhood and the loftiness of deity have their separate spheres. For just as God is not changed by the compassion exhibited, so the manhood is not absorbed by the dignity bestowed. Each form, in communion with the other, performs the function that is proper to it; that is, the Word performing what belongs to the Word, and the flesh carrying out what belongs to the flesh. The one sparkles with miracles, the other succumbs to injuries. And as the Word ceases not to be on an equality with the Father's glory, so the flesh does not forgo the nature of our race. For – a fact which must be repeated again and again – one and the same is truly Son of God, and truly Son of Man. "He is God", inasmuch as "in the beginning was the Word, and the Word was with God, and the Word was God." "Man" "because the Word was made flesh and dwelt among us." "God" "because all things were made through him, and without him nothing was made": "Man" "inasmuch as he was made of a woman, made under the law."

### 4.5.10  The Henotikon of Zeno

The *Henotikon* (or *Edict of Union*) of the emperor Zeno, published in 482, attempted to reconcile Monophysites with Chalcedonians by accepting the first three ecumenical councils but avoiding references to "one nature" or "two natures" of Christ. Not only was this attempt at unity unsuccessful, Zeno was excommunicated by the Pope.

*The Henotikon: Letter of Zeno to the Bishops, Monks and Laity of Egypt* (Evagrius, *Ecclesiastical History* 111.14)

[W.H.C. Frend, *The Rise of the Monophysite Movement: Chapters in the History of the Church in the Fifth and Sixth Centuries* (Cambridge: Cambridge University Press, 1972) pp. 360–3]

The emperor Caesar Zeno, pious, victorious, triumphant, supreme, ever worshipful Augustus, to the most reverend bishops and clergy, and to the monks and laity throughout Alexandria, Egypt, Libya, and Pentapolis. Being assured that the origin and constitution, the might and invincible defence, of our sovereignty is the only right and true faith, which, through Divine inspiration, the three hundred holy fathers assembled at Nicaea set forth, and the hundred and fifty holy fathers, who in like manner met at Constantinople, confirmed. . . . So long as our great God and Saviour Jesus Christ, who was incarnate and born of Mary, the holy Virgin, and *Theotokos*, approves and readily accepts our concordant glorification and service, the power of our enemies will be crushed and swept away, and peace with its blessings, kindly temperature, abundant produce, and whatever is beneficial to man, will be liberally bestowed. Since, then, the irreprehensible faith is the preserver both of ourselves and the Roman weal, petitions have been offered to us from pious archimandrites and hermits, and other venerable persons, imploring us with tears that unity should be procured for the churches, and the limbs should be knit together, which the enemy of all good has of old time been eagerly bent upon severing . . . that this state of things might be transformed into good, who would not pray? For this reason, we were anxious that you should be informed, that we and the churches in every quarter neither have held, nor do we or shall we hold, nor are we aware of persons who hold, any other symbol, or lesson, or definition of faith or creed, than the before-mentioned holy symbol of the three hundred and eighteen holy fathers, which the aforesaid hundred and fifty holy fathers confirmed; and if any person does hold such, we deem him an alien: for we are confident that this symbol alone is, as we said, the preserver of our sovereignty, and on their reception of this alone are all the people baptized when desirous of the saving illumination . . . We moreover confess, that the only begotten Son of God, himself God who truly assumed manhood, namely, our Lord Jesus Christ, who is con-substantial with the Father in respect of the Godhead, and con-substantial with ourselves as respects the manhood; that He, having descended, and become incarnate of the holy Spirit and Mary, the Virgin and *Theotokos*, is one and not two; for we affirm that both his miracles, and the sufferings which he voluntarily endured in the flesh, are those of a single person: for we do in no degree admit those who either make a division or a confusion, or introduce a phantom; inasmuch as his truly sinless incarnation from the *Theotokos* did not produce an addition of a son because the Trinity continued a Trinity even when one member of the Trinity, the God-Word, became incarnate. Knowing, then, that neither the holy orthodox churches of God in all parts; nor the priests, highly beloved of God, who are at their head, nor our own sovereignty, have allowed or do allow any other symbol or definition of faith than the before-mentioned holy lesson, we have united ourselves thereto without hesitation. And these things we write not as setting forth a new form of faith, but for your assurance: and every one who has held or holds any other opinion, either at the present or another time, whether at Chalcedon or in any synod whatever, we anathematize; and specially the before-mentioned Nestorius and Eutyches, and those who maintain their doctrines. Link yourselves, therefore, to the spiritual mother, the church, and in her enjoy the same communion with us, according to the aforesaid one and only definition of the faith, namely, that of the three hundred and eighteen holy fathers. For your all-holy mother, the church, waits to embrace you as true children, and longs to hear your loved voice, so long withheld. Speed yourselves, therefore, for by so doing you will both draw towards yourselves the favour of our Master and Saviour and God, Jesus Christ, and be commended by our sovereignty.

### 4.5.11 An apology for differences of opinion among Christians

Evagrius practiced law in Antioch during the sixth century and wrote a history of the church which drew on a rich variety of archival sources. In this passage he explains how Christianity benefits from doctrinal disputes. His discussion is cast as a counter-argument to polytheists who mock Christian disputes but have no true understanding of divinity.

Evagrius, *Ecclesiastical History* 11

[Evagrius, *Ecclesiastical History* (London: Samuel Bagster and Sons, 1846) pp. 20–2]

> And here let not any one of the deluded worshippers of idols presume to sneer, as if it were the business of succeeding councils to depose their predecessors, and to be ever devising some addition to the faith. For while we are endeavouring to trace the unutterable and unsearchable scheme of God's mercy to man, and to revere and exalt it to the utmost, our opinions are swayed in this or that direction: and with none of those who have been the authors of heresies among Christians, was blasphemy the first intention; nor did they fall from the truth in a desire to dishonour the Deity, but rather from an idea which each entertained, that he should improve upon his predecessors by upholding such and such doctrines. Besides, all parties agree in a confession which embraces the essential points; for a Trinity is the single object of our worship, and unity the complex one of our glorification, and the Word, who is God begotten before the worlds, and became flesh by a second birth in mercy to the creature: and if new opinions have been broached on other points, these also have arisen from the freedom granted to our will by our Saviour God, even on these subjects, in order that the holy catholic and apostolic church might be the more exercised in bringing opposing opinions into captivity to truth and piety, and arrive, at length, at one smooth and straight path.

### 4.5.12  Justinian on orthodoxy

In a long treatise, *Against the Monophysites*, sent to some Alexandrian monks in 541/2, Emperor Justinian spelled out the tenets of Orthodox Chalcedonian Christianity.

Justinian, *Against the Monophysites*, Conclusion

[Kenneth Paul Wesche, *On the Person of Christ: The Christology of Emperor Justinian* (Crestwood, NY: St Vladimir's Seminary Press, 1991) pp. 104–6]

> And so that you might have a clear understanding of the confession we uphold in accordance with the catholic and apostolic Church, we have set it down in concise chapters for you who have chosen the monastic life and for those with you in and around Alexandria.
>
> i. If anyone does not confess one essence of the Holy Trinity, that is to say [one] nature of the Godhead, worshipped in three *hypostases* or *prosopa*, that is, in the Father, and the Son, and the Holy Spirit, let him be anathema.
>
> ii. If anyone says that the Divine Logos of the Holy Spirit is a creature, or of another essence than the Father, let him be anathema.
>
> iii. If anyone says that the Father, Son, and Holy Spirit are the same, believing them to be one *prosopon* with different names or one *hypostasis*

140

carrying three names, we consider such a one Like the Jews and anathematize him.

iv. If anyone denies that there are two generations of the one *prosopon* of our Lord Jesus Christ, the only-begotten Son of God – the one [generation] of the Father before the ages in his divinity, the other of the same [*prosopon*] in these last days of the holy Virgin and Theotokos Mary in his humanity – and that he is one of the Holy Trinity, one *hypostases* of three *hypostases*, let him be anathema.

v. If anyone does not confess that the holy, glorious, and ever-Virgin Mary is *Theotokos*, let him be anathema.

vi. If anyone introduces two Sons, one of God the Father, the other of the Mother, or says that the man Jesus was acted upon [by the Logos] and was united [to the Logos] through the good pleasure of the only-begotten as though he were different from him as Paul of Samosata and Nestorius blasphemously taught, and does not confess that the one Lord Jesus Christ is the same only-begotten Son and Word of God, let him be expelled from the company of Christians.

vii. If anyone says that the Logos passed through the Virgin as through a channel, and that he was not fashioned in her in a divine and human manner divinely because he was [conceived in the womb] apart from man and humanly in that he followed the law of birth, this one also is godless.

viii. If anyone divides the expressions in the Gospels and the apostolic writings referring to Christ spoken either by the saints or by Christ himself concerning himself into two *prosopa* or *hypostases*, let him be anathema.

ix. If anyone does not confess that there is one *hypostasis* or one *prosopon* of Christ, constituted of divinity and humanity, let him be anathema.

x. If anyone says that before the union there were two natures of the only-begotten, and after the union there is produced one nature of divinity and his flesh, let him be anathema.

xi. If anyone does not confess that the two natures of divinity and humanity are united in one *hypostasis* and that they produce one Christ, and that he is known in both natures without confusion and without division, whereby we confess that the same is perfect in Godhead and perfect in humanity, and believe that the miracles and the Passion are of one and the same, let him be anathema.

## 4.5.13 The "Three Chapters" Controversy

In a futile effort to unify the Church by placating the non-Chalcedonian Monophysites, in 543 Justinian condemned posthumously the "Three Chapters," the writings of three theologians particularly despised by the Monophysites. The chief consequence was condemnation of Justinian by western bishops. The reaction of Facundus of Hermione, a North African bishop, is indicative of the strong, "hands off" point of view in the West.

Facundus of Hermione, *In Defense of the Three Chapters* 12.3
[Francis Dvornik, *Early Christian and Byzantine Political Philosophy. Origins and Background* II (Washington, DC: Dumbarton Oaks Press, 1966) p. 826]

See *1.2.12*, page 10, for passage text.

## 4.6 Martyrs and relics

### *4.6.1 The martyrdom of Timothy of Gaza*

Women and men who gave their lives for their Christian beliefs during periods of persecution were often made saints. The veneration of these martyrs was a significant aspect of Christian devotion in Late Antiquity. The fourth-century churchman Eusebius of Caesarea compiled a number of martyr stories with his *Ecclesiastical History*. This account describes the death in 305 of Timothy of Gaza.

Eusebius, *The Martyrs of Palestine* 3.1
[Eusebius, *The Ecclesiastical History and the Martyrs of Palestine*, trans. Hugh Jackson Lawlor and John E.L. Oulton (London: SPCK, 1927) pp. 340–1]

> Now when these orders from the emperors were put into operation, the blessed Timothy was delivered up at Gaza, a city of Palestine, to Urban when he was there, and was unjustly put into bonds, like a murderer. But he was not bound for anything that was worthy of blame, for in all his conduct and life he was blameless. And when he refused to submit to idol-worship, and did not worship dead, lifeless images (for he was in all respects a perfect man, and in his soul knew his God), and because of his temperance, and on the score of his virtuous ways, he had endured grievous sufferings, even before he was delivered up to the governor, from the inhabitants of the city, and lived there subject to great insult, frequent stripes and afflictions. For the men of Gaza were turbulent and accursed in their paganism. And when he approached the governor's tribunal this champion of righteousness triumphed in all excellence of endurance. And angrily the judge used against him grievous tortures, and showered upon his body unnumbered scourgings, and with fearful and indescribable lacerations did he torture his sides. But amid all these sufferings the wonderful martyr strove like a warrior, and at last attained victory in his contest by enduring death by a slow fire, for the fire was gentle and slow in which he was burnt, so that his soul should not easily leave his body and be at rest. And there was he tried like pure gold in a furnace of gentle fire, and displayed the perfection and genuineness of his piety towards his God; and was crowned with the crown wherewith the glorious conquerors of righteousness are crowned. And because he loved God he received the reward that matched his desire – that perfect life which he desired – to be with God the King of all.

## 4.6.2 Mar Kardagh: a martyr in Persia

After Christianity became a permitted religion in the Roman Empire, the opportunities for martyrdom dried up. Beyond Rome's borders, however, Christians still might die for their faith. This Syriac tale of the mid-seventh century relates the martyrdom of the Christian hero Mar Kardagh at the hands of Zoroastrians in Persia. Son of a noble pagan family, Kardagh earned great honor serving the king of Persia, but after a miraculous conversion to Christianity his career took a fatal turn. His rebellion in defence of Christians failed and he was put to death by the king.

*The History of the Heroic Deeds of Mar Kardagh the Victorious Martyr*, 1, 65–9 [Joel Walker, "'Your Heroic Deeds Give Us Pleasure!' Culture and Society in the Christian Martyrs: Legends of Late Antique Iraq" (Dissertation, Princeton University, 1998) pp. 207, 259–66]

1. Dearly beloved, the histories of the martyrs and saints of our Lord Jesus Christ are a banquet for the holy church! They are spiritual nourishment for the holy congregations of the cross. They are an ornament to the lofty beauty of Christianity which is bespattered with the blood of the Son of God. They are a heavenly treasure for all the generations who enter the holy church through the spiritual birth of baptism. They are a polished mirror in which discerning men see the ineffable beauty of Christ. They are the possessions of righteousness for the children of the church who are invited to the heavenly kingdom, and [they are] the fire of the love of Christ flaming in the souls of believers. Whoever longs for their reading and for their constant study is a beloved son of the saints, because in him the beauties of those who are with God are expressed . . .

65. . . . And immediately he kneeled down, and when the casting of stones upon him began, he shook them off and stood up bravely. And he did this also a second time. And while the cavalrymen and magi were urging the crowds to throw the rocks hard, the blessed one answered and said to them, "I will not die unless my father throws the stone against me."

And his father, who was drunk with the error of Magianism and was afraid of death and sought favor with the king and the nobles, took a veil and bound it around his face and threw the rock for the stoning of his son. And immediately the soul of the athlete of righteousness departed to eternal life.

66. And at that hour the odor of spices filled the air everywhere in the region in which the blessed one was stoned. And, behold, a voice was heard saying, "You have fought well and won a heroic victory, glorious Kardagh. Go gladly and take up the crown of victory."

67. And that holy Mar Kardagh was crowned in the forty-ninth year of king Shapur on Friday. And during the night on which he shined forth on the Sabbath, compassionate men gathered together and took the body of the holy one and buried it with great honor.

68. And each year on the day on which the blessed one was crowned, people gathered together at the place of his crowning. And they made a festival and a commemoration for three days. But because of the multitude of the gathering,

they began also to buy and sell during the days of the saint's commemoration. And after some time had passed, a great market was built on the place in which the blessed one was stoned. It remains up until this day. And the commemoration of the holy one lasts three days, and the market six days. And it is called the market of Melqi from the name of the fortress of the blessed one.

69. But later a great and handsome church was also built at great expense in the name of the holy one by believing men worthy of good memory. It was built on that tell on which the holy Mar Kardagh was stoned. Would that we were made worthy to be helped by his prayers in this world full of wretchedness, and in that new world which will not pass away. May we find mercy through his prayers and join him in delight through the grace and love of our Lord Jesus Christ and to Him, his Father, and the Holy Spirit glory and honor and exaltation for ever and ever, amen.

Thus ends the martyrdom of Mar Kardagh, the holy and victorious martyr.

### 4.6.3 Relics of martyrs

Maintaining control of the physical remains of martyrs was important for Christians, who understood contact with relics to serve as a bridge between heaven and earth. The Spanish poet Prudentius (304–c.405) describes how Christians treated the corpse of Saint Vincent, who had been tortured to death in 304.

Prudentius, *On the Crowns of the Martyrs* 5.333–44
[Michael Roberts, *Poetry and the Cult of the Martyrs* (Ann Arbor: University of Michigan Press, 1993) p. 14]

> You could see the throng of the faithful come together from the whole city, set up a soft bed, and dry his raw wounds. One ranges with kisses over the double furrows left by the claws, another rejoices to lick the red blood from his body. Many dip linen garments in the drops of blood so as to preserve in their homes a sacred source of protection for their descendants.

### 4.6.4 Martyrs in church art

Illustrations of martyrs' deaths painted on church walls inspired worshipers at prayer.

Prudentius, *On the Crowns of the Martyrs* 11.123–34
[Michael Roberts, *Poetry and the Cult of the Martyrs* (Ann Arbor: University of Michigan Press, 1993) p. 154]

> A painted wall carries a representation of the crime, on which pigments of many colors set out the whole outrage, and above the tomb a likeness is depicted powerful in its clear images, delineating the bleeding limbs of the man dragged to his death. I have seen the moist points of the rocks, best of fathers, and the purple stains on the brambles. A hand skilled in imitating green vegetation had also portrayed the red blood with vermilion. You could see the torn

frame and limbs scattered and lying randomly in unpredictable locations. The painter had included the saint's loyal friends following with tearful footsteps where his erratic course traced its fractured path.

### 4.6.5 Violation of tombs in search of relics

The demand for holy relics created a new way to make money. The government sought to suppress this illegal traffic.

*Theodosian Code* 9.17.7

> No person shall transfer a buried body to another place. No person shall sell the relics of a martyr; no person shall traffic in them. But if anyone of the saints has been buried in any place whatever, persons shall have it in their power to add whatever building they may wish in veneration of such a place, and such building must be called a martyry. [Gratian, Valentinian, and Theodosius, 386]

### 4.6.6 Send me the head of Saint Paul!

In an immensely tactful letter to the empress Constantina, Pope Gregory the Great (590–604) explains that he cannot comply with her request for Saint Paul's head. His letter reveals some of the risks of handling relics and explains differences between the cult of relics in the East and West.

Pope Gregory the Great, *Letter* 30
[Gregory the Great, *Selected Epistles*, trans. James Barmby, in *Nicene and Post-Nicene Fathers*, vol. XII, eds. Philip Schaff and Henry Wace (Grand Rapids, MI: Eerdmans, 1895/1995) pp. 154–6]

> Gregory to Constantina:
> The Serenity of your Piety, conspicuous for religious zeal and love of holiness, has charged me with your commands to send to you the head of Saint Paul, or some other part of his body, for the church which is being built in honour of Saint Paul in the palace. And, being desirous of receiving commands from you, by exhibiting the most ready obedience to which I might the more provoke your favour towards me, I am all the more distressed that I neither can nor dare do what you enjoin. For the bodies of the apostles Saint Peter and Saint Paul glitter with so great miracles and terrors in their churches that one cannot even go to pray there without great fear. In short, when my predecessor, of blessed memory, was desirous of changing the silver which was over the most sacred body of the blessed apostle Peter, though at a distance of almost fifteen feet from the same body, a sign of no small dreadfulness appeared to him. Nay, I too wished in like manner to amend something not far from the most sacred body of Saint Paul the apostle; and, it being necessary to dig to some depth near his sepulchre, the superintendent of that place found some bones, which were not indeed connected with the same sepulchre; but, inasmuch as he presumed to lift them and transfer them to another place, certain awful signs appeared, and he died suddenly.

... Moreover, let my most tranquil lady know that it is not the custom of the Romans, when they give relics of saints, to presume to touch any part of the body; but only a cloth is put into a box, and placed near the most sacred bodies of the saints: and when it is taken up it is deposited with due reverence in the church that is to be dedicated, and such powerful effects are thereby produced there as might have been if their bodies had been brought to that special place. Whence it came to pass in the times of Pope Leo, of blessed memory, as has been handed down from our forefathers, that, certain Greeks being in doubt about such relics, the aforesaid pontiff took scissors and cut this same cloth, and from the very incision blood flowed. For in the Roman and all the Western parts it is unendurable and sacrilegious for anyone by any chance to desire to touch the bodies of saints: and, if one should presume to do this, it is certain that this temerity will by no means remain unpunished. For this reason we greatly wonder at the custom of the Greeks, who say that they take up the bones of saints; and we scarcely believe it. For certain Greek monks who came here more than two years ago dug up in the silence of night near the church of Saint Paul, bodies of dead men lying in the open field, and laid up their bones to be kept in their own possession till their departure. And, when they were taken and diligently examined as to why they did this, they confessed that they were going to carry those bones to Greece to pass for relics of saints. From this instance, as has been already said, the greater doubt has been engendered in us whether it be true that they really take up the bones of saints, as they are said to do ...

But I trust in Almighty God that your most kind good will is in no way being stolen away from me, and that you will always have with you the power of the holy apostles, whom with all your heart and mind you love, not from their bodily presence, but from their protection.

Moreover, the napkin, which you have likewise ordered to be sent you, is with his body, and so cannot be touched, as his body cannot be approached. But since so religious a desire of my most serene lady ought not to be wholly unsatisfied, I will make haste to transmit to you some portion of the chains which Saint Peter the Apostle himself bore on his neck and his hands, from which many miracles are displayed among the people; if at least I should succeed in removing it by filing ...

## 4.7 Pilgrimage and relics

### 4.7.1 Relics in Jerusalem

Pilgrimage to holy sites throughout the Mediterranean, and especially to Palestine to view the places and relics of Jesus' life and death, began in earnest after Constantine's conversion. Pious travelers flocked to the backwater province of Palestine, turning the Holy Land into a prosperous tourist center. Rich buildings were constructed as the province discovered a new, holy landscape. Cyril, bishop of

Jerusalem (*c.*348–*c.*386), who argued forcefully for the continued theological significance of historical places, described how the inhabitants of Jerusalem shared
Constantine's vision of the Cross.

Cyril of Jerusalem, *Letter to the Emperor Constantius* 3–5

[William Telfer, ed., *Cyril of Jerusalem and Nemesius of Emesa* (*The Library of
Christian Classics*, vol. 4) (London: SCM Press, 1955) pp. 194–6]

> For, in the days of Constantine your father, most dear to God and of blessed
> memory, there was discovered the wood of the cross fraught with salvation,
> because the divine grace that gave piety to the pious seeker vouchsafed the
> finding of the buried holy places. But in your time, your Majesty, most
> religious of Emperors, victorious through a piety towards God greater even
> than that which you inherited, are seen wonderful works, not from the earth any
> more, but from the heavens. The trophy of the victory over death of our Lord
> and Saviour Jesus Christ, the only-begotten Son of God, I mean the blessed
> cross, has been seen at Jerusalem blazing with refulgent light!
>
> For in these very days of the holy feast of Pentecost, on the seventh of May,
> about the third hour a gigantic cross formed of light appeared in the sky above
> holy Golgotha stretching out as far as the holy Mount of Olives. It was not seen
> by just one or two, but was most clearly displayed before the whole population
> of the city. Nor did it, as one might have supposed, pass away quickly like
> something imagined, but was visible to sight above the earth for some hours,
> while it sparkled with a light above the sun's rays . . .

### 4.7.2 Constantine and Jerusalem's holy sites

Eusebius of Caesarea describes the first discoveries of holy places in Jerusalem and
how Constantine poured money into constructing shrines to glorify them.

Eusebius, *Life of Constantine* 3.25, 27–9

[Eusebius, *Life of Constantine*, in *Egeria's Travels*, trans. John Wilkinson
(London: SPCK, 1971) pp. 164–6]

> [25] Constantine realized that he ought to display the most blessed place of the
> Savior's Resurrection in Jerusalem in a worthy and conspicuous manner. So,
> without delay, he gave orders that a house of prayer should be erected . . . [27]
> As soon as he had issued his orders, this false device [a temple of Aphrodite]
> was cast to the ground . . . with its images and gods. The Emperor also
> commanded that the stone and timber of the ruins should be removed and
> dumped as far away as possible, and that a large area of the foundation soil,
> defiled as it was by devil-worship, should be dug away to a considerable depth,
> and removed to some distance. [28] At once the work was carried out, and, as
> layer after layer of the subsoil came into view, the venerable and most holy
> memorial of the Savior's resurrection, beyond all our hopes, came into view;
> the holy of holies, the cave, was, like our Savior, "restored to life" . . . by its
> very existence bearing clearer testimony to the resurrection of the Savior than

any words. [29] Thereupon the Emperor . . . gave orders that a house of prayer should be built in the precincts of the saving cave, rich, royal, and magnificent. It was as though he had long foreseen all this, and had by some superior acumen known what was going to happen. He ordered the governors of the eastern provinces to provide lavish supplies in order that the work should be extremely great and magnificent . . .

### 4.7.3 Paula – a pious Roman aristocrat in Jerusalem

In 404 Jerome wrote a letter of condolence to Eustochium on the death of her mother, Paula. Eustochium was a noble Roman lady who had gone to Jerusalem with Jerome to live as a nun and scholar. Jerome's account of her mother Paula's visit to Jerusalem reveals the special treatment given to aristocratic tourists as well as Paula's extreme piety.

Jerome, *Letter* 108 to Eustochium

[Jerome, *Letters and Select Works*, trans. W.H. Fremantle, *Nicene and Post-Nicene Fathers*, 2nd series, vol. VI, eds. Philip Schaff and Henry Wace (Grand Rapids, MI: Eerdmans, 1893/1995)]

> To make a long story short, leaving on her left the mausoleum of Helena queen of Adiabene who in time of famine had sent corn to the Jewish people, Paula entered Jerusalem, Jebus, or Salem, that city of three names which after it had sunk to ashes and decay was by Aelius Hadrianus [the emperor Hadrian] restored once more as Aelia. And although the proconsul of Palestine, who was an intimate friend of her house, sent forward his apparitors and gave orders to have his official residence placed at her disposal, she chose a humble cell in preference to it. Moreover, in visiting the holy places so great was the passion and the enthusiasm she exhibited for each, that she could never have torn herself away from one had she not been eager to visit the rest. Before the Cross she threw herself down in adoration as though she beheld the Lord hanging upon it: and when she entered the tomb which was the scene of the Resurrection she kissed the stone which the angel had rolled away from the door of the sepulchre. Indeed so ardent was her faith that she even licked with her mouth the very spot on which the Lord's body had lain, like one athirst for the river which he has longed for. What tears she shed there, what groans she uttered, and what grief she poured forth, all Jerusalem knows.

### 4.7.4 Egeria visits the Cross

Egeria was a wealthy woman, perhaps a nun, who visited the Holy Land during the years 381–384. She recorded detailed observations of her long journey from her home in Gaul or Spain. Here she describes viewing the Cross in Jerusalem.

Egeria, *Travels* 36.5, 37.1–3

[*Egeria's Travels*, trans. John Wilkinson (London: SPCK, 1971) pp. 136–7]

36.5 Then the bishop speaks a word of encouragement to the people. They have been hard at it all night, and there is further effort in store for them in the day ahead. So he tells them not to be weary, but to put their hope in God, who will give them a reward out of all proportion to the effort they have made. When he has given them as much encouragement as he can, he speaks to them as follows: "Now off you go home till the next service, and sit down for a bit. Then all be back here at about eight o'clock so that till midday you can see the holy Wood of the Cross, that, as every one of us believes, helps us attain salvation." . . .

37.1 . . . But it is not long before everyone is assembled for the next service. The bishop's chair is placed on Golgotha Behind the Cross (the cross there now), and he takes his seat. A table is placed before him with a cloth on it, the deacons stand round, and there is brought to him a gold and silver box containing the holy Wood of the Cross. It is opened, and the Wood of the Cross and the Title are taken out and placed on the table.

2. As long as the holy Wood is on the table, the bishop sits with his hands resting on either end of it and holds it down, and the deacons round him keep watch over it. They guard it like this because what happens now is that all the people, catechumens as well as faithful, come up one by one to the table. They stoop down over it, kiss the Wood, and move on. But on one occasion (I don't know when) one of them bit off a piece of the holy Wood and stole it away, and for this reason the deacons stand round and keep watch in case anyone dares to do the same again.

3. Thus all the people go past one by one. They stoop down, touch the holy Wood first with their forehead and then with their eyes, and then kiss it, but no one puts out his hand to touch it . . .

### 4.7.5 *The Piacenza Pilgrim*

A traveler known as the Piacenza Pilgrim composed a lively description of his trip to the Holy Land about 570. Though not completely accurate in all he describes, the pilgrim's pleasure in his journey is evident.

*The Piacenza Pilgrim* 1, 5, 11, 12, 18–20
[John Wilkinson, *Jerusalem Pilgrims Before the Crusades* (Warminster: Aris and Phillips, 1977) pp. 79, 81, 83]

1. Blessed Antoninus the Martyr was ahead of me from the time that I set out from Piacenza in all the places where I travelled, I mean, the holy places.

5. We travelled on to the city of Nazareth, where many miracles take place. In the synagogue there is kept the book in which the Lord wrote his ABC, and in this synagogue there is the bench on which he sat with the other children. Christians can lift the bench and move it about, but the Jews are completely unable to move it, and cannot drag it outside. The house of Saint Mary is now a basilica, and her clothes are the cause of frequent miracles.

11. I kept Epiphany at the Jordan, and on that night special miracles take place at the spot where the Lord was baptized. There is an obelisk there surrounded by a screen, and in the water, where the river turned back in its bed, stands a wooden cross. On both banks there are marble steps leading down to the water. The eve of Epiphany is a solemn vigil with an enormous congregation. They begin matins at the fourth or fifth cockcrow, and at dawn, when matins is over, the ministers come outside, and, accompanied by deacons, the priest goes down into the river. The moment he starts blessing the water the Jordan turns back on itself with a roar and the water stays still till the baptism is finished. All the ship owners of Alexandria have men there that day with great jars of spices and balsam, and as soon as the river has been blessed, before the baptism starts, they pour them out into the water, and draw out holy water. This water they use for sprinkling their ships when they are about to set sail. After the baptism every one goes down into the river to gain a blessing. Some wear linen, and some other materials which will serve as their shrouds for burial. And after the baptism the water returns to its place. From the point where the Jordan comes out of the Sea of Tiberias to where it ends at the Salt Sea is about 130 miles.

12. On the bank of the Jordan there is a cave in which are cells for seven virgins. They are placed there as small girls, and when one of them dies, she is buried in her cell, and another cell is hewn from the rock, so that another girl can be placed there to make up the number. They have people outside to look after them. We went in with great reverence to pray there, but we did not see the face of a single one of them. It is said that the cloth is there which the Lord wore on his face. By the Jordan, not far from where the Lord was baptized is the very large Monastery of Saint John, which has two guest-houses. On both banks of the Jordan below the mountains there are serpents from which people make antidotes against poisoning.

18. After we had prostrated ourselves and kissed the ground, we entered the Holy City and venerated the Lord's Tomb. The Tomb is hewn out of living rock, or rather in the rock itself . . . and in the place where the Lord's body was laid, at the head, has been placed a bronze lamp. It burns there day and night, and we took a blessing from it, and then put it back. Earth is brought to the tomb and put inside, and those who go in take some as a blessing. The stone which closed the Tomb is in front of the tomb door, and is made of the same coloured rock as the rock hewn from Golgotha. This stone is decorated with gold and precious stones, but the rock of the tomb is like a millstone. There are ornaments in vast numbers, which hang from iron rods: armlets, bracelets, necklaces, rings, tiaras, plaited girdles, belts, emperors' crowns of gold and precious stones, and the insignia of an empress. The Tomb is roofed with a cone which is silver, with added beams of gold. In front of the Tomb stands an altar.

19. From the Tomb it is eighty paces to Golgotha; you go up on one side of it by the very steps up which our Lord went to be crucified. You can see the place

where he was crucified, and on the actual rock there is a bloodstain. Beside this is the altar of Abraham, which is where he intended to offer Isaac, and where Melchizedech offered sacrifice. Next to the altar is a crack, and if you put your ear to it you hear streams of water. If you throw an apple into it, or anything else that will float, and then go to Siloam, you can pick it up there. I suppose it is a mile between Siloam and Golgotha. In fact Jerusalem has no water of its own except the spring at Siloam.

20. From Golgotha it is fifty paces to the place where the Cross was discovered, which is in the Basilica of Constantine, which adjoins the Tomb and Golgotha. In the courtyard of the basilica is a small room where they keep the Wood of the Cross. We venerated it with a kiss. The title is also there which they placed over the Lord's head, on which they wrote "This is the King of the Jews". This I have seen, and had it in my hand and kissed it. The Wood of the Cross comes from the nut-tree. At the moment when the Cross is brought out of this small room for veneration, and arrives in the court to be venerated, a star appears in the sky, and comes over the place where they lay the Cross. It stays overhead whilst they are venerating the Cross, and they offer oil to be blessed in little flasks. When the mouth of one of the little flasks touches the Wood of the Cross, the oil instantly bubbles over, and unless it is closed very quickly it all spills out. When the Cross is taken back into its place, the star also vanishes, and appears no more once the Cross has been put away. In that place are also the sponge and reed mentioned in the Gospel (from this sponge we drank water) and also the onyx cup which he blessed at the Supper, and many other marvellous things beside: a portrait of Blessed Mary on a raised place, her girdle, and the band which she used to have on her head. In that place there are also seven marble seats for the elders.

### 4.7.6 Heraclius restores the Cross to Jerusalem

One of the high points of the eventful career of the emperor Heraclius was bringing back to Jerusalem in 630 the remnants of the Cross that the Persian king had looted from there in 614. The return of the Cross represented the defeat of Persia, an additional cause to rejoice. The Armenian historian Sebeos records the event.

Sebeos, *History*, ch. 29, verse 99

[*Sebeos' History*, trans. Robert Bedrosian (New York: Sources of the Armenian Tradition, 1985) pp. 115–16]

Now when the holy Cross of the Lord had fallen to the venerable, pious, and blessed king Heraclius, he enthusiastically and joyfully assembled his troops. Then, taking all the royal attendants and revering the blessed, miraculous and divine discovery they took the Cross back to the holy city of Jerusalem. They also took there all the vessels of the church which had been saved from the enemy, in the city of Byzantium. And there was no small amount of joy on the day they entered Jerusalem, with the sound of sobbing and moaning, an outpouring of tears from their excited and moved hearts, and there was a tightening feeling in the king, the princes, all the troops and the inhabitants in the city. No one was capable of singing the sacred songs due to the tremendous and deep emotion felt by the king and the entire multitude. Heraclius took the Cross and re-established it in its place; he put each of the vessels of the churches back in its place; and he gave wealth and incense to all the churches and inhabitants of the city.

## 4.8 Asceticism

### 4.8.1 The Devil tempts Antony

The goal of ascetic life was to suppress all the physical impulses and societal ties so that God might fill the human body and work through it in miraculous ways. To achieve such a state required endless training through acts of self-discipline and fierce austerity. Whether living alone as hermits or in the midst of monastic communities, men and women devoted their lives to this new form of devotion in increasing numbers, and the ascetic movement spread quickly across the Roman world. Antony's asceticism, called "the discipline" because of the constant and rigorous concentration it required, keeps him "in shape" to struggle with the Devil. In contrast to "the discipline" was "the household," the repository of all the pleasures and social ties of daily life that Antony sought to push away. In this passage, Antony emerges unscathed from a wrestling match with the Devil. Antony's victory over temptation imitates that of Jesus. (See also *4.2.4*, page 113.)

Athanasius, *Life of Antony* 5–7

[*Athanasius: The Life of Antony and the Letter to Marcellinus*, trans. Robert C. Gregg (New York: Paulist Press, 1980) pp. 33–5]

5. The devil, who despises and envies good, could not bear seeing such purpose in a youth, but the sort of things he had busied himself in doing in the past, he set to work to do against this person as well. First he attempted to lead him away from the discipline, suggesting memories of his possessions, the guardianship of his sister, the bonds of kinship, love of money and of glory, the manifold pleasures of food, the relaxations of life, and finally, the rigor of virtue and how great the labor is that earns it, suggesting also the bodily weakness and the length of time involved. So he raised in his mind a great dust cloud of considerations, since he wished to cordon him off from his righteous intentions. But the enemy saw his own weakness in the face of Antony's resolve, and saw that he instead was being thrown for a fall by the sturdiness of this contestant, and being overturned by his great faith and falling over Antony's constant prayers. Then he placed his confidence in the weapons in the navel of his belly, and boasting in these (for they constitute his first ambush against the young), he advanced against the youth, noisily disturbing him by night, and so troubling him in the daytime that even those who watched were

aware of the bout that occupied them both. The one hurled foul thoughts and the other overturned them through his prayers; the former resorted to titillation, but the latter, seeming to blush, fortified the body with faith and with prayers and fasting. And the beleaguered devil undertook one night to assume the form of a woman and to imitate her every gesture, solely in order that he might beguile Antony. But in thinking about the Christ and considering the excellence won through him, and the intellectual part of the soul, Antony extinguished the fire of his opponent's deception ... 7. This was Antony's first contest against the devil – or, rather, this was in Antony the success of the Savior . . .

## 4.8.2 Extreme asceticism

In 343, a church council at Gangra in Paphlagonia (Asia Minor) attempted to stop some ascetic practices that it considered extreme. The focus of attention was Eustathius of Sebaste, one of the founders of the ascetic movement in the lands south of the Black Sea and in Armenia who was also associated with some heretical doctrinal positions. He eventually came into conflict with the church hierarchy, whose authority he refused to accept. The canons of the council illuminate points of contention.

*Canons of the Council of Gangra 343*
[*The Seven Ecumenical Councils of the Undivided Church, their Canons and Dogmatic Decrees*, trans. Henry R. Percival, *Nicene and Post Nicene Fathers*, vol. XIV, 1900 (Grand Rapids, MI: Eerdmans, 1956) pp. 92–9]

CANON I. If anyone shall condemn marriage, or abominate and condemn a woman who is a believer and devout and sleeps with her own husband, as though she could not enter the Kingdom of heaven, let him be anathema.

CANON II. If anyone shall condemn him who eats flesh which is without blood and has not been offered to idols nor strangled, and is faithful and devout, as though the man were without home of salvation because of his eating, let him be anathema.

CANON III. If anyone shall teach a slave, under pretext of piety, to despise his master and to run away from his service, and not to serve his own master with goodwill and all honour, let him be anathema.

CANON IX. If anyone shall remain a virgin or observe continence, abstaining from marriage because he abhors it, and not on account of the beauty and holiness of virginity itself, let him be anathema.

CANON X. If any one of those who are living a virgin life for the Lord's sake shall treat arrogantly the married, let him be anathema.

CANON XIII. If any woman, under pretence of asceticism, shall change her apparel, and instead of a woman's accustomed clothing, shall put on that of a man, let her be anathema.

CANON XIV. If any woman shall forsake her husband, and resolve to depart from him because she abhors marriage, let her be anathema.

CANON XV. If anyone shall forsake his own children and shall not nurture them . . ., under pretence of asceticism, let him be anathema.

CANON XVI. If under pretence of piety, any children shall forsake their parents, particularly if the parents are believers, and shall withhold becoming reverence from their parents, on the plea that they honour piety more than them, let them be anathema.

CANON XVII. If any woman from feigned asceticism shall cut off her hair, which God gave her as the reminder of her subjection, thus annulling as it were the ordinance of subjection, let her be anathema.

### 4.8.3 Simeon the Stylite: public ascetic acts draw crowds

Simeon the Stylite, a fifth-century Syrian monk, demonstrated his piety through repeated acts of mortification. He began his career living exposed to the elements in a hole in the ground for several years. When he moved to the top of a pillar on the outskirts of town he achieved lasting fame by performing such acts as standing on one foot for days, to the awe of admiring crowds. The first excerpt below shows how Simeon chose a more solitary life than monastic coexistence allowed. The second excerpt, from a Syriac homily of Jacob of Sarug (c.450–c.520), describes Simeon's last days.

Bedjan, *The Heroic Deeds of Mar Simeon, the Chief of the Anchorites* (*Acts of Martyrs and Saints*)

[Charles C. Torrey and Hanns Oertel, eds., *Journal of the American Oriental Society*, vol. 35, part II (New Haven, CT: The American Oriental Society, 1915) pp. 118, 132–3, 135–6]

[Other lives of Simeon are available in Robert Doran, *The Lives of Simeon Stylites* (Kalamazoo, MI: Cistercian Publications, 1992).]

The Blessed Mar Simeon had no care for anything except how he might please his Lord. And when he had been with the monks a long time, he separated from them and went and dug for himself a hole in a corner of the garden up to his breast, and he stood in it two years in the oppressive heat of summer and the severe cold of winter. When the monks saw his hard toil, and not one of them was able to vie with him in his ascetic practices, they were filled with jealousy, and said to the abbot, "If he is not placed on an equality with us, he can not live here." When the abbot saw the will of the monks, he entreated him either to mingle with the brothers or to diminish his toil; but he did not obey.

After these things he set up a stone, that he might stand upon it, that had four bases and was two cubits high . . . After these things the saint's fame began to be talked about in the world, and men began to flock to him from everywhere. For he stood upon that stone five years. And his fame began to spread abroad to all quarters, and men resorted to him from every place.

How many thousands and myriads who were even unconscious that there is a God, through the saint came to know God their Creator and became his worshippers and adorers! Again, how many unclean were sanctified, and how many licentious became chaste at sight of him! How many, also, who were not persuaded in the fear of our Lord, who came to hear him from distant places, when they saw his beautiful person and his discipline and never-ending toil, despised and left the transitory world with all that is in it, and became disciples of the word of truth, and many of them were vessels of honor! Again, how many harlots came there and from afar saw him, the Holy One, and renounced and left their places and the cities in which they had lived, and surrendered themselves to the Christ, and entering dwelt in convents and became vessels of honor, and with their tears they served their Lord and blotted out the list of their debts! How many distant Arabs who did not even know what bread is, but whose subsistence was the flesh of animals, when they came and saw the Blessed One, became disciples and were Christians and renounced the images of their fathers and served God! How many barbarians and Armenians and Aurtians and pagans of every tongue came continually, and every single day crowd upon crowd received baptism and confessed the living God! And there was no end to the Arabs and their kings and chiefs who there received baptism and believed on God and confessed the Messiah, and at the word of the Blessed One also built churches among their tents. How many oppressed were released by his word from their oppressors! How many bills of debt were torn up by his effort! How many maltreated were relieved from those who led them in bonds! How many slaves, too, were manumitted, and their documents torn up before the Holy One! How many orphans and widows were sustained and supported (after our Lord) by the standing of the Blessed One! Lord did these things by his hands. He also magnified the priests of God sedulously, and the regulations and laws of the church were established by his care. He also gave command regarding usury, that one half of the usury on everything should be taken; and every person in joy received his command, so that there were many who remitted the whole of it and did not exact usury after he had commanded.

Now concerning the healing which our Lord gave through his hands, and how much deliverance and benefit came to men through his prayer, and to how many afflicted lives which had been crushed and tortured by smitings of various sorts from the workings of the Devil, by the hands of the Blessed Mar Simeon God was pleased to give alleviation and free them from the servitude of the Fiend. This for the mouth of mortals is too great to talk about.

### 4.8.4 The death of Simeon

Jacob of Serug, *Homily on Simeon the Stylite* 655–6, 659–60, 664–5
[Jacob of Serug, *Homily on Simeon the Stylite*, trans. Susan Ashbrook Harvey, in Vincent L. Wimbush, *Ascetic Behavior in Greco-Roman Antiquity* (Minneapolis, MN: Trinity Press International, 1990) pp. 21, 23, 26, 27]

(655) But when the affliction grew strong and acted mightily on the holy one, his flesh decayed and his foot stood exposed. He lifted his voice and the angels marveled at his fortitude, while he sang with the harp of David on his pillar, "My foot stands straight and does not bend. For its Lord will sustain it that it may stand and support the burden of two. For lo, it bears the palace of the body like a pillar of that master-builder who fastens and supports it so that it will not be shaken. O Evil One, the hurt you are causing does not hurt me since it is sweet for me; you will tire yourself out as I am not going to leave my labor. (656) Increase the torment like a craftsman for good gold, so that I will grow bright, and as for you, your craftsmanship will have been exhausted. Strike me not only on the feet if you can: strike all my body and continue without boasting. A horse is not tamed without a bridle, so undertake to chastise the insolent one like savage youths would. Do not think that I am hindered by your blows, for I will not cease from the labor to which I have applied myself."

[...]

(659) The blessed one was occupied with this labor for a very long time, while he was standing on one foot, and he did not weaken. It is marvelous to speak, that there should even be a way of life like this pillar! For his foot stood firm, that foot of the blessed man, and it was not shaken. Who would withhold this work from the discerning, but one whose heart is blind of understanding? One moment a man might stand still, but hours he could not. But that chosen one was standing up day and night on his one foot. Thirty and ten years he endured as one day, heat and cold and vigils and fasts, and the contest with the Evil One. Never have I seen (660) one who stood like this just man, nor in books have I seen a story like his. Righteous men fasted for generations for a known period of days, from thirty weeks and sixty, each according to his strength. But who would count the fasting of this angel in the body? For he is not comparable with men but with angels. Forty days the divine Moses fasted. And also Elijah in his number of days fasted like Moses. Of these two men, one shone and one was taken up ...

(664) The disciples saw that their master had fallen asleep [died], and gave voice; and the rocks in the walls wept with them and the mountains quaked. They embraced the pillar and gave voice like jackals. They wet the ground with their tears bitterly. The corpse was standing on the pillar and everyone was looking. And the congregation were thinking that he had in fact fallen asleep. Creation stood still and groaned in pain in response to his disciples, while they were saying to him, "Our father you have left us like orphans. Where shall we go and with whom shall we seek refuge instead of you? Who like you will comfort us in our miseries? We left family and took refuge with you, O beautiful one. And you filled for us the place of family and siblings and father. Report of you went out in all places and we had heard about you, and when we came to (665) your fountain death stopped it up. We saw your light like a torch and came to visit it. And suddenly the breath of death breathed out and quenched its flame ...".

## 4.8.5 John Cassian's rules for monastic life

As the monastic movement grew, the ascetic communities required rules and regulations. All-powerful abbots determined the patterns of life of the people in their establishments. John Cassian founded monasteries in southern Gaul in the first decades of the fifth century. He followed the Egyptian model. The following excerpts from his *Institutes* illuminate aspects of monastic life.

John Cassian, *Institutes* 1.2, 4.5

[Philip Schaff and Henry Wace, eds., *A Select Library of Nicene and Post-Nicene Fathers of the Christian Church*, second series, vol. XI (Grand Rapids, MI: Eerdmans, 1955) pp. 202, 220, 241]

### Book 1, Ch. 2: Of the Monk's Robe

Let the robe also of the monk be such as may merely cover the body and prevent the disgrace of nudity, and keep off harm from cold, not such as may foster the seeds of vanity and pride; for the same apostle tells us: "Having food and covering, with these let us be content." "Covering," he says, not "raiment," as is wrongly found in some Latin copies: that is, what may merely cover the body, not what may please the fancy by the splendour of the attire; commonplace, so that it may not be thought remarkable for novelty of colour or fashion among other men of the same profession; and quite free from anxious carefulness, yet not discoloured by stains acquired through neglect. Lastly, let them be so far removed from this world's fashions as to remain altogether common property for the use of the servants of God. For whatever is claimed by one or a few among the servants of God and is not the common property of the whole body of the brethren alike is either superfluous or vain, and for that reason to be considered harmful, and affording an appearance of vanity rather than virtue . . .

### Book 4, Ch. 5

Wherefore each one on his admission is stripped of all his former possessions, so that he is not allowed any longer to keep even the clothes which he has on his back: but in the council of the brethren he is brought forward into the midst and stripped of his own clothes, and clad by the Abbot's hands in the dress of the monastery, so that by this he may know not only that he has been despoiled of all his old things, but also that he has laid aside all worldly pride, and come down to the want and poverty of Christ, and that he is now to be supported not by wealth, sought for by the world's arts, nor by anything reserved from his former state of unbelief, but that he is to receive out of the holy and sacred funds of the monastery his rations for his service . . .

## 4.8.6 Benedict on the twelve degrees of humility

Benedict of Nursia (480–547) was a founder of Christian monasticism in Italy and western Europe. He established twelve monasteries, of which the best known is

Monte Cassino, in the hills between Rome and Naples. The rule book that he wrote for his monks, composed *c.*535–540, stressed moderation and reasonableness and was widely adopted by monks in the Middle Ages.

Saint Benedict, *Rule for Monasteries* 7
[*St. Benedict's Rule for Monasteries*, trans. Leonard J. Doyle (Collegeville, MN: St. John's Abbey Press, 1948) pp. 20–8]

Chapter 7: On Humility
Holy Scripture, brethren, cries out to us, saying,
"Everyone who exalts himself shall be humbled,
and he who humbles himself shall be exalted."
In saying this it shows us
that all exaltation is a kind of pride,
against which the Prophet proves himself to be on guard
when he says,
"Lord, my heart is not exalted,
nor are mine eyes lifted up;
neither have I walked in great matters,
nor in wonders above me."
But how has he acted?
"Rather have I been of humble mind
than exalting myself;
as a weaned child on its mother's breast,
so You solace my soul."

Hence, brethren,
if we wish to reach the very highest point of humility
and to arrive speedily at that heavenly exaltation
to which ascent is made through the humility of this present life,
we must by our ascending actions
erect the ladder Jacob saw in his dream,
on which Angels appeared to him descending and ascending.
By that descent and ascent
we must surely understand nothing else than this,
that we descend by self-exaltation and ascend by humility.
And the ladder thus set up is our life in the world,
which the Lord raises up to heaven if our heart is humbled.
For we call our body and soul the sides of the ladder,
and into these sides our divine vocation has inserted
the different steps of humility and discipline we must climb.

The first degree of humility, then,
is that a person keep the fear of God before his eyes
and beware of ever forgetting it.
Let him be ever mindful of all that God has commanded;
let his thoughts constantly recur

to the hell-fire which will burn for their sins
those who despise God,
and to the life everlasting which is prepared
for those who fear Him.
Let him keep himself at every moment from sins and vices,
whether of the mind, the tongue, the hands, the feet,
or the self-will,
and check also the desires of the flesh.

The second degree of humility
is that a person love not his own will
nor take pleasure in satisfying his desires,
but model his actions on the saying of the Lord,
"I have come not to do My own will,
but the will of Him who sent Me."
It is written also,
"Self-will has its punishment, but constraint wins a crown."

The third degree of humility is that a person
for love of God
submit himself to his Superior in all obedience,
imitating the Lord, of whom the Apostle says,
"He became obedient even unto death."

The fourth degree of humility
is that he hold fast to patience with a silent mind
when in this obedience he meets with difficulties
and contradictions
and even any kind of injustice,
enduring all without growing weary or running away . . .

The fifth degree of humility
is that he hide from his Abbot
none of the evil thoughts
that enter his heart
or the sins committed in secret,
but that he humbly confess them.

The sixth degree of humility is that a monk be content
with the poorest and worst of everything,
and that in every occupation assigned him
he consider himself a bad and worthless workman . . .

The seventh degree of humility
is that he consider himself lower and of less account
than anyone else,

and this not only in verbal protestation
but also with the most heartfelt inner conviction . . .

The eighth degree of humility
is that a monk do nothing except what is commended
by the common Rule of the monastery
and the example of the elders.

The ninth degree of humility
is that a monk restrain his tongue and keep silence,
not speaking until he is questioned . . .

The tenth degree of humility
is that he be not ready and quick to laugh . . .

The eleventh degree of humility is that when a monk speaks
he do so gently and without laughter,
humbly and seriously,
in few and sensible words,
and that he be not noisy in his speech . . .

The twelfth degree of humility
is that a monk not only have humility in his heart
but also by his very appearance make it always manifest
to those who see him.
That is to say that whether he is at the Work of God,
in the oratory, in the monastery, in the garden, on the road,
in the fields or anywhere else,
and whether sitting, walking or standing,
he should always have his head bowed
and his eyes toward the ground . . .

Having climbed all these steps of humility, therefore,
the monk will presently come to that perfect love of God which casts out
fear . . .

### 4.8.7 The difficulties of monastic life

Romanos the Melodist's hymn *On Christian Life* addresses the difficulties of
monastic existence in the Greek east in the sixth century.

Romanos the Melodist, *On Christian Life*, strophes 22, 23, 25
[*Kontakia of Romanos, Byzantine Melodist*, vol. II: *On Christian Life*, trans.
Marjorie Carpenter (Columbia, MO: University of Missouri Press, 1973) pp. 257–8]

*Strophe 22:*
Again he says to you: "How are you able
to carry out the rules of the monastery?
The yoke is heavy and difficult to bear,
and the one who does not endure it is useless."

Immediately, you will answer the wily one:
"The rules make demands on me according to my strength.
If I do not succeed in this, I shall become master of something else.
If I am strong, I shall work at singing the psalm,
Hallelujah."

*Strophe 23:*
Hasten to labor along with the workmen
Whom the Lord has called to the vineyard;
thrust away the unsound life of the flesh,
And assume the life of the angels, in order that you may reach
the eleventh hour
Along with those who endure the intense heat,
For your inheritance is the reward.
Hallelujah.

*Strophe 25:*
Then, strengthened in the faith, take a stand;
bow down your necks,
And bend your bodies to the earth,
looking up in the spirit of Christ,
Watching eagerly, and hastening
to withdraw from this life;
And dwell in the abode of the holy angels along with them,
So that from there you may shout aloud the song, "Hallelujah."

### 4.8.8  Female founders of monasteries

Women founded monasteries (nunneries) and pursued ascetic lives with the same commitment and zeal as men. Olympias (*c*.361/8–408) came from the highest aristocracy. When her husband died she refused to remarry and devoted her great wealth to the cause of the church. She built a convent in the heart of Constantinople. (See also Chapter 7, Women.)

Sergia, *Narration Concerning Saint Olympias* 1, 4, 5, 9
[Elizabeth A. Clark, "Sergia's Narration," *Jerome, Chrysostom, and Friends: Essays and Translations* (New York: The Edwin Mellen Press, 1979) pp. 145, 147–8, 151]

> Narration of the pious friend of God, the superior Sergia, concerning the holy Olympias. Bless me, father.
>
> 1. We have come into knowledge in intimate detail of matters concerning the inspired and virtuous discipline and way of life of the pious and holy Olympias through previous trustworthy accounts. For the rest, even I myself Sergia the sinner, who through the concession of God was entrusted with the government, that is to say, the superiorship of the undefiled monastery named after her, i.e., Olympias, having received several of these accounts from my

pious mothers and students who died before, wish to pass them on to those succeeding me in the administration of the monastery. Accordingly, I have kept in view the idea of putting this also in the present book for the security and benefit of our souls and so that all men and women may know the tumult which was brought about by sins and, in contrast, the restoration of the present monastery through the grace of God.

4. But after some time, according to God's concession, I, Sergia, an unworthy sinner, received my leadership of the same monastery. There occurred the attack of the godless Persians who burned the monastery of Saint Thomas across from Brochthoi where the precious, awesome remains of the pious Olympias were placed, both the casket itself and her holy remains which had been carried on the waters, as has earlier been made clear . . .

5. I, Sergia, sinful and unworthy, fell into extreme faintheartedness when I learned that because of sins the aforementioned monastery of Saint Thomas had burned. With great haste I reached the spot and collected her holy remains which had been inundated by the waters. The waters in which they there were floating, if you are completely convinced, were filled with blood, so that I, struck down, glorified the benevolent God who shows grace to his saints and works wonders through them while they are alive and after their deaths, the God who glorifies those who glorify him, as Holy Scripture says . . . I Sergia the sinner took and gathered them all together in fear and with great assurance; at the same time I was afflicted with an immeasurable joy and I carried them into the monastery of her servants.

9. Why is it necessary to tell of the healings and miracles of this inspired and virtuous Olympias? For I well know that if I wished to write down in detail her virtues, time would not suffice for the discourse. And I fear lest in the abundance of things I have to say I bore the friends of God who hear and those who read the present book. To put it simply, many other cures took place before the deposition of her holy remains. And up to the present we see these things accomplished in many men, women, and children, both through incredible, manifest apparitions of her and by the authority of her holy remains, as has been said, in those who with a whole soul and a sincere faith call upon her to be granted release from afflictions with the cure for their sufferings.

### 4.8.9 Advice to young nuns

A chaste eroticism fills the advice to young nuns given by Evagrius Ponticus, a monk in the Egyptian desert who lived during the last decades of the fourth century.

Evagrius Ponticus, *Advice to a Young Woman*
[Translated by Susanna Elm]

1. Love your Lord and he will love you; serve him and he will illuminate your heart.
3. Love your sisters as your mother's daughters, and do not forsake the way of peace.

7. Christ is your beloved. Cast all men away from yourself, and you will never lead a life for which you could be reproached.

22. Laughter is shameful and impudence is disgraceful, and every virgin who engages in such things is a fool.

30. Do not say, this is mine and that is yours, for in Jesus Christ everything is held in common.

55. Virgin eyes will see the Lord,
And with their ears will virgins hear his words.
Lips of virgins will kiss their bridegroom,
and the virgin sense of smell will be filled with the scent of his perfume,
With their hands will virgins caress the Lord,
And purity of flesh will be received with honor.
The virgin soul will be garlanded,
And will live with her bridegroom forever.
She will be given a spiritual [baptismal] habit,
And will dance with angels in heaven.
The lamp she lights will never be extinguished,
And the oil in her vessel will not run out.
She will receive eternal riches,
And will inherit the kingdom of God.

### 4.8.10 Monks on a rampage: the destructive side of piety

Because their religious zeal often turned to violence against pagans and pagan shrines, monks earned the hatred of those who did not share their views. In a letter of complaint to the emperor Theodosius, the great Antiochene rhetorician Libanius drew an ugly picture of monks in action. (See *5.4.8*, page 197.)

## 4.9 Liturgy and prayer

### 4.9.1 Celebration of the Eucharist

Elaborate ceremonies of worship in churches developed as communities of the faithful grew in size in Late Antiquity. The Divine Liturgy as celebrated in Constantinople refers specifically to celebration of the Eucharist, the sacrament that symbolizes partaking of the body of Christ.

*The Divine Liturgy* 9.1

[John Clabeaux, "The Eucharist Prayers from *Didache* 9 and 10," in Mark Kiley, ed., *Prayer from Alexander to Constantine: A Critical Anthology* (New York: Routledge, 1997) pp. 263–4]

Now, regarding the Eucharist (Thanksgiving), this is how you are to give thanks:

2. First, regarding the cup:
We thank you, Our Father, for the holy vine of David your Servant, which you have made known to us through Jesus your servant.
– To you be glory forever. –

3.  Then regarding the broken bread:
    We thank you, Our Father, for life and knowledge which you have made known to us through Jesus your servant.
    – To you be glory forever.
4.  Just as this broken (bread) was scattered upon the mountains and, when gathered, became one, so may your church be gathered from the ends of the earth into your kingdom.
    – For yours is the glory and the power forever.
5.  But let no one eat nor drink from your Eucharist but those who have been baptized into the name of the Lord. For about this too has the Lord spoken, "Do not give what is holy to the dogs."

### 4.9.2 Prayers, priests and the people

John Chrysostom's description of the sacrament of the Eucharist illustrates the relation of the priest and the congregation.

John Chrysostom, *On the Second Letter to the Corinthians*, p. 61, xviii, col. 527
[Bishop Kallistos of Dioklea, "Teaching the Faith," in Rosemary Morris, ed., *Church and People in Byzantium* (Birmingham, UK: Center for Byzantine, Ottoman and Modern Greek Studies, 1990) p. 21]

It is not as in the Old Testament, when the priest ate one part of the offering and the people another, and the laity were not allowed to partake from the same part as the priest. But now it is different: one Body is set before us all, and one Chalice . . . Prayers are offered in common by priest and people, and all say the same prayer . . . We all exchange the Kiss of Peace together . . .

The priest prays for the people, and the people pray for the priest; for the words "And with your spirit" mean precisely this. Everything in the Eucharistic thanksgiving is shared in common; for the priest does not offer thanksgiving alone, but the whole people give thanks with him. For after he has replied to their greeting, they then give their consent that "it is just and right", and only then does he commence the Eucharistic thanksgiving.

### 4.9.3 The Akathistos Hymn

According to tradition, the *Akathistos Hymn* (sung with the entire congregation standing) was first sung during the Avar siege of Constantinople in 626. It is addressed to Mary the Mother of God, who was credited with saving the imperial city at this critical time. (See also *12.1.14*, page 341.)

*Akathistos Hymn*, Prooimion
[*The Akathist Hymn and Little Compline* (Akron, OH: Greek Orthodox Clergymen, Sixth Archdiocesan District, n.d.)]

To Thee, the Champion Leader, do I, thy city,
  ascribe thank-offerings of victory!

For thou, O Mother of God, hast delivered me from
  terrors;
But as Thou hast invincible power, do thou
  free me from every kind of danger,
So that to Thee I may cry: Hail, thou Bride unwedded!


## 4.10 Calendars and apocalyptic literature

From the days of the week to grand theories of the shape of history, Christianity attached new meanings to the passage of time and the significance of events. This reconfiguration of time according to Christian beliefs was one of the more far-reaching consequences of the spread of the new faith.


### 4.10.1 No litigation on Sundays

Emperor Constantine established Sunday as a day free from legal business and so invented the weekend:

*Theodosian Code* 2.8.1

> Just as it appears to Us most unseemly that the Day of the Sun (Sunday), which is celebrated on account of its own veneration, should be occupied with legal altercations and with noxious controversies of the litigation of contending parties, so it is pleasant and fitting that those acts which are especially desired shall be accomplished on that day. Therefore all men shall have the right to emancipate and to manumit on this festive day, and the legal formalities thereof are not forbidden. [Constantine, 321]


### 4.10.2 "Anno Domini" – the Christian calendar begins

In the middle of the sixth century, Dionysius Exiguus, a monk in Rome, invented a new way of naming the calendar year. He rejected the Roman system then in use. Instead of dating from the reign of Diocletian, he began from the incarnation of Jesus [anno domini: in the year of our Lord]. Though known to contemporaries, it took several centuries for the "AD" system to take hold.

Dionysius Exiguus, *Letter to Bishop Petronius* (*Patrologia Latina* 67.487)

> I do not want my calculations of Easter to perpetuate the memory of [Diocletian], an impious persecutor of Christians. I prefer to count and denote the years from the Incarnation of our lord Jesus Christ, in order to make the foundation of our hope better known and the cause of human redemption, the passion of our Saviour, more visible.

### 4.10.3 Providential history

The significance of events in providential history was variously interpreted. While Eusebius saw a steady progress toward the end of days marked most recently by Constantine's conversion, Augustine argued in the *City of God* that between the Incarnation and the Day of Judgment anything might happen and the meaning of events would remain uncertain; there was no fixed relationship between the Roman empire and the history of salvation. (See 2.6.2, page 56.)

### 4.10.4 Apocalyptic: the oracle of Baalbek

Apocalyptic visions of the end of time were a feature of Jewish and Christian traditions in Late Antiquity. Apocalyptic narratives enjoyed wide popularity with their combination of prophetic vision and historical narrative. The vision attributed to the Tiburtine Sibyl excerpted below was composed during the reign of the emperor Anastasius (491–518) in Syria near the region of Heliopolis-Baalbek. It combines thinly veiled references to historical figures and events with obscure and fanciful references. The author carries his account to the victory of Jesus over the Antichrist. The apocalyptic genre prospered in Byzantium and the medieval Latin West.

*The Oracle of Baalbek*, lines 136–227

[Paul J. Alexander, *The Oracle of Baalbek. The Tiburtine Sibyl in Greek Dress* (Washington, DC: Dumbarton Oaks Press, 1967) pp. 27–9]

> In the eighth generation there will arise an emperor named after a wild beast [the emperor Leo I, 457–474]. The birth pains of the world begin in his times, earthquakes, drownings of cities and countries, and there will be wars and burnings of cities. Thrace will be laid waste, and there will be no one to administer or to manage the Roman Empire. Taurocilicia will lift high her neck (head). There will arise Scylla, wife of the ruling wild beast, and she will bring forth two wombs, one of which will give birth to a male child; and they will call it by the name of the father. And he too will share the throne with his father of the beastly name and they will have one and the same likeness of earthly kingship. While he is king, an Isaurian will appear [Emperor Zeno, 474–491], and he will be worshipped by his father. And then those men will speak blasphemous words against the nature of the Son. And because of his saying his father will be brought down powerfully from his throne, but the power and domination of the womb will hold sway for fifty-two years. And after that an Isaurian will become king, and he will hate the inhabitants of his city and will flee to his country. And there will arise another king whose name is that of the trailing beast; the name of the beast begins with the letter *beta:* it is Basiliscus [a usurper in 475–476]. And he will speak blasphemy against the highest god, and because of his blasphemy he will be treated scornfully by a woman and will perish, both he and his entire kin. And after that an Isaurian will return to this kingship, except that his kingship is not given (to him) by heaven. His name stands in Roman letters at the end of the alphabet, but is written in Greek

(letters) beginning with the seventh letter (*zeta*) and his name is Greco-Latin [the emperor Zeno]. And his rule will be powerful and will be pleasing to the entire people; he will love the Poor and will humble the Powerful and Rich. And after this there will arise another king from the Western city of Epidamnos, which is (called) in Latin Dyrrhachium. The name of the king is hidden from the Gentiles, but his name resembles the last day (*i.e.* the day of the resurrection or *anastasis*) and begins with the eighteenth letter (*sigma*), but when he seizes his kingship, he will be called Anastasios. He is bald, handsome, his forehead (shines) like silver, he has a long right arm, he is noble, terrifying, high-souled and free (liberal?) and hates all the beggars. He will ruin many from among the people either lawfully or unlawfully and will depose those who observe godliness. And the Persians will arise in his times and will overturn with the sword the cities of the East together with the multitudes of the soldiers of the Roman Empire. And he will be king for thirty-one years.

And after that men will be rapacious, greedy, rebellious, barbarian, they will hate their mothers, and in lieu of virtue and of mildness they will assume the appearance of barbarians. They will raid their own ancestral cities, and there is none to resist their works and deeds; they work their land because of their great avarice. In the ninth generation the years will be shortened like months, and the months like weeks, and the weeks like days, and the days like hours. And two kings will arise from the East and two from Syria, and the Assyrians will be countless like the sand of the sea, and they will take over many lands of the East unto Chalcedonia. And there will be much shedding of blood, so that the blood will reach the chest of horses as it is commingled with the sea. And they will capture and set on fire the cities and despoil the East. And after that another emperor will arise from the East, whose name is Olibos. He will seize the four kings who preceded him and will slay them. And he will grant an exemption from paying a public tax and will restore all the people of the entire East and of Palestine. And after that there will arise another king who has a changed shape and he will rule thirty years and will rebuild the altars of Egypt. And he will wage war upon the king from the East and will kill him and all his army and will seize children from the age of twelve. And people will seize poisonous asps and suck milk from women with new-born babes and draw blood for the sake of the poison of arrows and the violence of wars. Woe to women with child and to those who suckle (their babes) in those days! And the cities of the East will become deserts. And he ("the king who has a changed shape") will be established by the foul nation of the Cappadocians and he will hiss and say: "Was there ever a city here?" And after that there will arise a woman. She will run from the setting to the rising of the sun and will not see a man; and she will long for the track of a man and will not find it. And she will find a vine and an olive-tree and say: "Where is he who planted these?" And she will embrace these plants and give up her spirit, and wolves will eat her. And after that there will arise another king from Heliopolis and he will wage war against the king from the East and kill him. And he will grant a tax-exemption to entire countries for three years and six months, and the earth will bring forth its fruits, and there is none to eat them. And there will come the ruler of perdition, he who is changed, and will smite and kill him. And he will do signs and wonders on earth. He will turn the sun into darkness and the moon into blood. And after that the springs and rivers will dry up, and the Nile of Egypt will be transformed into blood. And the survivors will dig cisterns and will search for the water of life and will not find it. And then there will appear two men who did not come to know the experience of death, Enoch and Elijah, and they will wage war upon the ruler of perdition. And he will say: "My time has come," and he will be angered and slay them. And then he who was crucified on the wood of the cross will come from the heavens, like a great and flashing star, and he will resurrect those two men. And he who was hung on the cross will wage war upon the son of perdition and will slay him and all his host. Then the land of Egypt will burn twelve cubits (deep), and the land will shout to God: "Lord, I am a virgin." And again the land of Judaea will burn eighteen cubits (deep), and the land will shout to God: "Lord, I am a virgin." And then the son of God will come with great power and glory to judge the nine generations. And then Christ will rule, the son of the living God, with his holy angels. Amen, so be it, amen.

### 4.10.5  Arabs in apocalyptic vision

After the initial Islamic conquests, the presence of Arab armies in apocalyptic writing followed naturally. The following excerpt comes from a seventh-century Syriac text which calls Arabs "The Children of Ishmael." (See also Chapter 15, Islam.)

*Apocalypse of Pseudo-Methodius*, "Children of Ishmael," 11.1–15

[*The Seventh Century in the West-Syrian Chronicles*, trans. Andrew Palmer and Sebastian Brock (Liverpool: Liverpool University Press, 1993) pp. 230–3]

> 11.1. In this last millennium, which is the seventh, during which the kingdom of the Persian will be extirpated, the Children of Ishmael will come out from the desert of Yathrib and all come and collect there at Gab 'ot Ramta [Yarmuk River]. 2. And there the word of our Lord will he fulfilled which says, "They resemble the wild animals of the wilderness and the birds of the sky"; and he will summon them, (saying) "Gather and come, for I am going to make a great sacrifice for you today; eat the flesh of fattened (men) and drink the blood of warriors." 3. For in Gab 'ot the fattened – the kingdom of the Greeks – will be devastated. Since they devastated the kingdom of the Hebrews and of the Persians, they too will be devastated at Gab 'ot by Ishmael, "the wild ass of the desert, who will be sent in the fury of wrath against mankind, against wild animals and domestic beasts, against trees and plants." 4. It is a merciless punishment. And these four heads will be sent before them over the whole earth: Destruction and the Destroyer, Devastation and the Devastator, destroying every town that he comes upon, and Devastation which devastates everything. 5. For he said through Moses, "It is not because the Lord your God

loves you that he is bringing you into the land of the Gentiles for you to inherit it, but because of the wickedness of its inhabitants." Similarly with these Children of Ishmael: it was not because God loves them that he allowed them to enter the kingdom of the Christians, but because of the wickedness and sin which is performed at the hands of the Christians, the like of which has not been performed in any of the former generations . . .

8. While I beheld and saw these four heads of punishments, Devastation and the Devastator, Destruction and the Destroyer, they cast lots over the land. 9. The land of the Persians was given to Devastation for him to devastate it, sending its inhabitants to captivity, slaughter and devastation; Syria was given to the sword of Devastation, its inhabitants to captivity and to slaughter; 10. Sicily was given to Destruction and to the sword, and its inhabitants to captivity and to slaughter; 11. Hellas was given to the sword of Devastation, and its inhabitants to captivity and to slaughter; the Roman empire was given to Devastation and to the sword, and its inhabitants to flight, plunder and captivity; the Islands of the (Aegaean) Sea were given to flight, and their inhabitants to captivity and destruction. 12. Egypt and Syria, and the regions of the Orient, shall be put under the yoke of tribute and taxation – seven times worse than the affliction of those in captivity. 13. The Promised Land will be filled with people from the four winds of heaven – like locusts gathering in a storm; there shall be famine there and affliction and plague. The Devastator shall grow strong and his horn will be raised: he will ride in exaltation and be wrapped in pride until the time of wrath. He will seize the entrances to the North, the roads of the East, and the crossings of the Sea . . . He will take a capitation tax from orphans, from widows, and from holy men. 15. They will have no mercy on the poor, nor will they give judgment to the afflicted; they will treat the old roughly and grieve the spirit of the oppressed. They will not spare the sick, or show mercy to the weak; rather, they will laugh at the wise, mock at lawgivers, and jeer at men of understanding. The veil of silence will be spread over all mankind, and all the inhabitants of the earth will live in stupor and in death-pangs. Their wisdom is from them and in them. The insignificant will be accounted as important, the despicable as someone of honour. Their words will cut as though with swords, and no one will be able to alter the argument of their words.

## 4.11 Reading the Bible

### 4.11.1 Translating the Bible

Augustine wrote a letter to Jerome in 403, discussing the difficulties of using different translations of the Bible:

Augustine, *Letter* 71

[Roy Deferrari, ed., *Saint Augustine: Letters*, vol. 1, trans. Sister Wilfrid Parsons, *The Fathers of the Church*, vol. 12 (New York: Fathers of the Church, 1951) pp. 325–7]

In this letter I add what I have since learned, that you have translated the Book of Job from the Hebrew, although we have had for some time your translation of that Prophet, rendered into Latin from the Greek tongue, wherein you have marked by asterisks what is found in the Hebrew version but not in the Greek and by obelisks what is found in the Greek but not in the Hebrew, with such extraordinary care that in some places we see stars appended to single words, indicating that these words are in the Hebrew but not in the Greek version. But, in this later translation, which is made from the Hebrew, there is not the same authority for the words, and it rouses no little disquiet when one wonders why in the former translation the asterisks are placed with such care as to show even the most insignificant parts of speech which are lacking in the Greek texts, but are found in the Hebrew, while in the later one, taken from the Hebrew, less care is shown in assigning these particles to their places. I should like to give you an example of this, but at the moment I have no text from the Hebrew. However, as you surpass me in quickness of mind, I think you understand not only what I say, but even what I want to say, and you can clear up what troubles me as if the case had been presented.

For my part, I would rather you translated the Greek Scriptures to us as they are presented in the Septuagint. It will be very difficult if they begin to read your translation more commonly in many churches, because the Latin churches will differ from the Greek, and especially because an objector is easily refuted by producing a Greek book, as that is the best known language. But, if anyone is disturbed by an unusual passage translated from the Hebrew, and claims that it is wrong, seldom or never is there an appeal to the Hebrew to sustain the passage challenged. Even if there were, who would allow so many Latin and Greek authorities to be overruled? In addition to this, Hebrew experts could conceivably give different answers, and you would then seem to be the sole indispensable critic to convince them, and I doubt that you could find any experts with that judge.

There was a certain brother bishop of ours who decided to read your translation in the church over which he presided, and he caused a sensation by some passage from the Prophet Jonas, which was very different from the version enshrined in the memory and hearing of all and sung for so many generations. There was such a disturbance made among the people by the Greeks arguing and stirring up passions with the charge of falsity, that the bishop – it was in the city of Oea – was forced to call on the testimony of the Jews. Was it through ignorance or malice that they answered that what the Greeks and Latins said and maintained was found in the Hebrew texts? To make a long story short, the man was forced to correct an apparently wrong statement, not wishing to run the great risk of remaining without a flock. After this, it seems to us that you, also, among others, can be wrong, and you see the sort of thing that can happen when a text cannot be corrected by comparison with the familiar languages.

## 4.11.2 Pope Gregory explains the Bible

In one remarkably long sentence, Pope Gregory I (*c*.540–604) describes his under-standing of what the Bible is and how it affects readers.

Pope Gregory I, *Moralia* 20.1.1

[*Gregory the Great*, trans. John Moorhead (London: Routledge, 2005) p. 49]

Although holy scripture incomparably transcends all knowledge and teaching, so that there is no need for me to say that it preaches the truth, that it issues a summons to the heavenly country, that it turns the heart of someone who reads it from earthly desires to embracing the things which are above, that it provides the strong ones with exercise in its obscure sayings and treats the little ones gently in its lowly speech, that its meaning is neither so inaccessible as to instill fear nor so obvious as to be held in contempt, that use of it takes away any dislike and that, the more it is meditated upon, the more it is loved, that it helps the mind of its reader with lowly speech and lifts it up with lofty meanings, that in some sense it grows with those who read it, that, while it can to some extent be investigated by ignorant readers, the learned can nevertheless always find it new, so, to say nothing about the importance of its subject matter, it nevertheless transcends all kinds of knowledge and teachings by the very way in which it says things, because in one and the same mode of discourse the piece of material it presents expresses a mystery, and it knows how to speak of the past in such a way as to be able to predict the future by the same subject, and without changing its way of speaking it knows how to describe things which have happened and to announce things which should be done in the same language, just as is the case with these very words of blessed Job, who, in speaking of his affairs, speaks of ours in advance, and in making his own griefs known in speech, gives voice through its meaning to the circumstances of the holy church.

## 4.11.3 Teaching the Bible through paintings in church

Paulinus of Nola, a Gallic aristocrat, churchman, and writer (*c*.354–431), spent the last half of his life in a monastery in Nola, a town near Naples that was the home of his patron saint Felix. He contributed generously to the construction of churches in the region. In this passage he describes the frescoes newly painted above the interior colonnades in the basilica at Nola. He explains what Bible stories are depicted and how they are meant to instruct illiterate church-goers. (See also *4.6.4* page 144.)

Paulinus of Nola, *Carmina* XXVII, 512–95

[Caecelia Davis-Weyer, *Early Medieval Art, 300–1150, Sources and Documents* (Toronto: University of Toronto Press in association with the Medieval Academy of America, 1986) pp. 18–19]

Now I desire thee to see the paintings on the porticoes decorated with a long series and to take the light trouble of bending thy neck backwards, taking stock of everything with head thrown back. He who on seeing this recognizes Truth from the idle figures, feeds his faithful spirit with a by no means idle image. For the painting contains in faithful order everything that ancient Moses wrote in five books.

Therefore it seemed to us useful work gaily to embellish Felix' houses all over with sacred paintings in order to see whether the spirit of the peasants would not be surprised by this spectacle and undergo the influence of the coloured sketches which are explained by inscriptions over them, so that the script may make clear what the hand has exhibited. Maybe that, when they all in turn show and reread to each other what has been painted, their thoughts will turn more slowly to eating, while they saturate themselves with a fast that is pleasing to the eyes, and perhaps a better habit will thus in their stupefaction take root in them, because of the painting artfully diverting their thoughts from their hunger. When one reads the saintly histories of chaste works, virtue induced by pious examples steals upon one; he who thirsts is quenched with sobriety, the result being a forgetting of the desire for too much wine. And while they pass the day by looking, most of the time the beakers are less frequently filled, because now that the time has been spent with all these wonderful things, but few hours are left for a meal.

## Further reading

Baldovin, John, *The Urban Character of Christian Worship: The Origins, Development, and Meaning of Stational Liturgy* (Rome: Pont. Inst. Studorium Orientalium, 1987)

Brown, Peter, *The Rise of Western Christendom. Triumph and Diversity AD* 200–1000, 2nd edn (London: Blackwell, 2003)

Chadwick, H., *The Church in Ancient Society. From Galilee to Gregory the Great.* (Oxford: Oxford University Press, 2001)

Doran, Robert, *The Lives of Simeon Stylites* (Kalamazoo, MI: Cistercian Publications, 1992)

Drake, H.A., *Constantine and the Bishops: The Politics of Intolerance* (Baltimore, MD: Johns Hopkins University Press, 2002)

Elm, Susanna, *"Virgins of God". The Making of Asceticism in Late Antiquity* (Oxford: Oxford University Press, 1994)

Elsner, Jas and Ian Rutherford, *Pilgrimage in Graeco-Roman and Early Christian Antiquity. Seeing the Gods* (Oxford: Oxford University Press, 2005)

*Encyclopedia of Early Christianity*, ed. Everett Fergusen, 2nd edn (New York: Garland, 1997)

Garnsey, Peter and Caroline Humfress, *The Evolution of the Late Antique World* (Cambridge: Orchard Academic, 2001)

Herrin, Judith, *The Formation of Christendom* (Princeton, NJ: Princeton University Press, 1987)

Klingshirn, William E. and Linda Safran, eds., *The Early Christian Book* (Washington, DC: Catholic University of America Press, 2007)

Lenski, Noel, *The Cambridge Companion to the Age of Constantine* (Cambridge: Cambridge University Press, 2006)

Markus, Robert, *The End of Ancient Christianity* (Cambridge: Cambridge University Press, 1990)

Meyendorff, John, *Imperial Unity and Christian Divisions: The Church, 450–680 AD* (Crestwood, NY: St. Vladimir's Seminary Press, 1989)

Pedersen, Olaf, "The Ecclesiastical Calendar and the Life of the Church," in G.V. Coyne, ed., *Gregorian Reform of the Calendar. Proceedings of the Vatican Conference to Commemorate its 400th Anniversary 1582–1982* (Vatican City, 1983) pp. 17–74 (esp. 49–54)

Rapp, Claudia, *Holy Bishops in Late Antiquity. The Nature of Christian Leadership in an Age of Transition* (Berkeley: University of California Press, 2005)

Rist, John, *Augustine: Ancient Thought Baptized* (Cambridge: Cambridge University Press, 1994)

Van Dam, Raymond, *The Roman Revolution of Constantine* (New York: Cambridge University Press, 2008)

Wimbush, Vincent and Valantasio, Richard with Gay L. Bryon and William S. Love, *Asceticism* (New York: Oxford University Press, 1995)

Young, Frances, *Biblical Exegesis and the Formation of Christian Culture* (Cambridge: Cambridge University Press, 1997)

# 5

# POLYTHEISM

## 5.1 Introduction

In antiquity most people did not identify themselves as followers of a faith. Men and women recognized that divinities of many sorts participated in all aspects of their lives – celebration of their cities' glory and imperial power, setting out on a business trip, having a baby, seeking philosophical enlightenment, or merely enjoying a meal – and they acknowledged these active divine forces however and whenever appropriate. To this extent everyone was "religious." Some individuals might be devotees of a particular god, but the idea of an exclusionary faith that could meet all religious needs had little currency. Monotheistic religions took a different approach. Christianity, which became the dominant religion in the Roman Empire in the course of Late Antiquity, claimed to embrace all of life's activities and defined communities in terms of religious practice. Consequently, Christians created a new group of people, pagans, by lumping together all those who were not Christians (except for Jews and Samaritans). "Pagans" (as they were called in Latin) or "Hellenes" (so called in Greek) constituted a group only in Christian eyes. With the coercive power of the government behind them, Christians forced the end of sacrificing to the old gods and closed their temples. But only when Christian religious practice could provide an alternative voice for all of the great variety of unconnected religious expressions found throughout society did the revolutionary turnabout that we call "the end of paganism" truly occur.

Some obvious turning points mark this transformation of religious sensibility. Constantine's conversion in 312 set the stage for the rapid erosion of non-Christian practice. The formal condemnation of polytheistic worship followed by the end of the fourth century. With the apparatus of the state to enforce legislation against them, polytheists had no chance of long-term survival. Professing Christianity became necessary to pursue public careers at any level. By the sixth century state-sponsored campaigns of forced conversion occurred, especially in the countryside. Similar policies were pursued in the successor states in western Europe, and Islam required that polytheists convert or die.

Because "pagans" were not a unified group, their responses took many forms. Acquiescence to the emerging Christian imperial order was not a matter of course. On the local level violence sometimes erupted against the heavy hand of the Church.

Fierce debates raged in intellectual circles at Rome and elsewhere about the need for tolerance and the historical importance of non-Christian worship to the welfare of the state. The emperor Julian (360–363) even tried to turn back the clock with a revived, synthetic kind of polytheistic worship derivative of Christianity in some ways. Old habits of life died hard, but lords and peasants eventually learned that in most of the important ways the business of getting on every day could continue in a Christian world.

## 5.2 Varieties of religious experience

### 5.2.1 A prayer to Hecate

In order to control his beloved, a man invokes the goddess Hecate, calling her by her many ancient names. This prayer, which might have been spoken at almost any time in the classical period, was preserved in the library of a fourth-century professional magician who lived in Egypt.

*Hymn to Selene–Hecate–Artemis* from a Greek magical handbook
[Christopher A. Faraone, "Hymn to Selene–Hecate–Artemis from a Greek Magical Handbook (*PGM* IV 2714–83)," in Mark Kiley, ed., *Prayer from Alexander to Constantine: A Critical Anthology* (New York: Routledge, 1997) pp. 196–7]

> Hither Hecate, giant who protects Dione, Persian Baubo, Phroune, goddess who pours forth arrows, unwedded Lydian, untamed, of noble father, torch-holder, leader who bends down the necks (of mortals), Kore, hear me, O Artemis, you who have completely closed the gates of unbreakable adamantine and who even before were the greatest overseer, Lady, earth-cleaver, leader of the hounds, subduer of all, worshipped in the streets, three-headed, light-bearing, august virgin, I call you, fawn-slayer, wily lady of the underworld, who appears in many forms.
>
> Hither Hecate, goddess of the crossroads, with your fire-breathing ghosts, you [i.e. the ghosts] who have got as your allotment horrible ambushes and irksome haunts, I call you, Hecate, with those who have died before their time and with those of the heroes, who hissing wildly with anger in their hearts have died without wife or children. You stand above the head and take sweet sleep from her. May her eyelids never be closely joined with each other, but rather let her be worn out over her wakeful thoughts about me. And if she is lying down with another man in her embrace, let her push that man away, let her put me down into her heart and let her immediately forsake him and quickly come stand near my doors, subdued in her soul for my wedding bed.

### 5.2.2 Divination

Attempts to foresee the future took many forms in Late Antiquity, ranging from astrology to opening books (including the Bible) and selecting a random word or passage. The excerpts below represent the casting of lots, a method in which a client

175

went to a diviner and stated his or her concern. Following this interview, the diviner would refer the client to the appropriate grouping of fixed responses (e.g. domestic, emotional, legal, military problems). Then the client would choose at random one of the responses, believing that some supra-human power was directing the choice. Another discussion would follow with the diviner in an attempt to make sense of the response, which could be quite cryptic. A good diviner would help steer the client to drawing conclusions that seemed appropriate. The excerpts below are taken from a divinatory manual dating from the late sixth or early seventh century called the "Lots of St. Gall" because the manuscript now rests in the Abbey Library of St. Gall in Switzerland.

*Sortes Sangallenses* 6, 14, 54, 57–60, 88, 106–7
[Translated by William E. Klingshirn]

### [6. Romantic problems]

VII   Do something else. You will [not be accepted.] You will not remain.
VIII  It will be good for you to receive what you desire, because she loves you with her whole heart.
IX    The woman you want shares your feelings with her whole heart.
X     The woman you want is deceiving you, for she promises herself to many men. Depart from there, foolish man!
XI    The woman you want does not share your feelings.
XII   She greatly shares your feelings and is willing.

### [14. Military problems]

I     You will not be able to go on campaign; beware!
II    Go on campaign with good fortune; you will return victorious.
III   You will not benefit by going on campaign; be careful not to be captured and killed.
IV    Go on campaign with good fortune, for victory is yours.
V     I warn you not to go on campaign.
VI    Go on campaign with good fortune and you will come back a victor with your spoils.
VII   Hurry to the campaign, for you will be very fortunate in victory.

### [54. Legal problems]

I     You will win your lawsuit through a patron. Pray to God.
V     You will have a lawsuit. Ask God that you win it.
VI    You will win your lawsuit through a patron after a long time, but you will be worn out by the expenses.
VII   You will indeed win the lawsuit that you have, but you will be worn out by expenses.

VIII  You will not now win the lawsuit that you have.
IX    You will win the lawsuit, but after a long time.
XII   You will win. . . .

### [57. Work problems]

II    [You are] not in favor with the lord's official.
III   Although you are angry, you are nevertheless arrogant. Therefore you are not in favor.
IV    The lord's official will support you, but not now.
V     When even foreigners (*extranei*) are in favor with the lord's official, do you doubt [that you are]?
VI    The lord's official neither loves nor hates you.
X     They too . . . will be in favor with the lord's official.
XI    You can be secure about the lord's account.

### [58. Slaves' problems]

I     You will be manumitted when you will have served well, but with a lawsuit.
II    Through a friend and your [good] behavior you will quickly be manumitted.
III   Be secure. You will be manumitted and you will have a good fate. But take care of everything.
IV    What [is this] to you? You will be manumitted, it is necessary, with a legacy.
V     You will be manumitted, it is necessary; liberty has been granted to you.
IX    You will [not] be manumitted and you will suffer [much].
X     You will not be manumitted now.

### [59. Inheritance problems]

I     You will not receive your mother's inheritance.
II    You will be her heir, because you are loved by your mother.
III   Your mother makes another her heir and you will be very involved in legal proceedings.
IV    You will lose your mother's inheritance through wicked men.
IX    You will not receive your mother's inheritance.

### [60.]

I     You will not receive your father's inheritance.
II    Do not offend your father and you will be his heir.
III   You will receive your father's inheritance, but with a lawsuit.
VIII  [If] your father is about [to die, quickly] see to it that you are his heir.

*[88. Health problems]*

I      You will now escape sickness.
II     You will escape sickness; why are you afraid?
VII    To avoid sickness, call in a physician and pray to God.
VIII   In a short while you will escape the sickness from which you are suffering.
IX     You have [suffered] much and [will lose] your effort; [you will not escape] sickness.

*[106. Children's problems]*

II     Your son does not have the mind for higher learning, but should learn a trade. For this will be beneficial to him and it has been granted to him.
III    Your son will be able to learn a professional skill (*ars*) if he wishes.

*[107. Education]*

I      You will not be able to learn literature more fully.
II     Your son does not have [the mind] for literature.

### 5.2.3 *Oracles*

Seeking to determine the fate of emperors through oracles was a crime. In this passage two aristocrats, Patricius and Hilarius, on trial for plotting against the emperor Valens, describe to their judges how they consulted an oracle.

Ammianus Marcellinus, *History* 29.1.29–32

[*Ammianus Marcellinus*, vol. III, trans. John C. Rolfe (London: Heinemann, 1958) pp. 203, 205, 207]

Hilarius said: "O most honoured judges, we constructed from laurel twigs under dire auspices this unlucky little table which you see, in the likeness of the Delphic tripod, and having duly consecrated it by secret incantations, after many long-continued rehearsals we at length made it work. Now the manner of its working, whenever it was consulted about hidden matters, was as follows. [30.] It was placed in the middle of a house purified thoroughly with Arabic perfumes; on it was placed a perfectly round plate made of various metallic substances. Around its outer rim the written forms of the twenty-four letters of the alphabet were skilfully engraved, separated from one another by carefully measured spaces. [31.] Then a man clad in linen garments, shod also in linen sandals and having a fillet wound about his head, carrying twigs from a tree of good omen, after propitiating in a set formula the divine power from whom predictions come, having full knowledge of the ceremonial, stood over the tripod as priest and set swinging a hanging ring fitted to a very fine linen thread and consecrated with mystic arts. This ring, passing over the designated intervals in a series of jumps, and falling upon this and that letter which detained it, made hexameters corresponding with the questions and completely finished in feet and rhythm, like the Pythian verses which we read, or those given out from the oracles of the Branchidae. [32.] When we then and there inquired, 'what man will succeed the present emperor?', since it was said that he would be perfect in every particular, and the rings leaped forward and lightly touched the two syllables 'the' and 'oh' adding the next letter, then one of those present cried out that by the decision of inevitable fate Theodorus was meant. And there was no further investigation of the matter; for it was agreed among us that he was the man who was sought."

### 5.2.4 The cult of Isis

The writings of Firmicus Maternus, a Sicilian aristocrat of the fourth century, span his conversion to Christianity. Before his conversion he composed a manual of astrology, the *Mathesis*. In his book *The Error of the Pagan Religions,* written after his conversion (*c.*343–347) he attacked divination, polytheistic mythology, and mystery cults. The following passages describe the venerable cults of Attis, a fertility god who promised salvation to his followers, and of Isis, a goddess popular throughout the Mediterranean world who also promised victory over death.

Firmicus Maternus, *The Error of the Pagan Religions* 2.3–6

[Firmicus Maternus, *The Error of the Pagan Religions,* trans. Clarence A. Forbes (Paramus, NJ: Newman Press, 1970) pp. 45–7, 93]

3. The following is the gist of the cult of Isis. Buried in their shrines they keep an image of Osiris, over which they mourn in anniversary lamentations, wherein they shave their heads so that the ugliness of their disfigured polls may show their grief for the pitiful lot of their king. Also they beat their breasts, tear their upper arms, and break open the scars of old wounds, so that the anniversary lamentations may ever renew in their hearts the memory of the death effected by gruesome and pitiable murder. And after performing these rites on set days, next they feign that they are questing for the remains of the mutilated corpse, and rejoice on finding them as if their sorrows were lulled. 4. O wretched mortals, soon to perish! In order to provide each year dismal rites of commemoration for your kings – neglecting the Supreme Deity, who has set all things aright by the guidance of His divine skill – you are wasting both your hope and your life; you are not converted by the splendor of the light revealed to you, nor do you reach for the tokens of liberty regained, nor recognize the gifts to you of the hope of salvation, nor repent and ask pardon for past offenses. 5. Vain is your supposition that this water which you worship is at times of benefit to you. Quite another thing is the water by which human beings are renewed and reborn. This water which you worship every year – why, a different power dries it up by overheating the channels of its veins; or at any rate the calamitous blood of your king befouls it. That water which you scorn is turned to fire and glorified by the power of the Worshipful

Spirit, so that from the water itself the healthiness of salvation, creeping through the old scars of conscience, is infused into those who believe. 6. But in these lamentations and funerals, which in very truth are funerals that once took place, of a body whose remains are still extant today (for the tomb of Osiris still exists in Egypt even today, and people see the remains of his cremated body), their apologists insist on adding a Scientific Theory, saying that Osiris is the seed of growing things, Isis the earth, Typhon heat. And because growing things matured by heat are harvested to support the life of many, thus being separated and taken away from the companionship of the earth, and are sowed again as winter draws near, they maintain that it is the death of Osiris when they store away the produce, and it is the finding of Osiris when growing things, conceived by the fostering warmth of mother earth, again begin to be produced by the annual procreation.

### 5.2.5  The mysteries of Attis

Firmicus Maternus, *The Error of the Pagan Religions* 22
[Firmicus Maternus, *The Error of the Pagan Religions*, trans. Clarence A. Forbes, (Paramus, NJ: Newman Press, 1970) p. 93]

> On a certain night, a statue [of the god Attis] is laid flat on its back on a bier, where it is bemoaned in cadenced plaints. Then when the worshippers have had their fill of feigned lamentation, a light is brought in. Next a priest anoints the throats of all who were mourning, and once that is done he whispers in a low murmur:
>
> Rejoice, O mystai [celebrants of the mystery rites], our god appears as saved!
>
> And we shall find salvation, springing from our woes.

### 5.2.6  Sacrificing a bull to Mithras

Mithras was a widely popular sun god who promised salvation to his followers. These were exclusively men who met in small groups for fellowship and worship. The focal point of the rite was the sacrifice of a bull in a special chamber called a Mithraeum. In the following inscription on an altar found at Rome and dated to 13 August 376, Sextilius Agesilaus Aedesius, an important imperial official, lists his rank in the Mithraic cult along with his other priestly responsibilities.

*Corpus of Latin Inscriptions* 6.510; H. Dessau, *Inscriptiones Latinae Selectae* II 1 (1902) No. 4152
[Frederick C. Grant, *Hellenistic Religions: The Age of Syncretism* (New York: The Liberal Arts Press, 1953) p. 147]

> To the Great Gods, to the Mother of the Gods, and to Attis, the honorable Sextilius Agesilaus Aedesius, the worthy Solicitor in the African court, Imperial Councilor, President of the Supreme Commission on Petitions and

Investigations, Head of the Chancellery, Captain of the Prefects in Spain in all the most important matters, Father of Fathers of the Invincible Sun God Mithras, Hierophant of Hecate, Chief Shepherd of Dionysus, reborn unto eternity through the sacrifice of a bull and a ram – has dedicated the altar, on the Ides of August, while our Lords Valens, for the fifth time, and Valentinian the younger, the Augusti, were consuls.

### 5.2.7 *The art and effects of prayer*

The Neoplatonic philosopher Iamblichus (*c.*250–*c.*325) describes the importance of prayers in religious rites.

Iamblichus, *On the Mysteries* 5.26

[Iamblichus, *On the Mysteries*, in Frederick C. Grant, *Hellenistic Religions: The Age of Syncretism* (New York: The Liberal Arts Press, 1953) pp. 175–6]

Since prayers are by no means the least part of sacrifice, but instead contribute something that is essential to its completion and thus supply to the whole rite its power and its effect, [and] since, moreover, they serve to enhance the general reverence for God and create a sacred, indissoluble bond of fellowship with the gods, it seems not inappropriate to say a few words upon the subject. Moreover, it is a subject that is worth knowing about in and for itself; further, it completes our knowledge of the gods. I therefore affirm that the first kind of prayer is that which brings [God and man] together, since it brings about the association with the divine and gives us the knowledge thereof. The second establishes a bond of fellowship founded upon like-mindedness and calls down gifts sent by the gods, which arrive before we can ask for them and perfect our efforts even without our knowledge. The third and most perfect form finally seals the secret union, which hands over every decision privately to the gods and leaves our souls completely at rest in them.

In these three stages, which embrace all that is divine, prayers gain for us harmonious friendship of the gods and also a threefold advantage from the gods: the first has to do with illumination, the second with fellowship in a common task, the third with the state of being filled with the [divine] fire. Sometimes this precedes the sacrifice; sometimes it interrupts the sacred rite; sometimes it comes as its conclusion.

No sacral act can be effective without the supplication of prayer. Steady continuance in prayer nourishes our mind, enlarges the soul for the reception of the gods, opens up to men the realm of the gods, accustoms us to the splendor of the divine light, and gradually perfects in us [our] union with the gods, until at last it leads us back to the supreme heights. Our mode of thinking is drawn gently aloft and implants in us the spirit of the gods; it awakens confidence, fellowship, and undying friendship [with them]; it increases the longing for God; it inflames in us whatever is divine within the soul; it banishes all opposition from the soul, and strips away from the radiant, light-formed spirit everything that leads to generation; it creates good hope and trust in the light. In brief, it gives to those who engage in it intercourse with the gods.

### 5.2.8 The importance of sacrifice

Sacrifice was an essential part of most cultic worship in the Roman Empire. In these passages the Neoplatonist writer Sallustius describes the importance of sacrifice in Neoplatonic terms. Some scholars identify Sallustius as Saturninius Secundus Salutius, a close friend of the emperor Julian.

Sallustius, *Concerning the Gods and the Universe* 15, 16

[Sallustius, *Concerning the Gods and the Universe*, trans. Arthur Darby Nock (Hildesheim: Georg Olms, repr. 1966) pp. 29, 31]

> 15. These considerations settle also the question concerning sacrifices and the other honours which are paid to the gods. The divine nature itself is free from needs; the honours done to it are for our good. The providence of the gods stretches everywhere and needs only fitness for its enjoyment. Now all fitness is produced by imitation and likeness. That is why temples are a copy of heaven, altars of earth, images of life (and that is why they are made in the likeness of living creatures), prayers of the intellectual element, letters of the unspeakable powers on high, plants and stones of matter, and the animals that are sacrificed of the unreasonable life in us. From all these things the gods gain nothing (what is there for a god to gain?), but we gain union with them.

> 16. I think it worth while to add a few words about sacrifices. In the first place, since everything we have comes from the gods, and it is just to offer to the givers first fruits of what is given, we offer first fruits of our possessions in the form of votive offerings, of our bodies in the form of hair, of our life in the form of sacrifices. Secondly, prayers divorced from sacrifices are only words, prayers with sacrifices are animated words, the word giving power to the life and the life animation to the word. Furthermore, the happiness of anything lies in its appropriate perfection, and the appropriate perfection of each object is union with its cause. For this reason also we pray that we may have union with the gods. So, since though the highest life is that of the gods, yet man's life also is life of some sort, and this life wishes to have union with that, it needs an intermediary (for objects most widely separated are never united without a middle term), and the intermediary ought to be like the objects being united. Accordingly, the intermediary between life and life should be life, and for this reason living animals are sacrificed by the blessed among men to-day and were sacrificed by all the men of old, not in a uniform manner, but to every god the fitting victims, with much other reverence. Concerning this subject I have said enough.

### 5.2.9  Worship in the countryside

Pre-Christian rites held on tenaciously in the countryside. Called "magic" and "devil worship" by church authorities, these forms of worship proved hard to root out. Maximus of Turin (after 405) describes the humble places of pagan religious practice.

Maximus of Turin, *Sermon* 107

[J.N. Hillgarth, ed., *Christianity and Paganism, 350–750: The Conversion of Western Europe* (Philadelphia: University of Pennsylvania Press, 1986) p. 56]

> If you entered a rustic shrine you would find there bleaching sods [the remains of a turf altar] and dead coals, a worthy devil's sacrifice when a dead god is worshiped with dead things. And if you went into the fields you would see wooden altars and stone images, suitable to a rite in which insensible gods are served at moldering altars. If you woke up earlier than you usually do you would see a rustic reeling with wine. You ought to know that he is what they call either a devotee of Diana [that is, an epileptic or one who is moonmad] or a soothsayer . . .

### 5.2.10  The end of the Secular Games

Zosimus, a historian of the late fifth century who was hostile to Christianity, felt certain that the end of the Secular Games, which had been celebrated for centuries, spelled ruin for the Roman Empire.

Zosimus, *New History* 2.7

[Zosimus, *New History*, trans. Ronald T. Ridley (Canberra: Australian Association for Byzantine Studies, 1982) p. 28]

> Therefore, as the oracle truly says, while all this was observed according to direction, the Roman empire was safe and Rome remained in control of virtually all the inhabited world, but once this festival was neglected after Diocletian's abdication, the empire gradually collapsed and was imperceptibly barbarised. The facts themselves show this, as I will prove from chronology. From the consulship of Chilo and Libo (204), when Severus celebrated the Secular Games, until Diocletian for the ninth time and Maximian for the eighth were consuls (304), one hundred years elapsed. Maximian wanted to celebrate the festival then, contrary to rule, but next year Diocletian became a private citizen instead of emperor and Maximian followed his example. When Constantine and Licinius were in their third consulship (313), the period of one hundred and ten years had elapsed and they ought to have kept up the traditional festival. By neglecting it, matters were bound to come to their present unhappy state.

### 5.2.11  Manichaeism

Manichaeism was an important religion of Late Antiquity that mixed Iranian, Jewish, and Christian beliefs. Its founder, Mani, a third-century Parthian prince, and prophet of the Forces of Light, offered his followers liberation from the Forces of Darkness. This Manichaean prayer was written in the early fourth century in Greek and was found in Egypt. Its forthright polytheism indicates that Christianity was not yet in ascendance.

*Prayer of the Emanations*

[Iain Gardner and Samuel N.C. Lieu, *Manichaean Texts from the Roman Empire* (Cambridge: Cambridge University Press, 2004) pp. 195–6]

> I worship and glorify the great Father of Lights from pure thought. With a guileless word you have been glorified and honoured: You and your majesty and the wholly blessed aeons. For you in glory have perfected their foundation. Your power and glory and your light and word and your majesty and the aeons of affirmation and all your counsel have been glorified. For you are God, the foundation of every grace and life and I worship and glorify all gods, all angels, all splendours, all luminaries, all powers: Those which are from the great and glorious father, those which subsist in his holiness, and in his light are nourished, purified from all darkness and malignance.
>
> I worship and glorify the great powers, the enlightening angels: Those, having advanced by their own wisdom and having subjected the darkness and its remorseless powers which were prepared to fight with the ruler of all; these are those who created heaven and earth and bound in them all the substance of contempt.
>
> I worship and glorify the offspring of the greatness, the enlightening mind, king and Christ: The one who came forth from the outer aeons into the upper creation, and from that to this lower creation; and having incomparably announced his wisdom and the ineffable mysteries to people on earth, and having displayed to the entire universe the way of truth, and having preached with all voices, and having distinguished truth from the lie and light from darkness and good from evil and the just from the wicked. From you every grace has become known to the universe, and life together with truth to every tribe has been interpreted with all voices. He himself has become for living souls the redeemer from the obligation of the inimical bonds.
>
> I worship and glorify the living God, virtuous and true: The one who, by his own power, raised up all things, this arrangement above and below.
>
> I worship and glorify the great luminaries, both the sun and the moon and the virtuous powers in them: Which by wisdom conquer the opponents and enlighten the entire arrangement, and of all observe and judge the world and conduct the victorious souls into the great aeon of light.
>
> I worship and glorify the five great lights: Through which the entire universe came into existence, and through which heaven and earth and through which by participation power and beauty and soul and life are present in all. And without these the universe could not exist.
>
> I worship and glorify all gods, all angels, the living and pure: Who support this whole creation with the permission of the great and virtuous light, who rules over all those now singing these hymns.

I worship and glorify all the enlightening angels: Who dominate the totality of the universe, and subject all demons and all evil, shielding righteousness and guarding it from the wicked demons and growing the good in it.

I worship and glorify all the righteous: Those who escape from all evil, those who both have existed before, exist now, are coming into existence and are ready to come into existence because they have recognised truth and all pre-eminence; the chaste and firm, in order that all those whom I have worshipped and glorified and invoked may assist me and bless me with favour and may deliver me from every bond and all constraint and oppression and every reincarnation, and provide me with access to the great aeon of light which all the wise and upright in knowledge hope to attain, where peace and the purest of the good rule, where there is no perception of evil but ambrosia and eternal life are present, where all the inhabitants are without any need and experience neither death nor corruption.

Blessed be he who prays this prayer frequently, or at least on the third day, with a pure heart and forthright speech, asking for forgiveness of sins committed.

The Prayer of the Emanations is ended.

### 5.2.12  *Imperial edict against Manichaeism*

The Roman and Persian governments persecuted Manichaeans. Diocletian issued the following edict probably in 296 in an effort to strengthen the traditional Roman religious cults. (See also *4.4.3*, page 121.)

*Comparison of Mosaic and Roman Law* 15.3

[Napthali Lewis and Meyer Reinhold, eds., *Roman Civilization*, vol. II, *Selected Readings. The Empire* (New York: Columbia University Press, 3rd edn, 1990) pp. 548–50]

The Emperors Diocletian and Maximian, August, and Constantius and Maximian, most noble Caesars, to Julianus, proconsul of Africa. Excessive idleness, my dear Julianus, sometimes drives people to join with others in devising certain superstitious doctrines of the most worthless and depraved kind. In so doing, they overstep the bounds imposed on humans. Moreover, they lure on many others to accept the authority of their erroneous doctrine.

But the immortal gods in their providence have deigned to dispose and arrange matters so that good and true principles should be approved and fixed by the wisdom and constant deliberation of many good, eminent, and very wise men. These principles it is not right to oppose or resist, nor ought the age-old religion be disparaged by a new one. For it is the height of criminality to re-examine doctrines once and for all settled and fixed by the ancients, doctrines which hold and possess their recognized place and course. Wherefore it is our vigorous determination to punish the stubborn depraved minds of these most worthless people.

We take note that those men concerning whom Your Sagacity has reported to Our Serenity, namely the Manichaeans, have set up new and unheard-of sects in opposition to the older creeds, with the intent of driving out to the benefit of their depraved doctrine what was formerly granted to us by divine Favor. We have heard that these men have but recently sprung up and advanced, like strange and unexpected portents, from the Persian people, our enemy, to this part of the world, where they are perpetrating many outrages, disturbing the tranquility of the peoples and also introducing the gravest harm to the communities. And it is to be feared that peradventure, as usually happens, they may try, with the accursed customs and perverse laws of the Persians, to infect men of a more innocent nature, namely the temperate and tranquil Roman people, as well as our entire Empire with what one might call their malevolent poisons. And since, as Your Sagacity has set forth in your report on their religion, all types of offenses against the statutes have very plainly been devised and falsehoods contrived, we have accordingly established for these people afflictions and deserving and condign penalties.

Now, therefore, we order that the founders and heads be subjected to severe punishment: together with their abominable writings they are to be burned in the flames. We instruct that their followers, and particularly the fanatics, shall suffer a capital penalty, and we ordain that their property be confiscated for our fisc [imperial treasury]. But if indeed any office-holders or persons of any rank or distinction have gone over to a hitherto unheard of, disgraceful, and wholly infamous sect, particularly to the creed of the Persians, you shall cause their estates to be added to our fisc, and the persons themselves to be sent to the Phaenensian or Proconnesian mines.

In order, then, that this plague of iniquity may be extirpated by the roots from this most happy age of ours, Your Devotion shall carry out with despatch the orders and enactments of Our Tranquility.

## 5.3  Suppression of polytheism

### 5.3.1  Roman legislation against polytheist practices

The following selection of laws issued in the fourth and fifth centuries by different emperors were kept in the *Code of Justinian*, issued in 534. The laws demonstrate the steady suppression of pagan worship. Making sacrifices was singled out as proof positive of pagan practice. Emperors took care to permit popular festivities not tainted by overtly pagan ritual.

Justinian, *Code* I.11.1–2, 4–7; *Theodosian Code* 16.10.4, 9, 17, 20, 24
[*The Civil Law*, trans. S.P. Scott (Cincinnati, OH: Central Trust, 1932) pp. 79–81]

CONCERNING THE PAGANS, THEIR SACRIFICES, AND THEIR TEMPLES.

1. We have determined that the temples shall be immediately closed in all cities, and access to them forbidden to all, so that permission for further offending may be refused to those who are lost. We also wish everyone to abstain from sacrifices, and if any person should do anything of this kind, he shall be laid low with the avenging sword; and We decree that his property, after having been taken from him, shall be confiscated to the Treasury, and that the Governors of provinces shall also be punished, if they have neglected to suppress these crimes. [Constantius, 354: *Theodosian Code* 16.10.4]

2. Let no mortal have the audacity to make sacrifices, and by the inspection of the liver of the victim, and by presages, obtain the hope of vain promise, or (which is even worse), endeavor to ascertain the future by means of a detestable consultation; for he will be liable to an even more severe punishment who, in opposition to what has been forbidden attempts to ascertain the truth of present or of future events. [Valentinian and Theodosius, 385: *Theodosian Code* 16.10.9]

[. . .]

4. As we have already abolished profane rites by a salutary law, We do not permit the common joy of all to be destroyed by abolishing the festive assemblies of the citizens; wherefore, We decree that the pleasures and convivial festivals of the people shall be conducted in accordance with the ancient customs, when the public wishes demand it, but that no sacrifices shall be offered, and no damnable superstition be observed. [Arcadius and Honorius, 399: *Theodosian Code* 16.10.17]

5. We order that all those places which the error of the ancients destined for sacred ceremonies shall be united with Our demesnes, and that such of them as, under any title whatsoever, the generosity of preceding Emperors or our Own Majesty has bestowed upon any private individuals shall forever form part of their estates; but that any property which, by various Constitutions, We have decreed shall belong to our venerated Church, the Christian religion shall very properly claim for itself. [Honorius and Theodosius, 415: *Theodosian Code* 16.10.20.1]

6. We especially direct those who are really Christians, or are said to be such, not to presume to employ any violence against Jews or Pagans who live quietly, and do not attempt to cause trouble, or perform any illegal acts; for if, abusing the authority of religion, they should display any violence against them, or plunder them of their property, when convicted they shall he compelled to restore not only what they took, but also double the value of the same; and the Governors of provinces and other officials and principal authorities are hereby notified that (if they do not punish offences of this kind, but permit them to be committed by the populace) they themselves will be subjected to punishment. [Honorius and Theodosius, 423: *Theodosian Code* 16.10.24.1]

7. No one, for the purpose of reverence or worship, shall reopen the temples of the Pagans, which have already been closed, in order that the honor which was formerly shown to their idols and their infamous and execrable rites may be removed from our age; for it is held to be sacrilege instead of religion to adorn the impious portals of shrines with garlands; to kindle profane fires on the altars; to burn incense upon the same; to slaughter victims there, and to pour out libations of wine from bowls. Anyone who attempts to perform sacrifices contrary to this Our decree, and against the prohibition of the most sacred ancient constitutions, can be lawfully accused of the crime before any judge, and, if convicted, shall suffer the confiscation of all his property, and the extreme penalty, and the accomplices of the crime as well as the ministers of the sacrifices shall undergo the same penalty to which he was sentenced; so that, terrified by the severity of this Our law, they may desist from celebrating forbidden sacrifices through the fear of punishment. If, however, the most illustrious Governor of the province as well as the judge himself, when the accusation has been lawfully made and the crime established, should, after proper examination, neglect to punish an offence of such gravity, they shall each immediately be compelled to pay fifty pounds of gold into Our Treasury. [Valentinian and Marcian, 451]

## 5.3.2  Christian resentment of pagan sacrifice

In a furious letter to a pagan notable, Shenute of Atripe, a fifth-century Egyptian abbot, describes how the public might be victimized by pagan priests.

Shenute, *Open Letter to a Pagan Notable*
["Shenute as a Historical Source," trans. John Barnes, in Jozef Wolski, ed., *Actes du X<sup>e</sup> Congrès International de Papyrologues, Varsovie/Cracovie 3–9* (September 1961) pp. 156–8]

Who shall be able to enumerate all your misdeeds? How you people slaughter your calf, because it is moribund or rejected as unfit for your work, and divide it up just as you please, and foist it upon them, even upon the widows, the old men and women, the orphans and the strangers, exacting exorbitant sums of money from them till you amass twice the price the calf was worth for wretched meat which is nothing but bones and worthless stuff. And again, how you people give them calves and cows to rear, distributing them among the holdings till they are full grown, and then take them, making some of them give them to you as gifts and giving no benefits in return, and making others of them maintain them for you; you do the same with horses and donkeys and sheep and calves and pigs. I wish you were content with that. For any whose cattle or any other goods you covet, you people seize them from them, some for no payment at all, some for some trifling price; to say nothing of bread and wine, and fodder and hay and barley for your beasts, and all the rest. And how you round them up to keep guard for you on the ships on the occasions when you are running away from the barbarians . . .

### 5.3.3 Destroying the temples

Zachariah, bishop of Mitylene (died after 536), describes how ancient statues of gods were publicly mocked and destroyed by churchmen, state officials and the public working in concert.

Zachariah, bishop of Mitylene, *Life of Severus* 27–35

[Walter E. Kaegi, "The Fifth Century Twilight of Byzantine Paganism," *Classica et Mediaevalia* (1966) 27, 1, pp. 252–3]

> We brought back their priest as well as their idols. It was possible for us, with God's aid, to capture him also. We had laden twenty camels with various idols even though we already had burned some at Menouthis, as we said. We brought them into the middle of the city on the orders which we received from the great Peter. He immediately convoked before the Temple of Fortune the Prefect of Egypt, commanders of the bodies of troops, and all those who were invested with some public duty, as well as the senate, the great men and the proprietors of the city. When he had sat down with them, he had the priest of the idols brought forth and ordered him to remain standing in a certain elevated place. Then, after the idols had been exhibited, he began to interrogate him. He asked him what this idolatry meant which was used on lifeless matter, ordered him to give the name of all of the demons and to tell what was the cause and the form of each of them. At that moment all of the people already had come to see. He listened to what was said and then mocked the infamous actions of the pagan gods which the priest revealed. When the altar of bronze had arrived together with the wooden serpent, the priest confessed the sacrifices which he had dared to complete, and declared that the wooden serpent was the One which had deceived Eve. He held this in effect, he said, by tradition from the first priests. He swore that the pagans adored the serpent. It was then delivered to the flames, along with the other idols. One could then in some manner hear all the people cry: "There is Dionysos the hermaphrodite god! There is Kronos who hated children! There is Zeus, the adulterer and lover of youths! This is Athena, the virgin who loved war, this is Artemis the huntress and enemy of strangers. Ares, that demon, made war and Apollo is the one who caused many people to perish. Aphrodite presided over prostitution. There was one among them who cared for theft. As for Dionysos, he protected drunkenness. And here among them is the rebel serpent! Among their number there are yet dogs and monkeys and moreover, families of cats, for these equally were Egyptian gods."

### 5.3.4 Churches built on pagan sites: the temple of Zeus Marnas in Gaza

Sometimes a church was erected on the site where a temple to earlier gods had stood. The main temple in the city of Gaza was the temple of Zeus Marnas. Wealthy citizens maintained it in open defiance of the law. Because of the rich taxes these notables paid regularly, the emperor hesitated for several years to close the shrine. After several years of hard lobbying, Porphyrius, the bishop of Gaza, persevered and the temple of Zeus Marnas (the Marneion) was destroyed in 402. When the resulting riots were put down, a great new Christian church was built on the spot. Attributed to "Mark the Deacon," the text below was actually composed in several stages and took its final form in the 450s.

Mark the Deacon, *Life of Porphyry* 75–6, 78
[Cyril Mango, *The Art of the Byzantine Empire, 312–1453* (Englewood Cliffs, NJ: Prentice-Hall Inc., 1972) pp. 30–2]

> 75. After the Marneion had been completely burnt down and the city been pacified, the blessed Bishop together with the holy clergy and the Christian people determined to build a church on the burnt site in accordance with the revelation he had had while he was at Constantinople: it was for this purpose that he had received money from the most pious empress Eudoxia . . . Some persons urged that it should be built on the plan of the burnt temple . . . As for the holy Bishop, he said, "Let us leave this, too, to the will of God." And while the site was being cleared, there arrived a special courier with imperial letters of Eudoxia of eternal memory. These letters contained greetings and a request for prayers on behalf of herself and of the Emperors, her husband and her son. On another sheet enclosed in the letter was the plan of the holy church in the form of a cross, such as it appears today by the help of God; and the letter contained instructions that the holy church be built according to this plan. The Holy Man rejoiced when he had read the letter and seen the plan . . . Furthermore, the letter announced the dispatch of costly columns and marbles.
>
> 76. When the ashes had been dug out and all the abominations removed, the holy Bishop ordered that the remaining debris from the marble revetment of the Marneion – these, they said, were sacred and pertained to a place into which access was forbidden, especially to women – would be used for paving the open space in front of the church so that they might be trodden on not only by men, but also by women, and dogs, and pigs, and cattle . . .
>
> 78. The holy Bishop had engaged the architect Rufinus from Antioch, a dependable and expert man, and it was he who completed the entire construction. He took some chalk and marked the outline of the holy church according to the form of the plan that had been sent by the most pious Eudoxia. And as for the holy Bishop, he made a prayer and a genuflection, and commanded the people to dig. Straightaway all of them, in unison of spirit and zeal, began to dig crying out, "Christ has won!" . . . And so in a few days all the places of the foundations were dug out and cleared.

### 5.3.5  *Saint Nicholas chops down sacred trees*

Saint Nicholas of Sion began his holy career destroying the sacred trees long worshiped before the advent of Christianity in his homeland Lycia, in Asia Minor. This sixth-century life contributed to the cult of the earlier Saint Nicholas of Myra, the original Santa Claus.

*The Life of Saint Nicholas of Sion* 15, 16, 18
[Ševčenko, Ihor and Nancy Patterson Ševčenko, *The Life of Saint Nicholas of Sion* (Brookline, MA: Hellenic College Press, 1984) pp. 35, 37, 39]

15. One day there came men from the village of Plakoma, who fell down before holy Nicholas and said: "O servant of God, on our land there is a sacred tree in which dwells the spirit of an unclean idol, that destroys both men and fields . . . we are unable to go unhindered about our business on account of it. May Your Holiness yield to our entreaties and deign to come with us and fell it, so that God, Lover of mankind, may through your prayers drive out the unclean spirit dwelling in that tree, and the fields and the district may be at peace and find respite."

16. Being so strongly urged by the inhabitants of the village of Plakoma, Nicholas, the servant of God, offered prayers, and came to the spot where the tree stood. Seeing the tree, holy Nicholas said: "Is this the sacred tree?" In response, the men of the aforementioned fields said to him: "Yes, Lord." And Nicholas the servant of God said: "What are those gashes in the tree?" They said to him: "Some man of old came to fell the tree with two hatchets, and an axe. And as he began to fell it, the unclean spirit snatched away the blades, and slaughtered the man, so that his grave was found at the roots of the tree." Offering prayers, the servant of God Nicholas – there being a crowd of nearly three hundred men, women and children to watch the workings of God, for none believed that such a tree, being sacred, was about to be felled – then the servant of God Nicholas knelt and prayed for two hours. And rising, he enjoined the men around saying: "In the name of our Lord Jesus Christ and of Holy Sion, come here, try and cut it down."

18. When he was about to fell this sacred tree, the servant of God said: "Assemble with one accord up the slope on the North side." For it was expected that the tree would fall to the West. The unclean spirit thought at that moment to frighten the crowd. And he made the tree lean toward the North, up the slope where the crowd stood watching, so that they all screamed with fear in one voice, saying: "Servant of God, the tree is coming down on top of us, and we will perish." The servant of God Nicholas made the sign of the cross over the tree, pushed it back with his two hands, and said to the sacred tree: "In the name of my Lord Jesus Christ I command you: turn back [in the other direction] and go down where God has ordained you." Forthwith, the tree swayed back by the will of God and moved toward the West, where it crashed. From that time on, the unclean spirit was no longer seen within those parts. And they all glorified God, saying: "One is God, who gave power to his servant against the unclean spirits."

### 5.3.6 *"Pagan" residues*

In a sermon of 451, Pope Leo (440–461) complained of the continuity of pagan habits even among practicing Christians.

Pope Leo I, *Sermon* 27.4

[*St. Leo the Great: Sermons*, trans. Jane Patricia Freeland and Agnes Josephine Conway (Washington, DC: The Fathers of the Church, Catholic University of America Press, 1996) p. 113]

> 4. From such customs as this has the following godlessness been engendered, where the sun – as it rises at daybreak – would be worshipped from the higher elevations by certain sillier people. Even some Christians think that they behave devoutly when, before arriving at the basilica of the blessed Apostle Peter (which has been dedicated to the one living and true God), they climb the steps which go up to the platform on the upper level, turn themselves around towards the rising sun, and bow down to honor its shining disk.
>
> This thing, done partly through the fault of ignorance and partly in a spirit of paganism, eats away at me and grieves me very much. Even if some of these perhaps revere the Creator of this beautiful light rather than the light itself, still we must refrain from even the appearance of this homage. When someone who has left behind the worship of the gods finds this among us, will they not bring this aspect of their former persuasion along with them, thinking it credible – upon having seen it to be something that both Christians and unbelievers hold in common?

### 5.3.7 *Non-religious festivals suppressed*

Festivals which even the relentless emperor Justinian (527–565) permitted to be celebrated as harmless occasions of public recreation were eventually proscribed in the sixty-second Canon of the Council "in Trullo" in Constantinople in 691–692. The Bota festival commemorates Pan, the protector of flocks. The Brumalia is the cult festival of Dionysus, the god of wine, and celebrates the final stage of winemaking. The Kalends festival lies in the first ten days of January and celebrates the winter solstice, and the Panegyris marks the end of the worst of winter weather.

Council "in Trullo" (691–692), Canon 62

[Frank Trombley, "The Survival of Paganism in the Byzantine Empire during the Pre-Iconoclastic Period (540–727)" (Dissertation, UCLA, 1981) p. 118]

> We wish the so-called Kalends, the so-called Bota, the so-called Brumalia and the *panegyris* festival celebrated on the first day of March to be removed completely from the way of life of believers. We reject the public dances of women which can cause great destruction and harm, still more the dances and rites done by men and in the name of those which are falsely called gods among the pagans, according to a certain custom ancient and alien to the way of life of Christians. We consequently define that no man dress himself in feminine garb nor a woman in that suitable to a man, nor wear comic, satiric, or tragic masks,

nor cry out the name of the abominable Dionysos while crushing the grapes in vats, nor provoke to laughter those who pour wine into jars: for they effect demonic error in the manner of ignorance or folly. We decree that those who attempt to celebrate any of the aforesaid cults, if they stand in knowledge of them, be deposed if clerics, suffer excommunication if laymen.

## 5.4 Difficulties of conversion

### 5.4.1 Neither pagan nor Christian

Converting the millions of people living in remote areas posed a great challenge. Sometimes the process of conversion stretched over several generations. Simeon the Mountaineer, a holy man who traveled to mountain villages east of the Euphrates, met people whose acquaintance with Christianity was limited but whose curiosity about it was strong.

John of Ephesus, *Life of Simeon the Mountaineer*

[John of Ephesus, *Lives of the Eastern Saints*, ed. E.W. Brooks (*Patrologia Orientalia* 17, 1923) pp. 234–6]

> He said to them, "And have you not heard the Scriptures, my children?" They answered, "We have heard about them from our fathers but the Scriptures themselves we have not seen" . . . He said to them, again: "Is it only you, my children, who are in this condition, or are all who are living on the mountains the same?" They said to him, "Sir, it is not only we who are so, but there are men on these mountains, who, unless they have heard from their fathers who carried them to church and had them baptized, do not know what a church is. And this same thing happens now also to those who have children born to them; on their account they go into a church and have them baptized; otherwise none of us has entered a church since he was born; but we live on the mountains like animals." Simeon replied, "You are unaware even of what Christianity is." And having spoken with them and warned them, he left them and departed . . . Then he reconsidered and he said in his heart as if from God, "Perhaps it was indeed for this reason that God's grace led me to the mountains here, in order that there may be salvation for these souls that are in the darkness of error . . ."

### 5.4.2 Tell your peasants what to do

At the end of the sixth century, Pope Gregory the Great (590–604) encouraged aristocratic landowners in Italy to convert their peasants.

Pope Gregory the Great, *Letter* 423

[Jeffrey Richards, ed., *Consul of God: The Life and Times of Gregory the Great* (London: Routledge, 1980) p. 236]

> I have learned from the report of my brother and fellow bishop Felix and my son the servant of God Cyriacus that nearly all of you have peasants on your

estates given to idolatry. And this has greatly saddened me because I know that the guilt of subjects weighs down the life of their superiors, and that, when sin in a subject is not corrected, the sentence rebounds on the master. Wherefore, my magnificent sons, I exhort that with all care and solicitude you be zealous for your souls and see what account you will render to Almighty God for your subjects. For indeed, they have been committed to you for this end, that they may serve for your advantage in earthly things and you, through your care for them, may provide for their souls in the things that are eternal. If then, they pay what they owe you, why do you not pay them what you owe them? That is to say, your Greatness should assiduously admonish them, and restrain them from the error of idolatry, so that by their being drawn to the faith you may make Almighty God propitious to yourselves.

### 5.4.3  Conversion, class, and coercion

Class distinctions inevitably affected the level of coercion thought appropriate in forcing conversion, as seen in this letter of Pope Gregory (599).
Pope Gregory the Great, *Letter* 9.204
[Jeffrey Richards, ed., *Consul of God: The Life and Times of Gregory the Great* (London: Routledge, 1980) p. 235]

> We vehemently exhort your fraternity to maintain your pastoral vigilance against idol-worshippers and soothsayers and magicians; to preach publicly among the people against the men who do such things and recall them by persuasive exhortation from the pollution of such sacrilege and from the temptation of divine judgment and peril in the present life. If, however, you find them unwilling to change their ways, we desire you to arrest them with a fervent zeal. If they are slaves, chastise them with blows and torments to bring about their correction. But if they are free men, let them be led to penitence by strict confinement, as is suitable, so that they who scorn to listen to words of salvation which reclaim them from the peril of death, may at any rate by bodily torments be brought back to the desired sanity of mind.

### 5.4.4  Mass conversions as imperial policy

John of Ephesus, who undertook missions of mass conversion on behalf of the emperor Justinian, describes in his *Ecclesiastical History* the fate of cults in Anatolia.
John of Ephesus, *Ecclesiastical History* (fragment)
[Frank R. Trombley, "Paganism in the Greek World at the End of Antiquity: The Case of Rural Anatolia and Greece," *Harvard Theological Review* 78 (1985) 3–4, pp. 327–52, here 333]

> In the year 542 the kindness of God visited Asia, Caria, Lydia, and Phrygia, thanks to the zeal of the victorious Justinian and by the activity of his humble servant John of Ephesus [John of Asia] . . . When God opened the minds of the

194

pagans and made them know the truth, he aided us in destroying their temples, in overturning their idols, in eradicating the sacrifices which were offered everywhere, in smashing their altars defiled by the blood of sacrifices offered to pagan gods, and in cutting down the numerous trees which they worshipped, and so they became estranged from all the errors of their forefathers. The saving sign of the cross was implanted everywhere amongst them, and churches of God were founded in every place.

### 5.4.5  Purge of intellectuals at Constantinople

In the same text, John of Ephesus describes a purge of intellectuals in Constantinople conducted by Justinian's agents in 546. While some of the individuals may have in fact still worshiped forbidden gods, it is as likely that the trials used the accusation of "paganism" to eliminate opponents of the regime. Under Justinian classical culture came under attack as religious attitudes became more intolerant of activities that were not cast in explicitly Christian terms.

John of Ephesus, *Ecclesiastical History* (fragment)
[F. Nau, "Analyse de la seconde partie inédite de l'Histoire ecclésiastique de Jean d'Asie," *Revue de l'Orient Chrétien* 2 (1897) pp. 481–2]

> In the nineteenth year of Justinian's reign (546), I was very deeply involved in the affair of the pagans discovered at Constantinople. These were illustrious and noble men, as well as a large group of grammarians, sophists, teachers, and doctors. After they were discovered and tortured they rushed to denounce one another; some were beaten, others flogged or put in prison, some turned over to the church where they accepted the Christian faith after admitting their false belief. They included patricians and nobles among their number. A rich and powerful man named Phocas, who was a patrician, was arrested. Since he knew that the men already apprehended had denounced him as a pagan, and since he knew that a severe judgment had been rendered against him because of the fervor of the emperor, he swallowed a deadly poison during the night and died. When the emperor heard of this, he rightly ordered that Phocas be buried like a donkey and that there be no funeral for him and no prayers offered for him. So Phocas' family collected him during the night on a cart and carried him to an open grave where they threw him like a dead animal.

### 5.4.6  Polytheists fight back

With different degrees of sophistication and force, non-Christians of different sorts resisted attacks against them. When the emperor Honorius forbade idol worship in 399 a crowd of Christians destroyed a statue of Hercules in the North African town of Sufes. In a violent counterattack, pagan citizens killed sixty Christians in revenge. Augustine, bishop of Hippo, sternly rebuked the leading citizens of Sufes.

Augustine, *Letter* 50
[*Saint Augustine, Letters*, trans. Sister Wilfrid Parsons, *The Fathers of the Church*, vol. XII (New York: Fathers of the Church, 1951) p. 237]

> Augustine, bishop, to the leaders and chiefs or elders of the colony of Sufes: The infamous crime and unspeakable cruelty of your savagery shakes the earth and strikes the heavens, when blood flows and murder cries aloud in your streets and shrines. By you Roman law is buried, respect for upright judges is trampled under foot; and among you there is surely neither respect nor fear for the emperors. The innocent blood of sixty brothers has been shed among you, and, if anyone killed more, he enjoyed praise and held high position in your government. Let us come, now, to the chief cause. If you say Hercules is yours, we will restore him; there is bronze, there is no lack of stone, there are several kinds of marble, and a supply of artisans is at hand. So, then, your god is carved carefully, he is smoothed off, and adorned; we add red clay to paint him red, so that your prayers may have the true ring of sacredness. For, if you say that Hercules is your god, we can take up a collection from everybody and buy you a god from the stone-cutter. You give us back the lives which your fierce hand wrested from us, and your Hercules will be restored to you exactly as the lives of so many are given back by you.

### 5.4.7 *Julian the Apostate and the Antiochenes*

Though raised as a Christian, Julian (a great-nephew of Constantine) was a devotee of traditional cults. While emperor (360–363) he attempted to suppress Christianity and revive worship of the old gods. His *Hymn to King Hellos* (see *11.1.5*, page 314) illustrates his sophistication as a religious thinker. The citizens of the empire, however, did not always take him seriously. For example, when he sought to rekindle enthusiasm for the old gods in Antioch, famous in antiquity for its temples and pagan worship, the crowds mocked him.

Ammianus Marcellinus, *History* 22.14.3
[*Ammianus Marcellinus*, vol. II, trans. John C. Rolfe (Cambridge, MA: Harvard University Press, 1958) pp. 273–5]

> For he was ridiculed as an ape; as a dwarf spreading his narrow shoulders and displaying a billygoat's beard, taking mighty strides, as if he were the brother of Otus and Ephialtes, whose height Homer describes as enormous. He was also called by many a slaughterer instead of high priest, in jesting allusion to his many [sacrificial] offerings; and in fact he was fittingly criticized because for the sake of display he improperly took pleasure in carrying the sacred emblems in place of the priests, and in being attended by a company of women. But although he was indignant for these and similar reasons, he held his peace, kept control of his feelings, and continued to celebrate the festivals.

## 5.4.8 Angry at the monks

In his angry speech "For the Temples," composed in 386 and addressed to the emperor Theodosius, Libanius, the great pagan orator of Antioch, wrote a scathing denunciation of Christian violence toward the worship of the old gods. He singles out monks, the "black-robed tribe," as ringleaders of the violence. His argument that traditional worship benefited the state fell on deaf ears. (See also *4.8.10*, page 163.)

Libanius, *Oration* 30 8–11, "For the Temples"

[*Libanius: Selected Works*, vol. 2, trans. A.F. Norman (Cambridge, MA: Harvard University Press, 1977) pp. 107–13]

> But this black-robed tribe, who eat more than elephants and, by the quantities of drink they consume, weary those that accompany their drinking with the singing of hymns, who hide these excesses under an artificially contrived pallor – these people, Sire, while the law yet remains in force, hasten to attack the temples with sticks and stones and bars of iron, and in some cases disdaining these with hands and feet. Then utter desolation follows, with the stripping of roofs, demolition of walls, the tearing down of statues and the overthrow of altars, and the priests must either keep quiet or die. After demolishing one, they scurry to another, and to a third, and trophy is piled on trophy, in contravention of the law.
>
> 9. Such outrages occur even in the cities, but they are most common in the countryside. Many are the foes who perpetrate the separate attacks, but after their countless crimes this scattered rabble congregates and calls for a tally of their activities, and they are in disgrace unless they have committed the foulest outrage. So they sweep across the countryside like rivers in spate, and by ravaging the temples, they ravage the estates, for wherever they tear out a temple from an estate, that estate is blinded and lies murdered. Temples, Sire, are the soul of the countryside: they mark the beginning of its settlement, and have been passed down through many generations to the men of today.
>
> 10. In them the farming communities rest their hopes for husbands, wives, children, for their oxen and the soil they sow and plant. An estate that has suffered so has lost the inspiration of the peasantry together with their hopes, for they believe that their labour will be in vain once they are robbed of the gods who direct their labours to their due end. And if the land no longer enjoys the same care, neither can the yield match what it was before, and if this be the case, the peasant is the poorer and the revenue jeopardized, for whatever a man's willingness, surely his inability frustrates him.
>
> 11. So the outrages committed by these hooligans against the estates bear upon vital matters of state. They claim to be attacking the temples, but these attacks are a source of income, for, though some assail the shrines, others plunder the wretched peasantry of what they have, both the produce stored from the land and their stock; and the invaders depart with the loot from the places they have stormed. Others are not satisfied with this but they appropriate the land too, claiming that what belongs to this or that body is temple property and many a man has been robbed of his family acres on this false title . . .

### 5.4.9  Obstacles to travel

In his *Life of Porphyry, Bishop of Gaza*, the author known as Mark the Deacon describes the obstacles to travel caused by angry villagers on a short trip in Gaza in 395.

Mark the Deacon, *Life of Porphyry, Bishop of Gaza* 17
[Marc Le Diacre, *Vie de Porphyre: Évêque de Gaza*, trans. Henri Grégoire and M.A. Kugener (Paris: Société d'Édition "Les Belles Lettres," 1930) p. 15]

> Two days later we set out. We slept the first night in Diospolis, and the next day, very late in the day we reached Gaza, after a lot of toil and trouble, thoroughly exhausted and irritated. This is the reason for our annoyance. All along the road, not far from Gaza we reached some villages where they still worship idols. There, by a prearranged signal, the villagers covered the entire road with brambles and logs, entirely blocking our passage. They also scattered filth on the road, a burning mix of foul matter. With their unhealthy odor the fumes nearly suffocated us and practically prevented us from seeing. We escaped with great difficulty and arrived in the city in the third hour of the night. These were the attacks of the devil against the holy man. But he (the holy man) was not disturbed because he knew that there went the ambushes of the devil who wished to prevent him from entering the city.

### 5.4.10  Resistance in North Africa

In North Africa in 408, Augustine records continued polytheistic practice in the face of the Church and imperial law.

Augustine, *Letter* 91
[*Saint Augustine, Letters*, vol. II, in *The Fathers of the Church*, vol. 18, trans. Sister Wilfrid Parsons (New York: Fathers of the Church, 1951) pp. 47–8]

> Contrary to the recent laws of June 1, an idolatrous worship was carried out at a pagan festival, without interference from anyone, and with such insolent daring that a most wanton band of dancers came into the neighborhood of the church and even to the very doors, something which had not happened in the times of Julian. When the clerics tried to put a stop to this most lawless and unseemly performance, the church was stoned. Then, about a week later, when the bishop had called the attention of public authority to these very well-known laws, and while the latter were making a semblance of enforcing the edicts, the church was stoned again. The next day, when ours were powerless to impose fear, as it seemed, and when they wished to make a public protest, they were refused their rights. Then came a hail of stones, but the offenders were so far from being frightened by celestial prodigies that, as soon as it was over, they at once engaged in a third stoning; and finally threw fire on the church roofs, and on men. They killed one of the servants of God, who lost his way and ran into them. Of the rest, some hid wherever they could, and some ran away wherever they could, and when the bishop had hidden himself, crowded and squeezed

into a certain place, he heard their voices calling for his death, and upbraiding him because they could not find him, and were thereby prevented from committing a further crime. This went on from the tenth hour until late in the night. Not one of those whose authority could have prevailed tried to restrain them; not one tried to help the victims, except one stranger who rescued several servants of God from the hands of those who were trying to kill them, and recovered a good deal of property from looters. From his act it is quite clear that it would have been easy to prevent these happenings entirely, or to stop them at the beginning, if the citizens, and especially the officials, had forbidden them to be done or to be continued.

### 5.4.11 The Altar of Victory dispute

In 382 the Christian emperor Gratian ended the period of official toleration of traditional religious practice. Government funding of public non-Christian religious ceremonies stopped, and pagan priests lost their exemption from public duties. A huge outcry arose in Rome when he ordered that the Altar of Victory be removed from the Senate house, where it had stood since the reign of Augustus. Senators swore allegiance to new emperors and regularly made offering at this altar. Gratian's act prompted an eloquent but unsuccessful plea for religious tolerance from the pagan aristocrat Symmachus who was the Prefect of the city of Rome in 384. He writes to the new emperor Valentinian II.

Symmachus, *Official Dispatch* 3.8–10
[Brian Croke and Jill Harries, *Religious Conflict in Fourth-Century Rome* (Sydney: Sydney University Press, 1982) pp. 37–8]

> 8. Everyone has their own custom, their own ritual. The divine purpose assigned different cults to different cities to protect them. Just as souls are given to men at birth, so nations are allotted a genius to preside over their destiny. There is also the question of services rendered, man's strongest argument for the existence of gods. For, as all reason moves in the dark over this, how can man gain greater recognition of the divine powers than from his recollection and factual proof of success? For if religions gain in authority from the passage of many years, we must keep faith with all the centuries we have known and follow in the footsteps of our fathers who followed their own with such good fortune.
> 9. Let us now imagine that the figure of Rome stands before you and addresses you thus: "Best of princes, father of your country, respect my length of years which pious observation of my ritual has ensured me. Let me employ the rites my ancestors used, for they are not a matter of regret. Let me live my own way, since I am free. Through this worship I brought the whole world under the rule of my laws, these sacred objects drove Hannibal from our walls, the Gauls from the Capitol. Have I been preserved then only to be reproached now for living so long?"

10. I will see what kind of reforms should be considered for implementation; yet correction of old age comes late and brings humiliation.

Therefore we ask that the gods of our fathers, our native gods, be left in peace. It is reasonable that all the different gods we worship should be thought of as one. We see the same stars, share the same sky, the same earth surrounds us: what does it matter what scheme of thought a man uses in his search for the truth. Man cannot come to so profound a mystery by one road alone. But such matters are for men at leisure to debate; we offer you now not arguments but prayers.

## Further reading

Ando, Clifford, *The Matter of the Gods. Religion and the Roman Empire* (Berkeley: University of California Press, 2008)

Chuvin, Pierre, *Chronicle of the Last Pagans*, trans. B.A. Archer (Cambridge, MA: Harvard University Press, 1990)

Flint, Valerie I.J., *The Rise of Magic in Early Medieval Europe* (Princeton, NJ: Princeton University Press, 1991)

Geffcken, Johannes, *The Last Days of Greco-Roman Paganism*, trans. S. MacCormack (trans. 1978 of 1929 edn, New York: Elsevier North-Holland)

Klingshirn, W.E., "Christian Divination in Late Roman Gaul: The *Sortes Sangallenses*," in *Mantikê: Studies in Ancient Divination*, ed. Sarah Iles Johnson and Peter T. Struck (Leiden: Brill, 2005) pp. 99–128

Matthews, Thomas F., *The Clash of Gods. A Reinterpretation of Early Christian Art* (Princeton, NJ: Princeton University Press, 1993)

Rives, J.B., *Religion and Society in Roman Carthage, Augustus to Constantine* (Oxford: Oxford University Press, 1995)

Rüpke, Jörg, *A Companion to Roman Religion* (Malden, MA: Blackwell Publishing, 2007)

Salzman, Michele, *The Making of a Christian Aristocracy. Social and Religious Change in the Western Roman Empire* (Cambridge, MA: Harvard University Press, 2002)

Tougher, Shaun, *Julian the Apostate* (Edinburgh: Edinburgh University Press, 2007)

Trombley, Frank, *Hellenic Religion and Christianization c.370–529*, 2 vols (Leiden: Brill, 1993–94)

# 6

# JEWS

## 6.1 Introduction

The emergence of Christianity as the Roman state religion in the course of the fourth century transformed the status of Jewish communities within the empire. No longer just an internal provincial population that had recovered from several unsuccessful rebellions against Rome in the first three centuries AD, Jews as the people of the Bible acquired a significance in Christian theology of the state. A Christian providential scheme of history placed on Jews responsibility for the death of Jesus, and the steady decline of their condition within the empire followed. From the fourth century Roman laws discriminated against Jews in a variety of ways. A notable exception was their right to remain members of the curial class – with all the financial burdens that the status entailed. Autonomous leadership of Jews as one group within the state ended in 429 when the position of Nasi, or Patriarch, ceased to be filled and the Roman state absorbed Jewish taxes that had been earmarked for the Patriarch. Each Jewish community continued to administer its own affairs under the leadership of rabbis. These men were not priests with a sacred function to perform, but experts in religious law.

Outside the empire legally sanctioned marginalization of Jews continued in the successor states in western Europe in the fifth century and later. Better conditions prevailed in Sasanian Persia, however, where the large Jewish community in Mesopotamia flourished. Jewish support of Persian kings and the significant presence of Jewish troops in the Persian army was noted by Procopius in the sixth century. In south Arabia and Ethiopia Jewish polities steadily lost ground. With the arrival of Islam in the seventh century, Jews, as fellow People of the Book, found themselves in a protected but inferior position within the new Islamic states.

The Jewish community transformed internally in the Late Antique period as well. The completion of the Mishnah (the final organization and transcription of a text of the Oral Law) by the end of the third century and the production of the Jerusalem and Babylonian Talmuds (commentaries on the Oral Law) by the end of the fourth and fifth centuries respectively marked the full emergence of rabbis and their courts at the center of community life. These leaders took measures to insulate and protect their communities. Women were not required to study the Law and did not have formal authority to interpret the Scripture or to acquire highly prized religious knowledge. Rabbinic texts legitimized their exclusion from these activities, as it also did their subordination to men in their traditional roles as daughters, wives, and mothers. Evidence from inscriptions, however, indicates that women sometimes served as leaders in some synagogues in this period when synagogue worship was developing.

## 6.2 Discrimination against Jews in Roman law

The following selection of laws issued from the fourth to the sixth centuries represents some of the measures taken to limit the legal rights and freedom of action of Jews and to penalize Christians who associated with them. Though the form and method of issuance of the laws conforms to standard Roman practice, the content of each is influenced by Christian belief. Many of them were compiled first in the Theodosian Code and kept in the Code of the emperor Justinian, demonstrating continuity of imperial policy regarding Jews. All of these laws were applicable throughout the empire.

### 6.2.1 *Jews may not circumcise Christian slaves*

*Theodosian Code* 16.9.1 [Justinian, *Code* 1.10.1]

1. If any Jew should purchase and circumcise a Christian slave or a slave of any other sect whatever, he shall not retain in slavery such circumcised person. But the person who endured such treatment shall obtain the privilege of freedom. [Constantine, 336]

### 6.2.2 *Jews and Christians may not marry one another*

*Theodosian Code* 3.7.2 [Justinian, *Code* 1.9.5]

2. No Jew shall receive a Christian woman in marriage, nor shall a Christian man contract a marriage with a Jewish woman. For if any person should commit an act of this kind, the crime of this misdeed shall be considered as the equivalent of adultery, and freedom to bring accusation shall be granted also to the voices of the public. [Valentinian, Theodosius, and Arcadius, 388]

### 6.2.3 *Christians may not become Jews*

*Theodosian Code* 16.8.7 [Justinian, *Code* 1.7.1]

In accordance with the venerable law which has been established, We command that if any person should be converted from Christianity to Judaism and should join their sacrilegious gatherings, when the accusation has been proved, his property shall be vindicated to the ownership of the fisc. [Constantius and Julian, 357]

### 6.2.4  Trials in Jewish courts

While Jews were permitted to refer matters of religious law to their rabbis (as all peoples in the empire were allowed to follow their customary laws), in all other matters they were bound by Roman law and obliged to settle their disputes before a Roman judge. If both parties agreed, and it was a civil matter, the case might be tried in Jewish courts.

*Theodosian Code* 2.1.10

> Jews who live under the Roman and common law shall approach the courts in the customary manner in those cases which concern not so much their superstition as the forum, the statutes, and the law; and they shall bring and defend all actions according to the Roman law; that is to say, they shall be subject to Our laws. Certainly, in the case of civil suits only, if any Jews should suppose that, by a mutual promise to abide by the decision in accordance with the agreement of both parties, they should litigate before Jews or patriarchs as though before arbitrators, they shall not be prohibited by public law from choosing the judgment of such men. The judges of the provinces shall execute their sentences as if such arbitrators had been assigned by the decision of a judge. [Honorius, 398]

### 6.2.5  Jews allowed in municipal senates

Municipal senates played such an important role in the administration of the empire (especially as tax collectors) that Jews were not excluded from them. This law of Constantine even permitted some exemptions to Jews.

*Theodosian Code* 16.8.3

> 3.  By a general law We permit all municipal senates to nominate Jews to the municipal council. But in order that something of the former rule may be left them as a solace, We extend to two or three persons from each group the perpetual privilege of not being disturbed by any nominations. [Constantine, 321]

### 6.2.6  Should translations of the Bible be used in synagogue worship?

Justinian's *Novel 146*, issued in 553, intervened in a Jewish dispute about the language of worship in synagogues. Jewish religious authorities preferred Hebrew to be the sole liturgical language, but many of their congregations preferred a currently spoken language, such as Latin or Greek, which they could more easily understand. Justinian decided that any language might be used in the Jewish liturgy, regardless of the wishes of Jewish authorities. The law forbade the use of the Mishnah by Jews, on the grounds that it was not a divinely inspired interpretation of the Bible.

Justinian, *Novel* 146, Preamble
[A. Linder, *The Jews in Roman Imperial Legislation* (Detroit, MI: Wayne State University Press, 1987) p. 408]

> It was right and proper that the Hebrews, when listening to the Holy Books, should not adhere to the literal writings but look for the prophecies contained in them, through which they announce the Great God and the Savior of the human race, Jesus Christ. However, although they have erred from the right doctrine till today, given as they are to senseless interpretations, when we learned that they dispute among themselves we could not bear to leave them with an unresolved controversy. We have learned from their petitions, which they have addressed to us, that while some maintain the Hebrew language only and want to use it in reading the Holy Books, others consider it right to admit Greek as well, and they have already been quarreling among themselves about this for a long time. Having therefore studied this matter we decided that the better case is that of those who want to also use Greek in reading the Holy Books, and generally in any language that is the more suited and the better known to the hearers in each locality.

### 6.2.7 Discrimination in church law

Church councils also established restrictions on Jews. The following were issued by a church council at Elvira, Spain, *c.*300. They unwittingly reveal a closeness between Christians and Jews in everyday activities that church officials wished to do away with.

Elvira Church Council, *Canons* 16, 49, 50
[Jacob R. Marcus, ed., *The Jew in the Medieval World. A Source Book: 315–1791* (New York: Athenaeum, 1972) pp. 101–2]

> *Canon* 16. Christian girls may not be married to infidels
> The daughters of Catholics shall not be given in marriage to heretics, unless these shall submit themselves to the Catholic church; the same is also decreed of Jews . . . since there can be no communion of one that believeth, with an infidel. And if parents transgress this command, they shall be excommunicated for five years.
>
> *Canon* 49. Jews may not bless the crops of Christians
> Landholders are to be admonished not to suffer the fruits, which they receive from God with the giving of thanks, to be blessed by the Jews, lest our benediction be rendered invalid and unprofitable. If any one shall venture to do so after this interdiction, let him be altogether ejected from the Church.
>
> *Canon* 50. Concerning Christians who eat with Jews
> If any person, whether clerical or one of the faithful, shall take food with the Jews, he is to abstain from our communion, that he may learn to amend.

### 6.2.8 Imperial protection of the Jewish community: synagogues and property rights

Not all legislation discriminated against Jews. Emperors also bore time-honored responsibility to protect the rights of their subjects. The following laws represent imperial efforts to ensure that Jewish property rights and customs were protected.

*Theodosian Code* 16.8.20 [Justinian, *Code* 1.9.10.13]

> 16.8.20  If it should appear that any places are frequented by assemblies of the Jews and are called by the name of synagogues, no one shall dare to violate or to occupy and retain such places, since all persons must retain their own property in undisturbed right, without any claim of religion or worship.
>
> 1.  Moreover, since indeed ancient custom and practice have preserved for the aforesaid Jewish people the consecrated day of Sabbath, We also decree that it shall be forbidden that any man of the aforesaid faith should be constrained by any summons on that day, under the pretext of public or private business, since all the remaining time appears sufficient to satisfy the public laws, and since it is most worthy of the moderation of Our time that the privileges granted should not be violated, although sufficient provision appears to have been made with reference to the aforesaid matter by general constitutions of earlier emperors. [Honorius and Theodosius, 412]

### 6.2.9 The State reserves the right of punishment for itself

*Theodosian Code* 16.8.21 [Justinian, *Code* 1.9.10.14]

> No person shall be trampled upon when he is innocent, on the ground that he is a Jew . . . Their synagogues and habitations shall not be burned indiscriminately, nor shall they be injured wrongfully without any reason, since, moreover, even if any person should be implicated in crimes, nevertheless, the vigor of Our courts and the protection of public law appear to have been established in Our midst for the purpose that no person should have the power to seek his own revenge.
>
> But just as it is Our will that the foregoing provision shall be made for the persons of the Jews, so We decree that the Jews also shall be admonished that they perchance shall not become insolent and, elated by their own security, commit any rash act in disrespect of the Christian religion. [Honorius and Theodosius, 412]

### 6.2.10 Ambrose challenges the emperor: the Callinicum affair

In 388 the destruction of a synagogue at Callinicum, a town on the Euphrates, by a Christian mob led by a local bishop resulted in a confrontation between Ambrose, the influential bishop of Milan, and the emperor Theodosius. When the emperor attempted to punish those responsible for breaking the law, Ambrose issued a stiff rebuke and forced the emperor to back down. This shows the growing force of Christian influence upon traditional governing practice. (See also *4.3.2*, page 119.)

Ambrose, *Letter* 40.1, 2, 6, 10, 13, 20, 21

[*Early Latin-Theology: Selections from Tertullian, Cyprian, Ambrose, and Jerome* (*The Library of Christian Classics*, vol. V), trans. S.L. Greenslade (London: SCM Press, 1956) pp. 229, 231–3, 235–6]

Bishop Ambrose to the most gracious prince and most blessed emperor, Theodosius Augustus.

1. My Lord Emperor, although I am constantly harassed by well-nigh unceasing cares, I have never been in such a fret of anxiety as now, when I see how careful I must be not to expose myself to a charge of high treason. I beg you to listen patiently to what I have to say. If I am not fit to have your ear, then I am not fit to make the offering for you or to have your prayers and petitions entrusted to me. You want me to be heard when I pray for you. Will you not hear me yourself? You have heard me pleading for others. Will you not hear me pleading for myself? Are you not alarmed at your own decision? If you judge me unfit to hear you, you make me unfit to be heard for you.

2. An emperor ought not to deny freedom of speech, and a bishop ought not to conceal his opinions. Nothing so much commends an emperor to the love of his people as the encouragement of liberty in those who are subject to him by the obligations of public service. Indeed the love of liberty or of slavery is what distinguishes good emperors from bad, while in a bishop there is nothing so perilous before God or so disgraceful before men as not to speak his thoughts freely . . .

6. The Count of the Eastern forces reported the burning of a synagogue at the instigation of the bishop. You ordered that the others should be punished and the synagogue be rebuilt by the bishop himself. I do not press the point that you should have waited for the bishop's own statement. Bishops check mobs and work for peace, except when they are themselves stirred by wrong done to God or insult offered to the Church. Suppose, however, that the bishop was too zealous in setting fire to the synagogue and suppose he is too timid when called to account. Do you feel no alarm at his acquiescence in your verdict, no apprehension at his fall?

10. So the unbelieving Jews are to have a place erected out of the spoils of the Church? The patrimony acquired by the favour of Christ for Christians is to be made over to the treasury of unbelief? . . .

13. What is your real concern? Is it that a public building of any kind has been set on fire, or specifically a synagogue? If you are concerned at the burning of a building of the cheapest sort (and what else could there be in so obscure a town?), do you not recall, Sir, how many Prefects' houses have been set on fire in Rome without any punishment? . . .

20. Will you give the Jews this triumph over the Church of God, this victory over the people of Christ? Will you give this joy to the unbeliever, Sir, this festival to the synagogue, these sorrows to the Church? The Jews will set this celebration among their feast-days and number it with the days of their triumph over the Amorites and the Canaanites, or the days of their deliverance from Pharaoh, King of Egypt, or from the hand of Nebuchadnezzar, King of Babylon. Now they will add this festival to commemorate their triumph over the people of Christ.

21. They say that they are not bound by the laws of Rome, even regarding the laws as criminal. Yet now they claim to be avenged by Roman law! Where were these laws when they burned the roofs of consecrated churches? If he did not avenge the Church because he was an apostate, will you, Sir, avenge the synagogue's wrongs because you are a Christian?

### 6.2.11 Julian and the temple in Jerusalem

Emperor Julian (361–363), called "the Apostate" because of his rejection of Christianity, in which he had been raised, promised to rebuild the Jewish temple in Jerusalem. He did this not out of fondness for Jews but to embarrass Christians who believed the temple would not be rebuilt until the second coming of Christ. Christians interpreted Julian's death and the failure of his plans to rebuild the temple as proof of the validity of their religion.

Julian, *Letter* 51, "To the Community of the Jews"
[*The Works of the Emperor Julian*, vol. 3, trans. W.C. Wright (New York: G.P. Putnam's Sons, 1923) pp. 177, 179, 181]

In times past, by far the most burdensome thing in the yoke of your slavery has been the fact that you were subjected to unauthorized ordinances and had to contribute an untold amount of money to the accounts of the treasury. Of this I used to see many instances with my own eyes, and I have learned of more, by finding the records which are preserved against you. Moreover, when a tax was about to be levied on you again I prevented it, and compelled the impiety of such obloquy to cease here; and I threw into the fire the records against you that were stored in my desks; so that it is no longer possible for anyone to aim at you such a reproach of impiety . . . And since I wish that you should prosper yet more, I have admonished my brother Iulus [Hillel II, died 365], your most venerable patriarch, that the levy which is said to exist among you [the taxes paid by world Jewry for support of the Palestinian patriarchate] should be prohibited, and that no one is any longer to have the power to oppress the masses of your people by such exactions; so that everywhere, during my reign, you may have security of mind, and in the enjoyment of peace . . . may offer more fervid prayers . . . to the Most High God, the Creator, who has deigned to crown me with his own immaculate right hand . . . This you ought to do, in order that, when I have successfully concluded the war with Persia, I may rebuild by my own efforts the sacred city of Jerusalem which for so many years you have longed to see inhabited, and may bring settlers there, and, together with you, may glorify the Most High God therein.

## 6.3 Christian justification of anti-Jewish behavior

### 6.3.1 What did Jews do wrong in Christian eyes?

Christians blamed Jews collectively for the crucifixion of Jesus and for failing to understand that Jesus' teachings had supplanted those of the Hebrew Bible. From this point of view the Hebrew Bible became the "Old" Testament while the Gospels became the "New" Testament. Here Augustine gives a representative explanation of Jewish guilt.

Augustine, *City of God* 4.34

[*Augustine: City of God*, trans. Henry Bettenson (New York: Penguin Books, 1981) p. 178]

> In fact the Israelites received from the one true God all the blessings for which the Romans thought it necessary to pray to all the hosts of false gods, and they received them in a far happier manner. And if they had not sinned against God by turning aside to the worship of strange gods and of idols, seduced by impious superstition as if by magic arts, if they had not finally sinned by putting Christ to death, they would have continued in possession of the same realm, a realm exceeding others in happiness, if not in extent. If today they are dispersed over almost all the world, amongst almost all the nations, this is part of the providence of the one true God . . .

### 6.3.2 Christian attraction to Judaism is condemned

In big cities like Antioch where Judaism was an old and respected religion, Christian clergymen struggled to break their congregants' attraction to the synagogue. John Chrysostom's shrill attacks speak not only for the close ties maintained between Jews and Christians but also for the tenuous position of the Christian community. The Church was not yet entirely triumphant in late fourth-century Antioch. Chrysostom's sermons had a great influence on medieval anti-Semitism.

John Chrysostom, *Homily Against the Jews* 1.3, 1.5

[Robert L. Wilken, *John Chrysostom and the Jews: Rhetoric and Reality in the Late Fourth Century* (Berkeley: University of California Press, 1983) pp. 79–80, 125]

> 1.3 Three days ago (believe me, I am not lying), I saw a noble and free woman, who is modest and faithful, being forced into a synagogue by a coarse and senseless person who appeared to be a Christian (I would not say that someone who dared to do such things was really a Christian). He forced her into a synagogue to make an oath about certain business matters which

were in litigation. As the woman passed by she kept calling out for help, hoping someone would stop this lawless show of force. Enraged and burning with anger, I roused myself and rescued her from this unjust abduction so that she would not be dragged into such lawlessness. When I asked her abductor whether he was a Christian he admitted he was. I reproached him severely.

1.5  We must return again to the sick. Do you realize that those who are fasting have dealings with those who shouted, "Crucify him! Crucify him!" [Luke 23:21]; and with those who said, "His blood be on us and on our children" [Matt. 27:25]? If a band of would-be revolutionaries were apprehended and then condemned, would you dare to go to them and talk with them? I certainly don't think so! Is it not absurd to be zealous about avoiding someone who had sinned against mankind, but to have dealings with those who affronted God? Is it not folly for those who worship the crucified to celebrate festivals with those who crucified him? This is not only stupid – it is sheer madness.

### 6.3.3  Forced conversion

Some Jews freely accepted Christianity, but many more were forced to do so. Bishop Severus of Minorca proudly tells how the Jews of Magona, a town on his island (off the Mediterranean coast of Spain), were compelled to abandon their faith in 418. Events such as these occurred in many communities throughout the empire when local Christian religious enthusiasm fanned by clergymen erupted into violence against non-Christians.

Severus of Minorca, *Letter on the Conversion of the Jews* 3.6–7, 6.1–4, 13.1–14, 24.1.10, 30. 1–2

[*Severus of Minorca: Letter on the Conversion of the Jews*, ed. and trans. Scott Bradbury (Oxford: Clarendon Press, 1996) pp. 83, 85, 93, 95, 117, 119, 123]

(3.6) Magona seethed with so great a multitude of Jews, as if with vipers and scorpions, that Christ's church was being wounded by them daily. (7) But that ancient, earthly favour was recently renewed for us in a spiritual sense, so that, as it is written, that generation of vipers [Luke 3:7], which used to attack with venomous stings, suddenly under the compulsion of divine power has cast aside the lethal poison of unbelief . . .

(6.1) The Jewish people relied particularly on the influence and knowledge of a certain Theodorus, who was pre-eminent in both wealth and worldly honour not only among the Jews, but also among the Christians of that town [Magona]. (2) Among the Jews he was a teacher of the Law and, if I may use their own phrase, the Father of Fathers. (3) In the town, on the other hand, he had already fulfilled all the duties of the town council and served as defender, and even now he is considered the patron of his fellow citizens. (4) The Christians, however, humble in heart as well as physical strength, yet superior by the force of truth, prayed for the assistance of Stephen, their patron, until the two armies separated, after they had agreed upon a day for their debate and concluded a truce for the present moment . . .

(13.1) Then we set out for the synagogue, and along the way we began to sing a hymn to Christ in our abundance of joy. (2) Moreover, the psalm was "Their memory has perished with a crash and the Lord endures forever" [Psalm 9:7–8], and the throng of Jews also began to sing it with a wondrous sweetness. (3) But before we reached the synagogue, certain Jewish women (by God's arrangement, I suppose) acted recklessly, and, doubtless to rouse our people from their gentleness, began to throw huge stones down on us from a higher spot. (4) Although the stones, marvellous to relate, fell like hail over a closely packed crowd, not only was none of our people harmed by a direct hit, but not one was even touched. (5) At this point, that terrible Lion took away for a short while the mildness from his lambs. (6) While I protested in vain, they all snatched up stones, and neglecting their shepherd's warning, since they were united in a plan suggested more by zeal for Christ than by anger, they decided that the wolves had to be attacked with horns, although no one could doubt that this was done with the approval of Him who alone is the true and good shepherd. (7) Finally, lest it seem that He had granted His flock a bloody victory, not one of the Jews pretended even to have been touched, not even to stir up ill will, as usually happens . . . (12) Therefore, after the Jews had retreated and we had gained control of the synagogue, no one, I won't say, "stole" anything, but no one even considered "looting" anything! (13) Fire consumed the synagogue itself and all of its decorations, with the exception of the books and silver. We removed the sacred books so that they wouldn't suffer harm among the Jews, but the silver we returned to them so that there would be no complaining either about us taking spoils or about them suffering losses. (14) And so, while all the Jews stood stupefied at the destruction of the synagogue, we set out for the church to the accompaniment of hymns and, giving thanks to the author of our victory, we poured forth our tears and beseeched the Lord to lay siege to the true dens of their unbelief and to expose to the light the faithlessness of their dark hearts.

(24.1) Consequently, only three women, although very noble women among the Jews, did Christ permit to hold out a little longer, in order to extend the glory of his power amidst the hardheartedness of their unbelief. (2) Artemisia, the daughter of Litorius, who recently governed this province and who is now said to be a Count, was distraught at the conversion of her husband Meletius. Without any thought for feminine frailty and with just one friend, a nurse, and a few servant girls, she deserted her husband's house and escaped to a cave, which, though located in a vineyard, was none the less in quite a remote spot. (3) In the vineyard, there was a small, new winepress, and a newly-made vat, which seemed somehow to serve as a symbol of a faithful people. (4) For we either believe or can see that the Jews have received the "must" of the New Testament not like "old wineskins", but like "new winevats" [Luke 5:37]. (5) This woman had passed two days in that spot, implacable and angry with her husband. As soon as the third day dawned, she ordered a maidservant to draw water for her so that she could wash her face in her usual way. The water came from the winevat, which was full from a rain shower. When she realized that the water resembled honey in the sweetness of its taste and smell, at first she began to grow angry with the servant and asked indignantly why she had put honey in the pitcher. (6) Afterwards, however, as if to disprove the servant's denials, she went to the vat, drew forth a little water with cupped hands, and found that the water she had been using for two days was changed into the sweetest, most delightful honey. (7) Then she called over all the women present and told them to taste the water, lest by chance a falsely sweet taste was deceiving her throat alone. (8) All of them tasted it and were stirred with such marvellous delight that they decided it was not water infused with honey, but the purest honey with only a resemblance to water. (9) Struck with wonder, they investigated more carefully while they were preparing to return to town and discovered that the dew, which was on much of the grass, also had a similar taste. (10) Accordingly, the previously mentioned lady set out for the town, reported these things to her husband, and through him made them known to everyone, and immediately, without resistance, she assented to faith in Christ . . .

(30.1) All the more joy should be felt at the following marvel, namely that we see the land of the Jewish people, barren for so long, producing manifold fruits of righteousness, now that the thorns of unbelief have been cut down and the seed of the Word implanted, so that we rejoice for ourselves in the hope of new crops. (2) Where we uprooted an infamous forest of unbelief, the most fertile works of faith have flourished. For not only are the Jews bearing the expense, first, for levelling the very foundations of the synagogue, and then, for constructing a new basilica, but they even carry the stones on their own shoulders . . .

### 6.3.4 Disappointment with a false Messiah – and conversion

In 431 a Jew claiming to be the Messiah appeared in Crete, where he won many followers. Instead of saving them, however, he encouraged mass suicide. When the Jewish community turned against him, he escaped. In disappointment and anger some Jews converted to Christianity.

Socrates Scholasticus, *Ecclesiastical History* 38

[Philip Schaff and Henry Wace, eds., *A Select Library of Nicene and Post-Nicene Fathers of the Christian Church*, second series, vol. II (New York: Eerdmans, 1890) pp. 174–5]

About this period a great number of Jews who dwelt in Crete were converted to Christianity through the following disastrous circumstance. A certain Jewish impostor pretended that he was Moses, and had been sent from heaven to lead out the Jews inhabiting that island, and conduct them through the sea: for he said that he was the same person who formerly preserved the Israelites by leading them through the Red Sea. During a whole year therefore he per-ambulated the several cities of the island and persuaded the Jews to believe such assurances. He moreover bade them renounce their money and other property, pledging himself to guide them through a dry sea into the land of promise. Deluded by such expectations, they neglected business of every kind, despising what they possessed, and permitting any one who chose to take it.

When the day appointed by this deceiver for their departure had arrived, he himself took the lead, and all followed with their wives and children. He led them therefore until they reached a promontory that overhung the sea, from which he ordered them to fling themselves headlong into it. Those who came first to the precipice did so, and were immediately destroyed, some of them being dashed in pieces against the rocks, and some drowned in the waters; and more would have perished, had not the providence of God led some fishermen and merchants who were Christians to be present. These persons drew out and saved some that were almost drowned, who then in their perilous situation became sensible of the madness of their conduct. The rest they hindered from casting themselves down by telling them of the destruction of those who had taken the first leap.

When at length the Jews perceived how fearfully they had been duped, they blamed first of all their own indiscreet credulity, and then sought to lay hold of the pseudo-Moses in order to put him to death. But they were unable to seize him, for he suddenly disappeared: which induced a general belief that it was some malignant fiend, who had assumed a human form for the destruction of their nation in that place. In consequence of this experience many of the Jews in Crete at that time, abandoning Judaism, attached themselves to the Christian faith.

### 6.3.5 Conversion to Islam

From the earliest biography of Muhammad, compiled by Ibn Ishaq (died AD 768–769) on the basis of oral tradition and some written accounts, which were in turn revised and edited by Ibn Hisham (died 833–834), comes this account of the first Jewish convert to Islam. He accepted Muhammad not as the Messiah, but as a prophet sent by God.

Ibn Hisham, *Biography of Muhammad*, vol. 1, 516–17
[*The Jews of Arab Lands*, trans. Norman A. Stillman (Philadelphia: Jewish Publication Society of America, 1979) pp. 113–14]

> Ibn Ishaq stated: The following is part of the story of Abd Allah b. Salam concerning him and his conversion as told to me by one of his relatives.
>
> He was a rabbi and a scholar. He said: When I heard about the Apostle of Allah – may Allah bless him and grant him peace – I realized from his description, his name, and his time, that he was the one whom we had been expecting. I was delighted by that, but kept silent until the Apostle of Allah came to Medina. When he alighted in Quba among Banu Amr b. Awf, a man

came to announce his arrival. I was working at the time on top of one of my palm trees, and my aunt Khalida b. al-Haritha was sitting below. When I heard the news of the Apostle's arrival I cried, "Allah is most great!" Hearing this, my aunt said to me, "By Allah, had you heard that Moses the son of Amram were coming, you could not have been more excited!"

I answered her. "Indeed, aunt, he is by Allah Moses' brother and follows his religion. He has been sent with the same mission."

She asked, "O nephew, is he the prophet who we have been told will be sent at this very time?"

"Yes," I replied.

"Then it is so," she said.

Then I went to the Apostle of Allah – may Allah bless him and grant him peace – and accepted Islam. Afterwards, I returned home and ordered the members of my household to convert as well, which they did.

He went on: "I concealed my conversion from the Jews. I then came to the Apostle and said to him, 'O Apostle of Allah, the Jews are a people given to falsehood. I would like you to take me into one of your apartments and hide me from them. Then ask them about me so that they will tell you how I am regarded among them before they learn of my conversion. For if they know about it already, they would slander and denounce me.' "

So the Apostle of Allah – may Allah bless him and grant him peace – took me into one of his apartments, and they came before him. They spoke with him and asked him questions. He in turn asked them, "What kind of a man is al-Husayn b. Salam among you?"

"He is our chief and the son of our chief, our rabbi and our leading scholar," they replied.

As they finished speaking, I came out in front of them and said, "O Jews, fear Allah and accept what he has sent you! For by Allah, you surely know that he is the Apostle of Allah. You will find him foretold in the Torah both by his name and his description. I bear witness that he is the Apostle of Allah. I believe in him. I declare him to be true. And I acknowledge him."

"You lie!" they cried, and went on to slander me.

Then I said to the Apostle of Allah – may Allah bless him and grant him peace, "Did I not tell you, O Apostle, that they were a slandering, treacherous, lying, and immoral people?"

I now proclaimed my conversion to Islam and the conversion of my household. My aunt Khalida b. al-Haritha converted too, and what a goodly conversion that was.

## 6.4 Jewish resistance

Jews did not accept oppression passively. Acts of resistance took different forms: violence against Jews who had converted to Christianity, symbolic destruction of their Christian persecutors, and outright military struggle.

### 6.4.1 Jewish anger at converts

*Theodosian Code* 16.8.1

> I. It is Our will that Jews and their elders and patriarchs shall be informed that if, after the issuance of this law, any of them should dare to attempt to assail with stones or with any other kind of madness – a thing which We have learned is now being done – any person who has fled their feral sect and has resorted to the worship of God, such assailant shall be immediately delivered to the flames and burned, with all his accomplices. [Constantine, 315]

## 6.4.2 Destruction of the symbols of persecution

The biblical Book of Esther (unknown to Honorius and Theodosius' lawyers) describes how the Jewish community in ancient Persia was saved from destruction at the hands of Haman, a minister of the Persian king, through the intervention of Esther, one of the king's wives. Jews celebrate this event in the annual holiday of Purim. Sometimes an effigy of Haman is destroyed in the festivities. Some Jews in the empire were accused of destroying Christian crosses as well.

*Theodosian Code* 16.8.18

> The governors of the provinces shall prohibit the Jews, in a certain ceremony of their festival Haman in commemoration of some former punishment, from setting fire to and burning a simulated appearance of the holy cross, in contempt of the Christian faith and with sacrilegious mind, lest they associate the sign of Our faith with their places. They shall maintain their own rites without contempt of the Christian law, and they shall unquestionably lose all privileges that have been permitted them heretofore unless they refrain from unlawful acts. [Honorius and Theodosius, 408]

### 6.4.3 Jews defend Naples in 535

When Belisarius began his siege of Naples in 535 as part of his effort to reconquer Gothic Italy for Justinian, the Jews of that city took an active role in resistance. They knew of Justinian's abusive policies toward Jews in reconquered North Africa and suffered no illusions about the fate awaiting them if he should win.

Procopius, *History of the Wars* 5.8.41–3, 10.24–6

[Procopius, *History of the Wars*, vol. III, trans. H.B. Dewing (London: Heinemann, 1968) pp. 81, 99]

> (5.8. 41–3) When they had finished speaking, Pastor and Asclepiodotus [the leaders of the opposition to Belisarius] brought forward the Jews, who promised that the city should be in want of none of the necessities, and the Goths on their part promised that they would guard the circuit-wall safely. And the Neapolitans, moved by these arguments, bade Belisarius depart from there with all speed. He, however, began the siege . . .

(5.10.24–26) But on the side of the circuit-wall which faces the sea, where the forces on guard were not barbarians, but Jews, the soldiers were unable either to use the ladders or to scale the wall. For the Jews had already given offence to their enemy by having opposed their efforts to capture the city without a fight, and for this reason they had no hope if they should fall into their hands; so they kept fighting stubbornly, although they could see that the city had already been captured, and held out beyond all expectation against the assaults of their opponents [the forces of Belisarius]. But when day came and some of those who had mounted the wall marched against them, then at last they also, now that they were being shot at from behind, took to flight, and Naples was captured by storm.

### 6.4.4 Jews help the Persians take Jerusalem

When Persian armies besieged Jerusalem in 614, Jews in the city helped them because they hoped for better treatment under new masters. Christians understood this as betrayal. This passage shows the bitter animosity between Christians and Jews in Jerusalem.

Antiochus Strategos, *The Sack of Jerusalem*

[F. Conybeare, "Antiochus Strategos' Account of the Sack of Jerusalem in AD 614," *English Historical Review* 25 (1910): 502–16, here 508]

Thereupon the Jews, enemies of the truth and haters of Christ, when they perceived that the Christians were given over into the hands of the enemy, rejoiced exceedingly because they detested the Christians; and they conceived an evil plan in keeping with their vileness about the people. For in the eyes of the Persians their importance was great because they were betrayers of the Christians. In this season, when the Jews approached the edge of the reservoir and called out to the children of God, while they were shut up therein, and said to them: "If you would escape from death, become Jews and deny Christ, and then you shall step up from your place and join us. We will ransom you with our money and you will be benefited by us." But their plot and desire were not fulfilled, their labors proved to be in vain; because the children of the Holy Church chose death for Christ's sake rather than to live in godlessness; and they reckoned it better for their flesh to be punished rather than their souls ruined, so that their portion was not with the Jews. And when the unclean Jews saw the steadfast uprightness of the Christians and their immovable faith, they were agitated with lively ire, like evil beasts, and thereupon imagined another plot. As of old they bought the Lord from the Jews with silver, so they purchased Christians out of the reservoir; for they gave the Persians silver and they bought a Christian and slew him like a sheep. The Christians, however, rejoiced because they were being slain for Christ's sake and shed their blood for His blood, and took on themselves death for His death . . . When the [Christian] people were carried into Persia, and the Jews were left in Jerusalem, they began with their own hands to demolish and burn such of the holy churches as were left standing . . .

## 6.5 Daily life in Jewish communities

### 6.5.1 Self-government

Within both the Roman and Persian empires, Jews were permitted to govern themselves within certain limits. The legal apparatus for doing so was in the hands of rabbis who established two major centers of law, in Jerusalem and in Babylonia. Legal study resulted in the compilation of several basic texts. The Mishnah, a redaction of oral law, was the essential foundation for the Talmuds which appeared by AD 200. The Jerusalem Talmud and the Babylonian Talmud drew general legal principles from the Mishnah and applied them to new problems that arose. The academies of Palestine and Babylonia which produced these works, though in constant contact with one another, often disagreed on interpretation of the Law. The following passages indicate contemporary Jewish awareness of these differences.

*The Babylonian Talmud*, Sanhedrin 4b–5a

[I. Epstein, ed., *The Babylonian Talmud, Seder Nizikin* (London: Soncino Press, 1936) pp. 15, 16]

> Said Rab: Whosoever wishes to decide monetary cases by himself and be free from liability in case of an erroneous decision, should obtain sanction from the Resh Galutha [Head of the Babylonian Jews]. And so said Samuel: It is clear that an authorization held from the Head of the Jews here in Babylonia holds good here. And one from the Palestinian authority there in Palestine is valid there. Likewise, the authorization received here is valid there, because the authority in Babylon is designated "sceptre", but that of Palestine, "law giver" [denoting a lower rank], as it has been taught: *The* sceptre *shall not depart from Judah*, this refers to the Exilarchs of Babylon who rule over Israel with sceptres.

### 6.5.2 Jews lose self-government: the end of the patriarchate

*Theodosian Code* 16.8.29 [Justinian, *Code* 1.9 16]

> The primates of the Jews, who are appointed in the sanhedrins [courts] of the two Palestines or who live in other provinces, shall be compelled to pay what they have received as tribute after the extinction of the patriarchate. But in the future, annual tribute shall be collected at the peril of the primates from all synagogues, under compulsion of the palatines and in the amount that the patriarchs formerly demanded in the name of crown gold. By skillful inquiry you shall ascertain what that amount is, and whatever was accustomed to be contributed to the patriarchs in the western part of the Empire shall now be paid to Our largesses. [Theodosius and Valentinian, 429]

### 6.5.3 Education

Study of the Law was considered a primary obligation for the males of the community, and rabbis took the lead in providing this education.

*The Jerusalem Talmud*, Hagigah 1.7.76c

[Lee I. Levine, "The Sages and the Synagogue in Late Antiquity," in *The Galilee in Late Antiquity*, ed. Lee I. Levine (New York/Jerusalem: The Jewish Theological Seminary of America, 1992) pp. 201–22, here 211]

> Rabbi Judah Nesiah sent Rabbi Hiyya, Rabbi Asi and Rabbi Ami to tour the towns of Palestine in order to check on teachers of Scriptures and Oral Law. In one place they found neither teacher of Scriptures nor of Oral Law, whereupon they said to the residents: "Bring us the guardians of the city." They brought them the sentries of the city. The sages responded: "These are not the guardians of the city, but rather its destroyers!" "And who are its guardians?" they asked. "The teachers of Scriptures and Oral Law."

### 6.5.4 Interpreting the Law

A typical discussion of a legal point from the Babylonian Talmud considers the problems that result when a husband dies while traveling overseas with his wife. Beginning with a passage from the Mishnah, it illustrates the method of pulling together the opinions of previous legal authorities. It also sheds light on the legal condition of women.

*The Babylonian Talmud*, Yebamoth 1 5, 114b

[I. Epstein, ed., *The Babylonian Talmud*, vol. 11: *Seder Nashim* (London: Soncino Press, 1936) p. 808]

> *Mishnah (c. AD 200)* If a woman and her husband went to a country beyond the sea at a time when there was peace between them and when there was also peace in the world, and she came back and said "my husband is dead," she may marry again; and if she said "my husband is dead and has left no issue," she may contract the levirate marriage (i.e. marry her brother-in-law). If, however, there was peace between him and her, but war in the world, or, if there was discord between him and her, but peace in the world, and she came back and said, "my husband is dead," she is not believed. Rabbi Judah said: She is never believed unless she comes weeping and her garments are torn. They [the Sages], however, said to him: she may marry in either case . . .

The reason why she is not believed in a time of war is given by Raba in the *Gemara* (a commentary on the Talmud).

> Raba stated: What is the reason why a wife is not believed in a time of war? Because she speaks from conjecture. "Could it be imagined," she thinks, "that among all those who were killed he alone escaped!" And should it be contended that since there was peace between him and her she would wait until

she saw what had actually happened to him, it may sometimes happen, it may be retorted, that he was struck by an arrow or spear and she would think that he was certainly dead, while in fact someone might have applied an emollient to his wound and he might have recovered.

### 6.5.5 Sabbath worship at sea

Judaism's strict prohibitions against work on the Sabbath and overriding injunctions to save life whenever necessary explain the actions of a Jewish sea captain – to the consternation of his aristocratic Roman passenger, Synesius of Cyrene (*c*.370–*c*.413). Synesius described his voyage in an amusing letter to his brother.

Synesius of Cyrene, *Letter* 4, "To His Brother"
[*The Letters of Synesius of Cyrene*, trans. Augustine Fitzgerald (London: Oxford University Press, 1926) pp. 81–4]

Hear my story then, that you may have no further leisure for your mocking wit, and I will tell you first of all how our crew was made up. Our skipper was fain of death owing to his bankrupt condition; then besides him we had twelve sailors, thirteen in all! More than half of them, including the skipper, were Jews – a graceless race and fully convinced of the piety of sending to Hades as many Greeks as possible. The remainder were a collection of peasants who even as late as last year had never gripped an oar, but the one batch and the other were alike in this, that every man of them had some personal defect. Accordingly, so long as we were in safety they passed their time in jesting one with another, accosting their comrades not by their real names, but by distinguishing marks of their misfortunes, as to call out "the Lame", the "Ruptured", the "Left-handed", the "Goggle-eyed". Each one had his distinguishing mark, and to us this sort of thing was no small source of amusement. The moment we were in danger, however, it was no laughing matter, but rather did we bewail these very defects. We had embarked to the number of more than fifty, about a third of us being women, most of them comely.

. . . a gale commenced to blow from the north, and the violent wind soon raised seas mountains high. This gust falling suddenly on us, drove our sail back, and made it concave in place of its convex form, and the ship was all but capsized by the stern. With great difficulty, however, we headed her in.

Then Amarantus (the captain) thunders out, "See what it is to be master of the art of navigation. I had long foreseen this storm, and that is why I sought the open. I can tack in now, since our sea room allows us to add to the length of our tack. But such a course as the one I have taken would not have been possible had we hugged the shore, for in that case the ship would have been dashed on the coast." Well, we were perforce satisfied with his explanation so long as daylight lasted and dangers were not imminent, but these failed not to return with approach of night, for as the hours passed the seas increased continually in volume. Now it so happened that this was the day on which the Jews make what they term the "Preparation", and they reckon the night, together with the day following this, as a time during which it is unlawful to work with one's hands. They keep this day holy and apart from the others, and they pass it in rest from labor of all kinds. Our skipper accordingly let go the rudder from his hands the moment he guessed that the sun's rays had left the earth, and throwing himself prostrate, "Allowed to trample on him what sailor so desired."

We who at first could not understand why he was thus lying down, imagined that despair was the cause of it all. We rushed to his assistance and implored him not to give up the last hope yet. Indeed the hugest waves were actually menacing the vessel, and the very deep was at war with itself. Now it frequently happens that when the wind has suddenly relaxed its violence, the billows already set in motion do not immediately subside; they are still under the influence of the wind's force, to which they yield and with which they battle at the same time, and the oncoming waves fight against those subsiding. I have every need of my store of flaming language, so that in recounting such immense dangers I may not fall into the trivial. To people who are at sea in such a crisis, life may be said to hang by a thread only, for if our skipper proved at such a moment to be an orthodox observer of the Mosaic law, what was life worth in the future? Indeed we soon understood why he had abandoned the helm, for when we begged him to do his best to save the ship, he stolidly continued reading his roll. Despairing of persuasion, we finally attempted force, and one staunch soldier – for many Arabs of the cavalry were of our company – one staunch soldier, I say, drew his sword and threatened to behead the fellow on the spot if he did not resume control of the vessel. But the Maccabean in very deed was determined to persist in his observances. However, in the middle of the night he voluntarily returned to the helm. "For now," he said, "we are clearly in danger of death, and the law commands."

### 6.5.6 Legal differences between men and women, c.500

Jewish law made precise distinctions between the rights of men and women. Women had fewer rights; men had harsher punishments. (See also Chapter 8, Domestic life)
*The Babylonian Talmud*, Kiddushin 29 a–b
[Ross S. Kraemer, ed., *Maenads, Martyrs, Matrons, Monastics: A Sourcebook on Women's Religions in the Greco-Roman World* (Philadelphia: Fortress Press, 1988) p. 67]

MISHNAH: What differences are there in law between a man and a woman? A man rends his clothes and loosens his hair, but a woman does not rend her clothes and loosen her hair . . . A man may sell his daughter, but a woman may not sell her daughter. A man may give his daughter in betrothal, but a woman may not give her daughter in betrothal. A man is stoned naked, but a woman is not stoned naked. A man is hanged, but a woman is not hanged. A man is sold for his theft, but a woman is not sold for her theft.

### 6.5.7 Public lives of women

Though severely limited in the scope of their public lives, women served as benefactors of synagogues. The following partial list of donors comes from Apamaea in Syria, about 391. The women mentioned paid for sections of the floor in fulfillment of vows they had made.

Apamaea Synagogue Floor Mosaic Inscription

[Ross S. Kraemer, ed., *Maenads, Martyrs, Matrons, Monastics: A Sourcebook on Women's Religions in the Greco-Roman World* (Philadelphia: Fortress Press, 1988) p. 116]

> 41. Alexandra, in fulfillment of a vow, gave 100 feet of floor for the welfare of her whole household.
> 42. Ambrosia, in fulfillment of a vow, gave 50 feet of floor for the welfare of her whole household.
> 51. Colonis, in fulfillment of a vow, gave 75 feet of floor for her welfare and that of her children.

### 6.5.8 Hebrew liturgy in synagogues

During the Late Antique period Hebrew liturgical poetry flourished in Palestine in the context of synagogue worship. Some of the works quickly became standard and are still recited today. Eleazar ben Killir (or Kallir), who probably lived in the sixth century, was the greatest and most influential of these poets. These excerpts from his cosmic *Battle between Behemoth and Leviathan* reveal messianic thought. Leviathan and Behemoth represent monstrous forces of chaos that will struggle in the age before the coming of the Messiah. Despite this battle, God will protect and save his people.

Eleazar ben Kallir, *Battle between Behemoth and Leviathan*

[T. Carmi, ed., *The Penguin Book of Hebrew Verse* (New York: Penguin Books, 1981) pp. 227–32]

> Then shall the gates of the garden of Eden be opened, and the seven preordained companies of righteous men shall be revealed within the garden, and the tree of life in the middle of the garden. They shall hear the sound of their Creator in the garden; and as once He moved about in the garden, so shall He now move amongst them in the garden.
>
> They shall see, and pointing a finger at his likeness, they shall say: "Such is God, our God, and we shall not die. He shall be our guide forever!" . . .
>
> Behemoth: his lair is upon the Thousand Mountains; he daily feeds upon the produce of the Thousand Mountains; and he drinks from the abundant waters of the River Yuval, which issues from Eden to become four rivers; his roar rends the mountains.
>
> See the strength in his loins; his deeds testify to his might; the power in the muscles of his belly proves it. Who can stand up to him? When he so wills, he raises his tail like a cedar, making room for all the beasts of the field to nestle

there. Then he gently lowers his tail, in the thicket of which he shelters the birds of the air, so that none shall be harmed by the beasts dwelling within him – for he is merciful in his ways. Thus he reclines like a king on his couch, till the appointed day, on which God shall sport with him and reveal him to the companies of the pious.

. . . Whereupon a divine voice calls out from the heights: "Blow upon my garden, let its fragrance be wafted abroad" to disperse the odour of its perfumes.

Then, at this signal, the north wind and the south wind awake and blow in all directions. Behemoth girds himself with strength and, gaining courage, turns back to Leviathan, who is prepared for battle. He moves at him, tensed for the combat, and again they grapple with each other. Behemoth, mad with rage, encircles him with his horns like a master warrior; while the Fish, facing him, wheels to the right, whetting his fins again and again, as he tries to gash him. Behemoth arches his horns, Leviathan rears his fins – but now he makes an end of the pair, to slaughter, prepare, and consecrate them. They shall be served up as a dish to the faithful people. Seeing that Israel has not been forsaken, they shall say: "Blessed is the Steadfast One. For everything that he ordained long ago, he accomplishes now, at the end of time!"

### 6.5.9 *Mourning the destruction of the Temple*

This anonymous dirge laments the destruction of the Temple in Jerusalem in AD 70 (on the ninth day of the Jewish month of Av), and is organized around the signs of the Zodiac. It claims that human sin brought divine punishment and yearns for divine redemption.

Anonymous, *Dirge for the Ninth of Av*
[T. Carmi, ed., *The Penguin Book of Hebrew Verse* (New York: Penguin, 1981) pp. 204–6]

How long will there be weeping in Zion and lamentation in Jerusalem? Have mercy on Zion and build anew the walls of Jerusalem!

Because of our sins the Temple was destroyed, because of our crimes the Palace was burnt. In the city that once was bound firmly together lamentations were heard, and the host of heaven sounded a dirge.

The Ram, first of all, wept bitterly, for his sheep were being led to the slaughter. The Bull howled on high, for we were all driven hard, with yokes upon our necks.

The Twins were seen to split asunder, for the blood of brothers was shed like water. The Crab would have fallen to earth, for we were fainting from thirst.

The Lion's roar filled heaven with terror, for our cry did not ascend to heaven. Virgins and young men were slaughtered, and the Virgin's face grew dark with grief . . .

The Balance tipped in supplication, for we preferred death to life. The Scorpion shuddered, for our enemies whipped us with lashes.

The Archer turned his bow away, for the Lord had drawn His bow like an enemy. The water rose high above our head, yet in the month of the Water-bearer our palates were parched.

We offered a sacrifice, but it was not accepted; the Goat would not present a he-goat as our sin-offering. Tender-hearted women boiled their own children, yet the Fish turned a blind eye.

With wayward hearts we forgot the Sabbath, and so the Lord did not remember our merits. O Lord, be most jealous for Zion's honour, and let Your radiance shine upon the city once so full of people!

### 6.5.10  Jews in the Islamic world

Some Arab communities before the rise of Islam were Jewish. To consolidate his power, Muhammad had to overcome the resistance of Arab Jewish communities that refused to convert. In 627 the Jews of Medina were destroyed, but after Muhammad's consolidation of power and in the first rapid expansion of Islam, Jews found a place in the new order. Protected as "People of the Book," they nonetheless had fewer rights than their Muslim neighbors. The Quran contains several pronouncements about their treatment. (See also Chapter 15, Islam.)

Quran, sura 9.29, 5.51

[*The Meaning of the Glorious Koran*, trans. Marmaduke Pickthall (New York: Alfred A. Knopf, 1930) pp. 126, 195]

> Fight against such of those who have been given the Scripture as believe not in Allah nor the Last Day, and forbid not that which Allah hath forbidden by His messenger, and follow not the religion of truth until they pay the tribute readily, being brought low.

> O ye who believe! Take not the Jews and the Christians for friends. They are friends one to another. He among you who taketh them for friends is (one) of them. Lo! Allah guideth not wrongdoing folk.

## Further reading

Becker, Adam H. and Annette Yoshiko Reed, *The Ways that Never Parted: Jews and Christians in Late Antiquity and the Early Middle Ages* (Tübingen: Mohr Siebeck, 2003)

De Lange, Nicholas, "Jews in the Age of Justinian," in *The Cambridge Companion to the Age of Justinian* (Cambridge: Cambridge University Press, 2005) pp. 401–26

Jacobs, Andrew S., *Remains of the Jews. The Holy Land and Christian Empire in Late Antiquity.* (Stanford, CA: Stanford University Press, 2004)

Kalmin, Richard Lee and Seth Schwartz, *Jewish Culture and Society Under the Christian Roman Empire* (Leuven: Peeters, 2003)

Lapin, Hayim, *Economy, Geography, and Provincial History in Later Roman Palestine* (Tübingen: Mohr Siebeck, 2001)

Levine, Lee, ed., *The Galilee in Late Antiquity* (New York/Jerusalem: The Jewish Theological Seminary of America, 1992)

Rutgers, Leonard Victor, *The Jews in Late Ancient Rome: Evidence of Cultural Isolation in the Roman Diaspora* (Leiden: Brill, 1995)

Sandwell, Isabella, *Religious Identity in Late Antiquity. Greeks, Jews, and Christians in Antioch.* (Cambridge: Cambridge University Press, 2007)

Schiffman, Lawrence, *From Tradition to Text* (New York: Ktav Pres, 1998)

Sharf, Andrew, *Byzantine Jewry: From Justinian to the Fourth Crusade* (London: Routledge and Kegan Paul, 1971)

Sivan, Hagith, *Palestine in Late Antiquity* (New York: Oxford University Press, 2008)

Stern, Menachem, ed., *Greek and Latin Authors on Jews and Judaism* (Jerusalem: Israel Academy of Sciences and Humanities, 1984)

Yuval, Israel Jacob, *Two Nations in Your Womb. Perceptions of Jews and Christians in Late Antiquity and the Middle Ages* (Berkeley: University of California Press, 2007)

# 7

# WOMEN

## 7.1 Introduction

Women's lives in the Roman Empire in Late Antiquity were carefully regulated by law and social convention. Wealth and status determined the quality of an individual's existence in the community. For most women, patriarchal family structures with their assumptions about female inferiority predominated, and traditional patterns of female subservience were the norm. Christianity made an enormous impact on the lives of women, especially through its emphasis on virginity, which in turn affected attitudes to marriage and domesticity. Patristic writings are a rich source of information about changing views of gender and social relations. Only a few women reached positions of power and influence beyond the family. These were consorts of great monarchs, such as Theodora, the wife of Justinian; Christian martyrs like Tarbo, whose deaths inspired the faithful; leaders of monastic communities, such as Melania or Olympias; and Hypatia the philosopher, who was murdered by a Christian mob. One way or another, these women were seen as threatening by the men whose writings about them are the source of most of our information about women's lives. This chapter for the most part deals with women beyond the domestic sphere, which is treated in the following chapter.

## 7.2 Powerful women

### 7.2.1 Helena – empress and Church benefactor

Helena, the mother of the emperor Constantine I, was made a saint because of her piety and donations to the Church. She took a special interest in the holy places and biblical sites of Palestine and contributed a great deal to the "rediscovery" of that province as a site of Christian pilgrimage and worship. In Jerusalem she found what was believed to be a fragment of the cross on which Jesus had been crucified. Her career demonstrates how a powerful woman could play a role of public service through the Church.

Sozomen, *Ecclesiastical History* 2.2
[*Nicene and Post-Nicene Fathers of the Christian Church*, vol. II, trans. Philip Schaff and Henry Wace (Grand Rapids, MI: Eerdmans, 1979) p. 259]

The emperor [Constantine], having determined upon erecting a temple in honor of God, charged the governors to see that the work was executed in the most magnificent and costly manner possible. His mother Helena also erected two temples, the one at Bethlehem near the cave where Christ was born, the other on ridges of the Mount of Olives, whence He was taken up to heaven. Many other acts show her piety and religiousness, among which the following is not the least remarkable: during her residence at Jerusalem, it is related that she assembled the sacred virgins at a feast, ministered to them at supper, presented them with food, poured water on their hands, and performed other similar services customary to those who wait upon guests. When she visited the cities of the East, she bestowed befitting gifts on the churches in every town, enriched those individuals who had been deprived of their possessions, supplied ungrudgingly the necessities of the poor, and restored to liberty those who had been long imprisoned, or condemned to exile or the mines. It seems to me that so many holy actions demanded a recompense; and indeed, even in this life, she was raised to the summit of magnificence and splendor; she was pro-claimed Augusta; her image was stamped on golden coins, and she was invested by her son with authority over the imperial treasury to give it according to her judgment. Her death, too, was glorious; for when, at the age of eighty, she quitted this life, she left her son and her descendants (like her of the race of Caesar), masters of the Roman world. And if there be any advantage in such fame – forgetfulness did not conceal her though she was dead – the coming age has the pledge of her perpetual memory; for two cities are named after her, the one in Bithynia, and the other in Palestine. Such is the history of Helena.

## 7.2.2 *The empress refuses to panic: Theodora during the Nika Riot*

Before meeting Justinian, whom she married in 525, Theodora supported herself as a prostitute and actress. When she became empress, however, she exerted a significant political influence at court and throughout the empire. During the Nika Riot of 532, when Justinian nearly lost his throne due to urban unrest fanned by political rivals who wanted to remove him from power, Theodora counseled her husband not to flee Constantinople. Emboldened by her speech, Justinian ordered the slaughter of perhaps ten thousand rioters and quelled the uprising. "Nika," which means "victory," was the slogan chanted by the rioters. Procopius gives an account of Theodora's inspiring words.

Procopius, *History of the Wars* 1.24.32–8

[Procopius, *History of the Wars*, vol. I, trans. H.B. Dewing (Cambridge, MA: Harvard University Press, 1971) pp. 231, 233]

Now the emperor and his court were deliberating as to whether it would be better for them if they remained or if they took to flight in the ships. And many opinions were expressed favouring either course. And the Empress Theodora also spoke to the following effect: "As to the belief that a woman ought not to be daring among men or to assert herself boldly among those who are holding back from fear, I consider that the present crisis most certainly does not permit us to discuss whether the matter should be regarded in this or in some other way. For in the case of those whose interests have come into the greatest danger nothing else seems best except to settle the issue immediately before them in the best possible way. My opinion then is that the present time, above all others, is inopportune for flight, even though it brings safety. For while it is impossible for a man who has seen the light not also to die, for one who has been an emperor it is unendurable to be a fugitive. May I never be separated from this purple, and may I not live that day on which those who meet me shall not address me as mistress. If, now, it is your wish to save yourself, O Emperor, there is no difficulty. For we have much money, and there is the sea, here the boats. However, consider whether it will not come about that after you have been saved you would gladly exchange that safety for death. For as for myself, I approve a certain ancient saying that royalty is a good burial-shroud." When the queen had spoken thus, all were filled with boldness, and, turning their thoughts towards resistance, they began to consider how they might be able to defend themselves if any hostile force should come against them.

### 7.2.3 Aristocratic female virtues

The tomb inscription of Anicia Faltonia Proba describes a Christian aristocrat of the very highest nobility of the city of Rome, the Anician family. She was the daughter and wife of consuls and was in Rome during the Visigothic siege in 410. She died in Africa by 432. Proba donated much of her wealth to the Church and to the poor. Her achievements link her family to the service of the state.

*Corpus of Latin Inscriptions*, 6.1755, Rome
[Brian Croke and Jill Harries, *Religious Conflict in Fourth-Century Rome: A Documentary Study* (Sydney: Sydney University Press, 1982) p. 116]

> To Anicia Faltonia Proba, trustee of the ancient nobility, pride of the Anician family, a model of the preservation and teaching of chastity, descendant of consuls, mother of consuls; her most loyal children Anicius Hermogenianus Olybrius, vir clarissimus ["Man of the Most Distinguished Senatorial Rank"], consul ordinarius ["consul elected at the beginning of the year"] and his wife Anicia Juliana, clarissima femina ["Woman of the Most Distinguished Senatorial Rank"] dedicated this.

### 7.2.4 Death of a scholar: Hypatia of Alexandria

Hypatia of Alexandria gave private classes and public lectures in philosophy, mathematics and astronomy in the tradition of late Platonic studies. She drew students from throughout the eastern Mediterranean and won great esteem for her brilliance and virtuous life. In 415 she became enmeshed in a quarrel between the prefect and the archbishop Cyril, and was murdered. The philosopher Damascius gives one account of her death.

Damascius, *Life of Isidore*, fragment 102
[Maria Dzielska, *Hypatia of Alexandria*, trans. F. Lyra (London: Harvard University Press, 1995) p. 18]

> Cyril, the bishop of the opposing party, went by Hypatia's house and noticed a great throng at her door, "a jumble of steeds and men." Some came, some went; others remained standing. He asked what this gathering meant and why such a tumult was being made. He then heard from his retainers that the philosopher Hypatia was being greeted and that this was her house. This information so pierced his heart that he launched a murderous attack in the most detestable manner. For when Hypatia was going out as usual, several bestial men, fearing neither divine vengeance nor human punishment, suddenly rushed upon her and killed her: thus laying their country both under the highest infamy and under the guilt of innocent blood.

## 7.3 Christianity and women

### 7.3.1 Olympias – aristocratic habits and spiritual values

The *Life of Olympias* reveals how the pursuit of a Christian life could bring power and a considerable measure of freedom from male influence. Olympias (*c.*361–408) was very highly born and had the ear of the emperor in Constantinople, but she used her wealth to help the poor. She was made a saint.

*The Life of Olympias* 2, 5
[Elizabeth A. Clark, *Jerome, Chrysostom, and Friends. Essays and Translations* (New York: Edwin Mellen Press, 1979) pp. 128, 130–1]

> 2. She was daughter according to the flesh of Seleucus, one of the Counts, but according to the spirit, she was the true child of God. It is said that she was descended from Ablabius who was governor and she was bride for a few days of Nebridius, the prefect of the city of Constantinople, but in truth she did not grace the bed of anyone. For it is said that she died an undefiled virgin, having become a partner of the divine Word, a consort of every true humility, a companion and servant of the holy, catholic and apostolic church of God. Left an orphan, she was joined in marriage to a husband, but by the goodness of God she was preserved uncorrupted in flesh and in spirit. For God, who watches over everything, who foresees the outcome of humans, did not deem it worthy for the one who was briefly her husband to live with her for a year. The debt of nature was shortly demanded of him and she was preserved a blameless virgin until the end . . .
>
> 5. The emperor, upon his return from the battle against Maximus, gave the order that she could exercise control over her own possessions, since he had heard of the intensity of her ascetic discipline. But she distributed all of her

unlimited and immense wealth and assisted everyone, simply and without distinction . . .

Then straightway after the distribution and sealing up of all her goods, there was rekindled in her the divine love and she took refuge in the haven of salvation, the great, catholic, and apostolic church of this royal city. She followed to the letter with intelligence the divinely-inspired teachings of the most holy archbishop of this sacred church, John, and gave to him for this holy church (imitating also in this act those ardent lovers and disciples of Christ who in the beginning of salvation's proclamation brought to the feet of the apostles their possessions) ten thousand pounds of gold, twenty thousand of silver and all of her real estate situated in the provinces of Thrace, Galatia, Cappadocia Prima, and Bithynia; and more, the houses belonging to her in the capital city, the one situated near the most holy cathedral, which is called "the house of Olympias"; together with the house of the tribune, complete with baths, and all the buildings near it; a mill; and a house which belonged to her in which she lived near the public baths of Constantinople; and another house of hers which was called the "house of Evander"; as well as all of her suburban properties.

### 7.3.2 The generosity and leadership of Melania the Younger

Melania the Younger (383–439) was made a saint because of her generosity and piety. The daughter of an enormously wealthy senatorial family in Rome, she married at an early age but remained loyal to ascetic principles. When in their early twenties, she and her equally noble husband decided to sell their estates and give the proceeds to charity and the Church. It took the help of the empress to overcome the objections of the Roman Senate – and Melania's own household slaves, who did not want to be sold. The couple went to Jerusalem where Melania built a nunnery, a monastery, and a cell for herself.

*Life of Melania the Younger* 22, 23, 30, 35

[*Life of Melania the Younger*, trans. Elizabeth A. Clark (New York/Toronto: Mellen Press 1984) pp. 48, 51]

> 22. Indeed in the beginning, Melania would just taste a little oil and take a bit of something to drink in the evening (she never used wine during her worldly life because the children of the Roman senatorial class were raised in this way). Then after that she began to mortify her flesh with strenuous fasting. At first she took food without oil every two days, then every three days, and then every five, so that it was only on Saturday and Sunday that she ate some moldy bread. She was zealous to surpass everyone in asceticism.

> 23. She was by nature gifted as a writer and wrote without mistakes in note-books. She decided for herself how much she ought to write every day, and how much she should read in the canonical books, how much in the collections of homilies. And after she was satisfied with this activity, she would go through the *Lives* of the fathers as if she were eating dessert. Then she slept for a period

of about two hours. Straightway after having gotten up, she roused the virgins who were leading the ascetic life with her, and said, "Just as the blessed Abel and each of the holy ones offered first-fruits to God, so we all in this way should spend the first-fruits of the night for God's glory. We ought to keep awake and pray at every hour, for, just as it is written, we do not know at what hour the thief comes." She gave strict rules to the sisters with her that no idle word or reckless laughter should come forth from their mouths. She also patiently inquired about their thoughts and refused to allow filthy imaginations to dwell in them in any way.

30. It was as if she hoped that by the virtuous practice of almsgiving alone she might obtain mercy; as the Lord said, "Blessed are the merciful, for they shall obtain mercy." Her love for poverty exceeded everyone else's. As she testified to us shortly before her departure for the Lord, she owned nothing at all on earth except for about fifty coins of gold for the offering, and even this she sent to a certain very holy bishop, saying, "I do not wish to possess even this much from our patrimony." Not only did she offer to God that which was her own; she also helped others to do the same. Thus many of those who loved Christ furnished her with their money, since she was a faithful and wise steward. She commanded these monies to be distributed honestly and judiciously according to the request of the donor.

35. Thus being much encouraged and praising God even more, they set sail for Jerusalem and hastened on to their destination. They stayed in the Church of the Holy Sepulcher. Since they themselves did not want to distribute with their own hands the gold left to them, they gave it to those who were entrusted with administering charity to the poor. They did not wish for people to see them doing good deeds. They were in such a state of poverty that the holy woman Melania assured us of this: "When we first arrived here, we thought of inscribing ourselves on the church's register and of being fed with the poor from alms." Thus they became extremely poor for the sake of the Lord, who himself became poor for our sakes and who took the form of a servant.

It happened that Melania was sick when we were first in Jerusalem and had nowhere to lie down except in her sackcloth. A certain well-born virgin presented her with a pillow as a gift. When she became healthy again, she spent her time in reading and prayer, sincerely serving the Lord.

### 7.3.3 Defying family expectations in Ireland

At the other end of Europe in the mid-fifth century, Patrick describes how an Irish woman's decision to live a new kind of Christian life challenged accepted behavior. Similar responses from horrified parents are noted across the empire.

Saint Patrick, *Declaration* 42

[A.B.E. Hood, *St. Patrick: His Writings and Muirchu's Life* (London: Phillimore, 1978) p. 50]

And there was also a blessed lady of native Irish birth and high rank, very beautiful and grown up, whom I baptised; and a few days later she found some reason to come to us and indicated that she had received a message from an angel of God, and the angel had urged her too to become a virgin of Christ and to draw near to God. Thanks be to God, six days later she most commendably and enthusiastically took up that same course that all virgins of God also do – not with their fathers' consent; no, they endure persecution and their own parents' unfair reproaches, and yet their number grows larger and larger (and we do not know the numbers of our family of faith who have been reborn there), not to mention widows and the self-denying. But it is the women kept in slavery who suffer especially; they even have to endure constant threats and terrorisation; but the Lord has given grace to many of His handmaidens, for though they are forbidden to do so, they resolutely follow His example.

### 7.3.4 *Saint Pelagia the Harlot: sin and salvation*

According to Christian belief, Eve, the first woman, successfully tempted Adam, and so God expelled them from the Garden of Eden. Consequently, all humanity lives in sin until saved through divine intervention. The fundamental evil of female sexuality was a mainstay of Late Antique Christian thought, and stories of whores who found redemption in Christian practice were particularly popular. Here Pelagia the Harlot wins sainthood not only by renouncing her profession, but also by pretending to be a eunuch. Written in Greek in the fifth century, this tale of sin and repentance was translated into many languages.

*The Life of Saint Pelagia the Harlot* 4–7, 18, 20–6, 53
[Helen Waddell, ed. and trans., *The Desert Fathers* (Ann Arbor: Michigan University Press, 1971) pp. 178, 181, 182, 183, 186, 187, 188]

And as we sat, certain of the bishops besought my master Nonnus [bishop of Antioch] that they might have some instruction from his lips: and straightway the good bishop began to speak to the weal and health of all that heard him. And as we sat marvelling at the holy learning of him, lo! on a sudden she that was first of the actresses of Antioch passed by: first of the dancers was she, and riding on an ass: and with all fantastic graces did she ride, so decked that naught could be seen upon her but gold and pearls and precious stones: the very nakedness of her feet was hidden under gold and pearls: and with her was a splendid train of young men and maidens clad in robes of price, with torques of gold about their necks. Some went before and some came after her: but of the beauty and the loveliness of her there could be no wearying for a world of men. Passing through our midst, she filled the air with the fragrance of musk and of all scents that are sweetest. And when the bishops saw her so shamelessly ride by, bare of head and shoulder and limb, in pomp so splendid, and not so much as a veil upon her head or about her shoulders, they groaned, and in silence turned away their heads as from great and grievous sin . . .

Now it befell, by the guiding of the Divine compassion, that to this very church should come that harlot of whom he had spoken to us: and for a marvel, she to whom never had come a thought of her sins and who never had been inside a church door was suddenly stricken with the fear of God . . .

[She wrote to Bishop Nonnus:]

"To Christ's holy disciple, the devil's disciple and a woman that is a sinner. I have heard of thy God, that He bowed the heavens and came down to earth, not for the good men's sake, but that He might save sinners, and that He was so humble that He drew near to publicans, and He on whom the Cherubim dare not look kept company with sinners. And thou my lord, who art a great saint, although thou hast not looked with the eyes of the flesh on the Lord Christ Himself, who showed Himself to that Samaritan woman, and her a harlot, at the well, yet art thou a worshipper of Him, for I have heard the talk of the Christians. If indeed thou art a true disciple of this Christ, spurn me not, desiring through thee to see the Saviour, that through thee I may come at the sight of His holy face."

Then the good bishop Nonnus wrote back to her: "Whatsoever thou art is known unto God, thyself, and what thy purpose is, and thy desire. But this I surely say to thee, seek not to tempt my weakness, for I am a man that is a sinner, serving God. If in very deed thou hast a desire after divine things and a longing for goodness and faith, and dost wish to see me, there are other bishops with me: come, and thou shalt see me in their presence: for thou shalt not see me alone."

[He received her in the church:]

She read it, this harlot, and filled with joy came hurrying to the basilica of the blessed Julian, and sent word to us that she was come. On hearing it, the good Nonnus called to him all the bishops who were in the place, and bade her come to him. She came in where the bishops were assembled, and flung herself on the pavement and caught the feet of the blessed Nonnus, saying, "My lord, I pray thee to follow thy master the Lord Christ, and shed on me thy kindness and make me a Christian. My lord, I am a sea of wickedness and an abyss of evil. I ask to be baptised."

Hardly could the good bishop Nonnus prevail on her to rise from his feet: but when she had risen, "The canons of the Church," he said, "provide that no harlot shall be baptised, unless she produce certain to go surety for her that she will not fall back into her old sins."

But on hearing such a judgment from the bishop, she flung herself again on the pavement and caught the feet of the good Nonnus, and washed them with her tears and wiped them with her hair, crying, "Thou shalt answer to God for my soul and on thee shall I charge all the evil of my deeds, if thou dost delay to baptise me in my foul sin. No portion mayst thou find in God's house among the saints, if thou makest me not a stranger to my sin. Mayst thou deny God and worship idols, if thou dost not this day have me born again, bride to Christ, and offer me to God."

[Eight days after her baptism she disappeared from Antioch. But the saga was not over, as the narrator reveals:]

And after some time the bishop of the city called all the bishops together, to dismiss them each to his own place. And after a space of three or four years I, James the Deacon, took a great longing to set out to Jerusalem that I might there adore the resurrection of our Lord Jesus Christ, and I asked my bishop if he would give me leave to go. And while giving me leave, he said to me, "I tell thee, brother deacon, when thou dost reach Jerusalem, inquire there for a certain brother Pelagius, a monk and a eunuch, who has lived these many years shut up and in solitude, if so be thou mightst visit him: for thou mightst well profit by him." And all the time he spoke of God's handmaid Pelagia, but I knew it not . . .

There was much talk among the monasteries of the fame of the holy Pelagius: and so I made up my mind to go back yet another time to visit him, and be quickened by his salutary speech. But when I had come again to his cell, and knocked, and even made bold to call upon him by name, there was no answer. I came again and waited a second day, and again a third, now and then calling, "Pelagius!" but I heard no one. So I said to myself, "Either there is no one here, or the monk who was here has gone away." And then, moved by some prompting from God, I said again to myself, "Let me make sure that he is not perhaps dead": and I opened the shutter of the window, and looked in, and I saw him dead. And I closed the shutter and carefully filled it up with clay, and came hurrying to Jerusalem and told the news that the good monk Pelagius who had wrought marvels was at peace. Then the good fathers came with the brethren of divers monasteries, and the door of the cell was opened: and they carried out the holy little body, reckoning it as precious as gold and jewels. And when the good fathers set about anointing the body with myrrh, they found that it was a woman. They would fain have hidden the miracle, but they could not: and they cried aloud with a shout, "Glory to Thee, Lord Christ, who hast many treasures hidden on the earth, and not men only, but women also." It was told abroad to all the people, and all the convents of virgins came, some from Jericho and some from Jordan where the Lord was baptised, with candles and torches and hymns: and so the holy relics of her were buried, and the good fathers carried her to her grave.

This is the story of a harlot, this the life of a desperate sinner: and may God grant that we find with her His mercy in the Day of Judgment: for to Him is the glory and honour, dominion and power, world without end. Amen.

### 7.3.5 Tarbo, a Christian martyr in Persia

Christians were sometimes persecuted in Zoroastrian Persia. The story of Tarbo's martyrdom in 340 at the hands of Persian officials won popularity in the Syriac-speaking world.

*Persian Martyrs*, "The Martyrdom of Tarbo, Her Sister, and Her Servant," 254–60 [*Holy Women of the Syrian Orient*, trans. Sebastian P. Brock and Susan Ashbrook Harvey (Berkeley: University of California Press, 1987) pp. 73–6]

At this time it so happened that the queen fell ill. Since she was favorably inclined to the enemies of the cross, the Jews, they told her, making their customary false accusation: "The sisters of Simeon have put spells on you because their brother has been put to death." Once this reached the queen's ears, Tarbo, a "daughter of the covenant," was arrested together with her married sister, who was living in continence, and her servant, who was also a "daughter of the covenant" and who had been instructed by Tarbo in the excellent teaching of Christ.

They brought the women to the queen's residence for interrogation. The head Mobed [a high-ranking Persian official] and two officers were sent for so that they could adjudicate their case. When the women were introduced into their presence, these men saw the valiant and holy Tarbo's beautiful looks and her fine appearance, excelling that of all other women. Straightaway all three of them conceived the same filthy thought and disgusting intentions concerning her, though none of them revealed anything to the others. They proceeded to speak harshly to the women, saying, "You deserve to die, seeing that you have brought these evil effects upon the person of the queen, the mistress of the entire orient."

The holy Tarbo replied, "What false charges are you bringing against us, charges that are quite out of keeping with our way of life? What wrong have we done you that you falsely accuse us of something quite alien to the truth for which we stand? Are you thirsting after our blood? If so, what prevents you from drinking it? Are you aiming at our death? Your hands are already befouled by killing us Christians every day: we may be put to death, but we will not renounce our religion. It is written down for us that we should serve one God alone, and not consider alongside him any likeness in heaven or on earth. Furthermore, the following is written down for us: 'If a sorcerer should be found, he is to die at the hands of this people.' How, then, could we perform sorcery? Sorcery is in the same category as the denial of God; in both cases the sentence is death."

Those evil judges sat there listening to her in silence, enjoying the occasion – that is, in their own bitter way, stunned as they were by her astonishing beauty and exceptional wisdom. Each one of them said to himself in the vain hope conjured up by his evil thoughts concerning her, "I'll rescue her from death so that she can be my wife."

The Mobed then spoke to the women: "In your anger over your brother being put to death you have gone so far as to transgress your own law, performing sorcery on the queen, despite the fact that you are not allowed to do this, as you yourself have said."

The glorious Tarbo spoke: "What bad or hateful thing has been done to my brother Simeon so that as a result we should risk losing our salvation at God's hands? For even though you may have killed him out of hatred and jealousy, he is nevertheless alive in the Kingdom on high – the Kingdom that will make your kingdom down here on earth pass away, and that will dissolve your position of authority and render useless this honor of yours that does not last."

After this they sent the three women off to prison, to be detained there. The next day the Mobed sent a message to Tarbo, saying, "I will intercede with the king and I will save the three of you from death – on the condition you become my wife." On hearing this the glorious woman was greatly shaken, replying, "Shut your mouth, you wicked man and enemy of God; don't ever again utter anything so disgusting. Your filthy words make no impression on ears that are pure, and your foul proposition does not have any effect on my mind, which is chaste and holy: for I am the betrothed of Christ. In his name I am preserving my virginity, and upon my hope in him I am hanging my sure conviction. I entrust my life to him since he is able to deliver me from your impure hands and from your evil intentions concerning me. I am not afraid of death or alarmed at the thought of being killed, seeing that you are marking out a path for me whereby I shall travel to behold my beloved and dearest brother Simeon, the bishop. In this way I shall receive consolation for all my pains and sufferings, as I follow on his footsteps."

The two officials likewise sent messages to her on the same lines, each concealing the matter from the other. With indignation and great anger she gave them an adamant refusal.

The three of them then decided together on a stratagem that would bear bitter fruit. Bringing totally false testimony, they gave a wicked verdict, saying that they were indeed witches. The king then sent word to the effect that, if they worshipped the sun, they need not be put to death, on the grounds that they might really not know how to cast spells. When the women heard this, they cried out, "We will not exchange our God for something created by him; we will not worship the created sun in place of our Creator, nor will we abandon our Savior Jesus just because of your threats."

The Magians immediately started making an uproar: "These women should perish from beneath the face of the heavens; they have cast spells on the queen and she has fallen ill." Permission was then given to the Magians to employ on the women whatever means of execution they liked. Now they said that their bodies should be cut in two and that the queen should pass between the two halves, after which she would be healed.

Once again, as the women were being taken out for execution, the Mobed sent a message to the glorious Tarbo to the effect that, if she listened to his proposal, neither she nor her companions would be put to death. The chaste woman, however, cried out with a loud voice, reviling him: "Foul and perverted man, why do you crazily rave after something that is neither proper nor permissible? I shall die a heroic death, for thus shall I obtain true life; I will not live in an ignominious way and then eventually die."

They took the three holy women outside the city and drove into the ground two stakes for each woman, and they stretched them out, attaching them by their hands and feet, like lambs about to be shorn. Thereupon they sawed their bodies in halves, cut them up into six portions, placing them in six baskets, which they suspended on six forked pieces of wood; these they thrust into the ground, three on each side of the road. These were shaped like half crosses, carrying half a body each. Hung upon them were fruits that blind those who pluck them, and they bore produce that is bitter to those who pick it.

This was a bitter spectacle that spoke for itself, girt with suffering; a grievous sight, carrying with it groans and lamentation. If anyone cannot weep, let him come here and bathe himself in tears; if anyone's eyes are dry, let him come here and wash himself in weeping, as he recalls the groans uttered by the pure and chaste bodies of those holy women. In their lifetime they were modestly dressed while in their own rooms, but in their death they were naked by the roadside. These are women who did not betray their freedom for a life of shame, whose chaste nature was handed over to be abused. How silent and quiet is Justice, who is normally not lenient or forgiving when she exacts the penalty. How daring and bold is Pride, which, once shattered, does not normally recover! These were merciless men, deprived of any pity or compassion; they resembled ravening wolves that tear out living flesh. The men who cut in half and strung up these women are cannibals who eat people alive; as it is written, "They swallowed us up alive." Who got any joy out of this lugubrious spectacle? Who took any pleasure in this awesome sight? Who could look on with dry eyes? Who could steel himself to turn round and look upon them? If any such person exists, his nature is not the same as our nature, and he cannot belong to the race of Adam.

They conveyed the queen along that road and made her get out in between the bodies. The entire entourage came out after her, for it was the time when the king was moving up to his summer residence.

The glorious women were crowned on the fifth of the lunar month Iyyar.

## 7.4 Male attitudes

### 7.4.1 Daughters of Eve

Ambrose, bishop of Milan from 374 to 397, illustrates a hostile attitude toward women, whom he sees as the inheritors of Eve's sin and not made in God's image.

Ambrose, *Commentary on Paul's First Letter to the Corinthians* 148
[Karl Frederick Morrison, "Rome and the City of God," *Transactions of the American Philosophical Society*, vol. 54, part I (Philadelphia: The American Philosophical Society, 1964) pp. 46–7]

Since she is not the image of God a woman ought, therefore, to veil her head, to show herself subject. And since falsehood began through her, she ought to have this sign, that her head be not free, but covered with a veil out of reverence for the bishop. For the bishop has the role of Christ. Because of the beginning of crime, she ought to appear subject before a bishop, since he is the vicar of the Lord, just as she would before a judge.

### 7.4.2 The pain of abandoning a concubine

When Augustine's mother arranged a marriage for him with a very young girl, his concubine left him, vowing to have no further sexual relationships. This prompted Augustine later in his life to speculate on what it means to have a good marriage. (See also Chapter 8, Domestic life.)

Augustine, *Confessions* 6.15.25

[*Saint Augustine: Confessions*, trans. Henry Chadwick (Oxford: Oxford University Press, 1991) p. 109]

> Meanwhile my sins multiplied. The woman with whom I habitually slept was torn away from my side because she was a hindrance to my marriage. My heart which was deeply attached was cut and wounded, and left a trail of blood. She had returned to Africa vowing that she would never go with another man. She left with me the natural son I had by her. But I was unhappy, incapable of following a woman's example, and impatient of delay. I was to get the girl I had proposed to only at the end of two years. As I was not a lover of marriage but a slave of lust, I procured another woman, not of course as wife. By this liaison the disease of my soul would be sustained and kept active, either in full vigor or even increased, so that the habit would be guarded and fostered until I came to the kingdom of marriage. But my wound, inflicted by the earlier parting, was not healed. After inflammation and sharp pain, it festered. The pain made me as it were frigid but desperate.

Augustine, *The Good in Marriage* 5.5.376–7

[Peter Brown, *The Body and Society. Men, Women and Sexual Renunciation in Early Christianity* (New York: Columbia University Press, 1988) p. 393]

> This problem often arises: If a man and a woman live together without being legitimately joined, not to have children, but because they could not observe continence; and if they have agreed between themselves to have relations with no one else, can this be called a marriage? Perhaps: but only if they had resolved to maintain until death the good faith which they had promised themselves . . . But if a man takes a woman only for a time, until he has found another who better suits his rank and fortune: and if he marries this woman, as being of the same class, this man would commit adultery in his heart, not towards the woman he wished to marry, but towards the woman with whom he had once lived.

## 7.5 Legal status

### 7.5.1 Women's right to prosecute in court

Roman law severely restricted women's right to prosecute in public suits.
*Theodosian Code* 9.1.3

> Since it is clear and manifest law that women do not have the right to prosecute public criminal suits, except in certain cases, that is, when prosecuting a case of outrage to themselves or to members of their families, the ancient statutes must be observed. For it is not right that the power to make an accusation should be entrusted generally to women. On the other hand, in public criminal trials at times their testimony or their authority as accusers has been admitted. Advocates also must be warned that they must not, in the interest of gain, rashly accept women as clients, who depend on the security of their sex and perhaps rush into unlawful action. [Constantine, 322]

### 7.5.2 The new status of celibacy

In pre-Christian Rome celibacy was a legal disadvantage because producing legitimate offspring was of primary importance, but with the advent of the new faith, attitudes and restrictions changed. This law of Constantine of 320 indicates the influence of Christianity on social legislation.
*Theodosian Code* 8.16.1

> *Annulment of the penalties for celibacy and childlessness*
>
> Those persons who were formerly considered celibates by the ancient law shall be freed from the threatening terrors of the law, and they shall live as though numbered among married men and supported by the bonds of matrimony, and all men shall have an equal status in that they shall be able to accept anything to which they are entitled. Nor indeed shall any person be considered childless, and the prejudices attached to that name shall not harm him. 1. We consider that the same provision shall be effective with respect to women, and We release all of them indiscriminately from the legal compulsion imposed as yokes on their necks. [Constantine, 320]

### 7.5.3 Protecting women

Roman law protected women from sexual exploitation by the males legally responsible for them.
*Theodosian Code* 15.8.2 [Justinian, *Code* 11.40.6]

> If fathers or masters should be procurers and should impose upon their daughters or female slaves the necessity of sinning, We do not allow such procurers to enjoy the right of ownership or to rejoice in the license of so great

criminality. It is Our pleasure, therefore, that such procurers shall be deprived by Our indignation, and they shall not be able to enjoy the right of control over their daughters or slaves, or to acquire any gain from them in this manner. But if the slaves and daughters so wish, as well as the persons hired on account of poverty and condemned to such a condition by their humble lot, they shall be permitted to implore the aid of bishops, judges, and defenders, to be released from all the bonds of their miseries. If the procurers should suppose that they may insist or if they should compel the women to undergo the necessity of sinning against their will, they shall not only forfeit all the power which they had over them, but they shall also be proscribed and delivered to the punishment of being assigned to exile in the public mines. Such a punishment is less severe than that of a woman who is compelled, at the command of a procurer, to tolerate the sordidness of a condition which she does not wish. [Theodosius and Valentinian, 428]

### 7.5.4 Legitimacy and inheritance

Legitimacy and inheritance remained intimately linked throughout the late Roman Empire. Justinian retained in his *Code* previous legislation on the subject and added his own rulings.

Justinian, *Code* 6.57.5

Where a woman of illustrious birth has a son born in lawful wedlock, and another one who is illegitimate, and whose father is uncertain, a doubt arose to what extent they would be entitled to their mother's estate, and whether it would only descend to legitimate children, or whether it would also go to those who are bastards. Therefore, We order that, while any legitimate children are living, no portion whatever of their estates shall pass from mothers of illustrious birth to their bastard offspring, either by will, on the ground of intestacy, or by donations to living people; for the preservation of chastity is the first duty of freeborn and illustrious women, and We hold that it would be unjust, and very oppressive and unworthy of the spirit of our age, for bastards to be acknowledged . . . [Justinian, 534]

### 7.5.5 Women benefit from Roman law

Motivated by concern to impose a uniform Christian law as well as to protect certain female rights, Justinian reformed inheritance law in Armenia in 536. (See also *9.2.2*, page 292.)

Justinian, *Novel* 21.1

[*The Civil Law*, vol. 16, trans. S.P Scott (Cincinnati, OH: Central Trust, 1932), p. 109]

Therefore We decree by this imperial enactment that the laws in force in Our Empire, which have reference to the right of women to succeed to estates, shall be observed in Armenia, and that no difference shall hereafter exist between the sexes in this respect; that women, in accordance with the rule laid down in Our laws, shall inherit from their parents, that is to say, in the ascending line, from their fathers and mothers, grandfathers and grandmothers, indefinitely; and in the descending line, from their sons and daughters, no matter in what way either of these transmit their property.

Hence the Armenians shall no longer be subject to laws different from those of the Empire; and if they form part of Our subjects, and are under Our government like many other peoples, and enjoy the benefits conferred by Us, their women shall not be the only ones deprived of Our justice; and they shall all enjoy the benefit of Our laws, whether the latter have come down to Us from former ages and have been inserted into Our *Institutes* and *Digest*, or whether they are called upon to obey the Imperial Constitutions promulgated by Ourself, or by Our predecessors.

## Further reading

Arjava, Antti, *Women and Law in Late Antiquity* (Oxford: Oxford University Press, 1996)

Clark, Gillian, *Women in Late Antiquity. Pagan and Christian Life-styles* (Oxford: Oxford University Press, 1993)

Connor, Carolyn L., *Women of Byzantium* (New Haven, CT: Yale University Press, 2004)

Evans, James Allan, *The Empress Theodora, Partner of Justinian* (Austin: University of Texas Press, 2002)

Evans-Grubbs, Judith, *Women and the Law in the Roman Empire: A Sourcebook on Marriage, Divorce and Widowhood* (London: Routledge, 2002)

Herrin, Judith, *Women in Purple. Rulers of Medieval Byzantium* (Princeton, NJ: Princeton University Press, 2001)

James, Liz, *Empresses and Power in Early Byzantium* (London: Leicester University Press, 2001)

Sivan, Hagith, "Why Not Marry a Barbarian? Marital Frontiers in Late Antiquity," in Ralph Mathisen and Hagith Sivan, eds., *Shifting Frontiers in Late Antiquity* (Aldershot: Variorum, 1996)

Smith, Julia M.H., "Did Women Have a Transformation of the Roman World?," *Gender and History* 12.3 (2000) Special Issue: *Gendering the Middle Ages*, ed. Pauline Stafford and Anneke B. Mulder-Bakker

Swan, Laura, *The Forgotten Desert Mothers. Sayings, Lives, and Stories of Early Christian Women* (New York: Paulist Press, 2001)

# 8

# DOMESTIC LIFE

## 8.1 Introduction

Roman ideas of family differed greatly from our own. In addition to the nuclear family of parents and children, the inhabitants of a household regularly included members of the extended family, slaves, and perhaps other dependants. The power relations among these different residents of a household, the emotional and economic ties that bound them together, the rituals that marked phases of their life cycle from birth to death and beyond, and the ways that the house itself was protected against supernatural forces rendered domestic life as rich and fascinating a phenomenon as the patterns of public life encountered in the Roman street. Great changes in domestic life in Late Antiquity resulted from the spread of Christianity. During the Late Antique centuries, Christian attitudes toward sexuality, gender relations, marriage, and the life cycle transformed the traditional domestic realm.

## 8.2 Sexuality, procreation, and birth

### 8.2.1 Sexual intercourse

Church leaders taught that sexual intercourse was acceptable only in marriage, and then only for the purpose of having children. This interpretation of sexual relations marked a radical change from earlier Roman practice.

Augustine, *On Christ's Grace and Original Sin* 2.38.43

["Marrying and the *Tabulae Nuptiales* in Roman North Africa from Tertullian to Augustine," trans. David G. Hunter in *To Have and to Hold: Marrying and its Documentation in Western Christendom, 400–1600*, ed. Philip L. Reynolds and John Witte, Jr. (Cambridge: Cambridge University Press, 2007) pp. 95–113, here 107]

> Marital intercourse, which according to the marriage contracts takes place "for the sake of producing children," is in itself a good without qualification, not merely in comparison with fornication. Even though, on account of the "body of death" which has not yet been renewed by the resurrections, this marital intercourse cannot take place without a kind of bestial motion, which causes

240

human nature to blush, nevertheless intercourse itself is not a sin, when reason uses lust for a good purpose and is not diverted to a bad purpose.

### 8.2.2 Conception

Nemesius of Emesa, a physician of the fourth century, articulated the belief widespread in Late Antiquity that women did in fact play a role in the conception of a child and were not merely vessels that carried the fetus, the commonly held view in earlier centuries. Nemesius also believed the sex of the fetus was determined by the relative force of the male and female seed and the fetus' position in the womb.

Nemesius of Emesa, *On the Nature of Man* 25

[Gillian Clark, *Women in Late Antiquity* (Oxford: Clarendon Press, 1993) pp. 72–3]

> Aristotle and Democritus want the woman's seed to contribute nothing to the procreation of children: they want the secretion of women to be a sweat from the part, rather than the seed. But Galen, criticizing Aristotle, says women do produce seed and the mixture of both seeds makes the embryo: that is why intercourse is called *mixis* [mixing]. But the woman's seed is not as perfect as that of the man, but still unrefined and moist; and since it is like that, the woman's seed is nourishment for that of the man.

### 8.2.3 Abortion and contraception

Churchmen opposed abortion. This sermon of Caesarius, bishop of Arles from 502 to 542, gives evidence of methods of contraception in use.

Caesarius of Arles, *Sermon* 44.2

[*Saint Caesarius of Arles. Sermons*, vol. I, trans. Mary Magdaleine Mueller (New York: Fathers of the Church, 1956) pp. 221–2]

> No woman should take drugs for purposes of abortion, nor should she kill her children that have been conceived or are already born. If anyone does this, she should know that before Christ's tribunal she will have to plead her case in the presence of those she has killed. Moreover, women should not take diabolical draughts with the purpose of not being able to conceive children. A woman who does this ought to realize that she will be guilty of as many murders as the number of children she might have borne. I would like to know whether a woman of nobility who takes deadly drugs to prevent conception wants her maids or tenants to do so. Just as every woman wants slaves born for her so that they may serve her, so she herself should nurse all the children she conceives, or entrust them to others for rearing. Otherwise, she may refuse to conceive children or, what is more serious, be willing to kill souls which might have been good Christians. Now, with what kind of a conscience does she desire slaves to be born of her servants, when she herself refuses to bear children who might become Christians?

241

### 8.2.4 Childbirth's pains

Ephrem the Syrian (*c.*306–373) attempts to represent a female point of view in this passage from a *Hymn on Paradise*. He emphasizes the violence of childbirth.

Ephrem the Syrian, *Hymn on Paradise* 8.8

[Peter Brown, ed., *The Body and Society: Men, Women, and Sexual Renunciation in Early Christianity* (New York: Columbia University Press, 1988) p. 330]

> There find their sweet repose
> Wives with bodies broken,
> Through pregnancy's dire curse,
> Through birth's hard labors.
> There do they see the babes,
> That they buried with sighs,
> Feed like the new born lambs,
> Deep in the green of the Garden.

### 8.2.5 Women's bodies and bearing children

The consequences of childbearing on women's bodies were harsh, a fact recognized by the male author of the following passage.

Pseudo-Athanasius, *Life of Syncletica* 42

[Gillian Clark, *Women in Late Antiquity* (Oxford: Oxford University Press, 1993) p. 91]

> Most women have a hateful time in the world. They give birth in pain and danger, they suffer in breast-feeding, when their children are ill they are ill too. They endure this without any end to their hard work. Either the children they conceive are maimed in body, or they are brought up in wickedness and plot to kill their parents. We know this: let us not be deceived by the Enemy into thinking that way of life is easy and trouble free. When they give birth they are damaged by labour, and if they do not, they are worn down by reproaches of barrenness.

### 8.2.6 Naming a baby girl

The Roman Empire was multi-ethnic in Late Antiquity, and naming practices varied from region to region and changed over time. In this papyrus fragment from Egypt, which dates to the fourth century, a woman (her signature is lost) writes to a friend or relative announcing the naming of her new baby girl.

*Military Papyrus* 2.84

[Roger S. Bagnall and Raffaella Cribiore, *Women's Letters from Ancient Egypt, 300 BC–AD 800* (Ann Arbor: University of Michigan Press, 2006) p. 271]

> I hope that I find you and your husband in good spirits. Andrias and Nikias greet you, and also little Lampiadis. If I had happened to give birth to a male,

I would have given it my brother's name. But now since it is female, it has been called by your name.

### 8.2.7 Exposure of unwanted infants

Abandoning unwanted infants by the roadside to die or be carried off by strangers was a common practice in Roman society. The jurist Paul (c.210) decried the practice, and his opinion was maintained in Justinian's *Digest*, as well as by Bishop Basil of Caesarea, a leading figure of the Greek Church in the fourth century.

Justinian, *Digest* 25.3.4

> Paul, *Views*, book 2: It is not just a person who smothers a child who is held to kill it but also the person who abandons it, denies it food, or puts it on show in public places to excite pity which he himself does not have.

Basil of Caesarea, *Letter* 199.33
[*Saint Basil, The Letters*, vol. III, trans. Roy J. Deferrari (Cambridge, MA: Harvard University Press, 1930) p. 125]

> (33) Let the woman who gave birth on the road and took no care of her offspring be subjected to the charge of murder.

## 8.3 Children

### 8.3.1 Raising abandoned children

In the following law Constantine ensures that the child could be raised as a slave or a free person, depending on the wish of the person who rescued it. Once abandoned in this way, a baby could never be reclaimed by its parents.

*Theodosian Code* 5.9.1

> If any person should take up a boy or a girl child that has been cast out of its home with the knowledge and consent of its father or owner, and if he should rear this child to strength with his own sustenance, he shall have the right to keep the said child under the same status as he wished it to have when he took charge of it, that is, as his child or as a slave, whichever he should prefer. Every disturbance of suits for recovery by those persons who knowingly and voluntarily cast out from home newly born children, whether slaves or free, shall be abolished. [Constantine, 331]

### 8.3.2 Parents prevented from selling their children

The government sometimes tried to help parents whose poverty forced them to sell their children as slaves. This law of Constantine reveals the compassionate side of imperial legislation.

*Theodosian Code* 11.27.2

We have learned that provincials suffering from lack of sustenance and the necessities of life are selling or pledging their own children. Therefore, if any such person should be found who is sustained by no substance of family fortune and who is supporting his children with suffering and difficulty, he shall be assisted through Our fisc before he becomes a prey to calamity. The proconsuls and governors and the fiscal representatives throughout all Africa shall thus have the power, they shall bestow freely the necessary support on all persons whom they observe to be placed in dire need, and from the State storehouses they shall immediately assign adequate sustenance. For it is at variance with Our character that We should allow any person to be destroyed by hunger or to break forth to the commission of a shameful deed. [Constantine, 322]

### 8.3.3 Girls

Jerome (*c.*347–430), a leader of the Latin Church in the fourth century, outlines a proper upbringing for a newly born girl, Pacatula. He advises that she be kept entirely apart from young men.

Jerome, *Letter* 128

["Jerome, Letter 128." *New Advent*. 2008. Kevin Knight. April 28, 2009 <http://www.newadvent.org/fathers/3001128.htm>]

A girl should associate only with girls, she should know nothing of boys and should dread even playing with them. She should never hear an unclean word, and if amid the bustle of the household she should chance to hear one, she should not understand it. Her mother's nod should be to her as much a command as a spoken injunction. She should love her as her parent, obey her as her mistress, and revere her as her teacher. She is now a child without teeth and without ideas, but, as soon as she is seven years old, a blushing girl knowing what she ought not to say and hesitating as to what she ought, she should until she is grown up commit to memory the psalter, and the books of Solomon; the gospels, the apostles and the prophets should be the treasure of her heart. She should not appear in public too freely or too frequently attend crowded churches. All her pleasure should be in her chamber. She must never look at young men or turn her eyes upon curled fops; and the wanton songs of sweet voiced girls which wound the soul through the ears must be kept from her. The more freedom of access such persons possess, the harder it is to avoid them when they come; and what they have once learned themselves they will secretly teach her and will thus contaminate our secluded Danae by the talk of the crowd. Give her for guardian and companion a mistress and a governess, one not given to much wine or in the apostle's words idle and a tattler, but sober, grave, industrious in spinning wool and one whose words will form her childish mind to the practice of virtue.

### 8.3.4  The benefits of beating children

Beating children was commonplace in Roman homes for infractions of rules of behavior, and it was considered a parent's right and duty to do so. Roman schoolmasters also used corporal punishment, and were notorious for their brutal teaching methods. In this passage Augustine comments on the benefits of this abusive behavior.

Augustine, *Letter* 104, *Patrologia Latina* 33

[Thomas Wiedemann, *Adults and Children in the Roman Empire* (London: Routledge, 1989) p. 106]

> If as small children, or even as rather bigger ones, we had successfully begged our parents or schoolteachers not to beat us, which of us would have grown up as a tolerable adult? Which of us would ever have learned anything? These things are done out of forethought, not cruelty.

### 8.3.5  A father's care for his son's education

About the year 400, the Roman aristocrat and intellectual Symmachus recorded his concern for his boy's education in a letter to a friend with an already grown son.

Symmachus, *Letter* 3.20

[Thomas Wiedemann, *Adults and Children in the Roman Empire* (London: Routledge, 1989) p. 107]

> Now that my son is beginning to learn Greek, I have been accompanying him in his studies for a second time, as though I were the same age. For the obligation to ensure that our children find pleasure in literature as well as labour bids us to become children again. As far as you are concerned, you have harvested, not just sown: your young man is such an accomplished speaker – as I found out when I spoke to him – that he seems to be treading hard on the heels of his father. You will be very fortunate, my friend, if he surpasses you. My own teaching is still concerned with creating a plant.

### 8.3.6  A teenager's love of learning

In his autobiography, the fourth-century rhetorician Libanius describes his early devotion to his studies – not the expected interest of a teenager. He shows how his studies fit into the urban life of his native town, Antioch in Syria.

Libanius, *Autobiography* 4, 5, 8, 19, 21, 22

[Libanius, *Autobiography and Selected Letters*, vol. I, trans. A.F. Norman (Cambridge, MA: Harvard University Press, 1992) pp. 57, 59, 61, 63, 75, 77, 79]

> 4.  My father took his bride from such a family and had three sons, of whom I am the middle one. He died before his prime when he had recovered a little of these great losses, and he was followed almost immediately by my maternal grandfather. My mother was a prudent woman and feared the dishonesty of

guardians and the litigation which would inevitably arise with them, and so she herself set out to be all to us. In general, she succeeded very well by dint of her exertions, but though she paid out fees to schoolmasters for us, she did not have the heart to get annoyed with her sleepyhead of a son, for she thought it was a loving mother's part never to upset her child. Thus it came about that we spent the greater part of the year in the countryside rather than in the study.

[. . .]

5. . . . when I was nearly fifteen my interest was kindled and an earnest love of study began to possess me. Hence the charms of the countryside were put aside: I sold my pigeons, pets which are apt to get a strong hold on a boy; the chariot races and everything to do with the stage were discarded, and I remained aloof, far from the sight of those gladiatorial combats where men, whom you would swear to be the pupils of the three hundred at Thermopylae, used to conquer or die. My attitude in this caused the greatest amazement both to young and old. The person responsible for the presentation of these shows was my maternal uncle, and though he invited me to the spectacle, I still stayed wedded to my books. The story goes that he, all that time ago, foretold for me the position of sophist that has actually come to pass.

[. . .]

8. Again, I was lucky as a pupil in that I attended the lectures of a teacher with a fine flow of oratory; my bad luck was that my attendance was not as regular as it should have been but occurred only in a most perfunctory fashion, and then, when my desire did spur me on to study, I found none to instruct me, for death had stopped his flow. So, though I longed for my dead teacher, I began to frequent the living, mere shadows of teachers, as men eat loaves of barley bread for want of anything better. However, when I found that I was making no progress but was running the risk of falling into the bottomless pit of ignorance through following blind guides, I had done with them. I restrained my mind from composing, my tongue from speaking, and my hand from writing, and I concentrated upon one thing only – the memorization of the works of classical authors – and studied under a man of prodigious memory who was capable of instilling into his pupils an appreciation of the excellence of the classics. I attached myself to him so wholeheartedly that I would not leave him even after class had been dismissed, but would trail after him, book in hand, even through the city square, and he had to give me some instruction, whether he liked it or not. At the time he was obviously annoyed at this importunity, but in later days he was full of praise for it.

[. . .]

19. From my boyhood, gentlemen, I had heard tales of the fighting between the schools which took place in the heart of Athens: I had heard of the cudgels, the knives and stones they used and of the wounds they inflicted, of the

resultant court actions, the pleas of the defence and the verdicts upon the guilty, and of all those deeds of derring-do which students perform to raise the prestige of their teachers . . .

[. . .]

21. Thus I took no part in the sallies, skirmishes, martial affrays, and pitched battles. In fact, even on the occasion of the great riot, when everyone was involved, even those excused by their age, I alone stayed in my seat far away from it all, hearing of the harm which befell each one and remaining aloof from the blows they dealt each other in their anger, giving none and receiving none, and with no intention of so doing, either . . .

22. Thus when I was present, everyone made a point of getting all to behave decently, for I never so much as touched a ball all the time I was in Athens, and I kept myself well away from the carousals and the company of those who raided the houses in the meaner quarters at night, and I made it quite clear too that the singing girls – Scylla's heads, or neighbours perhaps more dangerous than Siren – who have wrecked the career of many a man, sang to me in vain.

### 8.3.7 A grandfather's advice about study and relaxation

Although the fifth-century Gallo-Roman aristocrat Ausonius takes it for granted that his grandson should study hard to master the texts essential to framing the world view of a Roman grandee, he also realizes that it is necessary to relax and have fun. Not only are these aspects of life desirable for a teenager, they are among the perquisites of aristocratic life.

Ausonius, *Epistles* 22

[*Ausonius: Works*, vol. 2, trans. Hugh White (Cambridge, MA: Harvard University Press, 1919) p. 73]

To Ausonius my grandson:
The Muses also have their own sports: hours of ease find place among the Camenae, my honey-sweet grandson; nor does the sour schoolmaster's domineering voice always harass boys, but spells of rest and study keep each their appointed times. As for an attentive boy to have read his lessons willingly is enough, so to rest is lawful. "School" has been called by that Greek name, that the laborious Muses may be allowed due share of leisure. Wherefore the more assured that play follows work in turn, learn willingly: to beguile the weariness of long toil we grant spells of leisure. Boyish zeal flags unless serious work is interspersed with merriment and workaday with holiday. Learn readily, and loathe not, my grandson, the control of your grim teacher. A master's looks need never cause a shudder. Though he be grim with age and, ungentle of voice, threaten harsh outbursts with frowning brows, never will he seem savage to one who has tutored his face to habitual calm. A child will love its nurse's wrinkles, who shrinks from its mother; grandchildren when they

come at last, a new anxiety, prefer doddering grandsires and grandmas to their parents.

## 8.4 Marriage and divorce

### 8.4.1 Adolescence and betrothal

Gregory of Nyssa (*c.*331–*c.*394) was one of the Fathers of the Greek Orthodox Church. In his busy career he wrote a biography of his sister Macrina. This portion of the work shows how a young woman's adolescence and betrothal were handled in a Christian household, and how she managed to avoid marriage.

Gregory of Nyssa, *Vita Macrinae* 4–5

[W.K. Lowther Clarke, *The Life of St. Macrina* (London: SPCK, 1916)]

Filling her time with these and the like occupations, and attaining besides a considerable proficiency in wool-work, the growing girl reached her twelfth year, the age when the bloom of adolescence begins to appear. In which connection it is noteworthy that the girl's beauty could not be concealed in spite of efforts to hide it. Nor in all the countryside, so it seems, was there anything so marvellous as her beauty in comparison with that of others. So fair was she that even painters' hands could not do justice to her comeliness; the art that contrives all things and essays the greatest tasks, so as even to model in imitation the figures of the heavenly bodies, could not accurately reproduce the loveliness of her form. In consequence a great swarm of suitors seeking her in marriage crowded round her parents. But her father – a shrewd man with a reputation for forming right decisions – picked out from the rest a young man related to the family, who was just leaving school, of good birth and remarkable steadiness, and decided to betroth his daughter to him, as soon as she was old enough. Meantime he aroused great hopes, and he offered to his future father-in-law his fame in public speaking as if it were one of the bridegroom's gifts; for he displayed the power of his eloquence in forensic contests on behalf of the wronged.

But Envy cut off these bright hopes by snatching away the poor lad from life. Now Macrina was not ignorant of her father's schemes. But when the plan formed for her was shattered by the young man's death, she said her father's intention was equivalent to a marriage, and resolved to remain single henceforward, just as if the intention had become accomplished fact. And indeed her determination was more steadfast than could have been expected from her age. For when her parents brought proposals of marriage to her, as often happened owing to the number of suitors that came attracted by the fame of her beauty, she would say that it was absurd and unlawful not to be faithful to the marriage that had been arranged for her by her father, but to be compelled to consider another; since in the nature of things there was but one marriage, as there is one birth and one death. She persisted that the man who had been linked to her by her parents' arrangement was not dead, but that she considered him who lived to God, thanks to the hope of the resurrection, to be absent only, not dead; it was wrong not to keep faith with the bridegroom who was away.

With such words repelling those who tried to talk her over, she settled on one safeguard of her good resolution [not to marry], in a resolve not to be separated from her mother even for a moment of time.

### 8.4.2 Aristocratic courtship

Jerome was fast friends with an aristocratic woman called Marcella, whom he encouraged in her choice of an ascetic life and whose gifts to the Church he was happy to accept. In one of his letters he offers a lengthy description of Marcella. He describes how she rejected the suitors her mother found for her when she was a young widow.

Jerome, *Letter* 127

["Jerome, Letter 127." *New Advent*. 2008. Kevin Knight. April 28, 2009 <http://newadvent.org/fathers/3001127.htm >]

> Her father's death left her an orphan, and she had been married less than seven months when her husband was taken from her. Then as she was young, and highborn, as well as distinguished for her beauty – always an attraction to men – and her self-control, an illustrious consular named Cerialis paid court to her with great assiduity. Being an old man he offered to make over to her his fortune so that she might consider herself less his wife than his daughter. Her mother Albina went out of her way to secure for the young widow so exalted a protector. But Marcella answered: "Had I a wish to marry and not rather to dedicate myself to perpetual chastity, I should look for a husband and not for an inheritance"; and when her suitor argued that sometimes old men live long while young can die early, she cleverly retorted: "A young man may indeed die early, but an old man cannot live long." This decided rejection of Cerialis convinced others that they had no hope of winning her hand.

### 8.4.3 Penalties for failing to marry are abolished

In 320 Constantine issued a law that repealed Augustus' legislation of three centuries earlier that had penalized celibacy in an attempt to encourage marriage and procreation by imposing restrictions on inheritance. With his law, which was part of a larger effort to reform inheritance and related issues, Constantine sought to make inheritance easier among the empire's wealthy elite. Constantine probably did not issue this law under Christian influence, for the ascetic lifestyle was still not well known among the empire's upper classes. However, the law did eliminate some barriers to the spread of the ascetic movement in centuries to come.

*Theodosian Code* 8.16.1

[Judith Evans-Grubbs, *Law and Family in Late Antiquity: The Emperor Constantine's Marriage Legislation* (Oxford: Oxford University Press, 1999) p. 119]

Those who were classed by the old law as *caelibes* [unmarried] shall be freed from the looming terrors of the laws: let them live as if included among the married and supported by the treaty of matrimony: let all be equally able to inherit what they deserve. And let no one be classed as childless; the losses prescribed for this name shall do no harm. We think this also with regard to women, and we release all alike from the yoke imposed upon their necks by the commands of the law. [Constantine, 320]

### 8.4.4 Astrology and different sorts of marriage

Before his conversion to Christianity in the 340s, the Sicilian rhetorician and astrologer Julius Firmicus Maternus composed a book about astrology called *Mathesis*. In the passages below he relates astral configurations to various sorts of marriage. Ideas such as these were widespread.

Firmicus Maternus, *Mathesis* 7.14

[Jean Rhys Bram, *Ancient Astrology Theory and Practice: Matheseos Libri VIII* (Park Ridge, NJ: Noyes Press, 1975) p. 248]

If Venus is in the house or terms of Mars, and Mars is in the house or terms of Venus, aspected in opposition the full Moon in her own house or terms, husbands kill their wives with their own hands. If Mars is on one of the angles, they kill them with a sword. But if in a woman's chart Mars is in her own house or his terms, on the MC [*medium coeli:* the zenith of a path in the sky] or in opposition to Venus, husbands are killed by their wives. This happens if there is no influence of Jupiter.

If the house of the wife, found as we showed in the last books, is in the house of Jupiter, the husband will be separated from all illicit desires. If Jupiter is in aspect to this house (his own), or if he is found in this house, the husband's chastity is even stronger. But if the house of the wife is in the house of Saturn, this will make the native [subject of the horoscope] lustful. If Saturn is in aspect to this house, this makes men austere toward their women.

If the house of the wife is found in the sign of Mars, and Mars or Jupiter is in aspect to this house, or one of them is in the house itself and another is in aspect to it, this will make husbands cherish their wives forever with true affection. But if the house of the wife is found the house of Mercury, and Mercury is in it, or in aspect to it, this will make passive lovers. The Sun will make them royal, the Moon pleasing and lovable.

If the Moon is with Mars in the house of Mars, and Saturn is in opposition or square aspect to them, the natives will be impotent and consumptive without wives or children. If Jupiter is found with Venus on the descendant, men freely cohabit with older women and women with old men. But if Jupiter is found with Venus on the ascendant, men sleep with younger women and women with youth.

### 8.4.5 Betrothal

Property arrangements played a significant part in deciding on marriage. Sometimes the gifts exchanged between bride and groom or their families could be quite substantial. In this ruling Constantine insists that the gifts be entered into the public record.

*Theodosian Code* 3.5.1

> It was the will of Our father that no act of generosity should be valid unless it was entered in the public records. We decree also that, after the time of the promulgation of this law, gifts between betrothed persons, as well as those between all other persons, shall be valid only if they are accompanied by the attestation of the public records. [Constantine, 319]

### 8.4.6 Prenuptial agreements

Getting married was not a step to take without careful preparation. A cautious groom would investigate what would happen to his bride's dowry if she should die. Issues of inheritance were paramount, as John Chrysostom described near the end of the fourth century.

John Chrysostom, "The Sort of Wives that Ought to be Taken in Marriage," *Patrologia Graeca* 51, 226–7

[Peter Garnsey and Caroline Humfress, *The Evolution of the Late Antique World* (Cambridge: Orchard Academic, 2001) p. 68]

> Now say that you are about to get married. You enter into careful consultation with external legal experts, you resort to them frequently, making anxious inquiry into what will happen if your wife dies childless, or if she leaves a son, or two or three survive her, then again, what use will she have of her father's property should he be alive, or should he be dead, what out of the inheritance will go to any brothers of hers, and what to the husband; likewise, you will want to know when she will be in control of all her property, so that no part of it will have to be yielded to another, and when on the other hand she will have to yield the whole of it. You pester them with questions of this kind, inquiring into all the ins and outs of the business in order to make sure that none of the woman's property will go to any of her relations.

### 8.4.7 Dowry

This document records the dowry of Geminia Januarilla, a Roman woman who wed Julianus in North Africa, in late 493. Though North Africa was at that time ruled by Vandal kings, the dowry arrangements were made in the traditional Roman fashion. They are recorded in Latin on a small cypress plank about 15 cm by 10 cm. The dowry was certainly the result of careful negotiations between Julianus and Geminia Januarilla's father. A *follis* (pl. *folles*) is a bronze coin with a small percentage of silver. The amounts mentioned below indicate that the dowry was respectable but far from lavish.

*The Dowry of Geminia Januarilla*
[Christian Courtois, *Tablettes Albertini: Actes privés de l'époque vandale (fin du Ve siècle)* (Paris: Arts et Métiers Graphiques, 1952) p. 215]

In the ninth year of the most invincible king, on the fifteenth of the kalends of October, this tablet [records] the dowry of Geminia Januarilla, married to Julianus, with the intention of producing children. The dowry that the maiden brings with her is composed of the following three portions. First, 8,000 *folles* in cash. Second, a white African vestment worth 2,000 *folles*; a gown worth 400 *folles*; another dress worth 200 *folles*; bridal finery worth 100 *folles*; a sash worth 150 *folles*; necklaces, bracelets, and rings worth 100 *folles*; riding boots of bull hide worth 150 *folles*; a weaving loom for wool, with her effects of shells, earrings, and lambskin boots, worth 150 *folles*. The dowry amounts to 11,500 *folles*. Third, there are another 500 *folles* to top off the dowry. This makes a grand total of 12,000 *folles* that I, Julianus, the husband, have accepted.

### 8.4.8 Traditional wedding ceremonies

Through the veil of John Chrysostom's criticism, there emerges a picture of the merriment that accompanied traditional weddings among non-Christians.

John Chrysostom, *Sermon on Marriage*
[Translated by Catharine Roth in Catherine Roth and David Anderson, *St. John Chrysostom on Marriage and Family Life* (Crestwood, NY: St. Vladimir's Seminary Press, 1986) pp. 82–3]

Nowadays on the day of a wedding people dance and sing hymns to Aphrodite, songs full of adultery, corruption of marriages, illicit loves, unlawful unions, and many other impious and shameful themes. They accompany the bride in public with unseemly drunkenness and shameful speeches. How can you expect chastity of her, tell me, if you accustom her to such shamelessness from the first day, if you present in her sight such actions and words as even the more serious slaves should not hear!

### 8.4.9 Forbidden marriage

Influenced by Christian beliefs, imperial legislation regarding proper marriage began to appear by the middle of the fourth century.

*Theodosian Code* 3.12.1–2

1. If any man should be so abominable as to presume that a daughter of a brother or a sister should be made his wife, and if he should fly into her embrace, not as her paternal or maternal uncle, he shall be held subject to a sentence of capital punishment. [Constantius and Constans, 342]

2. Although the ancients believed it lawful for a man to marry his brother's wife after the marriage of his brother had been dissolved, and lawful also for a

man, after the death or divorce of his wife, to contract a marriage with a sister of the said wife, all men shall abstain from such marriages and they shall not suppose that legitimate children may be begotten from such a union. For it is established that children so born are spurious. [Constantius and Constans, 321]

### 8.4.10 Adultery

Questions of social standing emerge in the following decision about adultery made by the emperor Constantine. A lowly barmaid was assumed to be little more than a prostitute, and so laws protecting chastity would not apply to her.
*Theodosian Code* 9.7.1

If any woman should commit adultery, it must be inquired whether she was the mistress of a tavern or a servant girl and thus in the performance of her servile duty she herself frequently served the wines of intemperance. If she should be mistress of the tavern, she shall not be exempt from the bonds of the law. But if she should give service to those who drink, in consideration of the mean status of the woman who is brought to trial, the accusation shall be excluded and the men who are accused shall go free, since chastity is required only of those women who are held by the bonds of law, but those who because of their mean status in life are not deemed worthy of the consideration of the laws shall be immune from judicial severity. [Constantine, 326]

### 8.4.11 A husband returns from captivity

In the unsettled conditions of the fifth century, many men and women were captured by barbarian raiders and forced to live far from home for many years. Occasionally, some did manage to escape or be ransomed, only to find that their spouses had remarried in their absence, thinking them dead. In this passage Pope Leo I (440–461) became involved in sorting out the problem.
Pope Leo I, *Epistle* 159.1–4
[Translated by Charles Lett Feltoe in *Nicene and Post-Nicene Fathers*, second series, vol. XII, ed. Philip Schaff (Buffalo, NY: Christian Literature Publishing Co., 1890). Revised and edited for *New Advent* by Kevin Knight. <http://www. newadvent.org/fathers/3604159.htm>]

Leo, the bishop, to Nicetas, bishop of Aquileia, greeting.

#### I. Prefatory.

My son Adeodatus, deacon of our See, on returning to us has delivered your request, beloved, to receive from us the authority of the Apostolic See upon matters which seem indeed to be hard to decide, but which we must make provision for with a view to the necessities of the times that the wounds which have been inflicted by the attacks of the enemy may be healed chiefly by the agency of religion.

## II. *About the women who married again when their husbands were taken prisoners.*

As then you say that through the disasters of war and through the grievous inroads of the enemy families have in certain cases been so broken up that the husbands have been carried off into captivity and their wives remain forsaken, and these latter thinking their own husbands either dead or never likely to be freed from their masters, have contracted another marriage under stress of loneliness, and as, now that the state of things has improved through the Lord's help, some of those who were thought to have perished have returned, you seem, dear brother, naturally to be in doubt what ought to be settled by us about women thus joined to other husbands. But because we know it is written that a woman is joined to a man by God (Proverbs 19:14) and again, we are aware of the precept that what God has joined, man may not put asunder (Matthew 19:6) we are bound to hold that the compact of the lawful marriage must be renewed, and after the removal of the evils inflicted by the enemy, what each lawfully had must be restored to him; and we must take all pains that each should recover what is his own.

## III. *Whether he is blameworthy who has taken the prisoner's wife.*

But notwithstanding let him not be held blameworthy and treated as the invader of another's right, who took the place of the husband, who was thought no longer alive. For thus many things which belonged to those led into captivity happened to pass into the possession of others, and yet it is altogether fair that on their return their property should be restored. And if this is duly observed in the case of slaves or of lands, or even of houses and personal goods, how much more ought it to be done in the restoration of wives, that what has been disturbed by the necessities of war may be restored by the remedy of peace?

## IV. *The wife must be restored to her first husband.*

And, therefore, if husbands who have returned after a long captivity still feel such affection for their wives as to desire them to return to partnership, that, which necessity brought about, must be passed over and judged blameless and the demands of fidelity satisfied.

## V. *Women must be excommunicated who refuse to return.*

And if any women are so possessed by love of their later husbands as to prefer to remain with them than to return to their lawful partners, they are deservedly to be branded: so that they be even deprived of the Church's communion; for in a pardonable matter they have chosen to taint themselves with crime, showing that they have sought their own pleasure in their incontinence, when a rightful restitution could have obtained their forgiveness. Let them return then to their former state and make voluntary reparation, nor let that which a condition of necessity extorted from them be by any means turned into disgrace through evil desires; because, as those women who refuse to return to their husbands are to be held unholy, so they who return to an affection entered on with God's sanction are deservedly to be praised.

## 8.4.12 A wife returns from captivity

In 406, Pope Innocent I wrote a letter to Probus, a Christian aristocrat in Rome. The problem concerned Ursa, a Roman woman, who had been captured by invaders, and her husband Fortunius, who remarried during her captivity. It is likely that Probus was the patron of this couple and that the Pope hopes that he will be able to convince Fortunius to return to his first wife.

Pope Innocent I, *Epistle 36* (*Patrologia Latina* 30: 602–3)
[Translated by Kristina Sessa, with some changes]

> The disorder of the barbarian trouble has produced an emergency in the application of the laws. For although the marriage of Fortunius and Ursa had been properly established, the assault of captivity would have stained it if the holy decrees of religion did not [provide for it.] For when this Ursa was held in captivity, Fortunius is known to have entered into another marriage with Restituta. But when with the Lord's favor Ursa returned, she approached us and with no one denying it, she explained that she was the proper wife of this man. Because of this, my lord son deservedly *illustris*, we determine that, with the support of the Catholic faith, that first one is the marriage which had been previously constituted by divine grace; and the agreement with the second woman, since the prior one is alive and has not been dismissed through divorce, cannot be legitimate by any means.

## 8.4.13 Marriage and divorce

Marriage and divorce remained a constant concern of Roman legislators. These laws of Justinian, enacted in 535, deal with reasons for ending a marriage.

Justinian, *Novel* 22.3–7
[*The Civil Law*, vol. 16, trans. S.P. Scott (Cincinnati, OH: Central Trust, 1932), p. 112]

### 22.3 In what way marriage is effected and dissolved

> Reciprocal affection constitutes marriage, without it being necessary to enter into a dotal contract; for when the parties are once agreed and have been influenced by pure affection, it is not requisite to stipulate for a dowry, or a donation on account of marriage. We shall treat of this relation as regards both its origin and end, whether the latter is accompanied by the penalty or not, since every tie effected by men is capable of being dissolved.
>
> A penalty is also prescribed where marriages contracted without a dowry are dissolved; and these We shall consider first.

### 22.4 Concerning dissolutions of marriage and divorces which take place by common consent and in other ways

Marriages occasionally are dissolved by common consent during the lives of the contracting parties, but it is not necessary to examine this kind of separation, because the parties interested settle their affairs by agreement among themselves; at other times, they are dissolved for some good reason, and this kind of separation is called divorce by common consent; in other instances, separations take place without any cause whatever, and in others still, for one which is reasonable.

### 22.5 Concerning monasticism

Divorce takes place without blame whenever either the husband or the wife enters monastic life, and desires to live in chastity; for another law of Ours specially provides that either a man or his wife, who devotes himself or herself to a monastic life, is authorized to dissolve the marriage, and separate from his or her consort by serving a notice by way of consolation. And whatever the parties may have agreed upon in case of the death of either, as set forth in their marriage contract, shall endure to the benefit of the abandoned wife or husband. The reason for this provision is, that wherever anyone embraces a different mode of life from that of his or her companion, he or she is considered to have died, so far as the marriage is concerned.

### 22.6 Concerning impotence

Marriage is dissolved for a necessary and not unreasonable cause, when the husband is incapable of copulation with his wife, and cannot do what nature created him for; and, in conformity with the law which We have already promulgated, if two years should have elapsed after the marriage, and the husband still not be able to show that he is a man, either his wife or her parents shall be permitted to dissolve the marriage, and give notice of repudiation to her husband, even if the latter should be unwilling to consent; the wife shall be entitled to the dowry, if one was given, and the husband shall return it if he received it; and the latter, on the other hand, shall be entitled to the ante-nuptial donation, and shall suffer no loss of his property.

We amend this law by making a certain addition thereto; for We decree that not two years, but three, shall elapse from the date of the marriage; as We have ascertained that some persons who were impotent for the term of two years have afterwards shown that they are capable of the procreation of children.

### 22.7 Concerning captivity

The effect of captivity is to dissolve marriage by mutual consent, where one of two married persons is in the hands of the enemy; for where the husband suffers a misfortune of this kind, and his wife remains at home; or, on the other hand, the wife is reduced to captivity, and her husband remains in his country, the marriage is dissolved for a reason derived from the condition of slavery; as, where a person is once reduced to servitude, the inequality of condition does not permit the equality derived from the marriage state to continue to exist. Therefore, considering cases of this kind from an humane point of view, We desire that the marriage shall remain undissolved as long as it is clear that either the husband or the wife is still living . . .

### 8.4.14 Women's right to divorce

Women's right to initiate divorce was limited. This law of Constantine establishes criteria for divorce.
*Theodosian Code* 3.16.1

*Notices of divorce.*

It is Our pleasure that no woman, on account of her own depraved desires, shall be permitted to send a notice of divorce to her husband on trumped up grounds, as, for instance, that he is a drunkard or a gambler or a philanderer, nor indeed shall a husband be permitted to divorce his wife on every sort of pretext. But when a woman sends a notice of divorce, the following criminal charges only shall be investigated, that is, if she should prove that her husband is a homicide, a sorcerer, or a destroyer of tombs, so that the wife may thus earn commendation and at length recover her entire dowry. For if she should send a notice of divorce to her husband on grounds other than these three criminal charges, she must leave everything, even to her last hairpin, in her husband's home, and as punishment for her supreme self-confidence, she shall be deported to an island. In the case of a man also, if he should send a notice of divorce, inquiry shall be made as to the following three criminal charges, namely, if he wishes to divorce her as an adulteress, a sorceress, or a procuress. For if he should cast off a wife who is innocent of these crimes, he must restore her entire dowry, and he shall not marry another woman. But if he should do this, his former wife shall be given the right to enter and seize his home by force and to transfer to herself the entire dowry of his later wife in recompense for the outrage inflicted upon her. [Constantine, 331]

### 8.4.15 A father decides for his daughter

In this papyrus from sixth-century Egypt, an angry father tells his son-in-law that the marriage to his daughter Euphemia is dissolved. Her opinion on the matter is not deemed relevant.
Oxyrhynchus Papyrus I.129
[John Garrett Winter, *Life and Letters in the Papyri* (Ann Arbor: University of Michigan Press, 1933) p. 128]

... I, John, father of Euphemia, my unemancipated daughter, send the present deed of repudiation and dissolution to you, Phoebammon, my most honorable son-in-law, through Anastasius, the most illustrious advocate of this city of Oxyrhynchus, to wit: Inasmuch as it has come to my hearing that you are giving yourself over to certain lawless practices which are pleasing neither to God nor to men – and there is no need that these be set down in writing – I have considered it proper that the marriage between you and her, my daughter Euphemia, should be broken, because, as has been said, I have heard that you are giving yourself over to the said lawless practices and because I want my daughter to lead a peaceful and quiet life. On this account, then, I send you the present deed of repudiation of the marriage between you and her ...

## 8.4.16 *Jerome defends a woman who decides to divorce*

In the following letter, Jerome (died 419/420), a leading voice of Latin Christianity, defends a woman named Fabiola, who decided to divorce her first husband and remarry. His statement reveals many basic attitudes about marriage held by Christians in Late Antiquity. Noteworthy is his condemnation of the behavior of her first husband.

Jerome, *Letter* 77.2–3

["Jerome, Letter 77." *New Advent.* 2008. Kevin Knight. April 28, 2009 <http://www.newadvent.org/fathers/3001077.htm>]

2. Today you give me as my theme Fabiola, the praise of the Christians, the marvel of the gentiles, the sorrow of the poor, and the consolation of the monks ...

3. And because at the very outset there is a rock in the path and she is overwhelmed by a storm of censure, for having forsaken her first husband and having taken a second, I will not praise her for her conversion till I have first cleared her of this charge. So terrible then were the faults imputed to her former husband that not even a prostitute or a common slave could have put up with them. If I were to recount them, I should undo the heroism of the wife who chose to bear the blame of a separation rather than to blacken the character and expose the stains of him who was one body with her. I will only urge this one plea which is sufficient to exonerate a chaste matron and a Christian woman. The Lord has given commandment that a wife must not be put away "except it be for fornication, and that, if put away, she must remain unmarried." Now a commandment which is given to men logically applies to women also. For it cannot be that, while an adulterous wife is to be put away, an incontinent husband is to be retained. The apostle says: "he which is joined to an harlot is one body." Therefore she also who is joined to a whoremonger and unchaste person is made one body with him. The laws of Cæsar are different, it is true, from the laws of Christ: Papinianus commands one thing; our own Paul another. Earthly laws give a free rein to the unchastity of men, merely condemning seduction and adultery; lust is allowed to range unrestrained

among brothels and slave girls, as if the guilt were constituted by the rank of the person assailed and not by the purpose of the assailant. But with us Christians what is unlawful for women is equally unlawful for men, and as both serve the same God both are bound by the same obligations. Fabiola then has put away – they are quite right – a husband that was a sinner, guilty of this and that crime, sins – I have almost mentioned their names – with which the whole neighbourhood resounded but which the wife alone refused to disclose. If however it is made a charge against her that after repudiating her husband she did not continue unmarried, I readily admit this to have been a fault, but at the same time declare that it may have been a case of necessity. "It is better," the apostle tells us, "to marry than to burn." She was quite a young woman, she was not able to continue in widowhood. In the words of the apostle she saw another law in her members warring against the law of her mind; she felt herself dragged in chains as a captive towards the indulgences of wedlock. Therefore she thought it better openly to confess her weakness and to accept the semblance of an unhappy marriage than, with the name of a monogamist, to ply the trade of a courtesan. The same apostle wills that the younger widows should marry, bear children, and give no occasion to the adversary to speak reproachfully. And he at once goes on to explain his wish: "for some are already turned aside after Satan." Fabiola therefore was fully persuaded in her own mind: she thought she had acted legitimately in putting away her husband, and that when she had done so she was free to marry again. She did not know that the rigour of the gospel takes away from women all pretexts for re-marriage so long as their former husbands are alive; and not knowing this, though she contrived to evade other assaults of the devil, she at this point unwittingly exposed herself to a wound from him.

## 8.5 Life in the Roman household

### 8.5.1 *Slaves in the household*

In fourth-century Egypt Demetrius, a slave in the household of Flavianus, wrote a letter to his master expressing his heartfelt concern for the mistress of the house, Flavianus' wife, who had fallen seriously ill.

Oxyrhynchus Papyrus VI.939

[John Garrett Winter, trans., *Life and Letters in the Papyri* (Ann Arbor: University of Michigan Press, 1933) pp. 93–4]

To my lord Flavianus, Demetrius, greeting. As in many other instances so now in even greater measure was the regard of the Lord God for you revealed to us all, with the result that our mistress recovered from the illness which had seized her; and may we continue forever to acknowledge our thanks because He was gracious to us and gave heed to our prayers by preserving to us our mistress, for in her we all have our hopes. May you pardon me, my lord, and receive me kindly if against my will I cast you into such distress by writing about her the tidings which you received. For when she was in great pain, being beside myself with anxiety, I sent you the first letter, hoping that you should by all means be able to come to us, for duty demanded this. But since she seems to have taken a turn for the better I am making haste that another letter may reach you by Euphrosynus in order that I may put you in a more cheerful mood. For by your own well-being, my lord, which is my chief concern, if my son Athanasius had not then been ill himself, I should have sent him to you with Plutarchus when she was afflicted by the sickness. But now I am at a loss what more to write about her, for she seems, as I have said, to be more comfortable in that she has sat up, although she is still rather ill. But we comfort her by hourly expecting your arrival. I pray, my lord, to the Lord of the Universe for your continued health. Pharmouthi 6 [= the date].

### 8.5.2 Responsibilities of the wife of a Roman senator

In the late fifth or early sixth century an anonymous author wrote a Latin manual of conduct for Gregoria, the wife of a Roman senator. This work describes the traditional role of a powerful Roman matron toward her household combined with a Christian ideology of devotion to God. It examines the moral responsibilities of rich Christian women who hope for salvation but do not abandon the obligations of a life of wealth and influence. The author emphasizes that God will judge Gregoria's conduct towards those dependent upon her and that the Devil is waiting for her to abandon the virtues of Christian life that she is expected to uphold.

Anonymous, *To Gregoria* 18

[Kate Cooper, *The Fall of the Roman Household* (Cambridge: Cambridge University Press, 2007) pp. 268–9]

Take care, I beseech you, Lady, lest anyone see filthy limbs among the rags of any of your home-born slaves, lest any one belonging to you should freeze in the cold of winter on account of poverty; let none suffer hunger, none be wearied by starvation, none by beatings, for there is not one of your slaves – male or female – for whom you may believe that you will not have to give account before God. For to this end mortals were made masters over other mortals, that they might receive the care of the image of God during its sojourn in this world, and might keep safe the riches destined for souls, which daily the plunderer of all that is good bestirs himself to snatch away.

So then be a model for all your servants: let them see you boldly standing guard over the riches of truth in your mouth, and of the riches of purity with respect to your body, of reverence in your breast, of innocence in your hands, of integrity in your expression. Let them see your eyes continually lifted to the heavens . . . By this model you will secure your own salvation and that of those [women] over whom you have been worthy to rule. For what they have seen you love, they do; what they see delight you, they imitate.

### 8.5.3 Female modesty, rings, and the household

Clement of Alexandra (died 215) wrote well before the Late Antique period, but his ideas about the role of women in marriage and the propriety of wearing jewelry were widely accepted in Christian communities for many centuries.

Clement of Alexandria, *Paedagogus* 3.11

[Simon P. Wood, trans., *Clement of Alexandria. Christ the Educator*. Fathers of the Church, vol. XXIII (New York: Fathers of the Church, 1954) pp. 244–6]

> [Christ] permits women the use of rings made of gold, not as ornaments, but as signet rings to seal their valuables at home worth guarding, in the management of their homes. If all were under the influence of the Educator [Christ], nothing would need to be sealed, for both master and servant would be honest. But, since lack of education exposes men to strong inclination to dishonesty, we always stand in need of these seals.
>
> In some circumstances, it is best to relax this stricture. We must be sympathetic with women who sometimes do not succeed in finding restraint in their married lives and who therefore adorn themselves to keep themselves attractive to their husbands. But let the attempt to win their husband's admiration be their sole motive. For my part, I would not want them to cultivate bodily comeliness, but, instead, to offer their husbands a self-controlled love, a remedy that is powerful and honest. However, when they are tempted to be unhappy in mind, let them recall this thought, that, if they wish to continue self-controlled, they will gently appease the unreasonable desires and cravings of their husbands. They must lead them back to simplicity quietly, by accustoming them little by little to what is more restrained.
>
> Dignity in dress comes not from adding to what is worn, but from eliminating all that is superfluous. The unnecessary luxuries that women wear, in fact, like tail-feathers, must be clipped off, because they give rise only to shifting vanity and senseless pleasure. Because of such vanity and pleasure, women become flighty and vain as peacocks, and even desert their husbands. Therefore, we should take care that the women are attired properly, and clothed abundantly in the modesty of self-restraint, so that they will not break away from the truth through vanity.
>
> It is but right that husbands trust their wives and confide the care of their homes to them. It is for this purpose that wives have been given as helpmates. But if, while we are engaged in public affairs, or are attending to other businesses, as those of our fields, and need be away from our wives frequently, we find it necessary to seal anything for safety's sake, then He allows us a signet ring for this purpose. But we should not wear any other rings, because, according to the Scriptures, it is only learning that is "an ornament of gold to the prudent."

### 8.5.4 Mother–daughter tensions in the same household

In addition to his exegetical, doctrinal, and other religious works, Jerome (died *c.*419) wrote copious letters of advice and instruction to friends and suppliants in Italy, Spain, and Gaul in which he advocated an ascetic life-style, sexual abstinence, and close reading of religious texts. In this letter, written in 405 in response to a Gallic friend's request, Jerome urged a woman not to live apart from her widowed mother.

Jerome, *Letter* 117

["Jerome, Letter 117." *New Advent*. 2008. Kevin Knight. May 12, 2009 <http://www.newadvent.org/fathers/3001117.htm>]

> Mother and daughter are names of affection; they imply natural ties and reciprocal duties; they form the closest of human relations after that which binds the soul to God. If you love each other, your conduct calls for no praise: but if you hate each other, you have committed a crime. The Lord Jesus was subject to His parents. He reverenced that mother of whom He was Himself the parent; He respected the foster-father whom He had Himself fostered; for He remembered that He had been carried in the womb of the one and in the arms of the other. Wherefore also when He hung upon the cross He commended to His disciple the mother whom He had never before His passion parted from Himself.
>
> Well, I shall say no more to the mother, for perhaps age, weakness, and loneliness make sufficient excuses for her; but to you the daughter I say: Is a mother's house too small for you whose womb was not too small? When you have lived with her for ten months in the one, can you not bear to live with her for one day in the other? Or are you unable to meet her gaze? Can it be that one who has borne you and reared you, who has brought you up and knows you, is dreaded by you as a witness of your home-life? . . . Why must you live in a house where you must daily win a battle or be ruined? . . . Even though she is as you say, you will have the greater reward for refusing to forsake her with all her faults. She has carried you in her womb, she has reared you; with gentle affection she has borne with the troublesome ways of your childhood. She has washed your linen, she has tended you when sick, and the sickness of maternity was not only borne for you but caused by you.

### 8.5.5 The married life of Augustine's parents

One of the strongest influences on Augustine's life was his mother, Monica. In this passage from his *Confessions*, he draws a portrait of her life with his father, Patricius, an abusive husband.

Augustine, *Confessions* 9.9.19

[Translated by J.G. Pilkington in *Nicene and Post-Nicene Fathers*, first series, vol. 1, ed. Philip Schaff (Buffalo, NY: Christian Literature Publishing Co., 1887). Revised and edited for *New Advent* by Kevin Knight. <http://www.new advent.org/fathers/1101.htm>]

Being thus modestly and soberly trained, and rather made subject by You to her parents, than by her parents to You, when she had arrived at a marriageable age, she was given to a husband whom she served as her lord. And she busied herself to gain him to You, preaching You unto him by her behaviour; by which You made her fair, and reverently amiable, and admirable unto her husband. For she bore the wronging of her bed so never to have any dissension with her husband on account of it. For she waited for Your mercy upon him, that by believing in You he might become chaste. And besides this, as he was earnest in friendship, so was he violent in anger; but she had learned that an angry husband should not be resisted, neither in deed, nor even in word. But so soon as he was grown calm and tranquil, and she saw a fitting moment, she would give him a reason for her conduct, should he have been excited without cause. In short, while many matrons, whose husbands were more gentle, carried the marks of blows on their dishonoured faces, and would in private conversation blame the lives of their husbands, she would blame their tongues, monishing them gravely, as if in jest: *"That from the hour they heard what are called the matrimonial tablets read to them, they should think of them as instruments whereby they were made servants; so, being always mindful of their condition, they ought not to set themselves in opposition to their lords."* And when they, knowing what a furious husband she endured, marvelled that it had never been reported, nor appeared by any indication, that Patricius had beaten his wife, or that there had been any domestic strife between them, even for a day, and asked her in confidence the reason of this, she taught them her rule, which I have mentioned above. They who observed it experienced the wisdom of it, and rejoiced; those who observed it not were kept in subjection, and suffered.

### 8.5.6 Mothers-in-law

The bridegroom, Papais, writes to Nonna, presumably his future mother-in-law, in this papyrus fragment from Egypt, dating to the fourth century. He is clearly eager to win her affection.

*Private letter*
[John W.B. Barns and Henrik Zilliacus, eds., *Antinoopolis Papyri*, vol. 2 (London: Egypt Exploration Society, 1950) pp. 103–5]

To my most honourable Nonna, Papais, greeting.

Before all I salute you and the mistress, my bride. I explained to your goodness already through the reader Serenus that you should take pains to arrange a house for me – only near to your own dwelling. For it is fitting that we should not be separated from one another. For next to God I respect you as my mother and my sister and you mean everything to me, if only my bride is in good health. But if you do not like this and feel troubled by our remaining in the immediate neighbourhood of your house, let me know, so that I may write to my brother Cronius and he may get ready for me the house . . . or I may get the house . . . I send you the box for seven bottles filled with plain (?) oil and the pillows and whatever I find. Let me know whether you received the golden ring from Dorotheus, the assistant of Anysius, together with the pearl of Arethusius the teacher, so that you may buy perfumes. When I come I am also bringing the sandals of P. . . . .ia; and if you have thought of anything useful for the wedding, write to me so that I may bring it with me when I come; for there is no dissension (?) between her and the bride. I pray for your lasting health.

I salute everyone in your house together with (our) friends. Mesore 22nd.

## 8.6  The house itself

The population of the Roman Empire lived in many sorts of houses in Late Antiquity, ranging from huts and elite villas in the countryside to urban palaces and densely packed tenement slums. A few different kinds of houses are shown in the illustrations that follow.

### 8.6.1  Farmhouse

This farmhouse at Horvat Susiya, near Hebron in modern Israel, combined an enclosed courtyard that held a baking oven, water trough, and area for corralling sheep with a covered one-story house that included two shops facing the street. Between the shops and the courtyard were the living and sleeping spaces and a large hall (*triclinium*) for communal eating. The farmhouse dates from the sixth through the eighth century.

[Yizhar Hirschfeld, *The Palestinian Dwelling in the Roman-Byzantine Period* (Jerusalem: Israel Exploration Society, 1995) pp. 36–7]

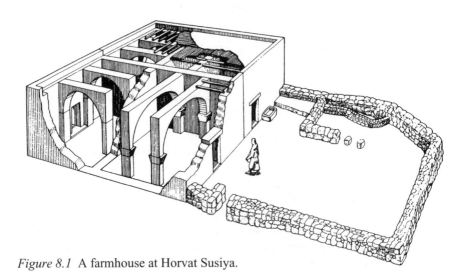

*Figure 8.1*  A farmhouse at Horvat Susiya.

### 8.6.2 Townhouse

This two-story townhouse in the city of Pergamon in Asia Minor was the home of a wealthy family that presumably had a large staff of slaves and other dependent workers. Built in the second half of the third through the fourth century, it had a colonnaded courtyard and boasted mosaic pavements, walls with fresco painting, a latrine, and two rectangular audience rooms.

[Isabella Baldini Lippolis, *La Domus Tardoantica. Forme e rappresentazioni dello spazio domestico nelle città del Mediterraneo* (Bologna: University Press, 2001) p. 249]

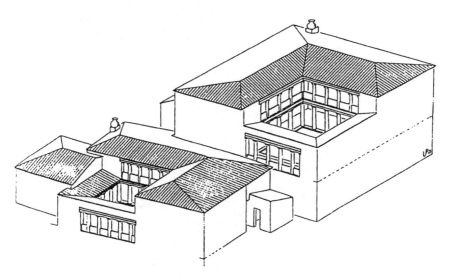

*Figure 8.2* A townhouse in the city of Pergamon.

### 8.6.3 Mansion

The mansion in Figure 8.3 in the North African city of Thuburbo Maius southwest of Carthage (in modern Tunisia) was called the House of the Animal Decorations (*Protomes*). It contains numerous large rooms decorated with elaborate floor mosaics and wall paintings, pools of water, and audience halls. It was built in the first quarter of the fourth century.

[Isabella Baldini Lippolis, *La Domus Tardoantica. Forme e rappresentazioni dello spazio domestico nelle città del Mediterraneo* (Bologna: University Press, 2001) p. 311]

### 8.6.4 Villa

Lullingstone Villa, in Kent in England, was built in stages over several centuries, reaching its greatest size and degree of luxury around 400 (see Figure 8.4). The

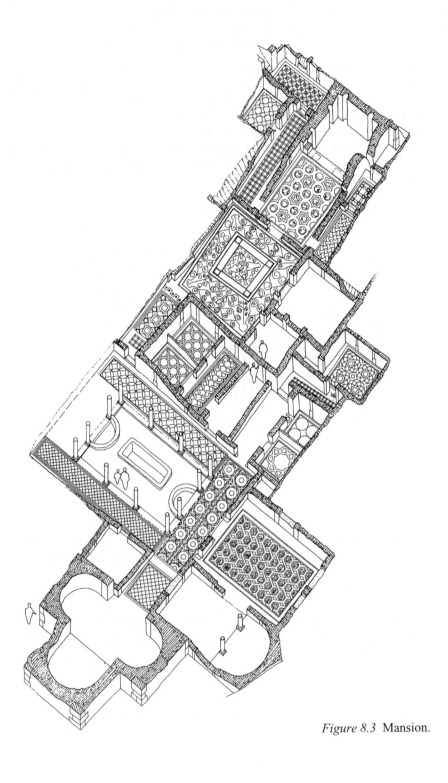

*Figure 8.3* Mansion.

*Figure 8.4* Villa. Reconstruction drawing of Lullingstone Villa and Temple-Mausoleum, *c.*360 by Alan Sorrell, Copyright English Heritage Photo Library.

complex of buildings was destroyed by fire around 500 and not rediscovered until the twentieth century. One of its rooms which had served as a pagan shrine became a small Christian chapel at an unknown date. A large dining room had two floor mosaics with mythological scenes. A series of very wealthy owners who doubtless had other properties possessed the property over the centuries of its occupation, and they profited from its use as a working farm.

### 8.6.5 Buying a house

The need for an expert to inspect a house for a prospective buyer was no less important in Late Antiquity than it is today.

Ambrose, *On Psalm 118 expositio sermo 13, littera* "mem" *7*
[Peter Garnsey and Caroline Humfress, *The Evolution of the Late Antique World* (Cambridge: Orchard Academic, 2001) p. 68]

> If you want to buy a tract of land, if you want to purchase a house, you get yourself someone more expert than yourself, you consider with care the legal regulations and, to avoid making some mistake, you do not trust in your own judgment.

### 8.6.6 Amulet to protect a house

The person who composed this text to protect a house in Egypt in the sixth century invoked deities from several traditions: Aphrodite (Greek), Horus (Egyptian), Yao Sabaoth Adonai (Judeo-Christian), and St. Phocas (Christian). At the beginning is the sign of the cross. The text is given a date at the very end. Dropping a letter from "Aphrodite" in each successive line would reduce an evil spirit until it vanished.

Oxyrhynchus Papyrus 1060
[Marvin Meyer and Richard Smith, *Ancient Christian Magic. Coptic Texts of Ritual Power* (Princeton, NJ: Princeton University Press, 1999) pp. 48–9]

> The door, Aphrodite
> Phrodite
> Rodite
> Odite
> Dite
> Ite
> Te
> E

> Hor Hor Phor Phor Yao Sabaoth Adonai, I bind you, Artemisian scorpion. Free this house of every evil reptile and annoyance, at once, at once. St. Phocas is here. Phamenoth 12, third indiction.

### 8.6.7  The sign of the cross, an emblem of protection

Although church leaders emphasized that the sign of the cross was only an emblem of safety, among the public the sign of the cross itself possessed magical qualities as a protective device against all forms of evil and danger. Private homes, public buildings, and individuals, too, found protection under the sign of the cross. The zealous application of crosses is described in the passages below.

*1.*

John Chrysostom, *Against Jews and Non-Christians* 9
[Eunice Dauterman Maguire, Henry Maguire, and Maggie J. Duncan-Flowers, *Art and Holy Power in the Early Christian House* (Urbana and Chicago: University of Illinois Press, 1989) pp. 18–19]

> No imperial crown can adorn a head in such a manner as the cross, which is in all the world more prized. This thing had largely been cause of horror to all, but now its image is so much sought after by all, that it is found everywhere, among rulers, among subjects, among women and slaves and freemen . . . One can see [the cross] celebrated everywhere, in houses, in marketplaces, in deserts, in streets, on mountains, in valleys, in hills, on the sea, in boats, on islands, on beds, on clothes, on weapons, in chambers, at banquets, on silverware, on objects in gold, in pearls, in wall paintings, on the bodies of much-burdened animals, on bodies besieged by demons, in war, in peace, by day, by night, in parties of luxurious livers, in brotherhoods of ascetics; so much do all now seek after this miraculous gift, this ineffable grace.

*2.*

Lintel of a house in Syria
[Eunice Dauterman Maguire, Henry Maguire, and Maggie J. Duncan-Flowers, *Art and Holy Power in the Early Christian House* (Urbana and Chicago: University of Illinois Press, 1989) p. 19]

> The lintel of a house in Sabbâ in Syria, dated to 547, had the following inscription with the sign of the cross (†):

> "† The Lord will protect the comings in and the goings out of this house; for as long as the cross is set in front of it the evil eye will not have power."

### 8.6.8  Household gods

In the following passage, Augustine mocks the multitude of gods associated with every aspect of domestic life in traditional religion. His view is hostile, but it reveals an important level of everyday religious expression in non-Christian households.

Augustine, *City of God* 4.11
[Jane F. Gardner and Thomas Wiedemann, *The Roman Household* (London: Routledge, 1991) pp. 34–5]

Should we also suppose that this ultimate godhead is visible in that multitude of so-called plebeian gods? Let him be in charge of men's seed in the person of *Liber*, and that of women as *Libera*; let him be *Diespater*, to bring children into the light of day; *Mena*, whom the Romans put in charge of women's monthly periods; *Lucina*, who is called on for help in childbirth. Let him be called *Ops* for helping the new-born by placing them on the surface of the earth; when he opens the infant's mouth for the first time to let him cry, let him be called *Vaticanus*; as *Levana*, let him look after the raising-up of the new-born child from the ground; as *Cunina* let him be said to guard the child's cradle. They say that one aspect of Jupiter is as the three fates, the *Carmentes*, who decide the new-born child's future; as *Fortuna*, let him be invoked as the god of chance. The breast was called "ruma" in archaic times: as *Rumina*, let him be the god of breast-feeding. When supervising children's drinking, they call him *Potina*, when supervising their eating, *Educa*. When children are scared he overcomes them as *Paventia*. When hope comes, let him be *Venilia*; when pleasure, *Volupia*; when there is activity, *Agenoria*, and when men are goaded to excessive activity, *Stimula*; when they work hard, *Strenia*. When they learn to count, call him *Numberia*; when they learn to sing, *Camena*. Let him be the god *Consus* who offers good advice, and *Sentia*, goddess of experience; let him appear as the goddess *Juventa* when a young man lays aside his child's toga, and as *Fortuna Barbata* when he first grows a beard. The heathen do not even bother to do their young men the honour of giving this divinity a masculine name; he might be called *Barbatus* (from "barba," as *Nodutus* from "nodus"), or be called *Fortunius* as a bearded god – but certainly not *Fortuna*. Let him be the god *Jugatinus* when joining man and wife in marriage; at the moment when the bride's girdle is removed, let him be called upon as *Virginensis*. Let him appear as *Mutunus* or *Tutunus*, the phallic god whom the Greeks call *Priapus*. If it causes no embarrassment, let Jupiter appear in all these aspects, and many that I have not listed here.

## 8.7 The end of life

### 8.7.1 The problems of old age

A dominant theme in the surviving poetry of Maximian, who lived in sixth-century Rome, is the author's old age. In the selections that follow, he vividly points out the tarnish on his golden years. Scholars have interpreted the mournful attitude that Maximian displays toward growing old as a kind of lament for the waning of classical culture and the evaporation of the pleasures it afforded.

Maximian, *Elegiacs* 1.1–16, 153–66, 191–204, 279–92
[Translated by Scott McGill]

*1–16:*

Jealous old age, why do you refrain from hurrying on my end?
Why do you come late to this worn-out body?
Please, release this wretched life from its prison;
for death now is a deliverance, and living a punishment to me.
I am not what I was, the better part of me has expired,                    5
and exhaustion and dread hold what remains.
Life, the greatest pleasure in happiness, is burdensome in sorrow;
and it is actually worse than any death to want to die.
While I had youthful appeal, while my mind and faculties were intact,
I was a universally celebrated orator.                                     10
Often I composed the sweet lies of the poets,
and fiction gave true honors to me.
Often I won the crown in a legal case I pled
and earned the welcome rewards of my eloquence.
Now that such things have gone the way of my failing limbs,               15
alas! what share of my life is left in my old age?

*153–66:*

Now come illnesses, now a thousand dangers.
Now enjoyable meals and delights bring harm.
I am forced to refrain from pleasurable things,                           155
and I stop living in order to go on living.
And the very foods by which I am sustained weigh me down,
me, whom nothing adverse ever used to harm.
It feels good to be full – soon I will regret it;
it seems better to abstain – then to have abstained brings me trouble.    160
The food that used to benefit me now does the opposite.
What used to be pleasing to eat now lies uneaten, disdained.
The gifts of Venus, of Bacchus bring me no joy,
nor does anything that is accustomed to distract us from life's woes.
Only the bare physical stuff remains, which hourly and on its own         165
fades away and is reduced by its afflictions.

*191–204:*

Hence above all else worries torture me in my agitation,
hence no rest is given to my soul.
I struggle to obtain the things I cannot, struggle to hold on to them always,
And, if I hold on to anything, I think that I have gotten nothing.
An old man exists uncertain and trembling and always distrusting,         195
and stupidly he fears what he himself does.
He praises bygone years and despises the present;

he thinks that only what he knows is right.
He estimates that he alone is learned, he alone knowledgeable,
and because he thinks himself so wise, he consequently becomes
    more foolish.                                      200
Although you do not want it, he, bringing up many things and
    repeating himself,
shakes and spatters his conversation with saliva.
Though he has no listener, he does not keep from talking:
O old men, vigorous only in your garrulity!

*279–92:*

And who could express the other troubles that old age brings?
This is also difficult for an old man to relate.               280
Disputes, contempt, and severe losses follow,
and none of one's many friends offers help.
The slaves and maids themselves – without punishment –
think it shameful to call me their master.
They laugh at my gait, they laugh at my face              285
and my trembling head, which once they feared.
Although I see nothing, nevertheless I will be permitted to see this,
so that this torment may be more grievous for wretched me.
Fortunate the man who has been granted the benefit of leading a
    peaceful life
and of bringing his secure days to a happy close.         290
All too harsh is the memory of past pleasures for the wretched,
and more heavily it falls from the highest peak, overwhelmed.

## 8.7.2 *The will of Gregory of Nazianzus*

Gregory of Nazianzus (*c*.330–*c*.390), known as "the Theologian," a highly influential churchman from Cappadocia and one of the Fathers of the Greek Church, served as bishop of Constantinople from 379 to 381. He inherited great wealth and property from his father, but had no heirs himself. His will, which is the first complete Roman will to have survived from antiquity, illustrates the many obligations that he fulfilled regarding relatives, slaves, and other dependants, and it also reveals the Church as a powerful institution that continued to benefit from Gregory's generosity of spirit even after his death.

Gregory of Nazianzus, *Will*
[Raymond Van Dam, "Self-Representation in the Will of Gregory of Nazianzus," *Journal of Theological Studies* 46.1 (1995): 118–48, here pp. 143–8]

"A copy of the will of the holy Gregory the Theologian, transcribed from the original document in which are preserved the autograph signatures of [Gregory] himself and the witnesses who signed."

During the consulships of the most distinguished Flavius Eucherius and the most distinguished Flavius Evagrius, one day before the Kalends of January.

I, Gregory, bishop of the Catholic church of Constantinople, alive and in my right mind, with sound judgment and sane reasoning, have composed this my will. I direct and I wish that it be legitimate and valid in every court and before every magistrate. For I have already openly revealed my intention, and I have dedicated all my possessions to the Catholic church at Nazianzus for the provision of the poor who are dependent upon the aforementioned church. In conformity with this preference of mine I have therefore appointed three men to be responsible for the management of poor-relief: the deacon and monk Marcellus; the deacon Gregorius, who was [a slave] of my household; and the monk Eustathius, who was also [a slave] of my household. Now I still maintain the same intention toward the holy church of Nazianzus, and I hold the same preference.

Whenever I happen to meet the end of my life, the aforementioned deacon and monk Gregorius, who was [a slave] of my household and whom I manumitted long ago, is to be heir of the entirety of all my possessions, both moveable and fixed, wherever my possessions are. All the others are to be disinherited. As a result, Gregorius may restore all my possessions, both moveable and fixed, to the holy Catholic church of Nazianzus, exempting nothing at all except whatever I specifically leave someone in this my will as a legacy or a trust. As I have already said, he may instead carefully preserve everything for the church, keeping the fear of God before his eyes and knowing that I have decided to add all my possessions to the provision of the poor of that same church and that I have designated him as heir so that he might completely preserve everything for the church.

With regard to the household slaves whom I have manumitted either by my own decision or in accordance with the instructions of my most blessed parents, I wish that all of them remain still now in freedom and that all their property remain guaranteed and undisturbed. I also wish that my heir the deacon Gregorius, along with the monk Eustathius, who were once [slaves] of my household, possess the estate in Arianzus that came to us from the possessions of Regunus. With regard to the herds and the flocks that I already instructed in person to be given to them and whose pasturage and ownership I granted to them, I wish that Gregorius and Eustathius retain them undisturbed for their lawful ownership. I furthermore especially wish that the deacon Gregorius, my heir who has faithfully served me, keep for his own lawful ownership fifty gold coins.

I have directed that a specified amount be given annually to the most venerable virgin Russiana, my relative, so that she might live independently. I wish and I direct that this entire amount, in accordance with the arrangement that I have established, be given to her annually without delay. In the past I did not decide about her residence, because I did not know where she preferred to live. But now I wish also this, that in whatever place she chooses a household might be prepared that is suitable for her, an independent woman, [and] for the respectable life of a virgin. She will of course possess this household for her use and sustenance without any disturbance until the end of her life; then it will revert to the church. I wish that two [slave] girls whom she has chosen also be given her on the understanding that the girls stay with her until the end of her life. And if she is satisfied with them, she is allowed to honour them with manumission; if not, they are to belong to the same church.

I have already manumitted Theophilus, the [former slave] boy who remains with me. Now I wish also to give him five coins as a legacy. I wish to manumit his brother Eupraxius and give him five gold coins as a legacy. I furthermore wish to manumit my secretary Theodosius and give him five gold pieces also as a legacy.

With regard to my very dear daughter Alypiana (the others, Eugenia and Nonna, whose lives are reprehensible, [deserve] little consideration), I wish her to forgive me if I have been unable to leave anything to her, for I have already promised everything to the poor. Or rather, I have followed the undertaking of my most blessed parents, to ignore whose intention I consider disrespectful and loyal. But with regard to whatever has survived from the possessions of my blessed brother Cesarius among the silk clothes, the linen clothes, the wool clothes, or the carriages, I wish to transfer this to her children. [I wish that] in no way is she or her sisters to give trouble either to my heir or to the church.

Let my son-in-law Meletius realize that he improperly possesses the estate at Apenzinsus that is part of the properties of Euphemius. I have already in the past often written to Euphemius concerning this property, accusing him of cowardice unless he retrieved the estate. But now I testify before all magistrates and subjects that Euphemius is being wronged. For it is necessary that the estate be returned to Euphemius.

I wish that the deed of sale for the property at Kanotala be delivered to my most venerable son, bishop Amphilochius. For the deed is [kept] in our papers, and everyone knows that the contract was paid, that I received the price, and that long ago I surrendered the pasturage and the ownership of the estate.

To Evagrius the deacon, who often toiled with me and shared my thoughts and in many instances offered his goodwill, I confess gratitude before both God and men. God will repay him with greater [rewards]. But so that we not neglect the small tokens of friendship, I wish that he be given one wool robe, one tunic, two cloaks, and thirty gold coins. Likewise I wish that our most delightful fellow deacon and brother Theodulus be given one wool robe, two of the tunics of my native land, and twenty of the gold coins from the account in my native land. I wish that Elaphius, who is a versatile secretary and who has well assisted us during the time he served, be given one wool robe, two tunics, three cloaks, a plain garment, and twenty of the gold coins in my native land.

I wish that this my will be legitimate and valid in every court and before every magistrate. If it is not valid as a will, I wish that it be valid as a final desire or a codicil. But whoever attempts to overturn this will give explanation on judgment day and will settle the account.

In the name of the Father and the Son and the Holy Spirit. I, Gregory, bishop of the Catholic church in Constantinople, have read the will and have approved all that is written. I signed with my own hand, and I direct and wish that it be valid.

I, Amphilochius, bishop of the Catholic church in Iconium, witnessed the will of the most venerable bishop Gregory. Having been summoned by him I signed with my own hand.

I, Optimus, bishop of the Catholic church at Antioch, witnessed the most venerable bishop Gregory making his will in the terms recorded above. Having been summoned by him I signed with my own hand.

I, Theodosius, bishop of the Catholic church in Ide, witnessed the will of the most venerable bishop Gregory. Having been summoned by him I signed with my own hand, Theodulus, bishop of the holy Catholic church at Apamea, witnessed etc.

I, Hilarius, bishop of the holy Catholic church at Isauria, witnessed etc.

I, Themistius, bishop of the holy Catholic church at [H]adrianopolis, witnessed etc.

I, Cledonius, presbyter of the holy Catholic church in Iconium, witnessed etc. "I, Joannes, reader and secretary of the most holy church in Nazianzus, have transcribed and published this copy of the sacred will of the holy and illustrious theologian Gregory that has been deposited with me in the most holy church."

### 8.7.3 The death and funeral of Proclus the Philosopher

Proclus (412–485), the Neoplatonic philosopher, had studied in Athens as a young man with Syrianus, another member of the Neoplatonic school, and became his favorite pupil. A biography of Proclus describes his funeral and informs us that Proclus and his teacher were buried together. (See also *11.1.8*, page 317.)

Marinus, *Life of Proclus* 36–7

[Kenneth Sylvan Guthrie, trans., *Proclus's Biography, Hymns and Works: Master-Key Edition: Putting the Reader in Full Command of the Whole Subject, and Giving the Full English Text of All Relevant Inaccessible Minor Works: Editio Princeps* (Newburyport, MA: Phanes Press, 1986) pp. 53–5]

36. Proclus left this world in the 124th year from Julian's accession to the empire [361] under the archonship of the younger Nicagoras in Athens on the seventeenth day of the month Munychion, or the seventeenth of April [485]. His body received the funerary honors usual among the Athenians, as he himself had requested; for more than any other did this blessed man have the knowledge and practice of funerary honors due the dead. Under no circumstances did he neglect to render the customary homage, and on fixed yearly dates he went to visit the tombs of the Attic heroes, those of the philosophers, of his friends, and acquaintances; he performed the rites prescribed by religion, and not through

some deputy, but personally. After having fulfilled this pious duty towards each of them, he went to the Academy, in a certain particular place, and by vows and prayers, he invoked the souls of his ancestors, collectively and separately; and, in another part of the building, in common with others, he made libations in honor of all those who had practiced philosophy.

After all that, this holy person traced out a third distinct space and offered a sacrifice to all the souls of the dead.

His body, clothed and arranged as I have said above, according to his own request, and carried by his friends, was buried in the most easterly part of the suburbs, near Mount Lycabettus, where rested the body of his teacher Syrianus. For it was Syrianus's own desire, expressed to the pupil, in view of which Proclus had caused a double funerary monument to be erected. But after Syrianus's death, Proclus wondered whether this was not contrary to respect and proprieties; but in a dream he saw Syrianus reproaching and threatening him for these questionings, and blamed him for harboring such thoughts. So [matters remained, and when Proclus died we] engraved on [the vacant part of the double monument] an inscription in four verses, which he himself had composed, as follows:

I, Proclus am of Lycian origin;
Syrianus here nourished me with his lessons, to succeed as teacher;
This same tomb has received our bodies,
May our two souls find the same abode!

37. A year before his death there were celestial prodigies, such as a solar eclipse which caused nocturnal darkness during daytime; the stars appeared, and it occurred at the moment when the sun was in the eastern center of Capricorn. The specialists who busy themselves with describing the daily weather mention a second one which was to occur exactly one year after his death.

These disorders to which the heavens are subject are said to be signs of events which happen on earth; in any case they suggested to us the disappearance and the eclipse of philosophy at that time.

### 8.7.4 Christian funerals

By the late fourth century, ordinary Christian dead as well as martyrs were being commemorated regularly in their graveyards by the entire Christian community in Rome and other cities of the empire.

*1.*

*Apostolic Constitutions* 6.30.2
[Anne Marie Yasin, trans., "Funerary Monuments and Collective Identity: From Roman Family to Christian Community," *The Art Bulletin* 87.3 (2005): pp. 433–57, here p. 448]

Gather together without fear [of pollution] in the cemeteries to read from the divine Scriptures and sing psalms for the martyrs who rest there, for all the saints and for your brothers who rest in the Lord; and celebrate the Eucharist, image of the royal body of Christ, in your churches and your cemeteries; and for funerals accompany the departed with psalms . . .

2.

Jerome describes the funeral of the wealthy woman Fabiola in which all the Christians of Rome participated. Participation in such rituals gave a sense of unity to a city's Christian community.

Jerome, *Letter* 77.11

[F.A. Wright, *Select Letters of St. Jerome* (Cambridge, MA: Harvard University Press, 1954) pp. 335–7]

> She had scarcely drawn her last breath and paid the debt of her soul to Christ, when flying rumor heralding such woe brought the peoples of the whole city to attend her funeral. Psalms re-echoed loudly and cries of "Alleluia" shook the gilded roofs of the temples . . . I hear it still; the crowds that went before the bier, the swaying multitude that attended her obsequies in throngs, no streets, no colonnades could contain, no overhanging roofs could hold the eager onlookers. On that day Rome saw all her peoples gathered together. Everyone flattered himself that he had a share in the glory of her penitence.

### 8.7.5  Burials and grave inscriptions

Directed by law and custom, Romans throughout the empire buried their dead outside the city walls. Wealthy individuals and families constructed grand tombs, often along the roads leading out of town. People of lower status formed burial associations which maintained portions of cemeteries for their members. Catacombs, or communal, underground cemeteries, were the final resting place of tens of thousands of the dead. Until the late fourth century, polytheists, Christians, and sometimes Jews, were buried in the same cemeteries. By the early fifth century Christian burial practices changed significantly with the spread of the cult of the martyrs. Christians wished to be buried as close to the martyrs' tombs as possible. Since the relics of martyrs and other saints were venerated in churches, graveyards quickly developed near churches and within cities, a revolutionary change in Roman practice. In the city of Rome, nearly 70,000 grave inscriptions survive, giving evidence of attitudes and beliefs about death.

*1.* A mother's grief

In the following passage, a mother expressed her deep grief on the tombstone of her child, a little boy called Boethius.

[Bertrand Lançon and Antonia Nevill, *Rome in Late Antiquity. Everyday Life and Urban Change, AD* 312–609 (Edinburgh: Edinburgh University Press, 2000) p. 128]

> Because of your death, your mother wanted to die: she would have been happy if she could have joined you.

## 2. The grave of a pagan couple

In addition to being a touching witness to a happy marriage, the funeral monument of the Roman senator Praetextatus (*c.*310–384) and his wife Aconia Fabia Paulina (*c.*325–after 384) reveals how important maintaining ancient cults was to members of the highest aristocracy. Praetextatus listed his many priesthoods before his equally illustrious public offices. His wife, Paulina, also was high priestess in important cults. This aristocratic couple embody an embattled and custodial sense of duty toward religious tradition in late fourth-century Rome.

*The Grave Inscription of Vettius Agorius Praetextatus and Aconia Fabia Paulina* [Brian Croke and Jill Harries, *Religious Conflict in Fourth-Century Rome. A Documentary Study* (Sydney: Sydney University Press, 1982), pp. 106–8]

*On The Front:*
To the Divine Shades. Vettius Agorius Praetextatus, augur, priest of Vesta, priest of the Sun, quindecemvir, curial of Hercules, consecrated to Liber and the Eleusinian mysteries, high priest, temple overseer, initiate of the taurobolium [the cult of Mithras], Father of the Fathers [priest of Mithras]; but in public office: quaestor designate, urban praetor, governor of Tuscia and Umbria, governor of Lusitania, proconsul of Achaea, Prefect of the City, seven times sent by the senate as ambassador, twice Praetorian Prefect of Italy and Illyricum, designated consul ordinarius, and Aconia Fabia Paulina, *clarissima femina* [most distinguished woman of senatorial rank], consecrated to Ceres and the Eleusinian mysteries, consecrated at Aegina to Hecate, initiate of the taurobolium, high priestess. These two lived together for forty years.

*On The Right:*
Vettius Agorius Praetextatus to his wife Paulina. Paulina, associate of truth and chastity, dedicated in temples and friend of the divine powers, putting her husband before herself, Rome before her man, modest, faithful, pure in mind and body, kind to all, a blessing to her household.

*On The Left:*
Vettius Agorius Praetextatus to his wife Paulina. Paulina partner of my heart, nurse of modesty, bond of chastity, pure love and loyalty produced in heaven, to whom I have entrusted the deep hidden secrets of my heart, gift of the gods who bind our marriage couch with friendly and modest ties; by the devotion of a mother, the gratitude of a wife, the bond of a sister, the modesty of a daughter, and by all the loyalty friends show, we are united by the custom of age, the pact

of consecration, by the yoke of the marriage vow and perfect harmony, helpmate of your husband, loving, adoring, devoted.

*On The Back:*

[Paulina to Praetextatus] The glory of my parents gave me nothing greater than to have seemed already worthy of my husband; but all light and glory is my husband's name. Agorius, sprung of proud lineage, you illumine your country, the senate and your wife by your integrity of mind, your character and your scholarship all at once. By these you attained the highest peak of virtue, for by translating whatever is proclaimed in either tongue by the thought of the wise; to whom the gate of heaven lies open, both the poems which the learned have composed and the prose works recited aloud, you have improved upon what you have found written down. Yet these things are of little account. You, a holy man, and priest of the mysteries, conceal in the secret places of your heart what you discovered in the sacred initiations and with your manifold learning you worship the divine power, uniting with your kindness your wife as your associate with the sacred objects, confidante of men and gods, and in one mind with you as she was. What may I now say of the offices and powers, joys sought by men in their prayers, which you who regard yourself as a priest of the gods and are marked out by your priestly headbands, always consider transient and trivial? You, O husband, deliver me pure and chaste from the lot of death by the goodness of your teaching, lead me into the temples and dedicate me to the gods as their handmaid. With you as witness I am initiated into all the mysteries. You, in your duty as husband, consecrate me as priestess of Didymenes [Cybele] and Attis through the rites of the bull. You instruct me, as a priestess of Hecate, in the threefold secrets and you prepare me for being worthy of the rites of Greek Ceres. Because of you everyone proclaims me holy and blessed, since it is you who spread my goodness throughout the world. Although unknown I am known to all. With you as my husband how could I fail to please? The matrons of Romulus' city seek me as a model and regard their offspring as beautiful if it resembles yours. Men and women alike both seek after and acclaim the honours which you, my teacher, have given me. Now, robbed of all this I, your grief-stricken wife, am wasting away. Happy would I have been had the gods granted that my husband had outlived me. Yet I am happy because I am yours, was yours and soon shall be yours after death.

### 3. A Christian epitaph

[J.S. Northcote, *The Catacombs or Christian Inscriptions in Rome during the First Four Centuries* (London: Longmans, Green, and Co., 1878) p. 109]

Gentianus, one of the faithful, in peace, who lived twenty-one years eight months and sixteen days. And in your prayers pray for us, because we know you to be in Christ.

### 8.7.6 Remembering the dead

Born in Bordeaux about 310 to an educated family, Ausonius became the tutor to the future emperor Gratian, who took the throne in 375. Ausonius' career flourished in imperial service until he retired to his family estates in Aquitania to pursue a leisurely life as a country gentleman and man of letters. Among his works is a collection of poems called the *Parentalia* that commemorates his deceased relatives. The examples below deal with the deaths of Ausonius' aged father, young wife, and small child. In Roman antiquity, it was all too common to die in the bloom or bud of life, and rare to enjoy the ample span that Ausonius' father did.

Ausonius, *Parentalia* 1, 9, 10
[Translated by Scott McGill]


*Parentalia* 1: Julius Ausonius, My Father

First in line is my father Ausonius. The natural order compels his son
    to place him first,
even if I should hesitate to do so.
He was God's special concern, as is clear from how he lived for twice
    eleven Olympiads,
and with the blessing of a calm old age.
He saw everything that he wanted fulfilled;          5
likewise, whatever he desired turned out for him as he wished.
This is not because he enjoyed the extreme favor of the Fates,
but because his wishes were so modest.
His own era compared him with the Seven Sages,
whose teachings he applied in his personal conduct,          10
so that he might live, rather than speak, in accordance with the
    knowledge of the Wise.
Even so, he was hardly unversed in the art of speaking.
So too he was given the ability to extend men's lives through the
    practice of medicine
and to lengthen the time that death had to wait.
Consequently, respect for him remains after his own life has ended,    15
as evidenced by the epitaph our age has given him:
"As Ausonius had no one whom he might follow,
so he has no one who now could equal him."


*Parentalia* 9: Attusia Lucana Sabina, My Wife

Thus far my dirge, performing its task, has sung in devout strains
of those who, while dear to me, were mourned after a mature death.
Now approaches my grief and my torture and a wound that cannot be
    expressed:

the death of my wife, snatched away from me, must be recalled.
Her line was noble, and she was born from senatorial stock;                    5
yet Sabina was distinguished more through her good character.
As a young man, cheated by your death in my early years, I mourned
    you,
and still, after 36 years, I weep for you, unmarried.
Nor can I dull the pain, obscured by old age.
For it always rages, a new torment to me.                                      10
Others who grieve allow time's balm to treat them;
the long day makes these wounds only heavier.
I tear out my white hair, which has escaped the notice of my unwed life,
and the more I live alone, the more I live in sadness.
That the still house is silent, that my bed lies cold,                         15
that I share experiences with no one, neither good nor bad –
all these things nourish the wound.
I grieve, if another man has a good wife, or on the contrary,
if he has a bad one; for I always compare the woman to you.
In either case, you come to torture me:                                        20
if a wife is bad, because you were unlike her, and if good, because
    you were like her.
I do not weep for the loss of wealth, an empty thing, or of hollow joys.
No, I weep because you, while young, were taken from youthful me.
Cheerful, modest, serious, renowned for your family and for your
    beauty,
you were both the despair and the distinction of your husband
    Ausonius.                                                                  25
About to complete your twenty-eighth December,
you left our two children, our pledges.
By god's mercy, they have flourished, just as you prayed,
and have been given the great goods that you desired.
And I pray that they may prosper, and that my dust may
    convey this to your ashes,                                                30
that each of them lives on.


## *Parentalia* 10: Ausonius, My Little Son

I will not deprive you, my son, of a memorializing lament,
you my first-born boy, called by my name:
whose death we mourned when he was preparing to put an end to his
    babbling
with his first words, a boy of ample intelligence.
You lie placed in the lap of your great-grandfather, sharing a common
    grave,                                                                     5
so that you not suffer the bitterness of your tomb.

### 8.7.7 What next? The afterlife in Late Antiquity

The idea of a life after death was commonly held in Late Antiquity, but with different degrees of clarity and importance in different regions and among followers of different religions. Polytheists had notions of the spirits of the dead existing as "shades" in the underworld, but ideas were not extensively developed. Some philosophers argued for forms of reincarnation as well as the return of the human soul to its celestial source.

In various Jewish apocalyptic writings it was held that there existed a timeless paradise in the heavens which would be the home of the dead. Christian writers developed the idea that the dead would be punished and the righteous rewarded at the end of time when humanity would be judged. Martyrs, however, without waiting might enter into that realm of eternal life where they would in some manner experience the presence of God. Zoroastrian heaven and hell were celestial realms, and in Islamic thought heaven was a delightful place of reward for the followers of God's law.

*1.*

An elegant inscription on a tombstone found in Algeria repeats a popular epitaph. It marked the final resting place of an otherwise unknown man named Euterpius who cherished no elaborate hopes of an afterlife:

*Epitaph*
[Claude Sintes and Ymouna Rebahi, *Algérie Antique* (Arles: Musée de l'Arles antique, 2003) p. 259]

> I did not exist.
> I existed.
> I no longer exist.
> Remember me!

*2.*

Ephrem the Syrian (*c.*306–373) was troubled by the relationship of the soul to the body in heaven. He believed that without the body, the soul cannot enter heaven and so must wait until the Resurrection when the body and soul will be rejoined. Until then, souls will wait on the outskirts of heaven.

Ephrem the Syrian, *Hymn on Paradise* VIII, Verses 2, 3, 4, 7, 11
[Sebastian Brock Crestwood, trans., *Saint Ephrem, Hymns on Paradise* (New York: St. Vladimir's Seminary Press, 1990) pp. 131–5]

> *Verse 2*
> I behold a dwelling thee
>    And a tabernacle of light,
> a voice proclaiming
>    "Blessed is the Thief

Who has freely received
   the keys to Paradise."
I imagined that he was already there,
   but then I considered
how the soul cannot have perception of Paradise
   without its mate, the body,
its instrument and lyre.

*Verse 3*

In this place of joys
   anguish seized me
as I realized that it is not profitable
   to delve into hidden things.
With respect to the Thief
   a dilemma beset me:
if the soul were able
   to see and to hear
without its body,
   why then is it confined therein?
And if the body is no longer alive,
   why should the soul be put to death with it?

*Verse 4*

That the soul cannot see
   without the body's frame,
the body itself persuades,
   since if the body become blind
the soul is blind in it,
   groping about with it;
see how each looks
   and attests to the other,
how the body has need of the soul
   in order to live,
and the soul too requires the body
   in order to see and to hear.

*Verse 7*

That blessed abode
   is in no way deficient,
for that place is complete and perfected
   in every way,
and the soul cannot
   enter there alone,
for in such a state it is in everything deficient –
   in sensation and consciousness;

but on the day of Resurrection,
   the body with all its senses,
will enter in as well, once it has been made perfect.

*Verse 11*
Thus in the delightful mansions
   on the borders of Paradise
do the souls of the just
   and righteous reside,
awaiting there
   the bodies they love,
so that, at the opening
   of the Garden's gate,
both bodies and souls might proclaim,
   amidst Hosannas,
"Blessed is He who has brought Adam from Sheol
   and returned him to Paradise in the company of many."

## Further readings

Bouston, Ra'anan S. and Annette Yoshiko Reed, eds., *Heavenly Realms and Earthly Realities in Late Antique Religions* (Cambridge: Cambridge University Press, 2004)

Bremmer, Jan N., *The Rise and Fall of the Afterlife: The 1995 Read-Tuckwell Lectures at the University of Bristol* (London: Routledge, 2002)

Brubaker, Leslie and Julia M.H. Smith, eds., *Gender in the Early Medieval World. East and West, 300–900* (Cambridge: Cambridge University Press, 2004)

Cooper, Kate, *The Fall of the Roman Household* (Cambridge: Cambridge University Press, 2007)

Evans-Grubbs, Judith, *Law and Family in Late Antiquity: The Emperor Constantine's Marriage Legislation* (Oxford: Oxford University Press, 1999)

Nathan, Geoffrey S., *The Family in Late Antiquity: The Rise of Christianity and the Endurance of Tradition* (London: Routledge, 2000)

Reynolds, Philip L. and John Witte, Jr., *To Have and to Hold. Marrying and Its Documentation in Western Christendom, 400–1600* (Cambridge: Cambridge University Press, 2007)

Stafford, Pauline and Anneke B. Mulder-Bakker, eds., *Gendering the Middle Ages*, Special Issue, *Gender & History* 12.3 (November, 2000)

# 9

# LAW

## 9.1 Introduction

Roman law continued to develop throughout the Late Antique period. Emperors continued to issue laws in great numbers. Sometimes laws were collected, as in the *Codex Gregorianus* in 291 and the *Codex Hermogenianus* in 293–294. The *Theodosian Code*, a more substantial effort completed in 429, gathered the laws issued by Christian emperors since Constantine. Roman law reached its high point in the *Corpus Iuris Civilis* [*Collection of Civil Law*] of the emperor Justinian. This great work summarized previous jurisprudence and sorted through previous legislation to establish an up-to-date code of law. In this Justinianic form Roman imperial law eventually passed to western Europe in the twelfth century, and through translations from its original Latin into Greek the *Corpus Iuris Civilis* became the foundation of law of the medieval Byzantine state. Profoundly influenced by Christianity and the strengthening of the imperial office, Justinian represented himself as the living law, its sole interpreter, and the sole source of human authority. Thus his legal work reflects changes in how the law was understood to function in society, what the sources of its authority were, and how it was commented upon and taught.

### 9.1.1 What is law?

The beginning of the *Institutes*, a textbook for law students completed by Justinian's top three legal officials, Tribonian, Theophilus and Dorotheus in 534, contains a precise definition of justice and law. It distinguishes among laws of nature, humanity, and individual nations.

Justinian, *Institutes* 1.1

[*Justinian's Institutes*, trans. Peter Birks and Grant McLeod (Ithaca, NY: Cornell University Press, 1987) 1.1, 1.2 (p. 37)]

### *1.1 Justice and law*

Justice is an unswerving and perpetual determination to acknowledge all men's rights. 1. Learning in the law entails knowledge of God and man, and mastery of the difference between justice and injustice. 2. As we embark on the exposition of Roman law after these general statements the best plan will be to give brief, straightforward accounts of each topic. The denser detail must be kept till later. Any other approach would mean making students take in a huge number of distinctions right at the start while their minds were still untrained and short of stamina. Half of them would give up. Or else they would lose their self-confidence – a frequent source of discouragement for the young – and at the cost of toil and tears would in the end reach the very standard they could have attained earlier and without overwork or self-doubt if they had been taken along an easier road. 3. The commandments of the law are these: live honorably; harm nobody; give everyone his due. 4. There are two aspects of the subject: public and private. Public law is concerned with the organization of the Roman state, while private law is about the well-being of individuals. Our business is private law. It has three parts, in that it is derived from the law of nature, of all peoples, or of the state.

### 1.2  The law of nature, all peoples, and the state

The law of nature is the law instilled by nature in all creatures. It is not merely for mankind but for all creatures of the sky, earth and sea. From it comes intercourse between male and female, which we call marriage; also the bearing and bringing up of children. Observation shows that other animals also acknowledge its force. 1. The law of all peoples and the law of the state are distinguished as follows. All people with laws and customs apply law which is partly theirs alone and partly shared by all mankind. The law which each people makes for itself is special to its own state. It is called "state law", the law peculiar to that state. But the law which natural reason makes for all mankind is applied the same everywhere. It is called "the law of all peoples" because it is common to every nation. The law of the Roman people is also partly its own and partly common to all mankind.

## 9.1.2  Legal education

The large bureaucracy created by the reforms of Diocletian and Constantine needed men trained in law to fill its ranks, and the role of law schools grew in importance. The chief schools were at Rome, Beirut, and Constantinople, with smaller academies, not sponsored by the state, scattered throughout the empire. Latin was the main language of instruction because laws were written in that language until the new legislation of Justinian (his *Novels*), but after 400 Greek was also used in the schools. In his famous introduction to the *Digest*, called *Constitutio Omnem* or *The Whole Body of Law* of 533, Justinian describes the changes he was making in legal education. Speaking directly to his leading professors of law ("wisdoms"), Justinian spells out the problems in legal training that he intends to correct.

Justinian, *Digest, The Whole Body of Law* 1–2, 6–7

["The Whole Body of Law," in *The Digest* of *Justinian*, trans. Alan Watson (Philadelphia: University of Pennsylvania Press, 1998), pp. xlvii, xlviii, 1]

## The Whole Body of Law

1. Earlier, indeed, as your wisdoms are aware, out of all the great multitude of legal writings, extending to two thousand books and three million lines, students, on the advice of their teachers, made use of no more than six books, and those confused and very rarely containing laws of practical use; the other books had gone out of use and become inaccessible to everyone . . . This then is the record of the method of education in former times, according to what is confirmed by your own testimony. 2. We, however, on discovering this great deficiency in the knowledge of the law, and deeming it a most unhappy state of affairs, are opening up to those who desire them the treasures of the law, by means of which, when your wisdoms have to some extent displayed them, your pupils may become the best endowed legal pleaders . . . 6. The students are to have nothing concealed from them, therefore, when these arcane matters have been revealed to them; and after perusing all the works we have composed through the agency of the eminent Tribonian and the others, they will prove themselves to be leading orators and servants of justice; in legal process they will be equally supreme as advocates and judges, successful everywhere and at all times. 7. We desire these three works which we have composed to be handed to students, as ordered now and by previous emperors, only in the royal cities and in the most excellent *civitas* of Berytus [the city of Beirut], which might well be called the nurse of the law, and not in other places which have earned no such privilege from our predecessors. We say this because we have heard that even in the most splendid *civitas* of Alexandria and in that of Caesarea and others there are unqualified men who take an unauthorized course and impart a spurious erudition to their pupils; we warn them off these endeavors, under the threat that if they should dare to perpetrate such deeds in future and act in this way outside the royal cities and the metropolitan city of Berytus, they are to be punished by a fine of ten pounds of gold and be driven from the *civitas* in which they commit a crime against the law instead of teaching it.

### 9.1.3 A hostile view of lawyers

In a famous diatribe, Ammianus Marcellinus accuses lawyers of a wide range of wrongdoings.

Ammianus Marcellinus, *History* 30.4.9–11, 13–15, 19

[*Ammianus Marcellinus*, vol. III, trans. John C. Rolfe (Cambridge, MA: Harvard University Press, 1956) pp. 325, 327, 329, 331]

9. Among these the first class [of lawyers] consists of those who, by sowing the seeds of all sorts of quarrels, busy themselves with thousands of recognisances, wearing out the doors of widows and the thresholds of childless men; and if they have found even slight retreats of secret enmity, they rouse deadly hatred among discordant friends, kinsfolk, or relatives. And in these men their vices do not cool down in course of time, as do those of others, but grow

stronger and stronger. Poor amid insatiable robbery, they draw the dagger of their talent to lead astray by crafty speeches the good faith of the judges, whose title is derived from justice.

10. By their persistence rashness tries to pass itself off as freedom of speech and reckless audacity as firmness of purpose; a kind of empty flow of words as eloquence . . .

11. A second class consists of those who profess a knowledge of law, which, however, the self-contradictory statutes have destroyed, and reticent as if they were muzzled, in never-ending silence they are like their own shadows. These men, as though revealing destinies by nativities or interpreting a Sibyl's oracles, assume a solemn expression of severe bearing and try to make even their yawning saleable . . .

13. A third group consists of those who, in order to gain glory by their troublous profession, sharpen their venal tongues to attack the truth, and with shameless brow and base yelping often gain entrance wherever they wish. When the anxious judges are distracted by many cares, they tie up the business in an inexplicable tangle, and do their best to involve all peace and quiet in lawsuits and purposely by knotty inquisitions they deceive the courts, which, when their procedure is right, are temples of justice, when corrupted, are deceptive and hidden pits: and if anyone is deluded and falls into those pits, he will not get out except after many a term of years, when he has been sucked dry to his very marrow.

14. The fourth and last class, shameless, headstrong, and ignorant, consists of those who have broken away too soon from the elementary schools, run to and fro through the corners of the cities, thinking out mimiambic lines, rather than speeches suitable to win lawsuits, wearing out the doors of the rich, and hunting for banquets and fine choice food.

15. When they have once devoted themselves to shady gain and to eagerness for money from any and every source, they urge all kinds of innocent people to involve themselves in vain litigations . . .

19. And when the contending parties are stripped of everything, and days, months and years are used up, at last the case, now worn out with age, is introduced, and those brilliant principals come forth, bringing with them other shadows of advocates. And when they have come within the barriers of the court, and the fortunes or safety of someone begins to be discussed, and they ought to work to turn the sword or ruinous loss from an innocent person, the advocates on both sides wrinkling their brows and waving their arms in semblance of the gestures of actors . . . stand for a long time opposite each other . . . when . . . after the semblance of a trial has gone on for three years allege that they are not yet fully informed; and after they have obtained a further postponement . . . they persistently demand the pay for their danger and toil.

### 9.1.4  Judges must be supervised

That disputes be heard and adjudicated fairly was a constant concern of Rome's emperors, as numerous laws indicate. The following law, issued in 389, illustrates the difficulties in maintaining a strong corps of judges.
*Theodosian Code* 1.5.9

> If your Sublimity should find any judges who are lazy in body and negligent, yawning with dreams of idleness, or any who are degenerate with the greed of servile thievery or involved in the disgrace of similar vices, you shall heap upon them the punishment of public vengeance, and you shall choose substitutes for those who have been removed, so that not their crimes but their punishments shall be referred to the knowledge of Our Clemency. [Valentinian, Theodosius, and Arcadius, 389]

### 9.1.5  The right of appeal

The right of appeal was an important element of Roman procedure, protected by imperial decree. Here Emperor Constantine reasserts the right of appeal to the Praetorian Prefect, his chief executive officer. (See also *1.3.8*, page 16.)
*Theodosian Code* 1.5.1

> By edict we remind all provincials that, if they have been treated with contempt when appealing to their own governor, they shall have the right to appeal to Your Gravity, so that, if it should appear that this mistreatment occurred by the fault or negligence of the governors, Your Gravity shall immediately refer the matter to Our Wisdom, in order that it may be possible for such governors to be fittingly punished. [Constantine, 325]

### 9.1.6  Law courts closed on Sunday

By closing the law courts on Sunday, Constantine, the first Christian emperor, helped invent the weekend.
*Theodosian Code* 2.8.1

> Just as it appears to Us most unseemly that the Day of the Sun (Sunday), which is celebrated on account of its own veneration, should be occupied with legal altercations and with noxious controversies of the litigation of contending parties, so it is pleasant and fitting that those acts which are especially desired shall be accomplished on that day. Therefore all men shall have the right to emancipate and to manumit on this festive day, and the legal formalities thereof are not forbidden. [Constantine, 321]

### 9.1.7 Codifications and reform

Through the centuries of imperial rule, mountains of often contradictory laws piled up and caused considerable confusion when it came time to cite precedents. In Late Antiquity there were several attempts at codifying the accumulated law. Toward the end of the third century Hermogenes and Gregorius compiled collections of imperial edicts issued as responses to individual queries between the reigns of Hadrian and Diocletian. On January 1, 439, when Theodosius II was on the throne, the massive *Theodosian Code* appeared. It selected and organized all the legislation of Christian emperors into one comprehensive body of law on a wide range of subjects. It is an invaluable historical source for social as well as legal history and is frequently cited in this Reader. The greatest codification, however, was that of Justinian. This colossal undertaking sorted through all the laws of the empire to produce the *Code* in 534, and all the jurisprudence to make the *Digest*. In the prefaces to the *Code*, Justinian describes his vast project.

Justinian, *Code*, "The First Preface"
[*The Civil Law*, vol. 12, trans. S.P. Scott (Cincinnati, OH: Central Trust, 1932) pp. 3, 4]

#### First preface, concerning the establishment of a new code

The Emperor Justinian to the Senate of the City of Constantinople. Those things which seem to many former Emperors to require correction, but which none of them ventured to carry into effect, We have decided to accomplish at the present time with the assistance of Almighty God; and to diminish litigation by the revision of the multitude of constitutions which are contained in the Three Codes; namely, the Gregorian, the Hermogenian, and the Theodosian, as well as in those other Codes promulgated after them by Theodosius of Divine Memory, and by other emperors, who succeeded him, in addition to those which We Ourselves have promulgated, and to combine them in a single Code, under Our auspicious name, in which compilation should be included not only the constitutions of the three above-mentioned Codes, but also such new ones as subsequently have been promulgated . . .

(3) Hence We have hastened to bring these matters to your notice, in order that you may be informed to what an extent Our daily care is occupied with matters having reference to the common welfare, by collecting such laws as are certain and clear, and incorporating them into a single code, so that, by means of this code, designated by Our auspicious name, the citation of the various constitutions may cause decisions to be more readily rendered in all litigation.

### 9.1.8 Jurisprudence

With the *Code* completed, Justinian turned the attention of his legal experts to the great jumble of interpretations of the law that had accumulated through the centuries. An introduction to the *Digest*, called the *Constitutio Deo Auctore* ("The Law Written by God"), explains why the work of previous jurisconsults must be systematized. The emperor usurps their function and claims the right to be the sole interpreter of law in the future.

Justinian, *Digest* 4, 12

["The Composition of the Digest," in *The Digest of Justinian*, vol. 1, trans. Alan Watson (Philadelphia: University of Pennsylvania Press, 1998) pp. xliv, xlv, xlvi]

*On the plan of* The Digest

4. We therefore command you to read and work upon the books dealing with Roman law, written by those learned men of old to whom the most revered emperors gave authority to compose and interpret the laws, so that the whole substance may be extracted from them, all repetition and discrepancy being as far as possible removed and out of them one single work may be compiled, which will suffice in place of them all . . .

12. We command that our complete work, which is to be composed by you with God's approval, is to bear the name of the *Digest* or *Encyclopaedia*. No skilled lawyers are to presume in the future to supply commentaries thereon and confuse with their own verbosity the brevity of the aforesaid work, in the way that was done in former times, when by the conflicting opinions of expositors the whole of the law was virtually thrown into confusion. Let it suffice to make some reminders by indexes alone and simple headings, in such a way that no offense arises through interpretation.

## 9.2  Christianity and the law

The extent to which Christianity influenced Roman legislation after Constantine was considerable in several areas. Most obviously, offensive sorts of entertainment were suppressed. The social behavior of women also was regulated in new ways.

### 9.2.1  Why is legislation always necessary?

Justinian added something new to Roman law when he claimed that Nature's constant innovations required constant imperial legislation in response. Since the emperor was God's chosen agent, his lawmaking played a role in a Christian scheme of universal order.

Justinian, *Novel* 84, Preface (539)

[*The Civil Law*, vol. 16, trans. S.P. Scott (Cincinnati, OH: Central Trust, 1932) p. 311]

Nature, everywhere inclined to the production of numerous innovations (this prelude has often been employed in legislation but will constantly be repeated as long as Nature persists in these practices), has induced Us to enact many laws.

Justinian, *Novel* 73, Preface (538)
[*The Civil Law*, vol. 16, trans. S.P. Scott (Cincinnati, OH: Central Trust, 1932)
p. 275]

> Therefore, as God rules the Empire of Heaven in order that He may afford good
> solutions to perplexing questions and interpret the laws in accordance with the
> varieties of Nature, We have thought it is proper to draw up this statute and
> render it generally applicable to Our subjects whom God has originally
> entrusted to our care.

### 9.2.2 Local law dies out

After 212, when the Antonine Constitution granted citizenship to all the free
inhabitants of the empire, everyone in the empire gained access to Roman law. This
undercut but did not abolish the different local laws that Rome had always permitted
her non-citizen subjects to follow. From the time of Diocletian local laws had steadily
diminished in force. Christianity's new models of community based on faith coupled
with old Roman beliefs about the superiority of Roman culture transformed the status
of local laws in the empire. Justinian did not hesitate to enforce uniformity, as seen
in this law of 536 regarding rights of women in Armenia. He equates Roman law and
Christian civilization. By the end of the sixth century local laws had virtually
disappeared in the East. (See also *7.5.5*, page 238.)

Justinian, *Novel* 21
*The Civil Law*, vol. 16, trans. S.P. Scott (Cincinnati, OH: Central Trust, 1932)
pp. 108, 109]

> The Emperor Justinian to Acacius, Proconsul of Armenia.
> Desiring that the country of Armenia should be governed by good laws, and in
> no respect differ from the rest of our empire, We have conferred upon it a
> Roman administration; have delivered it from its ancient customs; and have
> familiarized it with those of the Romans, ordering that it shall have no other laws
> than theirs. We think, however, that it is necessary, by means of a special
> enactment, to abolish a barbarous practice which the Armenians have preserved;
> for among them women are excluded not only from succession to the estates of
> their ascendants, but also from those of their own brothers and other blood-
> relatives; they are married without a dowry; and are purchased by their future
> husbands. These barbarous customs they have observed up to the present time,
> and they are not the only ones who act in this cruel manner, for there are other
> races that dishonor nature in the same way, and injure the female sex just as if it
> were not created by God, and took part in the propagation of the human race,
> and finally, as if it was utterly vile, contemptible, and not entitled to any honor.
>
> Chapter 1. Therefore we decree by this imperial enactment that the laws in
> force in our Empire, which have reference to the right of women to succeed to
> estates, shall be observed in Armenia, and that no difference shall hereafter
> exist between the sexes in this respect . . .

Hence the Armenians shall no longer be subject to laws different from those of the Empire; and if they form part of our subjects, and are under our government like many other peoples, and enjoy the benefits conferred by Us, their women shall not be the only ones deprived of our justice; and they shall all enjoy the benefit of our laws . . .

### 9.2.3 The comparison of Roman and Mosaic law

Probably written in Rome in the later fourth century by a Jewish author, this Latin treatise compares Roman and the biblical Law of Moses in a systematic fashion. The book demonstrates that its Jewish author could appreciate Roman law at a fairly sophisticated level. He was interested in the status of the law of his community within the larger context of Roman imperial law. A typical entry begins with a biblical quotation followed by the opinions of authoritative Roman jurists.

The Comparison of Roman and Mosaic Law 15
[*Mosaicarum et Romanarum Legum Collatio*, trans. M. Hyamson (London: Oxford University Press: 1913) pp. 127, 129]

Of astrologers, sorcerers, and Manichaeans Moses says:
Let there not be found in thee any one who purgeth thy son or daughter (by fire), nor a diviner with whom thou castest lots; nor shalt thou countenance makers of poisons, importers who say what it is that a woman has conceived, since these are misleading tales. Nor shalt thou give heed to prodigies, nor enquire of the dead.

Let there not be found in thee an augur, nor examiner of birds, nor sorcerer, nor enchanter, nor one that has a snake in his belly, nor a soothsayer, nor an enquirer of the dead, nor a watcher of portents.

For all these things as well as the doer of them are condemned by the Lord, thy God. For because of these abominations God will uproot the Canaanites from before thee.

But thou shalt be perfect before the Lord thy God.

For those nations which thou wilt possess listened to auguries, lots and divinations.

Ulpian, in the Seventh Book of the Proconsular Functions, under the title of "Astrologers and Soothsayers":
Moreover, a ban has been put upon the crafty imposture and persistent persuasion of the astrologers. Nor has this been forbidden them to-day for the first time; the prohibition is of long standing. In fact, a Decree of the Senate, passed in the Consulship of Pomponius and Rufus, is extant, which provides that astrologers, Chaldeans, soothsayers, and others who engage in the like practices, be interdicted from fire and water, and all their property confiscated, and if the offender be a foreigner, he shall be punished with death . . .

Nearly all the Emperors have indeed, time after time, issued interdicts which forbid meddling with such meaningless things, and those practicing them were punished in accordance with the character of the consultation. If the Emperor's health was the subject of the consultation, death or other severe punishment was inflicted; the penalty was lighter where the enquiry concerned the consulter's own health or that of his relatives. This last class also includes soothsayers, though they, too, must be punished because they sometimes exercise their reprehensible arts to the prejudice of the public peace and the Roman Empire . . .

### 9.2.4 The Syro-Roman Law Book

The *Syro-Roman Law Book is* a compendium of Roman laws with local customs mixed in. The author believes that Christian teaching as embodied in the laws of Christian Roman emperors has supplanted the laws of all other peoples. The *Law Book* thus represents a Roman–Christian universalism interacting with the traditions of a particular region. Compiled originally in Greek in the fifth century, the *Law Book* became widely popular in Syriac translation as well as Arabic and Armenian.

*The Syro-Roman Law Book*, introduction

[*The Syro-Roman Law Book*, vol. II, trans. Arthur Vööbus (Stockholm: Estonian Evangelical Lutheran Church, 1983) pp. 1–2]

Again the laws of the victorious and Christian kings Constantine, Theodosius and Leo, the kings of the Romans.

These are the excellent and good laws which our Lord and God has given to men since the beginning and has made them known. In the first book of the Torah he has shown to us that Adam generated Seth, Enosh and so on, the rows of the fathers until the flood. Noah generated Shem, and after that Shem generated Arpakshad, and the generation of the fathers follows in order and comes until Abraham. Abraham generated Isaac, Isaac Jacob, Jacob the twelve fathers.

This glorious and excellent law was given by God the Lord of all so that every man should leave his goods as an inheritance to his children. For this good reason, all the nations have taken over his law, namely, that every man shall have his goods as an inheritance for his children. If he has no children, he shall leave his goods as an inheritance to whom he wishes.

Whereas all the laws of the nations differ in other matters, this right of inheritance has not been changed by any nation, but has continued and come down (to the time) of our Lord Jesus Christ who has received body from the holy virgin and become a man according to his will, who has freed all men from error, those who so desired.

He has along with other benefits given an excellent law to the church and through his church he has given gifts of his grace to the Christian kings of the nation of the Romans. He has given them the knowledge of the faith and the truth and he has through his church subjugated the generation of all the nations to them; so that through the ordinances of the laws of Christ, they rule men according to the law which these kings have received from the church which is a gift for all men.

For every nation and all nations who wanted to be ruled by a law have taken their precedent from the law of Moses, have set up laws in their generations and imitated Israel which was ruled by the laws of God. For, also, not a single one of the nations had a writing or a book (of this kind) before Moses, but Moses and his laws, those which God gave to Israel, precede all the sages of the Greeks, the Athenians, the Romans, the Egyptians, as we have said above, and all nations and all languages. To Israel and the nations also was this gift given so that they would be ruled according to laws.

As the laws, however, were annulled by the coming of our Lord, among all nations the one law of Christ has been given through the Christian kings, which has begun with the glorious and blessed Constantine, the elect of God.

## 9.3 Torture

Augustine disliked torture, but he knew that it was a basic part of all courtroom procedures meant to uncover the truth. As the passage below shows, however, he realized that torture cannot be relied upon to find the truth, and may in fact produce unnecessary suffering. He did not argue for the elimination of torture, however, or say that Christians should not be judges.

Augustine, *City of God Against the Pagans* 19.6

[Augustine, *City of God Against the Pagans*, ed. and trans. R.W. Dyson (Cambridge: Cambridge University Press, 1998) pp. 926–7]

What of those judgments passed by men upon their fellow-men, which cannot fail to be present in cities no matter how peaceful they remain? Do we not consider these things miserable and deplorable? For indeed, those who give such judgment can never penetrate the consciences of those upon whom they pronounce it. Therefore they are often compelled to seek the truth by torturing innocent people merely because they are witnesses to the crimes of other men. And what of torture applied to a man in his own case? Here the question is whether he is guilty or not; but he is tortured even if he is innocent. Thus, he suffers, for a doubtful crime, a punishment which is very certainly not doubtful; and he suffers it not because he is found to have committed the crime, but because it is not known that he did not commit it. For this reason, the ignorance of the judge is very often a calamity to the innocent. And what is still more intolerable – a thing to be greatly lamented and, if it were possible bathed in fountains of tears – is the fact that the judge tortures the accused precisely so that he shall not, in his ignorance, slay an innocent man. In his wretched ignorance, therefor, he puts to death, tortured and innocent, the very man whom he had tortured to avoid putting the innocent to death. For if, acting according to the wisdom of the philosophers, the accused now chooses to flee from this life rather than endure those tortures any longer, he will confess to a crime which he had not committed. And when he has been condemned and put to death, the judge still does not know whether he has slain a guilty man or an innocent one, even after torturing him to avoid ignorantly slaying the innocent. In this case, he has tortured an innocent man in order to discover the truth, and has killed him while still not knowing it.

## Further reading

Evans-Grubbs, Judith, *Law and Family in Late Antiquity: The Emperor Constantine's Marriage Legislation* (Oxford: Oxford University Press, 1995)

Evans Grubbs, Judith, *Women and the Law in the Roman Empire: A Sourcebook on Marriage, Divorce and Widowhood* (London: Routledge, 2002)

Garnsey, Peter and Caroline Humfress, *The Evolution of the Late Antique World* (Cambridge: Orchard Academic, 2001)

Harries, Jill, *Law and Empire in Late Antiquity* (Cambridge: Cambridge University Press, 1999)

Harries, Jill and Ian Wood, eds., *The Theodosian Code. Studies in the Imperial Law of Late Antiquity* (Ithaca, NY, and London: Cornell University Press, 1993)

Honoré, Tony, *Tribonian* (London: Duckworth, 1998)

Humfress, Caroline, *Orthodoxy and the Courts in Late Antiquity* (Oxford: Oxford University Press, 2007)

Mathisen, Ralph W., *Law, Society and Authority in Late Antiquity* (Oxford: Oxford University Press, 2001)

Matthews, John F., *Laying Down the Law: A Study of the Theodosian Code* (New Haven, CT: Yale University Press, 2000)

Meyer, Elizabeth, *Legitimacy and the Law in the Roman World* (Cambridge, 2004)

Stein, Peter, *Roman Law in European History* (Cambridge: Cambridge University Press, 1996)

Swain, Simon and Mark Edwards, eds., *Approaching Late Antiquity* (Oxford: Oxford University Press, 2004)

# 10

# MEDICINE

## 10.1 Introduction

The study and practice of medicine flourished in Late Antiquity. Important steps were taken to develop and codify the Greco-Roman medical tradition. New handbooks and encyclopedias distilled ancient learning and added the fruits of new observation and experience with advances made particularly in pharmacology and surgery. At the same time, Christian healing, which depended more on faith, the power of holy men, and exorcism than clinical treatment, came to the fore, as many saints' lives testify. Though there was often conflict between practitioners of these different strategies of healing, the two approaches were not exclusive and patients consulted both sorts of specialist, just as doctors and holy men sometimes made referrals to one another. Hospitals associated with monastic communities developed, and in some of them a combination of faith healing and clinical medicine was pursued.

## 10.2 The medical profession

### 10.2.1 What is medicine?

Isidore, the polymath bishop of Seville from about 600 to 636, wrote a treatise *On Medicine*, which sums up the long tradition of Greco-Roman medicine. He adds references to the Bible and the history of medical terms. This passage defines the practice of medicine and describes the training of doctors.

Isidore of Seville, *On Medicine* 1.1–2; 4.1–2; 5.2–3; 9.1, 2, 3, 5; 13.1–5
[*Isidore of Seville: The Medical Writings*, trans. William D. Sharpe (*Transactions of The American Philosophical Society*, vol. 54, 1964) pp. 55–6, 61–2, 64]

*1. Medicine*

1. Medicine is that which either protects or restores bodily health: its subject matter deals with diseases and wounds.

2. There pertain to medicine not only those things which display the skill of those to whom the name physician is properly applied, but also food and drink, shelter and clothing. In short, it includes every defense and fortification by which our body is kept safe from external attacks and accidents.

### 4. The three sects of physicians

1. These three men founded as many sects. The first, or Methodist, was founded by Apollo, whose remedies are also discussed in poems. The second, or Empiric, that is, the most fully tested, was established by Aesculapius and is based upon observed factual experience alone, and not on mere signs and indications. The third, or Logical, that is, rational sect, was founded by Hippocrates.

2. For having discussed the qualities of the ages of life, regions and illnesses, Hippocrates thoroughly and rationally investigated the management of the art; diseases were searched through to their causes in the light of reason [and their cure was rationally studied]. The Empirics follow only experience; the Logical join reason to experience; the Methodists study the relationships of neither elements, times, ages, nor causes, but only the properties of the diseases themselves . . .

5.2 The word "disease" [*morbus*] is a general term which includes all bodily afflictions; our elders called it "disease" to indicate by this name the power of death [*mors*] which could arise therefrom. Healing consists in a middle course between health and disease for, unless *congruent* with the disease, it does not conduce to health.

3. All diseases arise from the four humors: that is, from blood and yellow bile, from black bile and phlegm. Healthy people are maintained by them and the ill suffer from them. When any of the humors increase beyond the limits set by nature, they cause illnesses. Just as there are four elements, so also there are four humors, and each humor imitates its own proper element: blood the air; yellow bile fire; black bile earth; and phlegm water. Thus, there are four humors as well as four elements which preserve our bodies . . .

### 9. Remedies and medications

1. The healing of medicine is not to be despised, for we also recall that Isaiah ordered a certain medication for Ezechiel when he was ill, and the Apostle Paul said that Timothy ought to take a little wine.

2. . . . The healing of disease is, however, of three sorts: pharmaceutical, which the Latins call "medications"; surgical, which the Latins call "operations using the hands," for hand is called *cheir* in Greek; and dietetic, which the Latins call "a rule," for it is careful attention to the laws of [daily] living. There are three species of cure, taken as a whole: the first group is dietetic, the second pharmaceutical, and the third surgical.

3. Dietetic consists in an observation of the laws of living; pharmacy is a cure using medicaments. Surgery is an *incision* using iron instruments, since those conditions not responding to treatment with drugs are excised with iron . . . .

5. Every cure is brought about either by the use of contraries or by the use of similars. By contraries, as a chilling disease is treated with heat, or a dry one with moisture, just as also it is impossible for pride to be cured except it be cured by humility.

### 13. The study of medicine

1. Some ask why the art of medicine is not included among the other liberal disciplines. It is because whereas they embrace individual subjects, medicine embraces them all. The physician ought to know literature to be able to understand or to explain what he reads.

2. Likewise also rhetoric, that he may delineate in true arguments the things which he discusses; dialectic also so that he may study the causes and cures of infirmities in the light of reason. Similarly also arithmetic, in view of the temporal relationships involved in the paroxysms of diseases and in diurnal cycles.

3. It is no different with respect to geometry because of the properties of regions and the locations of places. He should teach what must be observed in them by everyone. Moreover, music ought not be unknown by him, for many things are said to have been accomplished for ill men through the use of this art, as is said of David who cleansed Saul of an unclean spirit through the art of melody. The physician Asdepiades also restored a certain insane man to his pristine health through music.

4. Finally also, he ought to know astronomy, by which he should study the motions of the stars and the changes of the seasons, for as a certain physician said, our bodies are also changed with their courses.

5. Hence it is that medicine is called a second philosophy, for each discipline claims the whole of man for itself. Just as by philosophy the soul, so also by medicine the body is cured.

## 10.2.2 Medical experience vs. received opinion

Alexander of Tralles (525–605), a physician deeply involved in clinical practice, wrote a twelve-book medical encyclopedia. He knew the canonical texts of Galen (129–216) very well, but did not hesitate to correct the master. The following excerpt from Alexander's study On Viscous Humors and Thick Masses Found in the Lung explains his preference for medical experience over received opinion.

Alexander of Tralles, On Viscous Humors and Thick Masses Found in the Lung 5, 4
[John Scarborough, "Early Byzantine Pharmacology," in Dumbarton Oaks Papers 38: Symposium on Byzantine Medicine (Washington, DC: Dumbarton Oaks Press, 1984) p. 227]

And I would not have said this about such a learned man, unless Truth itself had not inspired me and urged me on, and did I not believe that keeping silent was sinful. For a doctor who does not speak his opinion commits a great sin and through his silence is greatly to be condemned. But one ought to follow that which Aristotle says he has stated: "Plato is my friend, but the Truth is also my friend; between the two, one must choose the Truth."

### 10.2.3 A great physician

Ionicus practiced medicine in Sardis in the second half of the fourth century. He won a brilliant reputation for his diagnostic and clinical skills, his experiments and his deep knowledge of medical history. Eunapius of Sardis describes this talented physician.

Eunapius of Sardis, *Lives of the Philosophers* (*Ionicus*) 499.2–3

[*Philostratus and Eunapius: The Lives of the Sophists*, trans. Wilmer Cave Wright (London: Heinemann; Cambridge, MA: Harvard University Press, 1922) pp. 537, 539]

> Ionicus was a native of Sardis, and his father was a celebrated physician. As a pupil of Zeno he attained to the highest degree of industry and diligence and won the admiration of Oribasius. While he acquired the greatest skill in the theory and practice of medicine in all its branches, he showed peculiar ability in every kind of experiment, was thoroughly acquainted with the anatomy of the body, and also made researches into the nature of man. Thus he understood the composition and mixture of every kind of drug that exists; he knew every sort of plaster and dressing that the most skilful healers apply to wounds, whether to stop a hemorrhage or to disperse what has gathered there. Also he was most inventive and expert in bandaging an injured limb, and in amputating or dissecting. He was so thoroughly versed in the theory and practice of all these arts that even those who prided themselves on their ability as healers were amazed at his accurate knowledge, and openly admitted that by conversing with Ionicus they really understood the precepts that had been uttered by the physicians of earlier times and could now apply them to their use, though before they had been like words whose meaning is completely obscured, save only that they had been written down.
>
> Such were his attainments in the science of his profession, but he was also well equipped in every branch of philosophy and both kinds of divination; for there is one kind that has been bestowed on man for the benefit of the science of medicine, so that doctors may diagnose cases of sickness; and another that derives its inspiration from philosophy and is limited to and disseminated among those who have power to receive and preserve it. He also studied the art of rhetoric with exact thoroughness, the complete art of oratory, and was an initiate in the art of poetry.

### 10.2.4 Military physicians

In an age without antisepsis or anesthetics, practicing medicine could be a grisly business, and nowhere more so than on the battlefield. Here Ammianus Marcellinus describes the labors of army doctors during the siege of the Syrian city Amida by Persian forces in 359.

Ammianus Marcellinus, *History* 19.2.15

[*Ammianus Marcellinus*, vol. I, trans. John C. Rolfe (London: Heinemann; Cambridge, MA: Harvard University Press, 1958) p. 483]

> Therefore each of the soldiers cured his wounds according to his ability or the supply of helpers; some, who were severely hurt, gave up the ghost slowly from loss of blood; others, pierced through by arrows, after vain attempts to relieve them, breathed out their lives, and were cast out when death came; others, whose limbs were gashed everywhere, the physicians forbade to be treated, lest their sufferings should be increased by useless infliction of pain; still others plucked out the arrows and through this doubtful remedy endured torments worse than death.

### 10.2.5  Faith healing

Bishop Gregory of Tours (540–593/4) was an aficionado of miracle cures, especially those performed by his hero, Saint Martin of Tours. This approach to healing had its roots in the long tradition of Greco-Roman medicine but in its Christian guise came to be seen as a superior alternative by devout Christians. Note that religious cures are attempted, however, only after other approaches have failed.

Gregory of Tours, *The Miracle of Saint Martin* 2.1, 4.36

[Loren C. MacKinney, *Early Medieval Medicine* (Baltimore, MD: Johns Hopkins University Press, 1937) pp. 24, 67]

> (4.36)  The people tried an appliance of herbs and verbal incantations, but were not able by medical skill to allay the malady . . . our daughter [Gregory's niece, Eustachia] coming to the sick woman and seeing her with the stupid herb dressing, poured oil from the holy sepulchre into her mouth. As a result the sick woman began to convalesce.
>
> (2.1)  . . . I had suffered so much [from dysentery] that I had no hope of life. The doctor's antidotes were absolutely ineffective. In desperation I called Armentarius the royal physician and said to him: "You have tried every expedient of your art, and your drugs are of no avail. One thing remains. I shall show you a marvelous cure. Take dust from the sepulchre of Saint Martin and make a drink from it" . . . After taking this drink my pain was eased and I recovered my health.

### 10.2.6  A medical specialist

Saint Theodore of Sykeon (c.540–613) was a monk who performed many healing miracles, yet his biographer shows that he was willing to send patients to an appropriate specialist. This indicates a synthesis of the Greco-Roman and Christian traditions of healing in late sixth-century Byzantium.

George the Monk, *Life of Theodore of Sykeon* 145–6
[Peregrine Horden, "Saints and Doctors in the Early Byzantine Empire. The Case of Theodore of Sykeon," in W.J. Sheils, ed., *The Church and Healing* (Oxford: Blackwell for the Ecclesiastical History Society, 1982) p. 1]

Again, if any required medical treatment for certain illnesses, or surgery or a purging draught or hot springs, this God-inspired man would prescribe the appropriate remedy to each like an experienced doctor trained in the art. He might recommend one to have recourse to surgery and would always state clearly which doctor he should employ. In other cases he would dissuade those who wished to have an operation or to undergo some other medical treatment, and would recommend rather that they should visit hot springs, and would name the springs to which they should go.

## 10.3 Care of the sick and cures

### 10.3.1 Hospitals

Christian charitable institutions that cared for the ill, the poor, the elderly, and the homeless were a common sight in Late Antiquity. Established by wealthy patrons to distribute alms, Christian hospices provided a necessary service and won many converts to the faith. The following passage describes the generosity of Bishop Masona of Mérida in Spain (570–*c.*600) who provided care for people of any faith.

*The Life and Virtues of the Holy Bishop Masona* 5.3.2–9
[Joseph N. Garvin, *The Vitae Sanctorum Patrum Emeretensium. Text and Translation, with an Introduction and Commentary* (Washington, DC: Dissertation, The Catholic University of America Press, 1946) pp. 193, 195]

5.3.2 This man is said to have lived a life of zeal in the basilica of the holy virgin Eulalia before he was made bishop and to have served God there irreprehensibly for many years. (3) As soon as he by the inspiration of God was moved thence where he had been in the mouth, eyes, and heart of everyone, and was ordained bishop, in the very beginning of his episcopate he founded many monasteries, enriched them with many farms, and with marvelous energy erected many basilicas and consecrated many souls to God therein.
(4) Then he built a hospice and enriched it with great estates and, assigning attendants and physicians, ordered that it serve the wants of travellers and the sick, (5) and gave order that physicians should unceasingly make the rounds of the entire city and bring to the hospital in their arms whomever they found sick, slave or free, Christian or Jew, and having neatly prepared beds lay the sick thereon and provide delicate and excellent food until with God's help they gave back to the sick person his former health.
(6) And although from the farms that were given to the hospice a large supply of delicacies were provided for many, this seemed to the holy man to be still

too little; therefore, adding to all these benefactions even greater ones, he ordered the physicians to see to it with watchful care that they received half of all the offerings that were brought to the Bishop's House by the actuaries from all the patrimony of the church to give them to the poor.

(7) Whenever any citizen of the town or rustic from the country came to the atrium because of need, asked the stewards for wine, oil, or honey, and held out a small vessel in which to carry it away and the holy man saw it, gracious of countenance and of pleasant mien as he always was, he would at once order the vessel broken and a larger one brought.

(8) His generosity in giving alms to the poor has been left to God alone to know; nevertheless let us say a little about that, too. (9) So great was his concern for the misfortunes of the wretched that he gave to the basilica of Saint Eulalia, to the venerable deacon Redemptus who was in charge there, 2,000 gold pieces from which anyone, when pressed by necessity, could, on drawing up an instrument, receive as much as he wanted without any delay or difficulty as soon as he came, and could thus provide for his straitened circumstances.

### 10.3.2 House calls

The following account (c.633–8) tells the story of a monk with medical training who was persuaded to leave his monastery to attend to a woman dying in childbirth. His sense of medical obligation took him from the quiet of his cell to the problems of the world.

*The Death and Miracles of the Bishops of Merida* 4.2.6–13
(Joseph N. Garvin, *The Vitae Sanctorum Patrum Emeretensium. Text and Translation, with an Introduction and Commentary* (Washington, DC: Dissertation: The Catholic University of America Press, 1946) pp. 165, 167]

(6) Her husband, knowing that no other physician's care would avail and that his wife was already almost dead, begged him earnestly with many tears not to send anyone there but to go himself and apply his knowledge with his own hands. (7) When he would not agree nor give his consent all the brethren came to him and with tears asked him to go. He replied: "I know that the mercy of the Lord is great and I am confident that if I go He will give back to the sick woman her former health and will at once forgive me for my presumption. But I shall have no doubt that wicked men will hereafter throw this matter up to me."

(8) When all the brethren answered: "Not one of us will say anything about it; but go, sir, and with all speed do that which will redound to your reward," finally, compelled by their prayers, he promised to go, provided however that he would first seek the will of the Lord lest, by proceeding rashly, he lightly do something for which he would be punished by the judgment of God and with difficulty receive forgiveness. (9) At once, therefore, he went to the basilica of the holy virgin Eulalia and lay there all day prostrate upon the pavement and continued perseveringly and untiringly in prayer during the night that followed.

(10) Then, advised by the voice of God, he at once arose and went unhesitatingly and with haste to the sick woman's home, uttered a prayer, laid his hands upon the sick woman in the name of the Lord and, (11) trusting in God, very carefully made a small incision with a sharp scalpel and withdrew in sections, member by member, the already corrupt body of the infant. The woman, already almost dead and only half-alive, he at once restored safely to her husband with the help of God (12) and bade her henceforth not to know her husband: for at whatever time she should know the embraces of her husband worse perils would come upon her. (13) Nevertheless they fell at his feet and thanked him and promised to observe in detail everything the man of God commanded, calling upon the Lord to send them worse ills thereafter if they should not keep their promise.

### 10.3.3 Baths

Bathing in pools of different temperatures was a precise and time-honored therapy in the classical world. Paul of Aegina, a talented doctor who lived in Alexandria until some time after 642, wrote on gynecology, toxicology, and general medicine. His last work, called the *Epitome of Medicine*, was a summary of medical knowledge in seven books that eventually played an important role in the development of Islamic medicine. In a passage on baths he describes the medical benefits of a good soak. (See also *2.3.11–12*, pages 46–7.)

Paul of Aegina, *The Seven Books of Paul of Aegina*, vol. 1, section 51, "On Baths" [*The Seven Books of Paulus Aegineta*, trans. Francis Adams (London: The Sydenham Society, 1844) pp. 67–8]

> I think well of the cold bath, and yet I do not say that it is proper for those who use no restriction as to diet, but only to those who live correctly, and take exercise and food seasonably. It may answer with most people very well, when they want to get much cooled, to swim in water during the season of summer, provided they are young and brawny, and have been previously heated by friction. They ought to attend, however, that they be not in a state of lassitude from venery, or any other cause, nor suffering from indigestion, nor after vomiting, nor after evacuation of the bowels, nor when in want of sleep. It may be attended with danger, if used at random. But the warm bath is the safest and best, relieving lassitude, dispelling plethora, warming, soothing, softening, removing flatulence wherever it fixes, producing sleep and inducing plumpness. It is expedient for all, man and woman, young and old, rich and poor.

### 10.3.4 Magical healing

Magic appealed to people of all religions and classes. Cures could be quite complex. This Jewish magical text combines fragrant spices, incantations, and an insistence upon spiritual purity.

*Sefer Ha-Razim [Book of Mysteries]* 1.28–3.4
[Robert L. Wilken, *John Chrysostom and the Jews: Rhetoric and Reality in the Late Fourth Century* (Berkeley: University of California Press, 1983) p. 86]

If you wish to perform an act of healing, arise in the first or second hour of the night and take myrrh and frankincense in your hand. Place the incense upon the burning embers of a fire while saying the name of the angel who rules over the first encampment, who is called Orpani'el, and say seven times the names of the seventy-two angels that minister to him, then say: "I, X the son of X, demand from you that you will bring success upon my hands in healing Y the son of Y." And anyone for whom you ask, whether in writing or verbally, will be healed. Purify yourself from all impurity and cleanse your flesh from all carnality and then you will succeed. These are the names of the angels of the second encampment who minister . . .

## 10.3.5 Dieting

People worried about losing weight in Late Antiquity. Caelius Aurelianus, a physician of the fifth century, translated from the Greek treatise of Soranus the following recommendation for overcoming obesity.

Caelius Aurelianus, *On Acute Diseases and Chronic Diseases* 11.129, 132–8
[Caelius Aurelianus, *On Acute Diseases and Chronic Diseases*, trans. I.E. Drabkin (Chicago: The University of Chicago Press, 1950) pp. 993, 995, 997, 999]

Bodies may keep acquiring additional flesh beyond what is needed; and it is because of the superfluous nature of these accessions that the Greeks call the condition obesity . . .

. . . The treatment of this disease takes two forms. One form of treatment seeks to restrain the excessive nourishment of the body. It relies on vigorous passive exercise, and employs, in limited amounts, foods that do not give much nourishment; in this way the body's growth will not exceed its actual intake. The other form of treatment employs the cyclical regimen and drastic metasyncritic measures for the purpose of altering the state of the body. But in order that our meaning may be understood and our instructions clear, we shall set forth our treatment of the parts.

The body should be given continual passive exercise. For this purpose the movement of a small carriage drawn by a team of animals is suitable; so also is riding on a horse or sailing. In addition, prescribe reading aloud; vigorous vocal exercise of the sort employed in practicing for contests in poetry and song; swift walking in order to exercise the calves of the legs; running; dry massage with bare hands or with a rough linen cloth, the body being sprinkled with sand; various types of vigorous exercise in the palaestra, including . . . a mock battle with heavy armor; physical training in which two participants are engaged, say wrestling or other forms of exercise for two . . . and vigorous and prolonged massage of the body, the massage to be dry, since it loses its vigor if the hands of the masseur become slippery with oil. Further, it is beneficial to bake the body in the sun; also to apply intense heat, using flames, hot coals, and dry steaming, in order to induce perspiration. Prescribe some hot baths, for these are very effective in reducing flesh, and also some cold baths, for these condense the body; in fact, the bodies of persons who bathe in cold water are found to be hard and like shells. In addition, let the patient bake his body with the hot sand of the beach. Also prescribe swimming in the sea or in waters that have natural curative properties. And in the hot baths, after sweating is completed, have the patient's body sprinkled with salt . . . Then rub the patient's body with a cleansing preparation of nitrum ground down and reduced to a powder.

After the bath, withhold food and drink for a long time. For then even the strongest appetite is weakened and its keenness is blunted by the delay in giving food, since at first the digestion is all ready for action, but becomes languid when the tinder is withheld. Never permit the patient to drink before he takes food; let him drink only a little altogether, and least of all while food is being taken. For when a considerable amount of fluid is imbibed, the food that has been eaten is dissolved, the flesh is rendered soft; and solid foods are more readily assimilated by digestion. But if a patient is very thirsty, let him have a little moderately tart wine. Do not give him such foods as spelt groats, starch, milk, pine kernels, brains, eggs, tender fish, or any fatty foods. Let him eat cold, leavened, whole-wheat bread, this being less nourishing, especially if it is stale. And give him dry food in particular; as a main dish give him vegetables, tough fish, the drier varieties of fowl or of game animals like hare and roe, or preserved pork, i.e., salted pork that has been dried for a long time. It is best for the patient to take only one food and, after eating, to stay up a long while, even if resting, so that as he remains awake his body may be used up by continual exhalation. For the body undergoes considerable increase in sleep: thus, when a person sleeps his body becomes more robust. Let the patient have only cold drink; and if the obesity persists, institute the cyclical treatment, first withholding food altogether, then permitting a little food and water, and then making the increases according to the regular procedure. Also begin vomitive treatment, having the patient vomit when the stomach is empty; radishes may be used for this purpose. Then employ successively the diet of acrid foods, foods of the middle class, fowl, and game animals. Do not prolong these diets, but employ them only for a few days, so that the cycles may be begun again and again at frequent intervals. Among the vegetables given to the patient include those with diuretic properties, e.g., asparagus, parsnip, parsley, fennel, wild carrot, scallions, and the like. In this way, by keeping in mind the general characteristics of the disease, we shall be able to promote metasyncrisis. But pay attention to the symptoms, too, and continue the reduction and thinning of the flesh.

## 10.4 Plague

### 10.4.1 The Great Plague

The greatest medical disaster in Late Antiquity was the outbreak of bubonic plague in 541 that halved the populations of the Mediterranean world. Evagrius, the sixth-century church historian and lawyer from Antioch, describes his first-hand experience of the plague and offers a discussion of its origins and pathology.

Evagrius, *Ecclesiastical History* 29

[Evagrius, *Ecclesiastical History* (London: Samuel Bagster and Sons, 1846) pp. 223–6]

> I will also describe the circumstances of the pestilence which commenced at that period, and has now prevailed and extended over the whole world for fifty-two years; a circumstance such as has never before been recorded. Two years after the capture of Antioch by the Persians, a pestilence broke out, in some respects similar to that described by Thucydides, in others widely different. It took its rise from Aethiopia, as is now reported, and made a circuit of the whole world in succession, leaving, as I suppose, no part of the human race unvisited by the disease. Some cities were so severely afflicted as to be altogether depopulated, though in other places the visitation was less violent. It neither commenced according to any fixed period, nor was the time of its cessation uniform; but it seized upon some places at the commencement of winter, others in the course of the spring, others during the summer, and in some cases, when the autumn was advanced. In some instances, having infected a part of a city, it left the remainder untouched; and frequently in an uninfected city one might remark a few households excessively wasted; and in several places, while one or two households utterly perished, the rest of the city remained unvisited: but, as we have learned from careful observation, the uninfected households alone suffered the succeeding year. But the most singular circumstance of all was this; that if it happened that any inhabitants of an infected city were living in a place which the calamity had not visited, these alone were seized with the disorder. This visitation also befell cities and other places in many instances according to the periods called Indictions [a fiscal period of 15 years]; and the disease occurred, with the almost utter destruction of human beings, in the second year of each indiction. Thus it happened in my own case – for I deem it fitting, in due adaptation of circumstances, to insert also in this history matters relating to myself – that at the commencement of this calamity I was seized with what are termed buboes, while still a school-boy and lost by its recurrence at different times several of my children, my wife, and many of my kin, as well as of my domestic and country servants; the several indictions making, as it were, a distribution of my misfortunes. Thus, not quite two years before my writing this, being now in the fifty-eighth year of my age, on its fourth visit to Antioch, at the expiration of the fourth indiction from its commencement, I lost a daughter and her son, besides those who had died previously. The plague was

a complication of diseases: for, in some cases, commencing in the head, and rendering the eyes bloody and the face swollen, it descended into the throat, and then destroyed the patient. In others, there was a flux of the bowels: in others buboes were formed, followed by violent fever; and the sufferers died at the end of two or three days, equally in possession, with the healthy, of their mental and bodily powers. Others died in a state of delirium, and some by the breaking out of carbuncles. Cases occurred where persons, who had been attacked once and twice and had recovered, died by a subsequent seizure.

The ways in which the disease was communicated were various and unaccountable: for some perished by merely living with the infected, others by only touching them, others by having entered their chamber, others by frequenting public places. Some, having fled from the infected cities, escaped themselves, but imparted the disease to the healthy. Some were altogether free from contagion, though they had associated with many who were afflicted, and had touched many not only in their sickness but also when dead. Some, too, who were desirous of death, on account of the utter loss of their children and friends, and with this view placed themselves as much as possible in contact with the diseased, were nevertheless not infected; as if the pestilence struggled against their purpose. This calamity has prevailed, as I have already said, to the present time, for two and fifty years, exceeding all that have preceded it. For Philostratus expresses wonder that the pestilence which happened in his time lasted for fifteen years. The sequel is uncertain, since its course will be guided by the good pleasure of God, who knows both the causes of things, and their tendencies.

## 10.4.2 *The Plague strikes Constantinople*

The historian Procopius of Caesarea (500–565), a first-hand witness, describes the spread and effects of the plague on Constantinople in 542.

Procopius, *History of the Wars* 2.22–23.1

[Procopius, *History of the Wars*, vol. 1, trans. H.B. Dewing (Cambridge, MA: Harvard University Press, 1971) pp. 451, 453, 455, 465]

In the second year it reached Byzantium in the middle of spring, where it happened that I was staying at that time . . . Now the disease in Byzantium ran a course of four months, and its greatest virulence lasted about three. And at first the deaths were a little more than the normal, then the mortality rose still higher, and afterwards the count of dead reached five thousand each day, and again it even came to ten thousand and still more than that. Now in the beginning each man attended to the burial of the dead of his own house, and these they threw even into the tombs of others, either escaping detection or using violence; but afterwards confusion and disorder everywhere became complete . . .

### 10.4.3 Plague in Gaul

In his *History of the Franks*, Bishop Gregory of Tours describes the effects of the plague in western Europe, where it flared up between 542 and 571.

Gregory of Tours, *The History* of *the Franks* 5.34

[Gregory of Tours, *The History of the Franks*, trans. Lewis Thorpe (Harmondsworth: Penguin, 1977) p. 296]

> A most serious epidemic followed these prodigies. While the Kings were quarrelling with each other again and once more making preparations for civil war, dysentery spread throughout the whole of Gaul. Those who caught it had a high temperature, with vomiting and severe pains in the small of the back: their heads ached and so did their necks. The matter they vomited up was yellow or even green. Many people maintained that some secret poison must be the cause of this. The country-folk imagined that they had boils inside their bodies; and actually this is not as silly as it sounds, for as soon as cupping-glasses were applied to their shoulders or legs, great tumours formed, and when these burst and discharged their pus they were cured. Many recovered their health by drinking herbs which are known to be antidotes to poisons. The epidemic began in the month of August. It attacked young children first of all and to them it was fatal: and so we lost our little ones, who were so dear to us and sweet, whom we had cherished in our bosoms and dandled in our arms, whom we had fed and nurtured with such loving care. As I write I wipe away my tears and I repeat once more the words of Job the blessed: "The Lord gave, and the Lord hath taken away; as it hath pleased the Lord, so is it come to pass. Blessed be the name of the Lord, world without end."

### 10.4.4 Farmers avoid plague-ridden cities

The terror inspired by the plague in the sixth century caused great rifts between city-dwellers most at risk and farmers reluctant to come to town with their produce.

*The Life of Saint Nicholas of Sion* 52

[*The Life of St. Nicholas of Sion*, text and trans. Ihor Ševčenko and Nancy Patterson Ševčenko (Brookline, MA: Hellenic College Press, 1984) p. 83]

> 52. And the plague came to people within forty days. It had its first beginning in the metropolis of Myra, and there was exceeding great affliction over the deaths of men. When the neighboring farmers living in the district saw the power of God, they feared to go into the city, saying: "If we give the city wide berth, we will not die of this disease." For the disease was bubonic and people were expiring right away, that is, within a single day. And the farmers were withdrawing from the city, and the survivors in the city had no means of livelihood. For the farmers brought down into the city neither grain, nor flour, nor wine, nor wood, nor anything else needed for sustenance. And there was hardship and exceeding great affliction over the provisions.

# Further reading

Crislip, Andrew T., *From Monastery to Hospital. Christian Monasticism and the Transformation of Health Care in Late Antiquity* (Ann Arbor: University of Michigan Press, 2005)

Horden, Peregrine, "Saints and Doctors in the Early Byzantine Empire: The Case of Theodore of Sykeon," in W.J. Sheils, ed., *The Church and Healing* (*Studies in Church History*, 19) (Oxford: Blackwell, 1982)

Horden, Peregrine, "Mediterranean Plague in the Age of Justinian," in Michael Maas, ed., *The Cambridge Companion to the Age of Justinian* (Cambridge: Cambridge University Press, 2005), pp. 134–60

Little, Lester K., ed., *Plague and the End of Antiquity. The Pandemic of 541–750* (Cambridge: Cambridge University Press, 2007)

Miller, Timothy, *The Birth of the Hospital in the Byzantine Empire* (Baltimore, MD: Johns Hopkins University Press, 1985)

Nutton, Vivian, *Ancient Medicine* (London: Routledge, 2004)

Nutton, Vivian, "Medicine in Late Antiquity and the Early Middle Ages," in Lawrence I. Conrad, *et al., The Western Medical Tradition 800 BC to 1800* (Cambridge: Cambridge University Press, 1995)

Scarborough, John, ed., *Symposium on Byzantine Medicine* (*Dumbarton Oaks Papers* 38) (1984)

Stathakopoulos, Dionysios C., *Famine and Pestilence in the Late Roman and Early Byzantine Empire. A Systematic Survey of Subsistence Crises and Epidemics* (Burlington, VT: Ashgate, 2004)

# 11

# PHILOSOPHY

## 11.1 Introduction

Philosophical and scientific investigations in Late Antiquity were marked by equal measures of creativity and consolidation. Philosophers accepted the authority of ancient traditions and assumed the fundamental agreement of Plato and Aristotle. A vigorous Neoplatonic tradition developed, not least by finding an accommodation with Christianity. Commentators on Aristotle produced original and rigorous arguments. In the Greek East, philosophy ceased to be taught by non-Christians during the reign of Justinian, and although Christian philosophers launched an attack on Aristotelian science in the later sixth century, specifically on the question of the pre-existence of matter and the creation of the world, the Greek philosophical tradition found a place in the schools of Byzantium. From the Greek (sometimes via Syriac) a great deal of classical philosophy passed to the Islamic world. In the West, knowledge of Greek philosophy came generally through Latin translation. Original work in Latin was not abundant. Handbooks and commentaries on all aspects of science and philosophy proliferated in East and West.

### 11.1.1 Plotinus and "the One"

For the Platonic philosopher Plotinus (205–270), the founder of Neoplatonism, "the One" or "the Good" is the ineffable and absolutely transcendent source and goal of all existence and values. It is the highest level of reality, while matter and the physical world of change constitute the lowest rank. In his *Enneads*, "the One" is the starting point for his entire conceptual system.

Plotinus, *Ennead* 5.4.1.5–16

[John Bussanich, "Plotinus' Metaphysics of the One," in Lloyd P. Gerson, ed., *The Cambridge Companion to Plotinus* (New York: Cambridge, 1996) p. 42]

> There must be something simple before all things, and this must be other than all the things which come after it, existing by itself, not mixed with the things which derive from it, and all the same able to be present in a different way to the other things, being really one, and not a different being and then one; it is false even to say of it that it is one, and there is "no concept or knowledge" of

it; it is indeed also said to be "beyond being." For if it is not to be simple, outside all coincidence and composition, it could not be a first principle; and it is the most self-sufficient, because it is simple and the first of all . . . A reality of this kind must be one alone.

### 11.1.2 The three hypostases: the One, Nous, and Soul

Plotinus outlined a clear hierarchy of transcendent principles. First is the One or the Good, and after that comes the Primal Intelligence, Nous, and after that, Soul. Linked together they tie the humblest forms of life to the transcendent principles of the intelligible world.

Plotinus, *Ennead* 5.2.1

[A.H. Armstrong, *Plotinus* (London: Allen & Unwin, 1953) pp. 54–5]

> The One is all things and not a single one of them: for the Source of all is not all things; yet It is all things, for they all, so to speak, run back to It: or, rather, in It they are not yet, but will be. How then do all things come from the One, Which is simple and has in It no diverse variety, or any sort of doubleness? It is because there is nothing in It that all things come from it: in order that being may exist, the One is not being but the Generator of being. This, we say, is the first of act of generation. The One, perfect because It seeks nothing, has nothing, and needs nothing, overflows, as it were, and Its superabundance makes something other than Itself. This, when it has come into being, turns back upon the One and is filled, and so becomes Its contemplator, Nous [Intellect]. Its halt and turning towards the One constitutes being, its gaze upon the One, Nous. Since it halts and turns towards the One that it may see, it becomes at once Nous and being. Resembling the One thus, Nous produces in the same way, producing a likeness of itself. This activity springing from being is Soul, which comes into being while Nous abides unchanged. . . . But Soul does not abide unchanged when it produces: it is moved and so brings forth an image. It looks to its source and is filled, and going forth to another opposed movement generates its own image, which is Sensation and the Principle of growth in plants. Nothing is separated, cut off from that which is before it. For this reason Soul seeks to reach as far as plants; and in a way it does reach so far, for the life principle in plants belongs to Soul . . .

### 11.1.3 A philosophical life

In his biography by Porphyry, Plotinus emerges as a philosopher keenly aware of the constraints of physical existence yet actively pursuing a gentle life of teaching in the world.

Porphyry, *On the Life of Plotinus and the Order of His Books* 1, 9

[A.H. Armstrong, ed., *Plotinus*, vol. I (Cambridge, MA: Harvard University Press, 1966) pp. 3, 31, 33]

1. Plotinus, the philosopher of our times, seemed ashamed of being in the body. As a result of this state of mind he could never bear to talk about his race or his parents or his native country. And he objected so strongly to sitting to a painter or sculptor that he said to Amelius, who was urging him to allow a portrait of himself to be made, "Why really, is it not enough to have to carry the image in which nature has encased us, without your requesting me to agree to leave behind me a longer lasting image of the image, as if it was something genuinely worth looking at?"

9. There were women, too, who were greatly devoted to him: Gemina, in whose house he lived, and her daughter Gemina, who had the same name as her mother, and Amphiclea, who became the wife of Ariston son of Iamblichus, all of whom had a great devotion to philosophy. Many men and women of the highest rank, on the approach of death, brought him their children, both boys and girls, and entrusted them to him along with all their property, considering that he would be a holy and god-like guardian. So his house was full of young lads and maidens, including Potamon, to whose education he gave serious thought, and would even listen to him revising the same lesson again and again. He patiently attended to the accounts of their property when their trustees submitted them, and took care that they should be accurate; he used to say that as long as they did not take to philosophy their properties and incomes must be kept safe and untouched for them. Yet, though he shielded so many from the worries and cares of ordinary life, he never, while awake, relaxed his intent concentration upon the intellect. He was gentle, too, and at the disposal of all who had any sort of acquaintance with him. Though he spent twenty-six whole years in Rome and acted as arbitrator in very many people's disputes, he never made an enemy of any of the officials.

### 11.1.4  Intellectual beauty and contemplation

In the World of the Primal Intelligence (*Nous*) reside Truth, Beauty and all Knowledge, separate yet fully partaking of one another. This World of Primal Intelligence is the object of contemplation of the Gods and should be that of the human philosopher as well, for it is the realm of pure Wisdom.

Plotinus, *Ennead* 5.8.4

[A.H. Armstrong, ed., *Plotinus*, vol. V (Cambridge, MA: Harvard University Press, 1978) p. 251]

This life in the World of Primal Intelligence is wisdom, wisdom not acquired by reasonings, but always all present, without any failing which would make it need to be searched for. It is the first, not derived from any other wisdom; the very being of Intellect is wisdom: it does not exist first and then become wise. For this reason there is no greater wisdom: absolute knowledge has its throne beside Intellect in their common revelation, as they say symbolically Justice is throned beside Zeus. All things of this kind there are like images seen by their own light, to be beheld by exceedingly blessed spectators. The greatness and the power of this wisdom can be imagined if we consider that it has with it and has made all things. All things follow it, and it is the real beings, and they came to be along with it, and both are one, and reality is wisdom there. We do not arrive at understanding this, because we consider that the different branches of knowledge are made up of theorems and a collection of proportions; but this is not true even of the sciences here below . . .

### 11.1.5  Julian's Hymn to Helios, god of the sun

Among the many writings of the emperor Julian (360–363), who made an ill-fated attempt to suppress Christianity and revive pagan worship, is an elegant hymn to the sun god, King Helios. It combines traditional names of gods with sophisticated Neoplatonic explanations.

Julian, *Hymn to King Helios, Dedicated to Sallust* 130, 132, 133
[*The Works of the Emperor Julian*, vol. 1, trans. Wilmer Cave Wright (Cambridge, MA: Harvard University Press, 1913) pp. 353, 359, 361]

What I am now about to say I consider to be of the greatest importance for all things "That breathe and move upon the earth," and have a share in existence and a reasoning soul and intelligence, but above all others it is of importance to myself. For I am a follower of King Helios. And of this fact I possess within me, known to myself alone, proofs more certain than I can give. But this at least I am permitted to say without sacrilege, that from my childhood an extraordinary longing for the rays of the god penetrated deep into my soul; and from my earliest years my mind was so completely swayed by the light that illumines the heavens that not only did I desire to gaze intently at the sun, but whenever I walked abroad in the night season, when the firmament was clear and cloudless, I abandoned all else without exception and gave myself up to the beauties of the heavens. . . .

This divine and wholly beautiful universe, from the highest vault of heaven to the lowest limit of the earth, is held together by the continuous providence of the god, has existed from eternity ungenerated, is imperishable for all time to come, and is guarded immediately by nothing else than the Fifth Substance whose culmination is the beams of the sun; and in the second and higher degree, so to speak, by the intelligible world; but in a still loftier sense it is guarded by the King of the whole universe, who is the centre of all things that exist. He, therefore, whether it is right to call him the Supra-Intelligible, or the Idea of Being, and by Being I mean the whole intelligible region, or the One, since the One seems somehow to be prior to all the rest, or, to use Plato's name for him, the Good; at any rate this uncompounded cause of the whole reveals to all existence beauty, and perfection, and oneness, and irresistible power; and in virtue of the primal creative substance that abides in it, produced, as middle among the middle and intellectual, creative causes, Helios the most mighty god, proceeding from itself and in all things like unto itself. Even so the divine Plato believed, when he writes, "Therefore said I when I spoke of this, understand that I meant the offspring of the Good which the Good begat in his own likeness, and that what the Good is in relation to pure reason and its objects in the intelligible world, such is the sun in the visible world in relation to sight and its objects." Accordingly his light has the same relation to the visible world as truth has to the intelligible world. And he himself as a whole, since he is the son of what is first and greatest, namely, the Idea of the Good, and subsists from eternity in the region of its abiding substance, has received also the dominion among the intellectual gods, and himself dispenses to the intellectual gods those things of which the Good is the cause for the intelligible gods. Now the Good is, I suppose, the cause for the intelligible gods of beauty, existence, perfection, and oneness, connecting these and illuminating them with a power that works for good. These accordingly Helios bestows on the intellectual gods also, since he has been appointed by the Good to rule and govern them, even though they came forth and came into being together with him, and this was, I suppose, in order that the cause which resembles the Good may guide the intellectual gods to blessings for them all, and may regulate all things according to pure reason.

Julian, *Hymn to the Mother of the Gods* 180
[*The Works of the Emperor Julian*, vol. 1, trans. W.C. Wright (Cambridge, MA: Harvard University Press, 1913) p. 503]

> ... And for myself, grant me as fruit of my worship of thee that I may have true knowledge in the doctrines about the gods. Make me perfect in theurgy. And in all that I undertake, in the affairs of the state and the army, grant me virtue and good fortune, and that the close of my life may be painless and glorious, in the good hope that it is to you, the gods, that I journey!

### 11.1.6 Pythagoras, the guide

Iamblichus (*c.*250–*c.*325) studied with Porphyry and eventually opened a school in Syria. He brought to Neoplatonism an interest in the teachings of Pythagoras, the semi-mythical philosopher of the sixth century BC. Iamblichus presented Pythagoras as a special soul sent by the gods to help lead man to salvation through a philosophic life, and he meant Pythagoras to be an inspiration for his students. Iamblichus' *Exhortation to Philosophy* describes the ascent of the soul made possible by careful instruction, and he presents Pythagoras as an agent of that process.

Iamblichus, *The Exhortation to Philosophy* 1
[*Iamblichus: the Exhortation to Philosophy*, trans. Thomas M. Johnson (Grand Rapids, MI: Phanes Press, 1988) p. 21]

> Of Pythagoras and the life in accordance with his doctrines, and of the Pythagoreans, we treated sufficiently in our first book: we will now explain the

remaining part of his system, beginning with the common preparatory training prescribed by his school in reference to all education and learning and virtue; a training which is not partial, only perfecting one is some particular good of all these but which, to speak simply, incites his cognitive powers to the acquirement of all disciplines, all sciences, all beautiful and noble actions in life, all species of culture – and, in a phrase, everything which participates in the Beautiful. For without an awakening, caused by exhortation, from the natural lethargy, it is not possible for one to apply himself suddenly to beautiful and noble studies; nor can one immediately proceed to the apprehension of the highest and most perfect good before his soul has been duly prepared by exhortation (which arouses his impulses to higher things, purifies his thoughts, and directs his actions).

But just as the soul gradually advances to the greater from the less, passing through all beautiful things, and finally reaches the most perfect good, so it is necessary that exhortation should proceed regularly, beginning from those things which are common. For exhortation will incite to Philosophy itself and to philosophizing in general, according to every system of thought, no particular school being expressly preferred, but all being approved according to their respective merits, and ranked higher than mere human studies, by a common and popular mode of exhorting.

## 11.1.7  The art of theurgy

Iamblichus taught another way to raise the soul from the evil world of matter and purify it, through theurgy. This technique used ritual and magical chants to help free the soul from the constraints of the material world. These excerpts from Iamblichus' treatise On the Mysteries illustrate his wedding of magic and philosophy.

Iamblichus, On the Mysteries 2.12, 5.23
[Iamblichus, On the Mysteries, 2nd edn, trans. Thomas Taylor (London: Bertram Dobell, 1895) pp. 55–6; 266–7]

> 2.12 . . . For the illumination which takes place through invocations is spontaneously visible and self-perfect; is very remote from all downward attraction; proceeds into visibility through divine energy and perfection, and as much surpasses our voluntary motion as the divine will of the Good transcends a deliberately chosen life. Through this will, therefore, the Gods, being benevolent and propitious, impart their light to theurgists in unenvying abundance, calling upwards their souls to themselves, procuring them a union with themselves, and accustoming them, while they are yet in the body, to be separated from bodies and to be led round to their eternal and intelligible principle.

> 5.23 . . . At the same time nothing prevents more excellent beings from being able to impart their light to subordinate natures. Neither, therefore, is matter separated from the participation of better causes; so that such matter as is

perfect, pure, and boniform, is not unadapted to the reception of the Gods. For, since it is requisite that terrestrial natures should by no means be destitute of divine communion, the earth also receives a certain divine portion from it, sufficient for the participation of the Gods. The theurgic art, therefore, perceiving this to be the case, and thus having discovered in common, appropriate receptacles, conformably to the peculiarity of each of the Gods, it frequently connects together stones, herbs, animals, aromatics, and other sacred, perfect, and deiform substances of the like kind; and afterwards, from all these, it produces an entire and pure receptacle.

## 11.1.8 The life and education of Proclus

Proclus (c.410–485), a Neoplatonic philosopher at the Academy of Athens, systematized a great deal of the work of earlier philosophers and created a curriculum of Neoplatonic texts fundamental to future generations in his Academy as well as to Christian Neoplatonists. He believed Plato and Aristotle to be entirely compatible, and he understood philosophy to be divine revelation to humans. By pursuing self-knowledge through reflection and a carefully organized life, the souls of men might return through a hierarchically organized cosmos to union with "the One," the ultimate source of all reality. Marinos of Neapolis (died 500) describes the education of the great philosopher and the ascetic principles that guided him and gave him the power to perform theurgic miracles. (See also *8.7.3*, page 275.)

Marinos of Neapolis, *Life of Proclus* 8–13, 19, 21, 29

[*Marinos of Neapolis, the Extant Works: Life of Proclus*, trans. A.M. Oikonomides (Chicago: Ares Publishers, 1977) pp. 27, 29, 31, 35, 37, 39, 49, 53, 67, 69]

> [8] For a very short while he attended a grammar school in Lycia, and then removed to Egyptian Alexandria, already imbued with the moral qualities which charmed the teachers he attended. The Isaurian sophist Leonas, the most celebrated among his fellow philosophers, not only admitted him to his courses, but invited him to become his house-guest, admitted him to intimacy with his wife and children as if he had been his own son. He introduced the youth to the magistrates of Egypt, who received him among their most intimate friends, charmed with the youth's mental vivacity and his manner's distinction and dignity. He frequented the school of the grammarian Orion . . . Then he attended the lessons of Roman teachers, and rapidly made great progress in their curriculum; for at the beginning he proposed to follow the legal career of his father, who had thereby made himself famous in the capital . . . [9] He was still studying when Leonas invited him to share his journey to Constantinople, which he had undertaken as a favor to Theodore, the Alexandrian governor, a man of great distinction, liberality, and friendliness to philosophy. The youth accompanied the philosopher with much pleasure so as not to interrupt his studies . . . On his arrival the goddess [Minerva] advised him to devote

himself to philosophy, and to attend the Athens schools. So he said farewell to rhetoric and to his other former studies, and first, returning to Alexandria, he attended only what philosophical courses were there given. To begin the study of Aristotle's philosophy he attended the instruction of the Younger Olympiodorus . . . for mathematics, he trusted himself to Hero . . . [10] After having studied under the teachers in Alexandria, and having profited by their lessons according to their talent and science, it seemed to him, on one day and on reading an author with his teacher, that the latter's explanation of the passage had failed to represent the author's meaning. So he looked upon those schools with scorn, and simultaneously remembering the divine vision that had visited him in Constantinople, had the command which it had brought him, he embarked for Athens, so to speak, under the escort of all the gods and good genii who watch over the preservation of the Oracles and philosophy. For he was being sent there by the gods protective of philosophy to preserve the school of Plato in its verity and pureness . . . [11] . . . Chance led him to hear first Syrianus, son of Philoxenus . . . [12] . . . Syrianus introduced him to the great Plutarch, son of Nestorius . . . With him Proclus read Aristotle's "Soul" and Plato's "Phaedo" . . . After the arrival of Proclus the old man [Plutarch] survived only two years; and, on dying, recommended him to his successor Syrianus . . . [13] . . . Syrianus led Proclus to direct and immediate vision of the really divine mysteries contained in this philosopher [Plato], "when the eyes of the soul are no longer obscured as by a mist, and reason, freed from sensation, may cast firm glances into the distance" . . . By an intense and unresting labor by day and night, he succeeded in recording in writing, along with his own critical remarks, the doctrine which he heard discussed, and of which he finally made a synoptic outline; making such progress that at the age of twenty-three years, he had composed many treatises . . .

Through these prolonged and inspiring studies, to science he added virtue, increasing the moral beauty of his nature . . . [19] As to the necessary pleasures of food and drink, for him they were no more than a solace from his fatigues, to prevent them from distracting and confusing him; for he made use of them with sobriety. He especially practiced abstinence from animal food; but if an imperious occasion compelled him to make use of it, he only tasted it, out of deference and respect. Every month he sanctified himself according to the rites devoted to the Mother of the Gods by the Romans . . . he observed the unlucky days observed among the Egyptians even more strictly than they did themselves; and especially he fasted on certain days, quite openly . . . It was a phrase he much used, and that was very familiar to him, that a philosopher should watch over the salvation of not only a city, nor over the national customs of a few people, but that he ought to be the common hierophant [interpreter of sacred knowledge] of the whole world. Such were the holy and purificatory exercises he practiced in his austere manner of life.

[21] So the soul of this blessed man went on gathering itself, and concentrating itself, separating itself, so to speak, from its body, during the very

time when it seemed contained in him. This soul possessed wisdom, no longer only the political wisdom which consists in good behavior in the realm of contingent things, and which can be otherwise than they are; but thought in itself, pure thought, which consists in return into oneself and in refusal to unite with the body to acquire conjectural knowledge. It possessed the temperance which consists in not associating with the inferior element of our being, not even in limiting oneself to setting limits to our passions but desiring to be absolutely exempt from all passion; it possessed the courage which for her consists in not fearing separation from the body. As in him reason and pure thought were the rulers, the lower faculties no longer resisting to purificative justice, they imparted to his whole life a perfect beauty.

[29] If we wished to do so, we might easily extend our observations on the theurgic labors of this blessed man. From among thousands, I will mention but one, which is really miraculous. One day Asklepigeneia daughter of Archiadas and my benefactor Theagenes's wife, Plutarcha, being still small, and being raised at her parents, became ill with a sickness pronounced incurable by the physicians. Archiadas was in despair, as the child was the family's only hope, and naturally uttered distressful lamentations. Seeing her abandoned by the physicians, the father, as in the gravest circumstances of life, turned to his last resort, and ran to the philosopher's as to the only person who could save her, and urgently besought him to come and pray for his daughter. [Proclus] ... ran to the Ascleius temple to pray to God in favor of the patient – for Athens was still fortunate to possess the temple, since it had not yet been sacked. While he was praying according to the ancient rite, suddenly a change manifested in the little girl's condition, and there occurred a sudden improvement – for the Savior [Asclepius], being a divinity, swiftly gave her back her health ...

### 11.1.9 Athenian philosophers go to Persia

In 529 the emperor Justinian forbade teaching of philosophy in Athens by pagans – a fatal blow to the Academy of Plato, though it lingered for another generation. About 532, a group of pagan philosophers went to Persia to escape the hostile environment created by Justinian. They were disappointed to discover that Chosroes was not a philosopher-king.

Agathias, *The Histories* 2.30.3–7, 2.31.1–4

[Agathias, *The Histories*, trans. Joseph D. Frendo (Berlin: de Gruyter, 1975) pp. 65, 66]

Not long before Damascius of Syria, Simplicius of Cilicia, Eulamius of Phrygia, Priscian of Lydia, Hermes and Diogenes of Phoenicia and Isidore of Gaza, all of them, to use a poetic turn of phrase, the quintessential flower of the philosophers of our age, had come to the conclusion, since the official religion of the Roman empire was not to their liking, that the Persian state was much superior. So they gave a ready hearing to the stories in general circulation according to which Persia was the land of "Plato's philosopher king" in which justice reigned supreme. Apparently the subjects too were models of decency and good behaviour and there was no such thing as theft, brigandage or any other sort of crime . . .

Elated therefore by these reports which they accepted as true, and also because they were forbidden by law to take part in public life with impunity owing to the fact that they did not conform to the established religion, they left immediately and set off for a strange land whose ways were completely foreign to their own, determined to make their homes there. But in the first place they discovered that those in authority were overbearing and vainglorious and so had nothing but disgust and opprobrium for them. In the second place they realised that there were large numbers of housebreakers and robbers, some of whom were apprehended while others escaped detection, and that every form of crime was committed. The powerful in fact ill-treated the weak outrageously and displayed considerable cruelty and inhumanity in their dealing with one another. But the most extraordinary thing of all was that even though a man could and did have any number of wives people still had the effrontery to commit adultery. The philosophers were disgusted by all these things and blamed themselves for ever having made the move.

The opportunity of conversing with the king proved a further disappointment. It was that monarch's proud boast that he was a student of philosophy, but his knowledge of the subject was utterly superficial. There was no common ground either in matters of religion, since he observed the practices I have already described. Finally the vicious promiscuity which characterized Persian society was more than the philosophers could stand. All these factors, then, combined to send them hurrying back home as fast as they could go. So despite the king's affection for them and despite the fact that he invited them to stay, they felt that merely to set foot on Roman territory, even if it meant instant death, was preferable to a life of distinction in Persia. Accordingly they resolved to see the last of barbarian hospitality and all returned home.

Nevertheless they derived from their stay abroad a benefit which was neither slight nor negligible, but which was to secure them peace of mind and contentment for the rest of their days. A clause was inserted in fact in the treaty which at that time was being concluded between the Romans and the Persians, to the effect that the philosophers should be allowed to return to their homes and to live out their lives in peace without being compelled to alter their traditional religious beliefs or to accept any view which did not coincide with them. Chosroes insisted on the inclusion of this point and made the ratification and continued observance of the truce conditional on its implementation.

### 11.1.10 Philoponus and the creation of the world

The eternity of the world was a basic tenet of Aristotelian and Neoplatonic science. In 529 the Christian Neoplatonist John Philoponus, a professor in Alexandria, attacked the Aristotelian view that the unmoving substance at the center of the universe (the fifth element or ether) was eternal. Philoponus argued instead that God had brought all creation into existence at a moment in time. In the following passage, the pagan philosopher Simplicius, who quarreled with Philoponus ("the Grammarian") on this topic, describes his opponent's views.

Simplicius, *On the Heavens* 119.7–9

[*Philoponus, Against Aristotle, on the Eternity of the World*, trans. Christian Wildberg (London: Duckworth, 1987) pp. 77–8]

> But again, he who entitles himself "Grammarian" pursues the clear aim of persuading people like himself to suppose that the world is destructible and has been generated at some time; in consequence, he is annoyed with those who prove that the heavens are ungenerated and indestructible, and stirs up a lot of verbal muck against what has been said by Aristotle in these passages. Let us invoke an assistant, the great Herakles, and descend to the cleansing of the ordure in his words. After having initially outlined the Aristotelian distinction of the senses of "ungenerated" and "generated" drawn at the end of the book, he then asks according to which sense Aristotle proves the heavens to be ungenerated now, and he writes as follows:
>
> "Neither the heavens nor the world would be ungenerated in the sense that they are in fact impossible to be generated. For they clearly exist and have received the perfection of their nature. Therefore, only one further hypothesis remains, if the heavens cannot have been generated in the sense of having a beginning of existence, not even a beginning which brought them into existence without a process of generation. Then, since Aristotle, as he wanted to reject this kind of generation of the world, used the axiom that everything generated is generated out of a contrary, one must ask if generation out of a contrary belongs indeed to everything generated in time."

### 11.1.11 The consolation of philosophy

The aristocrat Anicius Manlius Severinus Boethius (*c*.480–*c*.524) served the Ostrogothic king Theoderic as Consul and Master of Offices. His scholarly knowledge of Greek was unusual for an Italian in the sixth century, and he planned to translate the corpus of Aristotle and Plato into Latin. While awaiting execution for alleged participation in a senatorial conspiracy, he wrote *The Consolation of Philosophy*. This brilliant dialogue with Lady Philosophy, who appears to him in his prison cell, combines Christian ideas of free will and divine providence. Here, Lady Philosophy reminds Boethius of the nature of the philosophic quest.

Boethius, *The Consolation of Philosophy* 1.2–3, 1.6–7

[Boethius, *The Consolation of Philosophy*, trans. V.E. Watts (New York: Penguin Books, 1980) pp. 38–40, 51–3]

> "But it is time for healing, not lamenting" . . . [Philosophy] went on. Then, fixing her eyes intently upon me, she said, "You are the man, are you not, who

was brought up on the milk of my learning and fed on my own food until you reached maturity? I gave you arms to protect you and keep your strength unimpaired, but you threw them away. Surely you recognize me? And yet you do not speak. Is it shame or is it astonishment that keeps you silent? I should prefer it to be shame, but I see that it is not."

When she saw that it was not that I would not speak, but that, dumbstruck, I could not, she gently laid her hand on my breast and said, "It is nothing serious, only a touch of amnesia that he is suffering, the common disease of deluded minds. He has forgotten for a while who he is, but he will soon remember once he has recognized me. To make it easier for him I will wipe a little of the blinding cloud of worldly concern from his eyes" . . .

. . . In the same way the clouds of my grief dissolved and I drank in the light. With my thoughts recollected I turned to examine the face of my physician. I turned my eyes and fixed my gaze upon her, and I saw that it was my nurse in whose house I had been cared for since my youth – Philosophy. I asked her why she had come down from the heights of heaven to my lonely place of banishment.

"Is it to suffer false accusation along with me?" I asked.

"Why, my child," she replied, "should I desert you? Why should I not share your labour and the burden you have been saddled with because of the hatred of my name? Should I be frightened by being accused? Or cower in fear as if it were something unprecedented? This is hardly the first time wisdom has been threatened with danger by the forces of evil. In olden times, too, before the time of my servant Plato, I fought many a great battle against the reckless forces of folly. And then, in Plato's own lifetime, his master Socrates was unjustly put to death – a victorious death won with me at his side. After that the mobs of Epicureans and Stoics and the others each did all they could to seize for themselves the inheritance of wisdom that he left. As part of their plunder they tried to carry me off, but I fought and struggled, and in the fight the robe was torn which I had woven with my own hands. They tore off little pieces from it and went away in the fond belief that they had obtained the whole of philosophy. The sight of traces of my clothing on them gained them the reputation among the ignorant of being my familiars, and as a result many of them became corrupted by the ignorance of the uninitiated mob.

But even if you do not know the stories of the foreign philosophers, how Anaxagoras was banished from Athens, how Socrates was put to death by poisoning, and how Zeno was tortured, you do know of Romans like Canius, Seneca and Soranus, whose memory is still fresh and celebrated. The sole cause of their tragic sufferings was their obvious and complete contempt of the pursuits of immoral men which my teaching had instilled in them. It is hardly surprising if we are driven by the blasts of storms when our chief aim on this sea of life is to displease wicked men. And though their numbers are great, we can afford to despise them because they have no one to lead them and are carried along only by ignorance which distracts them at random first one way then another. When their forces attack us in superior numbers, our general conducts a tactical withdrawal of his forces to a strong point, and they are left to encumber themselves with useless plunder. Safe from their furious activity on our ramparts above, we can smile at their efforts to collect all the most useless booty: our citadel cannot fall to the assaults of folly.

"Now I know the other cause, or rather the major cause of your illness: you have forgotten your true nature. And so I have found out in full the reason for your sickness and the way to approach the task of restoring you to health. It is because you are confused by loss of memory that you wept and claimed you had been banished and robbed of all your possessions. And it is because you don't know the end and purpose of things that you think the wicked and the criminal have power and happiness. And because you have forgotten the means by which the world is governed you believe these ups and downs of fortune happen haphazardly. These are grave causes and they lead not only to illness but even death. Thanks, however, to the Author of all health, nature has not quite abandoned you. In your true belief about the world's government – that it is subject to divine reason and not the haphazards of chance – there lies our greatest hope of rekindling your health. You need have no fears then, now that this tiny spark has blazed with the fire of life. Still, as it is not yet time for stronger medicine, and as it is the accepted opinion that the nature of the mind is such that for every true belief it rejects, it assumes a false one from which the fog of distraction rises to blot out its true insight, I will try to lessen this particular fog little by little by applying gentle remedies of only medium strength. In this way the darkness of the ever treacherous passions may be dispelled, and you will be able to see the resplendent light of truth."

VII

"In dark clouds
Hidden
The stars can shed
No light.
If boisterous winds
Stir the sea
Causing a storm,
Waves once crystal
Like days serene
Soon turn opaque
And thick with mud
Prevent the eye
Piercing the water.
Streams that wander
From tall hills
Down descending
Often dash

Against a rock
Torn from the hillside.
If you desire
To look on truth
And follow the path
With unswerving course,
Rid yourself
Of joy and fear,
Put hope to flight,
And banish grief.
The mind is clouded
And bound in chains
Where these hold sway."

## 11.1.12 *Martianus Capella on the shape of the universe*

In the last decades of the fifth century, Martianus Capella, a Roman scholar in Vandal Carthage, wrote *The Marriage of Philology and Mercury* or *Philologia*. This was an encyclopedia of the seven liberal arts: grammar, dialectic and rhetoric, which constituted the medieval "trivium," and geometry, arithmetic, music and astronomy, the "quadrivium." This collection was a major conduit of ancient learning, especially Neoplatonism, to the medieval world. The following passage from his eighth book on astronomy provides a Neoplatonic view of the heavens.

Martianus Capella, *The Marriage of Philology and Mercury* 8.814

[William Harris Stahl and Richard Johnson with E.L. Burge, *Martianus Capella and the Seven Liberal Arts*, vol. 11: *The Marriage of Philology and Mercury* (New York: Columbia University Press, 1977) pp. 318–19]

[814] The universe is formed in the shape of a globe composed entirely of four elements. The heavens, swirling in a ceaseless and rotary motion, set the earth apart in a stationary position in the middle and at the bottom. I would not disdain, at the very outset of my discourse, to give heed to the physical philosophers who do not believe that the softness of rarefied bodies is drawn and divided by its very condensations into certain set paths and intervals of circles; but rather that the natures of these bodies, coalescing by their own surgings, are diffused the entire way around the globular layers. The physical philosophers declare that the first envelopment is that of water, the second of air, the third of fire, arranged about a midpoint which they call the center. And coming next is a fifth agglomeration of corporeal matter, in which the shining heavenly bodies have their courses, in a region where the inclined paths of the sun, moon, planets, and zodiac are drawn; in the philosophical schools the last is referred to as the "circular billow." The very calm of that realm keeps its position outermost and its course an encompassing one; it is called "starless" from the fact that it is studded with no constellations.

## 11.1.13 Macrobius on the descent of the soul

Macrobius was a scholar and administrator (he was Praetorian Prefect in Italy in 430) who wrote philosophical works which were very influential in the medieval Latin world. His *Commentary on Cicero's Dream of Scipio* brings to the text of Cicero a wealth of knowledge of all sorts. The following passage explains the Neoplatonic view of the descent of the soul.

Macrobius, *Commentary on the Dream of Scipio* 1.12.1–2, 4, 7, 9, 16, 17

[*Commentary on the Dream of Scipio*, trans. William Harris Stahl (New York: Columbia University Press, 1952) pp. 133–5, 137]

[1] At this point we shall discuss the order of the steps by which the soul descends from the sky to the infernal regions of this life. The Milky Way girdles the zodiac, its great circle meeting it obliquely so that it crosses it at the two tropical signs, Capricorn and Cancer. Natural philosophers named these the "portals of the sun" because the solstices lie athwart the sun's path on either side, checking further progress and causing it to retrace its course across the belt beyond whose limits it never trespasses.

[2] Souls are believed to pass through these portals when going from the sky to the earth and returning from the earth to the sky. For this reason one is called the portal of men and the other the portal of gods: Cancer, the portal of men, because through it descent is made to the infernal regions; Capricorn, the portal of gods, because through it souls return to their rightful abode of immortality, to be reckoned among the gods.

[4] So long as the souls heading downwards still remain in Cancer they are considered in the company of the gods, since in that position they have not yet left the Milky Way. But when in their descent they have reached Leo, they enter upon the first stages of their future condition.

[7] When the soul is being drawn towards a body in this first protraction of itself it begins to experience a tumultuous influx of matter rushing upon it. . . . [9] Now if souls were to bring with them to their bodies a memory of the divine order of which they were conscious in the sky, there would be no disagreement among men in regard to divinity; but, indeed, all of them in their descent drink of forgetfulness, some more, some less. Consequently, although the truth is not evident to all on earth, all nevertheless have an opinion, since opinion is born of failure of the memory. . . . [16] The difference between terrestrial and supernal bodies (I am speaking of the sky and stars and the other components) lies in this, that the latter have been summoned upwards to the abode of the soul and have gained immortality by the very nature of that region and by copying the perfection of their high estate; but to our terrestrial bodies the soul is drawn downwards, and here it is believed to be dead while it is shut up in a perishable region and the abode of mortality.

[17] Be not disturbed that in reference to the soul, which we say is immortal, we so often use the term "death." In truth, the soul is not destroyed by its death but is overwhelmed for a time; nor does it surrender the privilege of

immortality because of its lowly sojourn, for when it has rid itself completely of all taint of evil and has deserved to be sublimated, it again leaves the body and, fully recovering its former state, returns to the splendor of everlasting life.

## Further reading

Edwards, Mark J., *Culture and Philosophy in the Age of Plotinus* (London: Duckworth, 2006)

Lindberg, David, *The Beginnings of Western Science. The European Scientific Tradition in Philosophical, Religious, and Institutional Context, 600 BC to AD 1450* (Chicago: University of Chicago Press, 1992)

O'Meara, Dominic J., *Plotinus. An Introduction to the Enneads* (Oxford: Oxford University Press, 1993)

O'Meara, Dominic J., *Pythagoras Revived. Mathematics and Philosophy in Late Antiquity* (Oxford: Oxford University Press, 2004)

O'Meara, Dominic J., *Platonopolis: Platonic Political Philosophy in Late Antiquity* (Oxford: Oxford University Press, 2007)

Shaw, Gregory, *Theurgy and the Soul. The Neoplatonism of Iamblichus* (University Park: Pennsylvania State University Press, 1995)

Smith, Andrew, *Philosophy in Late Antiquity* (London: Routledge, 2004)

Smith, Andrew, ed., *The Philosopher and Society in Late Antiquity. Essays in Honour of Peter Brown* (Swansea: The Classical Press of Wales, 2005)

Sorabji, Richard, ed., *Aristotle and After* (London: Institute of Classical Studies, 1997)

Sorabji, Richard, *The Philosophy of the Commentators, 200–600 AD: A Sourcebook* (Ithaca, NY: Cornell University Press, 2005)

Watts, Edward, *City and School in Late Antique Athens and Alexandria* (Berkeley: University of California Press, 2006)

Wildberg, Christian, "Philosophy in the Age of Justinian," in Michael Maas, ed., *The Cambridge Companion to the Age of Justinian* (Cambridge: Cambridge University Press, 2005) pp. 316–42

# 12

# SASANIAN PERSIA

## 12.1 Introduction

Based on the Iranian plateau, the Sasanian Empire in Late Antiquity was an aggressive, polyethnic state covering a territory about the same size as the eastern Roman Empire (see Map 18). The two empires, which shared a border stretching from the Caucasus to the Red Sea, had much in common. Both were frequently preoccupied with the threat of northern steppe nomads (though this was a greater problem for Persia), and both cultivated client states among Arab tribes on their southern borders. The Mesopotamian agricultural land was densely urbanized like much of the Roman Empire, and both had a secular administrative system with fiscal machinery geared to extracting taxes. Persians had a state religion, Zoroastrianism, and used this faith as a major prop of the political order. Most importantly, Persia and Rome maintained an uneasy equilibrium that sometimes broke down in struggles over Armenia, Syria and the Mesopotamian frontier. Under the Sasanian dynasty (*c*.220–633) Rome had a fierce and worthy rival, for the two states were military equals. The official treatment of Christians in the Sasanian Empire and the handling of Bedouin Arab client states were contentious issues. A period of relatively good relations lasted for most of the fifth century, but the sixth century saw bitter, chronic warfare. After a protracted life-and-death struggle, Roman forces under Heraclius finally defeated Persia in 627. This conflict left both populations so exhausted that neither could mount an effective resistance against the armies of Islam. Persia was overrun by Arab armies (*c*.633–650) and slowly Islamicized. By 750, when the Abbasids established themselves at Baghdad, Persia had become an integral part of the Caliphate, and a new chapter in her history began.

### 12.1.1 The ideal Sasanian monarch

The Persian state exercised firm control over its subjects through its centralized administration, particularly its tax-collecting apparatus, and through the collaboration of the nobility. The King of Kings, the paramount ruler, depended for support upon a warrior aristocracy of Iranian clans. Subject peoples were ruled by their own kings, who were in turn strictly subordinated to the King of Kings. No attempt was made at enforcing cultural uniformity. In the *Shahnamah* or *Epic of the Kings* by Firdawsi, written in the tenth century but drawing upon documents of the Sasanian period, we find the *Letter of Tansar*. The letter is set in the days of Alexander the Great, who had conquered Persia in 333 BC, and it includes the imagined words of Aristotle. Nevertheless, the letter gives a glimpse of how the Sasanians idealized a good king (probably the sixth-century ruler Khosrau Anoshirwan – Chosroes to the Romans) and the social order he established within the Persian Empire. The government of subject peoples, the divisions of Persian society into different classes, the strict control of religious legitimization and worship, and the virtues of a good monarch are all matters of concern.

*Tansar's Letter to Gushnasp* 1–3, 12–13, 22–3, 27, 44

[Mary Boyce, trans., *The Letter of Tansar* (Rome: Istituto Italiano per il Medio ed Estremo Oriente, 1968) pp. 27–8, 37–8, 47–8, 52, 67]

> When the king [Alexander] had seized Iran all the princes and descendants of the nobility and the leader and rulers and provincial aristocracy gathered in his presence. Their splendor and numbers troubled him, and he wrote a letter to his minister, Aristotle: "By the Grace of great and glorious God our fortunes have prospered thus far. I wish to go to India and China and the farthest East, but fear to leave alive these Persian nobles, lest they create troubles in my absence which it will be hard to remedy and come to Greece to do harm to our land. It seems prudent to me to destroy them all, that I may carry out my purpose with untroubled mind."
>
> Aristotle wrote the following answer: "Truly the peoples of each of the world's climes are distinguished by some excellence, some talent and some dignity which those of other climes do not possess. The people of Persia are pre-eminent for courage and boldness and skill on the day of battle, qualities which form one of the mightiest tools of empire and instruments of power. If you destroy them, you will have overthrown one of the greatest pillars of excellence in the world. Moreover, when the noble among them have gone, you will be forced of necessity to promote the base to the same ranks and stations. Be assured that there is no wickedness or calamity, no unrest or plague in the world which corrupts so much as the ascending of the base to the stations of the noble . . . [Instead of killing them] you must make the heads of their first families and their men of rank and their lords and nobles rely upon your position and patronage, your sincerity and bounty; and through favors and kindness you must banish the causes of vexation and care from their hearts. For the ancients have said that no matter of moment will be brought about by force and harshness which cannot be accomplished by clemency and kindness. The best course is to divide the realm of Iran among their princes and to bestow throne and crown on whomsoever you appoint to any province; giving none precedence, as ascendancy, or authority over another, that each may be absolute on the throne of his own domain. For the title of king is a great pride, and none wearing a crown is ready to pay tribute to another, or to humble

himself before any man. There will appear among them so much disunity and variance and presumption and haughtiness, so much opposition and rivalry about power, so much bragging and vaunting about wealth, so much contention over degree, and so much ruffling and wrangling over retainers, that they will have no leisure to seek vengeance upon you. . . . Thus there would be security for you and for those who follow after you . . . .

[Tansar replies:]

Do not marvel at my zeal and ardor for promoting order in the world, that the foundations of the laws and of the [Zoroastrian] Faith may be made firm. For [Church] and State were born of the one womb and joined together and never to be sundered . . .

As for your especial case, my counsel to you is to take horse and come with crown and throne to the king's court. Know and understand that a crown is what the King of Kings sets upon your head, and a realm is that which he entrusts to you.

[pp. 37/38] . . . Know that according to our religion, men are divided into four estates. This is set down in many places in the holy books and established beyond controversy and interpretation, contradiction, and speculation. They are known as the four estates, and at their head is the king. The first estate is that of the clergy; and this estate is further divided among judges and priests, ascetics, temple-guardians and teachers. The second estate is that of the military, that is to say of the fighting-men, of whom there are two groups, cavalry and foot-soldiers. Within them there are differences of rank and function. The third estate is that of the scribes, and they too are divided into groups and categories, such as writers of official communication, accountants, recorders of verdicts and registrations and covenants, and writers of chronicles; physicians, poets and astronomers are numbered among their ranks. The fourth estate is known as that of the artisans, and comprises tillers of land and herders of cattle and merchants and others who earn their living by trade. It is through these four estates that humanity will prosper as long as it endures. Assuredly there shall be no passing from one to another unless in the character of one of us outstanding capacity is found . . .

[p. 47] . . . The truth is that after Darius each of the [lesser] "kings of the peoples" built his own fire-temple. This was pure innovation, introduced by them without the authority of any king of old. The King of Kings has razed the temples and confiscated the endowments, and had the fires carried back to their places of origin.

[p. 48] Next, for what you have said, that the King of Kings has forbidden people too lavish a way of life and too ample an expenditure. This he has made a binding law, his purpose being to make clear the divisions and distinctions among the people, that the appurtenances proper to each class may be plainly seen. The nobles are distinguished from the artisans and trades people by their dress and horses and trappings of pomp, and their women likewise by silken garments; also by their lofty dwellings, their trousers, headgear, hunting and whatever else is customary for the noble.

[p. 52] Know that we are called the Iranian people, and there is no quality or trait of excellence or nobility which we hold dearer than this, that we have ever showed humility and lowliness and humbleness in the service of kings, and have chosen obedience, devotion and fidelity.

[p. 67] The wonder lies in this, how, alone he pursued and won the lordship and kingdom of the world, though all the land surged with lions of whetted appetite. . . . In the space of fourteen years, through policy and strength and skill, he brought it about that he made water flow in every desert and established towns and created groups of villages, in a way not achieved in the 4,000 years before him. He found builders and inhabitants and caused roads to be made. He established customs concerning eating and drinking, and clothes for travel and home. He sets his hand to nothing without gaining the people's trust in his ability, and without accomplishing it surely. He has taken such pains for the future – up to a thousand years after his own day – that within that time no evil will befall. He has more joy in the future and more concern in the interest of those who will come after him than he has in his own auspicious age. Yet good order in the affairs of the people affects him more than the welfare of his own body and soul. Whoever considers his achievements during these fourteen years, and whoever sees and understands his excellence and learning, his powers of exposition and eloquence, his wrath and graciousness, his liberality and modesty, his sagacity and shrewdness, will agree that since the power of the world's Creator arched this azure sphere the world has not known so true a king. This gate to goodness and good order, set open by him for the people, will remain so for a thousand years . . .

### 12.1.2  The Zoroastrian creed

Zoroastrianism, the official religion of the Sasanian Empire, derived from the teachings of the prophet Zoroaster (Zarathustra) in the sixth century BC. It understood the world to be in the midst of a great conflict between Ahura-Mazda, the protector of good order, and Ahriman, the devil and promoter of discord and the negation of life. Ahura-Mazda was worshiped at fire altars. Like Judaism and Christianity, Zoroastrianism is a credal religion. The following is a statement of faith of Zoroaster's followers, written down shortly after the fall of the Sasanian Empire in the seventh century.

*The Book of the Counsel of Zartusht* 2–8

[R.C. Zaehner, *The Teachings of the Magi. A Compendium of Zoroastrian Beliefs* (New York: Macmillan, 1956) pp. 21–2]

So this one must know without venturing to doubt: I have come from the unseen world, but I was not always of this world. I was created and have not always been. I belong to Ahura-Mazda, not to Ahriman; to the gods, not the demons; to the good, not to the wicked. I am a man, not a demon, I am a creature of Ahura-Mazda, not of Ahriman . . . To perform my function and to do my duty means that I should believe that Ahura-Mazda is, was, and evermore shall be, that his Kingdom is undying, and that he is infinite and pure; and that Ahriman is not, and is destructible; that I myself belong to Ahura-Mazda and his Bounteous Immortals, and that I have no connection with Ahriman, the demons, and their associates. My first duty on earth is to confess the Religion, to practice it, and to take part in its worship and to be steadfast in it, to keep the Faith in the Good Religion of the worshippers of Ahura-Mazda ever in my mind, and to distinguish profit from loss, sin from good works, goodness from evil, light from darkness, and the worship of Ahura-Mazda from the worship of the demons. My second duty is to take a wife and to procreate earthly offspring, and to be strenuous and steadfast in this. My third duty is to cultivate and till the soil; my fourth to treat all livestock justly; my fifth to spend a third of my days and nights in attending the seminary and consulting the wisdom of holy men, to spend a third of my days and nights in tilling the soil and in making it fruitful, and to spend the remaining third of my days and nights in eating, rest, and enjoyment.

### 12.1.3 The struggle of light and darkness

The Zoroastrian creation myth reflects the basic principles of the religion.
*Greater Creation* 1.1–39
[Mary Boyce, ed., *Textual Sources for the Study of Zoroastrianism* (Totowa, NJ: Barnes and Noble, 1984) pp. 45–8]

About Ahura-Mazda, Ahriman and the spirit creation.
It is thus revealed in the Good Religion that Ahura-Mazda was on high in omniscience and goodness. For boundless time He was ever in the light. That light is the space and place of Ahura-Mazda. Some call it Endless Light . . .

Ahriman was abased in slowness of knowledge and the lust to smite. The lust to smite was his sheath and darkness his place. Some call it Endless Darkness. And between them was emptiness. They both were limited and limitless: for that which is on high, which is called Endless Light, . . . and that which is abased, which is Endless Darkness – those were limitless. But at the border both were limited, in that between them was emptiness. There was no connection between the two. Then both two Spirits were in themselves limited. On account of the omniscience of Ahura-Mazda, all things were within the knowledge of Ahura-Mazda, the limited and the limitless; for He knew the measure of what is within the two Spirits. Then the entire kingship of the creation of Ahura-Mazda, in the future body for ever and ever, that is limitless. The creation of Ahriman, at the time when the future body will be, shall be destroyed. That truly is limited. Ahura-Mazda by His omniscience knew that the Evil Spirit existed, what he plotted in his enviousness to do, how he would commingle, what the beginning, what the end; what and how many the tools with which He would make an end. And He created in the spirit state the creatures He would need as those tools. For 3,000 years creation remained in the spirit state. The Evil Spirit, on account of his slowness of knowledge, was not aware of the existence of Ahura-Mazda. Then he arose from the deep, and came to the boundary and beheld the light. When he saw the intangible light of Ahura-Mazda he rushed forward. Because of his lust to smite and his envious nature he attacked to destroy it. Then he saw valour and supremacy greater than his own. He crawled back to darkness and shaped many devs [spirits], the destructive creation. And he rose for battle. When Ahura-Mazda saw the creatures of the Evil Spirit, they appeared to Him frightful and putrid and evil; and He desired them not. When the Evil Spirit saw the creatures of Ahura-Mazda they appeared to him most profound and fully informed. And he desired the creatures and creation of Ahura-Mazda. Then Ahura-Mazda, in spite of His knowledge of creation and the end of the affair, approached the Evil Spirit and proffered peace and said: "Evil Spirit! Aid my creatures, and give praise, so that in recompense for that you may be immortal . . .". The Evil Spirit snarled: "I shall not aid your creatures and I shall not give praise, but I shall destroy you and your creatures for ever and ever. And I shall persuade all your creatures to hate you and to love me." And Ahura-Mazda said: "You are not all-powerful, Evil Spirit; so you cannot destroy me, and you cannot so influence my creatures that they will not return to being mine." . . . When He pondered upon creation, Ahura-Mazda saw by His clear vision that the Evil Spirit would never turn from the Assault; the Assault would not be made powerless except through creation; creation could not develop except through time; but if He created time, Ahriman's creation too would develop. And having no other course, in order to make the Assault powerless, He created time . . .

### 12.1.4 A trip to Hell and Heaven

In the Zoroastrian religion, men and women can choose to follow the ways of good or evil. The *Arda Viraz Nameh*, the *Book of the Vision of Arda Viraz*, is the story of a visit to Heaven and Hell. The narrator's guides, the spirits Srosh and Adar Yazad, explain how the dead receive appropriate rewards for the way they lived their lives. The virtues and vices described here illustrate basic values of everyday life in Sasanian Persia.

Arda Viraz, *A Vision of Heaven and Hell* 6.3.8–12, 15, 18

[Mary Boyce, *Textual Sources for the Study of Zoroastrianism* (Totowa, NJ: Barnes and Noble, 1984) pp. 87–9]

> 6.3.8 (1) I came to a place and saw the souls of generous people, who walked adorned and were above all other souls in all brightness. And Ohrmazd [Ahura Mazda] ever honoured the souls of the generous, which were bright and tall and strong. And I said: "Happy are you, who are the soul of a generous person,

exalted thus above other souls." And it seemed to me praiseworthy. (2) And I saw the souls of those persons who in the flesh had chanted the Gathas and performed acts of worship, and professed the Good Religion of the Mazda-worshippers which Ohrmazd had taught to Zardusht. And when I advanced, they were in garments adorned with silver and gold, the most embellished of all garments. And it seemed to me very praiseworthy.

6.3.9 ... And I saw the souls of "warriors", who went in the highest happiness and joyfulness of mind, and in kingly garments. And the wellmade caparisons of those heroes were made of gold, studded with jewels, very glorious, richly adorned; and they were in chariots with wondrous bodywork, in much splendour and strength and victoriousness. And it seemed to me praiseworthy ... (2) And I saw the souls of "herdsmen", in a brilliant place and glorious raiment, as they had stood before the spirits of Water and Earth and Plants and Cattle, and blessed them. And they utter praise and thanks and gratitude, and their position is great, and they occupy a good place. And it seemed to me praiseworthy. (4) And I saw the souls of those "artisans" who in the world had served their lords and masters, as they sat upon daises [thrones] which were well carpeted, large, brilliant and shining. And it seemed to me very praise-worthy.

6.3.10 ... And I saw the souls of those who love good, the intercessors and peace-seekers, from whom there ever shines a light like that of the stars and moon and sun; and, possessed of joy, they ever walked in the atmosphere of light. (2) And I saw the foremost existence of the just, light, with all ease and plenty, and many fragrant flowers of all colours, all in blossom – radiant, full of glory and every happiness and joy, from which none knows satiety.

6.3.11 (1) Then just Srosh and Adar Yazad took my hands, and brought me into a desolate place on the Peak of the Law, beneath the Chinvat Bridge; and they showed me hell in the midst of that desolate place, in the earth beneath the Chinvat Bridge. From that place there rose up the weeping and lamentation of Ahriman and the demons and she-devils and also the many souls of the wicked, concerning which I thought: "The seven regions of the earth would shake, if they should hear that lamentation and weeping." I was affrighted and entreated just Srosh and Adar Yazad: "Do not bring me here! Turn back!" (2) Then just Srosh and Adar Yazad said to me: "Fear not! for there will never be any dread for you here." And just Srosh and Adar Yazad went on before; and behind went I, just Viraz, fearlessly, further into that dark hell.

6.3.12 (1) And I saw the blackest hell, dangerous, fearful, terrible, holding much pain, full of evil, foul-smelling. Then I thought that it seemed like a pit, to whose bottom a thousand spears would not reach; and if all the firewood which is in the world were placed on the fire in the most evil-smelling, darkest hell, it would never give out fragrance. Again, as (close) as eye to ear, and as many as the hairs on a horse's mane, so (close) and many in number are the souls of the wicked therein. Yet they see not, and hear no sound from one another. Each one thinks: "I am alone." And they suffer gloom and darkness and stench and fearfulness and torment and punishment of diverse kinds, so that he who has been one day in hell cries out: "Are not those nine thousand years yet fulfilled, that they do not release us from this hell?"

6.3.15 (1) And I saw the souls of women whose heads were cut off and separated from their bodies, and their tongues kept up an outcry. And I asked: "Whose souls are those?" Just Srosh and Adar Yazad said: "These are the souls of those women who in the flesh made much lamentation and mourning, and beat their heads and faces."

6.3.18 (1) Then just Srosh and Adar Yazad took my hands and bore me out of that black place, dangerous and fearful, and carried me to the Endless Light and the assembly of Ohrmazd and the Amahraspands. (2) When I wished to do homage before Ohrmazd . . . He said: "You are welcome, just Viraz, messenger of the Mazda-worshippers! Go to the material world and as you have seen and understood, tell it truly to those who dwell therein. For I who am Ohrmazd am with you. Each man who speaks what is sound and true, I recognise and know him. Tell this to the wise." When Ohrmazd spoke in this way, I remained astonished, for I saw light, but I saw no one; and I heard a voice, and I knew that this was Ohrmazd. (3) And He, the Creator Ohrmazd, holiest of divine beings, said: "Speak, just Viraz, to the Mazda-worshippers of the world, saying: 'One is the path of righteousness, the path of the original doctrine, and all other paths are not paths. Take you that one path of righteousness, and turn not from it in prosperity, nor in adversity, and go not by any other path. Practise good thoughts, good words and good acts; and remain in that same faith which Spitaman Zardusht received from Me, and Vishtasp made current in the world.' . . . Well is it with you, Just Viraz! Depart in your prosperity; for whatever purity and purification you (men) perform and keep, and all which you keep lawfully, and the pure and holy acts of worship which you perform in like manner, mindful of the yazads [sacred beings] I know it all." (4) When I heard those words, I made deep obeisance to the Creator Ohrmazd. Then just Srosh conveyed me triumphantly and valorously to this carpeted place. May the Glory of the Good Religion of the Mazda-worshippers be victorious!

### 12.1.5 Expansion of Zoroastrianism

Zoroastrians sometimes attempted to impose their religion on conquered people. This Persian inscription from the late third century celebrates the deeds of the Zoroastrian high priest Kirdir, who introduced his religion to Roman lands seized by Persian armies. He also established control of Zoroastrian shrines that existed independently of Persian control in the Caucasus region.

Inscription of Kirdir at the Kaaba of Zoroaster, lines 11–13

[Mary Boyce, ed., *Textual Sources for the Study of Zoroastrianism* (Totowa, NJ: Barnes and Noble, 1984), in Michael H. Dodgeon and Samuel N.D. Lieu, eds., *The Roman Eastern Frontier and the Persian Wars (AD 226–363): A Documentary History* (New York: Routledge, 1991) p. 65]

And from the first, I, Kirdir, underwent much toil and trouble for the yazads [divine powers] and the rulers, and for my own soul's sake. And I caused many fires and priestly colleges to flourish in Iran, and also in non-Iranian lands. There were fires and priests in the non-Iranian lands which were reached by the armies of the King of kings. The provincial capital of Antioch and the province of Syria, and Cilicia, and the districts dependent on Cilicia; the provincial capital of Caesarea and the province of Cappadocia, and the districts dependent on Cappadocia, up to Pontus, and the province of Armenia, and Georgia and Albania and Balasagan, up to the "Gate of the Alans" – these were plundered and burnt and laid waste by Shapur, King of kings, with his armies. There too, at the command of the King of kings, I reduced to order the priests and fires which were in those lands. And I did not allow harm to be done them, or captives made. And whoever had thus been made captive, him indeed I took and sent back to his own land. And I made the religion and its good priests esteemed and honoured in the Mazda-worshipping land.

### 12.1.6  Christians in Roman–Persian negotiations

Intricate diplomatic maneuvers between Rome and Sasanian Persia went on throughout Late Antiquity, and the large communities of Christians in Persia often were a bargaining chip in negotiations. In his *Life of Constantine*, Eusebius of Caesarea describes a letter of the emperor Constantine in one such set of negotiations.

Eusebius, *Life of Constantine* 4.8–13
[Michael H. Dodgeon and Samuel N.D. Lieu, eds., *The Roman Eastern Frontier and the Persian Wars (AD 226–363). A Documentary History* (New York: Routledge, 1991) pp. 150, 152]

#### Letter of Constantine the Great to Shapur II [after 324?]

The king of the Persians also made known a desire to form an alliance with Constantine, by sending an embassy and presents as assurances of peace and friendship. The emperor, in negotiating this treaty, far surpassed the monarch who first paid him homage in the magnificence with which he acknowledged his gifts. When he heard, too, that there were many churches of God in Persia, and that large numbers there were gathered into the fold of Christ, he rejoiced at this information and resolved to extend his solicitude for the general welfare to that country also, as one whose aim it was to care for all alike in every nation. He demonstrated this in his own words through the letter which he dispatched to the king of the Persians, putting their [i.e. the Christians'] case in the most tactful and sensible manner. This royal missive, which the emperor himself composed, is in circulation among us in the Roman tongue [Latin] but has been translated into Greek so that it would be more accessible to the readers. The text is as follows:

*Letter of the Emperor to Shapur, king of the Persians, concerning his care over the people of God.*

By protecting the Divine faith, I am made a partaker of the light of truth . . .

"Imagine, then, with what joy I received information so accordant with my desire, that the finest provinces of Persia are filled with those men on whose behalf alone I am at present speaking, I mean the Christians. For abundant blessing will be to you and to them in equal amounts, for you will find the Lord of the whole world is gentle, merciful and beneficent. And now, because your power is great, I commend these persons to your protection; because your piety is eminent, I commit them to your care. Cherish them with your customary humanity and kindness; for by this proof of faith you will secure an immeasurable benefit both to yourself and us."

### 12.1.7 Julian's fatal invasion of Mesopotamia

In 363, the emperor Julian, overly confident of his military capabilities, invaded Persian territory hoping to overcome the Sasanian monarchy and put an end to the recurrent conflicts that had flared again in the reign of Constantine. Julian made a number of serious strategic errors, including cutting himself off from his own supply lines by burning his fleet. He was fatally wounded at the battle of Samarra and died on June 26. His soldiers chose Jovian, a Christian, to be their new emperor. He led them home after making a hasty truce with the Persians. Christians saw Julian's death as divine punishment, while polytheist writers suspected an assassination.

Ammianus Marcellinus, *History* 24.7.1, 3–6

[Beate Dignas and Engelbert Winter, *Rome and Persia in Late Antiquity. Neighbors and Rivals* (Cambridge: Cambridge University Press, 2007) p. 91, with some changes]

> 1. The emperor Julian therefore discussed a siege of Ctesiphon with his chief advisors and then followed the opinion of some well-informed men that this would be bold and inappropriate because not only was the city impregnable by its location but also because the king was expected to arrive any minute together with an enormous force . . . 3. But as usual he was greedy for more and did not respect the rods of those who warned him; he accused the generals of advising him to let go of the Persian kingdom, which was already almost won, because of laziness and a desire for leisure. With the river (Euphrates) on his left and untrustworthy guides leading the way he decided to march quickly into the interior . . .

### 12.1.8 The Persians sack Amida

In 502 Kavadh, the Persian King of Kings, suddenly attacked the Roman Empire. This passage describes the thoroughness and brutality with which the Persians sacked Amida, a rich town on the Tigris River. Zachariah, the Christian chronicler of these events, provides a glimpse of Persian motivations as seen through Roman eyes, as well as a very Christian twist: Jesus appears to the Persian king and grants him the city – to punish the Christian inhabitants for their sins.

Zachariah of Mitylene, *Syriac Chronicle* 7.3–4

[Zachariah of Mitylene, *Syriac Chronicle*, trans. F.J. Hamilton and E.W. Brooks (London: Methuen, 1899, reprinted AMS Press, 1979) pp. 152, 153, 155, 158, 159, 160]

[3] But Kavadh, who succeeded (Piroz) in the kingdom, and his nobles cherished hatred against the Romans, saying that they had caused the incursion of the Huns, and the pillage and the devastation of their country. And Kavadh gathered an army and went out against Theodosiopolis in Armenia of the Romans, and subdued the city; and he treated its inhabitants mercifully, because he had not been insulted by them. . . . And in the month of October he reached Amida of Mesopotamia. But though he assailed it with fierce assaults of sharp arrows and with battering-rams, which thrust the wall to overthrow it, and roofs of skin which protected those who brought together the materials for the besiegers' mound and raised it up and made it equal in height with the wall, for three months, day after day, yet he could not take the city by storm; while his own people were suffering much hardship through work and fighting, and he was constantly hearing in his ears the insults of disorderly men on the wall, and their ridicule and mockery, and he was reduced to great straits.

[4] When Kavadh and his army had been defeated in the various assaults which they had made upon the city, and a large number of his soldiers had perished, his hands were weakened; and he asked that a small gift of silver should be given to him and he would withdraw from the city. But Leontius, the governor, and Paul Bar Zainab the steward, by the messengers whom they sent to Kavadh, demanded from him the price of the garden vegetables which his army had eaten, as well as for the corn and wine which they gathered and brought away from the villages. And when he was greatly grieved at this and was preparing to withdraw in disgrace, Christ appeared to him in a vision of the night, as he himself afterwards related it, and said to him that within three days He would deliver up to him [Kavadh] the inhabitants of the city, because they had sinned against him . . .

[The siege was successful.]

And after three days and three nights the slaughter ceased by the king's demand. And men went in to guard the treasures of the Church and of the great men of the city, that the king might have whatever was found in them. But the order also was given that the corpses of those who were slain in the streets and of those whom they had crucified should be collected and brought round to the northern side of the city, so that the king, who was on the south side, might enter in. And they were collected, and they were numbered as they were brought out, eighty thousand . . . And the king entered the treasury of the Church, and seeing there an image of the Lord Jesus, depicted in the likeness of a Galilean, he asked who it was. And they answered him, "It is God"; and he bowed his head before it, and said, "He it was Who said to me, 'Stay and receive from Me the city and its inhabitants, for they have sinned against me.' " . . .

But the gold and silver belonging to the great men's houses, and the beautiful garments, were collected together and given to the king's treasurers. But they also took down all the statues of the city, and the sundials, and the marble; and they collected the bronze and everything that pleased them, and they placed them upon wooden rafts that they made and sent them by the river Tigris . . . But the king sought for the chiefs and great men of the city . . . They clothed Leontius and Cyrus in filthy garments, and put swine-ropes on their necks, and made them carry pigs, and led them about proclaiming and exposing them, and saying, "Rulers who do not rule their city well nor restrain its people from insulting the king, deserve such insult as this." But at last the great men, and all the chief craftsmen, were bound and brought together, and set apart as the king's captives; and they were sent to his country with the military escort which brought them down. But influential men of the king's army drew near and said to him, "Our kinsmen and brethren were killed in battle by the inhabitants of the city," and they asked him that one-tenth of the men should be given to them for the exaction of vengeance. And they brought them together and counted them, and gave to them in proportion from the men; and they put them to death, killing them in all sorts of ways.

### 12.1.9  The reforms of Khusro Anushirwan

Khusro Anushirwan (Chosroes "Of the Immortal Soul") ruled the Sasanian Empire from 531 to 579 and is best known for waging war against Justinian. Domestically he introduced a series of fiscal, agricultural, and administrative reforms that contributed to the centralization of the empire. The tax base was maintained and royal revenues greatly increased. Scholars today debate the details of these changes because of a lack of contemporary sources. The following passage, which purports to be the words of Khusro, comes from an eleventh-century Arabic text that draws upon sixth-century sources.

Ibn Miskawayh, *The Experiences of the Nations*
[Zeev Rubin, "The Reforms of Khosro Anushirwan," *The Byzantine and Early Islamic Near East III: States, Resources and Armies*, ed. Averil Cameron (Princeton, NJ: The Darwin Press, 1996) pp. 268–9, 275–7]

> Since I became concerned in my mind, during a review of my subjects' affairs, about removing from them the distress, the oppression, and whatever affliction they were suffering on account of the heavy land-tax, I realized that, among other things, this would serve to glorify the kingdom, and by adding to their resources, it would enable the ruler to levy from them whatever was necessary, whenever he needed it. I know that some of my ancestors had deemed it right to take off the burden of the tax from them for one year or two years, and to ease it occasionally, in order to restore their strength for the field works.

I therefore assembled the officials and the tax-payers, and from their confusion I realized that there was no remedy for the situation except making the taxes just and fixing their rates on every town, on every district, and on every rustaq [district], on every village, and on every man. I nominated men who in my mind were faithful and trustworthy to be in charge of their administration, and I placed in every village superintendents together with every official to watch over him, and I assigned to the judge of every district the supervision of the inhabitants of the district. I instructed the tax-payers to submit whatever complaint they required to make before us to the judges whom I empowered to oversee the affairs of the districts, so that no official should be able to add anything to the amount they owed. I also ordained that they pay the tax, in presence of their judge, and that the receipt be handed through him . . .

. . . I found out that the men at arms are of service to the men who till the ground, and I have likewise seen that those who till the ground are of service to the men at arms. As for the men at arms, they require their remuneration from the tax-payers and the inhabitants of the villages for defending them and beating back enemies who come after them. It is just that those who till the ground should provide for the men at arms, and that their crops should be available to them. For if they withhold their crops from the men at arms, they make them weak, and the enemies become stronger. I have also seen what is just for the tax-payers, that they should not keep more of their crops than what would provide for their livelihood and what would bring prosperity to their villages. I have realized that I should not exhaust them and drain all their possessions to the treasuries to be kept there and given to the men at arms . . . There can be no agriculture lest the surplus be left in the hands of the tax-payers . . .

### 12.1.10 An Armenian obituary of Khusro

Caught between the warring empires of Rome and Persia, the Christian kingdom of Armenia was strong and capable. An anonymous Armenian historian in the middle of the seventh century describes a defeat of the Persian monarch Khusro Anushirwan (called *Khosrov* in the passage below) by Armenian troops and offers a positive assessment of his reign. The Persian monarch's deathbed conversion to Christianity, however, was only a fantasy.

*Khusro's Obituary*

[R.W. Thompson, *The Armenian History attributed to Sebeos, Part I: Translation and Notes* (Liverpool: Liverpool University Press, 1999) pp. 7–9]

On the morning of the next day [the Persians and the Armenians] drew up contingent facing contingent and line to line, and engaged each other in battle. The battle grew intense over the face of the land, and the conflict became very dense. The Lord delivered the Persian king and all his army to defeat . . . But the king with a few men escaped by the skin of his teeth taking refuge in the elephants and cavalry. He fled through Aldznik and returned to his own residence. [The Armenians] seized all their camp with the royal treasures. They captured the queen and the women, and appropriated the entire [royal] pavilion, and the golden carriage of great value, which was set with precious stones and pearls and was called by them the "glorious carriage." Also seized was the Fire which the king continually took around with him for assistance, which was reckoned more important than all other fires; it was called by them *At'ash*. This was extinguished in the river with the [chief priest] and a further host of the most eminent persons. At all times God is blessed.

This Khosrov, who was called Anush Ěřuan during the period of his reign before this rebellion, restored the land because he was a lover of peace and a promoter of prosperity. When that rebellion occurred, thenceforth he was prompted and aroused to anger, reckoning himself blameless on the grounds that "I was a father to the whole country and not a master, and I cared for them all like sons and friends. So now," he said, "God will seek [vengeance for] this blood from them." . . . He held the throne for 48 years. At the time of his death the light of the divine Word shone splendidly around him; for he believed in Christ.

### 12.1.11  Huns: a common enemy

Persians and Romans agreed on the danger of Huns coming though the Caspian Gates in the Caucasus mountains. Both empires were vulnerable to such attacks.

Procopius, *History of the Wars* 2.10.19–24

[Procopius, *History of the Wars*, vol. 1, trans. H.B. Dewing (Cambridge, MA: Harvard University Press, 1971) pp. 349–51]

(See *14.2.9*, page 379, for passage text.)

### 12.1.12  Justinian breaks Persia's silk monopoly

Persian diplomatic and economic ties reached from Gaul to Central Asia. Persia stood at the crossroads of Asia, controlling the end of the silk route that led to China. Silk was a luxury item desired in the West, especially in the imperial court. As a gift it played a significant role in Roman diplomacy. Procopius describes how, in about 552, the Byzantines broke this Persian monopoly by smuggling live silkworms direct from Serinda, the region around modern Bokhara and Samarkand in Central Asia.

Procopius, *History of the Wars* 8.17.1–8

[Procopius, *History of the Wars*, vol. V, trans. H.B. Dewing (Cambridge, MA: Harvard University Press, 1928) pp. 227, 229, 231]

At about this time certain monks, coming from India and learning that the Emperor Justinian entertained the desire that the Romans should no longer purchase their silk from the Persians, came before the emperor and promised so to settle the silk question that the Romans would no longer purchase this article from their enemies, the Persians, nor indeed from any other nation; for they had, they said, spent a long time in the country situated north of the numerous nations of India – a country called Serinda – and there had learned accurately by what means it was possible for silk to be produced in the land of the Romans. Whereupon the emperor made very diligent enquiries and asked them many questions to see whether their statements were true, and the monks explained to him that certain worms are the manufacturers of silk, nature being their teacher and compelling them to work continually. And while it was impossible to convey the worms thither alive, it was still practicable and altogether easy to convey their offspring. Now the offspring of these worms, they said, consisted of innumerable eggs from each one. And men bury these eggs, long after the time when they are produced, in dung, and after thus heating them for a sufficient time, they bring forth the living creatures. After they had thus spoken, the emperor promised to reward them with large gifts and urged them to confirm their account in action. They then once more went to Serinda and brought back the eggs to Byzantium, and in the manner described caused them to be transformed into worms, which they fed on the leaves of the mulberry; and thus they made possible from that time forth the production of silk in the land of the Romans.

### 12.1.13  Roman hostility in the later sixth century

A hostile and strikingly inaccurate view of Zoroastrianism comes from Agathias (536–582/594), a historian at Constantinople with a strong interest in the mechanics of cultural change. His description is the product of the bitter wars between Rome and Persia that had occupied the better part of the sixth century.

Agathias, *The Histories* 2.24.5, 2.25.3

[*Agathias: the Histories*, trans. Joseph Frendo (New York: Walter De Gruyter, 1975) p. 58]

> (2.24.5) But the present-day Persians have almost completely abandoned their old ways; an upheaval which has been marked by the wholesale adoption of alien and degenerate manners, ever since they have come under the spell of the doctrines of Zoroaster the son of Horamasdes [Ahura-Mazda] . . .
> (2.25.3) Indeed I know of no other society which has been subjected to such a bewildering variety of transformations or which through its submission to an endless succession of foreign dominations has failed so signally to achieve any degree of continuity. Small wonder then that it still bears the stamp of many different forms and conventions.

### 12.1.14  The siege of Constantinople in 626

In 626, after seizing Egypt and sacking Jerusalem, the Persian King of Kings Chosroes launched an attack upon Constantinople itself, in co-ordination with an army of Avars and Slavs who assaulted the city from the European side. Led by the Patriarch Sergius because Emperor Heraclius was commanding imperial armies far to the east in the Caucasus, the citizens of the imperial city narrowly staved off the onslaught. They understood the intercession of the Virgin Mary to have been the deciding factor. (See also *4.9.3*, page 164.)

*Easter Chronicle* (AD 626)

[*Chronicon Paschale 284–628 AD*, trans. Michael Whitby and Mary Whitby (Liverpool: Liverpool University Press, 1989) pp. 169–71]

> It is good to describe how now too the sole most merciful and compassionate God, by the welcome intercession of his undefiled Mother, who is in truth our Lady Mother of God and ever-Virgin Mary, with his mighty hand saved this humble city of his from the utterly godless enemies who encircled it in concert, and redeemed the people who were present within it from the imminent sword, captivity, and most bitter servitude; no one will find a means to describe this in its entirety. For the accursed Salbaras, commander of the Persian army, while he was awaiting . . . the arrival of the utterly godless Khan of the Avars, had for these very many days been at Chalcedon; he impiously burnt all the suburbs and palaces and houses of prayer, and thereafter remained awaiting the advent of that man. And so on the 29th of the month of June of the present indiction 14, that is on the day of the Feast of the holy and glorious chief apostles, Peter and Paul, a vanguard of the God-abhorred Khan arrived, about 30,000 [men].

### 12.1.15  Heraclius triumphant

Roman perseverance paid off. By 628, the Roman emperor Heraclius and the armies he had raised and trained in Armenia and Lazica defeated the forces of the Persian King of Kings, Chosroes II, and made a treaty with his son Seiroe (Cabades II). In the following letter, preserved in the *Easter Chronicle*, Heraclius announces his victory to the people of Constantinople.

*Easter Chronicle* (AD 628)

[*Chronicon Paschale 284–628 AD*, trans. Michael Whitby and Mary Whitby (Liverpool: Liverpool University Press, 1989) pp. 182–3]

> Let all the earth raise a cry to God; serve the Lord in gladness, enter into his presence in exultation, and recognize that God is Lord indeed . . .
>
> And let all we Christians, praising and glorifying, give thanks to the one God, rejoicing with great joy in his holy name. For fallen is the arrogant Chosroes, opponent of God. He is fallen and cast down to the depths of the earth, and his memory is utterly exterminated from earth; he who was exalted and spoke injustice in arrogance and contempt against our Lord Jesus Christ the true God and his undefiled Mother, our blessed Lady, Mother of God and ever-Virgin Mary, perished is the profaner with a resounding noise. His labour has turned back upon his head, and upon his brow has injustice descended. For on the 24th of the past month February, of the current first tax period, disturbance came to him at the hands of Seiroe his first-born son, just as we signified to you in our other missive. And all the Persian officials and troops

who were there, along with all the army that had been amassed from diverse places by the cursed Chosroes, gathered to the side of Seiroe, together also with Gurdanaspa, the former commander of the Persian army. That God-abhorred Chosroes proposed to resort to flight and, being arrested, was cast in bonds into the new fort which had been built by him for protecting the wealth amassed by him.

And on the 25th of the same month February, Seiroe was crowned and proclaimed Persian king, and on the 28th of the same month, after keeping the God-abhorred Chosroes bound in iron for four days in utter agony, he killed the same ingrate, arrogant, blaspheming opponent of God by a most cruel death . . .

### 12.1.16  The Cross restored to Jerusalem

After years of struggle with Persia, Heraclius restored the True Cross to Jerusalem in 630, a fitting end to his crusade. Note that Theophanes, a ninth-century Byzantine historian, dates the event from the creation of the world (AM = *anno mundi*). He also includes dates from Jesus' Resurrection, regnal years of Roman and Persian kings and various patriarchs.

Theophanes, *Chronicle* (AM 6120)

[*The Chronicle of Theophanes Confessor*, trans. Cyril Mango and Roger Scott (New York: Clarendon Press, 1997) pp. 458, 459]

Year of the divine Incarnation 620
Heraclius [Emperor of Rome] – 19th year
Adeser [Emperor of the Persians] (7 months) – 1st year
Sergius [Patriarch of Constantinople] – 20th year
Zacharias – 20th year
George – 10th year

In this year, setting forth from the Imperial City in the early spring, the emperor proceeded to Jerusalem, taking with him the venerable and life-giving Cross so as to offer thanks to God. When he had come to Tiberias, the Christians there accused a certain man called Benjamin of oppressing them. For he was very rich and received the emperor and his army. The emperor censured him, saying: "For what reason do you oppress the Christians?" He replied, "Because they are enemies of my faith." For he was a Jew. Then the emperor instructed him and, after converting him, had him baptized in the house of Eustathios of Neapolis, a Christian who also received the emperor.

On entering Jerusalem, the emperor reinstated the patriarch Zacharias and restored the venerable and life-giving Cross to its proper place. After giving many thanks to God, he drove the Jews out of the Holy City and ordered that they should not have the right to come within three miles of the Holy City. And when he had reached Edessa, he restored the church to the orthodox: for, since the days of Chosroes, it had been held by the Nestorians. And when he came to Hierapolis, he was informed that Siroes, the emperor of the Persians, had died and that Adeser, his son, had succeeded to the empire of Persia. After the latter had ruled seven months, Sarbarazas rose up against him and, having smitten him, ruled over Persia for two months. But the Persians killed him and appointed queen the daughter of Chosroes, Borane, who ruled the Persian kingdom for seven months. She was succeeded by Hormisdas, who was driven out by the Saracens, and so the kingdom of Persia has remained under Arab sway to the present time.

## Further reading

Brosius, Maria, *The Persians: An Introduction* (London: Routledge, 2006)

Crone, Patricia, "Kavad's Heresy and Mazdak's Revolt," *Iran* 29 (1991) pp. 21–40

Daryaee, Touraj, *Sasanian Persia: The Rise and Fall of an Empire* (London/New York: I.B. Tauris, 2009)

Dignas, Beate and Engelbert Winter, *Rome and Persia in Late Antiquity: Neighbours and Rivals* (Cambridge: Cambridge University Press, 2007)

Greatrex, Geoffrey, *Rome and Persia at War, 502–532* (Leeds: Francis Cairns, 1998)

Greatrex, Geoffrey, "Byzantium and the East in the Sixth Century," in Michael Maas, ed., *The Cambridge Companion to the Age of Justinian* (Cambridge: Cambridge University Press, 2005) pp. 477–509

Howard-Johnston, James, "The Two Great Powers in Late Antiquity: A Comparison," in Averil Cameron, ed., *The Byzantine and Early Islamic Near East III: States, Resources and Armies* (*Studies in Late Antiquity and Early Islam 1*) (Princeton, NJ: Darwin Press, 1995)

Rubin, Zeev, "The Reforms of Khusro Anushirwan," in Averil Cameron, ed., *The Byzantine and Early Islamic Near East III: States, Resources and Armies* (*Studies in Late Antiquity and Early Islam I*) (Princeton, NJ: Darwin Press, 1996)

Yarshater, Ehasan, ed., *The Cambridge History of Iran*, vols 3.1 and 3.2: *The Seleucid, Parthian, and Sassanian Periods* (Cambridge: Cambridge University Press, 1983)

# 13

# INVADERS AND
# SUCCESSOR STATES

## 13.1 Introduction

The northern expansion of Rome came to a halt in the second century, more or less along the Rhine–Danube line. Romans sneered at the populations beyond their direct political and military control, calling them "barbarian," which meant uncivilized, hostile, and violent. Realities on the ground, however, were far more complex than suggested by this rhetoric of "us vs them." Whether as fierce enemies in open warfare, as allies bound by treaty to the empire, as a source of slaves and of recruits for the army, or as a market for Roman trade goods and ideas, Rome's northern neighbors remained a constant presence in imperial life. The Roman Empire and the societies of its neighbors developed in response to one another. During the fifth century, when Roman armies could no longer defend the frontier, many foreigners entered the empire. Roman authorities lost political control of western Europe, from Britain and the Atlantic coast to Dalmatia. After some time on Roman soil, the newcomers developed and grew to maturity as Rome's so-called "successor states": the Ostrogoths in Italy, the Visigoths in Aquitania and Spain, the Vandals in North Africa, Angles and Saxons in Britain, and a few smaller kingdoms in the old territory of the Roman Empire. These kingdoms represent a complex fusion of the many Roman provincial communities with the transplanted, still-evolving identities of the newcomers. The newcomers are frequently called Germans today, and the states that evolved under their direction are often called Germanic kingdoms because the languages of the newcomers had a relation to modern German. Nineteenth-century German nationalism imposed a false unity on these populations, claiming them as the ancestors of modern Germans. In fact, the various groups of newcomers did not share a spoken language and had no sense of common origin or shared identity. Always vastly outnumbered by Rome's huge provincial and urban populations, and never immune to the attractions of imperial power – especially tax collection – the new arrivals generally maintained close ties with the Roman elites in their new kingdoms and with the imperial court at Constantinople. One significant element dividing the new ruler-settlers from the Roman populations they ruled was the fact that the new masters were Arian Christians, unlike their subjects who followed Chalcedonian orthodoxy (Catholicism). Separate law codes helped maintain the formal distinction of the populations. When the kings of the successor states (and their administrative elites) converted to orthodox Christianity in the sixth and seventh centuries, however, full amalgamation with their subjects became a reality. Though many elements of Mediterranean life continued, such as literacy in Latin, ideology and the ritual of empire, and the role of the Christian church, the successor states neither re-created Roman society of the high empire nor followed the path of the New Rome in Constantinople. They created a new cultural and political synthesis, part of the evolution of group identities in the Late Antique world. (See also 3.6, page 97.)

### 13.1.1 Early Visigothic communities

Early in the fourth century, Bishop Ulfila translated the Bible into Gothic, a first step in the gradual conversion of the Goths to Arian Christianity. *The Passion of Saint Saba*, written in the later fourth century, tells the story of the Gothic Christian, Saba, living in the Gothic lands in modern Wallachia, who was executed in 372 by pagan Gothic leaders for refusing to eat sacrificial meat that had been offered to pagan gods. This passage demonstrates that despite occasional persecution of Christians, some Goths were willing to help their Christian neighbors.

*The Passion of Saint Saba* 3.3–5

[Peter Heather and John Matthews, *The Goths in the Fourth Century* (Liverpool: Liverpool University Press, 1991) p. 113]

> On another occasion when a time of trial was moved in customary fashion by the Goths, some of the pagans from the same village intended while offering sacrifices to the gods to swear to the persecutor that there was not a single Christian in their village. But Saba, again speaking out, came forward in the midst of their council and said, "Let no man swear on my account, for I am a Christian." Then in the presence of the persecutor, the villagers who were hiding away their friends swore that there was no Christian in the village, except one. Hearing this, the leader of the outrage ordered Saba to stand before him. When he stood there, the persecutor asked those who brought him forward whether he had anything among his possessions. When they replied, "Nothing except the clothes he wears", the lawless one set him at naught and said, "Such a man can neither help nor harm us", and with these words ordered him to be thrown outside.

### 13.1.2 Adrianople: an unexpected catastrophe in 378

In 376 the Roman emperor Valens permitted large numbers of Goths into the Balkans. Uprooted from their homes in South Russia by the Huns, they promised to serve in the Roman army in return for land. Grossly mistreated by Roman officials they rose in rebellion, and in 378 destroyed the Roman army at Adrianople. Valens died with tens of thousands of his men in the worst military disaster for Rome since the Hannibalic wars. Here Ammianus Marcellinus, a fourth-century historian who had been a soldier, describes the passage of the Goths across the Danube.

Ammianus Marcellinus, *History* 31.4.1–6

[*Ammianus Marcellinus*, vol. III, trans. John C. Rolfe (London: Heinemann; Cambridge, MA: Harvard University Press, 1956) pp. 401, 403, 405]

1. Therefore, under the lead of Alavivus, the Goths took possession of the banks of the Danube, and sending envoys to Valens, with humble entreaty begged to be received, promising that they would not only lead a peaceful life but would also furnish auxiliaries, if circumstances required. 2. While this was happening in foreign parts, terrifying rumours spread abroad that the peoples of the north were stirring up new and uncommonly great commotions: that throughout the entire region which extends from the Marcomanni and the Quadi to the Pontus, a savage horde of unknown peoples, driven from their abodes by sudden violence, were roving about the river Hister in scattered bands with their families. 3. In the very beginning this news was viewed with contempt by our people, because wars in those districts were not ordinarily heard of by those living at a distance until they were ended or at least quieted for a time. 4. But when the belief in what had taken place gained strength, and was confirmed by the coming of the foreign envoys, who begged with prayers and protestations that an exiled race might be received on our side of the river, the affair caused more joy than fear; and experienced flatterers immoderately praised the good fortune of the prince, which unexpectedly brought him so many young recruits from the ends of the earth, that by the union of his own and foreign forces he would have an invincible army; also that instead of the levy of soldiers which was contributed annually by each province, there would accrue to the treasuries a vast amount of gold. 5. In this expectation various officials were sent with vehicle to transport the savage horde, and diligent care was taken that no future destroyer of the Roman state should be left behind, even if he were smitten with a fatal disease. Accordingly, having by the emperor's permission obtained the privilege of crossing the Danube and settling in parts of Thrace, they were ferried over for some nights and days embarked by companies in boats, on rafts, and in hollowed tree trunks; and because the river is by far the most dangerous of all and was then swollen by frequent rains, some who, because of the great crowd, struggled against the force of the waves and tried to swim were drowned; and they were a good many. 6. With such stormy eagerness on the part of insistent men was the ruin of the Roman world brought in.

### 13.1.3 *Destruction of Visigothic draftees*

In the immediate aftermath of the Roman defeat at Adrianople the Visigothic troops in the eastern Roman garrisons posed a great threat to the shaken government at Constantinople. What if they should revolt and try to rejoin their kinsmen? Ammianus describes their fate.

Ammianus Marcellinus, *History* 31.16.8

[*Ammianus Marcellinus*, trans. John C. Rolfe (London: Heinemann; Cambridge, MA: Harvard University Press, 1958) pp. 503, 505]

At that time the salutary and swift efficiency of Julius, commander-in-chief of the troops beyond the Taurus, was conspicuous. For on learning of the ill-fated events in Thrace [the battle of Adrianople], by secret letter to their leaders, who were all Romans (a rare case in these times) he gave orders that the Goths who had been admitted before and were scattered through the various cities and camps, should be enticed to come without suspicion into the suburbs in the hope of receiving the pay that had been promised them, and there, as if on the raising of a banner, should all be slain on one and the same day. This prudent plan was carried out without confusion or delay, and thus the eastern provinces were saved from great dangers.

### 13.1.4  Visigothic quarrels

Between 379 and 382 the new emperor Theodosius fought a series of unsuccessful campaigns in an attempt to eject the Visigoths from the empire. In 382 he signed a treaty with them, recognizing them as federates and assigning them lands in Thrace. The Goths soon began to fight among themselves about how loyal they should be to the emperor.

Zosimus, *New History* 4.56

[Zosimus, New *History*, trans. R. Ridley (Canberra: Australian Association for Byzantine Studies, 1982) pp. 96–7]

> When Theodosius first came to the throne he accepted some barbarians as friends and allies, honouring them with gifts and promises and paying every attention to the leaders of each tribe, who were even allowed to share his table. Now a debate arose among them in which opinions differed: some said it was better to ignore the oaths given when they surrendered to the Romans, while others to the contrary said they ought in no way to break their contracts. Eriulphus was in favour of trampling on their bond and urged all his countrymen to do the same, while Fravitta vigorously supported their standing by their oaths. No one knew for a long time that they had had this dispute, until in fact they were invited to the emperor's table, where, under the influence of extended drinking, they quarrelled and revealed their views. Having ascertained the opinions of each, the emperor ended the banquet. But as the two left the palace they became so enraged that Fravitta lost control, drew his sword and killed Eriulphus. When the latter's soldiers moved to attack Fravitta, the imperial guard intervened and prevented the strife from going any further.

### 13.1.5  Improving relations with Rome

Sacking Rome did not solve the problems of the Goths who followed Alaric, the Visigothic king from 395 to 410. Unable to seize land for permanent settlement and outnumbered by Roman forces, compliance with Roman leaders was an attractive option. Alaric's successor, Athaulf (410–415), attempted to establish good relations with the Roman authorities and even posed as Rome's champion. (See also section 2.6, page 56.)

Orosius, *History Against the Pagans* 7.43

[Orosius, *The Seven Books of History against the Pagans*, trans. Irving Raymond (New York: Columbia University Press, 1936) pp. 395–6]

> 43. In the one thousand one hundred and sixty-eighth year of the City of Rome, Count Constantius, who was occupying the city of Arles in Gaul, drove the Goths from Narbonne, and by his vigorous actions forced them into Spain, especially by forbidding and completely cutting off the passage of ships and the importation of foreign merchandise. The Gothic peoples at that time were under the rule of King Athaulf, who, after the capture of Rome and the death of Alaric, had succeeded him on the throne and had taken to wife, as I said, Placidia, the captive sister of the emperor. This ruler, an earnest seeker of peace, as was often claimed and finally shown by his death, preferred to fight loyally for the emperor Honorius and to employ the forces of the Goths for the defense of the Roman state . . . It seems that at first he ardently desired to blot out the Roman name and to make all the Roman territory a Gothic empire in fact as well as in name, so that, to use the popular expressions, *Gothia* should take the place of *Romania*, and he, Athaulf, should become all that Caesar Augustus once had been. Having discovered from long experience that the Goths, because of their unbridled barbarism, were utterly incapable of obeying laws, and yet believing that the state ought not to be deprived of laws without which a state is not a state, he chose to seek for himself at least the glory of restoring the renown of the Roman name by the power of the Goths, wishing to be looked upon by posterity as the restorer of the Roman Empire, since he could not be its transformer. On this account he strove to refrain from war and to promote peace. He was helped especially by his wife, Placidia, who was a woman of the keenest intelligence and of exceptional piety; by her persuasion and advice he was guided in all measures leading to good government.

### 13.1.6 Settlement of the Goths in Aquitania

As part of their efforts to restore order in Gaul and Spain in 418, imperial officials arranged for the Visigoths to settle as federates in the rich farmlands of Aquitania. It was a mutually advantageous treaty. The Visigoths (now led by King Theoderic I) finally got land for farming, while the imperial government gained their military service for campaigns against Vandals and Alans in Spain. They would also guard against seaborne Saxon raiders and keep an eye on rebellious Bagaudae (groups of peasants resisting government control). This settlement rapidly developed into an independent kingdom. The treaty, by then a shallow fiction, was broken in 475.

The Visigothic presence in Gaul, though quite unpleasant, was not seen as a conquest, however, and Gallo-Roman aristocrats learned to cope. Here Paulinus of

Pella (376–c.460), a newly impoverished intellectual, describes one instance of relations with a new settler.

Paulinus of Pella, *Eucharisticus* 564–81

[*Ausonius*, vol. 2, trans. H.G. Evelyn White (Cambridge, MA: Harvard University Press, 1921) pp. 347, 349]

> Yet in this same state of life thou didst not suffer me long to drowse in doubt, but unasked, O God, did you speedily deign to comfort me. . . . For when you had shown I could no longer hope for further profit from my grandfather's property; and when all that also which in my poverty I was able to hold at Marseilles was retained by me under the terms of a written contract, the freehold now being lost – you did raise up for me a purchaser among the Goths who desired to acquire the small farm, once wholly mine, and of his own accord sent me a sum, not indeed equitable, yet nevertheless a godsend, I admit, for me to receive, since thereby I could at once support the tottering remnants of my shattered fortune and escape fresh hurt to my cherished self-respect.

### 13.1.7 A Frankish prince

The correspondence of Sidonius Apollinaris, a Gallo-Roman aristocrat, gives bright images of the realities of living under new masters. In this letter to an old friend he describes a Frankish lord and his retinue. The Franks were a society that had emerged in the lower Rhine region in the third century.

Sidonius Apollinaris, *Letter* 4.20

[*Sidonius, Poems and Letters*, vol. 2, trans. W.B. Anderson (London: Heinemann, 1965) pp. 137, 139]

> Sidonius to his friend Dominicus, greeting.
> 1. You who are so fond of looking at arms and armed men, what delight, methinks, you would have felt if you had seen the young prince Sigismer, decked out in the garb and fashion of his nation, as the chosen lover or as suitor paying a visit to the palace of his lady's father! Before him went a horse gaily caparisoned: other horses laden with flashing jewels preceded or followed him. But the most gracious sight in the procession was the prince himself marching on foot amid his runners and footmen, clad in gleaming scarlet, ruddy gold, and pure-white silk, while his fair hair, glowing cheeks, and white skin matched the colours of such bright dress.
> 2. The princelings and allies who escorted him presented an aspect terrifying even in peacetime. Their feet from toe to ankle were laced in hairy shoes; knees, shins, and calves were uncovered; above this was a tight-fitting many-coloured garment, drawn up high, and hardly descending to their bare houghs [elbows], the sleeves covering only the upper part of the arm. They wore green mantles with crimson borders. Their swords suspended from the shoulders by overrunning baldrics pressed against sides girded with studded deer-skins. 3. This equipment adorned and armed them at the same time. Barbed

lances and missile axes filled their right hands; and their left sides were protected by shields, the gleam of which, golden on the central bosses and silvery white round the rims, betrayed at once the warrior's wealth and ruling passion. The total effect was such that this bridal drama displayed a pageant of Mars no less than of Venus. But why say more about it? The fine show lacked only one thing – your presence. For when I saw that you were not seeing the sights your eye delights in, at that moment I wanted not to feel the want of you. Farewell.

### 13.1.8 An Italian ambassador at the Visigothic court

Euric ruled the Visigoths in southern Gaul from 460 to 484 and included expert Roman officials in his government. Bishop Epiphanius of Padua went to the Visigothic court as an ambassador from Julius Nepos (474–475), the last western emperor recognized by Constantinople. Epiphanius and Leo (Euric's chief advisor), both Romans, are depicted as cultured and articulate, while the Visigothic king can only speak in his own barbaric tongue. The passage illustrates Roman administrators serving new masters and in their clerical role functioning as go-betweens in diplomatic maneuvers.

Ennodius, *Life of Saint Epiphanius*

[Ennodius, *Life of St. Epiphanius*, trans. Genevieve Marie Cook in *Early Christian Biographies*, ed. Roy J. Deferrari (*The Fathers of the Church*, vol. 15, 1952) pp. 323–5]

[Bishop Epiphanius] entered the city of Toulouse, in which King Euric was then residing. The news of his sanctity, having preceded him, had come to the ears of the Gauls, especially of the priests in that region, whom it filled with amazement and deep curiosity concerning the new arrivals. Leo, at that time the moderator and arbiter of the king's council, whose eloquence had more than once carried off the prize in declamation, joyfully proclaimed to all the arrival of Bishop Epiphanius. At once the king summoned the bishop to his presence, who, when he had come before the monarch, looked at him, greeted him, and addressed him thus: "O awe-inspiring prince, although the fame of your might renders your name terrifying to the ears of man and although the swords with which you constantly devastate neighboring lands cut down a harvest, as it were, of your enemies' sons, no blessing from above accompanies your cruel desire for war, nor, if you do what offends God, will the sword suffice to protect your domain. Remember that you, too, are subject to a Sovereign whose pleasure you must consider . . . Then, it is also well for us to consider that he most effectively defends his own possessions who does not covet another's. Wherefore, Nepos, to whom Divine Providence has committed the governance of Italy, has commissioned me to bring about a restoration of mutual trust and a union in the bonds of charity of your adjoining realms. He does not fear battle, but he is eager above all for peace. You know, as well as he, how extensive was the domain of the former emperors; you know with what patient subjection the people of the regions lost to the empire have borne their new rulers. Let it suffice that he seeks, or at least is willing to be called friend, who ought to be called master." . . .

Then, Euric ceased to mumble in I know not what strange tongue, and the serenity of his countenance showed that the bishop's words had impressed him. . . . The king answered as follows through an interpreter: "The cuirass scarcely ever leaves my breast, the shield of bronze, my hand, the protecting sword, my side; yet I have found a man who with words can subdue me in all my armor . . . I shall, therefore, venerable father, do what you ask, since you as ambassador carry more weight with me than the power of him who sent you. Accept my pledge, then, and promise in the name of Nepos that he will preserve intact this peace; for you, to have promised is to have taken an oath." Then, the truce concluded, the venerable bishop said farewell and left the king's presence.

### 13.1.9 How strange to learn "German"!

For Sidonius, being a Roman meant knowing the Latin classics. But for his friend Syagrius, who served as a legal advisor at the Burgundian court at Lyons, the pursuit of power and influence required learning a new language. He was one of a long succession of Romans who kept the Roman administration and Roman law working for several generations after the empire fell.

Sidonius, *Letter* 5.5

[*Sidonius, Poems and Letters*, vol. 2, trans. W.B. Anderson (Cambridge, MA: Harvard University Press, 1965) pp. 181, 183]

Sidonius to his friend Syagrius, greeting.

1. You are the great-grandson of a consul, and in the male line too – although that has little to do with the case before us; I say, then, you are descended from a poet, to whom his literary glory would have brought statutes had not his magisterial glories done so, as even to this day this author's words enshrined in verse bear witness; and the culture of his successors has not declined one whit from his standard, particularly in this respect. I am therefore inexpressibly amazed that you have quickly acquired a knowledge of the German tongue with such ease. 2. And yet I remember that your boyhood had a good schooling in liberal studies and I know for certain that you often declaimed with spirit and eloquence before your professor of oratory. This being so, I should like you to tell me how you have managed to absorb so swiftly into your inner being the exact sounds of an alien race, so that now after reading Virgil under the schoolmaster's cane and toiling and working through the rich fluency of the varicose man from Arpinum [Cicero] you burst forth before my eyes like a young falcon from an old nest. 3. You have no idea what amusement it gives me, and others too, when I hear that in your presence the barbarian is afraid to

perpetrate a barbarism in his own language. The bent elders of the Germans are astounded at you when you translate letters, and they adopt you as umpire and arbitrator in their mutual dealings . . . 4. Only one thing remains, most clever of men: continue with undiminished zeal, even in your hours of ease, to devote some attention to reading; and, like the man of refinement that you are, observe a just balance between the two languages: retain your grasp of Latin, lest you be laughed at, and practise the other, in order to have the laugh of them. Farewell.

### 13.1.10 Romans deserve their fate! The interpretation of Salvian of Marseilles

Salvian, a priest at Marseilles, believed that the barbarians, even though they were Arian Christians, had gained the upper hand as a divine response to Roman sins. His book *On the Governance of God* (440) includes a ringing condemnation of the suffering of the poor in Roman society.

Salvian, *On the Governance of God* 5.4–7

[*The Fathers of the Church: The Writings of Salvian, The Presbyter*, trans. Jeremiah O'Sullivan (New York: CIMA, 1947) pp. 132–3, 135–7]

(4) Furthermore, insofar as it pertains to the way of life among the Vandals and Goths, in what way are we better than they, or can even be compared with them? First, let me speak of their love and charity which the Lord teaches is the chief of virtues and which He not only commends throughout Sacred Scriptures but even in his own words: "By this shall it be known that you are my disciples, that you love one another." Almost all barbarians, at least those who are of one tribe under one king, love one another; almost all Romans persecute each other. . . .

All the while, the poor are despoiled, the widows groan, the orphans are trod underfoot, so much so that many of them, and they are not of obscure birth and have received a liberal education, flee to the enemy lest they die from the pain of public persecution. They seek among the barbarians the dignity of the Roman because they cannot bear barbarous indignity among the Romans. Although these Romans differ in religion and language from the barbarians to whom they flee, and differ from them in respect to filthiness of body and clothing, nevertheless, as I have said, they prefer to bear among the barbarians a worship unlike their own rather than rampant injustice among the Romans.

Thus, far and wide, they migrate either to the Goths or to the Bagaudae [peasants in revolt], or to other barbarians everywhere in power; yet they do not repent having migrated. They prefer to live as freemen under an outward form of captivity than as captives under an appearance of liberty. Therefore, the name of Roman citizens, at one time not only greatly valued but dearly bought, is now repudiated and fled from, and it is almost considered not only base but even deserving of abhorrence.

### *13.1.11  Theoderic's wise rule in Italy*

Italy flourished under the rule of the Ostrogoths. Theoderic the Great (*c*.454–526), who established the kingdom in 493, cultivated the support of the Italian elite, which in turn appreciated the good order that he maintained. A fragment of a contemporary chronicle called *The Anonymus Valesianus* written around 527 describes town life continuing as usual under Ostrogothic rule.

*The Anonymus Valesianus* 12.65–7, 69–73

[*Ammianus Marcellinus*, vol. III, trans. John C. Rolfe (Cambridge, MA: Harvard University Press, 1956) pp. 549–55]

> 65. After peace was made in the city of the Church, King Theoderic went to Rome (in 500) and met Saint Peter (as a pilgrim to Saint Peter's) with as much reverence as if he himself were a Catholic. The Pope Symmachus, and the entire senate and people of Rome amid general rejoicing met him outside the city. 66. Then coming to Rome and entering it, he appeared in the senate, and addressed the people at The Palm [a section of the Roman Forum], promising that with God's help he would keep inviolate whatever the former Roman emperors had decreed.
>
> 67. In celebration of his *tricennalia* [thirtieth anniversary of rule] he entered the Palace in a triumphal procession for the entertainment of the people, and exhibited games in the Circus for the Romans. To the Roman people and to the poor of the city he gave each year a hundred and twenty thousand measures of grain, and for the restoration of the Palace and the rebuilding of the walls of the city he ordered two hundred pounds to be given each year from the chest that contains the tax on wine . . . 69. . . . At the request of the people he gave orders that the words of the promise which he had made to them should be inscribed upon a bronze tablet and set up in a public place.
>
> 70. Then returning to Ravenna, five months later, he gave Amalbirga, another sister of his, in marriage to Herminifred, king of the Turingi, and in that way gained peace with all the nations round about. He was besides a lover of buildings and restorer of cities. 71. At Ravenna he repaired the aqueduct which the emperor Trajan had constructed and thus brought water into the city after a long time. He completely finished the palace, but did not dedicate it. He completed the colonnades around the palace. He also built baths and a palace at Verona, and added a colonnade extending all the way from the gate to the palace; besides that he restored the aqueduct at Verona. . . .
>
> 72. He also showed many favours to the other cities. And he so won the good will of the neighbouring nations, that they offered to make treaties with him, in the hope that he would be their king. Indeed, merchants flocked to him from the various provinces, for his organization was such that if anyone wished to send consignments of gold or silver in his domain, it was deemed as good as if he were within the walls of a city.
>
> 73. And he followed this principle so fully throughout all Italy, that he gave no city a gate; and where there were already gates, they were never shut; and

everyone could carry on his business at whatever hour he chose, as if it were in daylight.

### 13.1.12 Theoderic's New World Order

King Theoderic used his influence to try to stop war among the other rulers of the new kingdoms in western Europe. The first letter below was written to the kings of the Heruli, the Warni, and Thuringians. It was composed in 506 by the Italian aristocrat Cassiodorus, Theoderic's chief court official, just before the outbreak of a war in which the Franks overran the Visigothic kingdom in Gaul. The second letter was written directly to Clovis, king of the Franks, urging him not to go to war against the Visigoths. The letter contains a call for restraint and a direct threat.

*1.*

Cassiodorus, *Variae* III.3
[Alexander C. Murray, *From Roman to Merovingian Gaul. A Reader* (Peterborough, Canada: Broadview Press, 2000) pp. 265–6]

> There is general agreement that measures should be taken against pride, a quality always hateful to the divinity. For whoever tries with deliberate unfairness to overthrow a renowned nation does not decide to treat others with justice. The worst habit is to disdain truth. If an arrogant man happens to conquer in a detestable war, he believes that all things will yield to him.
>
> You are ennobled by a sense of virtue but angered when you contemplate abominable presumption: send your envoys, along with mine and those of our brother King Gundobad (of the Burgundians) to Clovis, king of the Franks, to tell him to halt the war with the Visigoths out of a regard for justice and to have recourse to the law of nations; otherwise, he will suffer the invasion of all for holding the judgment of so many in contempt. What more does he want than to be granted complete justice? Let me state my opinion plainly, whoever tries to do without law is someone whose plan is to shatter the kingdoms of all. It is better if a dangerous enterprise is stopped in its early stages; in that way, what would be a struggle for each may be won without hardship for any. Recall now the good will of the elder Euric [c.466–484] and the many gifts with which he gave you assistance and how often on your behalf he warded off threats of war by neighboring peoples. Repay the favor to his son, recognizing that it also contributes to your own well-being. For whoever gets the better of so great a kingdom will dare to attack you without hesitation. . . .

*2.*

Cassiodorus, *Variae* III.4
[Alexander C. Murray, *From Roman to Merovingian Gaul. A Reader* (Peterborough, Canada: Broadview Press, 2000) pp. 266–7]

The god-given ties of affinity try to take root among kings to this end, that their pacifying spirit may bring forth the peace that peoples desire. This is sacred and must not be breached by any disturbance. What pledges guarantee good faith, if they lack the affective ties of nature? Rulers are linked by kinship so that separate peoples should glory in the same desire, and, as if through certain channels, the longing of nations for harmony can be united and joined together.

In these circumstances, I am astonished that your feelings are so roused by petty reasons of complaint that you want to sustain a serious collision with our son Alaric, just when many who fear you will find joy in your dispute. Both of you are the kings of great peoples, both of you are in the prime of life. You will not shake our kingdoms lightly, if you are both allowed to come into conflict. Let your bravery not be the unexpected destruction of a homeland, for the mighty fall of peoples attends the serious ill-will of kings in small disputes.

Let me state my opinion freely, let me state it in the spirit of friendship. To immediately assemble troops at the first embassy shows a lack of self control. What is being sought from kinsmen may be attained once adjudicators have been chosen. They are even agreeable to including among such mediators men you choose. What would you yourself think of me if you learned that I neglected your complaints? Avoid a clash where one of you will mourn your defeat. Put down the sword if you wish to contradict my reproach.

By the right of a father and a friend I threaten you. He who thinks such warnings are to be despised – and I do not imagine this – will have myself and my friends as enemies.

### 13.1.13  Tensions of acculturation

Under Ostrogothic rule, Romans were the administrators and Ostrogoths the warriors. Cultivating an uncouth warrior persona provided one way for the outnumbered Ostrogoths to retain their identity. Procopius tells the sad story of Atalaric, an Ostrogothic prince whose mother preferred that he read poetry instead of indulging in binge drinking.

Procopius, *History of the Wars* 5.2.6–19

[Procopius, *History of the Wars*, vol. III, trans. H.B. Dewing (Cambridge, MA: Harvard University Press, 1953) pp. 17–19]

Amalasuntha (Theoderic's sister, regent to the new boy-king) wished to make her son resemble the Roman princes in his manner of life, and was already compelling him to attend the school of a teacher of letters. And she chose out three among the old men of the Goths whom she knew to be prudent and refined above all the others, and bade them live with Atalaric. But the Goths were by no means pleased with this. For because of their eagerness to wrong their subjects they wished to be ruled by him more after the barbarian fashion. On one occasion the mother, finding the boy doing some wrong in his chamber, chastised him; and he in tears went off thence to the men's apartments. And some Goths who met him made a great to-do about this, and reviling

356

Amalasuntha insisted that she wished to put the boy out of the world as quickly as possible, in order that she might marry a second husband and with him rule over the Goths and Italians. And all the notable men among them gathered together, and coming before Amalasuntha made the charge that their king was not being educated correctly from their point of view nor to his own advantage. For letters, they said, are far removed from manliness, and the teaching of old men results for the most part in a cowardly and submissive spirit. Therefore the man who is to shew daring in any work and be great in renown ought to be freed from the timidity which teachers inspire and to take his training in arms. They added that even Theoderic would never allow any of the Goths to send their children to school; for he used to say to them all that, if the fear of the strap once came over them, they would never have the resolution to despise sword or spear. And they asked her to reflect that her father Theoderic before he died had become master of all this territory and had invested himself with a kingdom which was his by no sort of right, although he had not so much as heard of letters. "Therefore, O Queen," they said, "have done with these tutors now, and do you give to Atalaric some men of his own age to be his companions, who will pass through the period of youth with him and thus give him an impulse toward that excellence which is in keeping with the custom of barbarians."

When Amalasuntha heard this, although she did not approve, yet because she feared the plotting of these men, she made it appear that their words found favour with her, and granted everything the barbarians desired of her.

### 13.1.14 Care for the Roman legacy

The Italian aristocrat Cassiodorus served as Theoderic's prime minister. His official business papers and correspondence have survived. This letter (c.510), sent to the city senators of Estuni (possibly modern Ostuni near Brindisi), reveals the Ostrogothic regime's calculated concern for the legacy of Roman antiquity. Theoderic's capital at Ravenna was the true beneficiary.

Cassiodorus, *Official Correspondence* 3.9

[Magnus Aurelius Cassiodorus, *Variarum Libri XX*, ed. Å.J. Fridh (Turnholt: Brepols, 1973) p. 104]

Though our intention certainly is to construct new buildings, we are more deeply concerned to preserve old ones, since we can obtain equal glory from innovation and preservation. Consequently we wish to build modern buildings without causing any injury to their predecessors. It is plainly unacceptable to accept anything obtained at another's cost. Now, we have learned that there are columns and building blocks pulled down by the envy of time that are lying useless in your city. Since there is no point to keeping this mess on the ground, the blocks and columns ought to rise and be beautiful again and not be a regretful memento of an earlier age. Therefore, with our authority, we decree that you shall hand over these marble slabs and columns to be brought to the city of Ravenna by all possible means – as long as the men supervising the report are reliable and as long as none of this material can be reused in a public monument that still stands. In this way exquisite craftsmanship will restore the grandeur lost by the collapse of the marble, and façades shadowed in their former location will regain the luster that made them splendid long ago.

### 13.1.15 Vandalism

The Vandals crossed the Rhine in 406 and won a deserved reputation for causing mayhem as they wandered through Gaul and Spain. Unable to find a permanent home, they were pleased to accept an invitation to intervene in a civil war in North Africa in 429. By 439 they controlled Carthage and went on to build a pirate empire in the western Mediterranean while maintaining the fiction of being federates of the emperor in Constantinople. Victor of Vita, who chronicled the Vandal persecution of their Catholic subjects, describes the efforts of Deogratias, the bishop of Carthage, to help captives brought from Rome after the Vandals sacked the city in 455.

Victor of Vita, *History of the Persecution in the Province of Africa*, "The Charity of Deogratias, Bishop of Carthage, to the Captives Brought from Rome by the Vandals," 1.24–6

[B.J. Kidd, *Documents*, II, pp. 323–4, in J. Stevenson, ed., *Creeds, Councils, and Controversies: Documents Illustrative of the History of the Church AD 337–461* (London: SPCK, 1966) pp. 360, 361]

24. Deogratias was ordained for the church of Carthage. If anyone were to try bit by bit to enumerate the things that the Lord did by him, words would fail him before he could tell anything. No sooner had he been made bishop than, since our sins demanded it, Gaiseric, in the fifteenth year of his reign, captured Rome, that once noble and famous city; and, at the same time, brought captive from thence the riches of many kings, with their peoples.

25. When the multitude of captives reached the shores of Africa, the Vandals and Moors divided up the vast crowds of people; and, as is the way with barbarians, separated husbands from wives and children from parents. Immediately that man, so full of God and so dear to him, set about to sell all the gold and silver vessels of service, and set them free from enslavement to the barbarians, in order that marriage might remain unbroken and children be restored to their parents. And since there were no places big enough to accommodate so large a multitude, he assigned two famous churches, the Basilica Fausti and the Basilica Novarum, furnishing them with beds and bedding, and arranging day by day how much each person should receive in proportion to his need.

26. And since many were in distress owing to their inexperience of a voyage by sea and to the cruelty of captivity, there was no small number of sick people among them. Like a devoted nurse, that saintly bishop went the round of them constantly with doctors and food; so that the condition of each was looked into, and every man's need supplied, in his presence. Not even at night did he take a rest from this work of mercy . . .

### 13.1.16  Saint Severinus – hero of a crumbling frontier

Written in 511 by his disciple the monk Eugippius, this account of the life of Saint Severinus vividly describes the collapse of the Danube frontier north of the Alps in modern Austria. Severinus had good informants on both sides of the river and did much to alleviate the suffering of the provincials.

Eugippius, *The Life of Saint Severinus* 24.1, 4.1–5

[Eugippius, *The Life of Saint Severinus*, trans. George W. Robinson (Cambridge, MA: 1914) pp. 35–6, 74–5]

1.  There was a town of Joviaco, twenty miles and more distant from Batavis. Thither the man of God, impressed as usual by a revelation, sent a singer of the church, Moderatus by name, admonishing that all the inhabitants should quit that place without delay. For imminent destruction threatened them if they despised his commands. Some were in doubt over so great a presage, while others did not believe it at all. Therefore yet again he sent one unto them, a certain man of Quintanis, to whom he said, weeping, "Make haste! Declare unto them that if they stay there this night, they shall without delay be made captives!" He bade that Saint Maximianus too, a priest of spiritual life, should be urgently warned; that he at least, leaving the scorners behind, through the compassion of heaven might escape. The servant of God said that he was in great sorrow over him, lest haply he might postpone obedience to the saving command, and so be exposed to the threatening destruction. Accordingly the messenger of the man of God went and fulfilled his orders; and when the others in their unbelief hesitated, he did not tarry a moment, though the priest strove to keep him and wished to extend to him the courtesy of his hospitality. That night the Heruli made a sudden, unexpected onslaught, sacked the town, and led most of the people into captivity. They hanged the priest Maximianus on a cross. When the news came, the servant of God grieved sorely that his warnings had been disregarded.

[At another time he organized the recovery of stolen goods.]

4.  At the same time barbarian robbers made an unexpected plundering incursion, and led away captive all the men and cattle they found without the walls. Then many of the citizens flocked weeping to the man of God, recounted to him the destructive calamity that had come upon them, and showed him evidences of the recent rapine.

But he straitly questioned Mamertinus, then a tribune, who afterwards was ordained bishop, whether he had with him any armed men with whom to institute an energetic pursuit of the robbers. Mamertinus replied, "I have soldiers, a very few. But I dare not contend with such a host of enemies. However, if thou commandest it, venerable father, though we lack the aid of weapons yet we believe that through thy prayers we shall be victorious." And the servant of God said, "Even if thy soldiers are unarmed, they shall now be armed from the enemy. For neither numbers nor fleshly courage is required, when everything proves that God is our champion. Only in the name of the Lord advance swiftly, advance confidently. For when God in his compassion goes before, the weakest shall seem the bravest. The Lord shall fight for you, and ye shall be silent. Then make haste; and this one thing observe above everything, to conduct unharmed into my presence those of the barbarians whom thou shalt take."

Then they went forth. At the second milestone, by a brook which is called Tiguntia, they came upon the foe. Some of the robbers escaped by hasty flight, abandoning their weapons. The soldiers bound the rest and brought them captive to the servant of God, as he had commanded. He freed them from chains, refreshed them with food and drink, and briefly addressed them. "Go," he said, "and command your confederates not to dare to approach this place again in their lust for booty. For the judgment and retribution of heaven shall straightway punish them, since God fights for his servants, whom his supernal power is wont so to protect that hostile missiles do not inflict wounds upon them, but rather furnish them with arms." Then the barbarians were sent away; and he rejoiced over the miracles of Christ, and promised that through Christ's compassion Favianis should have no further experience of hostile pillage; only let neither prosperity nor adversity withdraw the citizens from the work of God.

### 13.1.17 The end of Roman Britain

Local Roman authorities invited Angles and Saxons from the North Sea coastlands to Britain after 410 to assist in struggles against Irish raiders. Britain could not control or absorb these Anglo-Saxon settlers peacefully, however, and they put an end to the Roman way of life by the end of the century. This account by Gildas written in the 540s looks back at a period of terrible destruction.

Gildas, *On the Ruin of Britain* 24

[Gildas, *On the Ruin of Britain*, trans. Michael Winterbottom (London: Phillimore, 1978) p. 27]

24.1 In just punishment for the crimes that had gone before, a fire heaped up and nurtured by the hand of the impious easterners spread from sea to sea. It devastated town and country round about, and, once it was alight, it did not die down until it had burned almost the whole surface of the island and was licking the western ocean with its fierce red tongue . . .

3. All the major towns were laid low by the repeated battering of enemy rams; laid low, too, all the inhabitants – church leaders, priests and people alike, as the swords glinted all around and the flames crackled. It was a sad sight. In the middle of the squares the foundation-stones of high walls and towers that had been torn from their lofty base, holy altars, fragments of corpses, covered (as it were) with a purple crust of congealed blood, looked as though they had been mixed up in some dreadful wine-press. 4. There was no burial to be had except in the ruins of houses or the bellies of beasts and birds . . .

### 13.1.18 *"Barbarian" law codes*

The Burgundian kingdom was established after 443 and destroyed by the Franks in 534. The *Burgundian Law Code* (compiled between 483 and 517) was influenced by Roman law as well as by concepts clearly of Germanic origin. Roman and Burgundian judges are mentioned, though the extent to which the legal distinction between Roman and Burgundian is a true measure of ethnic difference remains a matter of controversy. The *Code* demonstrates how Roman legislation continued in the vacuum left by the collapse of Roman authority. The *Code* also contains evidence of continuing Germanic practices of feuding and *wergeld* compensation.

*The Burgundian Code*, Preface 1, 2, 3, 8, 13; 2.1, 2

[*The Burgundian Code*, trans. Katherine Fischer Drew (Philadelphia: University of Pennsylvania Press, 1972) pp. 17–18, 20, 23]

#### Preface

1. In the name of God in the second year of the reign of our lord the most glorious king Gundobad, this book concerning laws past and present, and to be preserved throughout all future time, has been issued on the fourth day before the Kalends of April (29 March) at Lyons.

2. For the love of justice, through which God is pleased and the power of earthly kingdoms acquired, we have obtained the consent of our counts and leaders, and have desired to establish such laws that the integrity and equity of those judging may exclude all rewards and corruptions from themselves.

3. Therefore all administrators and judges must judge from the present time on between Burgundians and Romans according to our laws which have been set forth and corrected by a common method, to the end that no one may hope or presume to receive anything by way of reward or emolument from any party as the result of the suits or decisions; but let him whose case is deserving obtain justice and let the integrity of the judge alone suffice to accomplish this.

[. . .]

8. Since a similar condition has been forbidden among Romans in cases of the crime of venality, we command that Romans be judged by the Roman laws just as has been established by our predecessors; let them know that they must follow the form and statement of the written law when they render decisions so that no one may be excused on grounds of ignorance.

13. Let no Roman or Burgundian count, in the absence of the other judge, presume to decide any case however often they may desire it, so that consulting frequently they may not be in doubt concerning the provisions of the laws.

### 2. Of murders

1. If anyone presumes with boldness or rashness bent on injury to kill a native freeman of our people of any nation or a servant of the king, in any case a man of barbarian tribe, let him make restitution for the committed crime not otherwise than by the shedding of his own blood.

2. We decree that this rule be added to the law by a reasonable provision, that if violence shall have been done by anyone to any person, so that he is injured by blows of lashes or by wounds, and if he pursues his persecutor and overcome by grief and indignation kills him, proof of the deed shall be afforded by the act itself or by suitable witnesses who can be believed. Then the guilty party shall be compelled to pay to the relatives of the person killed half his wergeld according to the status of the person: that is, if he shall have killed a noble of the highest class, we decree that the payment be set at one hundred and fifty solidi [pieces of gold], i.e., half his wergeld; if a person of middle class, one hundred solidi; if a person of the lowest class, seventy-five solidi.

## 13.1.19  The rise of the Franks

Around 500 a warlord named Clovis (c.481–511) unified the various Frankish tribes that lived on the eastern bank of the lower Rhine. Crafty and ruthless, he converted to Chalcedonian Orthodoxy (Catholicism) and represented himself as an ally of the emperor in Constantinople, who made him consul. This began a relationship between the Frankish court and Constantinople that would last for centuries. Clovis went on to overwhelm all other kingdoms in Gaul. His Merovingian dynasty led the Franks to pre-eminence in western Europe. Gregory of Tours, a sixth-century churchman, tells an anecdote about Clovis.

Gregory of Tours, *The History of the Franks* 2.27

[*Gregory of Tours: The History of the Franks*, trans. Lewis Thorpe (New York: Penguin, 1977) pp. 139–40]

27. . . . At that time many churches were plundered by the troops of Clovis, for he still held fast to his pagan idolatries. The soldiers had stolen a ewer of great size and wondrous workmanship, together with many other precious objects used in the church service. The bishop of the church in question sent messengers to the King to beg that, even if he would not hand back any of the other sacred vessels, this ewer at least might be restored to the church. The King listened to them and replied: "Follow me to Soissons, where all the objects which we have seized are to be distributed. If this vessel for which your bishop is asking falls to my share, I will meet his wishes." They came to Soissons and all the booty was placed in a heap before them. King Clovis addressed his men as follows, pointing to the vessel in question: "I put it to you, my lusty freebooters, that you should agree here and now to grant me that ewer over and above my normal share." They listened to what he said and the more

rational among them answered: "Everything in front of us is yours, noble King, for our very persons are yours to command. Do exactly as you wish, for there is none among us who has the power to say you nay." As they spoke, one of their number, a feckless fellow, greedy and prompt to anger, raised his battle-axe and struck the ewer. "You shall have none of this booty," he shouted, "except your fair share." All present were astounded at his words. The King hid his chagrin under a pretence of long-suffering patience. He took the vessel and handed it over to the envoy of the church; but in his heart he resented what had happened. At the end of that year he ordered the entire army to assemble on the parade-ground, so that he could examine the state of their equipment. The King went round inspecting them all and came finally to the man who had struck the ewer. "No other man has equipment in such a bad state as yours", said he; "your javelin is in a shocking condition, and so are your sword and your axe!" He seized the man's axe and threw it on the ground. As the soldier bent forward to pick up his weapon, King Clovis raised his own battle-axe in the air and split his skull with it. "That is what you did to my ewer in Soissons", he shouted. The man fell dead. Clovis ordered the others to dismiss. They were filled with mighty dread at what he had done. Clovis waged many wars and won many victories.

### 13.1.20 *Venantius Fortunatus*

Born and educated in Italy during the period of Justinian's reconquest, Venantius Fortunatus (*c.*530–*c.*600), who was familiar with classical as well as Christian poetic traditions, became one of the most influential of Latin writers at the royal courts of Frankish Gaul. In addition to his poems meant to be read aloud at court in celebration of kingly achievements, he also composed a body of personal poetry that reveals complex psychological relationships within monastic and royal environments. The first of the poems below was written to Radegund, a Frankish queen who left her bloodthirsty husband Clothar to become a nun and establish the Convent of the Holy Cross near Poitiers in the early 550s. Agnes, the mother superior of the convent, lived a rigorously ascetic life quite in contrast to the lushness of Fortunatus' passionate imagery. His openly expressed affection for the women raised eyebrows, forcing him to explain that he loved Radegund as a mother and Agnes only as a sister. His love for Agnes is the subject of the second poem. The third poem below expresses his condolences to King Chilperic and Queen Fredegund, whose two sons had recently died. Toward the end of his life, Fortunatus became bishop of Poitiers.

Venantius Fortunatus, *Poems*
[Translated by: Joseph Pucci]


*To Radegund*

8.10
You've returned, Radegund –

when?
swathed in the radiance Moses knew.
What kept you?
Stealing my contentment
that you now return,
doubling Easter's sanctity.
Shoots poke through clumps of earth
to paint green furrows
that explode into fullness when I see you:
fruits, fleshy and full, bundled,
insist it's August when yesterday was March!
Buds and shoots scamper in fields
that droop with October's pregnant grapes when I see you.
Apple buds and pear-flowers out of reach
fan fragrances that become plump fruits
when I see you.
The field is nude, no grain spilling saffron shadows.
Radegund, when you walk by it's time to reap.

### To Agnes

11.6

Agnes, your honor makes you mother,
your love, a sweet sister,
I cherish you, heart and soul,
like a father his brood, all trust:
I love you like the angels
(I'm not fallen),
my spirit covets you,
my body is still.
Christ swears by it,
Mary, Paul, Peter,
the company of saints,
all know that I love you like
my own sister, Titiana.
If we were of Radegund's flesh,
nourished by the milk of her chastity,
would you doubt me?
Damn these rumors,
poisoning our love!
I'm standing my ground,
said how I feel.
Will you let me love you?

*Appendix 23*

Nectar flowing from an ageless crag
is no sweeter to me, Agnes, than your life,
cherishing you heart and soul (God knows!).
See: change is all around
as the ancient orbits, heavenly vaults, shift,
our lives a tuft of bird's down,
slighted by mindless breezes,
minutes and hours
a sop to uncertainty;
who divines beginnings and ends?
Snow as deep as trees,
winter brooking stiff conformity,
bows the branches,
rigidly deformed.
Tomorrow, perhaps, if the sun
flashes limpid in the east,
the cold will flow away.
We are fallen, Agnes,
beguiled by things we cannot know:
how we should live,
when we will die.
The ambit of all things yields, falls:
but the wise know eternity's embrace,
Christ be your dignity, hope,
your lover,
fasten on him,
exclude all else,
unhesitatingly turn to his love,
and after you are wed let
your chastity seduce him.
If sleep sneaks in, hold fast your heart
where Christ emboldens soldiers of the dark,
his love its bulwark:
no demon's fury stonger than his peace;
fall into his arms,
feel his embrace
like an extravagance,
nothing can harm you there.
Don't linger, Agnes!
And when the judge of the world
comes to your bed,
the flash of your eyes

will prove your purity
and light the way for the sisters
like a shining lamp,
led by Thecla and Susanna into songs of joy.
Words – so ordered, so written, Agnes.
Think of *me* when you read them again.


To King Chilperic and Queen Fredegund (after the death of their
two sons of dysentery)

9.3
Tempests, lowering clouds, withdraw,
earth's icy vise relents;
white-out days, wintry woes,
howling winds vexing the fields' stubble, recede.
Spring skips onto the scene,
whispering taunts to the warming day,
reviving fields that cough perfume,
every grove strutting green,
trees hunch-backed with savory fruits,
soil tickled by its green-growing hair.
Majesties, after all your griefs,
I wish for you a happier season.
Look! Easter is come. Christ pacifies a world
that murmurs prayers that refresh.
Let griefs melt away as you bundle your wounds,
bid the servants prepare a blessed feast.
God keep you, Majesties.
Tower over us forever!


## 13.2 Ethnogenesis: Where and how did ancient peoples come into being?

Roman writers devoted much thought to questions about the origin and identity of different peoples. Topics of discussion frequently included illustrious ancestors as "founding fathers"; specific places of origin in distant lands followed by long migrations up to the time of writing; and continuity of identity and distinctive customs throughout these centuries of movement. In Late Antiquity foreign peoples who came into the Roman orbit often concocted such fanciful pedigrees for themselves, combining Roman tropes with their own legends and sense of group history. Modern scholars continue to investigate the emergence of peoples in Late Antiquity and their ties to older communities. They do not accept ancient sources at face value in their attempt to explain the new social and political formations as well as the identities of these groups.

### 13.2.1  The origin of the Goths

Jordanes, a Gothic chronicler of the sixth century, perhaps writing at Constantinople, gives the first extant account of the Goths written from a Gothic perspective, but on a Roman model.

Jordanes, *The Gothic History* 4.25–29

[*The Gothic History of Jordanes*, trans. Charles C. Mierow (Princeton, NJ: Princeton University Press, 1915) pp. 57–8]

> Now from this island of Scandza, as from a hive of races or a womb of nations, the Goths are said to have come forth long ago under their king, Berig by name. As soon as they disembarked from their ships and set foot on the land, they straightway gave their name to the place. And even to-day it is said to be called Gothiscandza. Soon they moved from here to the abodes of the Ulmerugi, who then dwelt on the shores of Ocean, where they pitched camp, joined battle with them and drove them from their homes. Then they subdued their neighbors, the Vandals, and thus added to their victories. But when the number of the people increased greatly and Filimer, son of Gadaric, reigned as king – about the fifth since Berig – he decided that the army of the Goths with their families should move from that region. In search of suitable homes and pleasant places they came to the land of Scythia, called Oium in that tongue. Here they were delighted with the great richness of the country, and it is said that when half the army had been brought over, the bridge whereby they had crossed the river fell in utter ruin, nor could anyone thereafter pass to or fro. For the place is said to be surrounded by quaking bogs and an encircling abyss, so that by this double obstacle nature has made it inaccessible. And even to-day one may hear in that neighborhood the lowing of cattle and may find traces of men, if we are to believe the stories of travelers, although we must grant that they hear these things from afar.

### 13.2.2  Maintaining tribal identity

In the following passage, Procopius of Caesarea, the historian of Justinian's wars of reconquest of western Mediterranean lands, describes the peculiar survival of the Rugi, a people whom he also describes as being Goths. He wonders what it meant to be a Rugi and a Goth, and of how specific communities understand and preserve their unique identities over long periods of time. These remain fundamental questions in the ethnogenesis debate.

Procopius, *History of the Wars*, 7.2.1–3

[Procopius, *History of the Wars*, vol. IV, trans. H.B. Dewing (Cambridge, MA: Harvard University Press, 1924) p. 167]

> These Rugi are indeed a Gothic nation, but in ancient times they used to live as an independent people. But Theoderic had early persuaded them, along with certain other nations, to form an alliance with him, and they were absorbed into

the Gothic nation and acted in common with them in all things against their enemies. But since they had absolutely no intercourse with women other than their own, each successive generation of children was of unmixed blood, and thus they had preserved the name of their nation among themselves.

### 13.2.3 A view of the Franks from Constantinople

The Constantinopolitan historian Agathias (died 582/594) viewed the Franks through rose-tinted glasses. His depiction reveals the categories in which he is prepared to evaluate these "barbarians": religion, mode of government, and way of life. He shows an interest in their origins. Above all, the degree to which the Franks may share Roman (i.e. Constantinopolitan) attributes is of importance to him. Agathias writes in the aftermath of the reign of Justinian; orthodox Chalcedonian Christianity and *Romanitas* are closely linked in his mind.

Agathias, *Histories*, 1.2.1; 1.2.3–4

[*Agathias. The Histories*, trans. Joseph D. Frendo (Berlin: Walter de Gruyter, 1975) p. 10]

> The Franks have a common frontier with Italy. They may reasonably be identified with the people who in ancient times were called "Germans", since they inhabit the banks of the Rhine and the surrounding territory. . . . The Franks are not nomads, as indeed some of the barbarian peoples are, but their system of government, administration and laws are modeled more or less on the Roman pattern, apart from which they uphold similar standards with regard to contracts, marriage and religious observance. They are in fact all Christians and adhere to the strictest orthodoxy. They also have magistrates in their cities and priests and celebrate the feasts in the same way as we do, and, for a barbarian people, strike me as extremely well-bred and civilized and as practically the same as ourselves except for their uncouth style of dress and peculiar language. . . . I admire them for their other attributes and especially for the spirit of justice and harmony which prevails amongst them.

### 13.2.4 What gives different peoples their distinguishing characteristics?

Classical notions that the character of entire peoples was determined by climate and geography flourished in Late Antiquity. Isidore of Seville (died 636), a Spanish scholar and cleric, transmitted some of these ideas into the Middle Ages. (See *12.1.1.*, page 328.)

Isidore of Seville, *Etymologies* 9.2.105

[*The Etymologies of Isidore of Seville*, ed. and trans. Stephen A. Barney, W.J. Lewis, J.A. Beach, and Oliver Berghof, with the collaboration of Muriel Hall (Cambridge: Cambridge University Press, 2006) p. 198]

> People's faces and coloring, the size of their bodies, and their various temperaments correspond to various climates. Hence we find that the Romans are

serious, the Greeks easy-going, the Africans changeable, and the Gauls fierce in nature and rather sharp in wit, because the character of the climate makes them so.

# Further reading

Amory, Patrick, *People and Identity in Ostrogothic Italy, 489–554* (Cambridge: Cambridge University Press, 1997)

Drinkwater, John F., *The Alamanni and Rome 213–496 (Caracalla to Clovis)* (Oxford: Oxford University Press, 2007)

Geary, Patrick J., *Before France and Germany: The Creation and Transformation of the Merovingian World* (New York and Oxford: Oxford University Press, 1988)

Geary, Patrick J., *The Myth of Nations: The Medieval Origins of Europe* (Princeton, NJ: Princeton University Press, 2002)

Gillett, Andrew, *On Barbarian Identity: Critical Approaches to Ethnicity in the Early Middle Ages* (Turnhout, Belgium: Brepols, 2004)

Goetz, Hans-Werner, Jörg Jarnut, and Walter Pohl, eds., with the collaboration of Sören Kaschke, *Regna and Gentes: The Relationship Between Late Antique and Early Medieval Peoples and Kingdoms in the Transformation of the Roman World* (Leiden, Boston: Brill, 2003)

Goffart, Walter, *Barbarian Tides: The Migration Age and the Later Roman Empire.* (Philadelphia: University of Pennsylvania Press, 2006)

Halsall, Guy, *Barbarian Migrations and the Roman West, 376–568* (Cambridge: Cambridge University Press, 2007)

Heather, Peter, *The Goths* (Oxford: Blackwell, 1997)

Heather, Peter, *The Fall of the Roman Empire: A New History of Rome and the Barbarians* (New York: Oxford University Press, 2006)

James, Edward, *Europe's Barbarians AD 200–600* (Harlow: Pearson, 2009).

Kulikowski, Michael, *Rome's Gothic Wars: From the Third Century to Alaric* (New York: Cambridge University Press, 2007)

Lee, A.D., *Information and Frontiers. Roman Foreign Relations in Late Antiquity* (Cambridge: Cambridge University Press, 1993)

Miles, Richard, *Constructing Identities in Late Antiquity* (London: Routledge, 2002)

Mitchell, Stephen and Geoffrey Greatrex, *Ethnicity and Culture in Late Antiquity* (London: Duckworth and the Classical Press of Wales, 2000)

Moorhead, John, *Theoderic in Italy* (Oxford, 1991)

Murray, Alexander C., *From Roman to Merovingian Gaul. A Reader* (Toronto: Broadview Press, 2000)

Noble, Thomas F.X., *From Roman Provinces to Medieval Kingdoms* (London: Routledge, 2006)

Pohl, Walter, ed., *Kingdoms of the Empire: The Integration of Barbarians in Late Antiquity* (Leiden, Boston: Brill, 1997)

Pohl, Walter with Helmut Reimitz, eds., *Strategies of Distinction: The Construction of Ethnic Communities, 300–800* (Leiden, Boston: Brill, 1998)

Pohl, Walter, Ian Wood, and Helmut Reimitz, *The Transformation of Frontiers from Late Antiquity to the Carolingians* (Leiden, Boston: Brill, 2001)

Smith, Julia M.H., *Europe After Rome: A New Cultural History 500–1000* (Oxford: Oxford University Press, 2005)

Ward-Perkins, Bryan, *The Fall of Rome and the End of Civilization* (Oxford: Oxford University Press, 2005)

Wolfram, Herwig, *The Roman Empire and its German Peoples*, trans. Thomas Dunlop (Berkeley: University of California Press, 1997)

Wood, Ian, *The Merovingian Kingdoms, 450–751* (London and New York: Longman, 1994)

# 14

# STEPPE PEOPLES AND SLAVS

## 14.1 Introduction

The vast steppe lands of Central Asia were home to mounted pastoral nomads famous throughout antiquity for their violence, mobility, and ferocity in war. Several main corridors brought them to Europe and the Middle East. From passes through the Caucasus Mountains the mounted warriors could reach Armenia, Cappadocia, and Syria. Turning east from there they threatened Persia. The other main route stretched from the Russian steppe to the Hungarian plain, from which the Balkans and Central Europe lay open to attack. The riches of the classical world irresistibly attracted these herdsmen, used to a harsh life of bare subsistence. In frequently shifting tribal configurations the nomads pursued each other across the plains only to crash against the defenses of Rome and Persia. These stable empires could absorb the shock of nomadic attack and contain the menace, but not before enormous damage had been done.

## 14.2 Huns

### 14.2.1 Huns: unknown and terrible invaders

Ammianus Marcellinus provides a terrifying portrait of the Huns, whose onslaught upon the Gothic kingdoms of the south Russian steppe precipitated events that led to the battle of Adrianople in 378. His description contains many stereotypes about a non-settled way of life that were widely accepted in antiquity, but it is not entirely inaccurate.

Ammianus Marcellinus, *History* 31.2.1–12

[*Ammianus Marcellinus*, vol. III, trans. John C. Rolfe (Cambridge, MA: Harvard University Press, 1956) pp. 381, 383, 385, 387]

> 1. However, the seed and origin of all the ruin and various disasters that the wrath of Mars aroused, putting in turmoil all places with unwonted fires, we have found to be this. The people of the Huns, but little known from ancient records, dwelling beyond the Maeotic Sea near the ice-bound ocean, exceed every degree of savagery. 2. Since there the cheeks of the children are deeply

371

furrowed with the steel from their very birth, in order that the growth of hair, when it appears at the proper time, may be checked by the wrinkled scars, they grow old without beards and without any beauty, like eunuchs. They all have compact, strong limbs and thick necks, and are so monstrously ugly and misshapen, that one might take them for two-legged beasts or for the stumps, rough-hewn into images, that are used in putting sides to bridges. 3. But although they have the form of men, however ugly, they are so hardy in their mode of life that they have no need of fire nor of savory food, but eat the roots of wild plants and the half-raw flesh of any kind of animal whatever, which they put between their thighs and the backs of their horses, and thus warm it a little. 4. They are never protected by any buildings but they avoid these like tombs, which are set apart from everyday use. For not even a hut thatched with reed can be found among them. But roaming at large amid the mountains and woods, they learn from the cradle to endure cold, hunger, and thirst. When away from their homes they never enter a house unless compelled by extreme necessity; for they think they are not safe when staying under a roof. 5. They dress in linen cloth or in the skins of field-mice sewn together, and they wear the same clothing indoors and out. But when they have once put their necks into a faded tunic, it is not taken off or changed until by long wear and tear it has been reduced to rags and fallen from them bit by bit. 6. They cover their heads with round caps and protect their hairy legs with goatskins; their shoes are formed upon no lasts, and so prevent their walking with free step. For this reason they are not at all adapted to battles on foot, but they are almost glued to their horses, which are hardy, it is true, but ugly, and sometimes they sit them woman-fashion and thus perform their ordinary tasks. From their horses by night or day every one of that nation buys and sells, eats and drinks, and bowed over the narrow neck of the animal relaxes into a sleep so deep as to be accompanied by many dreams. 7. And when deliberation is called for about weighty matters, they all consult as a common body in that fashion. They are subject to no royal restraint, but they are content with the disorderly government of their important men, and led by them they force their way through every obstacle. 8. They also sometimes fight when provoked, and then they enter the battle drawn up in wedge-shaped masses, while their medley of voices makes a savage noise. And as they are lightly equipped for swift motion, and unexpected in action, they purposely divide suddenly into scattered bands and attack, rushing about in disorder here and there, dealing terrific slaughter; and because of their extraordinary rapidity of movement they are never seen to attack a rampart or pillage an enemy's camp. 9. And on this account you would not hesitate to call them the most terrible of all warriors, because they fight from a distance with missiles having sharp bone, instead of their usual points, joined to the shafts with wonderful skill; then they gallop over the intervening spaces and fight hand to hand with swords, regardless of their own lives; and while the enemy are guarding against wounds from the sabre-thrusts, they throw strips of cloth plaited into nooses over their opponents and so entangle them that they fetter their limbs and take from them the power of riding or walking. 10. No one in their country ever plows a field or touches a plow-handle. They are all without fixed abode, without hearth, or law, or settled mode of life, and keep roaming from place to place, like fugitives, accompanied by the wagons in which they live; in wagons their wives weave for them their hideous garments, in wagons they cohabit with their husbands, bear children, and rear them to the age of puberty. None of their offspring, when asked, can tell you where he comes from, since he was conceived in one place, born far from there, and brought up still farther away. 11. In truces they are faithless and unreliable, strongly inclined to sway to the motion of every breeze of new hope that presents itself, and sacrificing every feeling to the mad impulse of the moment. Like unreasoning beasts, they are utterly ignorant of the difference between right and wrong; they are deceitful and ambiguous in speech, never bound by any reverence for religion or for superstition. They burn with an infinite thirst for gold, and they are so fickle and prone to anger, that they often quarrel with their allies without provocation, more than once on the same day, and make friends with them again without a mediator. 12. This race of untamed men, without encumbrances, aflame with an inhuman desire for plundering others' property, made their violent way amid the rapine and slaughter of the neighboring peoples . . .

### 14.2.2 Attila at home

Based north of the Danube, Attila forged an empire of the Huns and tributary peoples that terrorized the Roman state for two decades. During his rule (434–453) Attila repeatedly sacked the Balkans and forced the government to pay large annual tributes of gold to buy him off, as much as 6,000 pounds of gold in 447. In 450 Attila turned west to invade Gaul and Italy, but after much destruction, his armies were defeated at the battle of the Catalaunian Fields in Gaul (near Chalons, France) in 451. When he died two years later, his empire crumbled, though smaller bands of Huns continued to play a role in international struggles for some time to come.

In 449, a diplomatic mission concerned with the return of fugitives traveled from Constantinople to Attila's camp. One of its members, the historian Priscus of Panium, recorded his sharp observations, which are very different from those of Ammianus. For Priscus, the Huns are strange but fully human enemies, not monsters.

Priscus, *Fragment* 11.2

[R.C. Blockley, *The Fragmentary Classicising Historians of the Later Roman Empire: Eunapius, Olympiodorus, Priscus and Malchus*, vol. II (Liverpool: Francis Cairns, 1983) pp. 247–51, 255, 257, 261–5, 277]

> Maximinus by his pleadings persuaded me to accompany him on this embassy. So, we set out together with the barbarians and reached Serdica, which is thirteen days from Constantinople for an unladen traveller . . .
>
> . . . When we arrived at Naissus, we found the city empty of people since it had been laid waste by the enemy. In the Christian hostels there were some

persons suffering from disease. A short distance away from the river we halted in a clean place (for all towards the river bank was full of the bones of men killed in the fighting) and on the following day we came to Agintheus, the general of the forces in Illyricum, who was not far from Naissus, to convey to him the Emperor's orders and to receive the fugitives. He was to hand over five of the seventeen about whom it had been written to Attila. We spoke to him and caused him to hand over the five fugitives to the Huns. He treated them kindly and sent them off with us.

Having spent the night we set out on our journey from the border at Naissus to the river Danube ... After this difficult ground we came to a plain which was also wooded. Here barbarian ferrymen received us and conveyed us across the river in boats which they had made from single trunks, themselves cutting and hollowing out the trees. They had not made these boats for our sake, but had already ferried across a force of barbarians, which had met us on the road, since Attila wished to cross over to Roman territory as if to hunt. But the royal Scythian was really doing this in preparation for war, on the pretext that all the fugitives had not been given up.

When we had crossed the Danube and travelled about seventy stades with the barbarians, we were compelled to wait on some flat ground while Edeco's attendants went to Attila to announce our arrival ...

[Only after many difficulties did the Roman ambassadors have an opportunity to meet Attila.]

While we were busy with these matters, Attila summoned us through Scottas, and we came to his tent, which was surrounded by a ring of barbarian guards. When we were granted entrance, we saw Attila seated on a wooden chair. We halted a little before the throne, and Maximinus advanced, greeted the barbarian, gave him the letters from the Emperor and said that the Emperor prayed that he and his followers were safe and well. He replied that the Romans would have what they wished for him. Then he immediately directed his words towards Vigilas, calling him a shameless beast and asking why he had wished to come to him when he knew the peace terms agreed between himself and Anatolius, which specified that no ambassadors should come to him before all the fugitives had been surrendered to the barbarians. When Vigilas replied that there was not one fugitive of the Scythian race amongst the Romans, for all who were there had been surrendered, Attila became even more angry and abused him violently, shouting that he would have impaled him and left him as food for the birds if he had not thought that it infringed the rights of ambassadors to punish him in this way for the shamelessness and effrontery of his words. He continued that there were many fugitives of his own race amongst the Romans, and he ordered the secretaries to read out their names, which were written on papyrus. When the secretaries had read out all the names, Attila told Vigilas to depart immediately, and he said that he would send with him Eslas to tell the Romans to return to him all the barbarians who had fled to them ...

[While traveling in Attila's lands, Priscus' party was frightened and scattered by a storm – he describes his reception in a Hun village.]

When the barbarians who were with us replied that we were panicked by the storm, they called to us and took us into their own homes and, burning a great quantity of reeds, gave us warmth.

The woman who ruled the village (she had been one of Bleda's wives; Bleda was Attila's dead brother) sent us food and attractive women for intercourse, which is a mark of honour amongst the Scythians. We plied the women generously from the foods placed before us, but refused intercourse with them. We remained in the huts and at about daybreak we went to search for our baggage and found it all, some in the spot in which we had happened to halt on the previous day, some at the edge of the pool, and some actually in the water. We gathered it up and spent the day in the village drying it all out, for the storm had ceased and the sun was shining brightly. When we had taken care of the horses and the rest of the baggage animals, we visited the queen, thanked her, and repaid her with three silver bowls, red skins, Indian pepper, dates and other dried fruits which the barbarians value because they are not native to their own country. Then we called blessings upon her for her hospitality and departed.

[Priscus' trip continued to Attila's main base.]

Since we were on the same journey, we waited for Attila to go ahead and followed with our whole party. Having crossed some rivers, we came to a very large village in which Attila's palace was said to be more spectacular than those elsewhere. It was constructed of timbers and smoothly planed boards and was surrounded by a wooden wall which was built with an eye not to security but to elegance. The buildings of Onegesius were second only to those of the king in magnificence, and they too had a circuit wall made of timbers but not embellished with towers, as was Attila's. Not far from this wall was a bath which Onegesius, whose power amongst the Scythians was second only to that of Attila, had built, fetching stones from Pannonia. For there is neither stone nor timber amongst the barbarians who inhabit this area, but the wood that they use is imported. The builder of the bath had been taken prisoner at Sirmium, and he hoped to gain his freedom as a reward for his inventive work. But he was disappointed and fell into greater distress than slavery amongst the Scythians. For Onegesius made him bath-attendant, and he waited upon him and his followers when they bathed.

... Then I walked to the other group of buildings, where Attila was living ... As I was standing in the midst of the whole throng (for I was known to Attila's guards and followers, and no one hindered me), I saw a group of persons advancing and heard murmuring and shouts around the place, since Attila was coming out. He came out of the house swaggering and casting his eyes around. When he had come out, he stood with Onegesius in front of the building, and many persons who had disputes with one another stepped forward and received his judgment. Then he re-entered the house and received the barbarian envoys who had come to him.

### 14.2.3 Attila looks west

For fifteen years Attila extorted steadily increasing tribute payments from Constantinople. In 450, however, when the emperor Marcian refused to pay, Attila unexpectedly turned westward.

Gregory of Tours, *The History of the Franks* 2.6–7

[Gregory of Tours, *The History of the Franks*, trans. Lewis Thorpe (New York: Penguin Books, 1974) pp. 115–16]

> 6. The Huns migrated from Pannonia and laid waste the countryside as they advanced. They came to the town of Metz, so people say, on Easter Eve. They burned the town to the ground, slaughtered the populace with the sharp edge of their swords and killed the priests of the Lord in front of their holy altars. No building in the town remained unburnt except the oratory of Saint Stephen, Levite and first martyr . . .
>
> 7. Attila the King of the Huns marched forward from Metz and ravaged a great number of other cities in Gaul. He came to Orleans and did all he could to capture it by launching a fierce assault with his battering-rams. At that time the Bishop of Orleans was the saintly Anianus, a man of great wisdom and admirable holiness, the story of whose miracles has been faithfully handed down to us. The besieged inhabitants begged their Bishop to tell them what to do. Putting his trust in God, he advised them to prostrate themselves in prayer and with tears to implore the help of the Lord, which is always present in time of need. As they carried out his orders and prayed to the Almighty the Bishop said: "Keep a watch from the city wall, to see if God in his pity is sending us help." His hope was that, through God's compassion, Aetius might be advancing, for Anianus had gone to interview that leader in Arles when he foresaw what was going to happen. They watched out from the wall, but they saw no one. . . . When their prayer was finished, they were ordered by the old man to look out a third time. Far away they saw what looked like a cloud of dust rising from the ground. This they reported to the Bishop. "It is the help sent by God," said he. The walls were already rocking under the shock of the battering-rams and about to collapse when Aetius arrived, and with him Theoderic, the King of the Goths, and his son Thorismund. They hastened forward to the city with their armies and drove off the enemy and forced them to retreat. Orleans was thus saved by the prayers of its saintly Bishop. They put Attila to flight, but he made his way to the plain of Moirey and there drew up his forces for battle. When they learned this, they bravely prepared to attack him . . .
>
> Meanwhile Aetius and his allies the Goths and the Franks had joined battle with Attila. When he saw that his army was being exterminated, Attila fled from the battlefield. Theoderic, the King of the Goths, was killed in this

conflict. No one has any doubt that the army of the Huns was really routed by the prayers of the Bishop about whom I have told you; but it was the patrician Aetius, with the help of Thorismund, who gained the victory and destroyed the enemy.

## 14.2.4  Why didn't Attila sack Rome?

Following his defeat in Gaul in 451, Attila turned toward Italy, where he could easily have taken the city of Rome. With his forces weakened by an outbreak of plague, however, he unexpectedly returned to his capital on the Danube. Christians attributed his decision to God and the intercession of the pope.

Prosper, *Epitoma Chronicon* for the year 452

[J. Stevenson, ed., *Creeds, Councils, and Controversies: Documents Illustrative of the History of the Church AD* 337–461 (London: SPCK, 1966) p. 359]

> No better plan presented itself to the Emperor, Senate, and People, than to send an embassy to seek peace with the savage king (Attila). With Avienus, a man of consular rank, and Trigetius, praetorian prefect, Leo the Pope, relying on God's help, which he knew had never failed to aid the actions of the faithful, undertook this task. The anticipation of his faith was fully justified. The whole embassy was received with honour, and the king so pleased at the presence of the chief Christian priest, that he gave orders to desist from the war, and, with a promise of peace, departed across the Danube.

## 14.2.5  A war of images

A mainstay of Roman iconography was the submissive barbarian – trampled underfoot, enslaved, utterly defeated. Attila had a keen understanding of such images and the attitudes about victory and barbarism they implied. Priscus tells how the "Scourge of God" subverted this symbol.

Priscus, *Fragment* 22.3

[R.C. Blockley, *The Fragmentary Classicising Historians of the Later Roman Empire: Eunapius, Olympiodorus, Priscus and Malchus*, vol. II (Liverpool: Francis Cairns, 1983) p. 315]

> Milan is a very populous city which Attila captured and enslaved. When he saw in a painting the Roman Emperors sitting upon golden thrones and Scythians lying dead before their feet, he sought out a painter and ordered him to paint Attila upon a throne and the Roman Emperors heaving sacks upon their shoulders and pouring out gold before his feet.

## 14.2.6  The death and burial of Attila

Attila died of a brain hemorrhage on the night of his wedding to a young woman in 453. Priscus describes the death and funeral.

Priscus, *Fragment* 24.1
[R.C. Blockley, *The Fragmentary Classicising Historians of the Later Roman Empire: Eunapius, Olympiodorus, Priscus and Malchus*, vol. II (Liverpool: Francis Cairns, 1983) pp. 317, 319]

Attila, after countless other wives, took in marriage according to the custom of his race a very beautiful girl named Ildico. At his wedding he gave himself up to excessive celebration and he lay down on his back sodden with wine and sleep. He suffered a haemorrhage, and the blood, which would ordinarily have drained through his nose, was unable to pass through the usual passages and flowed in its deadly course down his throat, killing him. Thus drunkenness brought a shameful end to a king who had won glory in war . . .

We shall not omit to describe a few of the many ways in which his spirit was honoured by his race. In the middle of a plain his body was laid out in a silken tent, and a remarkable spectacle was solemnly performed. For in the palace where he had been laid out the best horsemen of the whole Hunnic race rode around in a circle, as if at the circus games, and recited his deeds in a funereal chant as follows.

"Chief king of the Huns, Attila, son of Mundzuc, lord of the bravest peoples, who possessed alone the sovereignty of Scythia and Germany with power unheard of before him and who terrorised both empires of the city of Rome by capturing their cities and, placated by their prayers, accepted a yearly tribute lest he plunder the rest. When he had achieved all these things through his good fortune, he died not by an enemy's wound or through treachery of his followers, but painlessly while his people was safe and happy amidst his pleasures. Who, then, shall call this a death, which no one thinks needs be avenged?"

When they had bewailed him with such lamentations, over his tomb they celebrated with great revelry what they call a strava and abandoned themselves to a mixture of joy and funereal grief, displaying both extremes of emotion. They committed his body to the earth in the secrecy of night and bound his coffins, the first with gold, the second with silver and the third with the strength of iron, demonstrating by this means that all three metals were appropriate for the most powerful king of all: iron because he had subdued nations, gold and silver because he had taken the valuables of both Empires. They added the arms of enemies won in combat, trappings gleaming with various precious stones and ornaments of various types, the marks of royal glory. Moreover, in order that such great riches be kept safe from human curiosity, those to whom the task was delegated they rewarded abominably by killing them. Thus sudden death engulfed both the one who was buried and those who buried him.

### 14.2.7 *After Attila's death*

When Attila died, the different peoples that he had brought together under his command came to blows and the Hunnic empire soon disintegrated. This passage describes a critical battle at the river Nedao in Pannonia in 454, in which subject peoples defeated the forces of Attila's sons and broke away from the Hunnic empire.

Jordanes, *Getica L*, 261 = Priscus fr. 25

[*The Gothic History of Jordanes in English Version*, trans. Charles C. Mierow (Princeton, NJ: Princeton University Press, 1915) p. 125]

> There an encounter took place between the various nations Attila had held under his sway. Kingdoms with their peoples were divided, and out of one body were made many members not responding to a single impulse. Being deprived of their head, they madly strove against each other. They never found their equals ranged against them without harming each other by wounds mutually given. And so the bravest of nations tore themselves to pieces.

## 14.2.8 Hun raiding in the Middle East

This account of a Hunnic invasion that reached as far as the Persian capital in 395 demonstrates the extreme vulnerability of settled communities if border defenses were penetrated. The text, an anonymous Syriac Chronicle compiled before 734, takes its name from a list of Caliphs that it includes.

*The Book of Caliphs* (*CSCO Script. Syr.* Ser. 3, vol. 4.2, Leipzig, 1904), 106

[Otto J. Maenchen-Helfen, *The World of the Huns* (Los Angeles: University of California Press, 1973) p. 58]

> In this year the cursed people of the Huns came into the land of the Romans and ran through Sophene, Armenia, Mesopotamia, Syria, and Cappadocia as far as Galatia. They took many prisoners and withdrew to their country. But they descended to the banks of the Euphrates and Tigris in the territory of the Persians and came as far as the royal city of the Persians [Ctesiphon]. They did no damage there but devastated many districts on the Euphrates and Tigris, killed many people and led many into captivity. But when they learned that the Persians advanced against them, they turned to flight. The Persians chased them and killed a band. They took away all their plunder and liberated eighteen thousand prisoners.

## 14.2.9 Huns force Romans and Persians to co-operate

One thing Roman and Persian rulers could agree on was the need to contain Hunnic bands north of the Caucasus. These passes, known as the Caspian Gates, had been the subject of negotiations between the Roman and Persian empires since at least the fifth century. Because the Persians suffered more severely from these raids, Roman emperors often dragged their heels in negotiation. Procopius describes a treaty arranged between Justinian and Chosroes in 533.

Procopius, *History of the Wars* 2.10.19–24

[Procopius, *History of the Wars*, vol. 1, trans. H.B. Dewing (Cambridge, MA: Harvard University Press, 1971) pp. 349–51]

Finally Chosroes made the demand that the Romans give him a large sum of money, but he warned them not to hope to establish peace for all time by giving money at that moment only. For friendship, he said, which is made by men on terms of money is generally spent as fast as the money is used up. It was necessary, therefore, that the Romans should pay some definite annual sum to the Persians. "For thus," he said, "the Persians will keep the peace secure for them, guarding the Caspian Gates themselves and no longer feeling resentment at them on account of the city of Daras, in return for which the Persians themselves will be in their pay forever." "So," said the ambassadors, "the Persians desire to have the Romans subject and tributary to themselves." "No," said Chosroes, "but the Romans will have the Persians as their own soldiers for the future, dispensing to them a fixed payment for their service; for you give an annual payment of gold to some of the Huns and to the Saracens, not as tributary subjects to them, but in order that they may guard your land unplundered for all time." After Chosroes and the ambassadors had spoken thus at length with each other, they at last came to terms, agreeing that Chosroes should forthwith take from the Romans fifty centenaria, and that, receiving a tribute of five more centenaria annually for all time, he should do them no further harm . . .

### 14.2.10  Conversion of Huns and imperial ritual

Byzantine diplomatic endeavors to win allies among Huns eventually paid off. Nikephoros of Constantinople, the Patriarch of Constantinople in the early ninth century, records a successful conversion during the reign of Heraclius (610–641).

Nikephoros, *Short History After the Reign of Maurice* 9

[*Nikephoros Patriarch of Constantinople, Short History*. Text, trans., and commentary, Cyril Mango (Washington, DC: Dumbarton Oaks Press, 1990) pp. 49, 51]

> 9. After a lapse of time the chieftain of the Hunnic nation came to Byzantium in the company of his noblemen and bodyguard and requested the emperor that he be initiated in the Christian faith. The latter received him gladly: the Roman noblemen became baptismal fathers of the Hunnic noblemen, and the wives of the former did the same to the spouses of the latter.
>
> After they had thus been initiated in things divine, the emperor presented them with imperial gifts and dignities: for he honored their chief with the rank of patrician and so dismissed him graciously to the abode of the Huns.

## 14.3  Avars

From the sixth century, when they first appeared on the steppe north of the Black Sea, to the end of the eighth century, when they were utterly smashed by Charlemagne, the Avars displaced the Huns as the greatest nomadic threat to European peace. Unlike the Huns, the Avars were able to create a durable kingdom. These mounted warriors used sabers and long lances to great advantage because of the iron stirrup which they introduced into European warfare. The Avar khans controlled many subsidiary peoples, including Huns and Slavs, but were particular enemies of the Turks. At the peak of their power, they unsuccessfully attacked Constantinople itself in concert with the Persians in 626.

### 14.3.1 Characteristics of Avar society

To Roman eyes, Avars shared attributes of nomad raiders all too familiar to Romans. The description of the Avars offered by Maurice's *Treatise on Strategy* draws on general knowledge of steppe nomads as well as direct experience of the Avars.

Maurice, *Treatise on Strategy* 11.2

[Maurice, *Strategikon*, trans. George Dennis (Philadelphia: University of Pennsylvania Press, 1984) pp. 116–17]

> The Scythian nations are one, so to speak, in their mode of life and in their organization, which is primitive and includes many peoples. Of these peoples, only the Turks and the Avars concern themselves with military organization, and this makes them stronger than the other Scythian nations when it comes to pitched battles . . . The Avars, for their part, are scoundrels, devious, and very experienced in military matters.
>
> These nations have a monarchical form of government, and their rulers submit them to cruel punishments for their mistakes. Governed not by love but by fear, they steadfastly bear labors and hardships. They endure heat and cold and the want of many necessities, since they are nomadic peoples. They are very superstitious, treacherous, foul, faithless, possessed of an insatiate desire for riches. They scorn their oath, do not observe agreements, and are not satisfied by gifts . . . They prefer to prevail over their enemies not so much by force as by deceit, surprise attacks, and cutting off supplies . . .
>
> A vast herd of male and female horses follows them, both to provide nourishment and to give the impression of a huge army. They do not encamp within entrenchments, as do the Persians and the Romans, but until the day of battle, spread about according to tribes and clans, they continuously graze their horses both summer and winter. They then take the horses they think necessary, hobbling them next to their tents, and guard them until it is time to form their battle line, which they begin to do under cover of night. They station their sentries at some distance, keeping them in contact with one another, so that it is not easy to catch them by a surprise attack . . .

### 14.3.2 Avars at the Byzantine court

In his poem *In Praise of Justin II* (emperor 565–578) the Byzantine poet Corippus describes the reception of an Avar embassy in the glittering palace halls of Constantinople. The Avars were disappointed to learn that the new emperor, strapped for cash, would no longer pay them annual subsidies to ensure their good behavior as had his predecessor Justinian. Corippus reveals how carefully staged palace ritual could overawe visitors.

Flavius Cresconius Corippus, *In Praise of Justin II*, 3.191–270
[Averil Cameron, ed., Corippus, *In Laudem Iustini Augusti Minoris* (London:
Athlone Press, 1976) pp. 106–7]

A lofty hall stands in the huge building gleaming with a sun of metal, wondrous
in its appearance, and more wondrous in the aspect of the place and proud in its
splendour. The imperial throne ennobles the inmost sanctum, girded with four
marvellous columns over which in the middle is a canopy shining with liquid
gold . . . Guards stood at the high entrance and kept out the unworthy who
wanted to enter, massed together as they were in large numbers and frightening
in their disdain and their gestures. When the officials had filled the decorated
palace with their groups arranged in order, a glorious light shone from the inner
chamber and filled all the meeting place. The emperor came forth surrounded
by the great senate. A throng of eunuchs was there to serve him . . .

When the happy emperor had ascended the lofty throne and settled his limbs
high up with his purple robes, the master of offices ordered the Avars to enter
and announced that they were before the first doors of the imperial hall begging
to see the holy feet of the merciful emperor, and he ordered with gentle voice
and sentiment that they be admitted. The barbarian warriors marvelled as they
crossed the first threshold and the great hall. They saw the tall men standing
there, the golden shields, and looked up at their gold javelins as they glittered
with their long iron tips and at the gilded helmet tops and red crests. They
shuddered at the sight of the lances and cruel axes and saw the other wonders
of the noble procession. And they believed that the Roman palace was another
heaven. They rejoiced to be stared at and to appear carefree as they entered: as
Hyrcanian tigers when New Rome gives spectacles to her people, under the
direction of their trainer do not roar with their usual savagery but enter, go all
round the edge, and look up at the circus full of thousands of people, and by
their great fear learn gentleness: they lay down their fury and are happy to wear
the cruel chains, to come right into the middle, and they love in their pride
the very fact that they are stared at. Their eyes range over the benches and the
enthusiastic crowds and they lie down in adoration before the throne of the
emperor. But when the curtain was drawn aside and the inner part was
revealed, and when the hall of the gilded building glittered and Tergazis the
Avar looked up at the head of the emperor shining with the holy diadem, he lay
down three times in adoration and remained fixed to the ground. The other
Avars followed him in similar fear and fell on their faces, and brushed the
carpets with their foreheads, and filled the spacious halls with their long hair
and the imperial palace with their huge limbs. When the merciful emperor
ordered the envoys to rise, the officials raised them up as they lay there, at his
command and behest as he ordered. "What you ask", said the ruler kindly with
calm countenance, "tell me, teach us, and bring the message of your king."
When the emperor had said this with his tranquil voice the harsh and cruel Avar
began thus with sharp words . . .

### 14.3.3 Persians and Avars attack Constantinople

In 626 Avars and their Slav subjects attacked Constantinople in concert with Persian forces.

Nikephoros, *Short History After the Reign of Maurice* 13
[*Nikephoros Patriarch of Constantinople, Short History.* Text, trans., and commentary, Cyril Mango (Washington, DC: Dumbarton Oaks Press, 1990) pp. 59–61]

13. The Avars, for their part, broke the treaty which Herakleios, before taking up arms against Persia, had confirmed by means of gifts – indeed, he promised to pay them 200,000 *solidi* [gold coins] and gave them as hostages one of his own . . . sons as well as his nephew . . . So they took up arms and drew near the walls of Byzantium, and straightaway they set fire to all the suburbs. Dividing, as it were, between themselves the Thracian Bosporos, the Persians destroyed the Asiatic part, while the Avars devastated the Thracian side, and they made a mutual agreement to capture Byzantium. Now the Avars constructed siege engines, namely, wooden towers and "tortoise shells"; but when these machines approached the walls, a divine force undid them and destroyed the Avar soldiers who were inside. Furthermore, the Avars had brought along a multitude of Slavonic allies and gave them the following signal, namely, that when the latter saw pyres kindled by the forward wall of the Blachernai (a church in northwest Constantinople), the one called Pteron, they would immediately set out in their hollowed-out canoes with a view to producing a mighty disturbance in the City by their sea-borne sortie, while the Avars, seizing this opportunity, would climb up the walls and so get inside the City. When these moves became known to the patrician Bonos, he, too, fitted out biremes and triremes, which he armed and stationed at the spot where the signal was to be given; he also drew up some biremes near the opposite shore and immediately directed them to light fires. The Slavs, upon seeing this, put out from the river called Barbysses and advanced upon the City; but the Roman ships moved out against them and, catching them in the middle, slaughtered them forthwith so that the sea was dyed with much blood. Among the dead bodies one could observe even those of Slav women. When the barbarians beheld this, they gave up the siege and returned home. As for the archpriest of the City and Emperor Constantine, they proceeded to the church of the Mother of God at Blachernai to offer unto God their prayers of thanksgiving; and straightaway they erected a wall to protect that sacred church. So much, then, for the Avars.

## 14.4 Turks

### 14.4.1 An embassy to the Turks

The long relationship of Byzantine and Turk began in the sixth century. Turks put pressure on the Avars (whom they regarded as disobedient slaves), and outflanked

Persia from the north, making them a natural and useful ally for the Roman emperor. Diplomatic ties with Constantinople nevertheless remained uneasy, as this account of a Roman mission to the Turks at the end of the sixth century illustrates.

Menander the Guardsman, *Fragment* 19.1

[*The History of Menander the Guardsman*, trans. R.C. Blockley (Liverpool: Francis Cairns, 1985) pp. 171, 173, 175]

1. In the second year of the reign of Tiberius Caesar (575–576), shortly before the above transactions with Chosroes took place, another embassy was sent from the Romans to the Turks. Its leader was Valentinus, who was one of the imperial bodyguard ... From all of these embassies there had collected at Byzantium one hundred and six Scythians of the people called the Turks, and Valentinus took them all with him when he set out from the capital.

Taking fast merchant ships he travelled via Sinope and Cherson (which is situated on the western coast of the Crimea) and by Apatura and Phoubi, and crossing the sands of ..., he passed the mountains of Taurice which stretched out to the south. Valentinus and his companions rode across those plains covered with marsh water, crossed tracts of reeds, shrubs and swamp, and passed through the region called Akkagas, which is the name of the woman who rules the Scythians there, having been appointed at that time by Anagai, chief of the tribe of the Utigurs. In short, they travelled by many roads and difficult ways and came to the war camp of Turxanthus, who was one of the leaders of the Turks. The ruler of the Turkish people had divided up all the land there into eight parts. The senior ruler of the Turks was named Arsilas.

When Valentinus came before Turxanthus, who was the first of the leaders whom those travelling there met, he bade him rejoice with the Caesar of the Romans (for he had come there to address the leaders of the Turkish people when Tiberius had been elevated to the rank of Caesar). He also asked that they reconfirm just as strongly the friendship and the earlier treaty between the Romans and the Turks, which Silzibul and the Emperor Justin had made when Zemarchus first came there. On that occasion Silzibul had declared that the friend of the Romans was his friend and their enemy his enemy, and that this should be unbreakable and inviolable. Therefore, said Valentinus in his address, since at this time the Romans were at war with the Persians, Turxanthus, too, should attack the Persians at the right time.

When the envoy had made his speech, Turxanthus said, "Are you not those very Romans who use ten tongues and lie with all of them?" As he spoke he placed his ten fingers in his mouth. Then he continued, "As now there are ten fingers in my mouth, so you Romans have used many tongues. Sometimes you deceive me, sometimes my slaves, the Uarkhonitai (the Avars). In a word, having flattered and deluded all the tribes with your various speeches and your treacherous designs, when harm descends upon their heads you abandon them and take all the benefits for yourselves. You envoys come to me dressed with lies, and he who has sent you deceives me equally. I shall kill you immediately and without delay. To lie is foreign and alien to a Turk. And your Emperor shall pay me due penalty, for he has spoken words of friendship to me while making a treaty with the Uarkhonitai, our slaves (he meant the Avars) who have fled their masters. When I wish it, the Uarkhonitai shall come to me as subjects of the Turks. If they as much as see my horsewhip sent to them, they will flee to the lowest reaches of the earth. If they face me, they shall perish, as is proper, not by the sword but trampled under the hooves of our horses, like ants. For the Uarkhonitai, this you can be sure of.

"As for you, Romans, why do you take my envoys through the Caucasus to Byzantium, alleging that there is no other route for them to travel? You do this so that I might be deterred from attacking the Roman Empire by the difficult terrain. But I know very well where the river Danapris [Dnepr River] flows, and the Danube and the Hebrus, and from where our slaves, the Uarkhonitai, crossed into Roman territory. I know your strength. For the whole world is open to me from the farthest East to the very western edge."

## 14.5  Slavs

### 14.5.1  A glimpse of early Slavic society

Slavic people appear in the Roman historical record in the mid-sixth century; they were established on the Danube and made frequent raids into the Balkans. Settlements there began in the late sixth century. After 576 they became part of the Avar Empire and some groups developed a fleet that was active in the Aegean by 600, attacking Crete in 623 and Constantinople in 626 in concert with the Avars and Persians. In the following passage of the *Treatise on Strategy*, Maurice describes Slavs bordering the Roman Empire.

Maurice, *Treatise on Strategy* 11.4

[Maurice, *Strategikon*, trans. George Dennis (Philadelphia: University of Pennsylvania Press, 1984) pp. 120–3]

> The nations of the Slavs and the Antes live in the same way and have the same customs. They are both independent, absolutely refusing to be enslaved or governed, least of all in their own land. They are populous and hardy, bearing readily heat, cold, rain, nakedness, and scarcity of provisions. They are kind and hospitable to travelers in their country and conduct them safely from one place to another, wherever they wish. If the stranger should suffer some harm because of his host's negligence, the one who first commended him will wage war against that host, regarding vengeance for the stranger as a religious duty. They do not keep those who are in captivity among them in perpetual slavery, as do other nations. But they set a definite period of time for them and then give them the choice either, if they so desire, to return to their own homes with a small recompense or to remain there as free men and friends. They possess an abundance of all sorts of livestock and produce, which they store in heaps, especially millet . . . Their women are more sensitive than any others in the world. When, for example, their husband dies, many look upon it as their own

death and freely smother themselves, not wanting to continue their lives as widows . . .

Owing to their lack of government and their ill feeling toward one another, they are not acquainted with an order of battle. They are also not prepared to fight a battle standing in close order, or to present themselves on open and level ground . . .

They are completely faithless and have no regard for treaties, which they agree to more out of fear than by gifts. When a difference of opinion prevails among them either they come to no agreement at all or when some of them do come to an agreement, the others quickly go against what was decided. They are always at odds with each other, and nobody is willing to yield to another . . .

Since there are many kings among them always at odds with one another, it is not difficult to win over some of them by persuasion or by gifts, especially those in areas closer to the border, and then to attack the others, so that their common hostility will not make them united or bring them together under one ruler. The so-called refugees who are ordered to point out the roads and furnish certain information must be very closely watched. Even some Romans have given in to the times, forget their own people, and prefer to gain the good will of the enemy. Those who remain loyal ought to be rewarded, and the evildoers punished. Provisions found in the surrounding countryside should not simply be wasted, but use pack animals and boats to transport them to our own country. The rivers there flow into the Danube, which makes transportation by boat easy.

## Further reading

Barfield, Thomas, *The Nomadic Alternative* (Upper Saddle River, NJ: Prentice Hall, 1997)

Curta, Florin, *The Making of the Slavs: History and Archaeology of the Lower Danube Region, c.500–70* (Cambridge: Cambridge University Press, 2001)

Curta, Florin, *Borders, Barriers, and Ethnogenesis: Frontiers in Late Antiquity and the Middle Ages* (Turnhout: Brepols, 2005)

Curta, Florin and Roman Kovalev, *The Other Europe in the Middle Ages: Avars, Bulgars, Khazars, and Cumans* (Leiden and Boston: Brill, 2008)

Shaw, Brent, " 'Eaters of flesh, drinkers of milk': the ancient Mediterranean ideology of the pastoral nomad," *Ancient Society*, 13/14 (1982/3) pp. 5–31

Thompson, E.A., *The Huns*, revised by Peter Heather (Oxford: Blackwell, 1996)

Wiedemann, Thomas, "Between man and beasts. Barbarians in Ammianus Marcellinus," in I.S. Moxon, J.D. Smart, and A.J. Woodman, eds., *Past Perspectives: Studies in Greek and Roman Historical Writing* (Cambridge: Cambridge University Press, 1986)

# 15

# ISLAM

## 15.1 Introduction

The appearance of Islam in the seventh century reshaped the Late Antique world. Universalist and inclusive, this monotheistic religion drew more peoples into its community than the Arabs who originally carried it out of Arabia. The first conquests and conversions to the faith beyond Arabia occurred in lands that had been ruled by the great powers, Rome and Persia. Islam has much in common with Christianity, Judaism, and Zoroastrianism as they existed in Late Antiquity, but the message from God made known by the Prophet Muhammad was distinctive and original. While Muhammad understood himself to be the last in a line of prophets that included Moses and Jesus, thus linking him to the biblical tradition, he also initiated an entirely new religious movement. Islam was an alternative to Judaism, Christianity, Zoroastrianism, and polytheism that made sense in light of other Late Antique ideas of religion and community.

Like many other internal and external peoples marginal to Rome and Persia, the Arabs were drawn to the centers of wealth and power after many years of contact. Through long-distance trade, the urbanized portions of the Arabian peninsula where Islam began had long been in touch with Rome, Persia, and points further east. In north Arabia tribal groups serving as allies were deeply involved in the perennial conflicts between the Roman and the Sasanian empires. Muhammad harnessed the tremendous energies of the tribes of the Arabian interior and set a course that resulted in rapid expansion. After the shock of conquest, a slow process of Arabization of local cultures began. Arabic slowly spread and new customs of daily life took hold. Protected by law, Christian and Jewish communities adapted themselves to new rulers.

## 15.2 Arabs before Islam

### 15.2.1 Pre-Islamic oral poetry: a death lament

A rich tradition of oral poetry existed among Arabs before the rise of Islam. This poem by al-Khansa laments the passing of a man taken too soon by implacable death.

Al-Khansa, "Lament for a Brother"
[Elizabeth Warnock Fernea and Basima Qattan Bezirgan, eds., *Middle Eastern Muslim Women Speak* (Austin: University of Texas Press, 1977/1984) p. 5]

> What have we done to you, Death,
> that you treat us so,
> with always another catch
> one day a warrior
> the next a head of state;
> charmed by the loyal
> you choose the best.
> Iniquitous, unequalling death
> I would not complain
> if you were just
> but you take the worthy
> leaving fools for us.
>
> Fifty years among us
> upholding rights
> annulling wrongs,
> impatient death
> could you not wait a little longer.
> He still would be here
> and mine, a brother
> without a flaw. Peace
> be upon him and Spring
> rains water his tomb but
> could you not wait
> a little longer
> a little longer,
> you came too soon.

### 15.2.2 Warrior virtues

One role for men in Arab society was that of the warrior. This poem extols the man who knows when it is necessary to fight and how to fight bravely. The Ghassanid tribe was one of the two major Arab groups that lived on the Persian–Roman frontier. The Ghassanids allied with Rome, the Lakhmids with Persia.

Qais Ibn Al-Khatim, "The Day of Bu'ath"
[Ilse Lichtenstadter, *Introduction to Classical Arabic Literature* (New York: Schocken Books, 1976) p. 185]

> I called on the Banu 'Auf to prevent bloodshed, but when they refused to heed my plea, I participated in the Khatib war,
> For I am a man who does not provoke unjust war, but when they refused my offer, I kindled the fire of war on all sides.

I tried to prevent the war until I saw that instead of preventing, this would only
increase the possibility of its outbreak.

And since there is no defense against the finality of death, let it be welcome,
since it has always been welcome (with us in a good cause).

And when I realized this war to be a war with swords drawn I put the garment
of a warrior over the two striped burdas:

a double armor long enough to cover the fingertips, whose two pairs of nail-
heads look like the eyes of locusts.

Then came the troops of the two Jewish Kahin tribes, and also the two
"Excellent Tribes" Malik and Tha'laba of the clan of Ibn Ghalib.

Men who, when called to fight until death, would rush headlong towards it as
intractable camels would rush on.

When they are fearful lest the unsteady lines of the attacked tribe they rush to
their aid with vigorous support like the towering wave of a foaming
torrent.

Then you would see the splinters of the spears blown about as if they were
yard-long palm branch pieces in the hand of the women that strip them.

Early in the morning we stormed with them the forts around Muzahim, the tops
of our foremost line of helmets shining like stars . . .

And on the Day of Bu'ath our swords made us worthy to enter the shining
lineage of the ranks of Ghassan.

They were white when drawn from their sheaths, but when we hit our enemy,
they were red when replaced into the scabbard, honed thin at the edges
where they had struck.

### 15.2.3  *Arab allies of dangerous superpowers*

Al-Mundhir (Alamoundaras) led the Lakhmids of al-Hira, the other main Arab client
tribe and Persian ally. They lived in Mesopotamia. Here Procopius describes the
Roman attempt to pit Harith ibn Jabala (Arethas, son of Gabalas) against him.
Procopius, *History of the Wars*, "Al-Mundhir (Alamoundaras)," 1.17.40–7
[Procopius, *History of the Wars*, vol. 1, trans. H.B. Dewing (London: Heinemann,
1971) pp. 157, 159]

For Alamoundaras was most discreet, and well experienced in matters of
warfare, thoroughly faithful to the Persians, and unusually energetic, – a man
who for a space of fifty years forced the Roman state to bend the knee. For
beginning from the boundaries of Egypt and as far as Mesopotamia he
plundered the whole country, pillaging one place after another, burning the
buildings in his track and making captives of the population by the tens of
thousands on each raid, most of whom he killed without consideration, while he
gave up the others for great sums of money. And he was confronted by no one
at all. For he never made his inroad without looking about, but so suddenly did
he move and so very opportunely for himself, that, as a rule, he was already off
with all the plunder when the generals and the soldiers were beginning to learn

what had happened and to gather themselves against him. If, indeed, by any chance, they were able to catch him, this barbarian would fall upon his pursuers while still unprepared and not in battle array, and would rout and destroy them with no trouble; and on one occasion he made prisoners of all the soldiers who were pursuing him together with their officers ... And, in a word, this man proved himself the most difficult and dangerous enemy of all the Romans. The reason was this, that Alamoundaras, holding the position of king, ruled alone over all the Saracens in Persia, and he was always able to make his inroad with the whole army wherever he wished in the Roman domain; and neither any commander of Roman troops, whom they call "dukes", nor any leader of the Saracens allied with the Romans, who are called Tribal Chieftains, was strong enough with his men to array himself against Alamoundaras; for the troops stationed in the different districts were not a match in battle for the enemy.

### 15.2.4 Arabian religion before Islam

Drawing on earlier accounts, Ibn al-Kalbi (died 821/822) described the religions of Arabia before the rise of Islam. The Ka'ba was the focus of Islamic pilgrimage. Previously it had been a pagan site. Connected to the biblical patriarch Abraham, the father of Ishmael, the first Arab, the site became a legitimate focus for Islamic pilgrimage as part of the Islamic prophetic tradition. The Quraysh were the tribe of Muhammad.

Ibn al-Kalbi, *The Book of Idols* 3–23

[*The Book of Idols,* ed. and trans. Nabih Faris (Princeton, NJ: Princeton University Press, 1952)]

> Hisham ibn Muhammad al-Kalbi said: I was informed by my father and others, and I personally checked and ascertained their report, that when Ishmael, the son of Abraham, settled in Mecca, he begot many children. Their descendants multiplied so much that they crowded the city and supplanted its original inhabitants, the Amalekites. Later on Mecca became overcrowded with them, and dissension and strife arose among them, causing them to fight among themselves and consequently be dispersed throughout the land where they roamed seeking a livelihood.
>
> The reason which led them to the worship of images and stones was the following: No one left Mecca without carrying away with him a stone from the stones of the Sacred House (al-Haram) as a token of reverence to it, and as a sign of deep affection for Mecca. Wherever he settled he would erect that stone and walk around it in the same manner he used to walk around the Ka'ba before his departure from Mecca, seeking thereby its blessing and affirming his deep affection for the Sacred House. In fact, the Arabs still venerate the Ka'ba and Mecca and journey to them in order to perform the pilgrimage and visitation, conforming thereby to the time-honored custom which they inherited from Abraham and Ishmael.
>
> In time this led them to the worship of whatever took their fancy, and caused

them to forget their former worship. They exchanged the religion of Abraham and Ishmael for another. Consequently they took to the worship of images, becoming like the nations before them. They sought and determined what the people of Noah had worshipped of these images and adopted the worship of those which were still remembered among them. Among these devotional practices were some which came down from the time of Abraham and Ishmael, such as the veneration of the House and its circumambulation, the pilgrimage (hajj), the visitation or the lesser pilgrimage (al-'umra), the vigil on 'Arafah and Muzdalifah, sacrificing she-camels, and raising the voice in the acclamation of the name of the deity at the pilgrimage and the visitation, introducing thereinto things not belonging to it . . .

The Quraysh were wont to venerate [al-'Uzza]. The Ghani and the Bahilah, too, joined the Quraysh in her worship. The Prophet, therefore, dispatched Khalid ibn al-Walid, who cut down the trees, destroyed the house, and demolished the idol.

The Quraysh had also several idols in and around the Ka'ba. The greatest of these was Hubal. It was, as I was told, of red agate, in the form of a man with the right hand broken off. It came into the possession of the Quraysh in this condition, and they, therefore, made for it a hand of gold.

## 15.3 Muhammad and the Quran

According to the Islamic faith, God (Allah) revealed the Quran to Muhammad the Prophet, the last in a series that included Moses and Jesus. This sacred text contained God's good news for humanity as well as a warning about punishment for wrongdoing at the end of days. It required that God's power be praised. The text is in Arabic, which was understood in its context to be a sacred language. Chapters are called suras. The following excerpts illustrate these major themes.

### 15.3.1 God and His praise

The opening sura of the Quran describes God.
Quran, sura 1.1–7, "The Opening" (revealed at Mecca)
[*The Meaning of the Glorious Koran*, trans. Marmaduke Pickthall (New York: Alfred A. Knopf, 1930) p. 21]

In the name of God, the Beneficent, the Merciful.
Praise be to God, Lord of the Worlds,
The Beneficent, the Merciful.
Owner of the Day of Judgment,
Thee alone we worship; Thee alone we ask for help.
Show us the straight path,
The path of those whom Thou hast favoured; Not the path of
   those who earn
Thine anger nor of those who go astray.

### 15.3.2 *God is transcendent*

God's unique and transcendent character is made clear in sura 2. This verse is often quoted and placed in inscriptions to indicate God's omnipotence.

Quran, sura 2.255, "The Cow" (revealed at Al-Madinah)

[*The Meaning of the Glorious Koran*, trans. Marmaduke Pickthall (New York: Alfred A. Knopf, 1930) p. 59]

> God! There is no God save Him, the Alive, the Eternal. Neither slumber nor sleep overtaketh Him. Unto Him belongeth whatsoever is in the heavens and whatsoever is in the earth. Who is he that intercedeth with Him save by His leave? He knoweth that which is in front of them and that which is behind them, while they encompass nothing of His knowledge save what He will. His Throne includeth the heavens and the earth, and He is never weary of preserving them. He is the Sublime, the Tremendous.

### 15.3.3 *God's judgment*

In sura 81 the judgment of God is proclaimed.

Quran, sura 81.1–21, "The Overthrowing" (revealed at Mecca)

[*The Meaning of the Glorious Koran*, trans. Marmaduke Pickthall (New York: Alfred A. Knopf, 1930) pp. 636–7]

> In the name of God, the Beneficent, the Merciful.
> When the sun is overthrown,
> And when the stars fall,
> And when the hills are moved,
> And when the camels big with young are abandoned,
> And when the wild beasts are herded together,
> And when the seas rise,
> And when souls are reunited,
> And when the girl-child that was buried alive is asked
> For what sin she was slain,
> And when the pages are laid open,
> And when the sky is torn away,
> And when hell is lighted,
> And when the garden is brought nigh,
> Then every soul will know what it hath made ready.
> Oh, but I call to witness the planets,
> The stars which rise and set,
> And the close of night,
> And the breath of morning
> That this is in truth the word of an honoured messenger,
> Mighty, established in the presence of the Lord of the Throne,
> One to be obeyed, and trustworthy.

### 15.3.4 God's apostle

Sura 18 explains that God sends apostles to give warning.

Quran, sura 18.57–8, "The Cave" (revealed at Mecca)

[*The Meaning of the Glorious Koran*, trans. Marmaduke Pickthall (New York: Alfred A. Knopf, 1930) p. 301]

> We send not the messengers save as bearers of good news and warners.
> Those who disbelieve contend with falsehood in order to refute the Truth thereby. And they take Our revelations and that wherewith they are threatened as a jest.
> And who doth greater wrong than he who hath been reminded of the revelations of his Lord, yet turneth away from them and forgetteth what his hands send forward (to the Judgment)? Lo! on their hearts We have placed coverings so that they understand not, and in their ears a deafness. And though thou call them to the guidance, in that case they can never be led aright.

### 15.3.5 A criticism of Christianity

The Christian Trinity is obliquely criticized by insisting that God is One. Note also interest in whether God was brought into being.

Quran, sura 112, "The Unity" (revealed at Mecca)

[*The Meaning of the Glorious Koran*, trans. Marmaduke Pickthall (New York: Alfred A. Knopf, 1930) p. 676]

> In the name of God, the Beneficent, the Merciful.
> Say: He is God, the One!
> God, the eternally Besought of all!
> He begetteth not nor was begotten.
> And there is none comparable unto Him.

### 15.3.6 The prophetic tradition

The connection with Jews and Christians and the biblical prophetic tradition is made clear in sura 3.

Quran, sura 3.84–5, "The Family of Imran"

[*The Meaning of the Glorious Koran*, trans. Marmaduke Pickthall (New York: Alfred A. Knopf, 1930) pp. 76–7]

> Say (O Muhammad): We believe in God and that which is revealed unto us and that which was revealed unto Abraham and Ishmael and Isaac and Jacob and the tribes, and that which was vouchsafed unto Moses and Jesus and the Prophets from their Lord. We make no distinction between any of them, and unto Him we have surrendered.
> And whoso seeketh as religion other than the Surrender to God it will not be accepted from him, and he will be a loser in the Hereafter.

### 15.3.7 God's message

That the Quran was a unique message of God and could not have been written by Muhammad (as some must have charged) is explained in sura 10.

Quran, sura 10.38–9, "Jonah" (revealed at Mecca)

[*The Meaning of the Glorious Koran*, trans. Marmaduke Pickthall (New York: Alfred A. Knopf, 1930) p. 214]

> And this Quran is not such as could ever be invented in despite of God; but is a confirmation of that which was before it and an exposition of that which is decreed for mankind – Therein is no doubt – from the Lord of the Worlds.
> Or say they: He hath invented it? Say: Then bring a surah like unto it, and call for help on all ye can besides God if ye are truthful.

### 15.3.8 Rewards after death

Heavenly rewards await those who live properly.

Quran, sura 29.57–8, "The Spider"

[*The Meaning of the Glorious Koran*, trans. Marmaduke Pickthall (New York: Alfred A. Knopf, 1930) p. 409]

> 57. Every soul will taste of death. Then unto Us ye will be returned.
> 58. Those who believe and do good works, them verily We shall house in lofty dwellings of the Garden underneath which rivers flow. There they will dwell secure. How sweet the guerdon of the toilers.

### 15.3.9 From oral tradition to written text: how the Quran was assembled

Muhammad delivered the message of God orally, and his words were memorized. Inevitably it became necessary for the Quran to be written down. The following passage describes the process of establishing an authoritative text in the mid-seventh century.

Al-Bukhari, *Sahih* 3.392–4

[Bernard Lewis, ed., *Islam from the Prophet Muhammad to the Capture of Constantinople*, vol. II: *Religion and Society* (New York: Walker and Company, 1974) pp. 1–2]

> Zayd ibn Thabit said: Abu Bakr sent for me at the time of the battle of al-Yamama, and 'Umar ibn al-Khattab was with him. Abu Bakr said: 'Umar has come to me and said, "Death raged at the battle of al-Yamama and took many of the reciters of the Quran. I fear lest death in battle overtake the reciters of the Quran in the provinces and a large part of the Quran be lost. I think you should give orders to collect the Quran."
>
> "What?" I asked 'Umar, "Will you do something which the Prophet of God himself did not do?"

"By God," replied 'Umar, "it would be a good deed" . . .

Then I sought out and collected the parts of the Quran, whether written on palm leaves or flat stones or in the hearts of men . . .

The leaves were with Abu Bakr until his death, then with 'Umar as long as he lived, and then with Hafsa, the daughter of 'Umar . . .

Hudhayfa ibn al-Yaman went with 'Uthman when he was preparing the army of Syria to conquer Armenia and Azerbaijan, together with the army of Iraq. Hudhayfa was shocked by the differences in their reading of the Quran, and said to 'Uthman, "O Commander of the Faithful, catch this community before they differ about their book as do the Jews and Christians."

'Uthman sent to Hafsa to say, "Send us the leaves. We shall copy them in codices and return them to you."

Hafsa sent them to 'Uthman, who ordered Zayd ibn Thabit, 'Abdallah ibn al-Zubayr, Said ibn al-'As, and 'Abd al-Rahman ibn al-Harith ibn Hisham to copy them into codices. 'Uthman said to the three of them who were of the tribe of Quraysh, "If you differ from Zayd ibn Thabit on anything in the Quran, write it according to the language of Quraysh, for it is in their language that the Quran was revealed."

They did this, and when they had copied the leaves into codices, 'Uthman returned the leaves to Hafsa. He sent copies of the codex which they made in all directions and gave orders to burn every leaf or codex which differed from it.

### 15.3.10 Muhammad's ordinance for Medina

Muhammad put forward the basic notion of a community of Believers (the followers of Islam, or Muslims), sometimes called the "Constitution of Medina." It explains the relation of Muslims and Jews. "Emigrants" are those who first went from Mecca to Medina – the earliest converts to Islam. "Helpers" are Muslims converted in Medina.

*Muhammad's Ordinance for Medina*

[Norman A. Stillman, *The Jews of Arab Lands: A History and Source Book* (Philadelphia: The Jewish Publication Society of America, 1979) pp. 115, 118; from Ibn Hisham, *Al-Sira al-Nabawiyya*, vol. 1 (Cairo, 1375/1955) pp. 501–4]

The Apostle of God – may God bless him and grant him peace – drew up a document between the Emigrants and the Helpers, in which he made a pact and a covenant with the Jews, confirming them in their religion and their possessions, and he stipulated certain conditions for them and imposed certain duties upon them:

In the name of God, the Merciful, the Beneficent.

This is a document from Muhammad the Prophet, between the Believers and Muslims of Quraysh [Muhammad's tribe] and Yathrib [the pre-Islamic name for Medina] and whoever follows them and are attached to them and strives with them. They are a single community in the face of all other men.

The Emigrants of Quraysh shall pay the bloodwit among themselves according to their Custom. They shall redeem their captives with kindness and justice among the Believers . . .

The Believers are not to forsake any destitute individuals among them, but are to give him the means, as is considered proper, to pay for ransom or bloodwit.

A Believer may not become the ally of a client of another Believer against the latter.

The God-fearing Believers shall be against whoever does injustice, whoever seeks power or oppression, or sin, or enmity, or corruption among the Believers. Every man's hand shall be against him, even if he is the son of one of them.

A Believer shall not kill a Believer for the sake of an unbeliever, nor shall he aid an unbeliever against a Believer.

God's protection is one; He grants protection even to the least among them. The Believers are responsible for one another in the face of all other men.

Any Jew who follows us shall have aid and comfort. Such a Jew shall not be oppressed nor his enemies aided against him.

### 15.3.11 The Pact of 'Umar

This agreement, attributed to the caliph 'Umar (634–44), regulates the position of non-Muslim Peoples of the Book: Christians, Jews, and Zoroastrians. It introduces the idea of *dhimma*, the social condition that entails protection by the Muslim authorities as well as certain disabilities within it, particularly a poll tax. There is no idea that people should be equal. This document takes the form of a petition, answered in a way similar to Roman imperial decrees.

Al-Turtushi, *Siraj al-Muluk* 229–30

[Bernard Lewis, ed., *Islam from the Prophet Muhammad to the Capture of Constantinople*, vol. II: *Religion and Society* (New York: Walker and Company, 1974) pp. 217–19]

When 'Umar ibn al-Khattab, may God be pleased with him, accorded a peace to the Christians of Syria, we wrote to him as follows:

In the name of God, the Merciful and Compassionate.

This is a letter to the servant of God 'Umar [ibn al-Khattab], Commander of the Faithful, from the Christians of such-and-such a city. When you came against us, we asked you for safe-conduct for ourselves, our descendants, our property, and the people of our community, and we undertook the following obligations toward you:

We shall not build, in our cities or in their neighborhood, new monasteries, churches, convents, or monks' cells, nor shall we repair, by day or by night, such of them as fall in ruins or are situated in the quarters of the Muslims . . .

We shall not give shelter in our churches or in our dwellings to any spy, nor hide him from the Muslims.

We shall not teach the Quran to our children.

We shall not manifest our religion publicly nor convert anyone to it. We shall not prevent any of our kin from entering Islam if they wish it.

We shall show respect toward the Muslims, and we shall rise from our seats when they wish to sit.

We shall not seek to resemble the Muslims by imitating any of their garments, the headgear, the turban, footwear, or the parting of the hair. We shall not speak as they do, nor shall we adopt their honorific names.

We shall not mount on saddles, nor shall we gird swords nor bear any kind of arms nor carry them on our persons.

We shall not engrave Arabic inscriptions on our seals.

We shall not sell fermented drinks. . . .

We shall not display our crosses or our books in the roads or markets of the Muslims. We shall only use clappers in our churches very softly. We shall not raise our voices in our church services or in the presence of Muslims, nor shall we raise our voices when following our dead. We shall not show lights on any of the roads of the Muslims or in their markets. We shall not bury our dead near the Muslims.

We shall not take slaves who have been allotted to the Muslims.

We shall not build houses overtopping the houses of the Muslims . . .

We accept these conditions for ourselves and for the people of our community, and in return we receive safe-conduct.

If we in any way violate these undertakings for which we ourselves stand surety, we forfeit our covenant [*dhimma*], and we become liable to the penalties for contumacy and sedition.

### 15.3.12 *Rules of war*

Proper behavior on military campaign is at the heart of Abu Bakr's *Rules of War*, written in 632.

Al-Tabari, *The History of the Prophets and Kings* 1.1850

[Bernard Lewis, ed., *Islam from the Prophet Muhammad to the Capture of Constantinople*, vol. I: *Politics and War* (New York: Walker and Company, 1974) p. 213]

O people! I charge you with ten rules; learn them well!

Do not betray, or misappropriate any part of the booty; do not practice treachery or mutilation. Do not kill a young child, an old man, or a woman. Do not uproot or burn palms or cut down fruitful trees. Do not slaughter a sheep or a cow or a camel, except for food. You will meet people who have set themselves apart in hermitages; leave them to accomplish the purpose for which they have done this. You will come upon people who will bring you dishes with various kinds of foods. If you partake of them, pronounce God's name over what you eat. You will meet people who have shaved the crown of their heads, leaving a band of hair around it. Strike them with the sword.

Go, in God's name, and may God protect you from sword and pestilence.

### 15.3.13 Substitute soldiers

This unwilling warrior, a poet, paid someone else to fight in his place in campaigns in Central Asia very far away from home, about 674–678.

*Poem on the Call to Arms*
[Michael Bonner, *Aristocratic Violence and Holy War: Studies in the Jihad and the Arab-Byzantine Frontier* (New Haven, CT: American Oriental Society, 1996) p. 19]

> I received a threat from Abu Anas,
> and my flesh was consumed by the anger of al-Dahhak.

> I did not disobey the amir, I gave him no cause
> to doubt, and I began no quarrel with Abu Anas.

> But the call to arms had reached us, and we found ourselves caught
> between far-away destruction and the payment of fines.

> And my soul was afraid of the mountains
> of Soghd and of Khwarazm [Caucasia/Central Asia].

> So I cast lots with those who had been called up,
> and won as my lot the right to lie about at home.

> And I gave the substitution payment to one who bravely sought death,
> an ardent warrior, one not weighed down by property and family.

### 15.3.14 Conquest by treaty

When the Arab armies reached the gates of Damascus in 635, negotiations with the city's bishop established the terms of Damascus' surrender.

Al-Baladhuri, *The Book of the Conquest of the Regions*
[Philip K. Hitti, *The Origins of the Islamic State*, vol. I (New York: Columbia University Press, 1916) pp. 186–7]

> The bishop who had provided Khalid with food at the beginning of the siege was wont to stand on the wall. Once Khalid called him, and when he came, Khalid greeted him and talked with him. The bishop one day said to him, "Abu Sulayman, thy case is prospering and thou hast a promise to fulfill for me; let us make terms for this city." Thereupon, Khalid called for an inkhorn and parchment and wrote:
> "In the name of God, the compassionate, the merciful. This is what Khalid would grant to the inhabitants of Damascus, if he enters therein: he promises to give them security for their lives, property and churches. Their city-wall shall not be demolished; neither shall any Muslim be quartered in their houses. Thereunto we give to them the pact of God and the protection of his Prophet, the caliphs and the Believers. So long as they pay the poll-tax, nothing but good shall befall them."

## 15.3.15 A Christian's explanation of Islam before the capture of Jerusalem

Patriarch Sophronius of Jerusalem (died c.639) is a most important source for Christian understanding of the Arab conquests of the seventh century. In the following excerpt from one of his sermons delivered shortly before the Arab conquest of Jerusalem in 637, he describes followers of Islam as enemies of God. The notion of war for religious purposes was a development of Late Antiquity in the Roman world.

Sophronius of Jerusalem, *Sermon on the Epiphany*
[Robert G. Hoyland, *Seeing Islam as Others Saw it: A Survey and Evaluation of Christian, Jewish, and Zoroastrian Writings on Early Islam* (Princeton, NJ: Darwin Press, 1997) p. 73]

> That is why the vengeful and God-hating Saracens [Arabs], the abomination of desolation clearly foretold to us by the prophets, overrun the places which are not allowed to them, plunder cities, devastate fields, burn down villages, set on fire the holy churches, overturn the sacred monasteries, oppose the Byzantine armies arrayed against them, and in fighting raise up the trophies [of war] and add victory to victory. Moreover, they are raised up more and more against us and increase their blasphemy of Christ and the church, and utter wicked blasphemies against God.

## 15.3.16 Jerusalem surrenders, 636

After the fall Jerusalem in 636, the conquerors imposed these terms.

Al-Tabari, *The History of the Prophets and Kings*, vol. 1, pp. 2405–6
[Bernard Lewis, ed., *Islam from the Prophet Muhammad to the Capture of Constantinople*, vol. I: *Politics and War* (New York: Walker and Company, 1974) pp. 235–6]

> In the name of God, the Merciful and the Compassionate.
>
> This is the safe-conduct accorded by the servant of God 'Umar, the Commander of the Faithful, to the people of Aelia [Jerusalem].
>
> He accords them safe-conduct for their persons, their property, their churches, their crosses, their sound and their sick, and the rest of their worship.
>
> Their churches shall neither be used as dwellings nor destroyed. They shall not suffer any impairment, nor shall their dependencies, their crosses, nor any of their property.
>
> No constraint shall be exercised against them in religion nor shall any harm be done to any among them.
>
> No Jew shall live with them in Aelia.
>
> The people of Aelia must pay the poll tax in the same way as the people of other cities.
>
> They must expel the Romans and the brigands from the city. Those who leave shall have safe-conduct for their persons and property until they reach

safety. Those who stay shall have safe-conduct and must pay the poll tax like the people of Aelia.

Those of the people of Aelia who wish to remove their persons and effects and depart with the Romans and abandon their churches and their crosses shall have safe-conduct for their persons, their churches, and their crosses, until they reach safety.

The country people who were already in the city before the killing of so-and-so may, as they wish, remain and pay the poll tax the same way as the people of Aelia or leave with the Romans or return to their families. Nothing shall be taken from them until they have gathered their harvest.

This document is placed under the surety of God and the protection of the Prophet, the Caliphs and the believers, on condition that the inhabitants of Aelia pay the poll tax that is due from them.

Witnessed by Khalid ibn al-Walid, 'Amr ibn al-'As, 'Abd al-Rahman ibn 'Awf, Mu'awiya ibn Abi Sufyan, the last of whom wrote this document in the year 15 [636].

### 15.3.17  A clear choice for Jews: Arabs welcomed to Hebron

Jews welcomed the Islamic armies, preferring Muslim protection to Christian-Roman persecution. When Arab armies reached Hebron, in 638, Jews aided them.

*Treatise on the Relics of the Patriarchs at Hebron*

["Canonici Hebronesis Tractatus de inventione sanctorum patriarchum Abraham, Ysaac, et Jacob," *Sefer ha-Yishuv*, vol. 2, 6 in Norman A. Stillman, *The Jews of Arab Lands: A History and Source Book* (Philadelphia: The Jewish Publication Society of America, 1979) p. 152]

> But when the Arabs came to Hebron, they marveled at the strong and beautiful construction of its walls and that there was no opening by which they could enter it. Meanwhile, some Jews, who had remained under the Greeks in that region, came over to them and said: "Grant us security so that we would have a similar status among you, and may we be conceded the right to build a synagogue in front of the entrance to the cave of Machpelah. If you will do this, we will show you where you should make a gateway."
>
> And thus it was done.

### 15.3.18  Christian collusion

Civil strife among the Romans of Egypt led Cyrus, the Patriarch of Alexandria (the capital of Egypt), to admit the Muslim armies to Alexandria.

John, Bishop of Nikiu, *The Chronicle* 120.17–28

[*The Chronicle of John, Bishop of Nikiu*, trans. R.H. Charles (London: William and Norgate, 1916) pp. 193–4]

120.17. And subsequently the patriarch Cyrus set out and went to Babylon to the Muslim, seeking by the offer of tribute to procure peace from them and put a stop to the war in the land of Egypt. And 'Amr welcomed his arrival, and said unto him: "Thou hast done well to come to us." And Cyrus answered and said unto him: "God has delivered this land into your hands: let there be no enmity from henceforth between you and Rome: heretofore there has been persistent strife with you." 18. And they fixed the amount of the tribute to be paid. And as for the Ishmaelites, they were not to intervene in any matter, but were to keep to themselves for eleven months. The Roman troops in Alexandria were to carry off their possessions and their treasures and proceed (home) by sea, and no other Roman army was to return. But those who wished to journey by land were to pay a monthly tribute. 19. And the Muslim were to take as hostages one hundred and fifty soldiers and fifty civilians and make peace. 20. And the Romans were to cease warring against the Muslim, and the Muslim were to desist from seizing Christian Churches, and the latter were not to intermeddle with any concerns of the Christians. 21. And the Jews were to be permitted to remain in the city of Alexandria.

22. And when the patriarch had concluded this negotiation, he returned to the city of Alexandria, and he reported to Theodore and the general Constantine (the conditions of peace), to the intent that they should report them to the emperor Heraclius and support them before him. 23. And straightway all the troops and the people of Alexandria and the general Theodore came together to him and paid their homage to the patriarch Cyrus. And he acquainted them with all the conditions which he had made with the Muslim, and he persuaded them all to accept them. 24. And while things were in this condition, the Muslim came to receive the tribute, though the inhabitants of Alexandria had not yet been informed of the treaty. And the Alexandrians, on seeing them, made ready for battle. 25. But the troops and the generals held fast to the resolution they had adopted, and said: "We cannot engage in battle with the Muslim: rather let the counsel of the patriarch Cyrus be observed." 26. Then the population rose up against the patriarch and sought to stone him. But he said unto them: "I have made this treaty in order to save you and your children." And plunged in much weeping and grief he besought them. 27. And thereupon the Alexandrians felt ashamed before him, and offered him a large sum of gold to hand over to the Ishmaelites together with the tribute which had been imposed on them.

28. And the Egyptians, who, through fear of the Muslim, had fled and taken refuge in the city of Alexandria, made the following request to the patriarch: Let the Muslim promise that we may return to our cities and become their subjects. And he negotiated for them according to their request. And the Muslim took possession of all the land of Egypt, southern and northern, and trebled their taxes.

### 15.3.19 The new managers

Arabic papyri show that Arab administrators soon began issuing orders to the local authorities. This letter was written in 710 by the Arab governor of Egypt to a district commissioner named Basil.

*Letter of Qorra, Governor of Egypt*
[Adolf Grohmann, *From the World of Arabic Papyri* (Cairo: Al-Maaref Press, 1952) pp. 125–6]

> In the name of God, the Compassionate, the Merciful!
> From Qorra ibn Sharik to Basil, Commissioner of Eshqauh.
> I praise God to you, beside whom there is no god. Thereafter: As you know, the time has already passed, and you are still in arrears with the tribute, although the allowance for the troops, and the allowance for their families is due as well as the departure of the army, if God wills! Therefore when this letter comes to you, begin with the transfer of what is incumbent upon your district of the tribute, and hasten to send at the earliest convenience remittance upon remittance of what you have collected, and I will not learn that you are in arrear with that what you owe, and there may be no holding back. The people of your district have already finished their agricultural work. So may God help them respecting that which is incumbent upon them of the claim of the Commander of the Faithful [Muslim caliph].

### 15.3.20 Mosques, symbols of imperial power

The caliphs of the first Umayyad dynasty of the late seventh century built great mosques which celebrated their power, just as Roman emperors had built churches. In this anecdote the Umayyad Caliph al-Walid explains to his nephew Muqaddasi why he spent so much money on building the mosque of Damascus.

Al-Muqaddasi, *The Best Divisions for Knowledge of the Regions*
[Oleg Grabar, *The Formation of Islamic Art* (New Haven, CT: Yale University Press, 1973) pp. 64–5]

> O my little son, you do not understand. Verily al-Walid was right, and he was prompted to a worthy work. For he beheld Syria to be a country that had long been occupied by the Christians, and he noted there the beautiful churches still belonging to them, so enchantingly fair, and so renowned for their splendor, as are the Church of the Holy Sepulchre, and the Churches of Lydda and Edessa. So he sought to build for the Muslims a mosque that should be unique and a wonder to the world. And in like manner is it not evident that 'Abd al-Malik, seeing the greatness of the martyrium of the Holy Sepulchre and its magnificence, was moved lest it should dazzle the minds of the Muslims and hence erected above the Rock the Dome which is now seen there.

## 15.3.21 Arabic, the new administrative language

Arabic became the language of the state bureaucracy in 693, replacing Greek, which had been the language of Roman administration. This indicates the emergence of an Islamic civil service.

Al-Baladhuri, *The Book of the Conquests of the Regions*
[Philip K. Hitti, *The Origins of the Islamic State* (New York: Columbia University Press, 1916) p. 301]

> Greek remained the language of the state registers until the reign of 'Abd-al-Malik ibn-Marwan, who in the year 81 [693] ordered it changed. The reason was that a Greek clerk desiring to write something and finding no ink urinated into the inkstand. Hearing this, 'Abd al-Malik punished the man and gave orders to Sulayman ibn Sa'd to change the language of the registers. Sulayman requested 'Abd al-Malik to give him as subsidy the land tax of the Jordan province for one year. 'Abd al-Malik granted his request and assigned him to the governorship of the Jordan. No sooner had the year ended, than the change of the language was finished and Sulayman brought the registers to 'Abd al-Malik. The latter called Sarjun [Sergius] and presented to him the new plan. Sarjun was greatly chagrined and left 'Abd al-Malik sorrowful. Meeting certain Greek clerks, he said to them, "Seek your livelihood in any other profession than this, for God has cut it off from you."

## 15.3.22 Muslims reach Ethiopia

Word of the new faith spread to different lands. This description taken from the eighth-century biography of Muhammad, compiled from oral tradition by Ibn Ishaq (died 768/9) and revised by Ibn Hisham (died 833/83), describes the reaction of the Christian king (the Negus) of Ethiopia.

Ibn Ishaq, *Biography of Muhammad*
[*The Life of Muhammad*, trans. A. Guillaume (New York: Oxford University Press, 1984) pp. 151–2]

> When the Muslim refugees came into the royal presence they found that the king had summoned his bishops with their sacred books exposed around him. He asked them what was the religion for which they had forsaken their people, without entering into his religion or any other. Ja'far ibn Abu Talib answered, "O King, we were an uncivilized people, worshipping idols, eating corpses, committing abominations, breaking natural ties, treating guests badly, and our strong devoured our weak. Thus we were until God sent us an apostle whose lineage, truth, trustworthiness, and clemency we know. He summoned us to acknowledge God's unity and to worship him and to renounce the stone and images which we and our fathers formerly worshipped. He commanded us to speak the truth, be faithful to our engagements, mindful of the ties of kinship and kindly hospitality, and to refrain from crimes and bloodshed. He forbade us

to commit abominations and to speak lies, and to devour the property of orphans, to vilify chaste women. He commanded us to worship God alone and not to associate anything with Him, and he gave us orders about prayer, almsgiving, and fasting (enumerating the commands of Islam). We confessed his truth and believed in him, and we followed him in what he had brought from God, and we worshipped God alone without associating aught with Him. We treated as forbidden what he forbade, and as lawful what he declared lawful. Thereupon our people attacked us, treated us harshly and seduced us from our faith to try to make us go back to the worship of idols instead of the worship of God, and to regard as lawful the evil deeds we once committed. So when they got the better of us, treated us unjustly and circumscribed our lives, and came between us and our religion, we came to your country, having chosen you above all others. Here we have been happy in your protection, and we hope that we shall not be treated unjustly while we are with you, O King."

The Negus asked if they had with them anything which had come from God. When Ja'far said that he had, the Negus commanded him to read it to him, so he read him a passage from the sura of Mary [the mother of Jesus]. The Negus wept until his beard was wet and the bishops wept until their scrolls were wet, when they heard what he read to them. Then the Negus said, "Of a truth, this and what Jesus brought have come from the same niche. You two may go, for by God, I will never give them up to them and they shall not be betrayed."

### 15.3.23 Islam in Samaritan eyes

This Samaritan account, written in Arabic in the eighth century, draws on earlier Samaritan traditions of their first encounter with Muhammad. Samaritans were a monotheistic sect of about one million adherents living mainly in the mountains of central Israel. They rejected the Hebrew Bible and the importance of Jerusalem, and were not accepted by Jews. Like the Jews, among Christians the Samaritans enjoyed the status of a permitted religion in the Roman Empire. They often rebelled against Roman rule, until Justinian crushed their resistance and destroyed their synagogues and their altar on Mt. Gerizim. Samaritan communities survived after the Muslim conquest.

*The Continuatio of the Chronicle of Abu al-Fath* 1.1

[Milka Levy-Rubin, *The Continuatio of the Samaritan Chronicle of Abu al-Fath* (Princeton, NJ: Darwin Press, 2002)

At that time there were three astrologers who used to foretell coming events: the first, Sarmasa, a Samaritan from Askar; the second, Ka'b al-Ahbar, a Jew, and the third, 'Abdallah, a Christian from Ludd (Lydda). These three were aware of each other's skill, and they saw in their dreams that the rule of Byzantium had ended, and the rule of Isma'il [Ishmael, i.e. the Arabs] is beginning, and that a leader was arising for them from amongst the descendants of Hashim; his sign would be found on his back in the form of a yellow mole the size of a palm, and the first thing to occur would be that he would emerge from a city called "the city of the messenger" (Medina). The three met together and said: Let us go and see whether it is he or not; if it is he, we shall contemplate what we should do, so that we will not be hurt by him as we were by those who preceded him. The three departed and arrived at his city, where he was staying. When they approached him and saw him they said: "Who could overcome him?" They decided that Ka'b al-Ahbar would approach him. So he approached and greeted him, and Muhammad asked him: "Who are you?" And he answered: "I am one of the Jewish dignitaries, and I found in my Torah that one of the descendants of Isma'il will arise, who will rule, and will conquer the world, and no one will stand in his way. Then 'Abdallah said likewise: "I found in the Gospel [and so on . . .], and they did not recognize anything but his authority." When Sarmasa, the Samaritan, approached him he said to him: "You will profess Muslim faith and law; with it you will subdue the necks of the infidels and you will rule the world *through* it. We were told that there is a sign between your shoulders," and Muhammad stood up and revealed his back, and they saw the mole on his back. When Ka'b al-Ahbar heard Sarmasa's words he became a hypocrite in his religion [i.e. he became a Muslim]; 'Abd al-Salam too became a hypocrite. Muhammad was pleased with them, and also with the words he heard from Sarmasa. He said: "Why are you not doing the same as these two did?" Sarmasa had already gained from him a concession with respect to taxation and protection, before he proclaimed the message of Islam to him, so that he would not force him to do what he did not want to; and Sarmasa, the Samaritan, said to him: "My need is satisfied by that which I have – that is, the law and the faith," and Muhammad said to him: "If this is your answer, what do you want, O Samaritan?" . . .

### 15.3.24 An early non-Muslim view of Muhammad

An anti-Jewish booklet written in Greek about 634 when Heraclius was persecuting his Jewish subjects provides an early glimpse of how Muhammad was viewed from outside the Islamic tradition. Cast in the form of a letter from a Palestinian Jew named Abraham, this passage describes Muhammad as a Jewish messianic figure rejected by the Jews.

*The Instruction of Jacob, who was recently baptized*
[Patricia Crone and Michael Cook, *Hagarism; The Making of the Islamic World:* (Cambridge: Cambridge University Press, 1977) pp. 3–4]

A false prophet has appeared among the Saracens . . . They say that the prophet has appeared coming with the Saracens, and is proclaiming the advent of the anointed one who is to come. I, Abraham, went off to Sykamina and referred the matter to an old man very well versed in the Scriptures. I asked him: "What is your view, master and teacher, of the prophet who has appeared among the Saracens?" He replied, groaning mightily: "He is an impostor. Do the prophets come with swords and chariot? Truly these happenings today are the works of disorder . . . But you go off, Master Abraham, and find out about the prophet who has appeared." So I, Abraham, made enquiries, and was told by those who had met him: "There is no truth to be found in the so-called prophet, only bloodshed; for he says he has the keys of paradise, which is incredible."

### 15.3.25 Disaster for the Romans

For the Christian Roman state, Islam was a great disaster. AM stands for *anno mundi* and indicates the number of years since the creation of the world. Muhammad was not murdered; the text is corrupt here.

Theophanes, *Chronicle* AM 6121, 6122 (AD 628/9)

[Cyril Mango and Roger Scott, trans., *The Chronicle of Theophanes Confessor* (Oxford: Clarendon Press, 1997) pp. 462, 464–5]

#### AM 6121

And while the Church at that time was being troubled thus by emperors and impious priests, Amalek rose up in the desert, smiting us, the people of Christ, and there occurred the first terrible downfall of the Roman army, I mean the bloodshed at Gabithas, Hiermouchas, and Dathesmos. After this came the fall of Palestine, Caesarea and Jerusalem, then the Egyptian disaster, followed by the capture of the islands between the continents and of all the Roman territory, by the complete loss of the Roman army and navy at Phoinix, and the devastation of all Christian peoples and land, which did not cease until the persecutor of the Church had been miserably slain in Sicily.

#### AM 6122

In this year died Muhammad, the leader and false prophet of the Saracens, after appointing his kinsman Abourbacharos [Abu Bakr] to his chieftainship. At the same time his repute spread abroad and everyone was frightened. At the beginning of his advent the misguided Jews thought he was the Messiah who is awaited by them, so that some of their leaders joined him and accepted his religion while forsaking that of Moses, who saw God. Those who did so were ten in number, and they remained with him until his murder. But when they saw him eating camel meat, they realized that he was not the one they thought him to be, and were at a loss what to do; being afraid to abjure his religion, those wretched men taught him illicit things directed against us, Christians, and remained with him . . .

He taught his subjects that he who kills an enemy or is killed by an enemy goes to Paradise; and he said that this paradise was one of camel eating and drinking and intercourse with women, and had a river of wine, honey, and milk, and that the women were not like the ones down here, but different ones, and that the intercourse was long lasting and the pleasure continuous; and other things full of profligacy and stupidity; also that men should feel sympathy for one another and help those who are wronged.

## Further reading

Bulliett, Richard W., *The Camel and the Wheel* (New York: Columbia University Press, 1990)

Cameron, Averil, Lawrence Conrad, and Geoffrey King, eds., *The Byzantine and Early Islamic Near East*, vol. I: *Problems in the Literary Source Material*; vol. 11: *Land Use and Settlement Patterns* (1994); vol. III: *States, Resources, and Armies* (1995); vol. IV: *Patterns of Communal Identity in the Late Antique and Early Islamic Near East* (Princeton, NJ: Darwin Press, 2007)

Donner, Fred M., *The Early Islamic Conquests* (Princeton, NJ: Princeton University Press, 1981)

Donner, Fred M., "The Background to Islam," in Michael Maas, ed., *The Cambridge Companion to the Age of Justinian* (Cambridge: Cambridge University Press, 2005) pp. 510–33

Griffith, Sidney H., *The Church in the Shadow of the Mosque. Christians and Muslims in the World of Islam* (Princeton, NJ: Princeton University Press, 2008)

Hoyland, Robert G., *Seeing Islam as Others Saw It. A Survey and Evaluation of Christian, Jewish and Zoroastrian Writings on Early Islam* (Princeton, NJ: Darwin Press, 1997)

Hoyland, Robert, *Arabia and the Arabs: From the Bronze Age to the Coming of Islam* (London: Routledge, 2001)

Kaegi, Walter E., *Byzantium and the Early Islamic Conquests* (Cambridge: Cambridge University Press, 1992)

Millar, Fergus, *The Roman Near East, 31 B.C.-A.D. 337* (Cambridge, MA: Harvard University Press, 1993)

Shahid, Irfan, *Byzantium and the Arabs in the Fourth Century / Fifth Century / Sixth Century* (Washington, DC: Dumbarton Oaks, 1984–95)

# APPENDIX:
# LATE ANTIQUITY ON THE WEB

## Compiled by Daniel Abosso

### [accurate as of May 1, 2009]

Many primary sources as well as pioneering works on Late Antiquity are now in the public domain and can be accessed via Google Book Search *<http://books.google. com>* or Project Gutenberg *<http://www.gutenberg.org/wiki/Main_Page>*.

Students may also find the following sites helpful:

1. Lacus Curtius
   *http://penelope.uchicago.edu/Thayer/E/home.html*
   A useful site that includes a wealth of primary and secondary material pertaining to Late Antiquity.

2. De Imperatoribus Romanis: An Online Encyclopedia of Roman Rulers and Their Families
   *http://www.roman-emperors.org/*
   Contains biographies of Roman emperors written by scholars.

3. Internet Guide for History: Late Antiquity
   *http://www.fordham.edu/halsall/ancient/asbook10.html*

4. Byzantium: The Byzantine Studies Page
   *http://www.fordham.edu/halsall/byzantium/*

5. The Online Reference Book for Medieval Studies
   *http://www.the-orb.net*

6. Roman Law Resources
   *http://www.iuscivile.com/*
   Provides an introduction to scholarship on Roman law.

7. Suda On Line: Byzantine Lexicography
   *http://www.stoa.org/sol/*
   An online edition of the *Suda*, a tenth-century Byzantine encyclopedia containing much information about the Late Antique world. Many entries have been translated and annotated.

8. Tables of Contents of Journals of Interest to Classicists
   *http://www.chass.utoronto.ca/amphoras/tocs.html*
   Searchable tables of content of numerous Classics, Near Eastern Studies, and Religious Studies journals.

9. Women in Byzantium
   *http://www.doaks.org/research/byzantine/women_in_byzantium.html*
   Bibliography of works on women in the Byzantine period, including primary sources, secondary sources, and Web resources.

10. Catholic Encyclopedia
    *http://www.newadvent.org/cathen*
    Searchable encyclopedia with entries on Christian authors, some emperors (Constantine), certain regions of the empire (Gaul), and important moments in the history of Christianity, such as church councils and persecutions.

11. Early Church Fathers
    *http://www.ccel.org/fathers2/*
    Translations of Christian authors from the second to the sixth century, divided into Ante-Nicene and Post-Nicene Fathers.

# INDEX OF ANCIENT SOURCES

Abbinaeus *Archive* 3: 94; 45: 90
*Acts of Marcellus* 250–9: 105–6
Agapetus, *Exposition* l, 2, 30, 35, 37: 5–6
Agathias: *Greek Anthology* 16.36: 67–68;
16.380, "On Porphyrius of the Blue
Faction": 43; *The Histories* 1.2.1;
1.2.3–4: 368; 2.24:5, 2.25.3: 341;
2.30.3–7, 2.31.1–4: 319–20
*Akathistos Hymn*, Prooimion: 164–65
Alexander of Tralles, *On Viscous Humors
and Thick Masses Found in the Lung* 5,
4: 299–300
Ambrose of Milan: *Commentary on Paul's
First Letter to the Corinthians* 148:
235–36; *Letters* 40.1, 2, 6, 10, 13, 20, 21:
205–7; 51.4, 6, 11, 13: 119–20; *On
Psalm 118 expositio sermo 13, littera
"mem"* 7: 268
Ammianus Marcellinus, *History* 15.5.12–14:
12–13; 16.10.5–10: 2–3; 17.1.5–7: 85;
17.13.3: 98; 17.13.8–10: 81; 19.2.7–11;
19.4.1; 19.8.4–9: 87–88; 19.2.15: 89,
300–301; 20.4.17–18: 99; 22.2.3–5: 3;
22.14.3: 196; 24.7.1, 3–6: 336; 25.6.1–4:
80–81; 29.1.29–32: 178–79; 30.4.9–1 l,
13–15, 19: 287–88; 31.2.1–12: 371–73;
31.4.1–6: 346–47; 31.16.8: 347–48
Ananias of Shirak, *Autobiography*: 75–6
*The Anonymus Valesianus* 12.65–7, 69–73:
354–55
*Antinoopolis Papyri, Private Letter*: 263–64
Antiochus Strategos, *The Sack of Jerusalem*:
215–16
Apamaea Synagogue Floor Mosaic
Inscription: 220
Aphrodisias: Inscription 40: 40; Inscription
83: 39–40
*Apocalypse of Pseudo-Methodius*, "Children
of Ishmael," 11.1–15: 168–69

*Apostolic Constitutions* 6.30.2: 276–77
Arch of Constantine, Inscription: 112
Arda Viraz, A *Vision of Heaven and Hell*
6.3.8–12, 15, 18: 332–34
Arius, *Letter to Alexander of Alexandria*
2–5: 131–32
Athanasius of Alexandria: *History of the
Arians* 44, 6–8: 9; *Life of Antony* 2–3:
113; 5–7: 152–53
Augustine of Hippo: *On Christ's Grace and
Original Sin* 2.38.43: 240–41; *City of
God* 2.3: 57; 4.3.4: 208; 4.11: 269–70;
18.53: 58–59; 19.15: 34; *City of God
Against the Pagans* 19.6: 295–96;
*Confessions* 2.3.5: 66–67; 6.15.25: 236;
8.12.29: 113–14; 9.9.19: 262–63;
*Disputation against Fortunatus* 1, 35–7:
121–22; "The Election of Eraclius," *Acta
Ecclesiastica, Letter* 213.1–7: 121;
*Against Faustus* 22.74–5: 107; *The Good
in Marriage*, 5.5.376–7: 236; *On
Heresies* 88: 136–37; *Letters* 10.2:
34–35; 50: 195–96; 71: 169–70; 91:
198–99; 104: 245; 189.2.4, 6: 108
Ausonius: *Epistles* 22: 247–48; *Parentalia*
1,9, 10: 280–81

*The Babylonian Talmud*: Kiddushin 29 a–b:
219; Sanhedrin 4b–5a: 216; Yebamoth
15, 114b: 217–18
Al-Baladhuri, *The Book of the Conquest of
the Regions*: 398, 403
Basil of Caesarea: *Address to Young Men on
Reading Profane Literature*: 70–71; *On
the Holy Spirit* 20: 32–33; *Homilies*: 10.1
"A Psalm on the Lot of the Just Man":
73–74; 11.4: 74; *Letters*: 199.33: 243;
299: 17
Bedjan, *The Heroic Deeds of Mar Simeon*,

the Chief of the Anchorites (Acts of Martyrs and Saints): 154–55

Benedict of Nursia, Rule for Monasteries 7: 157–60

Boethius (child), burial inscription for: 277–78

Boethius (philosopher), The Consolation of Philosophy, 1.2–3, 1.6–7: 321–24

The Book of Caliphs (CSCO Script. Syr. Ser. 3, vol. 4.2, Leipzig, 1904), 106: 379

The Book of the Counsel of Zartusht 2–8: 330–31

Al-Bukhari, Sahih 3.392–4: 394–95

The Burgundian Code, Preface 1, 2, 3, 8, 13; 2.1, 2: 285, 361–62

Caelius Aurelianus, On Acute Diseases and Chronic Diseases 11.129, 132–8: 305–6

Caesarius of Arles, Sermon 44.2: 241

Cassiodorus: An Introduction to Divine and Human Readings I.1, 5–6: 74–75; Documents 6.5: 13–14; Official Correspondence 3.9: 357–58; Variae: III.3: 355; III.4: 355–56; XII.18: 19–20

Chalcedon, Council of (451), Definition of the Faith: 135

Clement of Alexandria, Paedagogus: 3.9: 46–47; 3.11: 261

The Comparison of Roman and Mosaic Law: 15: 293–94; 15.3: 185–86

Constantine, Speech of Thanks to, 5–6: 26–28

The Continuatio of the Chronicle of Abu al-Fath 1.1: 404–405

Corpus of Latin Inscriptions: 6.510: 180–81; 6.1189: 54–55; 6.1755: 226

"The Creed of Nicaea": 132

Cyril of Alexandria, Letter 96: 128–29

Cyril of Jerusalem, Letter to the Emperor Constantius 3–5: 146–47

Cyril of Scythopolis, Life of Sabas, ch. 71: 5

Damascius, Life of Isidore, fragment 102: 226–27

The Death and Miracles of the Bishops of Merida 4.2.6–13: 303–304

Description of the Entire World 35–7: 40

Diocletian, Edict on Maximum Prices, preamble: 21–22

Dionysius Exiguus, Letter to Bishop Petronius (Patrologia Latina 67.487): 165

Dirge for the Ninth of Av: 221–22

The Divine Liturgy 9.1: 163–64

Easter Chronicle 1, (AD 328): 59–60; (AD 626): 341–42; (AD 628): 342–43

Egeria, Travels 36.5, 37.1–3: 148–49

Eleazar ben Kallir, Battle between Behemoth and Leviathan: 220–21

Elvira Church Council, Canons 16, 49, 50: 204

Ennodius, Life of Saint Epiphanius: 351–52

Ephrem the Syrian, Hymn on Paradise: 8.8: 242; VIII, Verses 2, 3, 4, 7, 11: 282–84

Epitaph, Algeria: 282

Eudocia, Empress, Inscription of: 46

Eugippius, The Life of Saint Severinus: 20.1: 86–87; 24.1, 4.1–5: 359–60

Eumenius of Autun, For the Restoration of the Schools .20–.21: 18–19

Eunapius of Sardis, Lives of the Philosophers (Ionicus) 499.2–3: 300

Eusebius of Caesarea: Life of Constantine: 1.29: 111–12; 2.35, 27–29: 147–48; 4.8–13: 335–36; 4.15: 8; The Martyrs of Palestine 3.1: 142; Tricennial Oration: On Christ's Sepulchre 16.4–6: 56–57

Evagrius, Ecclesiastical History: 11: 139–40; 29: 307–308; 111.14: 138–39

Evagrius Ponticus, Advice to a Young Woman: 162–63

Facundus of Hermione, In Defense of the Three Chapters 12.3: 10, 141–42

Firmicus Maternus: The Error of the Pagan Religions: 2.3–6: 179–80; 22: 180; Mathesis 7.14: 250

Flavius Cresconius Corippus, In Praise of Justin 11, 3.191–270: 381–82

Gangra, Canons of the Council of, 343: 153–54

Geminia Januarilla, The Dowry of: 251–52

Gentianus, burial inscription for: 279

George the Monk, Life of Theodore of Sykeon 145–6: 301–2

Gerontius, Life of Melania the Younger 19: 41

Gildas, On the Ruin of Britain 24: 360

Greater Creation 1.1–39: 331–32

"The Greek Anthology" 16.48: 15

Gregory I the Great (pope): Book of Pastoral Rule 2.1: 123–24; Letters: 1.5, to Princess Theoctista: 130; 2.24, to Bishop Desiderius of Vienne: 71; 9.204:

194; 30: 145–46; 423: 193–94; *Moralia* 20.1.1: 171
Gregory of Nazianzus: *Concerning His Own Life* 1680–9: 126; *Oration* 4.80: 7; *Will*: 272–75
Gregory of Nyssa, *Life of Macrina/Vita Macrinae* 4–5: 248–49
Gregory of Tours: *The History of the Franks* 2.6–7: 376–77; 2.27: 362–63; 2.30: 115; 5.34: 309; VI.11: 20; *The Miracle of Saint Martin* 2.1, 4.36: 301

*The History of the Heroic Deeds of Mar Kardagh the Victorious Martyr*, 1, 65–9: 143–44
*History of the Monks in Egypt* 8.30–1: 30–31
*Hymn to Selene–Hecate–Artemis*, from a Greek magical handbook: 175

Iamblichus: *The Exhortation to Philosophy* 1: 315–16; *On the Mysteries* 2.12, 5.23: 316–17; 5.26: 181–82
Ibn Hisham, *Biography of Muhammad* vol. 1, 516–17: 212–13
Ibn Ishaq, *Biography of Muhammad*: 403–404
Ibn al-Kalbi, *The Book of Idols* 3–23: 390–91
Ibn Miskawayh, *The Experiences of the Nations*: 338–39
Innocent I (pope), *Epistle 36 (Patrologia Latina* 30: 602–3): 255
*The Instruction of Jacob, who was recently baptized*: 405–406
Isidore of Seville: *Etymologies* 9.2.105: 368–69; *On Medicine* 1.1–2; 4.1–2; 5.2–3; 9.1, 2, 3, 5; 13.1–5: 297–99

Jacob of Serug, *Homily on Simeon the Stylite*, 655–6, 659–60, 664–5: 155–56
Jerome, *Letters* 22.30 (to Eustochium): 69–70; 77.2–3: 258–59; 77.11: 277; 108 (to Eustochium): 148; 117: 262; 127: 249; 127.12: 56; 128: 244
*The Jerusalem Talmud*, Hagigah 1.7.76c: 217
John Cassian, *Institutes* 1.2, 4.5: 157
John Chrysostom: *Homily Against the Jews* 1.3, 1.5: 208–9; *Homily on Matthew* 37.6: 45; 61.3: 28–29; *Against Jews and Non-Christians*, 9: 269; *On the Second Letter to the Corinthians*, p. 61, xviii,

col. 527: 164; *Sermon on Marriage*: 252; "The sort of wives that ought to be taken in marriage": 251
John of Ephesus: *Ecclesiastical History* (fragment): 194–95; *Life of Simeon the Mountaineer*: 193
John Lydus, *On the Magistracies of the Roman State*: 3.26: 67; 3.59: 17–18
John Malalas, *The Chronicle* 7.7: 45–46
John, Bishop of Nikiu, *The Chronicle* 120.17–28: 400–401
Jordanes: *Getica L*, 261: 378–79; *The Gothic History*, 4.25–29: 367
Julian the Apostate: *Hymn to King Helios* 130, 132, 133: 196, 314–15; *Hymn to the Mother of the Gods* 180: 315; *Letters*: 36: 68–69; 51, "To the Community of the Jews": 207–8
Junillus Africanus, *The Basic Teachings of Divine Law*, Introduction: 72–73
Justinian: *Against the Monophysites*, Conclusion: 140–41; *Code*: "The First Preface": 290; 1.19.6: 216; 1.27.2.4, 8: 86; 6.57.6: 238; 11.40.6: 237–38; 11.48.23.2: 30; I.11.1–2, 4–7: 186–88; II.54.1: 28; *Digest: Constitutio Omnem/The Whole Body of Law* 1–2, 6–7: 286–87; *Constitutio Deo Auctore/The Law Written by God* 4, 12: 290–91; 25.3.4: 243; *Edicts: 1*, Preface: 15–16; *6*, "On the Regulation of Skilled Labor," Preface, 1: 22–23; *Institutes*: 1.1: 285–86; 1.3–5: 33–34; *Novels* 6: 9; 21: 292–93; 21.1: 238–39; 22.3–7: 255–57; 73, Preface: 291–92; 84, Preface: 291–92; 146, Preamble: 203–4

Al-Khansa, "Lament for a Brother": 387–88
*Khusro's Obituary*: 339–40
Kirdir, Inscription of, at the Kaaba of Zoroaster, lines 11–13: 334–35

Lactantius, *On the Death of the Persecutors* 7.1–8: 11–12; 48.1–11: 117–19
Leo I (pope): *Letters*: 28.4: 137–38; 159.1–4: 253–55; *Sermons* 3: 54–54; 27.4: 192; 54.2: 133–34
Libanius: *Autobiography* 4, 5, 8, 19, 21, 22: 245–47; *Orations* 7.1–3: 24; 11 "In Praise of Antioch," 133–7: 38–39; 18.289, 293: 25; 30 8–11, "For the Temples": 163, 197; 47, "On Protection Systems," 1, 3–12, 2.17, 18: 91–94

*The Life and Virtues of the Holy Bishop Masona* 5.3.2–9: 302–303

*Life of Melania the Younger* 22, 23, 30, 35: 228–29

*The Life of Olympias* 2, 5: 227–28

*The Life of Saint Nicholas of Sion* 15, 16, 18: 190–91; 52: 309

*The Life of Saint Pelagia the Harlot* 4–7, 18, 20–6, 5 3: 230–32

Macrobius, *Commentary on the Dream of Scipio*, 1.12.1–2, 4, 7, 9, 16, 17: 325–26

Majorian, *Novel* 4: 55

Marinus of Neapolis, *Life of Proclus* 8–13, 19, 21, 29: 317–19; 36–7: 275–76

Mark the Deacon, *Life of Porphyry, Bishop of Gaza* 17: 198; 75–6, 78: 189–90

Martianus Capella, *The Marriage of Philology and Mercury* 8.814: 324

Maurice, *Treatise on Strategy*: 1.2: 81–82; 2.18: 103–4; 8.2.4: 103; 11.2: 381; 11.3: 104; 11.4: 385–86

Maximian, *Elegiacs* 1.1–16, 153–66, 191–204, 279–92: 270–72

Maximus of Turin, *Sermon* 107: 183

Menander the Guardsman, *Fragment* 19.1: 383–85

*Midrash Ha-Gaddol*, Deuteronomy 32: 9: 31

*Military Papyrus* 2.84: 242–43

*Muhammad's Ordinance for Medina*: 395–96

Al-Muqaddasi, *The Best Divisions for Knowledge of the Regions*: 402

Nemesius of Emesa, *On the Nature of Man* 25: 241

Nestorius: *The Bazaar of Heracleides* 2.1: 126–28; *Second Letter to Cyril*: 132–33

Nicaea, Council of, *Canon* 4 (325): 120

Nikephoros, *Short History After the Reign of Maurice* 9: 380; 13: 383

Olympiodorus of Thebes, *Fragment* 41.2: 23

*On Riches* 6.3, 20.1–2: 23–24

*On Strategy* 9: 83–84

*The Oracle of Baalbek*, lines 136–227: 166–68

Orosius, *History Against the Pagans* 7.39–41: 57–58; 7.43: 348–49

*Oxyrhynchus Papyrus*: 1.130, lines 1–10:

29–30; 1060: 268; I.129: 257–58; VI.939: 259–60

*The Passion of Saint Saba* 3.3–5: 346

Patrick (St.): *The Confession* 1.1, 2, 17, 23, 41, 42, 50, 52: 115–17; *Declaration* 42: 229–30

Paul of Aegina, *The Seven Books of Paul of Aegina*, vol. 1, section 51, "On Baths": 304

Paul the jurist, *Views* book 2: 243

Paul the Silentiary, *Description of Hagia Sophia*: 64–66

Paulinus of Nola: *Carmina* 27, 512–595: 171–72; *Letter* 5.4: 114; *Poem* 19.53–75: 53

Paulinus of Pella, *Eucharisticus* 564–81: 349–50

*Persian Martyrs*, "The Martyrdom of Tarbo, Her Sister, and Her Servant," 254–60: 232–35

Philostorgius, *Suda*, A 254, Leontius: 124

*The Piacenza Pilgrim* 1, 5, 11, 12, 18–20: 149–51

Plotinus, *Ennead*: 5.2.1: 312; 5.4.1.5–16: 311–12; 5.8.4: 313–14

*Poem on the Call to Arms*: 398

Porphyry, *On the Life of Plotinus and the Order of His Books* l, 9: 312–13

*Prayer of the Emanations*: 183–85

Priscus of Panium, *Fragments* 11.2: 373–76; 22.3: 377; 24.1: 377–78; 25: 378–79

Procopius of Caesarea: *On Buildings* 1.1.23, 24, 27, 47–9: 61; 1.2.1–19: 60–61; 1.10.10–20: 63–64; *History of the Wars* 1.17.40–7: 389–90; 1.24.1–2, 7–10: 41–42; 1.24.32–8: 225–26; 2.10.19–24: 340, 379–80; 2.22–23.1: 308–9; 3.11.1–5: 98; 4.9.1–14: 61–62; 5.2.6–19: 356–57; 5.8.41–3, 10.24–6: 214–15; 7.2.1–3: 367–68; 8.17.1–8: 340–41; *Secret History* 3.1 and 5.1: 10–11; 9.20–2: 45; 26.5: 73

Prosper, *Epitoma Chronicon* for the year 452: 377

Prudentius: *On the Crowns of the Martyrs* 2.1–20, 413–562: 50–52; 2.517–28: 112; 5.333–44: 144; 9.5–60: 71–72; 11.123–34: 144–45; *Against Symmachus*, 506–25, 565, 578, 587: 52–53

Pseudo-Athanasius: *Life of Syncletica* 42: 242; *Patrologia graeca* 28.264: 47

Pseudo-Joshua the Stylite, *Chronicle*: 38–42: 25–26; 93–1: 100–101

Qais Ibn Al-Khatim, "The Day of Bu'ath": 388–89
*Qorra, Governor of Egypt, Letter of*: 402
Quran: sura 1.1–7, "The Opening": 391; sura 2.255, "The Cow": 392; sura 3.84–5, "The family of Imran": 393; sura 9:29 and 5:51: 222; sura 10.38–9, "Jonah": 394; sura 18.57–8, "The Cave": 393; sura 29.57–8, "The Spider": 394; sura 81.1–21, "The Overthrowing": 392; sura 112, "The Unity": 393

Romanos the Melodist: *On Christian Life*, strophes 22, 23, 25: 160–61; *On the Presentation in the Temple*, strophes 3, 4: 134–35
Rutilius Namatianus, "A Voyage Home to Gaul," lines 37–66: 48–49

Sabbâ, Syria, lintel inscription on house: 269
Sallustius, *Concerning the Gods and the Universe* 15, 16: 182
Salvian of Marseilles, *On the Governance of God* 5.4–7: 353
Sebeos, *History* 10: 43–44; ch. 29, verse 99: 151–52
*Sefer Ha-Razim [Book of Mysteries]* 1.28–3.4: 304–5
Sergia, *Narration Concerning Saint Olympias* 1, 4, 5, 9: 161–62
Severus of Minorca, *Letter on the Conversion of the Jews* 3.6–7, 6.1–4, 13.1–14, 24.1.10, 30. 1–2: 209–11
Shenute of Atripe, *Open Letter to a Pagan Notable*: 188
Sidonius Apollinaris, *Letters* 4.20: 350–51; 5.5: 352–53
Simplicius, *On the Heavens* 119.7–9: 320–21
Socrates Scholasticus, *Ecclesiastical History* 1.34: 124–26; 38: 211–12
Sophronius of Jerusalem, *Sermon on the Epiphany*: 399
*Sortes Sangallenses* 6, 14, 54, 57–60, 88, 106–7: 175–78
Sozomen, *Ecclesiastical History* 2.2: 224–25
Sulpicius Severus, *The Life of Saint Martin of Tours* 2: 106–7

Symmachus, Roman aristocrat, *Letters/Official Dispatches* 3.8–10: 199–200; 3.20: 245; 6: 42–43
Synesius of Cyrene: *On Kingship* 16: 6; 18: 91; *Letters* 4, "To His Brother": 218–19; 148: 31–32
Synod of Antioch, *Canon* 9 (341): 120
*The Syro-Roman Law Book*, introduction: 294–95

Al-Tabari, *The History of the Prophets and Kings* 1.1850: 397; 1.2050: 399–400
*Tansar's Letter to Gushnasp* 1–3, 12–13, 22–3, 27, 44: 327–30
Themistius, *Oration* 19 (227d, 228a): 7–8
Theodoret, *Letter* 2: 108–9
*Theodosian Code* 1.5.1: 16–17, 289; 1.5.9: 289; 1.15.1: 14–15; 1.27.1: 130; 2.1.10: 203; 2.8.1: 165, 289; 3.5.1: 251; 3.7.2: 202; 3.12.1–2: 252–53; 3.16.1: 257; 5.9.1: 243; 7.1.5: 96; 7.2.1: 15; 7.8.5: 99–100; 7.13.1: 96; 7.13.5: 96; 7.13.16: 97; 7.17.1: 84–85; 7.18.1: 96; 8.16.1: 237, 249–50; 9.1.3: 237; 9.7.1: 253; 9.17.7: 145; 11.24.2: 28; 11.27.2: 243–44; 12.1.144, 184: 38; 13.3.3: 97; 15.3.4: 19; 15.8.2: 237–38; 15.12.1: 44; 16.5.5: 135–36; 16.8.3: 203; 16.8.7: 202; 16.8.20: 205; 16.8.21: 205; 16.8.29: 216; 16.9.1: 202; 16.10.4, 9, 17, 20, 24: 186–88; 16.18.1: 214; 16.18.18: 214; "Minutes of the Senate," 5: 3–4
Theodosius, *Novel* 4.1: 83
Theophanes Confessor, *Chronicle* AM 5961 (AD 468–469): 82–83; AM 6120 (620): 343–44; AM 6121, 6122 (AD 628/9): 406–407
Theophilus of Alexandria, *A Homily on the Virgin*: 8
Theophylact Simocatta, *History* 2.6.10–12: 90
*To Gregoria* 18: 260
*Treatise on the Relics of the Patriarchs at Hebron*: 400
Trullo, Council in (691–2), Canon 62: 192–93
Al-Turtushi, *Siraj al-Muluk* 229–30: 396–397

Vegetius, *Epitome of Military Science*: 1.1: 101; 1.2–4: 95; 3.2: 88–89; 3.26: 102–103

Venantius Fortunatus, *Poems* 8.10, 9.3, 11.6: 363–66

*Vettius Agorius Praetextatus and Aconia Fabia Paulina, The Grave Inscription of*: 278–79

Victor of Vita, *History of the Persecution in the Province of Africa*, 1.24–6: 358

Zachariah of Mitylene: *Life of Severus* 27–35: 189; *The Syriac Chronicle*: 7.3–4: 336–38; 10.16: 49–50

Zosimus, *New History*: 2.7: 183; 2.34: 79–80; 3.3.4–5: 102; 4.12: 98–99; 4.56: 348

# INDEX

Page numbers in *italics* indicate illustrative matter. Arabic names beginning with "Al-" are sorted by their primary element; for instance, Al-Bukhari will be found under B. Late Antique names are indexed as they are written; thus Marinos of Neapolis is listed under M, not N.

abandonment/exposure of unwanted infants, 243

Abbinaeus, *Archive*: civilian policing duties of military, 90; tax collectors, military as, 94

'Abd-al-Malik ibn-Marwan (caliph), 403

abortion and contraception, 241

Abu al-Fath, Samaritan view of Islam presented by, 404–405

Abu Bakr (Abourbacharos), 406

Academy of Plato, 319

acclamations, imperial, 3–4

acculturation problems of Ostrogoths, 356–57

Aconia Fabia Paulina, grave inscription of, 278–79

administration: bishops as administrators, 120; imperial (*see* imperial administration); Islamic, 403

Adrianople, mutiny of Gothic troops at (378), 78, 346–47, 371

adultery, 253

Aedui, Gaul, 26–28

afterlife, different concepts of, 282–84, 332–34, 394, 406–407

Agapetus, on imperial duties, 5–6

Agathias: on celebrity charioteers, 43; on Franks, 368; on Heraklamon (educator), 67–68; on pagan Athenian philosophers in Persia, 319–20; on Zoroastrianism, 341

age, dying, and death, 270–84; afterlife, different concepts of, 282–84, 332–34, 394, 406–407; Arab death lament,

pre-Islamic, 387–88; children, death of, 277–78, 281, 309, 363, 366; commemorative poems for family members, 280–81; Julian the Apostate (emperor), death of, 25, 336; monastic vows taken in old age, 114; Muhammad, death of, 406; obituary of Khusro Anushirwan (Sasanian ruler), 339–40; problems of old age, elegiac lament on, 270–72; Proclus the Philosopher, death of, 275–76; Simeon the Stylite, death of, 155–56; wills, 273–75. *See also* funerals and funerary practices; martyrs and martyrdom

Agnes (Frankish nun), 363, 364–66

agriculture: exhaustion of land, 26–28; plague, problems arising from, 309; vine and olive cultivation map, *xlvii. See also* peasantry

Ahriman, 330–32

Ahura-Mazda, 330–32

*Akathistos Hymn*, 164–65

Alans, Visigothic troops in campaigns against, 349

Alaric (Visigothic king), sack of Rome by (410), 41, 56–59, 348

Albinus (patron of Aphrodisias), 39–40

Alexander of Tralles, on lung disease, 299–300

Alexander the Great, 328

Alexandria: Arius, *Letter to Alexander of Alexandria*, 131–32; Cyrus (patriarch), Islamic forces admitted to city by, 400–401; description of, 40–41; Hypatia,

death of, 226–27; Theophilus of
Alexandria, 8. *See also* Athanasius of
Alexandria; Clement of Alexandria;
Cyril of Alexandria
Altar of Victory dispute, 199–200
Amalasuntha (Ostrogothic princess),
356–57
Ambrose of Milan: on buying a house, 268;
Callinicum, destruction of synagogue at,
205–207; on massacre at Thessalonika,
119–20; on women, 235–36
Amida, siege and sack of (502), 87–88, 89,
301, 336–38
Ammianus Marcellinus: on elephant troops
fighting legionaries, 80–81; on emperors
entering cities, 2–3; on federates, 98; on
Gothic defeat of Valens at Adrianople,
346–48; on guarding the emperor, 81; on
Huns, 371–73; on imperial advisory
councils, 12–13; on Julian the Apostate's
efforts to revive old gods in Antioch,
196; on Julian the Apostate's invasion of
Sasanian Persia, 336; lawyers, hostile
view of, 287–88; on military medicine,
89, 300–301; on oracles, 178–79; on
raiding, 85; on Rome, 48; on siege of
Amida, 87–88, 89, 301; on stipend
granted to troops, 99
Ammon's salt, 31–32
amulets protecting houses, 268
Ananias of Shirak, on trying to find a
teacher, 75–76
Angles, 345, 360
Anicia Faltonia Proba, tomb inscription of,
226
Anno Domini system, inception of, 165
Anoup (Egyptian peasant), 29–30
anthropology. *See* ethnography
Antioch: Judaism, Christian attraction to,
208–209; Julian the Apostate's attempts
to revive old gods of, 175, 196; Leontius
of Antioch, 124; Pelagia the Harlot
(saint), 230–32; plague in, 307–308;
Synod of Antioch (341), on
administrative role of bishops, 120
Antiochus Strategos, on role of Jews in
Persian conquest of Jerusalem, 201,
215–16
*Antonine Constitution*, 292
Antony the Hermit: rejection of world by,
113; temptation of, 152–53
Apamaea Synagogue, floor mosaic
inscription from, 220

Aphrodisias (southwest Asia Minor),
inscriptions in praise of patrons, 39–40
apocalyptic literature, 166–69
Apollo (Egyptian monk), as patron, 30–31
apostles sent from God, Quran on, 393
*Apostolic Constitutions*, on funerary
practices, 276–77
appeal, right of, 289
Aquitania, settlement of Visigoths in,
349–50
Arabic as administrative language of Islam,
403
Arabs and Arabia, 387; death lament,
387–88; Ghassanids and Lakhmids,
alliances of, 388–90; Jews of, 389; map,
*lix*; religion of, before Islam, 390–91;
warrior virtues of, 388–89. *See also*
Islam
Arcadius (emperor), restoration of Roman
buildings under, 54–55
Arch of Constantine, Rome, inscription, 112
architecture: domestic (*see* houses); Hagia
Sophia, Constantinople, 61, 64–66;
mosques, building of, 402; Roman
buildings, restoration of, 54–55
Arda Viraz, on Zoroastrian afterlife, 332–34
Arethas son of Gabalas (Harith ibn Jabala),
Arab leader, 389–90
Arians and Arianism: bishops' controversy,
Constantine I's intervention in, 124–26;
on human nature of Christ, 131–32;
imperial intervention in church affairs, 9;
invaders and successor states, 345–46,
353; Justinianic crusades against, 79;
Leontius of Antioch, middle course taken
by, 124; Nicene Creed and, 132
aristocracy: Roman senator, responsibilities
of wife of, 260; study and relaxation,
advice regarding, 247–48; wealth of, 23;
women, virtues of, 224–27. *See also*
patronage system
Aristotle, 311, 317, 318, 320–21, 328
Armenia: Ananias of Shirak on trying to find
a teacher in, 75–76; Khusro Anushirwan
(Sasanian ruler), obituary of, 339–40;
map, *xlix*; Roman law, enforcement of,
292–93; Smbat, martyrdom of, 43–44
armies. *See* military
art: Attila the Hun, Roman barbarian
iconography reversed by, 377; biblical
teaching through church art, 171–72;
martyrs in church art, 144–45; Plotinus
on, 313

asceticism and monasticism, 111, 152–63;
Benedict of Nursia on twelve degrees of
humility, 157–60; celibacy, legal status
of, 237, 249–50; childbirth, monk
attending at, 303–304; difficulties of
monastic life, 160–61; divorce and, 256;
extreme asceticism, canonical attempts to
curtail, 153–54; habits, monastic, 157;
John Cassian, rule of, 157; Melania the
Younger, 228–29; pagan temples,
monastic destruction of, 163, 197;
papacy, Gregory I on accession to, 130;
patrons, monks as, 30–31; Paulinus of
Nola, monastic vows taken in old age by,
114; rules, monastic, 157–60; women
ascetics and nuns, 161–63. *See also*
Antony the Hermit; Simeon the Stylite
astrology and marriage, 250
Atalaric (Ostrogothic prince), 356–57
Athanasius of Alexandria: on conversion of
St. Antony, 113; on imperial interference
in church affairs, 9; on temptation of St.
Antony, 152–53
Athaulf (Visigothic king), attempting to
establish better relations with Rome,
348–49
Athens, pagan philosophers of, in Sasanian
Persia, 319–20
Attila the Hun, 373–79; Catalaunian Fields,
battle of (451), 373; death and funeral of,
377–78; described by Priscus of Panium,
373–76; disintegration of empire after
death of, 371, 378–79; Gaul and Italy,
invasion of, 371, 376–77; map of empire
under, *lv*; Roman barbarian iconography
reversed by, 377; Rome, failure to sack,
377
Attis, cult of, 180
Attusia Lucana Sabina (wife of Ausonius),
commemorative poem for, 280–81
Augustine of Hippo: on abusive relationship
of his parents, 262–63; on beating
children, 245; conversion of, 113–14;
Eraclius elected as successor bishop to,
121; Fortunatus the Manichaean, debate
with, 121–22; on household gods,
269–70; on Jewish guilt, 208; on just
war, 79, 107; on marriage, concubinage,
and sexuality, 236, 240–41; on military
vocation for Christians, 108; on
pagan/Christian rioting, 195–96;
Pelagianism condemned by, 136–37; on
polytheistic practice in North Africa,

198–99; on providential history, 57, 166;
on sack of Rome (410), 57, 58–59; on
secular education, 66–67; on slavery,
34–35; on torture, 295–96; on translating
the Bible, 169–70
Aurelius Prudentius Clemens. *See*
Prudentius
Ausonius: commemorative poems for family
members, 280–81; grandfatherly advice
on study and relaxation, 247–48
Avars, 380–83; at court of Constantinople,
381–82; described by Maurice, 381;
kingdom of, 380–81; map of empire of,
*lv*; Sasanian Persians, alliance with, 383;
Slavs and, 383, 385; Turks and, 383

*Baalbek, Oracle of*, 166–68
*The Babylonian Talmud*: creation of, 201;
on interpretation of the law, 216,
217–18
Bagaudae, 349
Al-Baladhuri: on Arabic as administrative
language, 403; on surrender of
Damascus, 398
"barbarians." *See* invaders and successor
states
Basil of Caesarea: on imperial
administrators, 17; on interpretation of
Bible, 73–74; on slavery, 32–33
baths and bathing, 46–47, 302, 304
battle. *See* military
beating children, 245
Bedjan, on public asceticism of Simeon the
Stylite, 154–55
Belisarius (general): in Chalke Gate mosaic,
64; frontier defenses, instructions for
establishing, 86; Naples, Jewish defense
of, 214–15; triumphal procession of,
61–62
Benedict of Nursia, on twelve degrees of
humility, 157–60
betrothal and courtship, 248–49, 251
Bible: interpretation of, 73–74; nature and
purpose of, 171; synagogue worship,
language used in, 203–204; translation
into Gothic, 346; translation into Latin,
73–74
billeting of troops, 99–101
birth control, 241
bishops: as administrators, 120; behavioral
standards for, 123–24; bribes given by,
128–29; conciliar debates of, 124–28;
election of Eraclius as successor bishop

to Augustine of Hippo, 121; imperial administration, role in, 15–16; legal authority of, 130; Nestorius, deposition of, 126–28; public debates with heretics and non-believers, 121–22; respect due to, 124. *See also* popes

black plague. *See* plague

the Blues (chariot team), 43

Boethius (child), burial inscription for, 277–78

Boethius (philosopher), on consolations of philosophy, 321–24

borders and frontiers: Amida, siege and sack of, 87–88, 89, 301, 336–38; Constantine I's de-emphasis of, 79–80; establishing frontier defenses, 86; forts, 83–84; raiding on, 85; river frontier patrols, 84–85; welfare of *limitanei* (border troops), 83. *See also* Danube border of empire

Bota festival, 192–93

bribes given by bishops, 128–29

Britain: Angles and Saxons in, 345, 349, 360; end of Roman way of life in, 360; Lullingstone Villa, Kent, 266–68, *267*

Britannic empire, rulers of, lxxvi

Brumalia festival, 45–46, 192–93

bubonic plague. *See* plague

Al-Bukhari, on creation of Quran, 394–95

Burgundian law code, 361–62

burial. *See* age, dying, and death

Byzantium. *See* Constantinople, *and specific Byzantine emperors by name*

Cabades II (Seiroe; Sasanian ruler), 343

Caelius Aurelianus, on dieting, 305–306

Caesarea, map of, *liii*

Caesarius of Arles, on contraception and abortion, 241

calendars: Anno Domini system, inception of, 165; apocalyptic, 166–69; creation of the world, dating from, 343, 406; festivals marking, 45–46, 192–93; providential history, 57, 166; Sundays, no litigation on, 165, 289

Callinicum, destruction of synagogue at, 205–207

canon law: on bishops as administrators, 120; extreme asceticism, attempts to curtail, 153–54; festivals with pagan origins, suppression of, 192–93; on Jews and Judaism, 204

captives: of Huns, 373–76; spouses as, 253–55, 256–57; of Vandals after sack of Rome, 358

Cassian (martyr), 71–72

Cassiodorus: Germanic kingdoms, Theoderic I's efforts to stop war between, 355–56; on integration of Christian and secular learning, 74–75; on Ostrogothic concern for Roman legacy, 357–58; on Quaestor, 13–14; on repair of Roman roads, 19–20

catacombs, 277, 279

Catalaunian Fields, battle of (451), 373

cavalry, training, 81–82

celibacy, legal status of, 237, 249–50

Chalcedonian Christianity: Council of Chalcedon (451), definition of the faith at, 133–34; *Henotikon* (or *Edict of Union*) of Zeno, 138–39; Justinian I on, 140–41; Leo I on unity of Christ's two natures, 133–34, 137–38; *Three Chapters* Controversy, 10, 141–42

Chalke Gate mosaic, Constantinople, 63–64

charioteers as celebrities, 43

Charlemagne, 380

childbirth: conception, 241; contraception and abortion, 241; effects on women's bodies, 242; monk attending at, 303–4; pains of, 242; souls, descent of, 325–26

Childebert (Frankish king), 20

children, 243–48; abandoned, 243; beating of, 245; death of, 277–78, 281, 309, 363, 366; divination in relation to, 178; girls: adolescent, 248; raising and education of, 244; infanticide, 243; legitimate and illegitimate, 238; mother–daughter relationships, 262; naming, 242–43; selling of, 219, 243–44. *See also* education

Chilperic (Frankish king), 20, 363, 366

Chosroes. *See entries at* Khusro

Christian Rome: Augustine of Hippo on Rome's place in God's plan, 58–59; conversion of citizens, 52–53; Eusebius of Caesarea on Rome's place in God's plan, 56–57; pagans blaming Christians for city's misfortunes, 57–58; Prudentius on Christianization process, 50–53; temples, abandonment of, 53; Zachariah of Mitylene on churches of, 49–50. *See also* popes

Christianity, 110–73; afterlife, concepts of, 282–84; Anno Domini system, inception of, 165; apocalyptic literature, 166–69;

bathing, Christian perspective on, 46–47; celibacy, legal status of, 237, 249–50; education and (*see under* education); empire, Christian theory of, 64–66; Eucharist, celebration of, 163–64; festivals, pagan, suppression of, 45; funeral practices, 276–77; gladiatorial games, efforts to suppress, 44; Judaism, Christian attraction to, 208–209; law and, 291–95; military and (*see under* military); Orthodox patriarchs of Constantinople, list of, lxxx–lxxxi; pagan habits, continuation of, 192; paganism as concept of, 174; prophetic tradition in Islam and, 393; providential history and, 57, 166; in Sasanian Persia, 335–36; sexual intercourse, view of, 240–41; Sundays, no litigation on, 165, 289; theatrical entertainment, disapproval of, 45; Trinity, implied Islamic critique of, 393; women in, 227–35; further reading, 172–73. *See also* asceticism and monasticism; Bible; bishops; canon law; Chalcedonian Christianity; Christian Rome; Christianity and the emperors; church-state relations; *entries at* conversions; councils of the church; heresies; Islam and Christianity; martyrs and martyrdom; paganism/polytheism, suppression of; pilgrimage to Jerusalem; Popes; prayers, Christian; priesthood; relics; theology, Christian

Christianity and the emperors: iconic images of emperors, 8; intervention in church affairs, 9, 10; piety expected of emperors, 8; priesthood, emperor as parallel to, 9; ruler cult, accommodation of, 7

Christology. *See* theology, Christian

chronology, lxxi–lxxiv

church-state relations: Arian controversy, emperor Constantine to bishops in, 124–26; Edict of Milan (313), 117–19; *Henotikon* (or *Edict of Union*) of the emperor Zeno, 138–39; heresy forbidden by state, 135–36; under Justinian I, 64, 66; Manichaeism, imperial edict against, 185–86; paganism/polytheism, legislation suppressing, 186–88; Thessalonika, emperor obliged to do penance for massacre at, 119–20. *See also* Christianity and the emperors

Cicero, 13, 69, 325–26, 352

cities, 37–77; Alexandria, description of, 40–41; baths, taking, 46–47; burial outside, 277; decurions (city senators), 37–39, 203; education in, 67–76; emperors arriving in, 2–3; imperial administration and, 38, 40; Jews as city senators, 203; military recruits from, 95; patrons, 39–40; plague, rural-urban conflict relating to, 309; rioting in, 41–42; Rome, 37, 47–59 (*see also* Rome); Theoderic I the Great (Ostrogothic ruler), continuation of Roman city life under, 354–55; further reading, 77

cities, entertainment in: celebrity charioteers, 43; festivals, 45–46; gladiatorial games, efforts to suppress, 44; martyrs as blood sport, 43–44; Roman expectations regarding, 42–43; theatrical, 45

classical literature. *See* literature, pagan/classical

Claudia (Vestal Virgin), 112

Clement of Alexandria: on bathing, 46–47; on women's jewelry, 261

climatological ethnography, 95, 368–69

Clothar (Frankish king), 363

Clotild (wife of Clovis the Frank), 115

Clovis (Frankish king): character of, 362–63; conversion of, 110, 115; Germanic kingdoms, Theoderic I's efforts to stop war between, 355–56

*Codex Gregorianus*, 285, 290

*Codex Hermogenianus*, 285, 290

codification of law, 285, 290–91; Burgundian law code, 361–62; *Codex Gregorianus*, 285, 290; *Codex Hermogenianus*, 285, 290; *Corpus Iuris Civilis (Collection of Civil Law)*, 285, 290 (*see also* Index of ancient sources, *under* Justinian); jurisprudence, systematization of, 290–91. *See also* *Theodosian Code*

colonate, 30

commerce. *See* economic life of Roman empire

conception of children, 241

Constantina (empress), request for head of St. Paul, 145–46

Constantine I the Great (emperor): on adultery, 253; on betrothal gifts, 251; border defenses and, 79–80; on citizens' right of access to emperor, 16–17;

Constantinople, founding of, 59–60; conversion to Christianity, 110, 111–12, 174; on divorce, 257; Edict of Milan (313), 117–19; equestrian statue of Justinian facing Persia, 60–61; gladiatorial games, efforts to suppress, 44; imperial administration of, 14; in Jerusalem in search of Cross, 146–48; natural disasters, response to, 26–28; piety of, 8; Sasanian Persia, negotiations with, 335–36; Secular Games neglected by, 183; on selling children into slavery, 243–44; Sunday, law courts closed on, 165, 289

Constantinople, 37, 59–66; Belisarius, triumphal procession of, 61–62; Chalke Gate mosaic, 63–64; charioteers as celebrities in, 43; empire, Christian theory of, 64–66; founding of, 59–60; Franks, *Romanitas* of, 368; Hagia Sophia, 61, 64–66; Julian (emperor), arrival of, 3; map, *li*; as New Rome, 59–60, 65–66; Nika riots, 41–42, 225–26; patriarchs, list of, lxxx–lxxxi; Persian siege of (626), 341–42, 383, 385; plague in, 308; purge of intellectuals, 195; Turks, embassy to, 383–85

Constantius II (emperor): church affairs, intervention in, 9; Limigantes as federate allies of, 98; military guard for, 81; Rome, arrival in, 2–3; Silvanus, framing of, 12–13

contraception and abortion, 241

conversions involving Jews and Judaism: Christian conversion to Judaism prohibited, 202; false Messiah, conversion to Christianity in response to, 211–12; forced conversion of Jews, 209–11; Islam, Jewish conversion to, 212–13; Jewish anger at converts to Christianity, 214

conversions to Christianity, 110, 111–17, 193–200; Altar of Victory dispute, 199–200; Antony the Hermit, rejection of world by, 113; of Augustine of Hippo, 113–14; of Clovis the Frank, 110, 115; of Constantine I, 110, 111–12, 174; of Huns, 380; Ireland, Saint Patrick in, 115–17, 229–30; mass conversion as imperial policy, 194–95; mountain people, limited Christianization of, 193; pagan resistance to, 195–99; Paulinus of Nola, monastic vows taken in old age by,

114; peasantry, patronage duties regarding, 193–94; of Pelagia the Harlot, 230–32; of Roman citizens, 52–53; social status and tactics for, 194; Vestal Virgin, last, conversion of, 112

conversions to Islam: by Jews, 212–13; Muhammad's Ordinance for Medina on, 395–96

Corippus (Flavius Cresconius Corippus), on Avar embassy to Justin II, 381–82

*Corpus Iuris Civilis* (*Collection of Civil Law*), 285, 290. *See also* Index of ancient sources, *under* Justinian

corruption in imperial administration, 12–13, 17–18

councils of the church: bishops, conciliar debates of, 124–28; Chalcedon (451), definition of the faith at, 133–34; Elvira (c.300), canons on Jews and Judaism at, 204; Ephesus (431), treatment of Nestorius at, 126–28; Gangra (343), attempts to curtail extreme asceticism at, 153–54; Synod of Antioch (341), on administrative role of bishops, 120; Trullo, Council in (691–692), suppression of festivals by, 192–93. *See also* Nicaea, Council of

countryside: farmhouse, Horvat Susiya (near Hebron), 264, *264*; military recruits from, 95; mountain people, limited Christianization of, 193; peasants of (*see* peasantry); plague, rural-urban conflict relating to, 309; survival of polytheism in, 183; villa, Lullingstone, Kent (England), 266–68, *267*

courts of law: Jewish courts, trials in, 203; Sundays, no litigation on, 165, 289; women's right of prosecution in, 237

courtship and betrothal, 248–49, 251

creation of the world: dating from, 343, 406; in Neoplatonism, 320–21; in Zoroastrianism, 331–32

Crete, conversion to Christianity in response to false Jewish Messiah on, 211–12

Cross (True Cross): Constantine I in Jerusalem in search of, 146–48; Cyril of Jerusalem on vision of, 146–47; Egeria, viewing of the Cross in Jerusalem by, 148–49; Helena (mother of Constantine I) and discovery of, 224; restoration to Jerusalem by Heraclius (630), 151–52, 343–44

crosses and crucifixes: protection provided

by, 269; Purim, alleged destruction of crucifixes during, 214

Cyril of Alexandria: bribes given by, 128–29; Hypatia of Alexandria, death of, 226–27; Nestorius, deposition of, 128; Nestorius' second letter to Cyril, 132–33

Cyril of Jerusalem, on Constantine's vision of Cross in Jerusalem, 146–47

Cyril of Scythopolis, on court ritual, 5

Cyrus (patriarch), Islamic forces admitted to Alexandria by, 400–401

Damascius, on death of Hypatia of Alexandria, 226–27

Damascus, surrender of (635), 398

Danube border of empire: collapse of, 86–87, 359–60; map of region, *lvii*; river frontier patrols, 84–85

death. *See* age, dying, and death

decurions (city senators), 37–39, 203

Demetrius (slave), 259–60

Deogratias (bishop of Carthage), attempts to assist Vandal captives by, 358

*Description of the Entire World*, 40

Desiderius of Vienne, Gregory I the Great (pope) on education to, 71

diets and dieting, 305–306

*Digest* (Justinian), 286, 290–91. *See also* Index of ancient sources

dioceses in the Roman empire, *xlvi*, 14–15

Diocletian (emperor): administrative reforms of, 11–12; economic reorganization of empire by, 21; Manichaeism, imperial edict against, 185–86; maximum prices, edict on, 21–22; military highway built by, 19; military reforms of, 78; Secular Games and, 183

Dionysius Exiguus and Anno Domini system, 165

discipline, military, 91, 102

disease. *See* medicine

divination, pagan, 80, 175–78

divorce and remarriage, 255–59

Dome of the Rock, Jerusalem, 402

domestic life, 240–84; divorce, 255–59; mother–daughter relationships, 262; will of Gregory of Nazianzus, family dynamics revealed in, 273–75; further reading, 284. *See also* age, dying, and death; childbirth; children; houses; marriage; sexuality; slavery; women

dowries, 251–52

drought, 25

Dulcitius (patron of Aphrodisias), 40

dying. *See* age, dying, and death

*Easter Chronicle*: on Constantinople as New Rome (328), 59–60; on defeat of Khusro II (628), 342–43; on siege of Constantinople (626), 341–42

eastern empire: maps, *xliv*, *xlviii*, *xlix*; patriarchs, list of, lxxx–lxxxi; rulers, list of, lxxviii. *See also* Constantinople

economic life of Roman empire, 20–35; maximum prices, Diocletian edict on, 21–22; poverty, attitudes towards, 24; silk trade, breaking of Persian monopoly on, 340–41; skilled labor, regulation of, 22–23; wealth, attitudes toward, 23–24; wealth inequality, 23. *See also* agriculture; natural disasters; patronage system; peasantry; slavery

Edessa, billeting of troops in, 100–101

Edict of Milan (313), 117–19

education, 66–76; Academy of Plato, 319; Bible, interpretation of, 73–74; Christian students reading pagan classics, 69–71; Christian teacher murdered by pagan students, 71–72; Christian teachers of classical curriculum, 68–69; divination in relation to, 178; of girls, 244; grandfatherly advice on study and relaxation, 247–48; for imperial service, 66, 67; importance of, 18–19; integration of Christian and secular materials, 74–75; intellectuals purged in Constantinople, 195; Jerome's crisis of conscience regarding, 69–70; Jewish, 217; legal, 286–87; love of learning, Libanius on, 245–47; medical, 299; military training, 81–82, 101; Ostrogothic acculturation problems and, 356–57; parental care for, 245; peasantry, ignorance of, 31–32; philosophical, 317–19; reduction of salaries of pagan teachers by Justinian I, 73; secular education, moral emptiness of, 66–67; Syrian Christian curriculum taught on classical model, 72–73; teachers, honoring, 67–68. *See also* literature, pagan/classical

Egeria, viewing of the Cross in Jerusalem by, 148–49

Egypt: exploitation of peasantry in, 28–29; Islamic governor, orders of, 402;

military, civilian policing responsibilities of, 90. *See also* Alexandria

Eleazar ben Kallir, *Battle between Behemoth and Leviathan*, 220–21

elephants, legionaries fighting, 80–81

Elijah, baths of, Gadara, 46

Elvira, Council of (*c*.300), canons on Jews and Judaism at, 204

emperors: acclamations, 3–4; cities, arrival in, 2–3; citizens' access to, 16–17; court ceremonial associated with, 5, 380–81; duties of, 5–6; head of St. Paul, imperial request for, 145–46; instability, as source of, 10–11; Jews and Judaism, 203–204, 205–206; law, as embodiment of, 7–8; law, duties regarding, 5; list of, lxxv–lxxviii; mass conversion as imperial policy, 194–95; massacre at Thessalonika, penance for, 119–20; military guards for, 81; oracles consulted about fate of, 178–79; Tetrarchy, lxxvi–lxxvii, 11, 14; war and peace, role in, 6. *See also* Christianity and the emperors; imperial administration

empire. *See* Roman Empire in Late Antiquity

empresses, respect due to bishops from, 124

England. *See* Britain

Ennodius, on Roman ambassador at Visigothic court, 351–52

entertainment, urban. *See* cities, entertainment in

Ephesus, Council of (431), treatment of Nestorius at, 126–28

Ephrem the Syrian: on the afterlife, 282–84; on pains of childbirth, 242

*Epic of the Kings* or *Shahnamah* (Firdawsi), 328

Epiphanius of Padua, as ambassador to Visigothic court, 351–52

episcopate. *See* bishops

Eraclius (successor bishop to Augustine of Hippo), election of, 121

Ethiopia: Islam in, 403–404; Jews in, 201; plague in, 307

ethnography: climatological, 95, 368–69; military, 95, 104; Roman theories of ethnogenesis, 366–69

Eucharist, celebration of, 163–64

Eudocia (empress), at baths of Elijah, Gadara, 46

Eugippius, on collapse of Danube border of empire, 86–87, 359–60

Eumenius of Autun, on importance of education, 18–19

Eunapius of Sardis, on Ionicus the physician, 300

Euric (Visigothic king), 351–52, 355

Eusebia (empress of Constantius II), chastised by Leontius of Antioch, 124

Eusebius of Caesarea: on Constantine's search for Cross in Jerusalem, 147–48; on martyrdom of Timothy of Gaza, 142; on negotiations with Sasanian Persia, 335–36; on piety of Constantine I, 8; on Rome, 56–57

Eutychius (patriarch), 64, 66

Evagrius Ponticus, advice for young nun from, 162–63

Evagrius Scholasticus: apology for Christian differences by, 139–40; on plague, 307–308

Eve, sin of, 230, 235–36

exemptions from military service, 97

exposure/abandonment of unwanted infants, 243

extortion/protection rackets run by military, 91–94

Fabiola (wealthy Roman): divorce and remarriage of, 258–59; funeral of, 277

Facundus of Hermione, on *Three Chapters* Controversy, 10, 141–42

faith healing/miracle cures, 301

families. *See* children; domestic life; marriage

famine: imperial administration's response to, 25–26; sack of Rome (410) and, 56

farmhouse, Horvat Susiya (near Hebron), 264, *264*

farms, farmers, and farming. *See* agriculture; peasantry

federates, 97–98

festivals: Justinian I's celebration of Brumalia festival, 45–46; marriage celebrations, 252; polytheistic practices at, 198; suppression of festivals with pagan origins, 192–93

Firdawsi, *Shahnamah* or *Epic of the Kings*, 328

Firmicus Maternus: on astrology and marriage, 250; on Attis cult, 179–80; on Isis cult, 179–80

Flaminian Way, 19–20

Flavius Apion III (Egyptian aristocrat), 29–30

Flavius Cresconius Corippus, on Avar embassy to Justin II, 381–82

Florentius, son of Nigrinianus (deputy master of the offices), 12–13

Fortunatus the Manichaean, date with Augustine of Hippo, 121–22

Fortunius (Roman aristocrat), remarriage while spouse in captivity, 255

Franks: Burgundian kingdom, destruction of, 361; Germanic kingdoms, Theoderic I's efforts to stop war between, 355–56; military anthropology of, 104; plague amongst, 309; Roman roads, use of, 20; *Romanitas* of, 368; Sigismer (Frankish prince) and his retinue, 350–51; Venantius Fortunatus, poems of, 363–66. *See also* Clovis

Fredegund (Frankish queen), 363, 366

freedmen: conversion of, 194; in law, 34

frontiers of the empire. *See* borders and frontiers

funerals. *See under* age, dying, and death

funerals and funerary practices, 277; Attila the Hun, death and funeral of, 377–78; burial inscriptions, 226, 276, 277–79, 282; catacombs, 277, 279; Christian, 276–77; Proclus the Philosopher, funeral of, 276. *See also* age, dying, and death

Gadara, baths of Elijah at, 46

Gallic empire, rulers of, lxxvi

Games, Secular, end of, 183

Gangra, Council of (343), attempts to curtail extreme asceticism at, 153–54

Gaul: Aedui, troubles of, 26–28; Aquitania, settlement of Visigoths in, 349–50; Catalaunian Fields, battle of (451), 373; Hun invasion of, 371, 376–77; plague in, 309; Rutilius Namatianus on his voyage home to, 48–49; Silvanus (military commander in Gaul and imperial pretender), 12–13. *See also* Franks

Gaza, Temple of Zeus Marnas in, 189–90

Geminia Januarilla, dowry of, 251–52

gender issues. *See* marriage; sexuality; women

Gentianus, burial inscription for, 279

George the Monk, on medical treatments of Theodore of Sykeon, 301–302

Germanic kingdoms: identity of, 345; maps of, *lvi, lvii*

Germanic language (Gothic), Romans learning, 352–53

Gerontius, on urban riots, 41

Ghassanids, 388–90

gifts at betrothals, 251

Gildas, on end of Roman Britain, 360

gladiatorial games, efforts to suppress, 44

"the Good" or "the One" in Neoplatonic philosophy, 311–12, 317

Goths: Adrianople, mutiny at (378), 78, 346–47, 371; billeted in Odessa, 100–101; Christian interpretation of military successes of, 353; ethnogenesis of, 367; Huns, pressure from, 346, 371; Rugi, 367–68; translation of Bible into Gothic, 346. *See also* Ostrogoths; Visigoths

government: decurions (city senators), 37–39, 203; Jews, self-government by, 201, 203, 216; Sasanian monarch, ideal concept of, 327–30. *See also* administration; church-state relations; emperors; imperial administration; law

Gratian (emperor), and Altar of Victory dispute, 199–200

"The Greek Anthology," 15

Gregoria (wife of Roman senator), 260

Gregorius, *Codex* of, 285, 290

Gregory I the Great (pope): on accession to papacy, 130; on behavioral standard for bishops, 123–24; on the Bible, 171; on conversion, 193–94; on education, 71; on imperial request for head of St. Paul, 145–46

Gregory of Nazianzus: on conciliar debates, 126; on ruler cult in Christianity, 7; will of, 273–75

Gregory of Nyssa, on efforts to betroth sister Macrina, 248–49

Gregory the Theologian. *See* Gregory of Nazianzus

Gregory of Tours: on Clovis the Frank, 115, 362–63; on miracle cures/faith healing, 301; on plague in Gaul, 309; on use of Roman roads by Franks, 20

Gundobad (Burgundian king), 355

Guntram (king of Burgundy), 20

habits, monastic, 157

Hagia Sophia, Constantinople, 61, 64–66

Harith ibn Jabala (Arethas son of Gabalas), Arab leader, 389–90

health. *See* medicine

heaven and hell, different concepts of, 282–84, 332–34, 394, 406–407

Hebron: farmhouse, Horvat Susiya (near Hebron), 264, *264*; Islamic forces welcomed by Jews of, 400

Helena (mother of Constantine I), 224–25

*Henotikon* (or *Edict of Union*) of Zeno, 138–39

Heraclius (emperor): Constantinople, siege of (626), 341; military under, 79; restoration of Cross to Jerusalem by (630), 151–52, 343–44; Sasanian Persia, defeat of, 79, 342–43

Heraklamon (educator), 67–68

heresies: apology for Christian differences addressed to polytheists, 139–40; Pelagianism, condemnation of, 136–37; state, forbidden by, 135–36. *See also* Arians and Arianism; Manichaeism; Nestorius and Nestorianism

Hermogenes, *Codex* of, 285, 290

Heruli, 355

Hillel II (Nasi), 207

Hippocrates, 298

history, providential, 57, 166

Honorius (emperor): idol worship prohibited by, 195; restoration of Roman buildings under, 54–55

Horvat Susiya (near Hebron), farmhouse, 264, *264*

hospitals, 302–303

household gods, 269–70

household life. *See* domestic life

houses, 264–70; buying, 268; farmhouse, Horvat Susiya (near Hebron), 264, *264*; mansion, Thuburbo Maius (near Carthage, in North Africa), 265, *266*; protecting, 268–70; townhouse, Pergamon, 265, *265*; villa, Lullingstone, Kent (England), 266–68, *267*

humility, twelve degrees of, 157–60

Huns, 371–80; Catalaunian Fields, battle of (451), 373; as common enemy of Rome and Persia, 340, 379–80; conversion to Christianity, 380; described by Ammianus Marcellinus, 371–73; described by Priscus of Panium, 373–76; disintegration of empire after death of Attila, 371, 378–79; Gaul and Italy, invasion of, 371, 376–77; Goths, pressure on, 271, 346; map of Attila's empire, *lv*; Rome, failure to sack, 377; in Sasanian Persia, 340, 379–80. *See also* Attila the Hun

Hypatia of Alexandria, murder of, 226–27

hypostases (the One, Nous, and Soul), 312

Iamblichus: on prayers, 181–82; on Pythagorean philosophy, 315–16; on theurgy, 316–17

Ibn Hisham, on conversion of Jews to Islam, 212–13

Ibn Ishaq, on Islam in Ethiopia, 403–404

Ibn al-Kalbi, on Arabian religious belief before Islam, 390–91

Ibn Miskawayh, on reforms of Khusro Anushirwan, 338–39

iconic images of emperors, 8

idols: in Arab religion before Islam, 390–91; Christians, destruction by, 163, 189–90, 195–96, 197, 198

illegitimacy and inheritance, 238

Illyrian emperors, lxxvi

imperial administration, 11–20; access to emperor by citizens, 16–17; advisory council, 12–13; bishops, role of, 15–16; cities and, 38, 40; corruption in, 12–13, 17–18; Diocletian's reforms, 11–12; education and, 18–19; education for, 66, 67; map of dioceses, prefectures, and provinces, *xlvi*; natural disasters, response to, 25–28; quaestor, role of, 13–14; roads, condition and use of, 19–20; social status of service in, 15, 17; Tetrarchy, lxxvi–lxxvii, 11, 14; vicars of dioceses, 14–15; at Visigothic court, 351–52; wealth spent in celebrating positions in, 23

impotence, divorce due to, 256

incestuous marriages, 252–53

infanticide, 243

inheritance law: legitimate and illegitimate children, 238; women and, 238–39

Innocent I (pope): in Ravenna during sack of Rome (410), 58; on return of captive spouse, 255

*Institutes* (Justinian), 285. *See also* Index of ancient sources

intellectuals purged in Constantinople, 195

invaders and successor states, 345–70; Alans, Visigothic troops in campaigns against, 349; Arianism of, 345–46, 353; Christian interpretation of military successes of, 353; ethnogenesis, Roman theories of, 366–69; German language, Romans learning, 352–53; law code, Burgundian, 361–62; military ethnography, 95, 104; military recruits,

non-Romans as, 78–79, 97–99, 346–48, 349; Scythians, 85, 367, 374–75, 377, 378, 381, 384; Slavs, 383, 385–86; Turks, Roman embassy to, 383–85; further reading, 369–70. *See also* Arabs and Arabia; Avars; Franks; Goths; Huns; Islam; Ostrogoths; steppe peoples; Vandals; Visigoths
Ionicus (physician), 300
Iran. *See* Sasanian Persia
Isidore of Seville: climatological ethnography of, 368–69; on medicine, 297–99
Isis, cult of, 179–80
Islam, 387–407; afterlife, concepts of, 282, 394, 406–407; Arabic as administrative language of, 403; Egypt, orders of governor of, 402; in Ethiopia, 403–404; map of Arabia Felix before Islam, *lix*; map of expansion of Islam, *lx*; Medina, Ordinance for, 395–96; mosques, building of, 402; Pact of 'Umar, 396–97; Samaritan account of, 404–405; Sasanian Persia and Roman Empire, struggle between, 327; substitute soldiers, use of, 398; further reading, 407. *See also* Arabs and Arabia; conversions to Islam; Islam and Christianity; Islamic military operations; Jews under Islam; Muhammad the Prophet; Quran
Islam and Christianity: apocalyptic literature, Arabs in, 168–69; Cyrus (patriarch), Islamic forces admitted to Alexandria by Christians, 400–401; Islam as disaster for Christianity, 406–407; Jerusalem, conquest of (636), 399–400; Muhammad viewed as messianic figure rejected by Jews, 405–406; Pact of 'Umar, 396–97; Sophronius of Jerusalem, Islam characterized by, 399; Trinity, implied Islamic critique of, 393
Islamic military operations: Arabs before Islam, warrior virtues of, 388–89; Cyrus (patriarch), Islamic forces admitted to Alexandria by Christians, 400–401; Damascus, surrender of (635), 398; dominance of, 79; Jerusalem, conquest of (636), 399–400; rules of war, 397; substitute soldiers, 398
Italy: Hun invasion of, 371, 376–77; Naples, Jewish defense of, 214–15; Ostrogothic

kingdom of (*see* Ostrogoths); Rome (*see* Rome)

Jacob of Serug, on death of Simeon the Stylite, 155–56
Jerome (saint): classical literature, crisis of conscience regarding, 69–70; on divorce, 258–59; on funerary practices, 277; girls, education and raising of, 244; on Marcella's avoidance of marriage, 249; military service endorsed by, 79; on mother–daughter relationships, 262; on Paula's pilgrimage to Jerusalem, 148; on sack of Rome, 56; translating the Bible, Augustine on, 169–70
Jerusalem: Dome of the Rock, 402; Helena (mother of Constantine I) in, *li*; Islamic forces, surrender to (636), 399–400; map, *lii*; Persian conquest of, role of Jews in, 215–16; relics brought back from, 146. *See also* Cross; Jerusalem Temple; pilgrimage to Jerusalem
*The Jerusalem Talmud*: creation of, 201; on education, 217; on interpretation of the law, 216
Jerusalem Temple: Julian's promise to rebuild, 207–208; lamentations for destruction of, 221–22
jewelry, women wearing, 261
Jews and Judaism, 201–23; afterlife, concepts of, 282; anger at converts to Christianity, 214; in Arabia before Islam, 389; Callinicum, destruction of synagogue at, 205–207; canon law on, 204; Christian attraction to Judaism, 208–209; Christian conversion to Judaism prohibited, 202; in city senates, 203; crucifixion and failure to accept Christianity, blamed for, 208; education, 217; false Messiah, conversion to Christianity in response to, 211–12; forced conversions, 209–11; imperial protections, 205–206; Jerusalem, role in Persian conquest of, 201, 215–16; language used in synagogue worship, 203–204; law, interpretation of, 216, 217–18; legal discrimination against, 202–208; legal trials in Jewish courts, 203; liturgical poetry, 220–21; magical healing text, 304–305; marriage between Christians and Jews, 202, 204; marriage, Jewish law regarding, 217–18; mass suicide, false Messiah encouraging,

211–12; Mishnah, 201, 203, 216, 217; Mosaic and Roman law, comparison of, 293–94; Naples, defense of, 214–15; Nasi (patriarch) position, end of, 201, 216; on patronage, 31; prophetic tradition in Islam and, 393; Purim, alleged destruction of crucifixes at, 214; resistance to discrimination, 213–16; Sabbath at sea, 218–19; in Sasanian Persia, 201; self-government by, 201, 203, 216; slaves, no circumcision of, 202; vigilantism against, prohibition of, 205; women, 201–202, 217–18; further reading, 222–23. *See also Babylonian Talmud*; conversions involving Jews and Judaism; *Jerusalem Talmud*; Jerusalem Temple; Jews under Islam; synagogues

Jews under Islam: conversion to Islam, 212–13; Hebron, Islamic forces welcomed in, 400; Muhammad viewed as Jewish messianic figure, 405–406; Ordinance for Medina on, 395–96; Pact of 'Umar, 396–97; Quran on, 222

John Cassian, on rules of monastic life, 157

John Chrysostom: on celebration of Eucharist, 164; on Christian attraction to Judaism, 208–209; on crosses, protection provided by, 269; on exploitation of peasantry, 28–29; on marriage, 251, 252; on theatrical entertainments, 45

John of Ephesus: on limited Christianization of mountain people, 193; on mass conversion as imperial policy, 194–95; on purge of intellectuals in Constantinople, 195

John Lydus: on corruption in imperial administration, 17–18; on education for imperial administrative service, 67

John Malalas, on Brumalia, 45–46

John, bishop of Nikiu, on admission of Islamic forces to Alexandria, 400–401

John Philoponus, on the creation of the world, 320–21

Jordanes: on disintegration of Hun Empire after death of Attila, 378–79; on Gothic ethnogenesis, 367

Jovian (emperor), 80, 336

Judaism. *See* Jews and Judaism

judges, supervision of, 289

judgment of God, Quran on, 392

Julian "the Apostate" (emperor): Constantinople, arrival in, 3; death of,

25, 336; on education, 68–69; *Hymn to King Helios*, 196, 314–15; *Hymn to the Mother of the Gods*, 315; Jerusalem Temple, promise to rebuild, 207–208; military discipline under, 102; polytheism, efforts to revive, 175, 196; Sasanian Persia, invasion of, 336; stipend granted to troops by, 99

Julius Nepos (emperor), ambassadors sent to Visigothic court by, 351–52

Junillus Africanus, on Syrian Christian curriculum taught on classical model, 72–73

just war, concept of, 79, 107

Justin I (emperor), Proculus as quaestor under, 15

Justin II (emperor), reception of Avar embassy by, 380–81

Justinian I the Great (emperor): Arians, crusades against, 79; on bishops' role in imperial administration, 15–16; Brumalia celebrated by, 45; Chalke Gate mosaic, Constantinople, 63–64; court ceremonial ignored by, 5; on divorce, 255–57; equestrian statue in Constantinople facing Persia, 60–61; frontier defenses, instructions for establishing, 86; Hagia Sophia, Constantinople, 61, 64–66; Huns, treaty with Persia regarding, 340, 379–80; instability, as source of, 10–11; Jews and Judaism, 203–204, 214–15; law as defined by, 285–86; on legal education, 286–87; mass conversion as imperial policy, 194–95; military under, 79; on need for new law, 291–92; Nika riots, 41–42, 225–26; on orthodox Chalcedonian Christianity, 140–41; pagan teachers, reduction of salaries of, 73; paganism/polytheism, suppression of, 186–88; priesthood, emperors as parallel to, 9; purge of intellectuals in Constantinople, 195; on regulation of skilled labor, 22–23; in Rome, 48; silk trade, breaking of Persian monopoly on, 340–41; *Three Chapters* Controversy, intervention in, 10, 141–42; universal enforcement of Roman law by, 292–93. *See also* Belisarius; Theodora

*Justinianic Code*, 285, 290. *See also* Index of ancient sources

Kalends festival, 192–93

Kardagh, martyrdom of, 143–44

Kavadh (Sasanian ruler), sack of Amida by, 336–38

Al-Khansa, pre-Islamic death lament by, 387–88

Khusro Anushirwan (Chosroes I; Sasanian ruler): Armenian obituary of, 339–40; Athenian philosophers in Persia and, 319–20; Huns, treaty with Rome regarding, 340, 379–80; idealization of, 328; reforms of, 338–39

Khusro II (Chosroes II; Sasanian ruler): Constantinople, siege of, 341–42; defeated by Heraclius, 342–43

Kirdir (Zoroastrian priest), 334–35

Koran. *See* Quran

Lactantius: on Diocletian's reforms, 11–12; on Edict of Milan (313), 117–19

Lakhmids, 388–90

languages: Arabic as administrative language of Islam, 403; Germanic language (Gothic), Romans learning, 352–53; Gothic, Bible translated into, 346; Latin, Bible translated into, 73–74; synagogue worship, language used in, 203–204

law, 285–96; adultery, 253; appeal, right of, 289; bishops, legal authority of, 130; celibacy, legal status of, 237, 249–50; Christianity and, 291–95; defined, 285–86; divination in relation to, 176; on divorce, 255–57; education in, 286–87; emperors as embodiment of, 7–8; heresy, prohibition of, 135–36; houses, buying, 268; imperial duties regarding, 5; infanticide, 243; Jewish courts, trials in, 203; Jewish law, interpretation of, 216, 217–18; Jews, legal discrimination against, 202–208; judges, supervision of, 289; jurisprudence, systematization of, 290–91; lawyers, hostile view of, 287–88; local law, disappearance of, 292–93; Manichaeism, imperial edict against, 185–86; marriage, abolition of penalties for failure to enter into, 237, 249–50; Mosaic and Roman law, comparison of, 293–94; new law, need for, 291–92; paganism/polytheism, legislation suppressing, 186–88, 198–99; slavery in, 33–34; Sundays, no litigation on, 165, 289; torture, use of, 13, 295–96; women, legal status of, 237–39; further reading, 296. *See also* canon law;

codification of law; courts of law; inheritance law

Laurence (martyr), on Christianization of Rome, 50–52

lawyers, hostile view of, 287–88

learning. *See* education

legitimacy and inheritance, 238

Leo I (emperor), military under, 79

Leo I the Great (pope): Attila the Hun's failure to sack Rome and, 377; on captive spouses, 253–55; on pagan habits, 192; on papal primacy, 54–54; relics distributed by, 146; on unity of Christ's two natures, 133–34, 137–38

Leo (Roman advisor to Visigothic court), 351–52

Leontius of Antioch, empress Eusebia chastised by, 124

Libanius: on city senators (decurions), 38–39; on destruction of temples by monks, 163, 197; on education and love of learning, 245–47; on effect of natural disasters on local economies, 25; on military protection/extortion rackets, 91–94; on poverty, 24

liberty, defined, 33

Licinius Augustus (emperor): Edict of Milan (313), 117–19; Secular Games neglected by, 183

Limigantes, 98

literature, pagan/classical: Basil of Caesarea on Christian students reading, 70–71; integration of Christian and secular materials, 74–75; Jerome's crisis of conscience regarding, 69–70; Julian the Apostate on Christian teaching of, 68–69

liturgy: Eucharist, celebration of, 163–64; language used in Jewish synagogue worship, 203–204; liturgical poetry, Jewish, 220–21. *See also entries at* prayers

Lullingstone Villa, Kent (Britain), 266–68, *267*

Macrina (saint), 248–49

Macrobius, on the descent of souls, 325–26

magic: amulets protecting houses, 268; medical healing via, 304–305; theurgy, 316–17, 319

Majorian (emperor), on protection of Roman public buildings, 55

Mani, 183–84

Manichaeism, 183–86; Augustine of Hippo

and Fortunatus, debate between, 121–22; founding and principles of, 183–84; imperial edict against, 185–86; *Prayer of the Emanations*, 183–85

mansion, Thuburbo Maius (near Carthage, in North Africa), 265, *266*

Mar Kardagh, martyrdom of, 143–44

Marcella (Roman aristocrat), 249

Marcellus (military martyr), 105–106

Marinos of Neapolis, on life and education of Proclus, 317–19

Mark the Deacon: on erection of church on site of Temple of Zeus Marnas, Gaza, 189–90; on travel obstacles laid down against Christians by pagans, 198

marriage, 248–59; abusive husbands, 262–63; adultery, 253; astrology and, 250; Augustine on marriage, concubinage, and sexuality, 236; avoidance of, 248–49; captive spouses, 253–55, 256–57; celebration of, 252; courtship and betrothal, 248–49, 251; divorce, 255–59; dowries, 251–52; failure to marry, abolition of penalties for, 237, 249–50; gifts at betrothals, 251; grave inscription of Vettius Agorius Praetextatus and Aconia Fabia Paulina, 278–79; impotence, 256; incestuous, 252–53; jewelry, wearing of, 261; Jewish law regarding, 217–18; between Jews and Christians, 202, 204; mothers-in-law, relationships with, 263–64; prenuptial agreements, 251; sexual intercourse in, 240–41. *See also* remarriage

Martianus Capella, on shape of universe, 324

Martin of Tours: military service, evasion of, 106–107; miracle cures of, 301

martyrs and martyrdom, 142–45; afterlife for, 282; burial near martyrs, 277; Cassian (Christian teacher murdered by pagan students), 71–72; in church art, 144–45; Laurence, on Christianization of Rome, 50–52; Mar Kardagh in Persia, 143–44; Marcellus, refusal to serve in military by, 105–106; North Africa, pagan resistance in, 195–96, 198–99; relics, 144, 145–46; Saba (saint and martyr) among the Visigoths, 346; Smbat of Armenia, 43–44; Tarbo, Persian martyrdom of, 232–35; Timothy of Gaza, 142

Mary, mother of Jesus: *Akathistos Hymn* addressed to, 164–65; Nestorian objections to Mary as *Theotokos* or mother of God, 132–33; presentation of Jesus in the Temple by, 134–35

Masona of Mérida, hospital of, 302–303

mass conversion as imperial policy, 194–95

mass suicide, false Messiah encouraging, 211–12

massacre at Thessalonika, 119–20

massacre of Visigothic troops after Roman defeat at Adrianople (378), 347–48

Maurice (emperor): Avars described by, 381; on battle cries and prayers, 103–104; on cavalry training, 81–82; military anthropology of, 104; pitched battles, dangers of, 103; Slavs described by, 385–86

Maxentius (emperor), 111, 112

Maximian (emperor) and Secular Games, 183

Maximian (poet), on old age, 270–72

Maximus of Turin, on survival of polytheism in countryside, 183

medicine, 297–310; baths, 302, 304; defined, 297–99; diets and dieting, 305–306; divination in relation to, 178; education in, 299; faith healing/miracle cures, 301; hospitals, 302–303; magical healing, 304–305; military, 88–89, 300–301; prescribing, 301–302; as profession, 297–304; remedies and medications, types of, 298–99; further reading, 310. *See also* childbirth; plague

Medina, Ordinance for, 395–96

Melania the Younger, 228–29

Menander the Guardsman, on embassy to Turks, 383–85

Milan, Attila the Hun in, 377

Milan, Edict of (313), 117–19

military, 78–109; Adrianople, battle of (378), 78, 346–47, 371; Amida, siege and sack of, 87–88, 89, 301, 336–38; Arabs and Arabia, warrior virtues of, 388–89; battle cries, dangers of, 103–104; billeting of troops, 99–101; Catalaunian Fields, battle of (451), 373; cavalry, training, 81–82; Christian interpretation of losses as wages of sin, 58, 336–38, 353; Christian prayers before battle, 103–104; Christian values and, 79; Christians in, 79, 105–109; civilian policing responsibilities, 90; Constantinople, siege of (626), 341–42,

383, 385; discipline in, 91, 102;
divination in relation to, 80, 176;
elephants, legionaries fighting, 80–81;
emperor's role in war and peace, 6;
ethnography of, 95, 104; exemptions
from service, 97; federates, 97–98;
Germanic kingdoms, Theoderic I's
efforts to stop war between, 355–56; just
war, concept of, 79, 107; medicine in,
88–89, 300–301; navy, 82–83; Nedao
River, battle of (454), 378–79;
non-Roman troops, 78–79, 97–99,
346–48, 349; organization of, 78, 80;
payment of troops, 99; pitched battles,
dangers of, 103; priests accompanying,
108–109; protection/extortion rackets run
by, 91–94; raiding, 85; rewards after
battle for, 90; strategy and tactics, 101;
substitute soldiers in Islam, 398; tax
collection by, 94; training, 81–82, 101.
*See also* borders and frontiers; Islamic
military operations; military
engagements with Sasanian Persia;
recruitment issues for military; rules of
war
military engagements with Sasanian Persia:
Constantinople, siege of (626), 341–42,
383, 385; Heraclian defeat of, 79,
342–43; Jerusalem, conquest of, 215–16;
Julian's invasion of, 336
Milvian Bridge, battle of (312), 111–12
Minorca, forced conversion of Jews of,
209–11
miracle cures/faith healing, 301
Mirrors for Princes, 5
Mishnah, 201, 203, 216, 217
Mithras, sacrifice of bull to, 180–81
monasticism. *See* asceticism and
monasticism
Monica (mother of Augustine of Hippo),
236, 262–63
Monophysites: *Henotikon* (or *Edict of
Union*) of the emperor Zeno, 138–39;
Justinian I on orthodox Chalcedonian
Christianity, 140–41; *Three Chapters*
Controversy, 10, 141–42
Mosaic and Roman law, comparison of,
293–94
mother–daughter relationships, 262
mothers-in-law, relationships with, 263–64
mountain people, limited Christianization of,
193
Muhammad the Prophet: death of, 406; as

Jewish messianic figure, 405–406;
Medina, Ordinance for, 395–96; role in
Islam, 387, 391
Al-Mundhir (Alamoundaras), Lakhmid
leader, 389–90
municipalities. *See* cities
Al-Muqaddasi, on mosque building, 402
mystery cults. *See* paganism/polytheism

naming children, 242–43
Naples, Jewish defense of, 214–15
Nasi (patriarch), Jewish, 201, 216
natural disasters: drought, 25; exhaustion
of land, 26–28; famine, 25–26, 56;
imperial administration's responses to,
25–28; susceptibility of local economies
to, 25
navy, 82–83
Nedao River, battle of (454), 378–79
Nemesius of Emesa, on conception of
children, 241
Neoplatonic philosophy. *See* philosophy
Nestorius and Nestorianism: Chalcedonian
Council (451) on, 135; defense of
theological ideas by, 132–33; Ephesus,
treatment of Nestorius at Council of
(431), 126–28
Nicaea, Council of (325): on administrative
role of bishops, 120; Arianism
condemned at, 132
Nicene Creed, 132
Nicholas of Sion: plague, rural-urban
conflict regarding, 309; sacred trees,
destruction of, 190–91
Nika riots, Constantinople, 41–42, 225–26
Nikephoros (patriarch): on conversion of
Huns, 380; on siege of Constantinople
(626), 383
*Ninth of Av, Dirge for*, 221–22
"Nobiscum" (battle cry), 103–104
non-Roman peoples. *See* invaders and
successor states; Islam; Sasanian Persia
Nonnus (bishop), 231
North Africa: Christian/pagan rioting in
Sufes, 195–96; Geminia Januarilla,
dowry of, 251–52; mansion, Thuburbo
Maius (near Carthage), 265, *266*;
polytheistic practice, continuation of,
198–99; Sufes, Christian/pagan rioting
in, 195–96; *Three Chapters* Controversy,
10. *See also* Vandals
Notitia Dignitatum, *xlvi*
Nous, Plotinus on, 312, 313–14

*Novels* (Justinian), 286. *See also* Index of ancient sources

nuns, 161–63

old age. *See* age, dying, and death

olive cultivation map, *xlvii*

Olympias (saint): founding of monastery by, 161–62; life of, 227–28

Olympiodorus of Thebes, 23

*On Riches*, 23–24

"the One" or "the Good" in Neoplatonic philosophy, 311–12, 317

oneness and unity of God, Quran on, 393

oracles, pagan, 178–79

Orosius: on Athaulf's efforts to improve Visigothic relationship with Rome, 348–49; on sack of Rome (410), 57–58

Orthodox Christianity, list of patriarchs for, lxxx–lxxxi

Ossius of Cordoba, on imperial interference in church affairs, 9

Ostrogoths, 345; acculturation problems of, 356–57; Ravenna, as beneficiary of concern for Roman legacy, 354, 357–58; Rugi, Gothic absorption of, 367–68. *See also* Theoderic I the Great

*Oxyrhynchus Papyrus*: amulet protecting a house, 268; divorce, 257–58; peasant dependence onpatrons, financial origins of, 29–30; slave's concern for family of master, 259–60

Pact of 'Umar, 396–97

paganism/polytheism, 174–200; Altar of Victory dispute, 199–200; apology for Christian differences addressed to, 139–40; Arab religion before Islam, 390–91; Athenian philosophers in Persia, 319–20; Attis, cult of, 180; as Christian concept, 174; Christian continuation of habits of, 192; Christians blamed for misfortunes of Rome, 57–58; countryside, survival of in, 183; divination, 80, 175–78; grave inscription of Vettius Agorius Praetextatus and Aconia Fabia Paulina, 278–79; household gods, 269–70; Isis, cult of, 179–80; Julian the Apostate's attempts to revive, 175, 196; Mithras, sacrifice of bull to, 180–81; North Africa, continued polytheistic practice in, 198–99; oracles, 178–79; sun worship, 192, 196, 314–15; further reading, 200. *See also entries at*

conversions; education; literature, pagan/classical; Manichaeism; paganism/polytheism, suppression of; prayers, pagan; sacrifice, pagan; temples, pagan

paganism/polytheism, suppression of, 186–93; destruction of temples, 163, 189–90, 195, 197; erection of churches on temple sites, 189–90; festivals prohibited, 192–93; idols, destruction of, 163, 189–90, 195–96, 197, 198; legislative, 186–88, 198–99; resistance to, 195–99; sacred trees, destruction of, 190–91, 195; sacrifice, Christian polemic against, 188; Secular Games, end of, 183

Palestine: Gaza, Temple of Zeus Marnas in, 189–90; Horvat Susiya (near Hebron), farmhouse, 264, *264*; Islamic forces welcomed by Jews of Hebron, 400; maps, *xlix, liv*; Samaritan account of Islam, 404–405. *See also* Jerusalem

Panegyris festival, 192–93

papacy. *See* popes

parents. *See* childbirth; children; *entries at* mother

patriarchate, Jewish (Nasi), end of, 201, 216

patriarchs of Constantinople, list of, lxxx–lxxxi

Patricius (father of Augustine of Hippo), 67, 262–63

Patrick (saint): on conversion of Irish women, 117, 229–30; in Ireland, 115–17

patronage system: city patrons, 39–40; conversion of peasants, duties regarding, 193–94; financial problems leading to dependence on, 29–30; finding a patron, 31; monks and holy men as patrons, 30–31; rise of, 28

Paul (apostle and saint), imperial request for head of, 145–46

Paul of Aegina, on medicinal bathing, 304

Paul the jurist, on infanticide, 243

Paul the Silentiary, description of Hagia Sophia, Constantinople, by, 64–66

Paula's pilgrimage to Jerusalem, 148

Paulinus of Nola: on abandonment of Roman temples, 53; on Biblical scenes in church paintings, 171–72; monastic vows taken in old age by, 114

Paulinus of Pella, on settlement of Visigoths in Aquitania, 349–50

payment of troops, 99

peasantry: Bagaudae, 349; colonate, 30; conversion of, 193–94; exploitation of, 28–29; financial crises leading to creation of, 29–30; rise of patronage system and development of, 28; sea, ignorance of, 31–32

Pelagia the Harlot (saint), 230–32

Pelagianism, Augustine's condemnation of, 136–37

Pergamon, townhouse in, 265, *265*

Persia. *See* Sasanian Persia

Philadelphia (Lydia), corruption of local officials in, 17–18

Philippicus (general), rewards after battle for soldiers of, 90

Philoponus the Grammarian, on the creation of the world, 320–21

philosophy, 311–26; Boethius on consolation of, 321–24; creation of the world, 320–21; pagan Athenian philosophers in Persia, 319–20; Proclus, life and education of, 317–19; Pythagoras, interest in, 315–16; souls, descent of, 325–26; "the One" or "the Good," 311–12, 317; theurgy, 316–17, 319; three hypostases (the One, Nous, and Soul), 312; universe, shape of, 324; further reading, 326. *See also* Plotinus

Philostorgius, on respect due bishops from empresses, 124

physicians, 297–304. *See also* medicine

Piacenza Pilgrim, 149–51

pilgrimage to Jerusalem, 111, 146–52; Constantine I's search for the Cross, 146–48; Egeria's viewing of the Cross, 148–49; Heraclius, restoration of Cross to Jerusalem by, 151–52; Jerome on Paula's pilgrimage, 148; Piacenza Pilgrim, 149–51

pitched battles, dangers of, 103

plague (sixth century), 307–309; in Antioch, 307–308; communication of, 308; in Constantinople, 308; distribution map, *lviii*; regulation of skilled labor following, 22–23; rural-urban conflict and, 309

Plato, 311, 317, 318, 319, 321, 322

Plotinus: life of, 312–13; on "the One" or "the Good," 311–12; on three hypostases (the One, Nous, and Soul), 312; on World of Primal Intelligence (Nous), 312, 313–14

politics. *See* church-state relations; emperors; government; imperial administration; law

polytheism. *See* paganism/polytheism

popes: Gregory I on accession to papacy, 130; list of, lxxix–lxxx; primacy of, 53–54

Porphyrius (celebrity charioteer), 43

Porphyry, on Plotinus and the philosophical life, 312–13

poverty, attitudes toward, 24

praise of God, Quran on, 391

*Prayer of the Emanations* (Manichaean), 183–85

prayers, Christian: *Akathistos Hymn*, 164–65; before battle, 103–104; Chalcedonian Creed, 133–34; Nicene Creed, 132

prayers, pagan: art and effects of, 181–82; to Hecate, 175

prefectures in the Roman empire, *xlvi*

prenuptial agreements, 251

priesthood: emperors as parallel to, 9; regimental priests, 108–109

Priscus of Panium, on the Huns, 373–79

Probus (Roman aristocrat), 255

Proclus (philosopher): death of, 275–76; life and education of, 317–19

Procopius of Caesarea: on federates, 98; on Huns, 340, 379–80; on imperial instability, 10–11; on Jewish defense of Naples, 214–15; on Al-Mundhir, 389–90; on Nika riots, 41–42, 225–26; on Ostrogothic acculturation problems, 356–57; on the plague, 308–309; on reduction of salaries of pagan teachers by Justinian I, 73; on Rugis and Goths, 367–68; on silk trade, breaking of Persian monopoly on, 340–41; on Theodora on stage, 45

Proculus (quaestor under Justin I), 15

prophetic tradition, Quran on, 393

Prosper, on Attila the Hun's failure to sack Rome, 377

protection/extortion rackets run by military, 91–94

providential history, 57, 166

provinces in the Roman Empire, *xlvi*, 11, 78

Prudentius (Aurelius Prudentius Clemens): on Christian teacher murdered by pagan students, 71–72; on Christianization of Rome, 50–53; on conversion of last Vestal Virgin, 112; on relics taken from corpse of St. Vincent, 144

Pseudo-Athanasius: on bathing, 47; on effect of childbirth on women's bodies, 242

Pseudo-Joshua the Stylite: on billeting of troops, 100–101; on famine, 25–26

*Pseudo-Methodius, Apocalypse of,* 168–69

Purim, alleged destruction of crucifixes at, 214

Pythagoras, philosophical interest in, 315–16

Qais Ibn Al-Khatim, Arab warrior virtues extolled by, 388–89

quaestor, 13–14

Quran, 391–95; on afterlife, 394; on apostles sent from God, 393; creation of, 394–95; on Jews living under Islam, 222; on judgment of God, 392; as message from God, 394; on praise of God, 391; on prophetic tradition, 393; on transcendent nature of God, 392; on unity and oneness of God, 393

Radegund (Frankish queen and nun), 363–64

raiding, 85

Ravenna, as beneficiary of Ostrogothic concern for Roman legacy, 354, 357–58

recruitment issues for military: draft evasion, 96; enforced recruitment, 96; exemptions from service, 97; non-Roman recruits, 78–79, 97–99; slaves, enlistment of, 97; sons of soldiers required to enlist, 96; where to find recruits, 95

relics: head of St. Paul, imperial request for, 145–46; Jerusalem, brought back from, 146; of martyrs, 144, 145–46; Vincent, relics taken from corpse of, 144; violation of tombs to recover, 145. *See also* Cross

religion. *See* Christianity; *entries at* conversions; Islam; Jews and Judaism; *entries at* paganism/polytheism; Zoroastrianism

remarriage: after divorce, 255–59; captive spouses and, 253–55, 256–57

rioting: Callinicum, destruction of synagogue at, 205–207; between Christians and pagans, 163, 189–90, 195–96, 197; Nika riots, Constantinople, 41–42, 225–26; urban, 41–42

roads, condition and use of, 19–20

Roman army. *See* military

Roman Empire in Late Antiquity, 1–36; Christian theory of empire, 64–66; chronology, lxxi–lxxiv; dates covered by, lxiii; dioceses, prefectures, and provinces, *xlvi*, 11, 14–15; Ghassanids allied with, 388–90; Huns as common enemy of Persia and, 340, 379–80; Islam as disaster for, 406–407; list of rulers, lxxv–lxxviii; maps of, *xliv–lx*; Ostrogothic concern for legacy of, 357–58; Sasanian Persia, relationship with, 327 (*see also* Sasanian Persia); vine and olive cultivation in, *xlvii*; online resources, 408–409; further reading, lxiv, lxvii–lxviii, 35–36 (*see also under more specific topics*). *See also* borders and frontiers; eastern empire; economic life of Roman Empire; emperors; imperial administration; travel in Roman Empire; western empire

Roman law. *See* law

Roman legacy: Franks, *Romanitas* of, 368; Ostrogothic concern for, 357–58

Romanos the Melodist: on difficulties of monastic life, 160–61; on presentation of Jesus by Mary in the Temple, 134–35

Rome, 37, 47–59; Altar of Victory dispute, 199–200; Ammianus Marcellinus on Rome in old age, 48; Arch of Constantine, 112; Attila the Hun's failure to sack, 377; Christians blamed by pagans for misfortunes of, 57–58; Constantinople as New Rome, 59–60, 65–66; Constantius II's arrival in, 2–3; entertainment expected by people of, 42–43; gladiatorial contests in, 44; Justinianic wars in, 48; map, *l*; quarries, public buildings used as, 55; restoration of, 54–55; rioting in, 41; Rutilius Namatianus on Rome as center of world, 48–49; senator, responsibilities of wife of, 260; Vandal sack of (455), 48, 358; Visigothic sack of (410), 41, 56–59, 349; Zachariah of Mitylene on wonders of, 49–50. *See also* Christian Rome

Rugi, 367–68

rules, monastic: Benedict of Nursia on twelve degrees of humility, 157–60; of John Cassian, 157

rules of war: Islamic, 397; just war, concept of, 79, 107; of Vegetius, 102–103

rural areas. *See* countryside

Rutilius Namatianus, on Rome as center of world, 48–49

Saba (saint and martyr) among the Visigoths, 346
Sabas (monk), greeted by Justinian, 5
Sabbâ, Syria, lintel inscription on house, 269
Sabbath, Jewish, at sea, 218–19
sack of Amida (502), 336–38
sacks of Rome: Attila the Hun's failure to undertake, 377; by Vandals (455), 48, 358; by Visigoths (410), 41, 56–59, 348
sacred trees, destruction of, 190–91, 195
sacrifice, pagan: Christian resentment of, 188; divinatory sacrifice, 80; importance of, 182; legislation against, 186–88; Mithras, sacrifice of bull to, 180–81
saints. See martyrs and martyrdom; relics; specific saints by name
Sallustius, on sacrifice, 182
salt, 31–32
Salvian of Marseilles, Christian interpretation of military successes of Vandals and Goths by, 353
Samaritan account of Islam, 404–405
Samarra, battle of, 336
Sasanian Persia, 327–44; Amida, siege and sack of (502), 87–88, 89, 301, 336–38; Avars, alliance with, 383; Christian communities in, 335–36; Constantinople, siege of (626), 341–42, 383, 385; Cross restored to Jerusalem after defeat of (630), 151–52; Heraclian defeat of (627), 79, 342–43; Hun invasion of, 340, 379–80; ideal king, concept of, 327–30; Islam and, 327; Jerusalem, conquest of, 215–16; Jews and, 201, 215–16; Julian's invasion of, 336; Justinian's equestrian statue in Constantinople facing, 60–61; Lakhmids allied with, 388–90; list of emperors, lxxviii–lxxix; maps, xliv, xlix, lxi; martyrdom of Mar Kardagh in, 143–44; pagan Athenian philosophers in, 319–20; Roman Empire, relationship with, 327; silk monopoly, breaking of, 340–41; Tarbo, martyrdom of, 232–35; further reading, 344. See also Khusro Anushirwan; Zoroastrianism
Saxons, 345, 349, 360
schools. See education
Scripture. See Bible
Scythians, 85, 367, 374–75, 377, 378, 381, 384

Sebeos (Armenian historian): on martyrdom of Smbat, 43–44; on restoration of Cross to Jerusalem, 151–52
Secular Games, end of, 183
secular literature. See literature, pagan/classical
Seiroe (Cabades II; Sasanian ruler), 343
senators, city (decurions), 37–39, 203
senators, Roman, wives of, 260
Sergia, on founding of monastery by Olympias, 161–62
Sergius (patriarch), 341
Severinus (saint) and collapse of Danube border, 86–87, 359–60
Severus of Minorca, on forced conversion of Jews, 209–11
Sextilius Agesilaus Aedesius, on sacrifice of bull to Mithras, 180
sexuality: abortion and contraception, 241; abusive husbands, 262–63; adultery, 253; Augustine on marriage, concubinage, and sexuality, 236; celibacy, legal status of, 237, 249–50; conception, 241; exploitation of women by their protectors, 237–38; impotence, 256; intercourse, 240–41; Pelagia the Harlot (saint), 230–32; Theodora (empress) on stage, 45
Shahnamah or Epic of the Kings (Firdawsi), 328
Shapur II (Sasanian ruler), letter of Constantine I to, 335–36
Shenute of Atripe, on pagan sacrifice, 188
sick, care of. See medicine
Sidonius Apollinaris: on Frankish prince Sigismer and his retinue, 350–51; on learning German, 352–53
Sigismer (Frankish prince) and his retinue, 350–51
silk trade, breaking of Persian monopoly on, 340–41
Silvanus (military commander in Gaul and imperial pretender), 12–13
Simeon the Mountaineer, on limited Christianization of mountain people, 193
Simeon the Stylite: death of, 155–56; public ascetic acts of, 154–55
Simplicius, on the creation of the world, 320–21
slavery, 32–35; abandoned children, 243; assumption of, 32–33; captive spouses, divorce of, 257; conversion of slaves, 194; divination in relation to, 177;

Gregory of Nazianzus, will of, 273–74; household, slaves as part of, 240, 259–60; international slave trade, 34–35; Jews not allowed to circumcise slaves, 202; in law, 33–34; military enlistment of slaves, 97; Patrick on Irish slave women, 117, 230; selling of children into slavery, 219, 243–44; sexual exploitation of women by their owners, 237–38; sin, as due to, 34

Slavs, 383, 385–86

Smbat (Armenian martyr), 43–44

social status: adultery and, 253; city senatorial families, 38; conversion tactics and, 194; of imperial administrators, 15, 17; wealth inequality in Roman empire, 23. *See also* aristocracy; peasantry

Socrates, 322

Socrates Scholasticus: on Constantine and bishops in Arian controversy, 124–26; on Jewish conversion to Christianity in response to false Jewish Messiah, 211–12

soldiers. *See* military

Sophronius of Jerusalem, on Islam, 399

*Sortes Sangallenses*, 175–78

Soul, Plotinus on, 312

souls, Macrobius on descent of, 325–26

Sozomen, on Helena (mother of Constantine I), 224–25

the state. *See* church-state relations; emperors; imperial administration; law

steppe peoples, 371–86; Scythians, 85, 367, 374–75, 377, 378, 381, 384; Slavs, 383, 385–86; Turks, Roman embassy to, 383–85; further reading, 386. *See also* Avars; Huns

Stilicho (general), 55

strategy and tactics, military, 101

successor states. *See* invaders and successor states

Sufes, North Africa, Christian/pagan rioting in, 195–96

suicide en masse, false Messiah encouraging, 211–12

sun worship, 192, 196, 314–15

Sundays, no litigation on, 165, 289

Symmachus (pope), 354

Symmachus (Roman aristocrat): on Altar of Victory dispute, 199–200; on education of his son, 245; on entertainment expected by people of Rome, 42–43;

Prudentius' treatise against, 52–53; wealth of, 23

synagogues: Apamaea Synagogue, floor mosaic inscription from, 220; Callinicum, destruction of synagogue at, 205–207; language used in synagogue worship, 203–204; liturgical poetry for worship in, 220–21

Synesius of Cyrene: on imperial duties, 6; on Jewish Sabbath at sea, 218–19; on military discipline, 91; on peasantry, 31–32

Synod of Antioch (341), on administrative role of bishops, 120

Syria: Christian curriculum taught on classical model in, 72–73; Damascus, surrender of (635), 398; exploitation of peasantry in, 28–29; map, *xlix*; military, protection/extortion rackets run by, 91–94; *Pseudo-Methodius, Apocalypse of*, 168–69; Sabbâ, lintel inscription on house, 269; *Syro-Roman Law Book*, 294–95

Syrianus (philosopher and teacher), 275, 276, 318

Al-Tabari: on conquest of Jerusalem (636), 399–400; on rules of war in Islam, 397

tactics and strategy, military, 101

Talmud. *See Babylonian Talmud; Jerusalem Talmud*

Tarbo, martyrdom of, 232–35

taxation: military, tax collection by, 94; natural disasters, taxes halted in response to, 25–28

teaching. *See* education

Temple, Jerusalem: Julian's promise to rebuild, 207–208; lamentations for destruction of, 221–22

temples, pagan: abandonment of Roman temples, 53; destruction of, 163, 189–90, 195, 197; erection of church on site of, 189–90; legislation against, 186–88

temptation of St. Antony, 152–53

Tetrarchy, lxxvi–lxxvii, 11, 14

Themistius, on emperor as embodiment of law, 7–8

Theoderic I (Visigothic ruler): Aquitania, settlement of Visigoths in, 349; Huns, invasion of Gaul by, 376–77

Theoderic I the Great (Ostrogothic ruler): education under, 357; quaestor under, 13–14; Roman city life under, 354–55;

Roman legacy, concern for, 357–58; Roman roads, repair of, 19–20; Rugi, Gothic absorption of, 367; war between Germanic kingdoms, efforts to stop, 355–56

Theodora (empress of Justinian I): Chalke Gate mosaic, Constantinople, 64; as intercessor for Constantinopolitan empire, 64, 65; during Nika riots, 225–26; on stage, 45

Theodore of Sykeon, medical treatments of, 301–302

Theodoret, on regimental priests, 108–109

*Theodosian Code*, 285, 290; appeal, right of, 289; on billeting of troops, 99–100; bishops, legal authority of, 130; on children, 243–44; city senators, 38; on enforced military recruitment and draft evasion, 96; on exemptions from military, 97; on gladiatorial contests, 44; heresy, prohibition of, 135–36; imperial acclamations from, 3–4; imperial administrators, standards for, 15; on Jews and Judaism, 202–203, 205, 214, 216; on judges, 289; on marriage and divorce, 237, 249–50, 251, 252–53, 257; paganism/polytheism, suppression of, 186–88; relics, on violation of tombs to recover, 145; river frontier patrols, 84–85; roads, construction and repair of, 19–20; on slaves in military, 97; Sundays, no litigation on, 165, 289; vicars of dioceses in, 14–15; on women's legal status, 237–38. *See also* Index of ancient sources

Theodosius I (emperor): entertainment expected by people of Rome, 42–43; law, emperor as embodiment of, 7–8; on *limitanei* (border troops), 83; Nestorius, deposition of, 128; Visigoths and, 348

Theodosius II (emperor): acclamations in honor of, 3–4; *Theodosian Code* and, 290

theology, Christian, 110; apology for Christian differences addressed to polytheists, 139–40; Arians on human nature of Christ, 131–32; *Henotikon* (or *Edict of Union*) of Zeno on, 138–39; Leo I on unity of Christ's two natures, 133–34, 137–38; Nestorian denial of Jesus the man as son of God, 132–33;

Nicene Creed, 132; Trinity, implied Islamic critique of, 393. *See also* Chalcedonian Christianity; heresies; Mary, mother of Jesus; Monophysites

theology, Islamic. *See* Quran

Theophanes Confessor: on disaster of Islam, 406–407; on the navy, 82–83; on restoration of Cross to Jerusalem (630), 343–44

Theophilus of Alexandria, 8

Theophylact Simocatta, on rewards after battle for soldiers, 90

Thessalonika, massacre at, 119–20

theurgy, 316–17, 319

*Three Chapters* Controversy, 10, 141–42

three hypostases (the One, Nous, and Soul), 312

Thuburbo Maius (near Carthage, in North Africa), mansion, 265, *266*

Thuringians, 355

timeline, lxxi–lxxiv

Timothy of Gaza, martyrdom of, 142

*Tome* of Leo, 137–38

torture, use of, 13, 295–96

townhouse, Pergamon, 265, *265*

towns. *See* cities

trade and commerce. *See* economic life of Roman Empire

transcendent nature of God, Quran on, 392

translation of Bible, 73–74

travel in Roman empire: approximate travel times, *xlvii*; pagans, obstacles laid down against Christians by, 198; roads, condition and use of, 19–20; Rutilius Namatianus on his voyage home to Gaul, 48–49

trees, sacred, destruction of, 190–91, 195

Trinity, implied Islamic critique of, 393

True Cross. *See* Cross

Trullo, Council in (691–692), suppression of festivals by, 192–93

Tully (Cicero), 13, 69, 325–26, 352

Turks, Roman embassy to, 383–85

Al-Turtushi, on Pact of 'Umar, 396–97

'Umar, Pact of, 396–97

unity of God: "the One" or "the Good" in Neoplatonic philosophy, 311–12, 317; Quran on oneness and unity of God, 393

universe, shape of, 324

urban life. *See* cities

Ursa (Roman aristocrat), remarriage of husband while in captivity, 255

Valens (emperor) defeated by Goths at Adrianople (378), 78, 346–47, 371

Valentinian I (emperor), non-Roman troops enlisted by, 99

Valentinian II (emperor): Altar of Victory dispute, 199–200; entertainment expected by people of Rome, 42–43

Valentinian III (emperor), acclamations in honor of, 3–4

Vandals, 345, 358; Belisarius' conquest of, 61–62, 64; Christian interpretation of military successes of, 353; sack of Rome by (455), 48, 358; Visigothic troops in campaigns against, 349

Vegetius: on military medicine, 88–89; on rules of war, 102–103; on strategy, tactics, and training of military, 101

Venantius Fortunatus, poems of, 363–66

Vestal Virgin, last, conversion of, 112

Vettius Agorius Praetextatus, grave inscription of, 278–79

vicars of dioceses in the Roman Empire, 14–15

Victor of Vita, on Vandals in North Africa, 358

villa, Lullingstone, Kent (Britain), 266–68, 267

Vincent (saint and martyr), relics taken from corpse of, 144

vine cultivation map, *xlvii*

Virgil, 352

Virgin Mary. *See* Mary, mother of Jesus

Visigoths, 345; Aquitania, settlement in, 349–50; Athaulf's efforts to establish better relations with Rome, 348–49; massacre of Visigothic troops after Roman defeat at Adrianople (378), 347–48; Roman ambassador at Visigothic court, 351–52; Saba (saint and martyr) among, 346; sack of Rome (410) by, 41, 56–59; Theodosius I and, 348

war. *See* military

Warni, 355

wealth. *See* economic life of Roman Empire

western empire: map, *xliv*; popes, list of,

lxxix–lxxx (*see also* popes); rulers, list of, lxxvii–lxxviii. *See also* Rome

will of Gregory of Nazianzus, 273–75

women, 224–39; abusive husbands, 262–63; aristocratic women, virtues of, 224–27; asceticism and monasticism for, 161–63; bathing by, 46–47; celibacy, legal status of, 237; Christianity and, 227–35; concubinage, 236; divorce, rights regarding, 257–59; Eve, sin of, 230, 235–36; exploitation by their protectors, 237–38; girls, adolescent, 248; girls, raising and education of, 244; inheritance law and, 238–39; jewelry, wearing of, 261; in Jewish community, 201–202, 217–18, 219–20; legal status of, 237–39; mother–daughter relationships, 262; mothers-in-law, relationships with, 263–64; Patrick on conversion of Irish women, 117, 229–30; Plotinus, female devotees of, 313; Roman senator, responsibilities of wife of, 260; soldiers disciplined by dressing as, 102; further reading, 239. *See also* childbirth; children; marriage; sexuality; *specific women by name*

World of Primal Intelligence (Nous), Plotinus on, 312, 313–14

Zachariah of Mitylene: on destruction of pagan temples, 189; on Rome, 49–50; on sack of Amida, 336–38

Zeno (emperor), *Henotikon* (or *Edict of Union*), 138–39

Zoroastrianism: afterlife, concepts of, 282, 332–34; Christian martyrs of, 143–44, 232–35; creation myth of, 331–32; creed of, 330–31; expansion of, 334–35; Pact of 'Umar, 396–97; Roman misconceptions regarding, 341; as state religion, 327

Zosimus: on Constantine I's de-emphasis of border defenses, 79–80; on end of Secular Games, 183; on military discipline, 102; on non-Roman troops, 98–99; on Visigoths and Theodosius I, 348